Third Edition

DESIGN AND ANALYSIS
A Researcher's Handbook

GEOFFREY KEPPEL

University of California, Berkeley

PRENTICE HALL
Englewood Cliffs, New Jersey 07632

Library of Congress Cataloging-in-Publication Data

Keppel, Geoffrey.

    Design and analysis: a researcher's handbook / Geoffrey Keppel.
    —3rd ed.
    p. cm.
    Includes bibliographical references and index.
    ISBN 0-13-200775-4
    1. Social sciences—Statistical methods. 2. Factorial experiment
    designs. 3. Social sciences—Research. I. Title.
HA29.K44   1991
300' .724—dc20   90-22248

Acquisition Editor: *Susan Finnemore*
Editorial/production supervision: *Edith Riker/Chris Nassauer*
Cover design: *CIRCA '86*
Prepress buyer: *Debra Kesar*
Manufacturing buyer: *MaryAnn Gloriande*

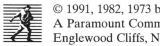 © 1991, 1982, 1973 by Prentice-Hall, Inc.
A Paramount Communications Company
Englewood Cliffs, New Jersey 07632

Printed in the United States of America

10 9 8 7 6 5

ISBN   0-13-200775-4

Prentice-Hall International (UK) Limited, *London*
Prentice-Hall of Australia Pty. Limited, *Sydney*
Prentice-Hall Canada Inc., *Toronto*
Prentice-Hall Hispanoamericana, S.A., *Mexico*
Prentice-Hall of India Private Limited, *New Delhi*
Prentice-Hall of Japan, Inc., *Tokyo*
Simon & Schuster Asia Pte. Ltd., *Singapore*
Editora Prentice-Hall do Brasil, Ltda., *Rio de Janeiro*

To Sheila

Contents

Chapter 17
The Mixed Two-Factor Within-Subjects Design:
The Overall Analysis and the Analysis of Main Effects
and Simple Effects

Chapter 18
The Mixed Two-Factor Within-Subjects Design:
Analysis of Interaction Comparisons

PART VI
HIGHER-ORDER FACTORIAL EXPERIMENTS

Chapter 19
The Three-Factor Design:
The Basic Analysis

Chapter 20
The Three-Factor Design:
Simple Effects and Interaction Comparisons

Preface

My major purpose in writing this book was to present the design and analysis of experiments from a researcher's point of view. The book was not intended to be a primary statistical reference, but rather to be a useful source of information and explanation of design and statistical matters rarely touched on by more mathematically sophisticated books. I wrote the book with a particular reader in mind, namely, a student who is about to engage in experimental research, but who possesses only the most fundamental mathematical skills and has little or no formal statistical background. What I offer in effect are *research tutorials* that provide the basic information necessary to design and to analyze meaningful experiments in the behavioral, social, and biological sciences. The emphasis is on the use of *the experiment as an inferential tool,* which a researcher employs to test theory and to build an empirical base for the science. Thus, a large proportion of the book is devoted to a detailed discussion of matters of experimental design and to the practical use of statistical procedures that will assist researchers in drawing inferences from experimental data. Statistical arguments are not neglected, however, but are covered in the context of data analysis and data interpretation; references to more mathematically oriented sources are liberally provided.

The major difference between my book and others at this level is its coverage of the detailed analysis of experiments. The book considers the reasons behind these analyses and provides numerous illustrations of their creative application to experimental problems. In contrast, most other books focus on the standard information available from experiments and spend relatively little time discussing the procedures that tailor the analysis to satisfy a researcher's specific needs. This book covers all the major designs commonly utilized by psychologists. I present these designs and the analyses appropriate to them in considerable detail. As a result, the book will provide you with a thorough appreciation for the richness of information obtainable from different experimental designs, and you should be in the position to take advantage of these procedures to plan your analyses in order to maximize the discovery and statistical assessment of this information.

The organization of this sort of book is dictated largely by the nature of the subject matter. I begin, therefore, with the simplest material and progress logically to the more complex. Because the analysis of variance consists of a number of design "building blocks" (a blending of simpler designs into more complex ones), I devote approximately one third of the book to the analysis of the simplest experimental design, the completely randomized single-factor design, and over 20 percent to the completely randomized two-factor design. This unique depth of coverage makes it possible for students and researchers to extend this knowledge to the analysis of the more complex designs.

This third edition represents a substantial revision of the second. I will highlight some of these changes:

1. The book has been reorganized to correspond more closely with how I currently teach this material. The analysis of the completely randomized single- and two-factor designs is considered first, followed by a discussion of two alternative procedures that help to increase the sensitivity of completely randomized experiments, namely, the blocking design and the analysis of covariance. The next major section focuses on designs in which subjects receive all the treatment conditions associated with an independent variable, the so-called within-subjects or repeated-measures design. The final section covers more complex factorial designs, including the completely randomized three-factor design and a design with two within-subjects factors.
2. Power and estimates of treatment magnitude are given expanded treatment in the third edition. Detailed examples of using power to estimate sample size have been added.
3. The new research on the effects of heterogeneity of variance has been given extensive coverage.
4. The analysis of simple effects and of interaction comparisons are considered in separate chapters; the discussion of interaction comparisons has been expanded to include the analysis of trend and of partial factorials.
5. My discussion of the analysis of experiments with unequal sample sizes has been expanded and is presented in a new chapter (Chap. 13).
6. I have increased the coverage of the mixed factorial design, which now appears in two chapters (Chaps. 17 and 18), and have added a new chapter on the analysis of the two-factor within-subjects design (Chap. 21).
7. A master plan for the analysis of complex factorial designs is presented in a new final chapter (Chap. 22).
8. The analysis of designs with random factors is considered in Appendix C.
9. Some new problems and exercises have been added. As in previous editions, extensive answers to the exercises are provided in Appendix B.
10. The notational system has been modified slightly to be more compatible with other design books, while retaining the use of capital letters to represent sums in the computational fomulas and the development of these formulas based on *df* statements.

This book is intended for use in a one-semester course or a two-quarter sequence in experimental design and statistical analysis. For a one-quarter course, an instructor might consider covering in detail Chapters 1–13, 15–18, and 21; this material constitutes what I feel graduate students should have mastered before becoming productively involved in experimental research. Because students require little supervision in working through most of the early chapters, instructors do not have to duplicate the presentation of the analyses in lecture. Instead, they are able to supplement the various topics with a development of statistical theory or with an amplification of the problems of experimental design—topics that are often neglected when an instructor must present the details of the analyses in class.

Because I have coauthored two other design books, which overlap to some degree the material covered in this book, I need to differentiate among them. This book presents a comprehensive coverage of the detailed analysis of basic experimental designs and is intended as a text at the graduate level and as a reference tool for researchers. The book by Keppel and Zedeck (1989), *Data Analysis for Research Designs,* was written to emphasize the equivalence of the analysis of variance and multiple correlation in the analysis of experiments; it considers the analysis of some of the same experimental designs that are covered in this book, but at a less detailed level. In addition, the book also includes such topics as the analysis of correlational studies and of nonexperimental designs. The book by Keppel and Saufley (1982), *Introduction to Design and Analysis,* is an introductory statistics text, intended for the undergraduate student or for students who have become a bit rusty on the "basics" usually taught at the undergraduate level or who have not been exposed to a course on experimental design as a sophomore or junior in college. I frequently refer such students in my graduate classes to this book for remedial or supplemental reading.

I am indebted to a number of individuals who provided advice and other assistance in the preparation of this book. I should mention first the useful comments I have received over the years from readers of the last two editions, including students in my undergraduate and graduate courses, individuals who have written to me with questions and ideas for improving the book, and the reviewers who offered useful suggestions for the third edition: Joseph S. Rossi, PhD, University of Rhode Island; Hugh J. Foley, Union College; John J. Bowell, University of Missouri in St. Louis; Thomas D. Wickens, University of California in Los Angeles; Steven L. Schandler, Chapman College. I should also mention some of the individuals who assisted in the production of this book. Susan Finnemore, the Psychology Editor for Prentice Hall, provided helpful advice and support at various stages of the project. Edith Riker and Chris Nassauer skillfully guided the manuscript through the many details of production. Finally, I wish to acknowledge the sabbatical leave I received from the University of California, which provided a semester free from teaching and committee service during which time I was able to complete a substantial portion of this edition.

Geoffrey Keppel

PART I

INTRODUCTION

This book was written for a relatively diverse audience—one ranging from advanced undergraduates to graduate students and professional researchers. As a result, some sections of the book, especially in the earlier chapters, may safely be omitted by the "seasoned" investigator, just as some sections in the later chapters may not be relevant to the immediate needs of the undergraduate.

A science is built on a large body of reliable facts and information. As most of you have discovered, or soon will discover, these facts are not easy to come by. They are established through many hours of patient observation, recording, and analysis of the behavior generated during the observation periods. A common method for establishing facts is the **experimental method.**

Basically, the experimental method consists of the contrast between two treatment conditions. The subjects in both of these conditions are treated identically, except for one feature that is different. I will refer to this difference as the **experimental treatment** or more commonly as the **independent variable.** (In this latter designation, *independent* stresses the point that the manipulation is under the control of the experimenter and *variable* indicates that the manipulation may take on two or more values.) Some aspect of the performance of the subjects in the two treatment conditions is measured and recorded after the treatment has been administered. This critical feature of the behavior of the subjects is referred to variously as the **dependent variable**, the **response variable**, or the **criterion variable**. Any difference between these two conditions that we observe on the dependent variable is called the **treatment effect** and is usually assumed to have been *caused* by the experimental treatment.

The experimental method is not the only method with which reliable scientific facts may be discovered. It is possible, for example, to show that two bits of behavior tend to appear together in nature and to use this fact to predict the occurrence of one from a knowledge of the other. Although relationships obtained by

1

this **correlational approach** may be reasonably accurate in their predictions—for example, the prediction of success in a job by means of scores on an aptitude test— we have not established a *causal* relationship with this procedure. For instance, to establish that cigarette smoking and the incidence of lung cancer tend to be related does not necessarily mean that smoking caused the cancer, as the cigarette manu- facturers have maintained for years. There is always the possibility that some other factor, a chemical imbalance, say, will account both for the smoking and for the occurrence of cancer as well.

The most important feature of the experimental method is that it is possible to infer a cause-effect relationship. That is, we can conclude that the difference we observe in the performance of the subjects in our two conditions was caused by the experimental treatment. This book will be concerned exclusively with the anal- ysis of data obtained from such controlled experiments. Chapter 1 describes the important features that must be considered in the design of an experiment.

1

Design of Experiments

An experiment consists of a carefully worked-out and executed plan for data collection and analysis. Treatment conditions are chosen to focus on particular features of the testing environment. These conditions are administered to subjects in such a way that observed differences in behavior can be unambiguously attributed to critical differences among the various treatment conditions. In essence, a well-designed experiment permits the inference of *causation*. This chapter describes a number of important features of experimentation—to place all readers on an equal footing. The steps required to establish causation are complicated, however, and will be considered in later chapters. Many of the points discussed in this chapter will be amplified and additional ones introduced throughout the remainder of the book. I will continually consider problems of experimental design along with the presentation of the formal statistical procedures. The design and statistical analysis of experiments are mutually serving and interdependent activities.

1.1   COMPONENTS OF EXPERIMENTATION

Experimentation begins by formulating a number of **research hypotheses.** These hypotheses may represent deductions or derivations from a more or less formal theoretical explanation of the behavioral phenomenon you wish to study, or they may represent simply hunches or speculations that you tentatively hold concerning this phenomenon. You may merely feel the need to collect additional facts about the behavior before developing a theory and deriving hypotheses from it. Research hypotheses are the questions you hope to answer by means of the experiment. They are what motivates your research. The introduction to a journal article generally contains the background information needed to set the experiment in proper theoretical and empirical perspective as well as an elaboration of the research hypotheses that are tested by the study.

The next stage in experimentation is the translation of the different research hypotheses into a set of treatment conditions and the selection of an appropriate experimental design within which to embody the different treatment conditions. The major requirement is that the particular treatment conditions chosen be capable of testing the research hypotheses. Are the treatment conditions relevant? Do the differences among them reflect the features of the experiment that we intended or have other features changed as well? The first question involves a consideration of the logical connection among the theory, the research hypotheses, and treatment conditions. The second question refers to a serious problem known as **confounding,** which I will discuss shortly. The details of the experimental design are presented in the methods section of a journal article.

The experiment is conducted, and the data are collected. We now have the two important tasks of summarizing the outcome of the experiment by means of statistical indices and procedures and evaluating the status of the research hypotheses. Our goal in this stage is to extract as much meaningful information as we can from the experiment. Our efforts at summarizing and analyzing the results of our experiment form the basis of the results section in a research report.

Since most of our time in this book will be spent in considering the statistical analysis of data, I should say a few more words about its place in experimentation. The statistical analysis provides a way of determining the *repeatability* of any differences observed in an experiment. If the same outcome is found when an experiment is repeated (or replicated) over and over again, we really do not need a statistical analysis to convince us that these differences are "real." A repeatable finding is really what we mean by a *fact* or a *phenomenon*. But rarely do we see replication used as a means for verifying the repeatability of findings, mainly because of the cost of conducting the same experiment more than once. Instead, we usually conduct a *single* experiment, and then we use statistical analysis to help us to decide whether it is likely that these same differences would be found if we repeated the experiment.

The final stage of experimentation, which is reported in the discussion section of an article, involves either the assimilation of the outcomes of the statistical tests of the research hypotheses into the theory that generated the hypotheses originally or the creation of a theoretical explanation if none is available in the literature. This process is a *reconstructive* phase, where facts that were not known before the experiment was conducted are now integrated into the research literature. If the experiment was conducted to test a theory and the outcome of the experiment is favorable to the theory, further tests of the theory (that is, new experiments) may be proposed. If the outcome is negative, the effect on the theory is a bit more complicated. At first glance, we might expect the theory to be discarded, revised, or perhaps even brought to further test. Actually, theories are much more entrenched than this suggests, and what happens is that the adequacy of the experiment is usually questioned instead. For example, its methodology may be reexamined, its supposed relation to the theory is reevaluated, a search for possible contaminating variables may be conducted, and so on. Only after considerable examination of the experiment is there much consideration of changing the theory. When it occurs, however, this complete sequence—research hypothesis, experiment, assimilation, research hypothesis—corresponds to the familiar **deductive** and **inductive** roles of science, namely, theory testing and theory building.

The completion of the assimilation stage is usually the beginning of another cycle, however. That is, your theoretical interpretations of these new findings now form the basis for a new set of research hypotheses, and a new research endeavor is launched.

1.2 PRINCIPLES OF EXPERIMENTAL DESIGN

The basic requirements of an experiment are simple: Differential treatments are administered to different groups of subjects (or to the same subjects in different orders), and performance on some response measure is observed and recorded following the administration of the treatments. In this section, I will elaborate on this relatively simple idea.

The Independent Variable

The independent variable implies several meanings in the context of experimental design. I have already mentioned one fundamental meaning, namely, the fact that the administration of the independent variable is under the direct control of the researcher and, consequently, is independent of the individual subjects who are serving in the experiment. A second meaning refers to the independence of the independent variable from all other potential variables that can affect the dependent variable; a lack of independence implies a confounding of the independent variable with any other variable that happens to have varied systematically with the experimental manipulation. A final meaning comes into play when we consider designs in which two or more independent variables are manipulated simultaneously in the same experiment. In these cases, we typically use a **factorial design,** in which the independent variables are manipulated in such a way that the manipulations are independent of each other and any effects associated with the independent variables—so-called main effects and interactions (which we will consider in later chapters)—are independent of each other as well.

Identifying Critical Features.   An experiment is made up of two or more treatment conditions, which in turn are characterized by a particular combination of potentially critical features. In an experiment, we compare the performance of subjects in the different treatment conditions and attempt to attribute differences in behavior to the feature (or features) that is (or are) different—that is, that vary—across the conditions. The independent variable is usually defined by the nature of the critical differences systematically varied among the treatment conditions. I will refer to an independent variable in a number of ways, for example, as a **manipulated variable,** a **treatment variable,** or a **factor.**
As an example, suppose that condition 1 consisted of a

SATIATED ADULT RAT given FOOD reward for solving a DIFFICULT maze.

In addition to the potentially critical features of this treatment condition, written in capital letters, I could list other features as well, such as the characteristics of the testing room, the apparatus and the experimenter, the time of testing, and so on. What can we conclude by studying subjects in this single condition? Very little, except to describe the situation. We can infer nothing about the relative importance of the various characteristics listed in influencing the speed with which the maze is learned.
On the other hand, let's add a second condition, which consists of a

SATIATED *YOUNG* RAT given FOOD reward for solving a DIFFICULT maze.

Although this condition suffers from the same problem as the first when the behavior of the subjects is considered alone, the purpose of the experiment springs immediately into focus when we *compare* the two treatment conditions. More specifically, the critical difference between the two conditions is age of the rats, and any difference observed between the two conditions will be attributed to this particular difference (adult versus young). Age is the independent variable.

Additional illustrations of independent variables are presented in Table 1–1, where separate experiments are defined by contrasting condition 1 with a different condition 2. Condition 2a, for example, focuses on a contrast between rats on the one hand (condition 1) and hamsters (condition 2a) on the other; any difference observed between the two conditions will be attributed to this particular difference. Species (rats versus hamsters) constitutes the independent variable. Condition 2b studies the effect of food deprivation (satiated versus hungry), condition 2c studies the effect of type of reward (food versus water), and condition 2d studies the effect of maze difficulty (difficult versus easy).

Each pair of conditions (condition 1 and one of the other conditions) constitutes an experiment. In each case, the two conditions are identical except for one critical difference, which defines the independent variable. Researchers usually refer to the different treatment conditions—"treatments" for short—in terms of the critical difference between conditions. Thus, for the experiment defined by the contrast between conditions 1 and 2, the treatments are adult and young. For the remaining experiments, the treatments would be rat and hamster, satiated and hungry, food and water, and difficult and easy, respectively.

Multiple Conditions. Most experiments consist of more than two treatment conditions. If we were interested in comparisons among species in a given learning task, for example, we might design an experiment in which various types of animals are represented, for example, rats, hamsters, mice, kangaroo rats, and so on. The choice of animal would be dictated by the questions we wanted to ask. If we were interested in the effects of food deprivation on learning, we would probably include several treatment conditions varying in the amount of time the animals have been without food, for example, 0, 12, 24, and 36 hours. Each one of the independent variables represented by the experiments specified in Table 1–1 could be expanded in a similar fashion.

Quantitative or continuous independent variables are variables that represent variation in *amount*—amount of food deprivation, variations in dosage, loudness of the masking noise, length of the learning task. Variables of this sort usually include treatment conditions that represent the full range of variation of the independent variable as well as several intermediate conditions to provide a picture of the effects of the variable in between the two extremes. **Qualitative or categorical independent variables**, on the other hand, represent variations in *kind*

Table 1–1   Examples of Treatment Conditions

Condition 1	A satiated adult rat given food reward for solving a difficult maze
Condition 2	A satiated YOUNG rat given food reward for solving a difficult maze
Condition 2a	A satiated adult HAMSTER given food reward for solving a difficult maze
Condition 2b	A HUNGRY adult rat given food reward for solving a difficult maze
Condition 2c	A satiated adult rat given WATER reward for solving a difficult maze
Condition 2d	A satiated adult rat given food reward for solving an EASY maze

or in *type* rather than in amount. Experiments designed to study species differences or the effects of type of reward or of different kinds of drugs are all examples of qualitative independent variables.

Qualitative manipulations can often be viewed as a collection of miniature experiments included within the context of a more general experiment. Suppose an experiment is designed to study the effects of different rewards on the speed of learning. Rats that have been deprived of food and water for a period of time are given one of the following three conditions:

Condition 1—food reward for solving the maze
Condition 2—water reward for solving the maze
Condition 3—food and water for solving the maze

A comparison between conditions 1 and 2 concentrates on the relative effects of food and water as rewards for learning. A comparison between conditions 1 and 3, on the other hand, focuses on the addition of water to the food reward. And a comparison between conditions 2 and 3 permits a similar determination of the effects of the addition of food to the water reward. Most experiments involving a qualitative independent variable can be analyzed as a set of smaller, more focused experiments. The primary characteristic of these miniature experiments is that they focus on a meaningful contrast between two (and sometimes more) treatment conditions. I will discuss the analysis of such manipulations in Chap. 6.

The effects of quantitative independent variables are usually analyzed differently. Rather than comparing miniature experiments in the data analysis, researchers concentrate instead on the overall relationship between the variation of the independent variable and changes in behavior. The goal of the analysis is to determine the nature or the shape of this relationship. Suppose that the independent variable is the number of hours of food deprivation and that we will be measuring the trials required to learn a difficult maze. How are we to describe the relationship? Presumably we will find an increase in performance as the animals become more hungry. But how will this increase in performance reveal itself? Will the increase occur steadily as the number of hours increases or will there be an absence of an effect at first followed by a steady increase? Specialized analyses are available that will permit us to distinguish between these two (and other) possibilities. I will discuss these procedures—called **trend analysis**—in Chap. 7. Although it may not be obvious at this time, the analysis of trend requires a reasonable number of treatment conditions to give any underlying relationship between variations of the independent variable and changes in behavior an opportunity to be revealed.

Classification Variables.   Experiments are frequently encountered that include the systematic variation of characteristics that are intrinsic to the subjects. The effect of intelligence on problem solving and the effect of gender on learning are examples of this type of study. Variables of this sort are variously referred to as **classification variables, subject variables, organismic variables**, and **individual-difference variables**. In the context of an experiment, classification variables are created by *selecting subjects* on the dimension to be included in the study. To "manipulate" intelligence, for example, we might segregate subjects into several groups on the basis of their IQ scores; these groups, then, would define the IQ variable for this experiment.

Manipulation of this sort does not constitute a true experiment since the administration of the "treatments" is obviously not under the control of the experimenter. In an experiment, the independent variable is the only feature of the situation that is allowed to vary systematically from condition to condition. It is this characteristic of an experiment that permits us to infer that a particular manipulation caused systematic differences in the behavior observed among the different groups. But when a classification variable is involved, the subjects may also differ systematically from group to group in characteristics other than the classification variable. Since such characteristics are not subject to a researcher's control, making an unambiguous statement about cause and effect is very difficult—if not impossible—when classification variables are under study.

In reality, this type of investigation is a *correlational* study, in which the classification variable is simply another dimension that is observed and recorded in addition to the dependent variable. In fact, it is generally advisable to study the relationship between the classification variable and behavior without selecting and grouping subjects, and to use the actual scores on the classification variable in the analysis, rather than lose this potentially valuable information by grouping. In some point in your training, you may wish to study the correlational techniques known as **multiple regression and correlation** (**MRC**), which consist of powerful and sophisticated procedures to assess the effects on a dependent variable of any number of classification variables (see, for example, Cohen & Cohen, 1983; Keppel & Zedeck, 1989; Pedhazur, 1982). In fact, Underwood (1975) has argued convincingly that experimentalists should introduce correlational designs into their research programs to provide critical assistance in theory development.[1]

We frequently do see classification variables introduced in conjunction with independent variables that *are* manipulated by the experimenter. Such designs, which I will consider in Chap. 14, can produce a more sensitive context in which to study the effects of the independent variable. Moreover, these designs permit researchers to examine these effects separately for each classification group and to determine whether the effects change or remain the same for the different groups of subjects. Underwood and Shaughnessy (1975, pp. 94–104) show how this approach can be used to study processes presumably "tapped" by a classification variable.

Dependent Variables

Suppose we have completed the first step in an experimental investigation: the development of a meaningful hypothesis and the choice of a particular experimental design. It is now up to us to work out the specific and minute details of the study and to collect the data. We will have to make a decision concerning the particular

---

[1] See Underwood (1957, pp. 112–125) for a general discussion of the problems surrounding the interpretation of correlational data.

aspect of the behavior we will observe and what measures of this behavior we will adopt. Each investigator will select measures that seem to "capture" the phenomenon being studied most accurately. Often these measures will overlap to some degree with those adopted by other investigators who have worked in this research area.

Even the behavior of a subject in an apparently simple experiment may be measured in a number of ways. Suppose we decide to study the effect of different types of food incentives on learning. Hungry rats will be used as the subjects, and their task will be to learn to approach a distinctive goal box, which has been consistently associated with food. Different groups of animals are given different types of food in the correct goal box. Since we are interested in learning efficiency, we would want to choose a dependent variable that reflects differences in time to learn. For example, we might record the total number of trials required for each animal to reach some predetermined level of performance—10 choices in a row of choosing the correct goal box. We might also want to compare the different groups of subjects at more than one criterion of mastery. For instance, we might want to see if the groups differ early in learning, for example, a criterion of 5 correct choices in a row, as well as late in learning. By requiring all of our subjects to attain the *highest* level of performance, 10 trials in a row, we are also able to compare the groups at levels of performance that reflect a lower degree of mastery. Alternatively, we might choose to give all animals a constant amount of training, 50 trials, say, and to compare the different treatment conditions in the total number of correct choices over the 50 trials. Again, if we want, we can also look at performance at different stages of learning, for example, the number of correct choices over the first 10 trials or over the second 10 trials. We can use any or all of these measures, just as long as all of the subjects have been tested on all 50 trials.

Up to this point, I have considered only measures that take into consideration the correctness of choice. Other aspects of behavior might be interesting to study. The time required by the rat to perform each trial is a commonly used measure. We could record the time for a rat to complete a given trial, from the opening of the start box to its entry into the goal box. More typically, we would probably choose to divide the total time period into subperiods and to record the duration of each subperiod separately. Common subperiods are (1) starting latency—time to leave the start box after the starting signal is given, (2) time spent within different segments of the approach to the discrimination choice point, (3) time spent at the choice point, and (4) time between the initiation of a choice and the entry into the goal box. In addition to time measures, we could record what the animal is doing during each trial. Does it stay oriented toward the patterns at the choice point at all times? What does it do at the choice point?

It is abundantly clear that any type of behavior that is singled out for study in an experiment may be indexed by a large number of response measures. With each measure, we can ask whether or not the independent variable was effective in producing differences among the treatment conditions. There is no simple rule to govern our actual selection of response measures. Some measures may provide redundant information, that is, give exactly the same picture of the effect of the independent variable. We would not have to include all these measures in our experiment since any one of them would give the same information. Some measures may be explicitly specified by a theory that is being tested in the experiment. Some measures may be easier to record or less subject to error either in measurement or in recording. In any case, it is most economical to attempt to include in any experiment a sufficient variety of response measures to ensure as complete a description as possible of the phenomenon under study.

Control of Nuisance Variables

A major effort in designing experiments is to control what are often called **nuisance variables.** Nuisance variables are potential independent variables, which if left uncontrolled, could exert a systematic influence on the different treatment conditions. When this occurs, the effects of the independent variable and the nuisance variables are intertwined and usually cannot be separated. Suppose, for instance, that we are interested in the effects of three drug dosages on the learning of a maze by rats. We may find it convenient, perhaps, to run the three different dosage groups in a maze at different times of day, with one dosage group run in the morning, another in the afternoon, and the final dosage group in the evening. Or we might decide to have each of the dosage groups run by a different laboratory assistant.

In the first case, the three dosage groups each learn at a different time of day. If time of day influences performance on the learning task—as it very well might, considering the diurnal cycles of rats—we will be unable to reach an unambiguous conclusion concerning the influence of drug dosage on learning. There will always be the problem of determining how much of this effect is due to the different times of day and how much to the different dosages. In the second case, each assistant runs the rats in only one of the dosage groups. If the assistants treat their animals differently, and if these differences in treatment are related to the rats' performance, again it will not be possible to attribute any differences in the behavior of the subjects in the three treatment groups to the experimental treatment. That is, how much of the treatment effect is due to the assistants and how much to the drug dosages?

Earlier, we referred to either state of affairs as a **confounding** of the independent variable (drug dosage) with some other feature of the testing situation (here, time of day or laboratory assistants). As another example of confounding, consider the various treatment conditions listed in Table 1–1. In an earlier section, you saw that a valid experiment was formed when condition 1 was contrasted with any one of the other conditions (2, 2a, 2b, and so on). As an obvious example of confounding, suppose the second condition were the following:

a HUNGRY YOUNG HAMSTER given WATER reward for solving an EASY maze.

It is clear that no meaningful inferences can be drawn from an experiment that includes the original condition 1 and this one. Each critical feature of the experiment—drive, age, species, type of reward, and maze difficulty—is varied between the two conditions; any difference in learning observed between the two treatment conditions may be due to any one or to any combination of the changes between the two conditions. A less flagrant confounding, but a confounding nevertheless, is created by comparing condition 2 with condition 2a. A close examination of the critical features reveals two changes between the two conditions, namely, age and species: Condition 2 specifies young rats whereas condition 2a specifies adult hamsters. In fact, no pair of the second conditions permits an unconfounded manipulation of a single independent variable. This only occurs when condition 1 is contrasted against one of the other conditions.

Confoundings in actual experiments are more subtle than the examples considered here. A significant amount of your training as a researcher will involve the development of an increased sensitivity to spot or identify potential confoundings. You can read about them in a variety of books, under the topic of **confounding of variables** or **internal validity** of experiments. See, for example, discussions of confounding in Neale and Liebert (1986, Chap. 5) and Underwood and Shaughnessy (1975). In addition, there are two useful undergraduate texts in paperback that are devoted entirely to the problem of internal validity (Huck & Sandler, 1979; Johnson & Solso, 1978). There is a more extensive and sophisticated discussion of these sorts of problems in books by Campbell and Stanley (1966), Cook and Campbell (1979), and Underwood (1957, Chaps. 4 and 5), which you are encouraged to study early in your scientific training.

Confoundings are controlled either by holding nuisance variables at a constant value throughout an experiment, by introducing important nuisance variables as a fundamental part of the experimental design, or by transforming systematic variation into unsystematic variation through randomization procedures. I will consider randomization later in this chapter.

Subjects

The critical issues concerning the subjects tested in an experiment are their nature and their number. What sort of subjects should you use for your experiment? How many subjects should you include in each treatment condition? The first question is usually answered by the overall purpose of the research. The most obvious decision is between animal and human subjects. But what sorts of animals, of what ages, of what early training or experience? Similar issues are relevant in research with humans. Undoubtedly, theoretical considerations will generally have an important impact on the eventual selection of subjects. Your decision might also be influenced by the relative cost or availability of subjects—for example, choosing animals from a departmental breeding stock rather than from a commercial laboratory supplier or using student volunteers enrolled in introductory psychology classes rather than paid subjects.

The question concerning the number of subjects required is usually unanswerable, for the simple reason that many factors influence the answer and some of these factors are generally unknown. Sometimes control features of the experimental design set the ultimate number. For example, suppose that the basic task presented to all subjects requires a series of judgments of stimuli presented in succession. Most researchers would present the stimuli in different orders to different subjects to avoid serial-order biases. If nine orders were constructed, the number of subjects required per condition would be some multiple of 9—9, 18, 27—assuming that each order was used an equal number of times.

The primary factor, however, is the desired sensitivity of the experiment in providing an adequate test of the research hypotheses. Sensitivity, known technically as **power** and discussed in Chap. 4, refers to the ability of an experiment to detect differences between treatment conditions when they are present. One way to increase the sensitivity in an experiment is to increase the number of subjects assigned to each condition. I will consider the problem of estimating sample size and other ways of increasing the sensitivity of an experiment in subsequent chapters.

1.3   CONTROL IN EXPERIMENTATION

In the ideal experiment, we can treat the subjects in the different conditions exactly alike in every respect except for the necessary variation of the independent variable. Unfortunately, this ideal experiment is never performed in real life. That is, it is virtually impossible to conduct an experiment in which the *only* difference among treatment groups is the experimental manipulation. Nonetheless, we are still able to conduct experiments and to draw meaningful conclusions from them.

Let us see how this is accomplished. First, certain features can in fact be held constant across the levels of the experiment. All the testing can be done in the same experimental room, by the same experimenter, and with the same equipment and testing procedures. Second, control of other features of the experiment, though not absolute, is sufficiently close to be considered essentially constant. Consider, for example, the mechanical devices that are used to hold various features of the environment constant. A thermostat, for instance, does not achieve an absolute control of the temperature at some fixed value, but it *reduces* the variation of the room temperature. An uncontrolled room would be subjected to a wider range of temperatures during the course of an experiment than a controlled room, but a variation will still be present. This variation may be sufficiently small to allow us to view the temperature as constant. Even with these features controlled, however, many variables that might influence the behavior we are studying remain uncontrolled.

I have not mentioned yet a major source of uncontrolled variability in any experiment, namely, the differences in performance among subjects. One obvious way to hold subject differences constant is to use the *same* subject in each treatment condition—a sort of biological analogue of absolute physical control. Unfortunately, even the same subject is not the same person each time he or she is tested. Moreover, there are potentially serious carryover effects from one treatment to another, resulting from the successive administration of the different treatments to the same subjects. To avoid this problem, we could try to *match* sets of subjects on important characteristics and then assign one member of each matched set to a different treatment, but matching would never be exact. Thus, neither attempt to control for individual differences among subjects guarantees that the treatment groups will contain subjects of the same average ability.

Control by Randomization

These considerations lead us to an alternative method for dealing with the problem of control. Specifically, it consists of an elimination of *systematic* differences among the treatment conditions by means of **randomization.** Consider again the control of room temperature. What might we do about controlling the temperature if the room were not equipped with a thermostat? We could try to match sets of subjects arriving at different times for the experiment, but for whom the temperature of the room is the same, and then place one of the subjects in one group, one in another group, and so on. But this is an unrealistic and cumbersome procedure. Suppose, instead, that we decide which of the different treatments a subject will receive by some random means at the time of his or her arrival for the experiment and that we continue to use this method until we have obtained the number of subjects we planned to run in each of the treatment conditions. What happens to the different room temperatures in this case? In a sense, the different temperatures of the experimental room have an equally likely "chance" at the start of each testing session of being assigned to *any one of the treatment levels.* If we follow this procedure with enough subjects, statistical theory tells us that the *average* room temperatures for the treatment groups will be equal. Under these circumstances, then, we will have effected a control of room temperature.

That is fine for temperature, but what about other features of the testing environment that also change from session to session? It may not be immediately apparent, but once we have controlled *one* environmental feature by randomization, we have controlled *all* other environmental differences as well. Suppose we list some of the characteristics of the testing session during the very first session in the experiment. The room will be at a certain temperature; there will be a certain humidity; the room illumination will be at a particular level; the noise from the outside filtering into the room will be of a certain intensity; the experiment will be given at a particular time of day, on a particular day, and by a particular experimenter; and so on.

When the experiment is about to begin, we choose a particular experimental treatment for the first subject in some random fashion. What this means is that at this point each of the treatment conditions has an equally likely chance of being the one chosen for the first experimental session. The implication is that the total composite of features that happens to be present at the time has an equally likely chance of being "assigned" to each of the experimental treatments. We come next to the second experimental session. The total composite of features at the second session will be different from the one at the first. The room will be at a different temperature, the noise level may not be the same, the session will be at a different time of day, and so on. Before the start of the session, we again choose randomly which treatment we will present. As with the first session, the composite of features present this time has an equally likely chance of being associated with each of the treatments.

Suppose this argument is continued until all of the subjects have been assigned to treatment conditions in the experiment. Then each and every feature of the experimental situation, which varies from session to session, has been assigned randomly to the different treatment conditions. There was no systematic bias leading to the running of one condition at the same time of day or only in warm rooms or only when the lights were bright or whatever. The assignment of the testing sessions to the experimental conditions in a random fashion eliminates from the experiment the possibility of systematic biases involving any of these factors.

Subject differences are also "controlled" by randomization. The subjects who are chosen to participate in an experiment will differ widely on a host of characteristics. Some of these will affect the behavior being studied and, hence, must be controlled. Suppose we could give all of our subjects numbers that represent their general abilities to perform on the sort of task being studied. This number will be a composite score, reflecting the influence of intelligence, emotionality, attitude, background and training, and so on. Now suppose that we assign the subjects to the different treatment conditions randomly. Subjects with high composite scores are just as likely to be assigned to one of the treatments as to any of the others. The same is true for subjects with low and with medium composite scores. Thus, random assignment of subjects to treatments will ensure in the long run that there will be an equivalence of subjects across the different treatments.

Suppose we take one final step in this argument. Somehow we select the first subject who will be run in the experiment; this may be the first subject who shows up as a volunteer for the experiment or the rat in the first cage that we come to. When we randomly assign this subject to one of the treatment conditions, we are essentially assigning jointly the subject *and* the environmental factors. By assigning the subject randomly to the treatment conditions, then, we are assigning randomly all of the ability and environmental factors as well—whatever the combination of ability and environmental factors may be for this subject. Random assignment of subjects to conditions essentially "guarantees" that subjects assigned to one group do not differ from those assigned to other groups in any intrinsic way. Until the experimenter treats them differently, then, the only differences between the groups are the results of random assignment. For these reasons, therefore, random assignment represents an indispensable method for controlling all nuisance variables in an experiment.

A serious problem presented by this argument has undoubtedly occurred to you. Specifically, we *never* run a sufficiently large number of subjects in our experiment to qualify for the statistician's definition of the "long run." In practice, we are operating in the "short run," meaning that we have no guarantee that our groups will be equivalent with regard to differences in environmental features or in the abilities of subjects. I will consider this problem in Chap. 2.

Methods of Random Assignment

Because of the fundamental importance of random assignment to the design and analysis of experiments, I will consider in detail methods by which randomization may be accomplished. Whatever method we use, we must be able to argue that *all* factors not involved in the manipulation of the independent variable have been neutralized by randomization. For example, suppose we conduct an experiment with three treatment conditions and we plan to run a total of 30 subjects in the experiment. For the first subject who shows up, we will determine which treatment he or she receives by some random process.[2] The treatment given to the second subject is determined in the same manner. This procedure is followed until all 30 subjects have served in the experiment. Note that each subject is randomly assigned to a treatment and each testing session is randomly assigned to a treatment. The critical features of the random assignment, then, are that each subject-session combination is equally likely to be assigned to any one of the three treatments and that the assignment of each subject is independent of that of the others. Following this procedure, then, we guarantee that each of the treatment conditions is equally likely to be assigned to a given subject and to whatever other uncontrolled factors might be present during any period of testing.

In actual practice, we would probably place a restriction on this random procedure of assigning treatments to subjects to ensure an *equal number* of subjects in each treatment condition. (Reasons for this decision are considered in Chap. 13.) When human subjects are appearing in the laboratory at their own convenience, that is, at a time that they choose, a typical approach is to make the random assignments so that any given treatment selected is not run again until all of the other treatments are represented *once*. In effect, this is the procedure of **sampling without replacement**. In the example, we would decide randomly which of the three treatments to administer to the first subject. For the second subject, we would randomly select the treatment from the two remaining treatments. The third subject will receive the remaining treatment by default, since there are only three conditions in the experiment. This completes a block of randomized treatments. The treatment given to the first subject in the next block (the fourth subject) is decided again by selecting randomly from the total pool of treatments, that is, three; the treatment given to the fifth subject is decided by selecting randomly from the remaining two treatments; and so on.

It is generally advisable to work with the smallest block, just as we did in the last paragraph. There is a good reason for following such a procedure. We can think of two general classes of variables that must be controlled in any experiment: those that really do fluctuate randomly from session to session and those that do not. We do not have to worry about the first class of variables—even if we run all the subjects in one treatment first and all the subjects in another treatment second, the particular values of these variables at each testing session occur randomly by definition. Thus, we turn to randomization to control the second class of variables, variables that do not fluctuate haphazardly.

We are usually unable to specify ahead of time exactly what the cycles of

---

[2]If there were only two treatment conditions, the treatment selected could be determined by the flip of a coin. If more than two conditions are included in the experiment, we usually give each condition a different number and then refer to tables of random numbers, which provide a source of random sequences of digits. Such tables may be found in many statistics texts and in experimental psychology texts.

fluctuation will be; however, we merely assume that they will be present. For example, subjects volunteering for an experiment do not represent a random flow of participants. There are undoubtedly different reasons why a subject volunteers early in the school term rather than late, and these reasons may reflect differences in abilities. The first subjects may be overly anxious or curious or smarter—who knows? The point is that we cannot assume that the flow of volunteers is random, nor is the fluctuation of room temperature or of time of day or of noise level outside the testing room. Randomizing in small blocks "helps" this control by ensuring that a block of three subjects, say, representing each treatment once, will not be placed in a room that is too different in temperature. Or three subjects appearing one after the other are likely to have the same reason for volunteering at that time.

Random Assignment versus Random Sampling

I should say a few words about the distinction between the **random assignment** of subjects to conditions and the **random sampling** of subjects from a known population.

Random sampling requires the specification of a population of subjects and then the assurance that each member of the population has an equally likely chance of being selected for the experiment. If these conditions are met, we will be able to *generalize* the results of our experiment to the population. It should be noted that even if we are able to obtain our subjects by randomly sampling from a population, we will still have to turn to randomization procedures in the assignment of treatments to subjects and to testing sessions. That is, even randomly selected subjects will come to the experiment one at a time and then be given one of the treatment conditions. Who receives which treatment must be determined by chance; otherwise, a systematic bias may result, and this bias will be damaging to any experiment whether the subjects are selected randomly from a population or not.

What about random sampling? Public opinion polls, voter preference polls, marketing research, and television ratings all depend on random sampling from a known population. Any findings from the sample are then extended to the population. Only rarely will we see random sampling in an experiment, however. And when we do, the population from which the sample was drawn may be so restricted as to be uninteresting in itself, for example, the rats in a laboratory animal colony, the students at a university taking a course in introductory psychology, or third-grade children in a particular school system. Almost invariably, our subjects are selected out of *convenience,* rather than at random. The failure to sample randomly from a known population means that we are not justified *statistically* in extending our results beyond the bounds of the experiment itself.

Since most researchers accept this "myopic" view of the results of an experiment, how can we ever discover results that *are* generalizable to a meaningful population of organisms? One answer is that past research in a number of laboratories with subjects chosen from different sources (for example, different breeding stocks, different suppliers of laboratory animals, and human subjects from different schools in different sections of the country) have shown that these differences are relatively unimportant in the study of various phenomena. Knowing this, an investigator working in this field may feel safe in generalizing the results beyond the single experiment.

The distinction, then, is between a *statistical* **generalization**, which depends on random sampling, and a *nonstatistical* **generalization**, which depends on knowledge of a particular research area. Cornfield and Tukey (1956) make this point quite clear:

> In almost any practical situation where analytical statistics is applied, the inference from the observations to the real conclusion has two parts, only the first of which is statistical. A genetic experiment on *Drosophila* will usually involve flies of a certain race of a certain species. The statistically based conclusions cannot extend beyond this race, yet the geneticist will usually, and often wisely, extend the conclusion to (a) the whole species, (b) all *Drosophila*, or (c) a larger group of insects. This wider extension may be implicit or explicit, but it is almost always present. (pp. 912–913)

Edgington (1966) makes a similar point.

In short, the generalizability of a given set of results is influenced by statistical considerations, such as the question of random sampling. For most experimenters, however, the extension of a set of findings to a broader class of subjects (or conditions for that matter) is dictated primarily by subject-matter considerations, that is, what is known in a particular field of research about the appropriateness of certain generalizations and the "length" of these generalizations. The availability of this information will depend on the state of development of the research area and the extent to which extrapolations beyond the particular subjects tested have been successful in the past.

1.4   BASIC EXPERIMENTAL DESIGNS

One useful feature of the procedures we will use to analyze experiments is the fact that the more complex designs are created from considerably simpler ones. In this book, I will cover the most common designs used in the behavioral sciences, taking advantage of the building-block nature of experimental designs. In this final section, we will look at three basic designs as a preview of the remainder of this book. I will start by describing two designs in which a single independent variable is manipulated, the so-called **single-factor designs.** (*Factor* has the same meaning as *independent variable.*)

Completely Randomized Design

The **completely randomized design** is characterized by the fact that subjects are randomly assigned to, and serve in only one of, the different treatment conditions.

Although it is not necessary, equal numbers of subjects are usually assigned to each treatment group. Since any differences in behavior observed between any one treatment condition and the others are based on the differences between independent groups of subjects, this sort of arrangement is also known as a **between-subjects design**. Completely randomized designs are simpler to understand conceptually, are easier to design and to analyze, and are relatively free from restrictive statistical assumptions. The main disadvantages are the large number of subjects required for even a modest experiment and a relative lack of sensitivity in detecting treatment effects when they are present.

Within-Subjects Design

A popular design in the behavioral sciences is one in which each subject serves in *all* the treatment conditions, rather than only in one. This type of design is commonly referred to in psychology as a **repeated-measures design**. The design is also known as the **within-subjects design** because any differences in behavior observed among the treatment conditions are based on the *same* set of subjects; that is, treatment effects are represented by differences *within* the single group of subjects serving in the experiment.

A within-subjects design requires fewer subjects and is more sensitive than a corresponding completely randomized or between-subjects design. Problems with the design center on relatively restrictive statistical assumptions and the fact that subjects can change while they are receiving the different treatment conditions.

Factorial Designs

Factorial designs permit the manipulation of more than one independent variable in the same experiment. The arrangement of the treatment conditions is such that information can be obtained about the influence of each of the independent variables considered *separately* and about how the variables *combine* to influence behavior. Factorial designs are widely used in behavioral research, and for good reason. The design permits us to move beyond a single-dimensional view of behavior—the restricted view provided by experiments with single independent variables—to a richer and more revealing multidimensional view.

The two single-factor designs described earlier in this section provide the building blocks with which factorial designs are constructed. There are three general possibilities. At one extreme, there is the **completely randomized factorial design**, in which each subject is assigned randomly to only *one* of the treatment conditions making up the basic design. At the other extreme is the **within-subjects factorial design**, with each subject receiving *all* of the required treatment conditions in a randomized order. Between these two extremes, we find designs that represent a "mixture" of the two basic single-factor designs, in which subjects receive *some*, but not all, of the treatment conditions defined by the basic factorial. This type of design is usually called a **mixed factorial design**.

Other Designs

I have only touched the surface. There are many more types of designs, each with a specialized function. I will cover the most common of these designs in this book. Kirk (1972, pp. 241–260; 1982, pp. 8–18) provides a useful classification scheme that describes a great number of experimental designs and the building blocks used in their construction. You may find this scheme useful not only to broaden your horizons but also to introduce you to the variety of experimental designs that are available to researchers in the behavioral sciences.

PART II

SINGLE-FACTOR EXPERIMENTS

A two-group experiment was used in Chap. 1 to illustrate the experimental method. In the not-too-distant past, this type of experiment represented the *modal* design in the behavioral sciences. Today, in its place, we see experiments in which a single independent variable is represented by more than two different treatments, and we find many cases in which two or more independent variables are manipulated concurrently in the same experiment.

The major reason for this increase in the complexity of the research is that the basic two-group design can only indicate the presence or the absence of treatment effects, whereas an experiment with more than two treatment conditions provides for a more *detailed* description of the relationship between variations in the independent variable and changes in behavior. Additionally, as our knowledge increases and more facts are established, our theoretical explanations of this knowledge become increasingly complicated and more elaborate designs are needed to test them. That is, to identify the mechanisms and processes that lie behind any given phenomenon, an experimenter frequently must increase the number of treatments and the number of independent variables that he or she includes in a single experiment.

In Part II, I will consider the analysis of experiments in which there is a single classification of the treatment conditions. By this I mean that the different treatments are classified only one way, on the basis of either *qualitative* differences or *quantitative* differences among the treatment conditions. Qualitative and quantitative independent variables were discussed in Chap. 1 (pp. 7–8). I will usually refer to either type of manipulation as a **factor** and to the specific treatment conditions represented in an experiment as the **levels** of a factor. In this book, I will also use the terms **levels, treatments**, and **treatment levels** interchangeably.

The general purpose of the single-factor experiment may be illustrated by a simple example. Suppose that we wanted to compare the relative effectiveness of

10 different methods of teaching a foreign language in elementary school and that we had no particular reason to expect any one method to be better than any other. How might we analyze the results of this experiment? One procedure would be to treat each of the possible two-group comparisons as a different *two-group experiment*. That is, we would compare method 1 versus methods 2, 3, . . . , 9, and 10; method 2 versus methods 3, 4, . . . , 9, and 10; and so on. There are 45 of these two-group comparisons. Obviously, this sort of analysis would require a considerable amount of calculation. Moreover, we should be concerned with the fact that we are using the same sets of data over and over again to make these comparisons. (Actually, we are using each group a total of 9 times.) We cannot think of these comparisons as constituting 45 *independent* experiments; if one group is distorted for some reason or other, this distortion will be present in all 9 of the comparisons in which it enters.

The single-factor analysis of variance allows us to consider all of the treatments in a *single* assessment. Without going into the details, this analysis sets in perspective any interpretations we may want to make concerning the differences we have observed. More specifically, the analysis will tell us whether or not it will be worthwhile to conduct any additional analyses comparing specific treatment groups.

I will first consider the logic behind the analysis of variance and then worry about translating these intuitive notions into mathematical expressions and actual numbers.

2

Specifying Sources of Variability

As described in Chap. 1, the first step in testing a research hypothesis is to design an experiment in which the influence of known and unknown variables is minimized. If uncontrolled, such variables could result in a systematic bias, that is, a confounding with the independent variable. Although it is possible to control nuisance variables by holding them constant, the most common procedure is to spread their effects randomly over all the treatment conditions. Unfortunately, however, the use of randomization to control the influence of nuisance variables—which is nearly unavoidable in experimentation—creates a new problem:

> **Differences observed among treatment means are influenced jointly by the actual differences in the treatments administered to the different groups *and* by chance factors introduced by randomization.**

The decision confronting the experimenter is to decide whether the differences associated with the treatment conditions are entirely or just partly due to chance. I will now consider, in general terms, a statistical solution to this disturbing problem.

2.1   THE LOGIC OF HYPOTHESIS TESTING

Suppose we have just completed collecting the data from an experiment. As a first step in the analysis of the data, we calculate summary statistics for each treatment condition—usually measures of "average" performance (the mean) and variability (the variance or standard deviation). Generally, we are not primarily interested merely in describing the performance of subjects in the different treatment conditions. Our main goal is to make *inferences* about the behavior of subjects who have not been tested in our experiment. Rarely will we choose to test all possible subjects in an experiment, such as all laboratory rats of a particular strain or all college students enrolled in an introductory psychology class at a particular university. Instead, we select samples from these larger groups, administer the experimental conditions to the samples, and make inferences about the nature of the population on the basis of the experimental outcome. We refer to these large groups as **populations**. Members of any population are identified by a set of rules of membership. A **sample** consists of a smaller set of observations drawn from the population. To be able to generalize to the population in a strict statistical sense, we must select the subjects constituting the sample *randomly* from the population. Summary descriptions calculated from the data of a sample are called **statistics**, and measures calculated from all the observations within the population are called **parameters**. In most cases, I will use Roman letters to designate statistics and Greek letters to designate parameters.

At this point, we can view the subjects in the treatment conditions as representing samples drawn from different treatment populations. Statistics, calculated on the scores obtained from the different groups of subjects, provide estimates of one or more parameters for the different treatment populations. We are now ready to consider the formal process of hypothesis testing, where we translate the research hypothesis into a set of **statistical hypotheses**, which we then evaluate in light of the obtained data.

Statistical Hypotheses

A research hypothesis is a fairly general statement about the assumed nature of the world that we translate into an experiment. Typically, but not always, a research hypothesis asserts that the treatments will produce an effect. (If it did not, we would probably not have performed the experiment in the first place!) Statistical hypotheses consist of a set of precise hypotheses about the parameters of the different treatment populations. We usually formulate two statistical hypotheses that are mutually exclusive or incompatible statements about the treatment parameters.

The statistical hypothesis we *test* is called the **null hypothesis**, often symbolized as H_0. The function of the null hypothesis is to specify the values of a particular parameter (the mean, for example) in the different treatment populations (symbolized as μ_1, μ_2, μ_3, and so on). The null hypothesis typically chosen gives the *same* value to the different populations—that is,

$$H_0 : \mu_1 = \mu_2 = \mu_3 = \text{etc.}$$

This is tantamount to saying that *no* treatment effects are present in the population. If the actual means obtained from the treatment groups are too deviant from those specified by the null hypothesis, H_0 is rejected in favor of the other statistical hypothesis, called the **alternative hypothesis**, H_1. The alternative hypothesis specifies values for the parameter that are *incompatible* with the null hypothesis. Usually, the alternative hypothesis states simply that the values of the parameter in the different treatment populations are *not* all equal. Specifically,

$$H_1 : \text{not all } \mu\text{'s are equal.}$$

A decision to reject H_0 implies an acceptance of H_1, which, in essence, constitutes support of our original *research* hypothesis. On the other hand, if the treatment means are reasonably close to those specified by the null hypothesis, H_0 is retained and not rejected. This latter decision can be thought of as a failure of the experiment to support the research hypothesis. You will see in a later discussion that a decision to retain the null hypothesis is not simple. Depending on the true state of the world, that is, the equality or inequality of the actual treatment population means, we can make an error of inference with *either* decision, rejecting H_0 or retaining H_0. (I will say more about these errors in Chap. 3.)

Experimental Error

The crux of the problem is the fact that we can always attribute some portion of the differences we observe among the treatment means to chance factors. All nuisance variables that we control in our experiment through random assignment of subjects to the treatment conditions are considered potential contributors to **exper-

imental error. In the behavioral sciences, the most important source of experimental error is that due to individual differences. In Chap. 1, I also mentioned variations in the various features of the testing environment as contributing to uncontrolled variability. Another source of experimental error is what may be called *measurement error*. A misreading of a dial, a misjudgment that a particular type of behavior has occurred, the variability in reaction time of an experimenter timing a given bit of behavior, and an error in transposing observations recorded in the laboratory to summary worksheets used in performing the statistical analyses are all examples of measurement error. Although it is not obvious, a given experimental treatment is not exactly the same for each subject serving in that treatment condition; the experimental apparatus cannot be counted on to administer the same treatment for successive subjects. An experimenter cannot construct an identical testing environment (the reading of instructions, the experimenter-subject interaction, and so on) for all subjects in any treatment group. We describe the contribution of all these different components of experimental error as *unsystematic*, stressing the fact that their influence is *independent* of the treatment effects.

Estimates of Experimental Error

Suppose we were able to estimate the extent to which the differences we observe among the group means are due to experimental error. We would then be in a position to begin to consider the evaluation of the hypothesis that the means of the treatment populations are equal. Consider the scores of subjects in any one of the treatment conditions. We certainly do not expect these scores to be equal. In the ideal experiment they would be. In an actual experiment, of course, all the sources of uncontrolled variability will also contribute to a subject's score, resulting in a difference in performance for subjects who are given the same treatment condition. The variability of subjects treated alike, that is, within the same treatment level, provides an estimate of experimental error. By the same argument, the variability of subjects within each of the other treatment levels also offers estimates of experimental error. If we assume that experimental error is the same for the different treatment conditions, we can obtain a more stable estimate of this quantity by pooling and averaging these separate estimates.

Assume that we have drawn random samples from a population of subjects, administered the different treatments, recorded the performance of the subjects, and calculated the means of the treatment groups. Further assume for the moment that the null hypothesis is *true*—that the population means associated with the treatment conditions are *equal*. Would we expect our *sample* means, the means calculated in the experiment, to be equal? Certainly not. From our discussion of the use of randomization to "control" unwanted factors in our experiment, it should be clear that the means will rarely be equal. If the sample means are not equal, the only reasonable explanation that we can offer for these differences is the operation of experimental error. All the sources of unsystematic variability, which contribute to the differences among subjects within a given treatment condition, will also be operating to produce differences among the sample means.

Take, for instance, error that results from the random assignment of subjects to treatments. If the assignment procedure is truly random, each subject will have an equal chance of being assigned to any one of the different treatments. But this in no way *guarantees* that the average ability of subjects assigned to these groups is equal. Similarly, for the other contributors to experimental error, there is no reason to expect these uncontrolled sources of error to balance out perfectly across the treatment conditions. In short, then, under these circumstances—an experiment conducted when the null hypothesis is true—differences among the sample means will reflect the operation of experimental error.

Estimates of Treatment Effects

So far in this discussion I have considered only the case in which the null hypothesis is true. Certainly we hope that we will discover at least a few situations in which the null hypothesis is *false*, in which case, there are real differences among the means of the treatment populations. Assuming that the subjects in each treatment group are drawn randomly from corresponding treatment populations, the means of the different groups in the experiment should reflect only the differences in the population means. The mere fact that the null hypothesis is false does not imply that experimental error has vanished, however. Not at all. The only change is that there is now an additional component contributing to the differences among the means, a systematic component as opposed to an unsystematic one, namely, **treatment effects**.

Thus, differences among treatment means may reflect *two different quantities*: When the population means are equal, the differences among the group means will reflect the operation of experimental error alone, but when the population means are not equal, the differences among the group means will reflect the operation of an unsystematic component and a systematic component, that is, experimental error and treatment effects, respectively.

Evaluation of the Null Hypothesis

You have seen that when the null hypothesis is true, we will have two estimates of experimental error available from the experiment. If we form a *ratio* of these two estimates, we will find that we have produced a useful statistic. More specifically, consider the following ratio:

$$\frac{\text{differences among treatment means}}{\text{differences among subjects treated alike}}$$

From this discussion, we can think of this ratio as contrasting an estimate of experimental error based on differences between groups with an estimate of experimental error based on pooled differences within groups. That is, we have

$$\frac{\text{experimental error}}{\text{experimental error}}$$

If we were to repeat this experiment a large number of times on new samples of subjects drawn from the same population, we would expect to find an average value of this ratio of approximately 1.0.

Consider now the same ratio when the null hypothesis is *false*. Under these circumstances, there is an additional component in the numerator, one that reflects the treatment effects. Explicitly, the ratio becomes

$$\frac{(\text{treatment effects}) + (\text{experimental error})}{\text{experimental error}}$$

Given this situation, if we were to repeat the experiment a large number of times, we would expect to find an average value of this ratio that is *greater* than 1.0.

You can see, then, that the average value of this ratio, obtained from a large number of replications of the experiment, depends on the values of the population means. If H_0 is true (that is, the means are equal), the average value will approximate 1.0; if H_1 is true (that is, the means are not equal), the average value will approximate a number greater than 1.0. A problem remains, however, since in any one experiment, it is always possible to obtain a value that is *greater* than 1.0 when H_0 is *true* and one that is *equal* to or *less* than 1.0 when H_1 is *true*. Thus, merely checking to see whether the ratio is greater than 1.0 does not tell us which statistical hypothesis is correct.

What we will do about this problem is to make a decision concerning the acceptability of the null hypothesis that is based on a consideration of the chance probability associated with the ratio we actually found in the experiment. If the probability of obtaining a ratio of this size or larger by chance is reasonably low, we will reject the null hypothesis. On the other hand, if this probability is high, we will not reject, or in essence, we will retain the null hypothesis. (I will have more to say about the **decision rules** we follow in making this decision in Chap. 3.)

2.2   THE COMPONENT DEVIATIONS

In the remainder of this chapter, you will see the abstract notions of variability *between* treatment groups and *within* treatment groups become concrete arithmetic operations extracted from scores produced in single-factor experiments. The next chapter indicates how we use this information to provide a test of the null hypothesis.

Suppose we were interested in the effect on reading comprehension of three different instructions. One group of children is asked to attempt to memorize an essay, a second group is asked to concentrate on the ideas in the essay, and a third group is given no specific instructions. I will refer to the independent variable, types of instruction, as **factor A**, and to the three levels of factor A (the three different instructional conditions) as levels a_1, a_2, and a_3. We draw the subjects from a fourth-grade class and randomly assign $n = 5$ different subjects to each of the levels of factor A. We allow all subjects to study the essay for 10 minutes, after which time we give them an objective test to determine their comprehension of the

Table 2–1   Numerical Example

	FACTOR A	
Level a_1	Level a_2	Level a_3
16	4	2
18	6	10
10	8	9
12	10	13
19	2	11

passage. The response measure—that is, the score for each subject (Y)—is the number of test items correctly answered by each student.

The data from this hypothetical experiment are presented in Table 2–1. The five Y scores for each treatment condition are arranged in three columns. Our first step in the analysis would be to compute the means for the three sets of scores. The three means are $\overline{Y}_{A_1} = 15$, $\overline{Y}_{A_2} = 6$, and $\overline{Y}_{A_3} = 9$. The grand mean of all three conditions, obtained by taking the average of the three treatment means, is $\overline{Y}_T = (15 + 6 + 9)/3 = 10$. (I will illustrate the calculations in the next section.) As explained previously, we cannot conclude that any differences among the group means represent the "real" effects of the different experimental treatments: The differences may have resulted from experimental error, the short-term siding of uncontrolled sources of variability with one treatment condition or another. You saw that the solution to this problem is to compare the differences among the group means against the differences obtained from subjects within each of the individual groups. Let us see how this is accomplished.

For the moment, I will focus on the worst score in condition a_2, which is two correct responses on the objective test given following the presentation of the essay. I will represent this score as $Y_{2,5}$, where the first subscript specifies the level of factor A (a_2 in this case) and the second subscript indicates the subject's ordinal position in the original listing of the scores. This subject happens to be the fifth score in level a_2 as listed in Table 2–1. (I will discuss the notational system in the next section.)

Consider now the deviation of this score $(Y_{2,5})$ from the grand mean $\overline{Y}_T$. This deviation $(Y_{2,5} - \overline{Y}_T)$ is represented geometrically at the bottom of Fig. 2–1 as the distance between the two vertical lines drawn from this score $(Y_{2,5} = 2)$ on the left and the grand mean $(\overline{Y}_T = 10)$ on the right, respectively. Consider next the vertical line drawn through the group mean for condition a_2 $(\overline{Y}_{A_2} = 6)$. From the figure, it is obvious that this deviation is made up of *two components*. One component consists of the deviation of the score from the mean of the group from which it was selected, that is, $Y_{2,5} - \overline{Y}_{A_2}$, the component deviation on the left. The other component consists of the deviation of the group mean from the grand mean, that is, $\overline{Y}_{A_2} - \overline{Y}_T$, the component on the right. This relationship may be written as

$$Y_{2,5} - \overline{Y}_T = (\overline{Y}_{A_2} - \overline{Y}_T) + (Y_{2,5} - \overline{Y}_{A_2})$$

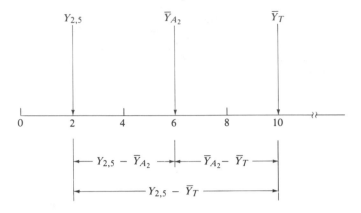

FIGURE 2–1   Geometric representation of the component deviations.

We can give each of the three deviations a name:

$Y_{2,5} - \overline{Y}_T$ is called the **total deviation**.

$\overline{Y}_{A_2} - \overline{Y}_T$ is called the **between-groups deviation**.

$Y_{2,5} - \overline{Y}_{A_2}$ is called the **within-groups deviation**.

This subdividing of the total deviation—or **partitioning**, as it is called—is illustrated with actual numbers in Table 2–2 under the heading, Level a_2. To illustrate again for the fifth subject, $Y_{2,5}$, we have

$$Y_{2,5} - \overline{Y}_T = (\overline{Y}_{A_2} - \overline{Y}_T) + (Y_{2,5} - \overline{Y}_{A_2})$$

Substituting for symbols ($Y_{2,5} = 2$, $\overline{Y}_{A_2} = 6$, and $\overline{Y}_T = 10$), we find

$$2 - 10 = (6 - 10) + (2 - 6)$$
$$- 8 = (-4) + (-4)$$

Table 2–2 summarizes these calculations for each of the five subjects in this group. A similar partitioning can be conducted for each of the subjects in the other two groups. These are also summarized in the table.

Thus, you have seen that the score for each subject in an experiment can be expressed as a deviation from the grand mean and that this deviation can be partitioned into two components, a between-groups deviation and a within-groups deviation. These two component deviations are what we have been after, a quantity that will reflect treatment effects in the population (the between-groups deviation), in addition to experimental error, and a quantity that will reflect experimental error alone (the within-groups deviation). You will next see how these deviations are translated into measures of variability.

Table 2–2   Analysis of Component Deviation Scores

SCORE	DEVIATIONS				
	Total	=	**Between**	+	**Within**
Y	$(Y - \bar{Y}_T)$	=	$(\bar{Y}_{A_i} - \bar{Y}_T)$	+	$(Y - \bar{Y}_{A_i})$
	Level a_1				
16	(6)	=	(5)	+	(1)
18	(8)	=	(5)	+	(3)
10	(0)	=	(5)	+	(−5)
12	(2)	=	(5)	+	(−3)
19	(9)	=	(5)	+	(4)
	Level a_2				
4	(−6)	=	(−4)	+	(−2)
6	(−4)	=	(−4)	+	(0)
8	(−2)	=	(−4)	+	(2)
10	(0)	=	(−4)	+	(4)
2	(−8)	=	(−4)	+	(−4)
	Level a_3				
2	(−8)	=	(−1)	+	(−7)
10	(0)	=	(−1)	+	(1)
9	(−1)	=	(−1)	+	(0)
13	(3)	=	(−1)	+	(4)
11	(1)	=	(−1)	+	(2)

2.3 SUMS OF SQUARES: DEFINING OR CONCEPTUAL FORMULAS

To evaluate the null hypothesis, it is necessary to transform the between-groups and within-groups deviations into more useful quantities, namely, **variances**. For this reason the statistical analysis involving the comparison of variances—in this case between-groups and within-groups variances—reflecting different sources of variability is called the **analysis of variance**. A variance is defined as follows:

$$\text{variance} = \frac{\text{sum of the squared deviations from the mean}}{\text{degrees of freedom}}$$

The quantity specified in the numerator, the **sum of the squared deviations from the mean,** usually shortened to **sum of squares** and abbreviated *SS*, reflects the degree to which the numbers in a set vary among themselves. When there is no variability, that is, when the numbers are all the same, each deviation from the mean will be zero (because the mean is equal to each number in the set), and the sum of the squared deviations (as well as the variance) will equal zero. On the other hand, when the numbers in a set are *different*, they spread out from the mean and the sum of the squared deviations becomes a positive value. As the spread increases, the deviations from the mean increase and the *SS* increases as well.

The quantity in the denominator, **degrees of freedom** (*df*), is approximately equal to the number of numbers in the set. This means, therefore, that the variance is basically an *average* of the squared deviations. I will consider variances and the concept of degrees of freedom in the next chapter. Our concern now is the calculation of component sums of squares.

Let's return to the component deviations developed in Sec. 2.2. You will recall that the deviation of each subject from the grand mean of the experiment can be divided into a between-group portion and a within-group portion. A similar additive relationship holds if we square the three deviations for each subject and then sum the squares over all of the subjects in the experiment. This important relationship may be stated as

$$SS_{total} = SS_{between\ groups} + SS_{within\ groups} \tag{2-1}$$

Translated into the numerical example from Table 2–1, Eq. (2–1) reads, "The sum of the squared deviations of all 15 subjects from $\overline{Y}_T$ may be broken down into two components, one obtained by summing all the squared deviations between individual group means and $\overline{Y}_T$ and the other by summing all the squared deviations of subjects from their respective group means." You will now see how these words are translated into formulas and numerical values.

Total Sum of Squares

The basic ingredients in the total sum of squares SS_T are the total deviations—that is, the deviations of all the scores in the experiment from the grand mean, $\overline{Y}_T$. The SS_T is formed by squaring the total deviation for each subject and summing the squares of the total deviations. In symbols,

$$SS_T = \Sigma (Y - \overline{Y}_T)^2 \tag{2-2}$$

As you undoubtedly know, the capital Greek letter Σ, sigma, is read, "the sum of . . . ." Thus, $\Sigma (Y - \overline{Y}_T)^2$ is read, "the sum of the deviations formed by subtracting the grand mean of the Y scores from all the Y scores in the experiment." We can calculate SS_T for the numerical example we have been considering by squaring each of the 15 total deviations presented in Table 2–2. More specifically,

$$SS_T = \Sigma (Y - \overline{Y}_T)^2$$
$$= (6)^2 + (8)^2 + \ldots + (3)^2 + (1)^2 = 380$$

Between-Groups Sum of Squares

You saw in Fig. 2–1 that one of the components of a subject's total deviation is the deviation of the subject's group mean from the grand mean $(\overline{Y}_A - \overline{Y}_T)$. If we square this component and sum the squares for all the subjects in the experiment, we will obtain the between-groups SS. (I will refer to this quantity as the SS_A, indicating that this sum of squares is based on the deviations involving the A means.) From the between-group deviations listed in Table 2–2,

$$SS_A = (5)^2 + (5)^2 + \ldots + (-1)^2 + (-1)^2 = 210$$

Alternatively, we can express this formula differently by taking advantage of the fact that the between-group deviation is the same for all subjects in any given group. In this example, the deviation is 5 for a_1, -4 for a_2, and -1 for a_3. We can obtain the same quantity by squaring these three between-groups deviations, multiplying the squared deviations by the number of subjects in each group (n), and then summing the three products. That is,

$$SS_A = n(\overline{Y}_{A_1} - \overline{Y}_T)^2 + n(\overline{Y}_{A_2} - \overline{Y}_T)^2 + n(\overline{Y}_{A_3} - \overline{Y}_T)^2$$

In general, the equation becomes

$$SS_A = \Sigma n(\overline{Y}_A - \overline{Y}_T)^2 \tag{2-3}$$

which may be simplified by placing n, the sample size, to the left of the summation sign; that is, it is simpler to square and sum the deviations first and then to multiply by n. With this example,

$$SS_A = n\Sigma (\overline{Y}_A - \overline{Y}_T)^2$$

$$= 5[(5)^2 + (-4)^2 + (-1)^2]$$

$$= 5(25 + 16 + 1) = 5(42) = 210$$

Within-Groups Sum of Squares

The final sum of squares is the within-groups sum of squares, denoted by $SS_{S/A}$. The subscript S/A is read "S within A" and stresses the fact that we are dealing with the deviation of subjects from their own group means. As illustrated in Fig. 2–1, the basic deviation involved in the definition of the $SS_{S/A}$ is expressed by $Y - \overline{Y}_A$. As a first step, we can obtain a sum of squares for *each group* by using these within-group deviations. From Table 2–2,

$$SS_{S/A_1} = (1)^2 + (3)^2 + (-5)^2 + (-3)^2 + (4)^2 = 60$$

$$SS_{S/A_2} = (-2)^2 + (0)^2 + (2)^2 + (4)^2 + (-4)^2 = 40$$

$$SS_{S/A_3} = (-7)^2 + (1)^2 + (0)^2 + (4)^2 + (2)^2 = 70$$

In the analysis of variance, we will average the different within-group variances to obtain a more stable estimate of experimental error. As a first step, then, we will want to add together the separate within-group sums of squares, a process often referred to as **pooling**. In this example,

$$SS_{S/A} = SS_{S/A_1} + SS_{S/A_2} + SS_{S/A_3}$$

$$= 60 + 40 + 70 = 170$$

The equation for the pooled sum of squares may be expressed as follows:

$$SS_{S/A} = \Sigma (Y - \overline{Y}_A)^2 \tag{2-4}$$

where it is understood that the summation sign refers to all of the within-group deviations.

2.4   SUMS OF SQUARES: COMPUTATIONAL FORMULAS

Although the defining formulas for the three sums of squares preserve the logic by which the component deviations are derived, we usually calculate the sums of squares with formulas that are equivalent algebraically but much simpler computationally.

Notation

Before presenting the different formulas, I should say a few words about the notational system adopted for this book. The basic job of any notational system is to express unambiguously the arithmetic operations in the most complex of designs as well as in the simplest. The system used in this book is designed specifically for the analysis of variance and to facilitate the calculation of sums of squares. You probably will not fully appreciate the pedagogical advantages of this system until we turn to the analysis of more complicated designs.

There are three major advantages of this system. First, the system uses different capital letters or different combinations of letters to designate basic quantities needed to calculate sums of squares. The confusion generated by the more usual notational systems—which consist of subscripts, parentheses, and multiple summation signs with subscripts and superscripts—is avoided, and the differences in the arithmetical operations are emphasized and made more distinct. Second, the system is designed to facilitate the reiterative computational sequences that are a part of the various calculations. As you will see in Chap. 10, the notational system works in conjunction with a general analysis scheme that can be applied to nearly all the designs I will consider in this book. Finally, the system adopted for this edition is compatible with the notation introduced by Keppel and Zedeck (1989), in which analysis of variance and multiple regression are applied to the analysis of the same experimental designs.[1]

A notational system is essentially a code. The symbols constitute a shorthand for specifying the operations to be performed on the data of an experiment. In the analysis of the completely randomized single-factor design, we need to designate only *three* basic quantities: the individual scores or observations (the *raw data*), the sum of these scores for each treatment condition (the *treatment sums* or *subtotals*), and the sum of all the scores or observations (the *grand sum* or *grand total*).

The Individual Scores.   Each subject provides a single numerical value that reflects his or her performance on the response measure. This basic score or observation is designated by a single capital letter, Y. Table 2–3 illustrates the use of this notation with numbers obtained from the numerical example of Table 2–1. I have

---

[1]For the benefit of those who are familiar with earlier editions of this book, the major changes are the use of Y to designate an individual score, of n to represent sample size, and of more standard symbols for means. I have retained the letter coding for sums and computational formulas.

Table 2–3 A Summary of the Notational System

	Level a_1		Level a_2		Level a_3		Total
	$Y_{1,1}$ = 16		$Y_{2,1}$ = 4		$Y_{3,1}$ = 2		
	$Y_{1,2}$ = 18		$Y_{2,2}$ = 6		$Y_{3,2}$ = 10		
	$Y_{1,3}$ = 10		$Y_{2,3}$ = 8		$Y_{3,3}$ = 9		
	$Y_{1,4}$ = 12		$Y_{2,4}$ = 10		$Y_{3,4}$ = 13		
	$Y_{1,5}$ = 19		$Y_{2,5}$ = 2		$Y_{3,5}$ = 11		
Sums	A_1 = 75		A_2 = 30		A_3 = 45		$T = \Sigma A = 150$
No. of Observations	n_1 = 5		n_2 = 5		n_3 = 5		$(a)(n) = 15$
Means	$\overline{Y}_{A_1}$ = 15		$\overline{Y}_{A_2}$ = 6		$\overline{Y}_{A_3}$ = 9		$\overline{Y}_T = 10$

used numerical subscripts so that each score is specified uniquely. The first number in the subscript designates the level of factor A and the second number designates the particular subject within that treatment condition. To refer to a score without specifying any particular one, I use Y without a subscript, or occasionally, with letters as subscripts, Y_{ij}. Technically, then, the subscript i refers to the levels of the independent variable, factor A, and can take on values of $i = 1, 2, \ldots, a$ and the subscript j can take on values of $j = 1, 2, \ldots, n$.

The Treatment Sums. As a first step in the analysis, we will calculate the sums of the scores in each of the treatment groups. These subtotals, or treatment sums, are designated by a capital A to stand for the sums of the scores obtained under the levels of factor A. A numerical subscript permits the specification of the treatment sum for a particular treatment condition. The meaning of this symbol and the subscript are illustrated in Table 2–3. To designate a treatment sum without specifying any sum in particular, I will use A without a subscript, or occasionally with an i as a subscript: A_i. As a numerical example, the respective treatment sums for the three groups at levels a_1, a_2, and a_3 are

$$A_1 = 16 + 18 + 10 + 12 + 19 = 75$$
$$A_2 = 4 + 6 + 8 + 10 + 2 = 30$$
$$A_3 = 2 + 10 + 9 + 13 + 11 = 45$$

To obtain a numerical summary of the outcome of the experiment, we use the treatment sums to calculate the **treatment means**, $\overline{Y}_A$, by dividing each treatment sum by the number of scores in each of the conditions. In this book, I use a lower-case n to designate **sample size**, that is, the number of subjects in a treatment condition.[2] Thus, the formula for a treatment mean is

$$\overline{Y}_A = \frac{A}{n} \tag{2-5}$$

[2] In most of the designs I will consider, equal sample sizes (n) are used in the treatment conditions. Although this represents a special case, it subsumes most of the experiments conducted in the behavioral sciences. The analysis of unequal sample sizes is presented in Chap. 13.

To refer to specific treatment means, I use the number subscript. From the data in Table 2–3,

$$\overline{Y}_{A_1} = \frac{A_1}{n} = \frac{75}{5} = 15.00$$

$$\overline{Y}_{A_2} = \frac{A_2}{n} = \frac{30}{5} = 6.00$$

$$\overline{Y}_{A_3} = \frac{A_3}{n} = \frac{45}{5} = 9.00$$

The Grand Sum.   I designate the **grand sum** of the scores—that is, the sum of all the scores in the experiment—as T. Computationally, T may be calculated by summing the entire set of Y scores or by summing the treatment subtotals (A). Expressing these operations in symbols,

$$T = \Sigma Y = \Sigma A$$

(The first summation, ΣY, is read, "the sum of all the Y scores," and ΣA is read, "the sum of all the A treatment subtotals.") When we translate this sum into a mean (the **grand mean**), the mean is designated $\overline{Y}_T$. We calculate $\overline{Y}_T$ as we would any arithmetic mean, by dividing the sum of the scores by the number of scores. This number can be calculated by multiplying the number of scores in each treatment group (n) by the number of treatment groups, which we will designate a. In symbols, the total number of scores is $a \times n$, and the grand mean is

$$\overline{Y}_T = \frac{T}{(a)(n)} \tag{2–6}$$

From the numbers in Table 2–3, where $T = 75 + 30 + 45 = 150$, $a = 3$ treatment groups, and $n = 5$ subjects per group,

$$\overline{Y}_T = \frac{150}{(3)(5)} = 10.00$$

Basic Ratios

Each of the sums of squares is calculated by adding and subtracting special quantities that I call **basic ratios**. Basic ratios represent a common step in the computational formulas for sums of squares in the analysis of variance. All basic ratios have the same form and are calculated in a series of simple arithmetic steps. For the present design, there are three basic ratios, one involving the individual observations (Y), another involving the treatment subtotals (A), and the other involving the grand total (T).

The *numerator term* for any basic ratio involves two arithmetic steps:

1. The initial *squaring* of a set of quantities—the Y's, the A's, or T
2. *Summing* the squared quantities if more than one is present

To calculate the three required numerators, we simply conduct the two operations of squaring and then summing on each of the Y's, A's, and T, that is, ΣY^2, ΣA^2, and T^2, respectively. To illustrate, the first quantity indicates that we are to sum the squared scores for all the subjects in the experiment; using the data from Table 2–3, we have

$$\Sigma Y^2 = (16)^2 + (18)^2 + \ldots + (13)^2 + (11)^2 = 1,880$$

The second quantity specifies the sum of all the squared treatment sums; using the subtotals from Table 2–3, we get

$$\Sigma A^2 = (75)^2 + (30)^2 + (45)^2 = 5,625 + 900 + 2,025 = 8,550$$

The final quantity involves the grand total, which merely needs to be squared since there is only one such quantity in an experiment. From Table 2–3,

$$T^2 = (150)^2 = 22,500$$

The *denominator term* for any basic ratio is found by applying a simple rule that depends on the particular term appearing in the numerator:

Whatever the term, we divide by the number of scores that contributed to that term.

For example, if the term is T, we divide by $(a)(n)$ because this is the number of scores that are actually summed to produce T. If the term is A, we divide by n because this is the number of scores that are summed to produce any one of the A treatment sums. Finally, if the term is Y, we divide by one, because a Y score is based on a *single* observation; this is equivalent, of course, to not dividing at all— that is, $\Sigma Y^2/1 = \Sigma Y^2$.

We are now ready to consider the formulas for the three basic ratios. For convenience in presenting computational formulas, I designate each basic ratio by a "bracket term"—a notational symbol consisting of a pair of brackets enclosing the letter appearing in the numerator of the basic ratio, that is, $[Y]$ for the Y scores, $[A]$ for the treatment sums, and $[T]$ for the grand total. The formulas for the three basic ratios are

$$[T] = \frac{T^2}{(a)(n)} \tag{2–7}$$

$$[A] = \frac{\Sigma A^2}{n} \tag{2–8}$$

$$[Y] = \Sigma Y^2 \tag{2–9}$$

Applying these new formulas to the partial answers we have already calculated, we find

$$[T] = \frac{22{,}500}{(3)(5)} = 1{,}500.00$$

$$[A] = \frac{8{,}550}{5} = 1{,}710.00$$

$$[Y] = 1{,}880$$

Sums of Squares

All that remains is to specify how the three basic ratios are combined to produce the three required sums of squares, SS_T, SS_A, and $SS_{S/A}$. This final step is accomplished simply by noting that each of the three deviations appearing in the defining formulas presented in Sec. 2.3 separately indicates how the basic ratios are combined to form the appropriate computational formulas. To illustrate, the total sum of squares is based on the following deviation:

$$Y - \overline{Y}_T$$

The computational formula combines the two basic ratios identified by this deviation, $[Y]$ and $[T]$, as follows:

$$SS_T = [Y] - [T] \tag{2–10}$$

or more completely,

$$SS_T = \Sigma Y^2 - \frac{T^2}{(a)(n)} \tag{2–11}$$

Substituting the quantities we calculated in the last section, we find

$$SS_T = [Y] - [T]$$
$$= 1{,}880 - 1{,}500.00 = 380.00$$

The treatment sum of squares, SS_A, is based on the deviation of the treatment means from the grand mean:

$$\overline{Y}_A - \overline{Y}_T$$

The computational formula combines the two ratios identified by this deviation as follows:

$$SS_A = [A] - [T] \tag{2–12}$$

or more fully,

$$SS_A = \frac{\Sigma A^2}{n} - \frac{T^2}{(a)(n)} \tag{2–13}$$

Substituting the quantities calculated previously, we find

$$SS_A = [A] - [T]$$
$$= 1,710.00 - 1,500.00 = 210.00$$

Finally, the within-groups sum of squares is based on the deviation of individual observations from the relevant treatment mean, that is,

$$Y - \overline{Y}_A$$

The computational formula combines the two ratios identified by these deviations as follows:

$$SS_{S/A} = [Y] - [A] \tag{2-14}$$

or

$$SS_T = \Sigma Y^2 - \frac{\Sigma A^2}{n} \tag{2-15}$$

Substituting the quantities from the last section, we obtain

$$SS_{S/A} = [Y] - [A]$$
$$= 1,880 - 1,710.00 = 170.00$$

As a computational check and as a demonstration of the relationship among these three sums of squares, we will apply Eq. (2–1) to these calculations:[3]

$$SS_T = SS_A + SS_{S/A} = 210.00 + 170.00 = 380.00$$

Comment

You can verify for yourself that the computational formulas produced exactly the same answers as those obtained with the defining formulas previously. The only time different answers are found is when rounding errors introduced in calculating the treatment means and the grand mean become magnified in squaring the deviations, but even then the differences will be small. Although we will focus almost entirely on the computational versions of the formulas because they are easy to use and can be generated by a simple set of rules, you should keep in mind that they are

---

[3]A complete check of all our calculations may be obtained in a number of ways. One obvious method is to perform the analysis again or, perhaps better still, to coax another person to go through the calculations independently. An alternative method is to add a constant, say, 1, to each Y score (that is, to use $Y + 1$) and to repeat the complete analysis. For example, the original scores in level a_1 (16, 18, 10, 12, and 19) would become 17, 19, 11, 13, and 20, respectively. If you have made no error in either set of calculations, you should end up with *identical* sums of squares in the two analyses. The addition of a constant does not change the basic *deviations*, on which the sums of squares are based, but it does change the actual numbers entering into the calculations when we use the computational formulas presented in this section.

equivalent to the defining versions, which reflect quite directly the logic behind the derivation of the sums of squares required for the analysis of variance.

2.5   SUMMARY

I considered first some of the logic underlying the process of hypothesis testing in a design where each subject serves in only one treatment condition. By way of summary, we can describe hypothesis testing as consisting of a contrast between two sets of differences. One of these sets is obtained from a comparison involving differences among the treatment means; these differences are often referred to as *between-groups* differences. The other set is obtained from a comparison involving differences among subjects receiving the same treatment within a treatment group; these differences are called *within-groups* differences. I argued that the between-groups differences are the result of the combined effects of the experimental treatment and of experimental error, whereas the within-groups differences represent the influence of experimental error alone. You saw that the comparison ratio,

$$\frac{\text{between-groups differences}}{\text{within-groups differences}}$$

provides a numerical index that is "sensitive" to the presence of treatment effects in the population. That is, with no treatment effects, the long-run expectation is that the ratio will approximate 1.0 since the treatment effects will be zero and we will be dividing one estimate of experimental error by the other. On the other hand, whenever there are treatment effects, the expectation is that the ratio will be greater than 1.0.

The statistical hypothesis we test, the null hypothesis, specifies the *absence* of treatment effects in the population. With the help of statistical tables and a set of decision rules, neither of which I have described yet, we can decide whether or not it is reasonable to reject the null hypothesis. If we reject the null hypothesis, we accept the alternative statistical hypothesis, which specifies the presence of treatment effects in the population. If we fail to reject the null hypothesis, essentially we conclude that the independent variable produced no systematic differences in the experiment.

The remainder of the chapter focused on the translation of these ideas into actual measures of variability based on the data of a single-factor experiment. You saw that between-groups and within-groups differences can be expressed as deviations from different means. I began by considering the deviation of Y scores from $\overline{Y}_T$ and established the fact that for each observation this deviation may be divided into a between-group deviation $\overline{Y}_A - \overline{Y}_T$ and a within-groups deviation $Y - \overline{Y}_A$. You saw that the defining formulas for the corresponding sums of squares were developed directly from these deviations. Our actual calculations, however, are performed with computational formulas, which are considerably easier to use and can be formed by using a set of simple rules. In the next chapter, I will complete the steps in the statistical evaluation of the null hypothesis.

2.6   EXERCISES[4]

1. In an experiment involving $a = 5$ treatment conditions, the following measures were obtained:

a_1	a_2	a_3	a_4	a_5
13	7	12	10	13
9	4	11	12	6
8	4	4	9	14
7	1	9	7	12
8	10	5	15	13
6	7	10	14	10
6	5	2	10	8
7	9	8	17	4
6	5	3	14	9
10	8	6	12	11

a. Calculate the sum of the scores and the sum of the squared scores for each of the treatment groups.

b. Calculate the treatment means.

c. Calculate the sums of squares for each of the sources of variability normally identified in the analysis of variance, that is, SS_A, $SS_{S/A}$, and SS_T. Reserve this information for problem 3 in the exercises for Chap. 3.

[4]The answers to this problem are found in Appendix B.

3

Variance Estimates and the Evaluation of the F Ratio

We are ready to complete the analysis of variance. As you will see, the remaining calculations are quite simple and easy to follow, whereas the theoretical justification of the procedures is complicated and considerably more abstract. Consequently, I will present the calculations quickly and devote a major portion of this chapter to an explanation of these procedures and a discussion of the possible consequences stemming from the evaluation of the null hypothesis.

3.1 VARIANCE ESTIMATES (MEAN SQUARES)

The complete analysis of variance is outlined in Table 3–1 in an arrangement called a **summary table**. The first column lists the sources of variances usually extracted from the analysis. The second column gives the three basic ratios that are combined in different patterns to produce the sums of squares. These patterns are indicated in the third column. To be useful in the analysis, the two component sums of squares must be converted to variances, or **mean squares**, as variances are called in the analysis of variance. In this context, a variance is defined by the equation

$$\text{variance} = \frac{SS}{df} \tag{3-1}$$

where SS refers to the component sum of squares and df represents the **degrees of freedom** associated with the SS.

Degrees of Freedom

The degrees of freedom, or df, associated with a sum of squares correspond to the number of scores with *independent information* that enter into the calculation of the sum of squares. Consider, for example, the use of a single sample mean to estimate the population mean. If we want to estimate the population variance as well, we must take account of the fact that we have already used up some of the independent information in estimating the population mean.

Let's examine a concrete example. Suppose that we have five observations in our experiment and that we determine the mean of the scores to be 7.0. This mean is used to estimate the population mean. With the number of observations set at

Table 3–1 Summary of the Analysis of Variance

Source	Basic Ratio	SS	df	MS	F
A	$[A] = \dfrac{\sum A^2}{n}$	$[A] - [T]$	$a - 1$	$\dfrac{SS_A}{df_A}$	$\dfrac{MS_A}{MS_{S/A}}$
S/A	$[Y] = \sum Y^2$	$[Y] - [A]$	$(a)(n - 1)$	$\dfrac{SS_{S/A}}{df_{S/A}}$	
Total	$[T] = \dfrac{T^2}{(a)(n)}$	$[Y] - [T]$	$(a)(n) - 1$		

five and the population mean set at 7.0, how much independent information remains for the estimate of the population variance? The answer is the number of
observations that are free to vary—that is, to take on any value whatsoever. The
number in this example is four, one less than the total number of observations. The
reason for this loss of "freedom" is that although we are free to select any value
for the first four scores, the final score is already determined. More specifically,
the total sum of all five must equal 35, so that the mean of the sample will equal
7.0; as soon as four scores are selected, the fifth score is fixed and can be obtained
by subtraction. In a sense, then, estimating the population mean places a restraint
on the values that the scores are free to take. The general rule for computing the df
of any sum of squares is

$$df = \begin{pmatrix} \text{number of} \\ \text{independent} \\ \text{observations} \end{pmatrix} - \begin{pmatrix} \text{number of} \\ \text{restraints} \end{pmatrix} \qquad (3\text{–}2)$$

or

$$df = \begin{pmatrix} \text{number of} \\ \text{independent} \\ \text{observations} \end{pmatrix} - \begin{pmatrix} \text{number of} \\ \text{population} \\ \text{estimates} \end{pmatrix} \qquad (3\text{–}3)$$

The df associated with each sum of squares in the analysis of variance are
presented in the fourth column of Table 3–1. We can calculate the df for each sum
of squares by applying Eq. (3–2). For the SS_A, there are a basic observations—that
is, a different sample means. Since 1 df is lost as a result of estimating the overall population mean μ_T from the grand mean $\overline{Y}_T$ of the experiment, $df_A = a$
$- 1$. For the $SS_{S/A}$, the calculation of the df is more complicated. This sum of
squares represents a pooling of separate estimates of experimental error obtained from the different treatment groups (see p. 33 for a demonstration of
this point). If we consider any one of these groups—the ith group—there are n
basic observations; we will lose 1 df, however, by estimating the mean of the
treatment population (μ_i). Thus, there are $df = n - 1$ for each of the treatment
groups. The total number of df for the $SS_{S/A}$ is found by pooling the df for each
group, just as we pool the corresponding sums of squares. The formula given in
Table 3–1,

$$df_{S/A} = (a)(n - 1)$$

simply has us multiply the df for any one of the groups ($n - 1$) by the number of
different groups (a). The df for the SS_T are obtained by subtracting 1 df from the
total number of independent observations, $(a)(n)$. As a check, we can verify that
the df's associated with the component sums of squares sum to df_T. That is,

$$df_T = df_A + df_{S/A}$$

and

$$(a)(n) - 1 = (a - 1) + (a)(n - 1) = a - 1 + (a)(n) - a = (a)(n) - 1$$

Mean Squares

The actual variance estimates, which, as I have already indicated, are called mean squares (MS), appear in the next column of Table 3–1. The mean squares for the two component sources of variance are given by the formula

$$MS = \frac{SS}{df} \tag{3–4}$$

or more specifically,

$$MS_A = \frac{SS_A}{df_A} \text{ and } MS_{S/A} = \frac{SS_{S/A}}{df_{S/A}}$$

The first mean square estimates the combined presence of treatment effects plus error variance, and the second mean square independently estimates error variance alone.

3.2   THE F RATIO

The final step in the calculations is the formation of the F ratio. The formula is listed in the last column of Table 3–1 and consists of the treatment mean square MS_A divided by the within-groups mean square $MS_{S/A}$. (The denominator of the F ratio, $MS_{S/A}$, is often called the **error term**, for obvious reasons.) From the arguments advanced in the last chapter, the average value of F, obtained by averaging an extremely large number of F's from imaginary experiments drawn repeatedly from the same theoretical treatment populations, is approximately 1.0 when the null hypothesis is true and is greater than 1.0 when the null hypothesis is false. I will return to this argument in the next section, following the completion of the numerical example we used in the last chapter to illustrate the calculation of the sums of squares.

The results of these earlier calculations are presented in Table 3–2. If you will recall, there were $a = 3$ treatment conditions and $n = 5$ subjects in this example; the original data may be found in Table 2–3.

The df's for the three sources of variance are obtained by simple substitution into the formulas listed in Table 3–1. The results of these substitutions are presented in the summary table. Specifically,

$$df_A = a - 1 = 3 - 1 = 2$$
$$df_{S/A} = (a)(n - 1) = 3(5 - 1) = (3)(4) = 12$$
$$df_T = (a)(n) - 1 = (3)(5) - 1 = 15 - 1 = 14$$

Table 3–2   Summary Table

Source	SS	df	MS	F
A	210.00	2	105.00	7.41
S/A	170.00	12	14.17	
Total	380.00	14		

We can check our separate calculations by verifying that the df's obtained for the component sums of squares equal the df obtained for the SS_T. That is,

$$df_T = df_A + df_{S/A} = 2 + 12 = 14$$

The two variance estimates (mean squares) are found by dividing the SS by the appropriate df. In this example,

$$MS_A = \frac{210.00}{2} = 105.00 \text{ and } MS_{S/A} = \frac{170.00}{12} = 14.17$$

These numbers are entered in the MS column of the table. Last, the F ratio becomes

$$F = \frac{MS_A}{MS_{S/A}} = \frac{105.00}{14.17} = 7.41$$

This value of F is larger than 1.0, bringing into question the correctness of the null hypothesis. On the other hand, we might have obtained a ratio this large (or larger) merely by virtue of the fact that the two mean squares are independent estimates of error variance when H_0 is true.

3.3   EVALUATING THE F RATIO

Sampling Distribution of F

In view of the minimal mathematical background assumed for the readers of this book, a reasonable approach to this topic is empirical rather than theoretical. Suppose we had available a large population of scores and that we drew at random three sets of 15 scores each. We can think of the three sets as representing the results of an actual experiment, with $a = 3$ and $n = 15$, for which we know the null hypothesis is *true*. That is, the scores placed in each "treatment" condition were in fact drawn from the *same* population. Thus, $\mu_1 = \mu_2 = \mu_3$. The two mean squares, MS_A and $MS_{S/A}$, are independent estimates of experimental error; we may estimate the operation of the same chance factors either by looking at the variability among the three sample means or by looking at the pooled variability of the scores within each of the samples.

Assume that we draw a very large number of such "experiments," each consisting of three groups of 15 scores each, and that we compute the value of F for each case. If we group the F's according to size, we can construct a graph relating F and frequency of occurrence. A frequency distribution of a statistic such as F is called a **sampling distribution** of the statistic.

This sort of empirical sampling study is called a *Monte Carlo* experiment. A sampling distribution of F, based on 1,000 experiments of the sort we have been discussing, is presented in Fig. 3–1. The population consisted of 6,000 scores; the sampling and calculations were performed on a high-speed computer.[1] The results

[1]The results of this sampling experiment were generously made available to me by Drs. Curtis D. Hardyck and Lewis F. Petrinovich.

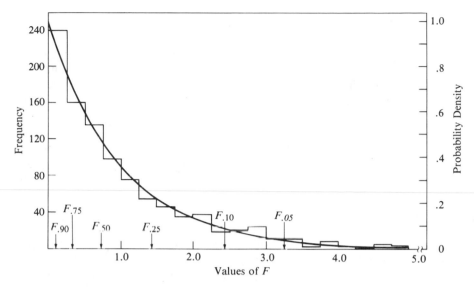

FIGURE 3–1   Empirical and theoretical sampling distributions of $F(2, 42)$.

of the experiments, which are plotted as a histogram, exhibit a regular trend, the frequency of cases tending to drop off rapidly with increasing values of F. The smoothed curve represents the *theoretical* sampling distribution of F. The approximation of the theoretical curve to the empirically obtained sampling distribution is extremely close. This correspondence provides a convincing intuitive meaning to the F distribution—namely, that it *is* the sampling distribution of F obtained when an infinitely large number of experiments, of the sort we have been discussing, are performed.

In evaluating the null hypothesis, we could use information drawn from either the empirical or the theoretical sampling distributions. The great advantage of knowing the mathematical properties of the F distribution is that the sampling distribution can be determined for any experiment of any size—that is, any number of groups and any number of subjects within these groups.

Let us return to Fig. 3–1 and see what useful information we can obtain from the F distribution. If we know the exact shape of the F distribution for a given experiment, we can make statements concerning how common or how rare an F observed in an actual experiment is. The F distribution is the sampling distribution of F when the population means are equal. If we consider a particular value of F, we can determine (with a working knowledge of the calculus) the probability of obtaining an F that large or larger by finding the percentage of the area under the curve that falls to the right of an ordinate erected at the value of F in question. Several values of F have been indicated in Fig. 3–1. The proportion of the curve falling to the right of F is indicated as a subscript. For example, only 10 percent of the time would we expect to obtain a value of F equal to or greater than 2.44 (symbolized $F \geq 2.44$). Stated another way, this probability represents the proportion of F's greater than or equal to 2.44 that will occur on the basis of chance factors alone.

The F Table.   The F distribution is actually a family of curves. The exact shape of any one of the curves is determined by the number of df's associated with the numerator and denominator mean squares in the F ratio. If we hold the numerator df (the number of treatment groups) constant and vary the denominator df (based on the number of subjects within groups), we will see relatively small changes in the shape of the curves. On the other hand, changing the number of treatment groups produces curves of quite different appearance. An example of another F distribution, with numerator and denominator df's equal to 4 and 10, respectively, is sketched in Fig. 3–2. As a shorthand way of referring to a particular F dististribution, we will use the expression $F(df_{num.}, df_{denom.})$, or in this case, $F(4, 10)$.

For our experiment, we do not have to know the exact shape of the F distribution. The only information we need is the value of F, to the right of which certain proportions of the area under the curve fall. These values have been tabulated and are readily available. An F table is found in Table A–1 of Appendix A. A particular value of F in this table is specified by three factors: (1) the numerator df (represented by the columns of the table), (2) the denominator df (represented by the main rows of the table), and (3) the value of α (represented by the rows listed for each denominator df), where α refers to the proportion of area to the right of an ordinate drawn at F_{α}.

For example, the value of $F(4, 10)$ is 3.48 at $\alpha = .05$. This F is found by locating the intersection of the column at $df_{num.} = 4$ and the row at $df_{denom.} = 10$. The different values of $F(4, 10)$ in this location represent critical points for a number of different α levels. The one we want is at $\alpha = .05$. What this value of F

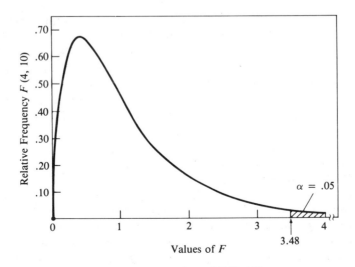

FIGURE 3–2   Theoretical sampling distribution of F (4, 10).

means is that an ordinate drawn at $F(4, 10) = 3.48$ will divide the sampling distribution of $F(4, 10)$ at a point where the proportion of the area under the curve to the right is .05. Said another way, $\alpha \times 100 = .05 \times 100$, which means that 5 percent of the area under the curve falls to the right of an ordinate drawn at $F(4, 10) = 3.48$. For $\alpha = .25$, $F(4, 10) = 1.59$, and for $\alpha = .01$, $F(4, 10) = 5.99$; 25 percent and 1 percent of the sampling distribution of $F(4, 10)$ fall to the right of these respective points.

Obviously, not all possible combinations of these three factors are listed in the table. The α levels, $\alpha = .25, .10, .05, .025, .01$, and $.001$, are ones most commonly encountered. Additional levels of α can be found in the different editions of Fisher and Yates (for example, 1953) and of Pearson and Hartley (for example, 1970) or in the more convenient tables of Dixon and Massey (1957). The intervals between successive columns and rows increase with the larger numerator and denominator df's. For instance, the $df_{num.}$ include entries for consecutive values of df from 1 to 10; the next columns are $df_{num.} = 12, 15, 20, 24, 30, 40, 60$, and ∞. The $df_{denom.}$ increase consecutively from 1 to 20, by 2's from 20 to 30, and then by the sequence 40, 60, 120, and ∞. Fine gradations are not needed for the larger df values since the numerical values of F do not change greatly from interval to interval.

I have only considered the sampling distribution of F when the null hypothesis is *true*—that is, when the population means are equal. Obviously, we do not intend to conduct many experiments in which this is the case. We perform an experiment because we expect to find treatment effects. Suppose we assume that H_0 is false. What should happen to the F ratio? From previous discussions, I have argued that the average or **expected value** of the ratio should be greater than 1.0 because the MS_A contains two components, treatment effects and experimental error, whereas the $MS_{S/A}$ is the result of experimental error alone. The sampling distribution of the F ratio under these circumstances is no longer the F distribution. Instead, the theoretical distribution is called F' or **noncentral F**. It would be nice to be able to draw the F' distribution and to compare it with a corresponding F distribution. Unfortunately, however, this is difficult to do since the F' distribution is a function of the *magnitude* of the treatment effects as well as the numerator and denominator df's. Thus, although there is only one F distribution at any combination of numerator and denominator df's, there is a family of F' distributions, one distribution for each value that the treatment effects may take. On the other hand, we can say that the F' distribution will be shifted to the right of the F distribution and will be centered over numerically larger values of F'. This means, then, that whenever the null hypothesis is false, we will expect to find values of F that on the average are larger than 1.0, the value expected when the null hypothesis is true.

Test of the Null Hypothesis

We are now ready to piece together this information concerning the sampling distributions of F and F' to provide a test of the null hypothesis. We start our testing procedure by specifying H_0 and H_1, the null and alternative statistical hypotheses. To review briefly an earlier discussion, the two hypotheses are

H_0 : all μ_i's are equal

H_1 : not all μ_i's are equal

The hypothesis we will test, the null hypothesis, assumes that the means of the treatment populations are equal. The alternative hypothesis is a mutually exclusive statement, which generally asserts simply that some of the population treatment means are not equal—that is, that some treatment effects are present. We choose this particular null hypothesis because it is usually the only hypothesis that we can state *exactly*. There is no ambiguity in the assertion that the population means are equal; there is only one way in which this can happen. The alternative hypothesis is an *inexact* statement—an assertion that the population means are not all equal. Nothing is said about the actual differences that are in the population. (If we had that sort of information, we would have no reason for conducting the experiment.) Another advantage of this particular null hypothesis is that the sampling distribution of F is known. Presumably the sampling distribution of F' can be worked out, but we will need a different distribution for treatment effects of different sizes. Just how we use the sampling distribution of F in evaluating the null hypothesis will be considered next.

Assume that we have conducted an experiment and that we have computed the value of F. What we have to decide is whether it is more likely that this value of F came from the F distribution or from the F' distribution. Logically, it could have come from only one, but which one? Since we are evaluating the null hypothesis, we will turn our attention to the F distribution. Although some values of F are less likely to occur than others, it is still possible theoretically to obtain any value of F in an experiment when the null hypothesis is true. From one point of view our situation is hopeless: If any value of F may have been the result of chance factors, we can never be certain that the F we observe in an experiment was *not* drawn from the F distribution. Agreed. If we were to take this attitude, however, we would never be able to use the experimental method as a way of finding out about the world. That is, if we maintain that any difference among the sample means may be due to chance, there is no way that we can conclude that our experimental manipulations influenced behavior differentially. As Fisher (1951) puts it, ". . . an experiment would be useless of which no possible result would satisfy [us]"(p. 13). We will not take this attitude. We must be willing to make mistakes in rejecting the null hypothesis when H_0 is true; otherwise, we can never reject the null hypothesis.

Suppose we could agree on a dividing line for any F distribution, where values of F falling above the line are considered to be unlikely and values of F falling below the line are considered to be likely. We would then see whether our observed F falls above or below this arbitrary dividing line. If the F falls above the line, we will conclude that the observed F is *incompatible* with the null hypothesis; that is, we will reject H_0 and conclude that the alternative hypothesis is true. If the F falls below the line, we will conclude that the observed F is *compatible* with the null hypothesis. Under these circumstances, then, we will retain H_0. Following such a set of rules means that we will be able to conclude that our independent variable was effective, provided an F ratio is obtained that falls within the region of incompatibility. But it also means that we are willing to make a mistake by rejecting a true null hypothesis a certain proportion of the time.

Decision Rules

The crux of the problem, of course, is to find a way of objectively defining the regions of "compatibility" and "incompatibility." If the null hypothesis is true, we can determine the sampling distribution of F. Suppose we find a point on this distribution beyond which the probability of occurrence is very, very small. (The probability is represented by the proportion of the total area under the curve that appears beyond this particular point.) We will arbitrarily consider values of F falling within this region as incompatible with the null hypothesis. We must identify such a region to be able to reject the null hypothesis. Our decision rule, then, is to reject the null hypothesis when the observed F falls within the region of incompatibility. We do so, knowing full well that we may be making the wrong decision, which would be the case if the null hypothesis really were true.

Suppose, now, that we begin to enlarge the region of incompatibility, by moving the critical point of transition to the left—toward the larger portion of the curve—and cumulate the probabilities associated with these new portions of the curve. As we increase the size of this region, we also increase the chance of observing values from this region. Said another way, increasing the region of incompatibility results in the inclusion of F's that are becoming increasingly more *compatible* with the null hypothesis. Theoretically, an investigator may pick any cumulative probability, just so long as the decision is made before the start of the experiment. In practice, however, there is fairly common agreement on a cumulative probability of $\alpha = .05$ to define the region of incompatibility for the F distribution. This probability is called the **significance level**.

We are now in a position to state more formally the decision rules that are followed after the calculation of the F ratio.[2] If the F value falls within the region of incompatibility, the null hypothesis is rejected and the alternative hypothesis is accepted. If the F value falls within the region of compatibility, the null hypothesis is not rejected. (These two regions are often called the regions of *rejection* and *nonrejection*.) The decision to reject or not is made by comparing the observed value of F with the value of F located at the critical point of transition. Symbolically, the rules are stated,

$$\text{Reject } H_0 \text{ when } F_{observed} \geq F_{(\alpha)}(df_{num.}, df_{denom.}); \qquad (3\text{--}5)$$
$$\text{otherwise, retain } H_0$$

In this statement, α refers to the significance level, and $df_{num.}$ and $df_{denom.}$ to the df's associated with the numerator and denominator of the F ratio, respectively.

There is often some confusion concerning the exact wording of the decision rules, stemming largely from the fact that we cannot *prove* a hypothesis, only *disprove* it. When we say that a particular hypothesis is "accepted," we do not mean

---

[2] Hays (1973, pp. 332–375) provides a detailed discussion of this decision process.

that it has been proved—just that it is consistent with the facts. Thus, if we reject H_0, this means that the results of the experiment are consistent with the alternative hypothesis that some of the treatment means are different; in this sense, then, we accept H_1. By the same token, if we retain H_0, this means that we consider the results of the experiment consistent with the hypothesis that the treatment means are equal. It is in this sense, too, that we are accepting the null hypothesis. We will consider further the issue of "proving" statistical hypotheses in Sec. 4.6.

I will illustrate the use of Eq. (3–5) with the F we calculated earlier in this chapter (see Table 3–2). In this example, $df_{num.} = 2$ and $df_{denom.} = 12$. If we set $\alpha = .05$, the critical value of F, which we find in the tabled values of the F distribution (Table A–1 of Appendix A), is 3.89. The rejection region consists of all values of F equal to or greater than 3.89. Substituting in Eq. (3–5), the decision rules become

Reject H_0 when $F_{observed} \geq 3.89$; otherwise, retain H_0

Since the F obtained in this example exceeded this value ($F = 7.41$), we would conclude that treatment effects were present in this experiment.

Other Significance Levels.   Although most researchers adopt $\alpha = .05$ as their personal significance level, occasionally you will see other probability levels reported in the research literature. A researcher will sometimes report that an F is significant at the 1 percent level of significance, for example, as a convenience for readers who may have adopted a more stringent criterion for rejecting the null hypothesis than 5 percent. To illustrate, I could have reported the outcome of the F test summarized in Table 3–2 as

$F(2, 12) = 7.41, p < .01$

which means that this value of F falls within a rejection region having an α level that is less than a probability (p) of .01. (An inspection of the F table indicates that the critical value of F at $\alpha = .01$ is 6.93.) This statement indicates that the null hypothesis would be rejected by any researcher who had adopted a significance level equal to 1 percent or larger. The main problem with this practice is that it tends to reinforce the false belief that a finding significant at $p < .01$ is somehow "better" or "stronger" than a finding significant at $p < .05$. As you will see in Chap. 4, comparisons of "strength" are more appropriately made by obtaining some measure of *effect magnitude* rather than by comparing significance levels in this manner.

Occasionally researchers will report the **exact probability** of $F_{observed}$, a value that is provided automatically by most statistical computer programs. (The exact probability refers to the proportion of the sampling distribution of the F statistic falling at or above the F found in an experiment.) The F of 7.41, for example, has an exact probability of $p = .008023$. Armed with this information, we do not need to consult an F table to determine significance, but instead we simply compare the exact probability with our personal significance level and reject H_0 if the exact probability is smaller than our chosen significance level. Assuming that this significance level is .05, we can state the decision rule quite simply, without specific reference to F as follows:

If $p \leq .05$, reject H_0; otherwise, retain H_0

In whatever manner a statistical test is reported, however, you must not forget that you choose your significance level *before* the start of an experiment and that alternative ways of reporting probabilities do not change this fundamental point. Some researchers make a practice of announcing their significance level before they present the results of an experiment in a research article, allowing them to report the outcome of statistical tests simply as "significant" or "not significant," which avoids the potential confusion created when different significance levels appear among a string of statistical tests.

Summary

You have seen that a statistical test begins with the specification of the null and alternative hypotheses. We then conduct our experiment and calculate an F ratio. Next, we judge whether we have obtained an F that is incompatible with the hypothesis that the means of the treatment populations are equal. Incompatibility is defined arbitrarily ahead of time as an F that would occur on the basis of chance, assuming H_0 is true, a small proportion of the time, for example, 1 time in 20 (5 percent). If the $F_{observed}$ falls within this region of incompatibility, we reject the null hypothesis; if it falls within the region of compatibility, we retain the null hypothesis.

3.4   ERRORS IN HYPOTHESIS TESTING

The procedures we follow in hypothesis testing do not guarantee that a correct inference will be drawn when we apply the decision rules enumerated in Eq. (3 5). On the contrary, whether or not we decide to reject the null hypothesis, we will be making either a correct decision or an incorrect decision, depending on the state of affairs in the real world—that is, the population. The two types of errors that we can commit are defined in Table 3–3. There are two states that "reality" can take: Either the null hypothesis is true or it is false. And there are two decisions that we may make: Either reject H_0 or do not. The four possible combinations of states of reality and types of decisions are enumerated in the table. Inspection reveals two situations in which we will make the correct decision, that is, no error of inference: (1) if we reject H_0 when it is false and (2) if we retain H_0 when it is true. On the other hand, in two complementary situations we will make an incorrect decision, that is, an error of inference: (1) if we reject H_0 when it is *true* and (2) if we retain H_0 when it is false. These errors of inference are called **type I and type II errors** or **α and β errors**, respectively. You should note that α and β are actually conditional

Table 3–3   Errors in Hypothesis Testing

	REALITY	
DECISION	H_0 *True,* H_1 *False*	H_0 *False,* H_1 *True*
Reject H_0, *Accept H_1*	Incorrect decision: type I error	Correct decision
Retain H_0, *Do not accept H_1*	Correct decision	Incorrect decision: type II error

probabilities since α is the probability of error given (that is, conditional) that H_0 is true and β is the probability of error given that H_1 is true.

To illustrate the two types of errors, we will consider a geometrical example. The upper panel in Fig. 3–3 represents the theoretical distribution of F when the null hypothesis is true—that is, when there are no treatment effects. The region of rejection, which is specified by the shaded area to the right of the ordinate at F_α, represents the magnitude of the type I error. That is, an F that falls within this region will lead to a rejection of the null hypothesis and thus constitutes a type I error. The probability with which this will occur is α. The unshaded area to the left of F_α represents the probability of making a correct inference and is equal to $1 - \alpha$.

The middle panel represents the theoretical distribution of F when the alternative hypothesis is true.[3] The region of rejection is again specified by the area to the right of F_α. It is clear that the critical value of F defining the beginning of the rejection region is the same in these two situations. The reason is that we set F_α with the null hypothesis in mind, and we are now considering the consequences of having set this rejection region when the alternative hypothesis is true. Consider, then, the rejection region—the area to the right of F_α. This area represents the probability of making a correct inference under these circumstances. The shaded area to the left of F_α (the region of nonrejection) represents the probability of making a type II error (β).

The bottom panel brings together the two separate distributions. The reciprocity of the two types of error is evident. Any change in the size of the rejection region (the area to the right of F_α) will produce changes in opposite directions for the two types of error. To be more specific, by moving the point of transition (F_α) to the right—that is, lowering the α level—we decrease the type I error and increase the type II error. By moving F_α to the left—that is, raising the α level—we increase the type I error and decrease the type II error.

It should be realized that a different display is needed for each particular alternative hypothesis we might consider. To make the point, however, it is sufficient to consider only one alternative hypothesis. The F distribution under the null hypothesis will not change with other alternative hypotheses. What does change is

---

[3]The exact shape and location of this distribution depends on a number of factors, including the actual difference between the population treatment means. In general, the noncentral F distribution is more spread out and more symmetrical than the F distribution, as we have depicted in the drawing. In any case, the argument still holds.

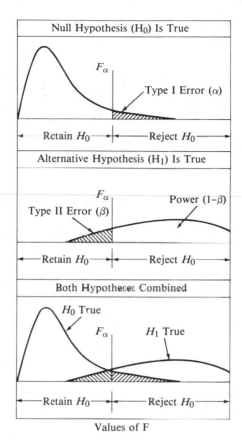

FIGURE 3–3   *Sampling distribution of the F ratio when the null hypothesis is true (top panel) and when the alternative hypothesis is true (middle panel). The two sampling distributions are shown together in the bottom panel.*

the location of the distribution of noncentral F. With an alternative hypothesis that specifies larger treatment effects than those depicted here, the noncentral F distribution will move to the right. Again, since F_α remains the same, this displacement of the distribution reduces the type II error. Similarly, a reduction in the treatment effects will move the distribution to the left and increase the type II error.

A quantitative index of the sensitivity of an experiment is its **power**. Power refers to the probability of rejecting the null hypothesis when an alternative hypothesis is true. Said another way, power represents the probability that a statistical test of the null hypothesis will result in the conclusion that the phenomenon under study exists. In this sense, power is interpreted as the probability of making a correct decision when the null hypothesis is false.

Power is usually defined in terms of the probability of making a type II error (β). Specifically,

$$\text{power} = 1 - \beta \tag{3–6}$$

Thus, the smaller the type II error (β), the greater the power and, therefore, the greater the sensitivity of the test. I will discuss this important concept in more detail in the next chapter.

As long as we are committed to making decisions in the face of incomplete knowledge, as every scientist is, we cannot avoid making these errors. We can, however, try to *minimize* them. We directly control the size of the type I error in our selection of significance level. By setting a region of rejection, we are taking a calculated risk that a certain proportion of the time (for example, $\alpha = .05$), we will obtain F's that fall into this region when the null hypothesis is true.

How can we control type II error? We have already considered an obvious procedure: to increase the rejection region. Of course, we do so at the cost of an increase in type I errors. Every researcher must strike a balance between the two types of error. If it is important to discover new facts, then we may be willing to accept more type I errors and thus *increase* the rejection region. On the other hand, if it is important not to clog up the literature with false facts, which is one way to view type I errors, then we may be willing to accept more type II errors and *decrease* the rejection region. Arguments can be made for both sides of this type I/type II coin (see, for example, Bakan, 1966; Keppel, 1973, pp. 153–155). We will return to the problem of balancing these two related errors in Chap. 8. As you will see in Chap. 4 and in subsequent chapters, we are able to control type II errors in a variety of other ways. For the time being, I will just mention two useful procedures for decreasing type II, namely, by adding to the number of observations in each treatment condition and by reducing error variance through the design of a more precisely controlled experiment.

3.5   A COMPLETE NUMERICAL EXAMPLE

Now that we have looked at each step of the one-factor analysis of variance, it is time to work through a numerical example from start to finish. Suppose a team of researchers is interested in the effect of sleep deprivation on the ability of subjects to perform a vigilance task, such as locating objects moving on a radar screen. They arrange to house the subjects in the laboratory so that they will have control over the sleeping habits of the subjects. There are $a = 4$ conditions, namely, 4, 12, 20, and 28 hours without sleep. There are $n = 4$ subjects randomly assigned to each of the different treatment conditions. The subjects have been well trained on the vigilance task before the start of the experiment. They are scored on the number of failures to spot objects on a radar screen during a 30-minute test period. The scores for each subject are presented in Table 3–4.

If you have a hand calculator designed to facilitate statistical calculations — generally available for under \$15 (at the present writing) — you would start the analysis with the basic summing and squaring operations performed on the scores

Table 3-4   Numerical Example

	HOURS WITHOUT SLEEP (FACTOR A)			
	4 hr. a_1	12 hr. a_2	20 hr. a_3	28 hr. a_4
	37	36	43	76
	22	45	75	66
	22	47	66	43
	25	23	46	62
Sum (A):	$\overline{106}$	$\overline{151}$	$\overline{230}$	$\overline{247}$
Mean ($\overline{Y}_A$):	26.50	37.75	57.50	61.75
ΣY^2:	2,962	6,059	13,946	15,825
Variance (s^2):	51.00	119.58	240.33	190.92
St. Dev. (s):	7.14	10.94	15.50	13.82

in each treatment condition.[4] The results of these calculations are also listed in the table. For the subjects in level a_2, for example,

$$A_2 = \Sigma Y_{2j} = 36 + 45 + 47 + 23 = 151$$

$$\overline{Y}_{A_2} = \frac{A_2}{n} = \frac{151}{4} = 37.75$$

$$\Sigma Y_{2j}^2 = (36)^2 + (45)^2 + (47)^2 + (23)^2 = 6,059$$

The means are the primary descriptive statistic of an experiment and are examined closely for any interesting trend or outcome. An examination of the means in Table 3–4 indicates that the average number of failures increases steadily as the number of hours of sleep deprivation increases. The means would be reported in a journal article either in a table or, more likely, in a figure because a quantitative independent variable is involved.

In addition to the mean, most researchers would calculate and report some measure of variability for each of the treatment conditions. The usual measure is the standard deviation (s), which can be easily calculated from the information in the table. The first step in calculating the standard deviation is to obtain the sum of squares (SS) for each treatment group. In terms of deviations from the mean ($Y - \overline{Y}_A$), the formula is

$$SS = \Sigma (Y - \overline{Y}_A)^2 \tag{3-7}$$

As an example of the calculations, the sum of squares for the four-hour group is equal to

$$SS = (37 - 26.5)^2 + (22 - 26.5)^2 + (22 - 26.5)^2 + (25 - 26.5)^2$$

$$= (10.5)^2 + (-4.5)^2 + (-4.5)^2 + (-1.5)^2 = 153.00$$

[4]Statistical calculators combine these two operations in a single step and, as a bonus, will provide the mean and standard deviation with the press of a button or two.

The computationally simpler formula for the sum of squares is given by

$$SS = \text{(sum of the squared scores)} - \frac{\text{(sum of the scores)}^2}{n} \tag{3-8}$$

As an example of the calculations, the sum of squares for the 4-hour group is equal to

$$SS = 2,962 - \frac{(106)^2}{4} = 153.00$$

The formula for the variance (s_i^2) was given by Eq. (3–1). Substituting the relevant data, we have

$$s_1^2 = \frac{SS}{df} = \frac{153.00}{4-1} = 51.00$$

The variances for each treatment condition are presented in Table 3–4. Finally, the standard deviation of a set of scores (s_i) is defined as follows:

$$\text{standard deviation} = \sqrt{\text{variance}} = s_i \tag{3-9}$$

For the four-hour group,

$$s_1 = \sqrt{51.00} = 7.14$$

The standard deviations for the different treatment conditions are also given in Table 3–4. The main reason for calculating measures of variability for each treatment condition is to determine whether the groups show comparable degrees of variability. Although an inspection of the variances and standard deviations of the treatment conditions indicates some differences in variability from group to group, these are well within the range of values one would expect if chance factors alone were operating.[5]

The steps in the analysis are summarized in Table 3–5. The upper half of the table details the operations for calculating the three basic ratios—[Y], [A], and [T]—and the lower half presents the summary table of the analysis of variance. From the formulas presented in Sec. 2.4, we combine the basic ratios to obtain the sums of squares as follows:

$$SS_A = [A] - [T] = 36,986.50 - 33,672.25 = 3,314.25$$

$$SS_{S/A} = [Y] - [A] = 38,792 - 36,986.50 = 1,805.50$$

$$SS_T = [Y] - [T] = 38,792 - 33,672.25 = 5,119.75$$

As a check,

$$SS_A + SS_{S/A} = 3,314.25 + 1,805.50 = 5,119.75 = SS_T$$

---

[5]I will discuss procedures for determining the significance of differences among treatment variances in Chap. 5.

Table 3–5 Summary of the Analysis

	Basic Ratios			

$[Y] = \Sigma Y^2 = (37)^2 + (22)^2 + \ldots + (43)^2 + (62)^2 = 38{,}792$

$[A] = \dfrac{\Sigma A^2}{n} = \dfrac{(106)^2 + (151)^2 + (230)^2 + (247)^2}{4} = \dfrac{147{,}946}{4} = 36{,}986.50$

$[T] = \dfrac{T^2}{(a)(n)} = \dfrac{(106 + 151 + 230 + 247)^2}{(4)(4)} = \dfrac{(734)^2}{16} = \dfrac{538{,}756}{16} = 33{,}672.25$

		Summary			
Source		SS	df	MS	F
A	$[A] - [T] =$	3,314.25	3	1,104.75	7.34*
S/A	$[Y] - [A] =$	1,805.50	12	150.46	
Total	$[Y] - [T] =$	5,119.75	15		

* p < .05.

The remainder of the analysis is based on the formulas listed in Table 3–1 (p. 43). The sums of squares we have just calculated are entered in Table 3–5. The df's associated with the different sums of squares are

$df_A = a - 1 = 4 - 1 = 3$

$df_{S/A} = (a)(n - 1) = 4(4 - 1) = 12$

$df_T = (a)(n) - 1 = (4)(4) - 1 = 15$

As an arithmetic check,

$df_A + df_{S/A} = 3 + 12 = 15 = df_T$

The between-groups and within-groups mean squares are formed by dividing the relevant sum of squares by the corresponding df. Specifically,

$$MS_A = \frac{SS_A}{a - 1} = \frac{3{,}314.25}{3} = 1{,}104.75$$

$$MS_{S/A} = \frac{SS_{S/A}}{(a)(n - 1)} = \frac{1{,}805.50}{12} = 150.46$$

The F ratio is obtained by dividing the first mean square by the second:

$$F = \frac{MS_A}{MS_{S/A}} = \frac{1{,}104.75}{150.46} = 7.34$$

The results of each of these steps are entered in the summary table. We will assume that the α level has been set at $p = .05$ before the start of the experiment.

To evaluate the significance of F, we locate the critical value of F at $\alpha = .05$, and $df_{num.} = 3$ and $df_{denom.} = 12$. From the F table (Table A–1 of Appendix A),

$$F(3, 12) = 3.49$$

The decision rules given in Eq. (3–5) may be stated as follows:

Reject H_0 if $F_{observed} \geq 3.49$; otherwise, retain H_0

Since $F_{observed} = 7.34$ exceeds this value, we reject the null hypothesis and conclude that the independent variable has produced an effect. The results of the statistical test are indicated by a footnote in the summary table.

In Chap. 2 (p. 33), you saw that the within-groups sum of squares $SS_{S/A}$ is in effect the sum of the individual sum of squares for the treatment groups; that is, $SS_{S/A} = \Sigma\, SS_{S/A_i}$. The within-groups mean square ($MS_{S/A}$), which is based on $SS_{S/A}$, can also be viewed as a composite or pooled source of variance. More specifically, the error term for the analysis of variance is literally an *average* of the separate variances of the separate groups (s_i^2). In symbols,

$$MS_{S/A} = \frac{\Sigma\, s_i^2}{a} \tag{3-10}$$

As an example, we can calculate the average within-groups variance with the variances presented in Table 3–4. More specifically,

$$MS_{S/A} = \frac{51.00 + 119.58 + 240.33 + 190.92}{4}$$

$$= \frac{601.83}{4} = 150.46$$

which is identical to the value we calculated with the standard formulas. Viewing the error term as an average of the group variances emphasizes the point that each group produces an estimate of experimental error for each condition, and that these estimates are then averaged to provide a more stable estimate of experimental error for the entire experiment. I will discuss this point again in Chap. 5.

3.6 SUMMARY

In this chapter, I considered the final steps in the analysis of a single-factor experiment, namely, evaluating the F ratio. From the tabled values of the F statistic, which are based on theoretical sampling distributions of F, we are able to obtain the critical value of F. This value sets the lower boundary of the range of F's within which we will reject the null hypothesis. If the F we obtain from an analysis falls within this range—if it is equal to or greater than the critical value of F—we reject the null hypothesis and conclude that some treatment effects are in the population. If the observed F is smaller than the critical value, we retain the null hypothesis.

Application of the decision rules will lead to errors of statistical inference at least part of the time. One such error, type I error, is that committed when the null hypothesis is falsely rejected. The magnitude of this error is called the significance level and is set by the researcher at a fairly low value (for example, $\alpha = .05$) before the start of the experiment. The other error, type II error (β), is that committed when the null hypothesis is not rejected and the alternative is true. The researcher controls this error indirectly by designing the experiment to be reasonably sensitive to the existence of treatment effects in the population.

3.7 EXERCISES[6]

1. Find the critical values of F for the following situations:
   a. $F(4, 30)$ at $\alpha = .05$
   b. $F(1, 120)$ at $\alpha = .001$
   c. $a = 7, n = 5, \alpha = .10$
   d. $a = 3, n = 9, \alpha = .25$

2. Perform an analysis of variance on the following set of scores:

a_1	a_2	a_3
8	9	2
0	4	0
9	8	5
4	1	7
2	8	7

   Reserve your calculations for problem 2 in the exercises of Chap. 4.
3. Complete the analysis of variance, using the data presented in problem 1 in the exercises of Chap. 2.
4. An experiment is conducted with $n = 5$ subjects in each of the $a = 6$ treatment conditions; in the following table, the sums are given in the first row of numbers and the sums of the squared Y scores are given in the second row of numbers.
   a. Perform an analysis of variance in the usual manner. Reserve your calculations for problem 1 in the exercises of Chap. 5.
   b. There is an alternative method for calculating the $MS_{S/A}$, which involves the individual group variances (see p. 60). Calculate the $MS_{S/A}$ by this other method.

	a_1	a_2	a_3	a_4	a_5	a_6
A:	15	10	25	35	25	20
ΣY^2:	65	35	130	275	150	102

[6] The answers to these questions are found in Appendix B.

4

The Sensitivity of an Experiment

Effect Size and Power

A researcher usually spends a great deal of time designing an experiment, taking great care in choosing exactly those treatment conditions that will provide the answers to the specific research questions that prompted the experiment in the first place. A researcher also attempts to design a *sensitive* experiment—one that is sufficiently powerful to detect any differences that might be present in the population. In general, we can create sensitive or powerful experiments by using large sample sizes, by choosing treatment conditions that are expected to produce sizable effects, and by reducing the uncontrolled variability in any study. We can also increase power by selecting a more sensitive experimental design, such as the randomized block design and the within-subjects design, or by using special statistical procedures, such as the analysis of covariance. Although I will consider these designs and procedures in later chapters, I mention them now to remind you that we do have ways to improve the sensitivity of our experiments and that you should be sufficiently familiar with these topics to take advantage of them when you design your own experiments.

This chapter focuses on three effective ways of improving the power of any experiment. I will begin by considering the role of effect size in designing an experiment. Next, I will discuss ways by which we can reduce the presence of error variance. Finally, I will show how to estimate power and how increases in sample size affect the sensitivity of an experiment. This is a critical chapter, which you should fully master so that you can take advantage of this information when you design your next research project. Researchers are beginning to realize that issues of power and design sensitivity must be carefully considered when they are designing their experiments and that failure to do so may greatly reduce their chances of detecting the treatment effects they have hypothesized.

4.1   ESTIMATING RELATIVE TREATMENT MAGNITUDE

Prediction is a primary goal of science. One index of our ability to predict behavior is the degree to which we can "force" it around with our experimental manipulations. Said another way, the importance of an experimental manipulation is demonstrated by the degree to which we can account for the total variability among subjects by isolating the experimental effects. It would be useful to have an index of the efficacy of experimental treatments, to guide us in our decision to follow or not to follow a certain direction in our research. It would point to manipulations that eventually must be included in any comprehensive theory of the behavior we are studying. In applied research, the importance of experimental treatments can be translated into dollars-and-cents language.

Many investigators already use one such index—the significance level associated with a given F test. Unfortunately, however, this index is simply not appropriate. All too frequently, researchers compare an F test that is significant at $p < .00001$ with one that is significant at $p < .05$ and conclude that the first experiment represents an impressive degree of prediction whereas the second experiment commands only passing interest. One problem with such a comparison of F statistics is that the size of the F ratio is affected by other factors in addition to the size of the treatment effects, the most obvious of which is *sample size*. Thus, a large F may imply that treatment effects are large or that sample size was large or that both factors are contributing to the observed value of F.

Suppose we approach this important point from another direction. Consider two experiments, one with a sample size of 5 and the other with a sample size of 20, in which both experiments produce an F that is significant at $p = .05$. Which set of results would be most impressive, the one with the small sample size or the one with the large sample size? Rosenthal and Gaito (1963) report that many researchers will choose the experiment with the *larger* sample size, because it suggests a larger or stronger effect. Actually, the experiment with the *smaller* sample size would be the correct choice. In view of the fact that power and sample size are positively correlated, we simply cannot use significance level alone as an index of the strength of an experimental effect. What we need is an index that is (1) responsive to the strength of the association between an experimental manipulation and changes in behavior and (2) independent of sample size.

A Measure of Relative Treatment Magnitude

Several measures of treatment magnitude have been proposed. The most popular is an index known as **omega squared** (ω^2).[1] When applied to the single-factor design, omega squared (ω_A^2) is based on two variances derived from the treatment populations, one based on the differences among the population treatment means (σ_A^2) and the other based on the variability within the treatment populations $(\sigma_{S/A}^2)$. More specifically,

$$\omega_A^2 = \frac{\sigma_A^2}{\sigma_A^2 + \sigma_{S/A}^2}$$

Defined in this way, $\omega_A^2 = 0$ when population treatment effects are absent and varies between 0 and 1.0 when they are present. Strength, as measured by ω_A^2, is clearly a *relative* measure, reflecting the proportional amount of the total population variance (represented by $\sigma_A^2 + \sigma_{S/A}^2$) that is attributed to the variation among

---

[1] Useful discussions of the history of the development of these measures, including comparisons between them, are provided by Camp and Maxwell (1983); Dwyer (1974); Glass and Hakstian (1969); Maxwell, Camp, and Arvey (1981); O'Grady (1982); and Vaughan and Corballis (1969).

the experimental treatments (represented by σ_A^2). This index is often referred to as the proportion of variation "explained" or "accounted for" by the treatment manipulation in an experiment, or more simply as "explained variance."

Estimating Omega Squared

Omega squared is estimated quite simply by using quantities already entered in the summary table of the analysis of variance. That is,

$$\hat{\omega}_A^2 = \frac{SS_A - (a - 1)(MS_{S/A})}{SS_T + MS_{S/A}} \tag{4-1}$$

where $\hat{\omega}_A^2$ is an estimate of treatment magnitude in the population. For example, consider the results of the experiment that was analyzed in Chap. 3 and summarized in Table 3–5 (p. 59). For this experiment, $a = 4$, $SS_A = 3,314.25$, $MS_{S/A} = 150.46$, and $SS_T = 5,119.75$. Substituting in Eq. (4–1), we find

$$\hat{\omega}_A^2 = \frac{3,314.25 - (4 - 1)(150.46)}{5,119.75 + 150.46} = \frac{2,862.87}{5,270.21} = .543$$

What this value indicates is that approximately 54 percent of the total variance is accounted for by the experimental treatments.

Other, algebraic equivalent formulas for estimating omega squared are available. One, for example, is written in terms of the observed F ratio:

$$\hat{\omega}_A^2 = \frac{(a - 1)(F - 1)}{(a - 1)(F - 1) + (a)(n)} \tag{4-2}$$

Entering the values from Table 3–5, we find

$$\hat{\omega}_A^2 = \frac{(4 - 1)(7.34 - 1)}{(4 - 1)(7.34 - 1) + (4)(4)} = \frac{19.02}{19.02 + 16} = .543$$

which is identical to the value we obtained with Eq. (4–1). Most readers find neither of these two equations particularly enlightening as they tend to obscure the fundamental logic of this index of relative treatment magnitude. A more illuminating approach is taken by Vaughan and Corballis (1969), who define $\hat{\omega}_A^2$ in terms of more meaningful population estimates. Regardless of how the index is calculated, however, its interpretation is the same, namely, a reflection of the proportion of the total variability in the experiment associated with the experimental treatments.

Some Properties of $\hat{\omega}_A^2$

The index omega squared provides a relative measure of the strength of an independent variable. Although logically the index can range from $\hat{\omega}_A^2 = .00$ to $\hat{\omega}_A^2 = 1.00$, there are certain realities that empirical data force on the measure. For example, negative values will be obtained when $F < 1$. In addition, it is highly unlikely that large values of $\hat{\omega}_A^2$ will be observed because of the relatively large contribution of error variance found in most behavioral research. Thus, the size of the error component will effectively limit the ultimate size of $\hat{\omega}_A^2$. Cohen (for example, 1977, pp. 284–288) suggests the following terms to describe the size of an effect in the behavioral and social sciences:

A "small" effect is an experiment that produces an $\hat{\omega}_A^2$ of .01.
A "medium" effect is an experiment that produces an $\hat{\omega}_A^2$ of .06.
A "large" effect is an experiment that produces an $\hat{\omega}_A^2$ of .15 or greater.

Although any admittedly arbitrary definition can be questioned, the rough "scale" offered by Cohen provides some perspective with which to interpret values of $\hat{\omega}_A^2$ reported in the literature.

The estimate of omega squared is not a test statistic, although in effect the "significance" of $\hat{\omega}_A^2$ is assessed by the regular F test. That is, a significant F implies that $\hat{\omega}_A^2$ is significantly greater than zero as well. On the other hand, $\hat{\omega}_A^2$ can provide useful information even when F is *not* significant, because $\hat{\omega}_A^2$ is unaffected by small sample sizes (and hence, low power), whereas the significance of the F test is so affected. The insensitivity of $\hat{\omega}_A^2$ to variations in sample size, which follows from its definition and is the critical reason for its use, has been demonstrated in several Monte Carlo sampling experiments (for example, Carroll & Nordholm, 1975, p. 550; Lane & Dunlap, 1978, p. 109).

Comments

Although $\hat{\omega}_A^2$ is the most commonly reported measure of relative magnitude in experimental studies, other indices are employed in correlational research. One of these, the squared multiple-correlation coefficient, R^2, is simply

$$R^2 = \frac{SS_A}{SS_T} \qquad (4\text{--}3)$$

the proportion of the total variation in the experiment (SS_T) that is associated with the variation in treatments (SS_A). In the present context, $R^2 = 3{,}314.25/5{,}119.75 = .647$. The R^2 measure will always be larger than $\hat{\omega}_A^2$, and in this example the difference is considerable (.543 vs. .647).[2]

How can we use estimates of relative treatment magnitude? First, the index might permit us to distinguish between a meaningful treatment effect and a trivial one. But how should we define what should be considered a "trivial" effect? One way to answer this question is to estimate the omega squared typically reported in the literature. Sedlmeier and Gigerenzer (1989), for example, reported that the average study in the *Journal of Abnormal Psychology* produced a "medium" effect ($\hat{\omega}_A^2 = .06$), a value that has been reported for other areas of study as well (Cooper & Findley, 1982). It appears, then, that many researchers regard effects of "medium" strength to be meaningful and certainly worthy of study. But at what point

---

[2]The difference between R^2 an $\hat{\omega}_A^2$ decreases as sample size (n) increases. A second measure, epsilon squared ($\hat{\epsilon}_A^2$), or "shrunken" R^2 as it is sometimes called (see Cohen & Cohen, 1983, pp. 105–107), is usually preferred over R^2 as a measure of strength in correlational studies. See Maxwell, Camp, and Arvey (1981) for a discussion of these two indices in the context of multiple regression.

below this "average" effect size should we begin to question the "importance" of a research finding? There seems to be some agreement among methodologists that Cohen's (1977) definition of "small" ($\hat{\omega}_A^2 = .01$) probably represents the lower limit of what we might call a meaningful effect.

On the other hand, we could argue that what should be termed a meaningful result depends largely on its implications for *theory*, not specifically on its estimated strength. Consider, for example, an investigator who begins work in a new and previously unanalyzed research area. A first strategy may be to search for independent variables that seem to produce "large" effects—in this case, *meaningful* refers to *large*. Now, consider what might happen once this researcher has discovered an independent variable that produces relatively large treatment effects. Subsequent research will usually not be concerned with the original finding but with a refinement of the discovery into component parts, each being responsive to a different collection of experimental manipulations. As theories develop to account for these findings and for the interrelationships among the components, a researcher eventually finds that he or she is no longer working with large effects but with small ones representing manipulations that are theoretically interesting. Under these circumstances, even small differences—as indexed by $\hat{\omega}_A^2$—may provide a decision between two competing theoretical explanations. Thus, we could say that one indication of a healthy and productive area of research is a preponderance of experiments with relatively *small* values of $\hat{\omega}_A^2$.

A number of criticisms have been leveled against the unqualified use of $\hat{\omega}_A^2$ in drawing inferences from the results of experiments (see O'Grady, 1982). One of these concerns the interpretation of a relative-strength measure when it is applied to strictly correlational data, on the one hand, and to the results of an experiment, on the other. With correlational data, none of the variables under scrutiny is manipulated by the researcher; the values observed with these variables are completely free to vary. With experimental data, the values of the independent variable—the actual treatment conditions—are usually under the direct control and manipulation of the investigator. As a result, the size of the relative-strength measure also is under at least the partial control of the experimenter. As an obvious example, the inclusion of an extreme group in an experiment, for example, a nontreatment control condition or a particularly deviant point on a stimulus dimension, will greatly increase $\hat{\omega}_A^2$ over what it would be without that group.

In summary, the presence of a significant F gives us some assurance that a *statistical association* (predictability between the treatment groups and the scores on the dependent variable) exists. The size of the F itself does not reflect the degree of this statistical association unambiguously. The index $\hat{\omega}_A^2$ provides this information and thus supplements any inference to be drawn from the outcome of an experiment. There is no question that both statistics, F and $\hat{\omega}_A^2$, contribute to a complete understanding of the outcome of the statistical test and both should be included in any research report.[3] Moreover, it is clear that we should be looking for

---

[3]Measures of statistical association are also useful to others when the results of similar experiments are being compared. In these cases, researchers often conduct what are called **meta-analyses** (see, for example, Hedges & Olkin, 1985; Hunter & Schmidt, 1990).

treatments that produce large estimates of statistical association. On the other hand, if we based *all* our actions on the size of $\hat{\omega}_A^2$ alone, we would be making a mistake. This is because a small statistical association may often be theoretically important.

4.2   CONTROLLING TYPE I AND TYPE II ERRORS

As discussed in the last chapter, we are able to control the magnitude of type I error (false rejection of the null hypothesis) through our choice of a rejection region for the F distribution (the α level). The control of the type II error (failing to reject the null hypothesis when it is false) and of power, unfortunately, is not this simple because power depends on several factors, including the size of the treatment effects, sample size, degree of error variance, and significance level.

You have already seen the reciprocity between the two types of error in Fig. 3–3 (p. 55)—that is, you know that any change in the size of the type I error will produce a change of opposite direction in the type II error. Given this reciprocity, then, one obvious way to decrease type II error (and to increase power) would be to increase the probability of a type I error. Unfortunately, however, we seem to be stuck with a rigidly set α level since rarely will it be set at any value greater than .05.

Why has type I error become fixed over the years? One answer is the absence of agreement concerning the relative seriousness of the two types of errors; in the absence of agreement, we must be arbitrary. It may be possible to establish a rational balancing of type I and type II errors in certain applied fields, however. In the medical sciences, for instance, researchers might be able to place a numerical value on the consequences of failing to recognize a new wonder drug (a type II error) and contrast this with the value placed on the consequences of switching to a new drug that is not better than the original one (a type I error). But in most research areas of the behavioral sciences, we are without such guidance. How serious is it if a new hypothesis is not recognized or if an old one is incorrectly rejected? Without explicit values to guide us, we must proceed by conventions. Thus, we fix the type I error at a level that will be acceptable to most researchers— that is, $\alpha = .05$ or lower—and allow the type II error (and power) to be what it has to be. We cannot answer the question of what is an acceptable level of power since we are usually not in a position to give weight to the relative consequences of the two types of error.

Why should we be concerned with controlling power? The answer is that power reflects the degree to which we can *detect* the treatment differences we expect and the chances that others will be able to *duplicate* our findings when they attempt to repeat our experiments. These are compelling reasons for us to pay strict attention to controlling power in our experiments. In spite of these arguments, however, the reality is that most researchers appear to pay little attention to power and that most experiments in the behavioral sciences are surprisingly lacking in power. To illustrate, Cohen (1962) surveyed all the research published in Volume 61 (1960) of the *Journal of Abnormal and Social Psychology* and found the studies to be substantially deficient in power. More specifically, if we assume that the overall effect size of studies reported in this journal was of "medium" strength (that is, $\hat{\omega}_A^2 = .06$), the average power calculated by Cohen was **.48**. You should note carefully exactly what this finding means: The significant effects reported in Volume 61 of this journal would have on average a 50–50 chance of being detected by others trying to duplicate these findings—a pretty dismal prognosis. A subsequent analysis 10 years later by Brewer (1972), who reviewed studies in a number of research journals, echoed Cohen's conclusion. Even more recently, an analysis by Sedlmeier and Gigerenzer (1989), who duplicated Cohen's examination of the same journal 24 years later, yielded almost exactly the same conclusion—the average power for detecting medium effects was **.50**.

The unfortunate conclusion from these findings is that research in the behavioral sciences is woefully lacking in power. This statement implies that a substantial number of research projects have been undertaken and then discarded when they failed to produce results at the accepted significance level of $\alpha = .05$. If power is truly equal to .50, as the evidence suggests, half of the research undertaken will not yield significant results even though there are real differences among the treatment means that should have been detected. This finding also means that the research outcomes that are published are unlikely to be duplicated by others who may attempt to repeat or to replicate these studies.

The puzzling aspect of these estimates of the power of published findings is that procedures are readily available to assist researchers in designing studies with respectable power, thus permitting them to avoid perpetuating this somewhat discouraging and dismal state of affairs. Let me state the problem once more. Why should we waste time and resources undertaking a project that has a relatively low probability of detecting treatment effects and producing significant results? We should be designing experiments that stand an excellent chance of detecting differences—power of .80 or higher—rather than repeat the actions taken by researchers in the past. Why haven't experimenters learned from the analyses of Cohen and others? Sedlmeier and Gigerenzer (1989) explore this puzzling question in some detail. I suspect that the answer lies in the training that researchers in the behavioral sciences have received. Most books on statistics and methodology tend to place more emphasis on significance testing and design issues than on considerations of statistical power. As Kraemer and Thiemann (1987) put it, "although, in principle, deriving power is as straightforward as deriving a significance level, researchers are routinely trained to deal with significance level, but rarely with power" (p. 16). Cohen (1988) is more optimistic, however, as he comments on the problem in the Preface to the second edition of *Statistical Power Analysis for the Behavioral Sciences* (see pp. xiii–xiv). He reports admittedly hearsay evidence that funding agencies are beginning to require power analyses to be included as an integral part of research proposals submitted to them. If true, I suspect that researchers will quickly correct any deficiencies they may have had in their statistical educations concerning power.

Another reason for conducting a power analysis is to avoid wasting resources by performing experiments with *too much* power. Not only does an experiment with an excessively large sample size cost more in time and money than one with a more appropriate sample size, but also the conclusions drawn are often misleading. Since the size of F depends in part on sample size, a particularly large sample size will produce a large F, which frequently is thought to reflect a "large" effect (see p. 64). This potential misinterpretation is one of the reasons why measures of relative treatment magnitude were developed and are reported in research articles. In addition, contemporary concerns for the rights of animals used as subjects in experiments usually involve the recommendation that animal studies be designed with the smallest sample sizes commensurate with acceptable power to keep any possible suffering and loss of life to a minimum.

In the remainder of this chapter, I will emphasize ways to facilitate the determination of power during the planning stage of an experiment. There is really no excuse for omitting this critical step in the design of an experiment. The stakes are simply too high for researchers to continue ignoring power when they design and interpret experiments.

4.3   REDUCING ERROR VARIANCE

It is of interest to see how the sensitivity of an experiment is related to the size of the error component. With treatment effects of a given magnitude, any increase in the size of the error variance reduces the size of the F ratio and lessens our chances of rejecting the null hypothesis; any decrease in error increases these chances.

There are three major sources of error variance: random variation in the actual treatments, unanalyzed control factors, and individual differences ("permanent" or "temporary" factors affecting a subject's performance during the course of the experiment). All these sources are reflected in a subject's score on the dependent variable and thus contribute to error variance, although certain steps can be taken to reduce their magnitude.

Reducing Treatment Variability

I have noted previously that no experimental treatment is exactly alike for every subject in a particular condition. The calibration of the equipment may change from session to session; the experimenter will not be perfectly consistent in the conduct of the experiment; and environmental factors such as noise level, illumination, and temperature will not be identical for each subject. To the extent that these factors influence the behavior under study, their variation from subject to subject contributes to the estimate of experimental error. I should add to this list any error of measurement and of recording that appear randomly in the data collection.

We can take certain steps to minimize these sources of variability: carefully calibrated equipment, automation, well-trained experimenters, and special testing rooms. In essence, this solution attempts to hold constant the specific conditions of testing in the experiment.

Unanalyzed Control Factors

Control factors are nuisance variables that are introduced into an experiment for a variety of reasons, but primarily for the removal of possible bias and for an increase in the generality of the results. For example, suppose an experimenter plans an experiment that requires far too many subjects for one assistant to test. If more than one assistant is employed, the researcher should make sure that each runs an equal number of subjects in each of the treatment conditions. To do otherwise would introduce a potential confounding of assistants and treatments into the experiment.

Most researchers would disregard these control factors—different laboratory assistants in the example—in the analysis of their experiments and simply analyze the results as a completely randomized single-factor design. Often this is a mistake because any variability associated with control factors contributes directly to error variance. That is, the variability of subjects within any group will now include differences associated with laboratory assistants, say, in addition to the usual factors contributing to experimental error. In short, a nonrandom source of variance, such as assistants, that is spread equally over all treatment conditions, as in this example, does not bias the treatment effects, but it does contribute to the size of the error term. The obvious solution to such a situation is to include control factors in the statistical analysis, using procedures that I will consider in later chapters of this book.

Reducing Subject Variability

Undoubtedly the major source of error variance in the behavioral sciences is that contributed by individual differences. The fact that subjects differ widely in performance on laboratory tasks means that when they are assigned randomly to the treatment conditions, this variability becomes an important source of error variance. The most obvious way of reducing subject variability is to select subjects who are relatively similar on some important and relevant characteristic, for example, IQ in a learning test, visual acuity in a perception experiment, socioeconomic status in an attitude-change study, and so on. A second type of matching is accomplished in small sets that consist of subjects matched *within* a set while generally differing widely *between* sets. Neither procedure is widely used in psychology, however, perhaps because there are more effective methods of reducing subject variability. These preferred procedures include the use of the same subject in all the treatment conditions and a statistical technique called the **analysis of covariance**, which adjusts estimates of error variance and of treatment effects on the basis of information obtained before the start of the study. Both of these procedures will be considered in subsequent chapters.

4.4 USING SAMPLE SIZE TO CONTROL POWER

The power of an experiment is determined by the interplay of three factors, namely, significance level α, the magnitude or size of the treatment effects, and sample size n. We will consider the influence of each factor on power in a moment. From a practical point of view, however, only one of these—sample size—is normally used to control power. This is because the α level is effectively fixed at

$p = .05$ by most researchers in the behavioral sciences and the effect size is frequently assumed to be as large as possible, given the specific interests of the researcher and the conditions surrounding his or her experimental design.

The relationship between sample size and power is presented in Table 4–1 for an experiment with $a = 4$ treatment conditions.[4] The entries in the upper half of the table are based on $\alpha = .05$, and those in the lower half are based on $\alpha = .01$. The three rows within each half of the table give the sample sizes n needed to achieve varying degrees of power for three different assumed or expected effect sizes, $\omega^2 = .01$ ("small"), .06 ("medium"), and .15 ("large"). We will examine this table carefully as it reveals some sobering facts about the sample sizes needed to obtain respectable amounts of power.

First, let's consider the sample sizes needed when the significance level is set at $p = .05$. Look carefully at the numbers appearing in the first row—that is, when the expected effect size is "small." As you can see, sample sizes are outrageously large if we want to obtain reasonable amounts of power. For example, if power is set at .80, we must assign 271 subjects to each of the four treatment conditions (a total of $(a)(n) = (4)(271) = 1{,}084$ subjects); if power is set at .90, we need 354 subjects (a total of 1,416). Consider next the sample sizes required when the expected effect size is "medium." The sample size we need for a power of .80 is 44 subjects (a total of 176 subjects) and for a power of .90 is 57 subjects (a total of 228 subjects). Obviously the situation is improved in the sense that there is a substantial drop in the sample sizes when the expected effect size increases from $\omega^2 = .01$ to .06, but still, these numbers will probably seem alarmingly large to most seasoned researchers. Finally, the sample sizes we need when we expect to find a "large" effect are more like those that we typically find in psychology research journals, namely, $n = 17$ for a power of .80 and $n = 22$ for a power of .90.

What effect will a more stringent significance level ($\alpha = .01$) have on the sample sizes, assuming that we want to maintain power at the same level we achieved at $\alpha = .05$? If you remember the relationship between significance level

Table 4–1   Sample Size (n) as a Function of Power, Effect Size (ω^2), and Significance Level (α)

EFFECT SIZE (ω^2)	POWER								
	.10	.20	.30	.40	.50	.60	.70	.80	.90
					$\alpha = .05$				
.01	21	53	83	113	144	179	219	271	354
.06	5	10	14	19	24	30	36	44	57
.15	3	5	6	8	10	12	14	17	22
					$\alpha = .01$				
.01	70	116	156	194	232	274	323	385	478
.06	13	20	26	32	38	45	53	62	77
.15	6	8	11	13	15	18	20	24	29

[4]These values were calculated by a computer program called PC-SIZE, described by Dallal (1986).

and power diagrammed in Fig. 3–3 (p. 55), you will realize that reducing the size of the rejection region guarantees that we will reject fewer null hypotheses when H_0 is true—we reduce type I error— but it also guarantees that we will reject fewer null hypotheses when H_0 is false (and H_1 is true), thus increasing type II error (and decreasing power). As a consequence, we will need to increase sample size to maintain power. You can see the effect of decreasing the rejection region from .05 to .01 simply by comparing the entries in the upper half of Table 4–1 with those in the lower half. To achieve power of .80 in an experiment with an expected effect size of $\omega^2 = .06$, for example, we need to increase sample size from $n = 44$ (for $\alpha = .05$) to $n = 62$ (for $\alpha = .01$).

What you have just observed has been called the power-sample size "facts of life" (Kraemer, 1985):

1. Increasingly larger sample sizes are needed to increase power a fixed amount.
2. Relatively small expected effect sizes require substantial sample sizes to achieve a reasonable power.
3. Adopting a more stringent significance level leads to a hefty increase in sample size to maintain power at the same level with a less stringent criterion.

Consider again how we reached this point in our discussion. Low power is poor science—we waste time, energy, and resources whenever we conduct an experiment that has a low probability of producing a significant result. What is the point of initiating an experiment that has low power? I have already indicated that we can directly translate the estimated power of an experiment into a probability statement that we will successfully reject the null hypothesis when it is false. When we design an experiment with an estimated power of .50, we stand a 50–50 chance of obtaining a significant F. Would you bet any money in a game of chance with these odds? Science must be based on solid research findings, findings that others can depend on and duplicate if they were to repeat the experiments. Experiments with low power do not produce reliable findings.

Estimating Effect Size

To estimate power or to achieve a certain power by selecting an appropriate sample size, we need to specify the sort of experimental outcome we wish to detect. This statement is usually expressed as a ratio that relates the variation of the anticipated population treatment means to an estimate of the variation within these populations. In many cases, researchers try to make realistic guesses of the expected outcomes by conducting preliminary or pilot studies in which a few selected treatment conditions are compared or from similar research published by others. One of my colleagues, for example, was able to determine the sample size he would need for an extensive series of related experiments on the basis of several preliminary studies in which two of the key conditions were compared. This, then, is the ideal situation—an educated guess about the specific patterns of differences that theory and a knowledge of the field suggest should occur. You should note that we do not have to estimate the absolute values of the population means, only the expected differences among them. Finally, if we estimate the population treatment effects from the means of an experiment, we should adjust these estimates for the unavoidable presence of random error. We can accomplish this most easily by calculating estimated omega squared ($\hat{\omega}_A^2$) from the sample data and substituting this value in one of the formulas I will soon present to begin the process of estimating power.

On the other hand, if we are unable to specify the exact pattern of differences, we might be able to specify simply the *range* of the population treatment means—the difference between the largest and smallest population mean—as well as a general pattern that the population means might take. Cohen (1977, pp. 276–280), for example, offers the following three patterns that a researcher might specify:

1. *Minimum variability*: One mean is at each extreme and the others at the midpoint between them.
2. *Intermediate variability*: The means are spaced equally over the range.
3. *Maximum variability*: Half the means fall at each extreme.

Cohen then shows how we can combine this information with an estimate of population variability to produce a useful measure of effect size.[5]

Finally, researchers might find it acceptable to specify the relative size of the expected treatment effects. A measure such as omega squared can provide the information needed to determine power and to fix sample size. We could, for example, estimate omega squared from previous research studies. Alternatively, we could simply specify the relative size of the expected effects by using Cohen's (1977) suggested labels, namely, "small," "medium," or "large," and his numerical values (ω^2 = .01, .06, and .15, respectively) to provide the quantitative estimate. There is a potential danger if we use Cohen's values indiscriminately, of course, as he points out: ". . . these qualitative adjectives . . . may not be reasonably descriptive in any specific area. Thus, what a sociologist may consider a small effect size may well be appraised as medium by a clinical psychologist" (p. 285).[6] On the other hand, Cohen also reminds us that researchers simply cannot shirk their responsibility to make at least a stab at estimating effect size. Again, in his words, "The investigator who insists that he has absolutely no way of knowing how large an [effect size] to posit fails to appreciate that this necessarily means that he has no rational basis for deciding whether he needs to make ten observations or ten thousand" (p. 285).

Usually, we base our power estimates on the *minimum* effect size that we wish to detect. Cohen (1977) suggests that a "small" effect size (ω^2 = .01) is the minimum for experimental research in the behavioral sciences. Most researchers

---

[5]Kirk (1982, pp. 144–145) describes a related procedure in which we estimate the *largest* difference we expect to detect, relate that difference to an estimate of error variance, and refer this information to a set of special tables.

[6]Cohen (1988) indicates that these values were chosen on the basis of his intuition and were intended only to serve as a guide to researchers who were unable to provide more accurate estimates of expected effect sizes. For additional views on this issue, see, for example, Feldt (1973), Hinkle and Oliver (1983), and O'Grady (1982).

would probably not adopt this value for their research because it is too small and would require far more subjects than they might wish to commit to a study (see Table 4–1). Our choice of effect size should represent a *realistic* estimate, one that is based on earlier research. We do not benefit by casually overestimating the expected effect size. The result of overestimating is an estimate of sample size that is far too small to allow us to detect the actual effect that may be present. If anything, we should be a bit cautious and *under*estimate the effect size so that our choice of sample size will be sure to afford reasonable power for our proposed study.

Choosing a Reasonable Value for Power

In addition to an estimate of effect size, we also need to select the degree of power we want our experiment to have. Although I have implied that a power of .50 is too low for the behavioral sciences, I have said nothing about what might be a reasonable or even a desirable level of power. Certainly there is no presumed agreement among researchers on the issue of what defines reasonable power, as there is with regard to significance level. In fact, one could conclude that many researchers tend to *ignore* the power of their experiments (see Sedlmeier & Gigerenzer, 1989). Interestingly, methodologists are beginning to agree that a power of about .80 represents a reasonable and realistic value for research in the behavioral sciences (Cohen, 1965, 1977; Hinkle & Oliver, 1983; Kirk, 1982, p. 144). A power of .80 is reasonable in the sense that it reflects a presumed general sentiment among researchers that type I errors are more serious than type II errors and that a 4:1 ratio of type II to type I error is probably appropriate (see Chase & Tucker, 1976).[7] This value is also realistic, particularly when we consider the sharp increase in the sample size required to increase power from .80 to .90 or higher (see Table 4–1).

The ultimate decision is ours, of course. No one wants to make any error of statistical inference, which is why we agree to set α at a fairly low level—that is, .05—although there are those who advocate reducing the probability of this error lower still (see, for example, Ryan, 1985). One of the main purposes of this chapter is to call attention to the importance of measuring and controlling the other error of statistical inference, β. By using relatively small sample sizes, researchers have unknowingly given relatively greater emphasis to controlling type I error than to controlling type II error. To be more specific, the ratio of type II error to type I error reflected in most experiments reported in the psychological literature is substantially *greater* than 4:1, perhaps closer to a ratio of at least 20:1 (Rosenthal & Rubin, 1985; Rosnow & Rosenthal, 1989b).

What if we cannot perform an experiment with the appropriate number of subjects required to achieve the power we want for our experiment? Some have suggested that one way to cope with this problem is to relax our control of type I error as an additional way of increasing power in an experiment (see, for example,

---

[7]Assuming that we set $\alpha = .05$ and power $= .80$, β thus becomes .20 and the ratio of type II to type I error is .20:.05 or 4:1.

Cohen, 1965, pp. 99–100; Cohen, 1977, pp. 15–16; Rotton & Schönemann, 1978; Stevens, 1986, p. 138). Simply by increasing the significance level from $\alpha = .05$ to .10, for instance, we can increase the probability with which we will reject the null hypothesis—because of this expanded rejection region, of course—and substantially increase power as a consequence.

You might find this option particularly attractive when you are entering a new research area and plan to replicate any significant result you may discover before you present your findings to the professional public. By relaxing your significance level to $\alpha = .10$, for example, you immediately increase your chances of discovering true differences among the treatment means, while the subsequent planned replication—based on this initial study and conducted at $\alpha = .05$—will help you guard against type I error. To elaborate, suppose you did commit a type I error in the first experiment, which is a real possibility because you set $\alpha = .10$ rather than at the more standard significance level of $\alpha = .05$. Because the probability is low that you will make the same type I error in two independent experiments, you stand a reasonable chance of catching this error by obtaining a nonsignificant F in the second experiment. Thus, by adopting a policy of replicating or repeating any experiment that we conducted with a "relaxed" significance level, we are able to protect ourselves from reporting a type I error while maintaining reasonable statistical power and sensitivity in an initial, exploratory investigation.

Using Power Charts to Determine Sample Size

Pearson and Hartley (1951, 1972) have constructed some helpful charts from which we can estimate a sample size that will ensure a particular degree of power. You will recall that four factors—power, significance level, effect size, and sample size—are interrelated and that fixing any three will fully determine the fourth. We estimate sample size with the Pearson-Hartley charts following a somewhat indirect procedure that starts with a trial sample size, which we will refer to as n' to distinguish it from the actual sample size (n) of an experiment. Next, we estimate the smallest effect size we wish to detect and select a significance level. We then use this information to determine the power associated with this particular combination of trial sample size, effect size, and significance level. If the estimated power is either too low or too high, we adjust n' accordingly and determine the power associated with this new combination. We continue this process until we find the sample size that produces the desired level of power. Let's see how this works in practice.

Suppose we propose to conduct an experiment with four treatment conditions and that we can make reasonable estimates of the minimum expected treatment effects, which we base on theoretical considerations and on data obtained from related studies. We will assume that the population treatment means μ_i are the following:

$$\mu_1 = 18, \mu_2 = 21, \mu_3 = 22, \text{ and } \mu_4 = 19$$

The grand mean μ_T is an average of the four population means $(\mu_T = 20)$. In addition, we will assume that an accurate estimate of the common population variance is available, namely $\sigma^2_{S/A} = 16$. These two pieces of information—population treatment means and population variance—are converted into a statistic ϕ^2_A, which is calculated by the following formula:

$$\phi^2_A = n' \, \frac{\Sigma(\mu_i - \mu_T)^2/a}{\sigma^2_{S/A}} \tag{4-4}$$

where n' = the trial sample size

μ_i = the population treatment means

μ_T = the mean of the population treatment means

a = the number of treatment means

$\sigma^2_{S/A}$ = the average or common variance in the treatment populations

The expression to the right of n' is a ratio of treatment variance relative to error variance. Substituting in Eq. (4–4), we find

$$\phi^2_A = n' \, \frac{[(18 - 20)^2 + (21 - 20)^2 + (22 - 20)^2 + (19 - 20)^2]/4}{16}$$

$$= n' \, \frac{10/4}{16} = .1563\, n'$$

Taking the square root of ϕ^2_A gives us

$$\phi_A = \sqrt{.1563\, n'} = .395\sqrt{n'}$$

With ϕ_A expressed in this form, we can now begin the process of choosing a trial sample size, n'.

Let's start with $n' = 16$ as a trial sample size and assume that we want to set power at .90 and $\alpha = .05$. Solving for ϕ_A, we find

$$\phi_A = .395\sqrt{16} = (.395)(4) = 1.58$$

We are now ready to use one of the Pearson-Hartley charts, which is presented in Fig. 4–1. The first thing to notice is that there are two sets of power functions within the body of the chart, one for $\alpha = .05$ and the other for $\alpha = .01$. Within either set, there are 11 different power functions, each associated with a different value of the *denominator* degrees of freedom of the F ratio. As you can see, $df_{denom.}$ = 6, 7, 8, 9, 10, 12, 15, 20, 30, 60, and ∞. Intermediate values may be interpolated visually. The baseline is marked off in increasing values of ϕ; this baseline is used in conjunction with the set of power functions for $\alpha = .05$. (I have omitted the baseline used with the set of power functions for $\alpha = .01$ to simplify this example.) Once all these factors are coordinated on the chart—α, $df_{denom.}$, and ϕ—we can read the power value directly off the ordinate.

The particular power function we need is the one on the left ($\alpha = .05$) associated with $df_{denom.} = (a)(n' - 1) = (4)(16 - 1) = 60$. I have highlighted this function in Fig. 4–1. We now locate $\phi = 1.58$ on the baseline and visually extend a vertical line upward from this point until it intersects with the appropriate power curve. From this point of intersection, we visually extend a horizontal line to the

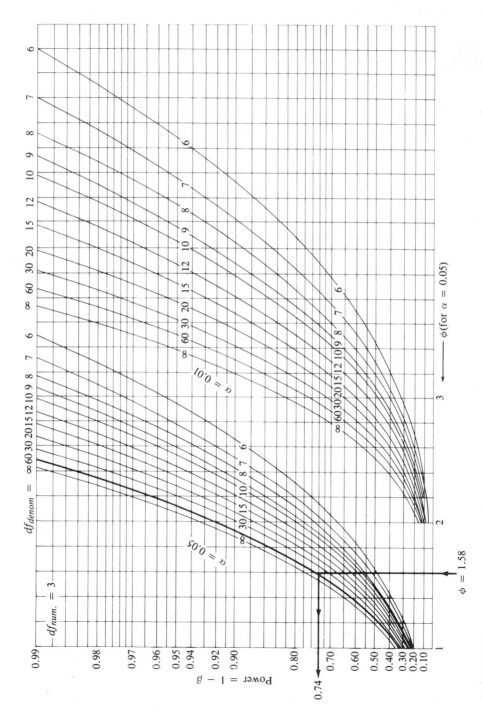

FIGURE 4–1 Illustrating the use of the Pearson-Hartley power charts for $a = 4$ ($df_{num.} = 3$), $\alpha = .05$, $\phi = 1.58$, and $df_{denom.} = 60$.

left until it intersects with the ordinate, where we can then read the estimated power for this combination of factors off the ordinate; I have illustrated these steps in the figure. As you can readily see, power = approximately .74. Since we were aiming for power = .90, however, we need to increase n' and repeat the process. If we try $n' = 24$, for example, we determine

$$\phi_A = .395\sqrt{24} = (.395)(4.899) = 1.94$$

To find out which power function to use with this new trial sample size, we again have to calculate the $df_{denom.}$. In this case, $df_{denom.} = (a)(n' - 1) = (4)(24 - 1) = 92$. This time we visually interpolate between the power functions for $df_{denom.} = 60$ and ∞ and find that the power associated with $\phi = 1.94$ is reasonably close to .90.

To recapitulate, estimating sample size with the Pearson-Hartley charts involves what amounts to a trial-and-error operation. We estimate the minimum treatment effects (or effect size) we wish to detect, decide on the α level, and use this information to solve for ϕ_A expressed in terms of the trial sample size, n'. We then estimate the power of the F test for the trial sample size by obtaining a numerical value for ϕ_A and entering this value appropriately in the relevant power chart. If the resultant power estimate is unsatisfactory (too low or too high), we change the trial sample size in the correct direction and repeat the operations.

We can reduce the number of repetitive calculations in this process by beginning our calculations with a realistic starting value for n'. I will describe how to determine this initial trial size as a series of steps.

1. We identify a particularly likely power function—one that is close to the final function we will use; I suggest using the power function for $df_{denom.} = 60$ for most situations.
2. From this function, we determine the value of ϕ that is associated with the power we seek. In our example, we were striving for a power of .90. Extending a line from .90 on the ordinate to the power function for $df_{denom.} = 60$ and then reading the value of ϕ on the baseline directly below the point of intersection, we find ϕ equal to approximately 1.92.
3. We take the value for ϕ_A^2 we obtained from Eq. (4–4), namely, $\phi_A^2 = .1563\, n'$, and then solve for n'; more specifically,

$$n' = \frac{\phi_A^2}{.1563}$$

4. We substitute our estimated value for ϕ (1.92) into this equation and calculate our first trial sample size as follows:

$$n' = \frac{(1.92)^2}{.1563} = 23.59$$

5. We would use a value of 23 or 24 as our starting point. Since these numbers are actually very close to the value we determined earlier, we have substantially reduced the number of times we would need to recycle through the calculations.

The entire set of Pearson-Hartley power charts is found in Appendix Table A–2. You will find 10 different charts, which are distinguished by the degrees of freedom in the *numerator* of the F ratio; these consist of $df_{num.} = 1, 2, 3, 4, 5, 6, 7,$

8, 12, and 24—a reasonable range for most experimental situations. Please note that there are two scales for ϕ on the baseline, one for $\alpha = .05$, of course, and the other for $\alpha = .01$. You should also note that for all charts *except the first*, the set of power curves on the left and the first set of ϕ values on the baseline are for $\alpha = .05$, whereas the charts on the right and the second set of ϕ values are for $\alpha = .01$. These relative positions are *reversed* for the first chart ($df_{num.} = 1$). Many users of these charts have misread critical information by failing to notice this reversal.

Using a Power Analysis as a Planning Tool

There are alternative ways of approaching the determination of an appropriate sample size that you may find useful during the planning stage of an experiment. One approach, for example, consists of working out the relationship between sample size and power over a useful range of values, rather than focusing on the sample size required for a certain degree of power. Suppose you started with a sample size that is typical for similar or related experiments in your research field and then calculated the power associated with a systematic variation of sample sizes around this value. Let's say that $n = 15$ is a reasonable number for the numerical example we have been using in this section. You could determine the power associated with various trial sample sizes around this value. Alternatively, you could start with the minimum sample size you would consider—the value below which you would begin to question the stability of your treatment means—and then determine power for different values of n above this number. Kraemer and Thiemann (1987, p. 28) define this number as "the minimum sample size necessary for the credibility of a study," which depends, of course, on one's research field.

Suppose that $n = 10$ is our minimum sample size and we will vary sample size in increments of 5 up to $n = 30$, which represents the largest sample size we can possibly afford. Table 4–2 summarizes the results of this analysis. The first row gives the values of ϕ_A for the different trial sample sizes, which we may easily obtain from the formula we calculated previously (see pp. 76–77), namely, $\phi_A = .395\sqrt{n'}$. The second row gives the $df_{denom.}$ for each value of n, which determines the power function we will consult in reading the power chart; the formula for $df_{denom.}$ is, of course, $df_{S/A} = (a)(n - 1)$. The third row contains the power estimates we obtain when we coordinate the values of each ϕ_A with the appropriate power functions in the chart. I have plotted these values in Fig. 4–2. As you can see, we can easily use this curve to obtain reasonable estimates of sample size over a wide range of power. If we need a more accurate determination of power, we can use this curve to make realistic choices for trial sample sizes.

Table 4–2   Power as a Function of Sample Size

	TRIAL SAMPLE SIZES (n')				
	10	**15**	**20**	**25**	**30**
ϕ_A	1.25	1.53	1.77	1.98	2.16
$df_{S/A}$	36	56	76	96	116
Power	.33	.68	.84	.92	.96

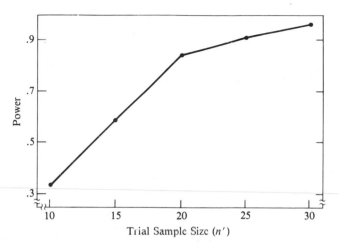

FIGURE 4–2   *Power as a function of sample size.*

Another way we can use a power analysis is to compare the relationship between sample size and power for a number of different plausible outcomes of our experiment or for different estimates of the common population variance. Under these circumstances, we would need to enter these new values into Eq. (4–4) and solve for ϕ_A as a function of n', duplicating the steps we followed in the numerical example (see pp. 76–80). Once we have calculated this formula, we can easily create a table or a graph depicting the relationship between power and sample size for these new estimates. You should find this information helpful in designing an experiment that is reasonably sensitive to several possible outcomes.

Another use of these power-sample size curves is to examine the trade-off between significance level and power over an extended range of trial sample sizes. Researchers generally have not considered relaxing the standard significance level ($\alpha = .05$) and adopting less stringent levels (for example, $\alpha = .10$ or .25), but this option most certainly is a reasonable possibility (see, for example, Cohen, 1977, pp. 15–16). The widespread use of .05 as the standard of statistical significance in the behavioral sciences is simply a convention and we should be willing to break with this convention when the situation calls for it. If careful analysis on our part reveals that we cannot attain reasonable power without relaxing the rejection standard, we should consider doing so. We can view a power analysis as a form of statistical "contract" in which we specify exactly the circumstances under which we will obtain a certain effect. The significance level is part of that contract. I am *not* recommending that we loosen our control of type I error in general, but only when we have integrated a power analysis into our experimental research plan and data analysis. If the effects we seek are significant, we can immediately plan a replication as a responsible response on our part to the use of a more liberal significance level. On the other hand, if the effects are not significant, we will at least have some guarantee—having set power at .80 or higher—that our research hypotheses have been given a fair and sensitive test.

The power charts of Pearson and Hartley cover only two levels of significance, $\alpha = .05$ and $.01$, and thus do not allow us to make power estimates with other levels. Fortunately, Rotton and Schönemann (1978) have prepared a detailed table for less stringent significance levels that supplements the Pearson-Hartley charts. More specifically, their table provides information on power for six levels of significance, namely, $\alpha = .05, .10, .20, .30, .40,$ and $.50$. You use this table by locating your estimate of ϕ, obtained in the usual fashion, in the appropriate part of the table—which is determined by α, $df_{num.}$, and $df_{denom.}$—and then reading the value of power found at that point.[8]

Finally, we can sometimes increase power substantially by reducing the number of treatment conditions included in an experiment to increase the sample size for the remaining conditions (see Cohen, 1977, pp. 362–363, 402–403). We would not consider this option, of course, if all the conditions in the experiment are necessary and critical for the study. On the other hand, we may have been overly ambitious and have included additional conditions that provide either supplemental information or information of secondary importance to the main purpose of the study. Under these circumstances, then, we could drop these conditions without damaging the integrity of the experiment. A power analysis is essential for this decision, of course. We must estimate power with the original experimental design, including the original choice of sample size, and then determine the effects on power of discarding certain groups and redistributing the subjects among the conditions that remain. A power analysis is the only rational way to make this sort of decision.

Using Other Estimates of Effect Size

As I mentioned earlier in this section, we can estimate the anticipated effect size for a proposed experiment in a variety of ways. Once we have this estimate, we can translate this information into ϕ_A and then use this index in conjunction with the Pearson-Hartley charts to determine sample size.

Using Cohen's f Statistic. I illustrated the general process of determining sample size by estimating the population treatment means and error variance (the common within-group variance). You may find it difficult, however, to estimate your expected outcome with this degree of specification. If you are unable to provide such a detailed estimate, you might be able to estimate the range between the largest and smallest treatment means and to specify some expected pattern they might reflect. This information, in addition to an estimate of error variance, can be used to produce Cohen's (1977, pp. 276–280) index of effect size f^2, which is related to ϕ^2 as follows:

$$\phi^2 = n'f^2 \tag{4-5}$$

Central to Cohen's formulas for this index is d, which he defines as the range of

[8]You may have to use linear interpolation to determine power for combinations that fall between the values listed in the table.

the means divided by the standard deviation in the treatment populations.[9] More specifically,

$$d = \frac{\mu_{max.} - \mu_{min.}}{\sigma_{S/A}} \tag{4–6}$$

where $\mu_{max.}$ = the largest population treatment mean
$\quad\quad\mu_{min.}$ = the smallest population treatment mean
$\quad\quad\sigma_{S/A}$ = the standard deviation in the treatment populations

Armed with an estimate of d and some idea of how the treatment means are distributed between the two extremes, we can estimate Cohen's f. Table 4–3 gives the formulas for calculating f for the three different dispersion patterns of the means, which we described earlier in this section (p. 74).

To illustrate with the current example, suppose that we were able to estimate only the range of the means ($\mu_{max.} - \mu_{min.} = \mu_3 - \mu_1 = 22 - 18 = 4$) and the population standard deviation ($\sqrt{16} = 4$) and that we anticipated that the other two means would fall in the middle between them (Cohen's "minimum" variation among the means). Using Eq. (4–6), we find

$$d = \frac{4}{4} = 1.00$$

Substituting $d = 1.00$ into the formula listed in the first row of Table 4–3, we calculate

$$f = d \sqrt{\frac{1}{(2)(a)}} = 1.00 \sqrt{\frac{1}{(2)(4)}}$$

$$= 1.00 \ \sqrt{.125} = .354$$

We can now use Eq. (4–5) to calculate ϕ; that is,

$$\phi_A^2 = n'f^2 = n'(.354)^2 = .125 \ n'$$

$$\phi_A = .354 \ \sqrt{n'}$$

Table 4–3 Calculating Cohen's f Statistic for Three Different Patterns of the Population Means

Dispersion Pattern	Formula
Minimum variation	$f = d \sqrt{\dfrac{1}{(2)(a)}}$
Intermediate variation	$f = d \sqrt{\dfrac{a + 1}{(12)(a - 1)}}$
Maximum variation	$f = d \dfrac{\sqrt{a^2 - 1}}{(2)(a)}$

[9] Cohen calls this d statistic the **standardized range of the population means**, which is defined as the range of the means divided by the population standard deviation.

We would now begin the process of varying the trial sample size n' until we achieved the level of power we want. As a reminder, we first turn to the third power chart ($df_{num.} = 3$). Using the method described in the last section to select a starting value for n', we find that $\phi = 1.92$ when power is .90 and $df_{denom.} = 60$. Solving for the first trial sample size,

$$n' = \frac{\phi_A^2}{.125} = \frac{(1.92)^2}{.125} = 29.49$$

If we use $n' = 30$,

$$\phi_A = (.354) \sqrt{30} = (.354)(5.477) = 1.94$$

and power is approximately .90.[10]

Using Omega Squared.   Even if we are unable to estimate the range of the means and the population standard deviation, we can still conduct a power analysis simply by estimating the population omega squared, ω_A^2. We could obtain such an estimate from pilot work we have conducted or from the work of others appearing in related studies reported in the literature. The relationship between ϕ_A^2 and ω_A^2 is as follows:

$$\phi_A^2 = n' \frac{\omega_A^2}{1 - \omega_A^2} \tag{4-7}$$

Even if we could find no estimate of ω_A^2, we could simply guess at a realistic effect size. Suppose we hoped to detect a "medium" effect, which happens to reflect the average effect size reported in psychological research (see Sedlmeier & Gigerenzer, 1989). You will recall that Cohen (1977) has defined a "medium" effect as $\hat{\omega}_A^2 = .06$. Substituting this value in Eq. (4–7), we find

$$\phi_A^2 = n' \frac{.06}{1 - .06} = n' \frac{.06}{.94}$$

$$= .0638 \, n'$$

Taking the square root of ϕ_A^2 gives us $\phi_A = .253 \sqrt{n'}$, which we can use to estimate the sample size required to achieve a particular degree of power. Without showing the steps, I determined that n must be approximately 58 to provide us with a power of .90 to detect a "medium" effect.[11]

Summary of Formulas.   Table 4–4 provides a summary of the various formulas by which ϕ^2 may be calculated. These formulas will permit you to shift from

---

[10] If we simply cannot specify a pattern for the minimum treatment effects we wish to detect, we can use the d statistic alone to estimate sample size. Under these circumstances, we can turn to a convenient table prepared by Hinkle and Oliver (1983) for exactly this situation. In the present example, we would locate the column for $d = 1.00$, which is designated 1.0 σ in the table, and find the sample size for $a = 4$ groups, $\alpha = .05$, and power .90; the estimated value from their table is $n = 29$.

[11] See problem 6b in the exercises if you want to determine this value yourself.

Table 4–4   Calculating ϕ^2 for the Pearson-Hartley Power Charts

General formula:	$\phi^2 = n \dfrac{\Sigma (\mu_i - \mu_T)^2 / a}{\sigma_{S/A}^2}$
Relation to f:	$\phi^2 = nf^2$
Relation to ω^2:	$\phi^2 = n \dfrac{\omega^2}{1 - \omega^2}$

one measure of effect size to another and to use information available in other power charts and tables that are based on one of these measures.

Using the Cohen Power Tables

Cohen (1977) provides a useful set of tables for calculating the sample size needed to control the power of an experiment (pp. 381–389).[12] He presents three basic tables, one for three different significance levels ($\alpha = .10, .05,$ and $.01$). Each basic table consists of 11 subtables, which are differentiated by the number of degrees of freedom associated with the numerator of the F ratio ($df_{num.} = 1, 2, 3, 4, 5, 6, 8, 10, 12, 15,$ and 24). For our example, we would need the subtable for $df_{num.} = 3$ (Table 8.4.4). Each of these subtables lists a range of values for Cohen's f statistic ($.05, .10, .15, .20, .25, .30, .35, .40, .50, .60, .70,$ and $.80$) and a range of values for power ($.10, .50, .70, .80, .90, .95,$ and $.99$). Since $f^2 = \phi_A^2 / n'$, we can use the value for ϕ_A^2 we calculated previously for our original example (see p. 77). More specifically, we found that $\phi_A^2 = .1563\ n'$. Thus, $f^2 = .1563$ and $f = \sqrt{.1563} = .395$. If we coordinate $f = .395$ with power $= .90$ for the $\alpha = .05$ significance level, using Cohen's Table 8.4.4 (p. 384), we find a sample size of approximately $n = 23$, which is identical to the one we obtained by using the Pearson-Hartley charts.

You may find Cohen's tables a useful way to estimate sample size. They encompass a wide variety of experimental situations and there is the added bonus of a less stringent significance level ($\alpha = .10$), if you are willing to increase type I error from $\alpha = .05$ to $\alpha = .10$ as a way of achieving greater power. One possible drawback is the need to use linear interpolation for entries that fall between those categories of f and power that are provided in the table.

Using Computer Programs to Estimate Sample Size

Software programs are beginning to appear that greatly facilitate the estimation of power and sample size. I can easily envision the time when tables and charts will be replaced by computer programs that provide the same information with greater speed and more accuracy. When we reach that time, there will be no good excuse

---

[12] The most recent version of Cohen's book (1988) provides updated references and includes some new material. The chapter dealing with the analysis of variance (Chap. 8) received only minor revisions, however, thus allowing researchers to use the material in the revised edition (1977) and the second edition (1988) interchangeably.

for researchers to fail to take power into consideration during the planning stages of their experiments. Although it is true that researchers will still have to provide estimates of the minimum effect sizes they wish to detect—for many, this is a serious stumbling block—the programs will inform them quickly what the sample size must be or what power will be achieved. Researchers will be able to try out different values for α, power, and n to determine an optimal course of action, that is, a feasible combination of significance level, power, and sample size for their studies. I find it difficult to offer specific recommendations here because information about the availability of programs is rapidly changing and any advice will soon be out of date. You will probably find out about useful programs from your friends and colleagues. This source of information is particularly appealing because you will have someone who may be willing to help you learn how to use these specialized programs, not a minor consideration when working with a new computer program.

Where else might you find out about statistical software programs? First, there are several software directories, which should be kept reasonably up to date. The American Psychological Association, for example, publishes a software directory for psychologists (Stoloff & Couch, 1988). A more useful directory, which lists over 200 statistical software packages, is also available (Woodward, Elliot, Gray, & Matlock, 1988). Second, certain professional journals provide a timely source of information. *Behavior Research Methods, Instruments, & Computers* and *Educational and Psychological Measurement*, for example, publish announcements of new programs developed by researchers, which are usually available from the author for a nominal sum. The *American Statistician* also publishes announcements of new programs as well as substantial reviews of established statistical software packages. Detailed reviews may also be found in two other journals, the *British Journal of Mathematical and Statistical Psychology* and *Multivariate Behavioral Research*. Finally, some computer magazines, such as *Byte* and *PC Magazine*, periodically publish in-depth reviews of statistical programs.

I do want to mention several programs that are currently available for power determination, although I cannot guarantee they will be available when you read this paragraph. Jacob Cohen, who has devoted much of his professional life to the power-sample size problem, has published a software package with Michael Borenstein entitled Statistical Power Analysis (Borenstein & Cohen, 1988). A useful program called Ganova 4—Power Computations has been developed by researchers in the Psychology Department at the University of California, Los Angeles (Brecht, Woodward, & Bonett, 1988). Another program, PC-Size, is available at nominal cost from its author (see Dallal, 1986). A final program, called STAT POWER, is written for the Apple computer (Anderson, 1981). Additional programs designed for determining sample size and power with MS/PC-DOS computers have been reviewed and compared by Goldstein (1989).

4.5   ESTIMATING THE POWER OF AN EXPERIMENT

Our focus up to this point has centered on the use of power to provide a rational basis for choosing an appropriate sample size. There is another use for power, which usually takes place *after* an experiment has been completed, a procedure sometimes called a **post hoc power analysis**. The power analyses reported by Cohen (1962), Sedlmeier and Gigerenzer (1989), and others, which supported the conclusion that many of the studies reported in our journals are underpowered, are examples.

These analyses were conducted on studies reporting significant statistical tests. Post hoc power analyses are frequently useful when we attempt to interpret an *F* test that is not significant. Does a nonsignificant test mean that the null hypothesis is true in the sense that the differences are either trivial or nonexistent, or does a nonsignificant test mean that there may be differences present but that there was insufficient power to detect them? One way to resolve this ambiguity is to estimate omega squared or some other index of relative treatment magnitude. Since estimated omega squared is essentially uninfluenced by sample size, its magnitude will provide useful information regardless of the underlying power of the experiment on which it based. It is for this reason that editors and reviewers urge that we estimate relative treatment magnitude for *all* statistical tests we perform. A "small" but significant *F* might suggest the presence of a "trivial" effect that was detected by a particularly powerful experiment, whereas a "medium" but nonsignificant *F* might suggest the possible presence of an "important" effect that was not detected because of a serious lack of power.[13]

Estimating Power from the Pearson-Hartley Charts

We can easily estimate the power of an experiment from the Pearson-Hartley charts by estimating omega squared and then using other information to enter the charts and determine power. Let's see how this is done. Suppose that we came across an interesting experiment with the following characteristics:

$$F = 3.20, a = 3, \text{ and } n = 5$$

Since the critical value of $F(2, 12) = 3.89$, the *F* is not significant ($\alpha = .05$). Using Eq. (4–2), we find

$$\hat{\omega}^2_A = \frac{(a - 1)(F - 1)}{(a - 1)(F - 1) + (a)(n)}$$

$$= \frac{(3 - 1)(3.20 - 1)}{(3 - 1)(3.20 - 1) + (3)(5)} = \frac{4.40}{4.40 + 15} = .227$$

Simply by estimating omega squared we have made an important discovery, namely, there is a potentially important effect (falling well within Cohen's "large" category) reflected in these data. The reason the researcher failed to reject the null hypothesis is probably because of the low power afforded by the relatively small sample size ($n = 5$).

---

[13]For an example of the importance of considering power when interpreting nonsignificant results, see Stevens (1986, p. 137).

To use the Pearson-Hartley charts, we need to calculate ϕ. From Table 4–4, we find that

$$\phi^2 = n \frac{\omega^2}{1 - \omega^2}$$

Substituting in this equation the value for omega squared we estimated for this experiment ($\hat{\omega}_A^2 = .227$), we obtain

$$\hat{\phi}_A^2 = n \frac{\hat{\omega}_A^2}{1 - \hat{\omega}_A^2} \tag{4–8}$$

$$= 5 \frac{.227}{1 - .227} = (5)(.2937) = 1.469$$

and $\hat{\phi}_A = \sqrt{1.469} = 1.21$. We now turn to the second chart in Table A–2 ($df_{num.} = 2$) and find the power curve for $df_{denom.} = 12$. For $\phi = 1.21$, power is approximately .36. You can understand now why the F test was not significant—power was simply too low to detect an effect even this large.

What sort of sample size would we need to detect this effect? We can use this same information to estimate the sample size we would need to reject the null hypothesis at $\alpha = .05$, but at a more comfortable power of .80. From Eq. (4–8), we obtain

$$\hat{\phi}_A^2 = n' \frac{.227}{1 - .227} = .294 \, n' \text{ and } \hat{\phi}_A = .542 \, \sqrt{n'}$$

If we try $n' = 12$ as a trial sample size,[14] we find

$$\hat{\phi}_A = .542 \sqrt{12} = (.542)(3.464) = 1.88$$

Since $df_{denom.} = (a)(n - 1) = (3)(12 - 1) = 33$, we will use the power function for $df_{denom.} = 30$. Locating $\phi = 1.88$ on this curve, I estimate power to be approximately .80. Assuming that this particular sample size does not exhaust our resources, we would design a new experiment with $n = 12$ as the sample size and know that the study will be reasonably sensitive (power $= .80$) for detecting an effect of this relative magnitude ($\hat{\omega}_A^2 = .227$).

Estimating Power from the Cohen Tables

Since Cohen's (1977, 1988) tables are familiar to many researchers, I will show how to estimate the power of an experiment by using his system of calculation. Cohen's extensive tables (pp. 289–354) require the calculation of f rather than $\hat{\phi}_A$. We can calculate f^2 with the following formula:

---

[14] I used the procedure I outlined earlier in this chapter for arriving at this starting sample size (see p. 79). To illustrate briefly, I first determined the value of ϕ associated with a power of .80 from the power function for $df_{denom.} = 60$; the value I found was $\phi = 1.83$. By expressing the formula, $\hat{\phi}_A^2 = .294 \, n'$, in terms of n'—that is, $n' = \hat{\phi}_A^2 / .294$—and substituting $\phi = 1.83$ in the new expression, I determined $n' = (1.83)^2 / .294 = 11.39$. I chose to use $n' = 12$ as a convenient starting value.

$$f^2 = \frac{\hat{\omega}_A^2}{1 - \hat{\omega}_A^2} \tag{4-9}$$

Substituting $\hat{\omega}_A^2 = .227$ in Eq. (4-9), we find

$$f^2 = \frac{.227}{1 - .227} = .294 \text{ and } f = \sqrt{.294} = .542$$

Consulting Cohen's Table 8.3.13 (p. 313) for $\alpha = .05$, $f = .54$, $df_{num.} = 3$, and n = 5, I find power to be approximately .37, very close to the value we obtained with the Pearson-Hartley charts.

4.6 "PROVING" THE NULL HYPOTHESIS

When researchers obtain a nonsignificant F, many are tempted to conclude that the independent variable produced no systematic effects on the dependent vari- able. Or stated more strongly, they are tempted to conclude that there are no treat- ment effects in the population, that they have in effect "proved" that the null hypothesis is true. What exactly can we conclude under these circumstances? Failing to reject the null hypothesis means that the differences we observed in our experiment were *too small* to permit us to conclude that the population treatment means are dif- ferent. We do not conclude that treatment differences are absent or lacking, but that the experiment is not sufficiently sensitive to detect them if they did exist.

Is there any way we can determine whether treatment effects are truly ab- sent? Technically, no—we cannot *prove* that the population treatment means are identical. On a more practical level, however, we could specify a band or set of values that we consider "trivial," "unimportant," or "negligible," which we are willing to assert is functionally equivalent to the complete absence of treatment effects. Some methodologists refer to this band as the **null range** (for example, Greenwald, 1975; Hays, 1973, pp. 850–853). Suppose we conducted an experiment with sufficient power to allow us to detect an effect just outside the null range. By creating an experiment with a low degree of risk for both type I *and* type II error, we could reasonably conclude that treatment effects are "trivial" (or functionally nonexistent) when we fail to reject the null hypothesis.[15]

It is important to note how this procedure I just described parallels the more familiar procedure of hypothesis testing. In both cases, we set up a situation in which we specify the risks involved when we reject the null hypothesis (α) and when we fail to reject the null hypothesis (β). We establish the risk of a type I error (α) by choosing an appropriate significance level and of a type II error (β) by esti- mating the size of the minimum treatment effects we wish to detect and choosing a sample size to achieve it. The "minimum treatment effects" in the more typical case of hypothesis testing refer to the smallest set of differences of any interest to us, whereas in the case of proving the null hypothesis they refer to the largest set of differences that we would still consider functionally equivalent to zero.

[15]The steps involved in accepting the null hypothesis are described in an interesting article by Greenwald (1975).

Experiments designed to prove the null hypothesis are rare in psychology. Moreover, many of these are deficient in the sense that they have failed to establish convincing degrees of power (Sedlmeier & Gigerenzer, 1989). As I have argued, it is not sufficient simply to fail to reject the null hypothesis to "prove" it, but you must do so under conditions of high power. Most researchers are unwilling to commit the resources necessary to achieve this experimental state of affairs. As an example, suppose we consider an effect size of $\omega^2 = .01$ as representing the transition between a negligible effect and one of some interest. Let's assume that we have only two conditions and that we would like to establish the same risk for both types of error, namely, $\alpha = .05$ and $\beta = .05$, which seems most appropriate under the circumstances. To use the Pearson-Hartley charts (Table A–2), we need to calculate ϕ_A, which we can obtain by means of Eq. (4–8):

$$\phi_A^2 = n' \frac{\omega_A^2}{1 - \omega_A^2} = n' \frac{.01}{1 - .01}$$

$$= .0101 \, n'$$

Taking the square root of this value gives us $\phi_A = .1005\sqrt{n'}$. We can facilitate the process of finding the trial sample size n' by finding the value of ϕ that is associated with a power of .95; we will use the power function for $df_{denom.} = \infty$, which should give us a reasonable approximation for any large value of n'. From the first chart ($df_{num.} = 1$), we determine that for a power of .95, we will need a ϕ of 2.55 (please note that the power functions for $\alpha = .05$ are drawn on the right and the appropriate scale on the baseline is the lower one). Solving for n', we find

$$n' = \frac{\phi_A^2}{.0101} = \frac{(2.55)^2}{.0101} = 643.81$$

Thus, we will need a sample size of around $n' = 644$ subjects to provide the desired power for detecting this minimum effect. Perhaps you can understand now why few researchers ever take these steps to "prove" the null hypothesis. Even if we relax our target power to .90 or .80, we still would need large numbers of subjects ($n = 519$ and 384, respectively).

The purpose of this section is to point out the misconception that many researchers harbor that a nonsignificant difference between two groups implies that there is no difference between the two groups. I argued that the appropriate conclusion in such a situation, which revolves around a specification of and a concern for power, is that the experiment may have not been sufficiently sensitive to detect a true difference. I also indicated that an experiment that is specifically designed to prove the null hypothesis usually requires a huge commitment of subjects and, as a consequence, is likely to be undertaken only when it is vitally important to show that a particular effect does not exist (for an example of such an undertaking, see Gillig & Greenwald, 1974).

4.7 EXERCISES[16]

1. Table 3–2 (p. 45) summarizes the analysis of a single-factor experiment.
   a. Calculate $\hat{\omega}_A^2$ from these data, using both Eq. (4–1) and Eq. (4–2).
   b. Using the same data, calculate R^2.
   c. What do these two quantities tell you about the outcome of this experiment?
2. a. Calculate $\hat{\omega}_A^2$ with the data presented in problem 2 in the exercises for Chap. 3.
   b. What does this quantity tell you about the outcome of this experiment?
3. Consider the analysis of variance obtained from two single-factor experiments summarized in the accompanying table.
   a. Calculate $\hat{\omega}_A^2$ for these two studies.
   b. What has this index told you about the relative outcomes of these two experiments?

Summary Tables for Two Experiments

Source	SS	df	MS	F
A	233.33	2	116.67	6.52*
S/A	376.00	21	17.90	
Total	609.33	23		
A	233.33	2	116.67	6.52*
S/A	1,557.30	87	17.90	
Total	1,790.63	89		

*$p < .05$.

4. Suppose an experimenter is planning an experiment with $a = 5$ different treatments and is able to assume the following population data: $\mu_1 = 10$, $\mu_2 = 10$, $\mu_3 = 14$, $\mu_4 = 16$, $\mu_5 = 15$. On the basis of past research, the experimenter estimates the population error variance to be 15.
   a. What sample size will the researcher need to achieve power of .80 at $\alpha = .05$?
   b. What sample size is needed to achieve power of .90?
   c. Suppose the researcher prefers to work at the .01 significance level. What sample sizes would be needed to achieve power of .80 and .90?
5. Cohen (1977) proposed a simplified way of specifying a pattern of results, which we considered in Sec. 4.4. Let's see how this procedure works with a a numerical example. We will assume that $a = 8$, $n = 9$, and the population error variance 27.56. We next estimate the smallest and largest population means, $\mu_{min.} = 5$ and $\mu_{max.} = 12$, and then assign values to the remaining means according to one of three possible patterns, which follow. Estimate power for each of these patterns, assuming that $\alpha = .05$.
   a. The pattern of means reflects *minimum variability* (the six remaining means are placed at the midpoint between the two extremes).
   b. The pattern of means reflects *intermediate variability* (the six means are spaced equally between the two extremes).

[16]The answers to these problems are found in Appendix B.

    c. The pattern of means reflects *maximum variability* (half of the remaining means are given the minimum value and the other half are given the maximum value).

6. Another way to estimate the sample size needed to obtain a certain degree of power is to express the minimum treatment effects we expect to find in terms of omega squared. Let's assume we plan an experiment with $a = 4$ treatment conditions and would like to choose a sample size that will detect a small treatment effect at the .05 level of significance. You will recall that Cohen (1977) suggests that a "small" effect is an experiment that produces an omega squared of .01 (see p. 66).

    a. What sample size would we need to achieve power of .90?

    b. Suppose we convince ourselves that an omega squared of .01 is an unrealistically small value and decide that a "medium" effect ($\omega_A^2 = .06$) is more appropriate. What sample size would we need to obtain the same degree of power?

5

Assumptions
and
Other Considerations

In this chapter, I consider a variety of important points and details that surround the use and interpretation of the analysis of variance. I begin with a brief discussion of the statistical model on which the F test is based. I then examine supplemental indices that add useful information to the interpretation of a set of results. These will include interval estimates of the population treatment means and the assessment of the differences among the within-group variances. I follow this discussion with a detailed consideration of the effects of violating one of the statistical assumptions underlying the analysis of variance, namely, that the population treatment variances are equal.

5.1   THE STATISTICAL MODEL

The logic of the F test was discussed in Chaps. 2 and 3 without reference to the statistical model underlying the analysis of variance. In this section, I describe certain critical features of this model, attempting to maintain a level of explanation that is in keeping with the purpose of this book. If you desire a more thorough description of this model and a specification of the steps involved in the statistical derivations based on the model, I recommend the discussion offered by Myers (1979, pp. 59–66).[1]

Our discussion begins with the assumption of an infinitely large population of individuals. Let's assume that these individuals are randomly assigned to the different treatment conditions. The set of scores obtained from subjects receiving the same treatment is called a **treatment population**. There is a different treatment population for each condition of the experiment. The mean of a treatment population is μ_i, and the overall mean of the treatment populations is μ_T, obtained by averaging the μ_i's. For statistical purposes, an experiment is assumed to consist of samples of size n that are drawn randomly from the treatment populations. The null hypothesis represents one possible statement about the population treatment means, namely, that they are equal. The data from the experiment are used to test the reasonableness of this particular hypothesis.

The Linear Model

The linear model, which underlies the analysis of variance, is a mathematical statement expressing the score of any subject in any treatment condition as the linear sum of the parameters of the population. In the case of the completely randomized single-factor design, the model states

$$Y_{ij} = \mu_T + \alpha_i + \epsilon_{ij} \qquad (5\text{--}1)$$

where Y_{ij} = one of the observations in any one of the treatment groups
$\quad\mu_T$ = the grand mean of the treatment populations

---

[1]A more comprehensive treatment of the statistical model is offered by Kirk (1982, Chap. 5); the discussion is technical and will be best appreciated if you have a working knowledge of matrix algebra.

$\alpha_i = \mu_i - \mu_T$, known as the **treatment effect** for condition a_i

$\epsilon_{ij} = Y_{ij} - \mu_i$, assumed to reflect experimental error

We make certain assumptions concerning the distribution of the treatment populations, which I mention only briefly here. First, we assume that the scores are mutually *independent*, which means in essence that we assigned subjects randomly to the different treatments. Second, we assume that the scores in the treatment populations are *normally distributed*. Finally, we assume that the *variances* of the scores in the treatment populations are *equal*. (This common variance, σ_{error}^2, is called **error variance**.) Keeping these assumptions in mind, we can now consider the internal structure—known as the **expected values**—of the two mean squares we normally obtain in the analysis of variance.

Expected Mean Squares

Statistical theory provides information about the theoretical expectations, or contents, of statistics calculated from data. More specifically, the expected value of a statistic is the mean of the sampling distribution of that statistic obtained from repeated random sampling from the population. In the case of the two mean squares of interest, the expected values are the average values of MS_A and $MS_{S/A}$ calculated from an extremely large number of replicated experiments based on independent random sampling from the treatment populations. Let's look at the expected values of these two mean squares.

The within-groups mean square $MS_{S/A}$ provides an unbiased estimate of error variance, σ_{error}^2. That is, repeated random samplings would produce a sampling distribution of $MS_{S/A}$ with a mean equal to the variance in the population. Stated in symbols,

$$E(MS_{S/A}) = \sigma_{error}^2 \tag{5–2}$$

where $E(MS_{S/A})$ is read, "the expected value of the within-groups mean square."

The expected value of the treatment mean square, $E(MS_A)$, is not equal to the treatment component but rather represents a combination of the treatment component and error variance. You can see this point quite vividly by considering the expected value for the treatment mean square, namely,

$$E(MS_A) = \sigma_{error}^2 + n\,\frac{\Sigma\,(\alpha_i)^2}{a - 1} \tag{5–3}$$

I will designate the second term on the right of the equal sign $n\,(\theta_A^2)$, where θ_A^2 is the treatment component, $\Sigma\,(\alpha_i)^2\,/(a - 1)$, and n is the number of observations contributing to the estimate of each treatment population mean. More compactly,

$$E(MS_A) = \sigma_{error}^2 + n\,(\theta_A^2) \tag{5–4}$$

The symbol θ_A^2 is used to indicate that this particular quantity is based on an additional assumption that refers to the way in which the levels of the treatment variable have been selected for the experiment. That is, Eqs. (5–3) and (5–4) reflect the

fixed-effects model, which is appropriate when the levels of the treatment variable have been selected *arbitrarily*—as they are in most experiments. A different model, the **random-effects model**, applies when the treatment levels have been selected *randomly*. I will discuss random models and the effects of randomly chosen treatment levels on the analysis of variance in later chapters.

The essential logic of the analysis of variance lies in the construction of ratios having the form

$$\frac{MS_{effect}}{MS_{error}}$$

where the expected value of the MS_{error} matches the expected value of the MS_{effect} in all respects except for the component reflecting the effect. In the present case,

$$E(MS_A) = \sigma_{error}^2 + n\,(\theta_A^2)$$

$$E(MS_{S/A}) = \sigma_{error}^2$$

Under the null hypothesis,

$$H_0\colon \mu_1 = \mu_2 = \mu_3 = \text{etc.} = \mu_T$$

Since $\alpha_i = \mu_i - \mu_T$, the null hypothesis can also be stated as follows:

$$H_0\colon \alpha_1 = \alpha_2 = \alpha_3 = \text{etc.} = 0$$

Either way, the "effect" component, θ_A^2, or the **null-hypothesis component**, as it is often called, equals zero, and the ratio

$$F = \frac{MS_A}{MS_{S/A}}$$

is distributed as $F(df_A, df_{S/A})$, provided the assumptions we mentioned earlier are satisfied. We can then relate the observed value of F to the tabled values of F and assess its significance through the application of the decision rules.

Violating the Assumptions of the Analysis of Variance

As I have indicated already, certain assumptions concerning the distribution of scores within groups must be met if the analysis of variance is to work as described. The values listed in the F table are based on the theoretical F distribution. These values are appropriate for an analysis only when these distribution assumptions are satisfied. If they are not, we have no simple way of determining whether or not $F_{observed}$ falls within the rejection region of the theoretical sampling distribution of this statistic—whatever it might be with a particular set of violations. The critical question for us, of course, is to see how our conclusions are affected by a failure of our experiment to meet these assumptions. Such a consideration is extremely important since rarely will we find all the assumptions satisfied in the experiments we conduct. If even the slightest violation can result in a considerable change in the sampling distribution of the F statistic, we are in trouble.

Independence of Scores.   The first assumption of the analysis of variance is that the Y scores are independent *within* treatment groups as well as independent *between* treatment groups. Independence here means that each observation is in no way related to any other observations in the experiment. We achieve independence by randomly assigning subjects to conditions and testing them individually.[2] This is not only a statistical assumption but a basic requirement of experimental design as well. With nonindependence of scores between treatment groups, there is a confounding of variables, and we are unable to make unambiguous inferences concerning the independent influence of our independent variable on the behavior we are studying. This assumption, then, emphasizes the critical importance statistically, as well as experimentally, of ensuring the random assignment of subjects to the treatment groups.

Normally Distributed Treatment Populations.   The second assumption states that the individual treatment populations, from which the members of each treatment group are assumed to be randomly drawn, are normally distributed. As a rough test of this assumption, we could look at the Y scores within each group and estimate the general shape of the distributions. Suppose the distributions are not reasonably bell-shaped, or normal? What effects do violations of this assumption have on the sampling distribution of the F statistic and on our decision-making process? Methodologists and applied statisticians have approached this problem by conducting Monte Carlo studies in which computers are used to draw scores at random from populations with characteristics differing from those assumed in the analysis and to conduct analyses of variance on them. These populations are constructed to have the same mean but different shapes. The resultant *empirical* sampling distribution of the F's obtained from these "experiments" will equal the *theoretical* distribution of F only if the violations of the assumptions are unimportant. The degree to which the empirically derived sampling distribution deviates from the theoretical distribution provides an assessment of the practical consequences of these violations.

The general conclusion we can draw from the Monte Carlo studies reported in the literature is that the F test is not particularly affected when the distribution of scores are symmetrical, but not normal, and when the sample sizes are equal and are greater than $n = 12$ (Clinch & Keselman, 1982; Tan, 1982). If we consider asymmetrical distributions, the situation becomes quite complicated (Bradley, 1980a, 1980b) and obvious solutions to the problem appear to be ineffective (Wike & Church, 1982a, 1982b). If your data appear to be asymmetrical, you should seek statistical advice or shift your significance level from the typical $\alpha = .05$ to a more stringent criterion, for example, $\alpha = .025$ or .01; this new significance level should

---

[2]A common way in which the independence assumption is violated is by testing subjects in small groups rather than as individuals. Stevens (1986, pp. 203–204) provides a useful discussion of this problem.

provide a reasonable correction for any distortions that might occur under these particular circumstances.

Homogeneity of Variance. Considerably more attention has been given to the effects of violating the assumption of equal variances than of violating the assumption of normality. Early work on this problem by Box (1954a) suggested that the F test was relatively insensitive to the presence of variance heterogeneity, except when unequal sample sizes were involved (for an excellent review of this older literature, see Glass, Peckham, & Sanders, 1972). More recent work summarized by Wilcox (1987a, pp. 30–32) clearly questions this earlier conclusion, however. More specifically, the F test becomes seriously biased in the positive direction when the largest within-group variance divided by the smallest within-group variance, which we will refer to as $F_{max.}$, is 9 or greater. What this means is that the actual significance level revealed by Monte Carlo studies is substantially greater than the level chosen by researchers to evaluate an obtained F; with the significance level set at $\alpha = .05$, for instance, the actual significance level may be as high as .08 or even higher. The degree of discrepancy between the chosen, or **nominal**, level and the actual level revealed by Monte Carlo studies depends on a number of factors. Rogan and Keselman (1977), for example, found that the discrepancy between the nominal and the actual significance levels increases as the degree of heterogeneity increases. They also found a tendency for the discrepancy to decrease but not disappear with larger sample sizes; others have reported similar findings (for example, Brown & Forsythe, 1974c; Wilcox, Charlin, & Thompson, 1986). The pattern of heterogeneity is also important. In general, the discrepancy is larger when the heterogeneity is associated with one deviant group than when it is spread among all the groups. To illustrate, Wilcox, Charlin, and Thompson (1986) sampled from two sets of treatment populations, one with standard deviations of 1, 2, 3, and 4 and the other with standard deviations of 1, 1, 1, and 4. With a sample size of $n = 11$, the actual significance levels were .068 and .109, respectively; with $n = 21$, the corresponding levels were .069 and .097. Finally, the effects of heterogeneity are even more serious with unequal sample sizes. The findings reveal a complex relationship between the patterns of heterogeneity and the sample sizes allocated to the specific variances included in any given set.[3]

One difficulty with these studies is in relating them to actual experiments. Since standard deviations are frequently not provided in research reports, we cannot determine what sorts of variance heterogeneity are typically found in behavioral studies. Wilcox (1987a) examined several volumes of the *American Educational Research Journal* and found only 14 studies in which standard deviations were reported; of these, 3 exhibited values of $F_{max.} > 16$. Although it may be true that the degree of heterogeneity found in most experiments is less than the heterogeneity included in the typical Monte Carlo study, the inflation in type I error resulting from the heterogeneity is still a serious matter of concern. Even studies in which the degree of heterogeneity was purposely chosen to represent

---

[3]There may even be additional complications when one or more of the treatment populations is asymmetrical (Bradley, 1980a, 1980b).

what is found in most typical experiments, the discrepancy between the chosen significance level and the actual level is still in the range of 1 or 2 percent (Rogan & Keselman, 1977; Tomarken & Serlin, 1986).

How do we cope with this problem? Applied statisticians have proposed a number of solutions, including abandoning the analysis of variance altogether (Wilcox, 1987a). I will consider this important topic in Sec. 5.2.

Estimating the Population Treatment Means

Estimation procedures usually associated with survey studies can be applied to the data of an experiment to provide interval estimates of the population treatment means. Interval estimates that are formed in consideration of the degree of risk are called **confidence intervals**. The degree of confidence is given by the expression

$$\text{confidence} = 100(1 - \alpha) \text{ percent}$$

If we allow the proportion of erroneous interval estimates—intervals that do not include the population mean—we may ever make to be $\alpha = .05$, say, our interval estimates are referred to as

$$100(1 - .05) = 100(.95) = 95 \text{ percent confidence intervals}$$

The formula for establishing the lower and upper limits of a confidence interval of a treatment population mean is

$$\hat{\mu}_i \pm (t)(\hat{\sigma}_M), \tag{5-5}$$

where $\hat{\mu}_i$ is the **point estimate** of the population mean, t is a standardized deviate from the t distribution, and $\hat{\sigma}_M$ is a point estimate of the standard deviation of the sampling distribution of the mean (also known as the **standard error of the mean**). We obtain the quantities specified in Eq. (5–5) as follows:

$\hat{\mu}_i$ is the mean of the treatment group (Y_{A_i}).
t is found in Table A–3, to be explained in a moment.
$\hat{\sigma}_M$ is obtained by Eq. (5–6).

More specifically,

$$\hat{\sigma}_M = \sqrt{\frac{MS_{S/A}}{n}} \tag{5-6}$$

The numerator of this fraction—$MS_{S/A}$, the within-group mean square from the overall analysis—is actually an average of the individual variances for the treatment groups; this quantity provides an estimate of the variability in the treatment populations, which are assumed to be equal in the analysis of variance.[4]

---

[4]Some researchers prefer to estimate $\hat{\sigma}_M$ separately for each treatment group, which is a good idea if you have reason to question the homogeneity assumption. The calculations are then based on standard deviations (s_i) for each group; that is, $\hat{\sigma}_{M_i} = s_i / \sqrt{n}$. The formula for the confidence interval becomes $\hat{\mu}_i \pm (t)(\hat{\sigma}_{M_i})$; the value for t, which is discussed in the next paragraph, will be based on the degrees of freedom associated with the within-group variance, namely, $df = n - 1$.

As an example, we will calculate a confidence interval based on the data presented in Table 3–4 (p. 57) and the analysis summary given in Table 3–5 (p. 59). The mean for the four-hour condition (a_1) is 26.50; the sample size is 4; and the pooled within-groups variance, $MS_{S/A}$, is 150.46. From this information, we can obtain the three quantities specified in Eq. (5–5), $\hat{\mu}_i$, t, and $\hat{\sigma}_M$. The first quantity has already been calculated; that is, $\hat{\mu}_i = \overline{Y}_{A_1} = 26.50$. The second term, t, depends on two quantities, the degrees of freedom associated with $MS_{S/A}$, namely, $df = (a)(n - 1)$, and α. If we set $\alpha = .05$, we can find t in a table of the t distribution, Table A–3 of Appendix A. This is accomplished by locating the row where $df = (4)(4 - 1) = 12$ and the column where $\alpha = .05$. This value is 2.18. For the standard error of the mean, $\hat{\sigma}_M$, we substitute in Eq. (5–6) and find

$$\hat{\sigma}_M = \sqrt{\frac{MS_{S/A}}{n}}$$

$$= \sqrt{\frac{150.46}{4}} = \sqrt{37.62} = 6.13$$

From Eq. (5–5), we can obtain the two limits of the 95 percent confidence interval:

$$\hat{\mu}_i \pm (t)(\hat{\sigma}_M) = 26.50 \pm (2.18)(6.13)$$

$$= 26.50 \pm 13.36$$

The value for the lower limit is

$$26.50 - 13.36 = 13.14$$

and the value for the upper limit is

$$26.50 + 13.36 = 39.86$$

The primary function of confidence intervals is to provide an index of the relative precision with which the treatment means are measured. A small confidence interval reflects greater precision than a larger one.

5.2   DEALING WITH HETEROGENEITY OF VARIANCE

For most of us, our research hypotheses are couched in terms of differences that may be observed among the treatment means. Usually, our interest in the within-group variances does not extend beyond a concern for the homogeneity assumption underlying the analysis of variance; even then, most researchers do not assess the validity of this assumption statistically. One reason for this lack of interest in testing for variance heterogeneity is the relatively long-held belief that violations of this assumption (and the normality assumption) have little or no consequences for the F test.[5] Another reason is the confusion surrounding the choice of proce-

---

[5] See Bradley (1978) for an interesting discussion of the extent of this belief and how it persisted even after Monte Carlo studies began to show convincing evidence to the contrary.

dure to use to test for variance heterogeneity; many of the available tests are overly sensitive to violations of the normality assumption, rendering them essentially useless for assessing variance heterogeneity. We will consider a relatively simple test that does not suffer from this problem. I will then discuss what steps we might take if we suspect that the assumption of homogeneous treatment variances is not tenable.

There are also reasons for examining the within-group variances in their own right, not just for a test of the homogeneity assumption. Important changes in behavior caused by the different treatments may not differentially affect average performance but influence the *variability* of subjects instead. Or if we look for them, systematic differences among the treatment conditions might be reflected in average performance and in the variability of the subjects within these conditions. We will consider some examples of situations in which treatment effects may be reflected in the group variances. We will then see how to test for variance differences in an experiment.

Examples of the Variance Reflecting Treatment Effects

Suppose, for example, that subjects employ a number of different strategies in performing a particular task. If they are asked to study a prose passage for an eventual test of comprehension, some may try to extract basic idea units and others may attempt to commit the entire passage to memory. The variability of their performance will reflect any differential efficiency that may be associated with these strategies—extracting idea units may be more efficient in general than learning by rote—in addition to any difference in ability that may exist among subjects. Suppose that subjects in a standard, noninstructed condition are contrasted with subjects in a condition in which they are required to perform the task with a particular strategy. Conceivably, such a comparison would not show much of a difference between the means of the two treatment groups, and a statistical analysis might lead to the conclusion that no treatment effects were present. On the other hand, the subjects in the "restricted" or instructed condition might be more variable in performance than the subjects in the "free" or uninstructed condition. Subjects forced to abandon their usual strategy might experience great difficulty in switching to the new strategy, which, moreover, might even be incompatible with the old one. Any such negative transfer resulting from a forced switch in strategies would show up as an increase of within-group variability for the instructed condition.

Consider another experiment, focused on the effect of administering a mild electric shock to college students each time they make an error on a motor-tracking task. Suppose that the task consists of tracking a moving object with some sighting device. The score for each subject is the number of errors made during a 10-minute tracking period. There are two groups; one receives a shock each time a subject loses track of the object, and one does not. How might the experiment turn out? Subjects differ greatly in how they respond even to the threat of shock—some try harder, whereas others "freeze" and perform poorly. If subjects reacted differentially in this experiment, there should be a marked increase in variance for the shock group, with some subjects reducing their tracking errors and others increasing them. In fact, it is conceivable that the number of subjects responding "positively" to shock would be equal to the number of subjects responding "negatively," the result being no effect on the average tracking errors for the two conditions.

Thus, a comparison of variances may lead to some interesting speculations about individual differences and the way in which subjects within a group respond to the experimental treatments. These comparisons may reveal important clues to the processes responsible for whatever effects are observed among the treatment means.[6]

Testing the Differences Among Variances

The statistical hypotheses evaluated in testing the differences among variances are similar to the ones we evaluate when comparing means. In effect, we are interested in determining whether the different treatment conditions affect the *variability* of the subjects differently. The null and alternative hypotheses are

$H_{0:}$ $\sigma_1^2 = \sigma_2^2 = \sigma_3^2 = $ etc.

H_1: not all σ_i^2's are equal

The problem now is to find a statistical procedure with which we can evaluate this null hypothesis.

Most researchers are familiar with the Hartley, Cochran, and Bartlett tests, which were designed to assess differences among variances. The Hartley test is the simplest of the three; it requires the $F_{max.}$ statistic, which is formed by dividing the largest within-group variance by the smallest, and referring $F_{max.}$ to a special table. As indicated earlier, I cannot recommend these tests because they are affected by departures from normality as well as by the presence of heterogeneity of variance. Conover, Johnson, and Johnson (1981) evaluated 56 different tests that have been proposed to assess variance heterogeneity. These tests were compared on their ability to detect variance heterogeneity when it was present (power) and their insensitivity to departures from normality. The test I will describe was one of those recommended.

Brown and Forsythe (1974b) proposed a test that is based on *transformed Y* scores, which I will refer to as Z scores. A Z score is defined as the deviation of a Y score from the *median* of the Y scores in the relevant treatment group, with the sign of the deviation disregarded (the absolute value of the deviation). That is,

$$Z_{ij} = |Y_{ij} - Md_i| \qquad (5\text{--}7)$$

where Y_{ij} = a score in one of the treatment groups
Md_i = the median of that particular treatment group

---

[6]Martin and Games (1977) offer several examples of studies from education that test hypotheses about variances. Birch and Lefford (1967) and Johnson and Baker (1973) represent interesting examples of the use of variance as a descriptive statistic in other areas of research.

The two vertical lines designate the absolute value of the deviation. Once we have calculated Z scores for each subject, we simply conduct an ordinary analysis of variance, treating the transformed scores as if they were the original Y scores obtained in the experiment. If the F is significant, we conclude that heterogeneity is present.

The Brown-Forsythe procedure tests for heterogeneity indirectly by focusing on the transformed Z scores, which provide a reasonable index of within-group variability—that is, the Z scores will be small when there is a small degree of within-group variability and they will be large when there is a large degree of variability.[7] By the same argument, the average Z scores for each group provide an index of within-group variability. Thus, a significant F indicates that the differences among the group averages exceed chance expectations, allowing us to conclude that the group variances are different. We will now consider a numerical example.

The example is based on data originally given in Table 2–1 (p. 29). These scores are presented again in the upper portion of Table 5–1. To the right of each Y score is the deviation of that score from the relevant group median. The medians

Table 5–1 Numerical Example of the Brown-Forsythe Test for Heterogeneity of Variance

Y Scores and Deviations from Group Medians					
a_1		a_2		a_3	
Y_{1j}	$Y_{1j} - Md_1$	Y_{2j}	$Y_{2j} - Md_2$	Y_{3j}	$Y_{3j} - Md_3$
16	$16 - 16 =\ \ \ 0$	4	$4 - 6 = -2$	2	$2 - 10 = -8$
18	$18 - 16 =\ \ \ 2$	6	$6 - 6 =\ \ \ 0$	10	$10 - 10 =\ \ \ 0$
10	$10 - 16 = -6$	8	$8 - 6 =\ \ \ 2$	9	$9 - 10 = -1$
12	$12 - 16 = -4$	10	$10 - 6 =\ \ \ 4$	13	$13 - 10 =\ \ \ 3$
19	$19 - 16 =\ \ \ 3$	2	$2 - 6 = -4$	11	$11 - 10 =\ \ \ 1$

Transformed Scores			
	a_1	a_2	a_3
	0	2	8
	2	0	0
	6	2	1
	4	4	3
	3	4	1
A_i:	15	12	13
ΣZ_{ij}^2:	65	40	75

Summary of the Analysis				
Source	SS	df	MS	F
A	.93	2	.47	.08
S/A	72.40	12	6.03	
Total	73.33	14		

[7]The Brown-Forsythe procedure is based on a test developed by Levene (1960), who defined Z in terms of deviations from the mean rather than the median of a treatment group. Subsequent Monte Carlo studies revealed that the Levene test has some serious deficiencies, which the Brown-Forsythe test does not (Church & Wike, 1976; Conover, Johnson, & Johnson, 1981).

for the three groups in order are 16, 6, and 10.[8] The transformed deviations, Z, are found in the middle portion of the table. For example, for the first subject in the second group,

$$Z_{2,1} = |Y_{2,1} - Md_2| = |4 - 6| = |-2| = 2$$

The next step is to conduct an analysis of variance on the Z scores, treating them as we would any other set of scores. For this test, we will let A_i be the sum of the Z scores for any treatment group and T be the grand sum of the Z scores. From the data in Table 5–1, we calculate the three basic ratios as follows:

$$[Z] = \Sigma Z^2 = 65 + 40 + 75 = 180$$

$$[A] = \frac{\Sigma A^2}{n} = \frac{15^2 + 12^2 + 13^2}{5} = \frac{538}{5} = 107.60$$

$$[T] = \frac{T^2}{(a)(n)} = \frac{(15 + 12 + 13)^2}{(3)(5)} = \frac{1,600}{15} = 106.67$$

We then combine the basic ratios to obtain the sums of squares. That is,

$$SS_A = [A] - [T] = 107.60 - 106.67 = .93$$

$$SS_{S/A} = [Z] - [A] = 180 - 107.60 = 72.40$$

$$SS_T = [Z] - [T] = 180 - 106.67 = 73.33$$

The remainder of the analysis is summarized in the bottom portion of Table 5–1. The F ratio is formed in the usual way:

$$F = \frac{MS_A}{MS_{S/A}}$$

and is evaluated in the F table, with $df_{num.} = 2$ and $df_{denom.} = 12$. This analysis indicates that the variances are homogeneous.

Evaluating Differences Among the Means When Heterogeneity Is Present

How should we proceed when we suspect that the variances are not equal? The problem, to repeat, is that variance heterogeneity leads to an increase in type I error. If we have adopted the 5 percent level of significance for our research, for example, our actual significance level may be several percentage points higher—6 to 8 percent (or higher)—depending on the degree of heterogeneity; the pattern of differences among the variances; the shape of the distributions of scores in the treatment populations; and the presence of unequal sample sizes, which usually magnifies the discrepancy between our chosen significance level (α) and the actual

---

[8]The median, you will recall, is the score that divides a distribution in such a way that half of the scores are smaller and half are larger than the median. When the number of scores is odd, as they are in this example, the median is the value of the middle-most score; when the number of scores is even, the median is the average of the two scores in the middle.

significance level. I will consider several alternatives to the usual F test that have been proposed to deal with this problem and then follow this presentation with some recommendations on how to proceed.

Statisticians have developed a number of procedures that test the null hypothesis of equal population treatment means without being unduly influenced by the presence of heterogeneity of variance. Unfortunately, none is ideal. Two tests, the **Welch W test** (Welch, 1951) and the **Brown-Forsythe F^* test** (Brown & Forsythe, 1974c), recommended by various reviewers (see, for example, Tomarken & Serlin, 1986), now appear to be unsatisfactory when the number of treatment conditions is greater than $a = 4$ (see Wilcox, 1988; Wilcox, Charlin, & Thompson, 1986).[9] A test developed by James (1951), called **James's second-order method**, appears to avoid these problems (Wilcox, 1988); however, the test is computationally complex and thus an unrealistic alternative for most researchers—at least until the test becomes available in statistical software packages.

An alternative approach, called the **two-stage method**, was proposed by Bishop and Dudewicz (1978) and is discussed in detail by Wilcox (1987b, pp. 161–168). The advantage of this procedure is that it appears to be insensitive to violations of the assumptions of normality and of variance homogeneity and allows control of the power of the test as well. The procedure consists of conducting an experiment in two stages. In the first stage, we plan an experiment, specifying the anticipated effect size and the power we want for rejecting the null hypothesis. We randomly assign a "reasonable" number of subjects to the treatment conditions and conduct the experiment. After collecting the data, we then use this information to determine how many subjects must be added to each treatment group in the second stage to achieve the power we specified during the planning stage of the experiment. We administer the treatments to these additional subjects and then perform some special calculations on all the data from the two stages combined. Numerical examples of the calculations required by this two-stage procedure are provided by Bishop and Dudewicz (1978) and by Wilcox (1987b). What the procedure does is to add more subjects to the more variable treatment groups.

Recommendations

As you can see, the analysis and interpretation of experiments with heterogeneous variances is complicated. It appears that none of the alternatives to the ordinary F test, which have been subjected to careful examination in Monte Carlo studies, has survived unscathed. Just when reviewers strongly urged the use of the Welch test (Tomarken & Serlin, 1986), new evidence was reported that questioned its use in experiments with more than $a = 4$ treatment conditions (see, for example, Wilcox, 1988). The currently favored procedure, James's second-order method, is simply too complicated for general use. Even if computer programs were readily available

---

[9]Both tests involve rather complicated calculations. Formulas for the two tests may be found in a number of readily accessible sources (for example, Clinch & Keselman, 1982; Tomarken & Serlin, 1986; Wilcox, 1987b). A worked example of the two tests appears as exercises in Wilcox (1987b, p. 168), with the answers provided in an appendix (p. 413). Welch (1951) provides a numerical example of his test (p. 335).

for this method, we should still probably wait until the procedure is subjected to the same intensive study as have the other tests we briefly considered in this section. Finally, most researchers will find the two-stage procedure too time-consuming and unwieldly, although one could argue that considerable time will be wasted by researchers working in any given field if studies are reported to be significant because of an inflated type I error or are underpowered because of unequal group variances.

One serious problem in evaluating the Monte Carlo studies is a lack of agreement among applied statisticians about what constitutes the degree of heterogeneity we may normally expect to find in actual experimentation. The values of $F_{max.}$ investigated by Box (1954a), whose findings contributed to the widely held belief that unequal variances did not present a problem for the F test, were relatively small ($F_{max.} = 3$), whereas a great deal of the contemporary research that brought the homogeneity assumption into question is based on relatively large values of $F_{max.}$ (for example, $F_{max.} \geq 16$). Since the problem of increased type I error for the F test and the problematic performance of the Welch and other tests are tied directly to the degree of heterogeneity present, I find it difficult to place these various investigations into perspective. In addition, the patterns of heterogeneity are important as well, both for type I error and for the power of the test. This is particularly evident when there are unequal sample sizes.

What we need is some way to relate the heterogeneity we observe in our experiments to the results of the Monte Carlo studies conducted by applied statisticians and methodologists. Until this sort of information is readily available, we might simply adopt a more stringent significance level—for example, $\alpha = .025$ or .01—whenever the ratio of the largest to the smallest variance is greater than 3:1.[10] By setting $\alpha = .025$, say, we may produce an *actual* significance level fairly close to $\alpha = .05$, or at least within the range around .05 that most researchers would accept as "close enough" (see Bradley, 1978).

As an illustration, consider the results of two Monte Carlo studies that included the same degree of variance heterogeneity ($F_{max.} = 9$). One study examined the effects of variance heterogeneity for $a = 3$ groups (Bishop, 1976, reported in Wilcox, 1987a, p. 31), and the other examined the effects for $a = 4$ and 6 treatment groups (Brown & Forsythe, 1974c). Portions of these studies are presented in Table 5–2. The first column of the table indicates the number of treatment conditions; the second column gives the sample size, n, investigated in any given experiment; and the third column lists the patterns of heterogeneity studied. The actual significance levels when nominal significance level was set at $\alpha = .05$ and .01 are given in the last two columns.

As you can see from Table 5–2, the actual significance levels observed in these studies varied from .063 to .083 when $\alpha = .05$ and from .017 to .030 when $\alpha = .01$. Consider now what would happen if we were to follow my suggestion of adopting a nominal significance level of $\alpha = .01$ when we observe the sorts of variance heterogeneity as those reported in the table in an experiment of ours. You

---

[10]Alternatively, we might decide to take this action whenever the Brown-Forsythe test for heterogeneity is significant. If we adopt this strategy, we should probably use a less stringent significance level in evaluating the Brown-Forsythe F as an effective way of increasing the power of the test.

Table 5–2 Actual Significance Levels Found in Selected Monte Carlo Studies

Number of Groups[a]	Sample Size (n)	Pattern of Variances	Nominal Significance Level $\alpha = .05$	$\alpha = .01$
3	6	1,4,9	.066	.018
	6	1,1,9	.082	.029
	11	1,1,9	.081	.030
4	4	1,4,4,9	.067	.017
	11	1,4,4,9	.063	.018
6	4	1,1,4,9,9	.083	.025
	6	1,1,4,4,9,9	.071	.022
	11	1,1,4,4,9,9	.073	.024
	16	1,1,4,4,9,9	.072	.022
	21	1,1,4,4,9,9	.069	.020

[a]The data for a = 3 are from Bishop (1976), reported in Wilcox (1987a); the data for a = 4 and 6 are from Brown and Forsythe (1974c).

can see that our *actual* significance level would never exceed .05—precisely the significance level we wanted to adopt in the first place. You probably noticed that this strategy actually produced an overcorrection; that is, rather than working at the .01 level, we should be working at about the .025 level to bring the actual significance level closer to the nominal level of α = .05. What we need are Monte Carlo studies that explore the effects of setting the significance level between .05 and .01. It is entirely possible that a nominal significance level of α = .025 will effectively achieve our goal of operating at an actual significance level of α = .05.

One problem is created if we deal with variance heterogeneity by adopting a slightly more stringent significance level, namely, an inevitable loss of power. The basis for this loss of power (or increase in type II error) may be readily understood if you refer back to Fig. 3–3 (p. 55). Looking first at the upper panel, you can see that to increase the significance level, we must use a larger critical F to evaluate the null hypothesis; this is accomplished by shifting the vertical line at F_α to the right. Referring now to the middle panel, which locates β (or type II error) on the noncentral F distribution, you can readily see what happens to β (the shaded area to the left of F_α); that is, moving F_α to the right necessarily increases the area associated with β.

We can compensate for this loss of power by increasing the sample size, n. Let's consider an example. In Chap. 4, we determined that with α = .05, we would need n = 24 to achieve power of .90 for a particular set of hypothetical results. Suppose we decided to compensate for variance heterogeneity by increasing the significance level to α = .025; as a result of this change, we would now need n = 28 to maintain the same degree of power. Table 5–3 gives the sample sizes needed for this example to achieve constant power at three levels (.70, .80, and .90) at three different significance levels (.05, .025, and .01). For this example, at least, the increase in sample size needed to restore the power lost by using α = .025 rather than α = .05 is relatively small and would probably be feasible and well within our experimental "budget."

I hope you do not interpret my comments as a recommendation to ignore the problem of variance heterogeneity. You should always calculate and report your

Table 5–3   Sample Size (n) Needed to Achieve Different
Levels of Power at Three Levels of Significance[a]

	Significance Levels (α)		
Power	.05	.025	.01
.70	16	19	23
.80	19	22	27
.90	24	28	33

[a]Sample sizes were calculated by PC-SIZE (Dallal, 1986).

group standard deviations and be prepared to take some corrective action if the degree of heterogeneity falls into the questionable range of $F_{max.} \geq 3$; it is exactly at this point that variance heterogeneity begins seriously to affect the probability of making type I and type II errors. If we do not examine our data for possible variance heterogeneity or if we fail to take steps to rectify the situation when it is present—such as using a more stringent significance level or conducting an alternative statistical test—our attempts to control type I error and to establish power may have been for nought.

Finally, you should also realize that the excessive type I error resulting from unequal variances can be dealt with in another way—through *replication*. We use statistical procedures as a tool with which we establish the facts of our science. Researchers have adopted one way of admitting new facts to the literature by using a significance level of $\alpha = .05$. The null hypothesis is rejected when the variation among a set of treatment means equals or exceeds this standard of risk. If we are operating under a more liberal criterion for rejecting the null hypothesis, either because of the presence of variance heterogeneity or as a deliberate choice, a reasonable next step is to repeat the study. Our statistical procedures help us decide whether the results of a single experiment are dependable, in the sense that they are repeatable. By actually repeating an experiment operating under increased type I error, we attack the problem directly by attempting to show that the findings in fact are reliable. If we find the same results on two independent occasions, we in essence validate the initial outcome of the study, which was somewhat in doubt because of the excessive type I error.

5.3   EXERCISES[11]

1. With the data from problem 4 in the exercises for Chap. 3, calculate the 95 percent confidence intervals for the population treatment means.
2. We conducted an analysis of variance of the data in Table 3–4 (p. 57) without considering whether the assumption of homogeneous group variances was met.
   a. Use the Brown-Forythe (1974b) test to determine if the variances are heterogeneous.
   b. On the basis of the arguments developed in this chapter, how should we proceed with the analysis?

[11]The answers to these problems are found in Appendix B.

6

Analytical
Comparisons Among
Treatment Means

For most researchers, the completion of the statistical analysis of the completely randomized single-factor experiment as outlined in the previous chapters is only a first step in the analysis of their data. The next three chapters will consider additional analyses we can use in the comprehensive examination of the data we have collected. In this chapter, I concentrate on the analysis of experiments in which the independent variable consists of *qualitative* differences among the treatment conditions, where the interest is in isolating and assessing meaningful comparisons between specific treatment conditions. Chapter 7 focuses on the analysis of experiments in which a *quantitative* independent variable has been manipulated. In this case, we examine the mathematical nature of the relationship between variations in the amount of factor A and changes in behavior. Although this approach may sound formidable, we utilize the same statistical procedures that I discuss in the present chapter. Chapter 8 considers the complications resulting from these additional analyses and offers some recommendations for a plan of analysis that will help to deal with them.

6.1   THE NEED FOR ANALYTICAL COMPARISONS

An **analytical comparison** refers to a meaningful comparison between two or more treatment conditions that are components of a larger experimental design. In some circumstances, analytical comparisons are undertaken following a significant F test conducted on the entire experiment. In other circumstances, they are conducted *instead of* the overall F test, in which case they are often referred to as **planned comparisons**.

The Composite Nature of SS_A

The between-groups sum of squares, SS_A, was defined in Chap. 2 in terms of the deviation of the group means from the grand mean:

$$SS_A = n\Sigma (\overline{Y}_A - \overline{Y}_T)^2$$

An alternative form of this equation shows that SS_A reflects the degree to which the group means differ from one another:

$$SS_A = \frac{n \sum_{\text{pairs}} (\overline{Y}_{A_i} - \overline{Y}_{A_{i'}})^2}{a} \tag{6-1}$$

where i and i' represent different levels of factor A and the summation refers to all *unique* pairs.

For example, consider the data presented in Table 2–3. There were three levels of factor A and $n = 5$ observations per group. The three means were as follows: $\overline{Y}_{A_1} = 15$, $\overline{Y}_{A_2} = 6$, and $\overline{Y}_{A_3} = 9$. Substituting in Eq. (6–1), we have

$$SS_A = \frac{5[(15 - 6)^2 + (15 - 9)^2 + (6 - 9)^2]}{3}$$

$$= \frac{5[(9)^2 + (6)^2 + (-3)^2]}{3} = 210$$

This value is identical to the one obtained by the standard defining formula:

$$SS_A = n \Sigma (\bar{Y}_A - \bar{Y}_T)^2$$

$$= 5[(15 - 10)^2 + (6 - 10)^2 + (9 - 10)^2]$$

$$= 5[(5)^2 + (-4)^2 + (-1)^2] = 210$$

You have seen, then, that the between-groups sum of squares is really an *average* of the differences observed between the pairs of means and as such does not provide unambiguous information about the nature of the treatment effects. In fact, it may have occurred to you that the overall variation among the treatment means reflected in SS_A may be better understood by examining these contributing parts, namely, the comparisons between pairs of means. The composite nature of SS_A has led some authors to refer to an F ratio based on more than two treatment levels as the **omnibus** or **overall** F test.[1]

The Omnibus F Test. The analysis outlined in the preceding chapters provides a procedure to guide us in drawing inferences about differences that we observe among the treatment means. With a nonsignificant omnibus F, we are prepared to assert that there are no real differences among the treatment means and that the particular sample means we have observed show differences that are reasonably accounted for by experimental error. We will stop the analysis there. Why analyze any further when the differences can be presumed to be chance differences?

In contrast, a *significant F* allows, if not demands, a further analysis of the data. By accepting the alternative hypothesis, we are concluding that differences among the treatment means are present. But which differences are the real ones and which are not? As I have noted before, the alternative hypothesis is inexact and, consequently, so must be our conclusion. Suppose, for example, we are contrasting the following four means: 5.25, 4.90, 5.10, and 10.50, and that the F from the single-factor analysis is significant. What have we been told? Simply that the four population means are not equal to one another. Nothing is said about *particular* differences among the means. An inspection of the means in this example suggests that the treatment effects are not spread equally over the four means— one group deviates from the other three, and these latter three do not deviate greatly from one another. The single-factor analysis does not locate the source (or sources) of the treatment effects. All that the analysis does is to indicate that there are real differences among the treatment means—somewhere. It is our job in this

---

[1]This composite nature of SS_A is also revealed when the total between-groups sum of squares is divided among a complete set of orthogonal comparisons, which I will consider later in this chapter.

and the next two chapters to see how we can identify the sources contributing to the significant overall F.

Planned Comparisons

Most research begins with the formulation of one or more research hypotheses—statements about how behavior will be influenced if such and such treatment differences are manipulated. Experiments are designed specifically to test these particular research hypotheses. Most typically, it is possible to design an experiment that will provide information relevant to *several* research hypotheses. Tests designed to shed light on these particular questions are planned before the start of an experiment and clearly represent the primary focus of analysis. A researcher is not interested in the omnibus F test; this test is more appropriate in the absence of specific hypotheses. Thus, most researchers form, or at least imply, an analysis plan when they specify their research hypotheses and design experiments to test them. This plan consists of a set of analytical comparisons chosen to extract information critical to the status of the research questions responsible for the initiation of the experiment in the first place. As you will see, analytical comparisons can be conducted directly on a set of data without reference to the significance or non-significance of the omnibus F test.

6.2   AN EXAMPLE OF PLANNED COMPARISONS

Consider a concrete example of an experiment designed with some explicit comparisons in mind. Suppose that subjects are given a list of 40 common English words to learn and that the method used allows them to recall these words in any order they want. The list is presented for six trials, each trial consisting of a study portion, in which the words are presented to the subjects, and a test portion, in which the subjects attempt to recall the words. Thus, each subject sees the list six times and is tested six times. Subjects are randomly assigned to five different conditions of training, which are summarized in Table 6-1.

For the first two groups, the words are presented all at once on a piece of paper for 2 minutes; different orderings of the 40 words are used on the six trials. The groups differ with regard to the arrangement of the words on the sheet of paper—for one group the words appear in a column and for the other group they are scattered around on the paper. The remaining three groups also study the list for a total of 2 minutes, but the words are presented one at a time, at a constant rate, on a mechanical device called a memory drum. For groups 3 and 4, each word is presented once for 3 seconds; the total presentation time for the whole list of words is 120 seconds (3 seconds × 40 words). The two groups differ with regard to the presentation of the words on successive trials. Group 3 receives the same presentation order on all six trials, whereas group 4 receives different presentation orders. The final group also receives the materials on the memory drum, but at a faster rate of presentation (1 second per word). However, to equate total study time per word, the words are presented three times before the recall test is admin-

Table 6–1   An Example of Planned Comparisons

Features	Group 1	Group 2	Group 3	Group 4	Group 5
Mode:	Paper	Paper	Drum	Drum	Drum
Order:	Varied	Varied	Same	Varied	Varied
Array:	Column	Scattered	–	.	–
Rate:	–	–	3-sec.	3-sec.	1-sec.
Comp. 1	+	+		–	.
Comp. 2	+	–			
Comp. 3				+	–
Comp. 4			+	–	

istered. As with group 4, the presentation order is changed at the start of each study trial. In summary, there are five different conditions of training. What they all have in common is that the list of words is presented for a total of 2 minutes before recall is tested.

The hypothesis under test is the *total-time hypothesis*. This hypothesis states that learning will be the same for these different groups just as long as the total time for study is held constant. It does not matter how the words are presented, all at once or one at a time, at a fast rate or at a slow rate, in the same order on successive study trials or in different orders, scrambled on a page or in a neat column array. The expectation, then, is that the groups will not differ in performance over the six training trials.

We could test this hypothesis by comparing the five groups simultaneously in an overall analysis of variance. If this omnibus F were significant, we would know that the total-time hypothesis did not hold in this experiment. We would not know, however, which of the groups were responsible for its failure. The way in which the experiment was designed suggests a number of meaningful comparisons, which represent more analytical tests of the total-time hypothesis.

Four such comparisons are indicated in Table 6–1. The first comparison contrasts the two groups receiving the words on a sheet of paper (groups 1 and 2) with two of the groups receiving the words on the memory drum (groups 4 and 5). The question asked here is whether or not performance will be affected by forcing subjects to study the words in a rigid pattern. The total-time hypothesis would say no. On the other hand, it would seem reasonable to expect that subjects who are free to distribute their study time among the 40 words as they wish may be able to organize the material in such a way as to aid recall; subjects who are studying the words one at a time for a fixed 3-second period may not be able to organize the material as effectively. Thus, an organizational theory of learning and memory would predict better performance by groups 1 and 2, relative to groups 4 and 5. (Groups 1 and 2 and groups 4 and 5 have been combined to provide more stable estimates of the paper and drum methods of presentation, respectively. The plus and minus signs denote the groups to be contrasted.) Group 3 was not included in this comparison, because the subjects in that group received the words in the same order on successive trials, whereas subjects in the other four groups received the words in different orders.

The second comparison focuses on the two "paper" groups and asks whether or not the *type of array* will affect performance. The total-time hypothesis would again say no. There is some suggestion in the literature that subjects will form more organizational groupings of the words in the scattered condition than in the column condition. An organizational theory maintains that the formation of these organizational groupings will aid performance. Thus, this latter theory would predict higher recall by the group receiving the scattered array.

The next comparison involves groups 4 and 5, groups differing in the rates at which the words are presented. This comparison asks whether or not performance will be affected when the exposure time is varied. The total-time hypothesis would say no. On the other hand, it is conceivable that subjects given a more leisurely study of each word (group 4) may have time to create organizational groupings, whereas subjects given a fast exposure (group 5) may not be able to do so, even though they are given the same total time to study each word. If this speculation is correct, an organizational theory would predict a difference in favor of the longer presentation rate.

The final comparison contrasts groups 3 and 4. The only difference between these two conditions is the use of the same or different orderings of the words on successive study trials. Although the total-time hypothesis again would predict no difference in performance, there are other hypotheses that do. For example, some investigators have speculated that a constant presentation order provides the subject with stable serial-position cues, which are not possible when the order varies from trial to trial. It is thought that this additional set of cues will aid the subject in recall. Thus, these researchers would predict better performance for group 3.

The object of this example is to illustrate that experiments are designed with meaningful comparisons in mind. The planned comparisons enumerated in Table 6–1 provide detailed information concerning the success or failure of the total-time hypothesis. If we knew only that the omnibus F was significant, we would not know *where* the hypothesis was deficient. The use of planned comparisons allows us to pinpoint the specific conditions under which the hypothesis does and does not hold.

6.3   COMPARISONS BETWEEN TREATMENT MEANS

In this and in subsequent sections, I will be considering procedures for making contrasts that essentially reduce to comparisons between *two means*. In some cases, these comparisons will involve simple comparisons between pairs of treatment means; in others, they will involve averages of two or more treatment means. In either case, however, the comparisons represent miniature experiments, each of which consists of $a = 2$ conditions and is based on a single df. I will refer to comparisons of this sort variously as **comparisons, contrasts,** or **single-*df* comparisons.**

Not all questions we will want to ask of our data reduce to comparisons between two means, however. Occasionally, we will want to test the significance of subsets of three or more means, simply asking whether the means differ among themselves. For instance, suppose there are four treatment conditions, one a control condition and the others experimental treatments of some sort. It might make sense to ask two questions: (1) Do the combined experimental groups differ from the control condition—that is, is there a general or average experimental effect? (2) Do the experimental groups differ among themselves? In the first case, we have a comparison between two means (the control mean versus an average of the three experimental means), whereas in the second case, we have a comparison among the three experimental means. I will consider the first type of comparison in this section and the second type in Sec. 6.5.

A Comparison as a Sum of Weighted Means

Suppose we have three treatment groups; group 1 is a control condition, and groups 2 and 3 receive different experimental treatments. One comparison that we might consider making is a contrast between the mean for the control group and the average of the means for the two experimental groups. The statistical hypotheses for this comparison are

$$H_0: \mu_1 = \frac{\mu_2 + \mu_3}{2}$$

$$H_1: \mu_1 \neq \frac{\mu_2 + \mu_3}{2}$$

It is convenient to express this comparison as a difference between two means. In this case, the statistical hypotheses become

$$H_0: \mu_1 - \frac{\mu_2 + \mu_3}{2} = 0$$

$$H_1: \mu_1 - \frac{\mu_2 + \mu_3}{2} \neq 0$$

Either way, you can see that the rejection of the null hypothesis leads to the conclusion that this particular difference between the two means is significant.

In general, I will use the symbol ψ (read "sigh") to represent the difference between two means. In the present case,

$$\psi_1 = \mu_1 - \frac{\mu_2 + \mu_3}{2}$$

Expressed slightly differently, this comparison becomes

$$\psi_1 = (+1)(\mu_1) + (-\tfrac{1}{2})(\mu_2) + (-\tfrac{1}{2})(\mu_3)$$

The numbers multiplied by each mean are called **coefficients**. Any comparison between two means can be represented in this manner: (1) the multiplication (or weighting) of the means by a set of coefficients and (2) the algebraic summation of these weighted means. In other words, a comparison between two means can be expressed as a sum of weighted means. The reason for this particular formulation will not be obvious at this time, but it will prove useful when we calculate the sum of squares for this sort of comparison.

A second comparison of interest in this experiment is a contrast between the two experimental groups. More specifically,

$$\psi_2 = \mu_2 - \mu_3$$

This difference can also be written as a sum of weighted means as follows:

$$\psi_2 = (0)(\mu_1) + (+1)(\mu_2) + (-1)(\mu_3)$$

In this case, the coefficient associated with the control group, which does not enter into this particular comparison, is equal to *zero*.

As a general formula, we can express any such comparison between two means as

$$\psi = (c_1)(\mu_1) + (c_2)(\mu_2) + (c_3)(\mu_3) + \ldots$$

or more compactly as

$$\psi = \Sigma (c_i)(\mu_i) \tag{6–2}$$

where the c_i's represent the coefficients appropriate for a particular comparison. For a sum of weighted means to qualify as a comparison, *the sum of the coefficients must equal zero*. That is,

$$\Sigma c_i = c_1 + c_2 + c_3 + \ldots = 0 \tag{6–3}$$

Both sets of coefficients in the preceding paragraph, $(1, -\frac{1}{2}, -\frac{1}{2})$ and $(0, 1, -1)$, sum to zero, which satisfies the requirements of Eq. (6–3), and they "perform" the comparison that we intended—that is, they result in the appropriate contrasts between means.

Usefulness of the Coefficients and Eq. (6–2)

These examples illustrate the fact that comparisons involving a set of treatment means may be specified by different sets of coefficients. You also saw that by using these coefficients to weight the corresponding treatment means, we could produce the comparison represented by the coefficients. There are several reasons why it is useful to express comparisons in terms of a sum of weighted means—that is, in terms of Eq. (6–2); these points will be illustrated later with actual examples. I simply list them at this time to justify the amount of attention I will give to this particular procedure in the sections that follow.

First, the procedure is general; it may be used to compare the means of two groups as well as for more complicated comparisons between combined means in experiments with any number of levels. Second, special sets of coefficients are available for the analytical analysis of experiments in which quantitative independent variables are present—that is, in which the levels of the independent variables differ in amount. Third, the statistical evaluation of these different comparisons is easily accomplished by using the coefficients to compute the sums of squares associated with the comparisons. Fourth, you will see that the independence of two or more comparisons is readily determined by comparing the sets of coefficients. Thus, it will be possible to ascertain whether several planned comparisons are mutually independent by comparing the coefficients associated with the comparisons we plan to make. Finally, sets of coefficients may be used to represent sources of variance in designs with two or more independent variables. We will consider comparisons of this sort in Chap. 12.

Constructing Coefficients

An appropriate set of coefficients can be obtained simply by using information available when we express a comparison as a difference between two means.[2] As an example, consider an experiment with five treatment conditions. Suppose we wanted to compare the average mean for groups 2 and 4 with the average mean for groups 1, 3, and 5. This is an example of a **complex comparison**, in which an average of two or more groups is compared with either a single group or an average of two or more other groups. (A comparison between two single groups is called a **pairwise comparison**.) Expressed as a difference, this complex comparison becomes

$$\psi = \frac{\mu_2 + \mu_4}{2} - \frac{\mu_1 + \mu_3 + \mu_5}{3}$$

The coefficient for the two means to the left of the minus sign is $+\frac{1}{2}$; the coefficient for the three means to the right of the minus sign is $-\frac{1}{3}$. Thus, the coefficients representing this comparison are the set c_i: $-\frac{1}{3}$, $+\frac{1}{2}$, $-\frac{1}{3}$, $+\frac{1}{2}$, $-\frac{1}{3}$. The coefficient is 1 (plus or minus) when a single mean is involved and 0 when a mean is not involved in a comparison. A comparison such as

$$\psi = \mu_1 - \frac{\mu_3 + \mu_5}{2}$$

is expressed by the set of coefficients c_i: $+1$, 0, $-\frac{1}{2}$, 0, $-\frac{1}{2}$.

This method of selecting coefficients produces what I will call a *standard set*. Standard sets express the differences between means directly and are used to calculate confidence intervals for these comparisons (see Myers, 1979, pp. 305–306). In calculating the sum of squares for a comparison, however, fractional coefficients introduce rounding errors as well as frequent arithmetical errors. Since the computational formula for a comparison sum of squares may be used with any set of coefficients—provided that the *relative weights* of the groups remain the same—we can eliminate fractional coefficients altogether by multiplying the set of coefficients by the lowest common denominator. In the first example, the lowest

---

[2]Loftus and Loftus (1988, pp. 485–486) describe a procedure by which coefficients are derived from hypothetical population treatment means predicted by a particular theory.

common denominator is 6 and the resulting coefficients are c_i: -2, $+3$, -2, $+3$, -2; in the second, it is 2 and the coefficients are c_i: $+2$, 0, -1, 0, -1.

Sums of Squares for Comparisons Between Treatment Means

The data of the experiment are used to evaluate the significance of a comparison. The comparison itself is given by the formula

$$\hat{\psi} = \Sigma\,(c_i)(\overline{Y}_{A_i}) \qquad\qquad (6\text{--}4)$$

The formula for the sum of squares for a comparison is not too many steps removed from Eq. (6–4). Specifically,

$$SS_{A_{comp.}} = \frac{n\,(\hat{\psi})^2}{\Sigma\,c_i^2} \qquad\qquad (6\text{--}5)$$

where n = the number of subjects per treatment condition[3]
$\quad\quad\ \hat{\psi}$ = the difference between the two means being compared
$\quad\ \Sigma\,c_i^2$ = the sum of the squared coefficients

The role of the term in the denominator of Eq. (6–5) is to adjust the quantity in the numerator so that the value for the sum of squares does not depend on the absolute magnitude of the coefficients used to represent the comparison. This is why we could transform fractional coefficients into whole numbers and not change the value of the sum of squares for a comparison.

As an example of these calculations, I will use the data originally listed in Table 2–3. In this example, $a = 3$ and $n = 5$. For illustrative purposes, let's assume that level a_1 represents a control condition and levels a_2 and a_3 represent experimental groups receiving two different drugs. Two obvious comparisons are suggested by this design, namely, a comparison between the control group and the average of the two drug groups and a comparison between the two drug groups. The means for the three groups are presented again in Table 6–2, along with the coefficients representing these two comparisons.

The first comparison shows a sizable difference in favor of the control condition. More specifically,

$$\hat{\psi}_1 = \Sigma\,(c_i)(\overline{Y}_{A_i})$$

$$= (1)(15.00) + (-\tfrac{1}{2})(6.00) + (-\tfrac{1}{2})(9.00)$$

$$= 15.00 - 3.00 - 4.50 = 7.50$$

The sum of squares associated with this difference between the two means ($\hat{\psi}_1 = 7.50$) is found by substituting in Eq. (6–5):

---

[3]Students frequently confuse n, which designates the group sample size, with the *total* number of subjects in the experiment, which is frequently designated as N and in this design is equal to $(a)(n)$.

Table 6-2   Numerical Example of Two Comparisons

	TREATMENT LEVELS		
	a_1	a_2	a_3
Means	15.00	6.00	9.00
Comparison 1	1	$-\frac{1}{2}$	$-\frac{1}{2}$
Comparison 2	0	1	-1

$$SS_{comp.\ 1} = \frac{n\,(\hat{\psi}_1)^2}{\Sigma\,c_i^2}$$

$$= \frac{5(7.50)^2}{(1)^2 + (-\frac{1}{2})^2 + (-\frac{1}{2})^2}$$

$$= \frac{5(56.25)}{1 + .25 + .25} = \frac{281.25}{1.50}$$

$$= 187.50$$

The second comparison reveals a smaller difference in favor of the second drug condition. That is,

$$\hat{\psi}_2 = (0)(15.00) + (1)(6.00) + (-1)(9.00) = -3.00$$

For the sum of squares associated with this difference,

$$SS_{comp.\ 2} = \frac{5(-3.00)^2}{(0)^2 + (1)^2 + (-1)^2}$$

$$= \frac{5(9.00)}{0 + 1 + 1} = \frac{45.00}{2}$$

$$= 22.50$$

Evaluating Comparisons

The two sums of squares we have just calculated have been entered in a new summary table, Table 6-3. If the comparisons listed in Table 6-2 were *planned* comparisons, we might not even bother to perform the omnibus F test. Table 6-3 also presents the SS_A calculated in Chap. 3 (see Table 3-2, p. 45). You should note that the two comparisons we have just computed completely account for or "use up" the total between-groups sum of squares. That is,

$$SS_{comp.\ 1} + SS_{comp.\ 2} = 187.50 + 22.50 = 210.00 = SS_A$$

This result will occur only when we have calculated a complete set of **orthogonal comparisons**. (I will discuss how to determine orthogonality in Sec. 6.4.)

Since each comparison in effect represents a miniature experiment in which $a = 2$, the *df* for each comparison sum of squares is 1; the mean square is calcu-

Table 6–3   Analysis of Variance

SOURCE	SS	df	MS	F
Treatment (A)	(210.00)	(2)		
Comp. 1	187.50	1	187.50	13.23*
Comp. 2	22.50	1	22.50	1.59
Within (S/A)	170.00	12	14.17	
Total	380.00	14		

*$p < .05$

lated in the usual way (SS/df). The F ratio is formed by dividing the comparison mean square by the error term from the *overall* analysis; that is,

$$F_{comp.} = \frac{MS_{A_{comp.}}}{MS_{S/A}} \tag{6-6}$$

We justify the use of $MS_{S/A}$ as the error term by assuming that the population treatment variances are equal. The F is evaluated in the usual manner by comparing $F_{comp.}$ with the value listed in the F table, with $df_{num.} = 1$ and $df_{denom.} = (a)(n - 1)$.

Although it can be shown that these two comparisons use independent information in their construction, I should mention that the two F ratios are not, strictly speaking, *statistically* independent. The reason is that we use the $MS_{S/A}$ to test both of the comparisons. It appears, however, that this lack of statistical independence of the tests does not present a practical problem as long as the df for the denominator of the F ratio are reasonably large—about 40, for example (see Games, 1971b).

The within-groups mean square for these data, previously calculated in Chap. 3, is presented in Table 6–3. The results of the two F tests, indicated in the table, show that variability among the treatment means is produced primarily by the difference between the mean of group 1 (the control in our example) and the mean of groups 2 and 3 combined (the experimental groups in our example). The great advantage of this analysis is in the additional information that it provides. If we had looked at the overall F ratio, as we did in Chap. 3, we would have rejected the null hypothesis and concluded that the three treatment means are not all the same. With the present analysis, we are able to pinpoint the locus of the differences contributing to the significant omnibus F.

Directional Alternative Hypotheses

The alternative hypotheses I have considered so far have been *nondirectional* in the sense that differences between two means in either the positive or negative direction are considered to be incompatible with the null hypothesis. That is, with H_0: $\mu_1 = \mu_2$ and H_1: $\mu_1 \neq \mu_2$, the null hypothesis will be rejected whenever $F_{comp.}$ falls within the rejection region, which obviously can occur if $\mu_1 > \mu_2$ or if $\mu_2 > \mu_1$. Thus, rejecting the null hypothesis in this case permits the conclusion that the observed difference between the two means—in whatever direction it may be—is significant. This type of alternative hypothesis, which is most common in psychology, is called a **nondirectional hypothesis**.

A test with a nondirectional hypothesis is also known as a *two-tailed* test. The "tail" refers to rejection regions used in conjunction with the **t test,** a statistical procedure frequently employed by researchers to analyze the results of two-group studies. To illustrate, the formula for the *t* test is

$$t = \frac{\overline{Y}_{A_1} - \overline{Y}_{A_2}}{\hat{\sigma}_{\overline{Y}_{A_1} - \overline{Y}_{A_2}}} \tag{6-7}$$

where $\overline{Y}_{A_1}$ and $\overline{Y}_{A_2}$ = the two means being compared

$\hat{\sigma}_{\overline{Y}_{A_1} - \overline{Y}_{A_2}}$ = the standard error of the difference between the two means

This last quantity may be calculated as follows:

$$\hat{\sigma}_{\overline{Y}_{A_1} - \overline{Y}_{A_2}} = \sqrt{\frac{s_1^2}{n_1} + \frac{s_2^2}{n_2}} \tag{6-8}$$

where s_1^2 and s_2^2 are the variances for the two groups and n_1 and n_2 are the corresponding sample sizes. Assuming that the population treatment variances are equal, we can use $MS_{S/A}$ as the average group variance and rewrite Eq. (6-8) to obtain

$$\hat{\sigma}_{\overline{Y}_{A_1} - \overline{Y}_{A_2}} = \sqrt{\left(\frac{1}{n_1} + \frac{1}{n_2}\right)MS_{S/A}} \tag{6-9}$$

Let's apply the *t* test to the first comparison, which contrasts the control mean (15.00) with the average of the means for the two experimental conditions (7.50); these means are based on $n_1 = 5$ and $n_2 = 10$ observations. Substituting in Eq. (6-9), we find

$$\hat{\sigma}_{\overline{Y}_{A_1} - \overline{Y}_{A_2}} = \sqrt{\left(\frac{1}{5} + \frac{1}{10}\right)(14.17)} = \sqrt{2.834 + 1.417} = 2.062$$

The value for *t* is

$$t = \frac{15.00 - 7.50}{2.062} = 3.637$$

We compare $t = 3.637$ with the critical value of the *t* statistic, which we find in Table A-3 under $df_{S/A} = 12$ and $\alpha = .05$. This value is 2.18, and we conclude that the difference between the control mean and the combined mean of the experimental groups is significant.

The interesting point is that the *t* test is actually a special case of the *F* test. That is, exactly the same information is derived from either test. We can translate from one statistic to the other by noting that when *F* is based on $df_{num.} = 1$ and $df_{denom.} = df_{S/A}$ and when *t* is based on $df_{S/A}$,

$$F = t^2 \text{ and } t = \sqrt{F}$$

Using the value of t we just calculated (3.637), we find that $t^2 = 13.23$, which is the same value we calculated for F (see Table 6–3). Because the two tests are algebraically equivalent, we simply remind ourselves when we see a reference to a t test that the conclusions are interchangeable: If the t is significant, F is significant; if t is not significant, F is not significant.

This relationship between the t and F tests is illustrated in the upper portion of Fig. 6–1; the t distribution is on the left and the corresponding F distribution is on the right. Since a value of t can be either positive or negative depending on the direction of the difference between the two means, the rejection region is located in *both* tails of the t distribution, with one-half of the significance level ($\alpha / 2 = .025$) located in the extreme positive portion of the t distribution and the other half in the extreme negative portion. On the other hand, the F test deals with *squared* values, which treats positive and negative values equivalently, leaving us with only one rejection region ($\alpha = .05$), for which half of the F's are produced by positive differences between the two means and half by negative differences.

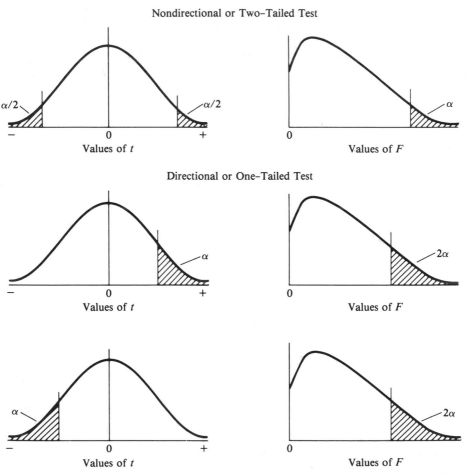

FIGURE 6–1   A comparison of the t and F distributions for nondirectional and directional tests.

In contrast, it is possible to choose an alternative hypothesis that specifies a particular direction of the difference, that is, H_1: $\mu_1 > \mu_2$ or H_1: $\mu_2 > \mu_1$. Since the direction of the difference is important, this type of alternative hypothesis is called a **directional hypothesis.** A test with a directional hypothesis is also known as a *one-tailed* test because there is a single rejection region, which is located in the positive or the negative tail of the t distribution. The two possibilities are depicted in the lower part of Fig. 6–1. As you can see, the entire rejection region specified by $\alpha = .05$ is located in either the positive or negative extreme. The equivalent F test, which is depicted on the right, creates a substantially larger rejection region, with a directional test being evaluated at $p = 2(\alpha)$, where α is a researcher's usual rejection probability. That is, rather than evaluating the significance of $F_{comp.}$ at $\alpha = .05$, say, we would use $\alpha = 2(.05) = .10$ instead. In the numerical example, the critical value of F would be $F(1, 12) = 3.18$ for a directional test, $p = .05$, as compared with $F(1, 12) = 4.75$ for a nondirectional one at the same significance level.[4]

Several disadvantages are associated with directional tests. First, a strict interpretation of a directional test means that a true difference in the *opposite* direction must be ignored. In some fields, a new therapy or drug or teaching method is compared with an older, established one, with an eye toward adopting the new approach only if it improves on the one currently in use. In this case, a researcher may not be concerned that negative effects of the new approach will not be tested statistically by a directional test. Second, directional tests are not particularly suited for use in basic or theoretical research. Generally, theories are only temporary explanations, tentative ideas about cause and effect. A significant effect in a predicted direction might provide positive support for one theory, whereas a significant effect in the negative direction frequently will be evidence against that theory, or even support for another theory. In addition, as we discover more information, our theories will be modified and our explanations will be changed. Given this transitional nature of theoretical research, then, we usually can justify only the use of nondirectional tests. Conducting a directional test under these circumstances is equivalent to adopting a more liberal significance level—$\alpha = .10$ rather than .05—which is why most journal editors question or refuse to publish research that is based largely on directional tests. Finally, nondirectional tests are also found in applied research, for example, when a researcher is comparing a set of products (books, packaging, advertising layouts, and so on) and the researcher's interest lies in establishing which is best, with no firm theoretical expectation concerning which one that may be.

Unequal Variances

The use of the within-groups mean square to evaluate the significance of a single-*df* comparison assumes homogeneity of variance. You will recall that this same assumption underlies the evaluation of the omnibus F, where the occurrence of

---

[4]Since the sampling distribution of F includes differences between means in both directions, the doubling of α adjusts for this difference between the F and t distributions and focuses attention on F's reflecting the direction specified by the directional alternative hypothesis.

$F_{max.} > 3$ (the ratio of the largest to the smallest variance) may increase type I error sufficiently for us to take corrective action. Variance heterogeneity creates an even more serious problem for the evaluation of analytical comparisons. For example, let's consider an experiment in which we find the following variances for $a = 5$ treatment conditions:

$$s_1^2 = 1, \; s_2^2 = 1, \; s_3^2 = 3, \; s_4^2 = 4, \; \text{and} \; s_5^2 = 6$$

Let's assume that these variances reflect differences that are present in the population. The error term from the overall analysis of variance is an average of these five variances; that is,

$$MS_{S/A} = \frac{\Sigma s_i^2}{a} = \frac{1 + 1 + 3 + 4 + 6}{5} = 3$$

Suppose we wanted to compare the means for the first two groups. Because of the heterogeneity in this example, the overall error term ($MS_{S/A} = 3$) overestimates the error term that should be appropriate for this comparison, namely, $(1 + 1)/2 = 1$. By the same token, $MS_{S/A}$ underestimates the error term that should be appropriate for a comparison between the last two groups, $(4 + 6)/2 = 5$. In short, heterogeneity of variance brings into serious question our use of $MS_{S/A}$ as the error term with which to evaluate all comparisons in this experiment.[5]

A reasonably adequate solution to this problem is a test proposed by Welch (1947) and modified by others for single-df comparisons (see Games, 1978a; Games & Howell, 1976; Kohr & Games, 1977). The **Welch test**, as I will call it, includes two sets of operations, those involved in calculating the error term and those involved in determining the degrees of freedom that we will use for selecting the critical value of F. The error term is an average of the variances of the specific groups (s_i^2) entering into the comparison, weighted by the relevant coefficients. More specifically,

$$MS_{error} = \frac{\Sigma (c_i^2)(s_i^2)}{\Sigma c_i^2} \tag{6-10}$$

When a *pairwise* comparison involves the difference between two treatment means, Eq. (6–10) produces an error term that literally is an average of the two within-group variances.[6] To illustrate, suppose there were three conditions in an experiment and the comparison involved the difference between the means of the first two groups $(1, -1, 0)$. The error term for this comparison would be

$$MS_{error} = \frac{(1)^2(s_1^2) + (-1)^2(s_2^2) + (0)^2(s_3^2)}{(1)^2 + (-1)^2 + (0)^2} = \frac{s_1^2 + s_2^2}{2}$$

---

[5]The biasing effects of variance heterogeneity on specific contrasts were confirmed in a Monte Carlo study reported by Games and Howell (1976, p. 119).
[6]The formulas presented by Games and Howell (1976) and by Kohr and Games (1977) are written in terms of the t statistic and unequal sample sizes. I have adapted the formulas to provide F ratios instead; these new formulas assume equal sample size.

The error term for a *complex* comparison is more complicated. To illustrate, the error term for the comparison $(1, 1, -2)$, for example, would be

$$MS_{error} = \frac{(1)^2(s_1^2) + (1)^2(s_2^2) + (-2)^2(s_3^2)}{(1)^2 + (1)^2 + (-2)^2} = \frac{s_1^2 + s_2^2 + 4(s_3^2)}{6}$$

The F ratio in either case is formed by substituting in the formula

$$F_{comp.} = \frac{MS_{A_{comp.}}}{MS_{error}} \tag{6-11}$$

The degrees of freedom for the numerator remain unchanged ($df_{num.} = 1$), whereas the degrees of freedom for the denominator must be calculated by a relatively complex formula developed by Welch (1947) and presented by Games (1978a, p. 664).[7] More specifically,

$$df_{error} = (n + 1) \frac{[\Sigma\,(c_i^2)(s_i^2)]^2}{\Sigma\,(c_i^4)(s_i^4)} - 2 \tag{6-12}$$

I do not expect you to understand the "logic" behind Eq. (6–12). Although the formula involves familiar quantities—sample size (n), coefficients (c_i), and group variances (s_i^2)—they are manipulated in unfamiliar ways. Perhaps the best way to proceed is simply to illustrate the steps involved with a numerical example.

Therefore, we will consider the data from Table 2–3, the critical features of which are presented in Table 6–4. Suppose we wanted to compare the mean of the first group with an average of the other two group means; coefficients for this comparison are given in column 3 and the squared coefficients in column 4. First, we will calculate the comparison sum of squares. The weighted treatment means are given in column 5. The sum of the squared coefficients and the sum of the weighted means ($\hat{\psi}$) are given at the bottom of the relevant columns. Using Eq. (6–5), we find

$$SS_{A_{comp.}} = \frac{n\,(\hat{\psi})^2}{\Sigma\,c_i^2} = \frac{5(15.0)^2}{6} = 187.50$$

Because this is a single-df comparison, $MS_{A_{comp.}} = 187.50$. The error term for this analysis is given by Eq. (6–10); an inspection of the formula indicates that we need the sum of the products of the squared coefficients and the corresponding variances. This information is provided in column 6 of the table. To illustrate the calculations for the first group, $(c_1^2)(s_1^2) = (2^2)(15.0) = 60.0$. The sum of these prod-

---

[7]A slightly different formula is recommended by Kirk (1982, p. 101), in which the quantity $(n + 1)$ is replaced by $(n - 1)$ and the "-2" in Eq. (6–12) is dropped, to produce the following:

$$df_{error} = (n - 1) \frac{[\Sigma\,(c_i^2)(s_i^2)]^2}{\Sigma\,(c_i^4)(s_i^4)} \tag{6-12a}$$

The two formulas give similar estimates of df_{error}, with Eq. (6–12a) producing slightly larger values. On the other hand, Eq. (6–12) appears to be more accurate (Winer, 1971, p. 42) and has been more thoroughly studied (see Kohr & Games, 1977).

Table 6–4 Numerical Example of the Welch Test

Group	(1) $\overline{Y}_{A_i}$	(2) s_i^2	(3) c_i	(4) (c_i^2)	(5) $(c_i)(\overline{Y}_{A_i})$	(6) $(c_i^2)(s_i^2)$	(7) $(c_i^4)(s_i^4)$
a_1	15.0	15.0	+2	4	30.0	$(4)(15.0) = 60.0$	$(60.0)^2 = 3{,}600.00$
a_2	6.0	10.0	−1	1	−6.0	$(1)(10.0) = 10.0$	$(10.0)^2 = 100.00$
a_3	9.0	17.5	−1	1	−9.0	$(1)(17.5) = 17.5$	$(17.5)^2 = 306.25$
				$\Sigma c_i^2 = 6$	$\hat{\psi} = 15.0$	$\Sigma (c_i^2)(s_i^2) = 87.5$	$\Sigma(c_i^4)(s_i^4) = 4{,}006.25$

ucts is given at the bottom of the column. Substituting the relevant quantities in Eq. (6–10), we find

$$MS_{error} = \frac{\Sigma (c_i^2)(s_i^2)}{\Sigma c_i^2} = \frac{87.5}{6} = 14.58$$

The F for this comparison becomes

$$F_{comp.} = \frac{MS_{A_{comp.}}}{MS_{error}} = \frac{187.50}{14.58} = 12.86$$

The Welch test requires us to calculate the degrees of freedom for the error term, which is based on the variances of the actual groups entering into the comparison. If you refer to Eq. (6–12), you will see that we need only to calculate a new set of products, namely, $(c_i^4)(s_i^4)$, which is most easily obtained by squaring the products we have already calculated in column 6; that is, $(c_i^4)(s_i^4) = [(c_i^2)(s_i^2)]^2$. The results of these calculations are presented in column 7. We are ready to calculate df_{error}. Substituting in Eq. (6–12),

$$df_{error} = (n + 1) \frac{[\Sigma (c_i^2)(s_i^2)]^2}{\Sigma (c_i^4)(s_i^4)} - 2$$

$$= (5 + 1) \frac{(87.5)^2}{4{,}006.25} - 2$$

$$= (6) \frac{7{,}656.25}{4{,}006.25} - 2 = 11.47 - 2 = 9.47$$

Rounding this value to the nearest whole number, we have $df_{error} = 9$. Thus, we find the critical value of F in the table to be $F(1, 9) = 5.12$ ($\alpha = .05$). Since $F_{comp.} = 12.86$, we would conclude that the comparison between the first group and the combined other two groups is significant.

Let's see what changes occurred as a result of using the Welch test. Table 6–5 summarizes the critical points. You will notice that although the $MS_{A_{comp.}}$ is identical under the two tests, the other features—namely, the error term, $F_{comp.}$, $df_{denom.}$, and $F_{critical}$—are different. You should realize that this example does not dramatize the changes that can occur with the Welch test because the group variances are relatively homogeneous in this example (that is, $F_{max.} = 17.5/10.0 = 1.75$). With

Table 6–5   A Comparison of the *F* Test and the Welch Test

	F Test	Welch Test
$MS_{A_{comp.}}$	187.50	187.50
Error term	$MS_{S/A} = 14.17$	$MS_{error} = 14.58$
$F_{comp.}$	13.23	12.86
$df_{denom.}$	$df_{S/A} = 12$	$df_{error} = 9$
$F_{critical}$	4.75	5.12

larger differences among the variances, we can expect two things to occur. First, MS_{error} will vary depending on the variances associated with the groups involved in a particular comparison: If the comparison isolates the groups with the smaller variances, MS_{error} will be smaller than $MS_{S/A}$; if the comparison isolates the groups with larger variances, MS_{error} will be larger than $MS_{S/A}$. Second, the df_{error} can drop severely. Regardless of the nature of the comparison, df_{error} can be as low as $n - 1$ when severe heterogeneity is present among the groups involved in a comparison (Brown & Forsythe, 1974a). Given this property of the Welch correction, we could first determine whether the $F_{comp.}$ is significant with the *minimum* value for df_{error} (that is, $n - 1$). If the F is significant, we do not need Eq. (6–12) to calculate the df_{error}; if it is not significant under these circumstances, we would then use the equation to calculate the appropriate df_{error}.

Recommendations.   It should be clear that unequal variances present a serious problem for the evaluation of single-*df* comparisons.[8] As I have already noted, $MS_{S/A}$ may underestimate or overestimate the error variance associated with a given comparison; the extent of this distortion depends on the degree of variance heterogeneity present and the variances of the groups involved in the comparison. One possible course of action is summarized in Fig. 6–2. First, we determine whether the variances are heterogeneous. I recommend the use of the Brown-Forsythe test (pp. 102–104) with α set at .25; the larger value of α helps us to increase the power of the Brown-Forsythe test. If the test is not significant, we can proceed fairly safely in the usual fashion and use $MS_{S/A}$ as the error term and $df_{S/A}$ to find $F_{critical}$. On the other hand, if the test is significant, we would conduct the Welch test, beginning with the calculation of MS_{error} for each of our comparisons. To save some calculations, we can see whether the comparison is significant when we use the minimum value for $df_{denom.}$—that is, $df_{error} = n - 1$. If the F is significant, we know that it will also be significant if we were to use Eq. (6–12) to calculate df_{error}. If the F is not significant, we need to continue with the Welch test and calculate df_{error}.

Most spreadsheet programs available for personal computers may be easily programmed to calculate a series of Welch tests. Briefly, you would simply duplicate the layout of Table 6–4 as a spreadsheet and program the multiplications and

---

[8]The situation is even more serious when there are unequal sample sizes. I consider the analysis of experiments with unequal sample sizes in Chap. 13.

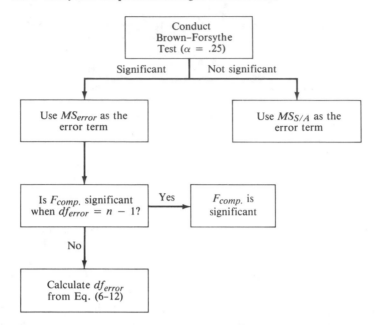

FIGURE 6–2. A strategy for conducting single-*df* comparisons when group variances are not equal.

sums as they are represented in the table. You can now use the four sums at the bottom of columns 4 through 7 to complete the necessary calculations. Once you have created a spreadsheet for one single-*df* comparison, you can conduct the Welch test for other comparisons simply by entering the relevant coefficients in column 3. If you are more ambitious, you could enter the formulas into the spreadsheet as well and have the program calculate $SS_{A_{comp.}}$, MS_{error}, $F_{comp.}$, and df_{error} for each comparison; all you will need to do is to look up the critical value of F.

Strength of a Comparison

In Chap. 4, I argued that the F statistic does not provide a useful index of the strength or magnitude of the treatment effects for the simple reason that it is influenced by sample size as well as by treatment magnitude. An index of relative treatment magnitude, such as omega squared ($\hat{\omega}_A^2$), overcomes this difficulty. By the same token, the size of $F_{comp.}$ does not unambiguously reflect the magnitude of the difference between two means. Unfortunately, however, we cannot use $\hat{\omega}_A^2$ to provide information about the relative contribution of particular single-*df* comparisons since this index reflects only the relative size of the *overall* or *average* treatment effects. What we need, then, is an analogous index that estimates the magnitude of single-*df* comparisons.

Methodologists have proposed several ways to measure the size of a comparison. I will illustrate these with the squared multiple regression coefficient R^2, which is an alternative measure of treatment magnitude. Let's start by considering the R^2 representation of the overall treatment effects, namely,

$$R_A^2 = \frac{SS_A}{SS_T} \tag{6-13}$$

In this case, R^2 relates the overall treatment effects (SS_A) to the total variability in the experiment (SS_T). One measure of the strength of a comparison, then, substitutes the comparison sum of squares $(SS_{A_{comp.}})$ for SS_A in Eq. (6–13); that is,

$$R_{A_{comp.}}^2 = \frac{SS_{A_{comp.}}}{SS_T} \tag{6-14}$$

As you can see, then, the strength of a comparison is also measured with respect to the total sum of squares. To illustrate with the first comparison in Table 6–3, $R_{A_{comp.}}^2 = 187.50/380.00 = .493$. A second measure, proposed by Huberty and Morris (1988), is identical to the first except that we define SS_T differently. More specifically, instead of the usual definition of SS_T $(SS_A + SS_{S/A})$, we use $SS_{A_{comp.}} + SS_{S/A}$. That is,

$$R_{A_{comp.}}^2 = \frac{SS_{A_{comp.}}}{SS_{A_{comp.}} + SS_{S/A}} \tag{6-15}$$

Using the same data, we find $R_{A_{comp.}}^2 = 187.50/(187.50 + 170.00) = 187.50/357.50 = .524$. A final measure of magnitude defines strength with reference to the overall treatment effects themselves rather than to the total sum of squares. More specifically,

$$R_{A_{comp.}}^2 = \frac{SS_{A_{comp.}}}{SS_A} \tag{6-16}$$

With reference to our example, $R_{A_{comp.}}^2 = 187.50/210.00 = .893$.

Each measure provides slightly different information. The first is most analogous to the measure of the overall treatment effect but has the disadvantage of being affected by the presence of other treatment effects. The second measure addresses this problem by using a denominator that focuses on the comparison itself, without reference to any of the other comparisons. As a result, this measure comes close to providing an index of strength that estimates what might be found in an actual two-group experiment involving this comparison. The last measure provides an assessment of the degree to which a particular comparison "explains" or "accounts for" the overall treatment effects. You may have noticed that the three measures have identical numerators and that the denominators decrease in size from Eq. (6–14) to Eq. (6–16); as a result, the values for $R_{A_{comp.}}^2$ will be smallest for the first formula and largest for the last. Because of these differences, we must clearly identify our choice of measure when we report this information to others.

We can use omega squared to provide similar estimates of the size of comparison effects. If our reference is the entire experiment, Maxwell, Camp, and Arvey (1981, p. 529) recommend

$$\hat{\omega}^2_{A_{comp.}} = \frac{SS_{A_{comp.}} - MS_{S/A}}{SS_T + MS_{S/A}} \tag{6-17}$$

To illustrate with the same data set, we find

$$\hat{\omega}^2_{A_{comp.}} = \frac{187.50 - 14.17}{380.00 + 14.17} = \frac{173.33}{394.17} = .440$$

The corresponding value for $R^2_{A_{comp.}}$ was .493. At the other extreme, we can express omega squared with reference to the overall treatment effects. The formula for this quantity comes from Vaughan and Corballis (1969, p. 211):

$$\hat{\omega}^2_{A_{comp.}} = \frac{SS_{A_{comp.}} - MS_{S/A}}{(a - 1)(MS_A - MS_{S/A})} \tag{6-18}$$

Substituting the relevant data from our example, we obtain

$$\hat{\omega}^2_{A_{comp.}} = \frac{187.50 - 14.17}{(3 - 1)(105.00 - 14.17)} = \frac{173.33}{181.66} = .954$$

The corresponding R^2 value was .893. To my knowledge, no one has proposed a formula for omega squared that corresponds to the $R^2_{A_{comp.}}$ specified by Eq. (6–15), which provides an estimate of strength that is not contaminated by the presence of other treatment effects.

Recommendation. I agree with Huberty and Morris (1988) that researchers should follow the practice of reporting estimates of comparison magnitude, particularly when single-*df* comparisons form an integral part of a study. As I have already pointed out, estimates of the magnitude of overall treatment effects are not very informative or revealing when our interest lies in analytical components of the omnibus effect. Your choice of index and the reference against which you are assessing your comparisons should be made clear when you report these estimates, of course. As a general approach, I favor the one suggested by Huberty and Morris in which the focus is the size of a particular comparison, uninfluenced by any other comparisons that might be present.[9]

Power of a Comparison

Considerations of power can be applied to comparisons during the planning stage of an experiment. Power estimates for specific comparisons force us to specify the smallest difference between two means (ψ) we are willing to detect and to estimate the sample size necessary to achieve acceptable power to detect this minimum difference. In fact, basing sample sizes on the power of the critical comparisons, which constitute the primary basis for an experiment, may make more sense than basing this decision on an estimate of the *overall* treatment effects. The strategy

---

[9]I will recommend an analogous approach when we consider estimates of treatment magnitude in more complicated designs.

would be to estimate the minimum differences for these critical comparisons and determine the sample size needed to achieve a certain level of power for each one. The sample size you would then choose would be the largest n you obtained from this analysis. By choosing the largest n, you will be guaranteed that all the critical comparisons will be evaluated at your chosen level of power (or higher).[10]

The calculations required to determine the necessary sample size are quite similar to those presented in Chap. 4 for the omnibus test (see pp. 76–79). We will use the Pearson-Hartley power charts provided in Table A–2. To use these charts for determining the sample size needed to achieve a certain degree of power, we must estimate ϕ for the comparison of interest ($\phi_{A_{comp.}}$) and experiment with different values of n until we achieve the desired amount of power. We start the process by using a special formula to calculate $\phi_{A_{comp.}}$.[11]

$$\phi^2_{A_{comp.}} = n' \frac{(\psi)^2}{(2)(\sigma^2_{S/A})(\Sigma c_i^2)} \qquad (6\text{-}19)$$

where n' = the trial sample size

ψ = the numerical value of the minimum difference for a particular comparison

$\sigma^2_{S/A}$ = the estimate of error variance based on previous research

Σc_i^2 = the sum of the squared coefficients specified in the comparison

The most difficult step in this process is in coming up with an estimate of the minimum size of the comparison we wish to detect. Perhaps the most common comparison we will consider in a power analysis is a pairwise comparison (the difference between two treatment means). We could estimate the absolute size of this difference from previous research and, if the research is applied, from practical considerations as well (for example, a difference that might be cost effective).

Suppose we wanted to study the effects of a drug on learning by rats. We know from previous research that animals in one of the drug conditions learned a particular task an average of 4.0 trials faster than did animals in the no-drug control condition. We plan to extend this research with an experiment using a control and three drug conditions, which include the original drug condition and two additional drug dosages, one larger than the original dosage and one smaller. We want to duplicate the original finding and to determine whether the advantage of the original drug condition is the same or changes with lower and higher dosage levels. The study consists of $a = 4$ groups (control and three drug conditions), and we want to determine the sample size we will need to replicate the original finding with power = .80. Our estimate of error variance, $MS_{S/A} = 10.0$, is obtained from the earlier study, and for a pairwise comparison, we know that $\Sigma c_i^2 = 2$.

We now have all the information we need to conduct a power analysis. Substituting in Eq. (6–19), we find

---

[10]Kraemer and Thiemann (1987, p. 49) also recommend this strategy.

[11]The formula we will use is based on the one proposed by McFatter and Gollob (1986); the one given in Keppel (1982, p. 118) is incorrect.

$$\phi^2_{A_{comp.}} = n' \frac{(\psi)^2}{(2)(\sigma^2_{S/A})(\Sigma c^2_i)}$$

$$= n' \frac{(4.0)^2}{(2)(10.0)(2)} = n' \frac{16}{40} = .4 \, n'$$

To use the Pearson-Hartley power charts, we need to calculate $\phi_{A_{comp.}}$:

$$\phi_{A_{comp.}} = \sqrt{\phi^2_{A_{comp.}}} = \sqrt{.4 \, n'}$$

We now begin a trial-and-error procedure of choosing different values for n', entering the power charts and determining the power associated with that choice of sample size; we then increase or decrease n' until we achieve the power of .80. If we were conducting a power analysis for the omnibus F test in this example, we would use the third power chart ($df_{num.} = a - 1 = 3$). However, since we are examining only a portion of this study, namely, a portion with $df_{A_{comp.}} = 1$, we use the first power chart ($df_{num.} = 1$). If we try $n' = 10$, we obtain[12]

$$\phi_{A_{comp.}} = \sqrt{(.4)(10)} = \sqrt{4} = 2.0$$

Before we can use this information, we must determine which power function to use by setting the significance level ($\alpha = .05$) and calculating the df for the error term. Since we will use the overall error term to evaluate single-df comparisons, $df_{S/A} = (a)(n - 1) = (4)(10 - 1) = 36$. We locate $\phi_{A_{comp.}} = 2.0$ on the lower baseline ($\alpha = .05$) and extend a line vertically from this point until it intersects the power function for $df_{denom.} = 30$; power is nearly .80 (.78). If we use $n' = 11$, we would obtain a value for power (.82), which slightly overestimates our target value of .80.

Estimating sample size for particular comparisons is not a common practice in the behavioral sciences, although it certainly should be. In fact, most researchers should base their estimates of sample size on the comparisons of specific interest, rather than on the omnibus F test. This latter determination is simply not relevant for specific comparisons. As I have already indicated, the most rational strategy would be to base sample size on the comparison that is expected to produce the smallest difference between means. If acceptable power is achieved for the smallest comparison of interest, it will be achieved for all the other comparisons planned for the experiment.

6.4   ORTHOGONAL COMPARISONS

A central concept underlying the analysis of variance is the fact that a sum of squares can be subdivided into separate and independent components. We already considered one example of this process when we divided SS_T into the between-

---

[12]I chose $n' = 10$ by following the procedure outlined in Chap. 4 for finding a reasonable value to start the process (see p. 79).

groups sum of squares, SS_A, and the within-groups sum of squares, $SS_{S/A}$. In general, we can divide any sum of squares into as many independent sums of squares as there are *df*. We have already considered how we can extract meaningful comparisons out of the omnibus analysis. I have said nothing about the relationship between the various comparisons we might examine in our analysis of an experiment, however. In this section, we consider a special set of comparisons, known as **orthogonal comparisons**, which collectively enjoy a unique status in statistics and in data analysis.

Meaning of Orthogonality

The valuable property of orthogonal comparisons is that they reflect *independent* or *nonoverlapping* pieces of information. What this means is that the outcome of one comparison gives no indication whatsoever about the outcome of another orthogonal comparison.

For example, consider the two comparisons I have been discussing throughout this chapter, namely, a complex comparison between a control and the two combined drug conditions, and a pairwise comparison between the two drug conditions. Suppose the two means in the first comparison are equal—for example, the mean for the control group is 5 and the mean for the combined drug groups is 5. What I want to show is that knowing that the difference between these two means is zero still tells us absolutely nothing about the status of the other comparison. That is,

> The means for the two groups may be *identical*, in which case, they would both be 5.
> The mean for the first group may be *greater* than the mean for the second group—for example, 7 versus 3 or 6 versus 4 (actually, any two numbers that average to 5).
> The mean for the first group may be *smaller* than the mean for the second group—for example, 2 versus 8 or 1 versus 9 (again, any two numbers that average to 5).

Please note that the first comparison remained the same regardless of the outcome of the second comparison. In this sense, the information provided by the two comparisons is independent.

The same point can be made if we assume that the first comparison now shows a difference—for example a mean of 6 for the control group and a mean of 4 for the combined drug groups. Again, this fact gives us no hint concerning how the second comparison will turn out:

> The two drug groups may be *equal*, in which case, they would both be 4.
> The mean for the first group may be *greater* than the mean for the second group—for example, 6 versus 2 (any two numbers that average to 4).
> The mean for the first group may be *smaller* than the mean for the second group—for example, 1 versus 7 (again, any two numbers that average to 4).

It is clear, then, that orthogonality means independence of information.

Definition

A numerical test of the orthogonality of any two comparisons is provided by the following relationship between the two sets of coefficients:

$$\Sigma \, (c_i)(d_i) \; = \; 0 \tag{6-20}$$

where c_i and d_i are corresponding coefficients in the two comparisons. As an illustration of Eq. (6–20), consider the two comparisons from the last section, c_i: $+1$, $-\frac{1}{2}$, $-\frac{1}{2}$ and d_i: 0, $+1$, -1. To test for orthogonality, we substitute corresponding coefficients into Eq. (6–20), calculate the product of each pair, and determine the sum of these products. To illustrate the operation of this formula, I have entered the two sets of coefficients according to the levels of factor A in the following table:

	a_1	a_2	a_3
ψ_1	$+1$	$-\frac{1}{2}$	$-\frac{1}{2}$
ψ_2	0	$+1$	-1
$(c_i)(d_i)$:	0	$-\frac{1}{2}$	$+\frac{1}{2}$

The test for orthogonality requires that we first obtain corresponding products for each treatment condition, which has been accomplished in the last row beneath the box. We then determine whether the sum of these products equals zero; in this case, $0 - \frac{1}{2} + \frac{1}{2} = 0$. According to Eq. (6–20), then, these two comparisons are orthogonal.[13]

In contrast, consider two comparisons that are not orthogonal, such as c_i: $+1$, -1, 0 and d_i: $+1$, 0, -1. Translated to our example, the first set of coefficients provides a comparison between the control and the first drug group, and the second set provides a comparison between the control and the second drug group. Although these two comparisons both ask meaningful questions, they are not orthogonal, which we discover by substituting in Eq. (6–20):

$$\Sigma \, (c_i)(d_i) = (+1)(+1) + (-1)(0) + (0)(-1)$$
$$= 1 + 0 + 0 = 1$$

Orthogonality and the Analysis of Variance

Just so many questions reflecting independent pieces of information can be asked of any given set of data. The number of such comparisons is equal to the *df* for the SS_A—that is, $a - 1$. Formally, we can say that

---

[13]Mathematically, orthogonality means *uncorrelated*. You can demonstrate this property by treating one set of coefficients as X scores and the other as Y scores and then calculating the product-moment correlation between these two sets of numbers. The correlation for orthogonal comparisons will be zero; the correlation for nonorthogonal comparisons will be some value other than zero.

With a treatment means, the total number of comparisons that are orthogonal to each other and to $\overline{Y}_T$ is equal to $a - 1$.

If we have three means, for example, it is possible to construct only two orthogonal comparisons.

An important point that should be mentioned is that the sums of squares produced by a complete set of orthogonal comparisons account for the SS_A completely. That is, if we calculate the sums of squares associated with a $- 1$ mutually orthogonal comparisons, we exhaust all the independent information in our data. In symbols,

$$SS_A = \Sigma SS_{A_{comp.}} \tag{6–21}$$

where $\Sigma SS_{A_{comp.}}$ represents the sum of a complete set of orthogonal comparisons.

As an example, consider the sums of squares for the two comparisons we calculated in Sec. 6.3 (see Table 6–3). Earlier, I showed that these two comparisons are orthogonal. From Eq. (6–21), we find that

$$SS_{A_{comp. 1}} + SS_{A_{comp. 2}} = 187.50 + 22.50 = 210.00 = SS_A$$

Suppose we apply two *non*orthogonal comparisons to the same set of data, where $a = 3$ and $n = 5$.

	a_1	a_2	a_3	
Mean:	15.00	6.00	9.00	$\hat{\psi}$
Comp. 1:	+1	−1	0	9.00
Comp. 2:	+1	0	−1	6.00

The two comparisons are not orthogonal; that is,

$$\Sigma (c_i)(d_i) = (1)(1) + (-1)(0) + (0)(-1) = 1 + 0 + 0 = 1$$

From the formula for a single-*df* comparison, Eq. (6–5),

$$SS_{A_{comp.}} = \frac{n(\hat{\psi})^2}{\Sigma c_i^2}$$

we find

$$SS_{comp.1} = \frac{5(9.00)^2}{(1)^2 + (-1)^2 + (0)^2} = 202.50$$

$$SS_{comp.2} = \frac{5(6.00)^2}{(1)^2 + (0)^2 + (-1)^2} = 90.00$$

The sum of these two comparisons, $202.50 + 90.00 = 292.50$, greatly exceeds the total for the SS_A given in Table 6–3 ($SS_A = 210.00$).

Only orthogonal comparisons have the equality stated in Eq. (6–21). What is being said is that the sum of the squares obtained from a set of a treatment means is a *composite* of the sums of squares associated with a set of $a - 1$ mutually orthogonal comparisons. This fact and the related property of complete *nonredundancy*, or *independence*, makes them especially attractive to researchers. A detailed analysis involving a properly constructed set of orthogonal comparisons represents an efficient way to examine the results of an experiment. But efficiency is not everything, and we will form incomplete sets of orthogonal comparisons and sets of nonorthogonal comparisons when they are dictated by the nature of the questions we want to ask of our data. I will pursue this point in the next section.

This property of orthogonal comparisons can be extended to the entire analysis of variance. That is, each one of the degrees of freedom in an experiment, $df_T = (a)(n) - 1$, can be used to represent an independent facet of the total sum of squares. This point adds a new meaning to the concept of degrees of freedom: The degrees of freedom associated with an experiment specify the maximum number of independent pieces of information that can be derived from the particular set of data.[14]

Orthogonality and Planned Comparisons

As noted earlier in this chapter, planned comparisons are a desirable alternative to the omnibus F test. What is not clear, however, is whether any restrictions are placed on the nature of those comparisons we may plan to test. Authors of statistical sourcebooks for psychologists are not in agreement on this issue. Some maintain that planned comparisons must be independent in the sense that they should provide nonredundant information. At one point in his discussion, Hays (1973), for example, refers to this property of independence as a *requirement* (p. 606). In contrast, Winer (1971) states that "in practice the comparisons that are constructed are those having some meaning in terms of the experimental variables; whether these comparisons are orthogonal or not makes little or no difference" (p. 175).

Consider again the comparisons I outlined earlier for a study contrasting methods of presentation in a learning experiment. These comparisons, which were originally summarized in Table 6–1, are listed again in the upper portion of Table 6–6. As I have noted previously, the absolute value of the coefficients are not critical. What has to be present is the desired relative weights. Comparison 1, for example, could be written as $(-1, -1, 0, 1, 1)$ or as $(\frac{1}{2}, \frac{1}{2}, 0, -\frac{1}{2}, -\frac{1}{2})$ and still produce the same sum of squares. Each of the four comparisons qualifies as a contrast—that is, the coefficients sum to zero, as shown in the last column on the right. The six different tests of independence are enumerated in the bottom half of the table. Each test involves a different pair of comparisons. As an example of the calculations, consider the test of comparisons 1 and 3:

$$\Sigma (c_i)(d_i) = (1)(0) + (1)(0) + (0)(0) + (-1)(1) + (-1)(-1)$$

These products are listed in the row labeled $(c_{1i})(c_{3i})$, and the sum of these products, zero, is indicated in the last column of the table. An inspection of the sums for the

---

[14]This important property of the analysis of variance is illustrated in the earlier editions of this book (Keppel, 1973, pp. 567–575; 1982, pp. 618–625); I omitted this discussion in this edition because of space limitations. Keppel and Zedeck (1989) explore the relationship between orthogonal comparisons and analysis of variance in depth.

Table 6-6   Example of a Test for Mutual Orthogonality

	a_1	a_2	a_3	a_4	a_5		
			FEATURES				
Mode:	Paper	Paper	Drum	Drum	Drum		
Order:	Varied	Varied	Same	Varied	Varied		
Array:	Column	Scattered	—	—	—		
Rate:	—	—	3-sec.	3-sec.	1-sec.		
			COMPARISONS				Σc_i
Comp. 1 (c_{1i}):	$+1$	$+1$	0	-1	-1	$=$	0
Comp. 2 (c_{2i}):	$+1$	-1	0	0	0	$=$	0
Comp. 3 (c_{3i}):	0	0	0	$+1$	-1	$=$	0
Comp. 4 (c_{4i}):	0	0	$+1$	-1	0	$=$	0
		TESTS FOR ORTHOGONALITY[a]					$\Sigma (c_i)(d_i)$
$(c_{1i})(c_{2i})$:	$+1$	-1	0	0	0	$=$	0
$(c_{1i})(c_{3i})$:	0	0	0	-1	$+1$	$=$	0
$(c_{1i})(c_{4i})$:	0	0	0	$+1$	0	$=$	$+1$
$(c_{2i})(c_{3i})$:	0	0	0	0	0	$=$	0
$(c_{2i})(c_{4i})$:	0	0	0	0	0	$=$	0
$(c_{3i})(c_{4i})$:	0	0	0	-1	0	$=$	-1

[a] Test for Orthogonality: $\Sigma (c_i)(d_i) = 0$.

different pairs of contrasts reveals that comparison 4 is not orthogonal either to comparison 1 or to comparison 3. The remaining comparisons, however, are all orthogonal (1×2, 1×3, 2×3, and 2×4). If we just consider comparisons 1, 2, and 3, we can say that they are *mutually* orthogonal since each possible pair of comparisons is orthogonal.

A fourth comparison ($4'$) which would be orthogonal to the first three is one that compares group 3 with the average of the remaining groups. In terms of coefficients, the set is -1, -1, 4, -1, -1 or, with fractions, $-\frac{1}{4}$, $-\frac{1}{4}$, 1, $-\frac{1}{4}$, $-\frac{1}{4}$. To test for orthogonality,

$$
\begin{aligned}
1 \times 4' : \Sigma (c_i)(d_i) &= (1)(-1) + (1)(-1) + (0)(4) + (-1)(-1) + (-1)(-1) \\
&= -1 - 1 + 0 + 1 + 1 = 0 \\
2 \times 4' : \Sigma (c_i)(d_i) &= (1)(-1) + (-1)(-1) + (0)(4) + (0)(-1) + (0)(-1) \\
&= -1 + 1 + 0 + 0 + 0 = 0 \\
3 \times 4' : \Sigma (c_i)(d_i) &= (0)(-1) + (0)(-1) + (0)(4) + (1)(-1) + (-1)(-1) \\
&= 0 + 0 + 0 - 1 + 1 = 0
\end{aligned}
$$

Thus, we have constructed a set of mutually orthogonal comparisons. But what usable information do we obtain from this new comparison? One difference in treatment between group 3 and the others is the order of the words on successive trials—the same order is used for group 3 and different orders are used for the other groups. There are other treatment differences as well, however. Group 3 receives the words on a memory drum; two of the remaining groups receive the words on the drum and two on a piece of paper. Group 3 receives the material at a three-second rate of exposure per word; the same rate is used for group 4, but group 5 receives the words at a one-second rate and groups 1 and 2 receive the words all at once. Since more than one treatment difference is reflected in this new contrast, any difference in behavior that is observed cannot be unequivocally attributed to one of the differences in treatment. The comparison is useless.

This demonstration with comparison 4' stresses the fact that the *meaningfulness* of a comparison is of critical importance in the analysis of an experiment and not its inclusion in an orthogonal set of comparisons. But what about the issue of including nonorthogonal comparisons among a set of planned comparisons? There are just so many meaningful comparisons that we can plan before the start of an experiment; most of these will provide independent information. Occasionally, we will think of comparisons that are partially redundant—such as comparison 4 in this example—but that provide important information that is not completely obtainable from the other orthogonal comparisons. Each of the four comparisons in Table 6–6 asks an important and interesting question, however, even though the comparisons themselves are not mutually orthogonal. The "ideal" experiment is one that is designed so that interesting questions can be easily interpreted. To this end, researchers must exercise judgment in the planning stages to guarantee that the important questions studied in an investigation can be answered unambiguously by the proposed experimental design. This is true for orthogonal as well as nonorthogonal comparisons. Nonorthogonal comparisons require special care to avoid logical ambiguities that can arise when information is shared between partially redundant questions.

6.5   COMPARING THREE OR MORE MEANS

Occasionally an analysis plan will include the examination of a subset of three or more means that represent a part of a larger experimental design. Studies with control or baseline conditions are common examples. Suppose we were interested in the effects of different incentives on the solving of problems by fifth-grade students. Groups receiving three forms of incentives—verbal praise (a_1), monetary reward (a_2), and extra credit (a_3)—are included, in addition to a control group (a_4) receiving no incentives. An obvious plan would be to compare the three incentive groups among themselves to see if the different rewards differ in effectiveness. Depending on the outcome of this analysis, we would then conduct additional comparisons to analyze the results of this experiment fully.

The simplest way to compare the three incentive conditions is to treat them as an independent experiment, where $a = 3$, in this case, rather than the 4 in the original design, and then to use the standard formula for the between-groups sum of squares from Chap. 3. More specifically, there would be three conditions in this analysis (levels a_1, a_2, and a_3 —omitting a_4, of course). The treatment sums are A_1, A_2, and A_3, and the new grand sum is $T = A_1 + A_2 + A_3$. For this analysis, $a = 3$, but sample size continues to be n. The computational formula for the sum of squares representing variation among these three conditions is

$$SS_{A_{set}} = \frac{A_1^2 + A_2^2 + A_3^2}{n} - \frac{T^2}{(a)(n)}$$

where the subscript *set* refers to the set of means included in this analysis. The degrees of freedom are 1 less than the number of means being compared; that is, $df_{A_{set}} = 3 - 1 = 2$. The mean square is formed in the usual way; that is,

$$MS_{A_{set}} = \frac{SS_{A_{set}}}{df_{A_{set}}}$$

The *F* ratio is formed by dividing the mean square by the error term obtained from the overall analysis based on all the treatment conditions:

$$F_{set} = \frac{MS_{A_{set}}}{MS_{S/A}}$$

The statistical hypotheses for this test are as follows:

H_0: $\mu_1 = \mu_2 = \mu_3$
H_1: Not all μ_i's are equal

The critical value of *F* is found in Table A–1 under the appropriate numerator and denominator degrees of freedom and significance level. The *df* associated with the numerator are 2. The *df* associated with the error term come from the larger analysis, where there are four groups, rather than three groups, contributing to this source of variance. Thus, if $n = 6$, $df_{S/A} = 4(6 - 1) = 20$ in this particular example.

This type of analysis is generally limited to experiments in which the formation of subgroups makes logical sense and the outcome of the statistical test may influence subsequent analyses. Suppose, for example, that the F_{set} is *not* significant. We would probably then average the three incentive conditions and compare this combined mean with the mean for the single control condition. On the other hand, if the F_{set} *is* significant, we have to probe further to determine in what ways the incentive conditions differ among themselves and also probably compare each of the incentive means with the control mean individually.

6.6 EXERCISES[15]

1. An experimenter is investigating the effects of two drugs on the activity of rats. Drug A is a depressant, and drug B, a stimulant. Half of the subjects receiving either drug are given a low dosage, and half, a high dosage. The experimenter also runs a control group that is given an injection of an inert substance, such as a saline solution. Five different groups are represented in the experiment, each containing $n = 4$ rats assigned randomly from the stock of laboratory rats on hand. The animals are injected

[15]The answers to these problems are found in Appendix B.

and then their activity is observed for a fixed period of time. The treatment sums for each group of four rats follow:

Control	DRUG A		DRUG B	
	Low	High	Low	High
a_1	a_2	a_3	a_4	a_5
60	55	32	66	92

The within-groups mean square $MS_{S/A}$ is found to be 37.00.
  a. Perform a one-way analysis of variance on these data.
  b. Construct a set of coefficients that will provide the following comparisons:
    (1) Control versus combined experimental groups
    (2) Drug A versus drug B
    (3) Low versus high dosage for drug A
    (4) Low versus high dosage for drug B
  c. Show that these four comparisons are mutually orthogonal.
  d. Extract the sums of squares associated with these comparisons and test their significance.
  e. Verify that the sum of the comparison sums of squares equals the SS_A.
2. In Sec. 6.2, I described a memory experiment and a set of planned comparisons that could be used to analyze the data. Let's assume that the experiment was conducted with $n = 5$ subjects in each of the five treatment conditions. The treatment sums obtained on the response measure were as follows:

a_1	a_2	a_3	a_4	a_5
63	84	47	48	42

We will assume that $MS_{S/A} = 13.50$.
  a. Conduct the four planned comparisons indicated in Table 6–1 (p. 113). What conclusions do you draw from this analysis?
  b. The comparisons in this set are not mutually orthogonal (see Table 6–6, p. 137). Show that the sum of the comparison sums of squares does not equal the SS_A.
3. The experiment described in Sec. 6.5 was concerned with the effects of different incentives on the solving of problems by fifth-grade students. There were three incentive groups, verbal praise (a_1), monetary reward (a_2), and extra credit (a_3), and a no-incentive control group (a_4). The experiment was conducted with $n = 10$ children. The response measure consisted of the number of problems solved in 20 minutes. The following treatment sums were obtained:

a_1	a_2	a_3	a_4
48	53	47	32

Assume that $MS_{S/A} = 4.11$.
  a. Determine whether the three incentives were differentially effective in influencing the number of problems solved.
  b. Conduct a single-*df* comparison between the control condition and the combined incentive conditions.
  c. Is the omnibus *F* based on all four conditions significant? Is this finding compatible with the conclusions you drew from the other two analyses? Explain.

7

Analysis of Trend

The procedures covered in the last chapter dealt with independent variables that were conveniently translated into comparisons between treatment means. The analyses, summarized in Table 6–6 (p. 137), of an experiment comparing five different methods of presenting words is a good example of a multilevel study analyzed as a set of component two-group experiments. When a *quantitative* independent variable is manipulated, however, we typically employ a specialized form of single-*df* comparisons called **trend analysis**—the topic of this chapter.

With a quantitative independent variable, the treatment levels represent different amounts of a single common variable. The levels can be ordered or spaced along a dimension in terms of the amount of the variable. Examples of quantitative or scaled, independent variables are the number of hours of food deprivation, different dosage levels of a particular drug, rates of stimulus presentation, and the intensity of the unconditioned stimulus in a conditioning experiment. In analyzing this sort of experiment, we are not particularly interested in comparing one treatment mean with another. Instead, we usually plot the entire set of treatment means on a graph, connect the points, and examine the display for any underlying *shape* or *trend*. Since we are interested in the general form of the relationship between the independent and dependent variables, we usually are not interested in testing differences between adjacent means.

I will introduce you to trend analysis through a numerical example. You will see how easily we can adapt the formulas from Chap. 6 to test for the underlying trend components that may be present in a set of data. We will then consider in more detail the methods by which we accomplish trend analysis and the different ways we can use the analysis in research.

7.1   ISOLATING TREND COMPONENTS

As an example of trend analysis, consider an experiment designed to test the proposition that subjects learn better when training is distributed over a period of time than when the training is massed all at once. If we wished, we could investigate this question with just two groups, one group receiving massed training and another distributed training of some sort. Consider, instead, a more comprehensive investigation in which we include several distributed conditions. The advantage of this approach is that it provides information about the *form* of the relationship between spaced training and learning. The two-group experiment allows only a restricted glimpse of this relationship. In fact, all we would know from this study is whether there is a significant difference between the massed condition and the spaced condition; we would know nothing about the effects of other conditions of spacing, amounts larger and smaller than the particular one included in the experiment.

Assume the following experiment: Subjects are given some material to learn for 10 trials, with the independent variable, the *intertrial interval* (the interval between successive trials), being manipulated at intervals of 0 seconds (the massed condition) and 20, 40, and 60 seconds (the spaced conditions). This means that one group of subjects receives no spacing between successive trials, another group receives 20 seconds between trials, another group 40 seconds, and a final group 60 seconds. Suppose that $n = 20$ subjects are randomly assigned to each of the four independent groups. The results of this hypothetical experiment, expressed in terms of the number of correct responses over the 10 learning trials, are given in the top part of Table 7–1. You should note that I have not listed the individual Y scores but rather the group sums, means, and sums of the squared scores—sufficient information to conduct the analysis.

As an initial step, it is generally a good idea to perform the overall analysis of variance, even though you may not be particularly interested in the outcome of the omnibus F test. You do need to calculate $MS_{S/A}$ in any case, and this is a convenient way to do so. This analysis is summarized in the lower parts of the table, and the overall $F = 10.72$ is significant. The means for the four treatment groups are plotted in Fig. 7–1. As you can see, although there is a general tendency for the learning scores to increase as the length of the spacing variable increases, this is true only up to a point (40 seconds), after which they begin to drop. A trend analysis attempts to verify these observations in a systematic fashion.

Table 7–1 Numerical Example: Overall Analysis

	BASIC DATA				
	Intertrial Interval (A)				
	0 sec. a_1	20 sec. a_2	40 sec. a_3	60 sec. a_4	Sum
Sum (A_i)	304	427	456	401	1,588
n	20	20	20	20	80
Mean ($\bar{Y}_{A_i}$)	15.20	21.35	22.80	20.05	19.85
ΣY_{ij}^2	5,175	9,461	10,551	8,529	33,716

BASIC RATIOS

$$[T] = \frac{T^2}{(a)(n)} = \frac{(1,588)^2}{(4)(20)} = 31,521.80$$

$$[A] = \frac{\Sigma A^2}{n} = \frac{(304)^2 + (427)^2 + (456)^2 + (401)^2}{20} = 32,174.10$$

$$[Y] = \Sigma Y^2 = 5,175 + 9,461 + 10,551 + 8,529 = 33,716$$

SUMMARY OF THE ANALYSIS

Source			SS	df	MS	F
A	$[A] - [T]$	$=$	652.30	3	217.43	10.72*
S/A	$[Y] - [A]$	$=$	1,541.90	76	20.29	
Total	$[Y] - [T]$	$=$	2,194.20	79		

*$p < .05$.

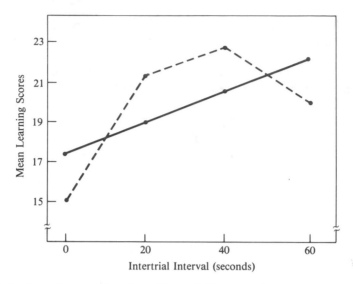

FIGURE 7–1   Learning as a function of intertrial interval: An example of linear trend.

Linear Trend

The analysis usually begins with the simplest mathematical way to describe a set of data—a straight line. In addition to plotting the four means in Fig. 7–1, I have also drawn a straight line through them. This particular line is called the line of "best fit" because it minimizes the discrepancies between the line and the actual data points.[1] To say that a function is linear means that the curve either rises or drops at the same rate along the extent of the independent variable. The data plotted in Fig. 7–1 seem to be reasonably described by a linear function. On the other hand, we can also see that the linear function does not fit the data of Fig. 7–1 all that well. We will consider this observation after we finish our discussion of linear trend.

Testing for Linear Trend.   The test for linear trend is simply an extension of the tests of single-*df* comparisons considered in the last chapter. More specifically, we start with a set of coefficients, which in this case reflects linear trend; determine the degree to which these coefficients describe the relationship among the means in our experiment; and then test the significance of this relationship. How might we use coefficients to represent linear trend? Since the presence of a linear trend implies a difference between the two end points, we could simply assess the significance of the difference between them, using the set c_i: $-1, 0, 0, 1$ as coefficients. Alternatively, we could use sets that concentrate on other differences also implied

[1]Technically, the mathematical operations that establish this line may be shown to satisfy the **criterion of least squares**. What this means is that the sum of the squared deviations of the means from the line are at a minimum value; any other line will produce a larger sum. I will illustrate how to determine this line later in this section.

by the presence of linear trend—for example, c_i: -1, -1, 1, 1 or c_i: 0, -1, 1, 0. In each case, we would expect to find a significant difference if linear trend is present in the data.

A more satisfactory way of assessing linear trend, however, is to use a set of coefficients that represents an idealized version of a straight line. You will find such sets in Appendix Table A–4, which lists coefficients for different types of trends for experiments with varying numbers of treatment groups. For the current example, we look up the linear coefficients under $a = 4$ groups in Table A–4 and find c_i: -3, -1, $+1$, $+3$. You can see that the coefficients themselves represent a straight line—each successive level of factor A increases steadily by two units. This set is preferable to the ones we considered in the preceding paragraph because the coefficients give progressively more weight to the treatment conditions located far- ther away from the center of the independent variable. The other sets of coeffi- cients do not represent the linear trend to its fullest.

We are now ready to return to the numerical example. At this point, the anal- ysis duplicates the analyses of single-df comparisons considered in the last chap- ter—that is, we use the linear coefficients in conjunction with the general formula for single-df comparisons, Eq. (6–5), and calculate a sum of squares that reflects the degree to which the variation among the treatment means may be described by a straight line. The first step is to calculate $\hat{\psi}$, the sum of the weighted treatment means. Using the linear coefficients, we find

$$\hat{\psi}_{linear} = \Sigma (c_i)(\overline{Y}_{A_i})$$

$$= (-3)(15.20) + (-1)(21.35) + (1)(22.80) + (3)(20.05)$$

$$= 16.00$$

We next substitute the relevant values into Eq. (6-5) as follows:

$$SS_{A_{linear}} = \frac{n\,(\hat{\psi}_{linear})^2}{\Sigma\,c_i^2}$$

$$= \frac{20(16.00)^2}{(-3)^2 + (-1)^2 + (1)^2 + (3)^2} = 256.00$$

Finally, we test the significance of this comparison by forming F_{linear},

$$F_{linear} = \frac{MS_{A_{linear}}}{MS_{S/A}} = \frac{256.00}{20.29} = 12.62$$

and evaluating the F with $df_{num.} = 1$ and $df_{denom.} = 76$; the linear trend is signifi- cant.

The linear coefficients satisfy the same requirement of all sets of coefficients representing single-df comparisons, namely, $\Sigma\,c_i^2 = 0$. Also, changing the signs of the coefficients does not alter their ability to detect linear trend. That is, the set c_i: 3, 1, -1, -3 produces $\hat{\psi}_{linear} = (3)(15.20) + (1)(21.35) + (-1)(22.80) + (-3)$ $(20.05) = -16.00$, which when squared in Eq. (6–5), produces exactly the same $SS_{A_{linear}} = 256.00$. Finally, you may be puzzled by the fact that linear trend is associated with 1 *df*. One explanation is that this comparison also reduces to a difference between two means, one mean based on the sum of the means weighted by *positive* coefficients and the other mean based on the sum of the means weighted by *negative* coefficients. This same argument holds for all single-*df* comparisons in general.

Determining the Regression Equation.   What did we discover from this analysis? The significant F_{linear} indicates that the data exhibit an overall linear trend—there is a significant tendency for learning to increase as the time between successive trials increases from 0 to 60 seconds. We can express this relationship by determining the best-fitting straight line that underlies this analysis. The equation for this line, which we call the **linear regression equation**, is given by

$$\overline{Y}'_{A_i} = \overline{Y}_T + (b_1)(c_i) \tag{7-1}$$

where $\overline{Y}'_{A_i}$ = the mean for level a_i determined by this equation

$\overline{Y}_T$ = the grand mean

b_1 = the **slope** of the line (the equation follows)

c_i = the linear trend coefficient for level a_i

The formula for the slope of the best-fitting line is as follows:

$$b_1 = \frac{\hat{\psi}_{linear}}{\Sigma c_i^2} \tag{7-2}$$

which we can calculate with information we have already obtained in conducting the test for linear trend. Substituting in Eq. (7–2), we find

$$b_1 = \frac{16.00}{20} = .80$$

The linear regression equation, Eq. (7–1), then becomes

$$\overline{Y}'_{A_i} = 19.85 + (.80)(c_i)$$

This equation represents the idealized linear relationship between the intertrial interval (factor A) and the dependent variable (learning scores)—our prediction of the outcome of the experiment if only a linear trend were present in the population. Usually, we would want to draw this line on a graph, along with the actual treatment means. We can do so by using the equation to calculate the two end points on the line ($\overline{Y}'_{A_1}$ and $\overline{Y}'_{A_4}$) and connect them. To illustrate the procedure, however, I will calculate all four points on the regression line:

$$\overline{Y}'_{A_1} = 19.85 + (.80)(-3) = 19.85 - 2.40 = 17.45$$

$$\overline{Y}'_{A_2} = 19.85 + (.80)(-1) = 19.85 - .80 = 19.05$$

$$\overline{Y}'_{A_3} = 19.85 + (.80)(1) = 19.85 + .80 = 20.65$$

$$\overline{Y}'_{A_4} = 19.85 + (.80)(3) = 19.85 + 2.40 = 22.25$$

You should verify that these values do fall on the regression line drawn in Fig. 7–1. Another way to think about the test for linear trend is that it tests the null hypothesis that the population regression coefficient is zero. That is, if no linear trend is present, $b_1 = 0$, and the straight line will have no slope; it will be parallel to the baseline.

Quadratic Trend

Although we have statistical evidence for the presence of a linear trend, it is clear that a straight line does not fully capture the total relationship between the independent and dependent variables. In fact, the linear trend seems to hold best up to a certain point (somewhere between 40 and 60 seconds), after which performance tends to decline. A **quadratic trend** is one that displays *concavity*—a single bend either upward or downward. In our example, we see what is sometimes called an *inverted U*, a function with a downward bend, that is, an increase fo!lowed by a decrease. Trend analysis permits us to determine whether an idealized quadratic trend is also present in these data. Let's see how we accomplish this task.

Testing for Quadratic Trend.   The statistical procedure is identical to the one outlined for the linear trend. We start by obtaining the *quadratic* coefficients from Table A–4: c_i: 1, -1, -1, 1. These coefficients reflect an idealized quadratic trend (concave upward, or U-shaped).[2] Our first step is to calculate $\hat{\psi}_{quadratic}$:

$$\hat{\psi} = \Sigma (c_i)(\overline{Y}_{A_i})$$

$$= (1)(15.20) + (-1)(21.35) + (-1)(22.80) + (1)(20.05)$$

$$= -8.90$$

Next, we use Eq. (6–5) to find the sum of squares associated with the quadratic trend:

$$SS_{A_{quadratic}} = \frac{n\,(\hat{\psi}_{quadratic})^2}{\Sigma c_i^2}$$

$$= \frac{20(-8.90)^2}{(1)^2 + (-1)^2 + (-1)^2 + (1)^2} = 396.05$$

---

[2]It does not matter that the coefficients reflect a trend opposite to that exhibited by the data since the formulas we use compensate for the signs given to the coefficients. That is, a reversal of the signs of these coefficients (c_i: -1, 1, 1, -1) will produce exactly the same information as the original set of coefficients.

Finally, we test the significance of this comparison by forming $F_{quadratic}$,

$$F_{quadratic} = \frac{MS_{A_{quadratic}}}{MS_{S/A}} = \frac{396.05}{20.29} = 19.52$$

which is evaluated with $df_{num.} = 1$ and $df_{denom.} = 76$. The quadratic trend is significant.

Determining the Regression Equation.   We can obtain a regression equation for the quadratic function that underlies the analysis just completed by following the same steps that we employed with the linear component. The formula for the quadratic function is based on Eqs. (7–1) and (7–2):

$$\overline{Y}'_{A_i} = \overline{Y}_T + (b_2)(c_i) \tag{7–3}$$

where the only change is a replacement of the linear regression coefficient b_1 in Eq. (7–1) by a quadratic regression coefficient b_2; the coefficient c_i refers to the quadratic trend coefficient for level a_i. The formula for b_2 is given by

$$b_2 = \frac{\hat{\Psi}_{quadratic}}{\Sigma c_i^2} \tag{7–4}$$

Substituting in Eq. (7–4), we find

$$b_2 = \frac{-8.90}{4} = -2.225$$

The quadratic regression equation, Eq. (7–3), then becomes

$$\overline{Y}'_{A_i} = 19.85 + (-2.225)(c_i)$$

With this equation, we find the four points that correspond to the treatment conditions in our experiment:

$$\overline{Y}'_{A_1} = 19.85 + (-2.225)(1) = 19.85 - 2.225 = 17.625$$

$$\overline{Y}'_{A_2} = 19.85 + (-2.225)(-1) = 19.85 + 2.225 = 22.075$$

$$\overline{Y}'_{A_3} = 19.85 + (-2.225)(-1) = 19.85 + 2.225 = 22.075$$

$$\overline{Y}'_{A_4} = 19.85 + (-2.225)(1) = 19.85 - 2.225 = 17.625$$

I have plotted this function along with the actual group means in Fig. 7–2. Just as the linear function did not fully capture the variation among the means, neither does the quadratic function. Clearly, we need both components to provide an adequate mathematical description of the data.

Higher-Order Trend Components

It is certainly possible to search for trend components that are more complex than the linear and the quadratic. The complexity of a trend component refers to the

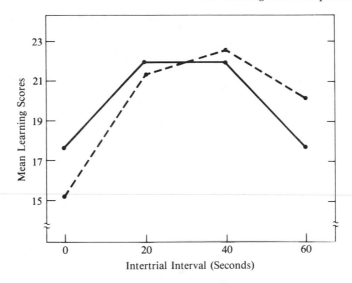

FIGURE 7-2   An example of quadratic trend.

number of bends or reversals it exhibits. A linear component has no bends, of course, and a quadratic component has one—the curve either rises and then falls (an inverted U) or it falls and then rises (a U). A curve that has two reversals is called a **cubic trend component**, and one that has three reversals is called a **quartic trend component**. Examples of both functions are given in Fig. 7–3. The only restriction to the number of possible components is the number of treatment groups. When $a = 2$, only a linear trend is detectable; when $a = 3$, linear and quadratic trends are detectable; when $a = 4$, linear, quadratic, and cubic trends are detectable; and when $a = 5$, linear, quadratic, cubic, and quartic trends are detectable.

Most existing theories in psychology make predictions about linear and quadratic components only, although there are some notable exceptions.[3] The most obvious reason researchers postulate only linear and quadratic trends is their simplicity. Another reason for stopping a trend analysis at this point is the relative absence of more complicated trend components in the behavioral sciences. In any case, the analysis of higher-order trends follows the same steps as did the analyses of the linear and quadratic components—all that changes is the set of coefficients. Table A–4 gives sets of coefficients for components ranging in complexity from linear (no reversal) to **quintic** (four reversals) for experiments in which the number of treatment conditions ranges from 3 to 10. More extensive tables are available in Fisher and Yates (for example, 1953) and Pearson and Hartley (for example, 1970).

I will illustrate the process with the same numerical example. Since $a = 4$, we can only extract three trend components, namely, linear, quadratic, and cubic. The coefficients for the cubic component come from Table A–4 (c_i: $-1, 3, -3, 1$). Substituting in Eq. (6–5), we find

[3]See Hayes-Roth (1977) for an interesting example of the theoretical prediction of higher-order trends.

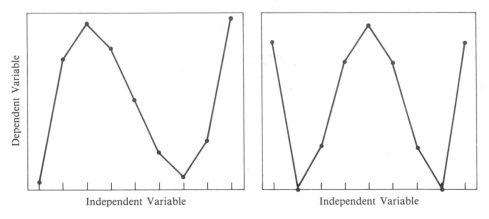

FIGURE 7–3   Examples of a cubic trend (left graph) and a quartic trend (right graph).

$$\hat{\psi}_{cubic} = (-1)(15.20) + (3)(21.35) + (-3)(22.80) + (1)(20.05) = .50$$

$$SS_{A_{cubic}} = \frac{20(.50)^2}{(-1)^2 + (3)^2 + (-3)^2 + (1)^2} = .25$$

The $F_{cubic} = .25/20.29 = .01$ is not significant.

Combining Trend Components

Now that we have determined that only two trend components are significant, namely, linear and quadratic, we can combine them to produce a composite curve that reflects both of them. A formula for this curve is given by

$$\overline{Y}'_{A_i} = \overline{Y}_T + (b_1)(c_{1i}) + (b_2)(c_{2i}) \tag{7-5}$$

where $\overline{Y}_T$ = the grand mean ($\overline{Y}_T = 19.85$)

$\quad b_1$ = the linear regression coefficient ($b_1 = .80$)

$\quad c_{1i}$ = the *linear* coefficient for level a_i

$\quad b_2$ = the quadratic regression coefficient ($b_2 = -2.225$)

$\quad c_{2i}$ = the *quadratic* coefficient for level a_i

We now calculate the points on this curve ($\overline{Y}_{A_i}$) by entering the appropriate pairs of linear and quadratic coefficients in Eq. (7–5):

$$\overline{Y}'_{A_1} = 19.85 + (.80)(-3) + (-2.225)(1) = 19.85 - 2.40 - 2.225 = 15.225$$

$$\overline{Y}'_{A_2} = 19.85 + (.80)(-1) + (-2.225)(-1) = 19.85 - .80 + 2.225 = 21.275$$

$$\overline{Y}'_{A_3} = 19.85 + (.80)(1) + (-2.225)(-1) = 19.85 + .80 + 2.225 = 22.875$$

$$\overline{Y}'_{A_4} = 19.85 + (.80)(3) + (-2.225)(1) = 19.85 + 2.40 - 2.225 = 20.025$$

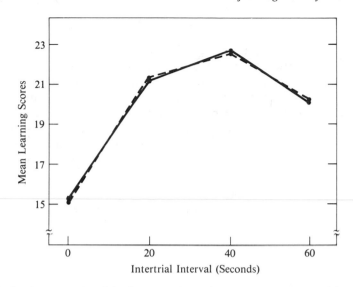

FIGURE 7–4   An example of the linear and quadratic components combined.

This composite curve is plotted in Fig. 7–4. As you can see, the combined linear and quadratic components match the actual treatment means quite closely.

7.2   METHOD OF ORTHOGONAL POLYNOMIALS

The purpose of trend analysis is to find a mathematical expression to relate changes in the treatment means (the dependent variable) to changes in the treatment variable (the independent variable). The trend analysis illustrated in the last section takes advantage of orthogonal polynomials. A polynomial is a mathematical function that is made up of a number of terms. The **method of orthogonal polynomials** permits us to assess each trend component without contamination from the others. Consider the coefficients we used to extract the linear component (c_{1i}: -3, -1, 1, 3) and the quadratic component (c_{2i}: 1, -1, -1, 1). These two sets of coefficients are *orthogonal*; that is,

$$\Sigma(c_{1i})(c_{2i}) = (-3)(1) + (-1)(-1) + (1)(-1) + (3)(1)$$
$$= -3 + 1 - 1 + 3 = 0$$

Similarly, both of these sets of coefficients are orthogonal to the set we used to determine the cubic component (c_{3i}: -1, 3, -3, 1), which you may wish to verify for yourself. This means, then, that each trend component is *independent* of the others—that is, each set of coefficients captures a different trend component in the data. You may recall that one property of a complete set of orthogonal comparisons is that the component sums of squares combine to equal SS_A. This is true for our example:

$$SS_{A_{linear}} + SS_{A_{quadratic}} + SS_{A_{cubic}} = 256.00 + 396.05 + .25 = 652.30$$

which equals the between-groups sum of squares (that is, $SS_A = 652.30$).

The trend coefficients in Table A–4 assume that the means are based on *equal numbers* of observations and that the levels of the independent variable are *equally spaced* on some continuum. I used equal intervals in the numerical example in that a difference of 20 seconds separates each successive level of the independent variable—0, 20, 40, and 60 seconds. Other examples of equally spaced intervals are exposure durations of 50, 250, and 450 milliseconds; noise levels of 20, 50, and 80 decibels; and drug dosages of 1, 2, and 3 grains. Using the tabled coefficients when the intervals are not equal will distort the trend analysis. Suppose, for example, that we conduct a memory experiment in which subjects are tested at different times after exposure to some learning material. One group is

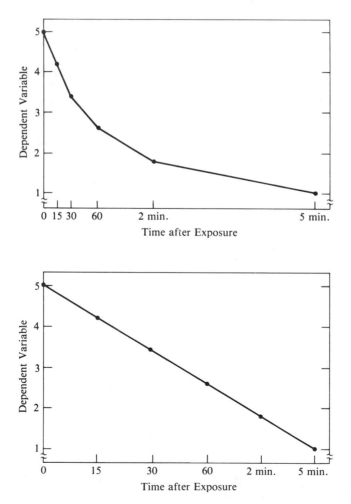

FIGURE 7–5 Upper graph: Intervals spaced according to actual time values. Lower graph: Intervals spaced equally.

tested immediately after exposure (0 seconds), and other groups are tested 15 seconds, 30 seconds, 60 seconds, 3 minutes, or 5 minutes after exposure. The hypothetical results of this experiment are presented in the upper portion of Fig. 7–5. As you can see, the amount remembered decreases rapidly at first (between 0 and 60 seconds) and then begins to level off over the longer time delays (between 1 and 5 minutes). But what do the data look like if we assumed that the intervals between adjacent conditions were *equal*, which is what would happen if we used the coefficients from Table A–4 to conduct the trend analysis? I have plotted the data this way in the lower portion of Fig. 7–5. Do you see how the trend analysis would change? Instead of a gradual reduction in the amount of forgetting occurring after the longer intervals, this analysis would show a perfect linear trend, that is, a *constant* decline from 0 seconds to 5 minutes.

To analyze the data appropriately, then, we cannot use the coefficients listed in Table A–4—which assume equal intervals—but must construct sets of trend coefficients that are appropriate for the particular spacings of the levels represented in our experiment. A detailed explanation of how this can be accomplished may be found in earlier editions of this book (Keppel, 1973, pp. 581–588; 1982, pp. 629–633). Another approach to unequal intervals is to conduct the trend analysis within the context of multiple regression and correlation, which is described in a number of sources (for example, Cohen, 1980; Keppel & Zedeck, 1989, pp. 500–505). Alternatively, you could turn to various software programs available on both mainframe computers (for example, SPSSX MANOVA and BMDP5V) and personal computers (for example, Systat), which will perform orthogonal trend analyses for equal and unequal intervals.

7.3 PLANNING A TREND ANALYSIS

We will now consider the special considerations that go into the planning of an experiment with a quantitative independent variable, in which a trend analysis is a likely possibility. We will consider first the choice of the intervals separating adjacent levels of the independent variable.

Choosing the Intervals

There are two questions that surround the choice of intervals, namely, the nature of the spacing between adjacent levels and the number of intervals. We will discuss the question of spacing first.

Spacing the Intervals.   Suppose we conduct an experiment in which we include five points on some stimulus dimension. We probably will include two groups at the extremes of the dimension to ensure that we "capture" the full range of effectiveness of the independent variable. How should we locate the other three groups?

Our first reaction might be to space them equally between the two extremes. Although many factors influence the choice of the specific intervals, the overriding consideration is the selection of levels that will "pick up" important changes in the response measure. Only if the function relating the independent and dependent variables is *linear* will equally spaced intervals be the most efficient choice. This may be seen in Fig. 7–6. The function plotted in the two left-hand graphs is linear. Equally spaced intervals (upper graph) result in equal changes between successive intervals, whereas unequal intervals (lower graph) result in small changes where the intervals are closely spaced and large changes where they are more spread out. In a sense, then, no interval is "wasted" in the first situation, whereas two of the intervals are wasted in the second. But what happens when the underlying function is not linear? One possible outcome is depicted in the two graphs on the right. Here, the situation is reversed. An equal spacing of intervals (upper graph) results in three intervals that show very little change and one interval that brackets around the point in the function where the maximum change is occurring. Unequal spacing (lower graph) does not waste any of the intervals since they are closely spaced where there is a precipitous change and widely spaced where only small changes occur.

The trick in designing an experiment, of course, is to know the general shape of the function ahead of time so that we can make efficient use of our intervals. In most research applications, we usually do have enough information to provide a basis for a rational choice in the spacing. Without such information, however, it is better to use equal intervals.

The Number of Intervals.   If the object of an experiment is to study trend components, you should include a reasonable number of intervals—for example, 5 to 7—so that the underlying relationship between the independent and dependent

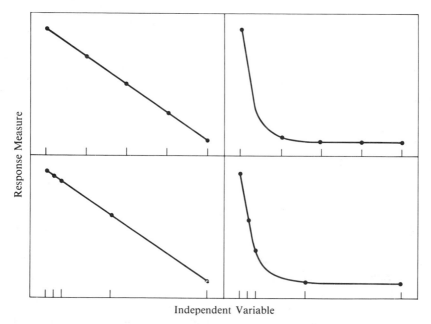

FIGURE 7–6   *Spacing of points along a stimulus dimension.*

variables is finely traced. Consider the results of an experiment reported by Hayes-Roth (1977), which are presented in Fig. 7–7. If she had reduced the number of levels between 0 and 10 correct verifications (her independent variable), the detailed curvature of the underlying relationship would have been lost.

This example illustrates another reason for including 5 to 7 intervals, namely, the detection of higher-order trend components. When an experiment includes relatively few treatment conditions, we can detect only lower-order trends. With three conditions, for example, Hayes-Roth would not have been able to detect the complex function depicted in Fig. 7–7 because all she would have been able to isolate would have been a linear and a quadratic component. Even when you expect to find only lower-order trend components, you should still include a reasonable number of intervals in order to convince yourself (and others) that there is no higher-order trend masked by your choice of intervals. If you find only a linear trend in an experiment with five or more well-spaced conditions, for example, you will feel quite confident that the basic relationship between the independent and dependent variables is linear.

In short, any researcher who is planning to study the nature of the relationship involving a quantitative independent variable should seriously consider investing in a substantial experiment. By substantial, I mean an experiment that includes a sufficient number of treatment conditions to provide convincing evidence of a linear or quadratic trend component—if only lower-order trends are present—and to provide a reasonable opportunity of detecting higher-order trends should they be present.

Predicting Trend Components

Researchers occasionally undertake trend analyses for theoretical reasons. Consider, for example, the classic study reported by Grant (1956) in which subjects

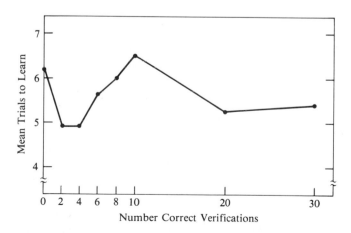

FIGURE 7–7   An example of a complex function. From B. Hayes-Roth, Evolution of cognitive structures and processes, *Psychological Review,* 1977, *84,* 260–278. Copyright 1977 by the American Psychological Association. Adapted by permission.

were trained to respond to a 12-inch circle.[4] Following training, they were randomly assigned to $a = 7$ different groups, each of which was tested with a different stimulus. One group was tested with the original training circle (12 inches), whereas the others were tested with circles differing in size—three were smaller than the original circle (circles with diameters of 9, 10, and 11 inches) and three were larger (circles with diameters of 13, 14, and 15 inches).

For theoretical reasons, Grant (1956) expected to find two trend components relating the independent variable (size of the testing stimulus) and the dependent variable (response to the test stimulus). More specifically, he predicted that subjects would tend to respond more vigorously as the size of the testing circle increased—that is, a linear component. His second prediction, which was his main interest in the study, was that the response would be greatest among subjects for whom the testing stimulus was the training stimulus itself (the 12-inch circle) and would taper off gradually among subjects tested with circles increasingly different in size from the training circle—that is, a *quadratic* component.

Statistical analysis revealed that only the quadratic trend component was significant. (The linear component was significant at $\alpha = .10$.) Let's see how well the two trend components match the actual data for this experiment. I have plotted the means and drawn the best-fitting straight line in the upper portion of Fig. 7–8 and the corresponding information for the quadratic component in the lower portion of the figure. Thus, the trend analysis generally supported the theoretical predictions on which this study was based. For more information about this analysis, see problem 1 at the end of this chapter.

Using Trend Analysis for Descriptive Purposes

Most researchers turn to trend analyses to simplify the description of their data. That is, they use trend analysis as a tool that systematically searches for significant trend components, the primary purpose of which is simplification. Thus, an analysis begins with an assessment of the linear component, in an attempt to see whether this simplest mathematical function will reasonably describe the data. Regardless of how this test turns out, researchers must also decide if they want to probe further with systematically more complex trend components—the quadratic, followed by the cubic, and so on. Some researchers will examine only the linear and quadratic trend components since trends of greater complexity are likely to be relatively weak or nonexistent and would probably defy theoretical explanation anyway. Other researchers have adopted a rule for stopping a trend analysis. We will consider two such rules next.

When there is no theory to guide the trend analysis and we are simply interested in discovering the trend components that will jointly describe the outcome of an experiment fairly accurately, we start by testing the overall F for significance. If significant, we would first calculate the linear sum of squares and test the signifi-

---

[4]The original experiment by Grant and Schiller (1953) used the classical conditioning procedure in which the subjects are conditioned to give a galvanic skin response (GSR) upon the presentation of the stimulus.

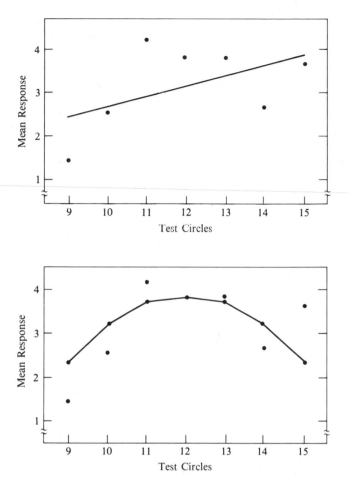

FIGURE 7–8   An example of two trend components (from Grant, 1956).

cance of this component. (In contrast, a theoretically driven analysis would usually omit the omnibus test and turn directly to an evaluation of the specific trend
component or components that are of theoretical concern.) We are now in a position to decide whether to continue searching for other significant trend components. One approach bases this decision on the significance of the variation among
the treatment means that remains after the linear component has been removed.
This is easily accomplished by subtracting the sum of squares for the linear component from the between-groups sum of squares:

$$SS_{A_{residual}} = SS_A - SS_{A_{linear}} \tag{7–6}$$

This residual sum of squares reflects the variability remaining after we remove the
variation associated with the linear component. We then test its significance to see
whether any additional trend components are present. This procedure is analogous

to the omnibus F test that proceeded the trend analysis. That is, the linear component was not examined unless the omnibus F was significant. By the same token, the quadratic component will not be examined unless the residual F is significant.

To illustrate, I will assume that the trend analysis we performed on the numerical example was not theoretically motivated.[5] Since the overall F was significant (see Table 7–1), we would be justified in isolating the linear component. The sum of squares from this analysis, $SS_{A_{linear}} = 256.00$, was significant. We now would calculate the residual sum of squares. Substituting in Eq. (7–6), we find

$$SS_{A_{residual}} = 652.30 - 256.00 = 396.30$$

The degrees of freedom for this sum of squares are also obtained by subtraction:

$$df_{A_{residual}} = df_A - df_{A_{linear}} \tag{7–7}$$

For this example, $df_{A_{residual}} = 3 - 1 = 2$. Completing the analysis, we have

$$MS_{A_{residual}} = \frac{SS_{A_{residual}}}{df_{A_{residual}}} \tag{7–8}$$

$$= \frac{396.30}{2} = 198.15$$

$$F_{residual} = \frac{MS_{A_{residual}}}{MS_{S/A}} \tag{7–9}$$

$$= \frac{198.15}{20.29} = 9.77$$

which, with $df_{num.} = 2$ and $df_{denom.} = 76$, is significant. This outcome suggests that there is still more variation that we can legitimately isolate.

Given this outcome, we would now test the quadratic trend component. Our earlier calculations showed that this trend component is significant. To decide whether to continue any further, we would test a new residual sum of squares—one from which the linear *and* the quadratic sums of squares have been removed from SS_A:

$$SS_{A_{residual}} = SS_A - SS_{A_{linear}} - SS_{A_{quadratic}} \tag{7–10}$$

which gives us $SS_{A_{residual}} = 652.30 - 256.00 - 396.05 = .25$; this new residual sum of squares is associated with

$$df_{A_{residual}} = df_A - df_{A_{linear}} - df_{A_{quadratic}} = 3 - 1 - 1 = 1$$

The F for this residual ($.25/20.29 = .01$) is not significant. We would stop.

An alternative rule for stopping is to perform the residual test with $df_{A_{residual}} = 1$ in all cases, regardless of the number of potential trend components contained

---

[5] Actually, this example was based on a theory that predicts exactly the analysis we did conduct (see Underwood, 1961).

within the residual sum of squares.[6] The rationale for this rule is the possibility that all the residual sum of squares may be associated with *one* of the remaining trend components. Thus, each test of the residual variation would define

$$MS_{A_{residual}} = \frac{SS_{A_{residual}}}{1} = SS_{A_{residual}} \tag{7-11}$$

Applying this procedure to our numerical example and the residual test we would conduct after the linear component had been extracted, we would find

$$F_{residual} = \frac{MS_{A_{residual}}}{MS_{S/A}} = \frac{396.30}{20.29} = 19.53$$

which is significant. The *F* for the first stop rule was 9.77. In most cases, the two stop rules will lead to the same course of action. The alternative rule guarantees that we will not "overlook" a potentially significant trend component simply because it has been averaged with other nonsignificant components, which can occur when we calculate $MS_{A_{residual}}$ with Eq. (7–8) rather than with Eq. (7–11).

I should point out that usually little is gained in behavioral insight when we find significant higher-order trend components. The main purpose of this sort of analysis is to see how well fairly simple trend components (linear and quadratic) fit the data as a first approximation. One index of the success of this approach is the degree to which these simpler functions account for the overall treatment variability observed in the experiment. We considered two such indexes in Chap. 6, one based on R^2 and one based on omega squared—Eqs. (6–16) and (6–18), respectively. I will illustrate with R^2. Adapted to trend analysis, Eq. (6–16) becomes

$$R^2_{A_{trend}} = \frac{SS_{A_{trend}}}{SS_A} \tag{7-12}$$

In the present example, the linear component accounts for $256.00/652.30 \times 100 = 39.2$ percent of the between-groups variation, and the quadratic component accounts for $396.05/652.30 \times 100 = 60.7$ percent.

7.4   LIMITATIONS OF TREND ANALYSIS

I should mention several limitations of trend analyses. First, we must continually remind ourselves that our only knowledge about the underlying function for the population comes from the limited number of points we have selected for the experiment. We assess the importance of different trend components on the basis of the means we do have. How do we know that the same underlying trend would be suggested if other points had been selected for the experiment? Is it accurate to draw a continuous function between the points that we do have? Would values of the independent variable falling between the ones included in the experiment give

---

[6] I am indebted to Dr. Charles Thompson for bringing this alternative stop rule to my attention.

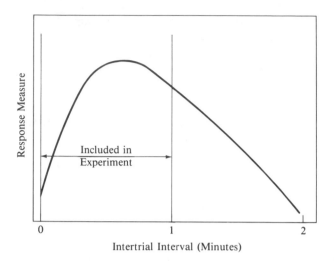

FIGURE 7–9 Hypothetical function relating the length of the intertrial interval to some measure of learning.

us the same picture? In our example, we are asking whether we can safely predict the treatment means for such values on the independent variable as an intertrial interval of 10 seconds, say, or of 50 seconds. In most cases, such predictions are reasonably accurate provided we have included a reasonable number of levels in the experiment.

A related and more serious question concerns the extrapolation of the function *outside* the two extreme values on the independent variable included in the experiment. Translated to our experiment, we are asking about the shape of the function beyond the shortest and the longest intervals included in the study. Consider the function depicted in Fig. 7–9. We will assume that it represents the function in the population. Our experiment has focused on one portion of the continuum, the band between 0 and 60 seconds. On the basis of a trend analysis, we concluded that there is a linear and a quadratic component. But the true function is *primarily quadratic*. We would have seen this clearly had we included a two-minute intertrial interval in the experiment, for instance. All that we can say about this function is what we have found within the band we have selected for the experiment. We did have a clue that a quadratic trend was present from the reversal of trend between 40 and 60 seconds. On the other hand, the reversal of trend does not necessarily mean that performance will continue to drop as we increase the intertrial interval; perhaps it will level off. We cannot tell from this experiment.

Other limitations are not as serious as the ones we have just considered. I have already mentioned that the orthogonal trend coefficients found in Table A–4 assume equal spacings on the independent variable and equal sample sizes. We can deal with the problem of unequal intervals by calculating sets of orthogonal polynomial coefficients that are appropriate to the actual spacings represented in an experiment. I will discuss the problem of unequal sample sizes in Chap. 13. Finally, the analysis is based on the assumption that the polynomial is the appropriate mathematical function to describe a set of data. In some areas of the behavioral sciences, certain phenomena are better described by an exponential function or by a logarithmic function. Nevertheless, the method we considered in this chapter still can approximate these alternative functions fairly well.

7.5   EXERCISES[7]

1. In Sec. 7.3, I described an experiment reported by Grant (1956) in which he predicted the emergence of linear and quadratic trend components (see pp. 155–156). Subjects were trained to respond to a 12-inch visual stimulus and then were tested on stimuli of different sizes (9, 10, 11, 12, 13, 14, and 15 inches); the response measure was the degree to which subjects responded on the first test trial. There were $n = 14$ subjects in each group. The means for the $a = 7$ groups are as follows:

9 in.	10 in.	11 in.	12 in.	13 in.	14 in.	15 in.
1.52	2.64	4.28	3.86	3.86	2.79	3.70

   a. Conduct an analysis of the linear and quadratic trends. (The within-groups mean square was 5.84.)
   b. The linear and quadratic components derived from this analysis are plotted in Fig. (7–8) (p. 157). Calculate the two corresponding regression equations and compare your answer with the predicted group means plotted in the figure.
2. Theorists have postulated a complicated relationship between anxiety level and performance on a complex task. Basically, they predicted that an inverted U-shaped function (concave downward) should result, with performance best at medium levels of anxiety and relatively poor at low and at high levels of anxiety. To test this prediction, an investigator attempted to measure the backward memory span (a rather difficult task) of subjects, who were given special instructions designed to create various degrees of anxiety. There were six sets of instructions (levels a_1 to a_6), where $a_1 =$ low anxiety instructions, $a_6 =$ high anxiety instructions, and the remaining conditions representing intermediate levels of anxiety. There were five subjects in each of the anxiety levels. The span lengths obtained were as follows:

a_1	a_2	a_3	a_4	a_5	a_6
1	2	3	3	4	3
0	1	4	5	3	2
1	1	2	2	2	3
1	2	5	5	4	4
1	2	3	3	3	2

   a. Perform an overall analysis of variance on these data, although the test is not necessary given the quadratic trend component predicted by theory.
   b. Test the quadratic component for significance, assuming that the levels of the anxiety variable are equally spaced.

---

[7]The answers to these problems are found in Appendix B.

c. Determine whether there is any point in testing for the presence of additional trend components.

d. Since the residual variation tested in part c is significant, test the significance of the linear component. Is there any basis for assessing the significance of any higher-order components?

e. What can you conclude from this experiment?

8

Correction for Cumulative Type I Error

One of the more complex and perhaps most confused topics in statistical inference concerns an unfortunate byproduct of the conscientious and detailed analysis of an experiment, namely, an increased vulnerability to type I error. That is, type I errors *cumulate* with each statistical test performed in a predictable and unavoidable fashion—unavoidable, unless steps are taken to correct it. This chapter examines this problem and the solutions designed to solve it. My coverage will be selective, focusing on particular recommendations rather than presenting a comprehensive description of the topic. If you wish to study the problem in more depth, you might read first two early discussions (Ryan, 1959; Wilson, 1962) and then three informative and useful papers by Games (1971b, 1978a, and 1978b).[1]

8.1   CUMULATIVE TYPE I ERROR

The major problem resulting from the performance of a series of analytical comparisons on a set of data is the unpleasant fact that the more comparisons we conduct, the more type I errors we will make when the null hypothesis is true. In talking about this relationship, I will distinguish between the type I error **per comparison (*PC*)** and the error rate **familywise (*FW*)**. The *PC* error, which I will continue to call α, uses the *comparison* as the conceptual unit for determining type I error. If we evaluated several comparisons in an experiment, each at $\alpha = .05$, our probability of making a type I error would be .05 for each of the separate comparisons. In contrast, the type I *FW* error rate, α_{FW}, considers the probability of making *one or more* type I errors in the *set of comparisons* under scrutiny.

The relationship between the two kinds of type I error is expressed by the formula

$$\alpha_{FW} = 1 - (1 - \alpha)^c \tag{8–1}$$

where c represents the number of orthogonal comparisons that are conducted. With the *PC* error set at $\alpha = .05$ and with $c = 3$ comparisons contemplated, the *FW* type I error rate is

$$\alpha_{FW} = 1 - (1 - .05)^3 = 1 - (.95)^3 = 1 - .857 = .143$$

If we were working at the 1 percent significance level,

$$\alpha_{FW} = 1 - (1 - .01)^3 = 1 - (.99)^3 = 1 - .970 = .030$$

The familywise error rate is approximated by

$$\tilde{\alpha}_{FW} = (c)(\alpha) \tag{8–2}$$

However, the approximation $\tilde{\alpha}_{FW}$ will always overestimate α_{FW}, though less for

---

[1] The 1971b paper should be read in conjunction with Games (1971a), which corrects a number of typographical errors in the original article. A more recent, but mathematically demanding, treatment of this topic may be found in a useful book by Hochberg and Tamhane (1987).

small values of α and for small numbers of comparisons (less than 6). In the present example, with α = .05,

$$\tilde{\alpha}_{FW} = (3)(.05) = .15$$

as compared with the α_{FW} = .143 obtained with Eq. (8–1). For the smaller α level, p = .01, the two values are identical when carried out to two decimal places.

When several comparisons are involved in the analysis of an experiment, researchers have different attitudes about which conceptual unit for the error rate is most appropriate. The point to be emphasized now is that when we conduct a number of comparisons on a set of means, there is an *FW* error rate with which we must contend and this error rate increases directly with the number of comparisons we test.

The relationship between the *FW* error rate and the number of analytical comparisons is not an exclusive property of orthogonal comparisons, however, but holds for nonorthogonal comparisons as well. Although the calculation of the *FW* rate is not simple when nonorthogonal comparisons are involved in an analysis plan, it is still accurate to say that the *FW* error rate increases with the number of comparisons we conduct regardless of orthogonality (see Harter, 1957, for a discussion of the problem).

8.2   PLANNED COMPARISONS

Experiments are usually designed with specific hypotheses in mind, and most researchers conduct analyses relevant to these hypotheses directly without reference to the outcome of the omnibus *F* test. (Although the omnibus test may be computed, its significance or nonsignificance does not modify this particular course of action.) Unplanned comparisons, in contrast, refer to the analysis of *unexpected* findings, outcomes that are revealed only after we have collected and partially analyzed the data. These **post hoc** or **multiple comparisons**, as they are also called, can sometimes be critically important in the development of a field of research.

Although both planned and post hoc comparisons lead to an increase in *FW* error, they are usually treated differently in any attempt to reduce or to control the *FW* error rate. The most widely used strategy is to evaluate the planned comparisons in the normal way—at the usual *PC*, or α, level—and to exercise control of the *FW* rate for post hoc comparisons through special evaluation procedures designed to cope with the problem. Not all commentators on the problem of *FW* error agree that planned comparisons should be left uncorrected, however. The correction they usually recommend for planned comparisons is the Bonferroni, or Dunn, test, which we will consider shortly.

We specify planned comparisons in the initial planning of an experiment. Collectively, they represent the answers we hope to obtain to the research questions that generated the experiment in the first place. Planned comparisons are special in that they bring the greatest amount of extrastatistical information to the analysis—specific hypotheses derived from theory—and, as such, they support the strongest inferences. The word *planned* is not the critical point in this discussion, however. *Planned* refers to the conciseness and the separability of the questions. Planned comparisons are pivotal and essential tests (Rule, 1976). Saying that you intend to compare every mean with every other mean is rarely an instance of planned comparisons; rather, it is usually an example of poor planning!

Although the definition of planned comparisons is clear, the restrictions suggested by various authors are not. The two major areas of concern are the orthogonality of the set of planned comparisons and the number of comparisons to be included in the set. I will consider both issues in some detail.

The Issue of Orthogonality

I have already discussed this issue in Chap. 6 (pp. 136–138). Consensus seems to favor a set of meaningful comparisons that, more often than not, contains some nonorthogonal comparisons—that is, a set of comparisons that are not mutually orthogonal. As you saw in Chap. 6, complete orthogonal sets do not necessarily contain comparisons that are all psychologically meaningful, on the one hand, nor do they completely enumerate the total set of meaningful comparisons associated with an experiment, on the other. The value of orthogonal comparisons lies in the independence of *inferences*, which of course is a desirable quality to achieve. That is, orthogonal comparisons are such that any decision concerning the null hypothesis representing one comparison is uninfluenced by the decision concerning the null hypothesis representing any other orthogonal comparison (see p. 133).

The potential difficulty with nonorthogonal comparisons, then, is in interpreting the different outcomes. If we reject the null hypothesis for two nonorthogonal comparisons, which comparison represents the "true" reason for the observed differences? If we reject one null hypothesis and not the other, what can we make of the results? I do not mean to say that such ambiguities always arise when nonorthogonal comparisons are involved or that they are unresolvable when they do; I simply suggest that nonorthogonal comparisons be interpreted with particular care to avoid this sort of problem.

The Number of Planned Comparisons

Although everyone seems to agree that planned comparisons should be limited in number, there is no agreement on what this number should be. One obvious possibility is to restrict the number of comparisons to the number of degrees of freedom associated with the treatment source of variances ($df_A = a - 1$). But this suggestion, or any other recommendation for that matter, is an arbitrary restriction. The point I wish to make is simply that many researchers do limit the number of planned comparisons, and depending on the research hypotheses and on the complexity of the experiment, the number of planned comparisons will range slightly above or below df_A.

In most situations, the number of planned comparisons is constrained by the nature of treatment conditions constituting any given experiment. Thus, we usually achieve a "natural" limit to the number of planned comparisons we will consider in our research plan simply by restricting ourselves to meaningful and theoretically focused questions. As an illustration of this point, consider again the example in Chap. 6 in which $a = 5$ different methods of presenting words in a learning task were studied (see Table 6–1, p. 113). Although it is possible to create a total of 90 single-*df* comparisons from this design—10 pairwise comparisons and 80 complex comparisons involving combinations of conditions—I only considered *four* of them to be central to the experiment.[2] A few of the remaining comparisons are secondary in importance, and the majority are virtually meaningless. In general, then, theoretically motivated research designs support a limited number of important comparisons that are central to the purposes of the experiment.

The Bonferroni, or Dunn, Test

Although I recommend no special correction for a reasonable number of planned comparisons, others do not agree. The most common suggestion is to apply a correction designed to maintain the *FW* error at a given level for the entire set of planned comparisons. Suppose we decided on five orthogonal comparisons. If we evaluated each comparison at the usual, per comparison, level of significance—for example, $\alpha = .05$—the *FW* error could be as high as $\tilde{\alpha}_{FW} = .25$. That is, the probability of a type I error for each comparison is .05 and the combined or cumulative probability of at least one type I error within the entire set is approximately the sum of the individual probabilities $(.05 + .05 + .05 + .05 + .05 = .25)$, which we can also determine with Eq. (8–2): $\tilde{\alpha}_{FW} = (c)(\alpha) = (5)(.05) = .25$. We can reduce this cumulative type I error simply by choosing a smaller value for α. For example, if we set $\alpha = .01$ for each of the five comparisons, the *FW* error will now be $\tilde{\alpha}_{FW} = (5)(.01) = .05$. This method of adjusting the *PC* error to control the *FW* error is known as the **Bonferroni test** or the **Dunn test** (Dunn, 1961).

The simplest form of the Bonferroni correction starts with the desired *FW* error (α_{FW}) and divides that probability equally among all of the c comparisons:

$$\alpha_B = \frac{\alpha_{FW}}{c} \tag{8–3}$$

where α_B is the new per comparison significance level we will use to evaluate the planned comparisons. One difficulty with the Bonferroni test is the need to determine the critical value of F when α_B falls between the probabilities provided in the standard F tables. Since the F's associated with most planned comparisons will involve 1 *df* in the numerator, it is possible to use the unit normal distribution and approximate the value of t, which when squared will give us the corresponding critical value of F. The value of t at an α level of significance is found by the formula

---

[2]The total number of single-*df* comparisons is $1 + (3^a - 1)/2 - 2^a$, where a is the number of treatment conditions. For the present example $(a = 5)$, we find the total to be

$$1 + \frac{(3^5 - 1)}{2} - 2^5 = 1 + \frac{243 - 1}{2} - 32 = 1 + 121 - 32 = 90$$

$$t(df_{S/A}) = z + \frac{z^3 + z}{(4)(df_{S/A} - 2)} \tag{8-4}$$

where z represents the point on the unit normal distribution above which $\{\frac{1}{2}(\alpha) \times 100\}$ percent of the curve falls.[3] Squaring the value for t gives us the corrected value for F, F_B, against which we would evaluate each of the planned comparisons.

As an example, I will work with a calculation we can verify in the F table. Suppose we planned to conduct $c = 4$ comparisons and to set $\alpha_{FW} = .10$. Entering this information into Eq. (8-3), we find

$$\alpha_B = \frac{.10}{4} = .025$$

From a table of the unit normal curve, available in most introductory texts, the value of z above which $\frac{1}{2}(.025) \times 100 = 1.25$ percent of the area of the curve falls is 2.24. Substituting in Eq. (8-4) and assuming $df_{S/A} = 40$,

$$t(40) = 2.24 + \frac{(2.24)^3 + 2.24}{(4)(40 - 2)}$$

$$= 2.24 + \frac{11.24 + 2.24}{152} = 2.33$$

We would then use $F_B = t^2 = (2.33)^2 = 5.43$ to evaluate each of the four planned comparisons. We can verify the goodness of the approximation provided by Eq. (8-4) by comparing $F_B = 5.43$ with the value of $F(1, 40)$ from Table A-1 at $\alpha = .025$; the tabled value is 5.42.

Specialized tables are available for the Bonferroni test (see, for example, Dunn, 1961; Kirk, 1982; and Myers, 1979). If you are using a computer to perform these analyses, you can apply the Bonferroni test simply by comparing the descriptive, or exact, probability of each comparison, which is provided as part of the output obtained from most software programs, with the adjusted significance level (α_B). If this probability is equal to or less than α_B, you will reject the null hypothesis. In this example, the critical probability is $\alpha_B = .025$. Thus, any $F_{comp.}$ with a descriptive probability $\le .025$ would be declared significant.

I believe that many researchers will balk at applying any correction for the FW error, particularly when they have designed an experiment around a limited number of central comparisons. O'Brien (1983) expresses this point of view for medical researchers as follows:

> It seems ironic that when many investigators publish their separate findings in the medical literature, per-comparison error rates are routinely accepted. However, when one investigator takes on the entire job himself, the same approach may no longer be deemed valid. Rather, he is required to achieve a considerably higher level of signifi-

---

[3]Dividing α by 2 provides a critical value of z corresponding to a *nondirectional* test in which one-half of the rejection region is located in the positive tail and the other half of the rejection region is located in the negative tail of the unit normal distribution.

cance with each comparison, virtually as a penalty for undertaking such an extensive effort. (p. 788)

The "cost" of the Bonferroni test is a loss of power, which we can see directly by the use of a new significance level that is appreciably smaller than .05. To control FW at $\alpha_{FW} = .10$ in the preceding example, we needed to set the rejection region at $\alpha_B = .025$. By adopting this more stringent level of significance, we make it more difficult to detect true differences in the treatment populations. You should realize, of course, that we are seeing again the difficult trade-off between type I and type II errors that we have discussed in a number of contexts. In this case, the issue involves the power associated with planned comparisons.

A Modified Bonferroni Test

Earlier I suggested that researchers might agree on a limit to the number of planned comparisons that may be evaluated without adjusting the normal significance level. More specifically, I proposed that we might choose our threshold of concern for the FW error somewhere near the "natural" limit set by the number of degrees of freedom. Suppose we use this number—the df associated with the between-groups mean square—to determine the FW standard for planned comparisons and to introduce corrections only when the number of comparisons *exceeds* df_A. This strategy has the advantage of preserving the attractiveness of reserving a reasonable number of critical comparisons for evaluation without adjusting the significance level and introducing an FW protection when this limit is exceeded.

We begin by calculating the α_{FW} associated with $a - 1$ orthogonal comparisons and then dividing this probability by the *actual* number of planned comparisons included in the analysis plan.[4] The resulting probability is a new PC rate to be used in assessing these comparisons that maintains α_{FW} at this presumably acceptable standard. In symbols, we use Eq. (8–2) to calculate the maximum FW error for planned comparisons,

$$\tilde{\alpha}_{FW_{planned}} = (df_A)(\alpha) \tag{8–5}$$

and divide this value by the number of comparisons actually planned (c):

$$\tilde{\alpha}_{planned} = \frac{\tilde{\alpha}_{FW_{planned}}}{c} \tag{8–6}$$

For example, consider an experiment with $a = 5$ conditions. Assuming that the maximum number of planned comparisons we will conduct without correction is equal to $df_A = 4$, and adopting the standard significant level $\alpha = .05$, we obtain

---

[4]These calculations are based on orthogonal comparisons, which will tend to cause overestimation of the FW error when nonorthogonal comparisons are involved; however, this "overcorrection" makes little practical difference in an actual research application.

Table 8–1   The Modified Bonferroni Test for Planned Comparisons

Number of Comparisons (c)	Rejection Probability ($\tilde{\alpha}_{planned}$)	Approximate Familywise Error ($\tilde{\alpha}_{FW}$)
1	.05	.05
2	.05	.10
3	.05	.15
4	.05	.20
5	.040	.20
6	.033	.20
7	.029	.20
8	.025	.20
9	.022	.20
10	.020	.20

an approximate probability for this "acceptable" *FW* rate by substituting in Eq. (8–5):

$$\tilde{\alpha}_{FW_{planned}} = (4)(.05) = .20$$

This *FW* rate of .20, then, represents the assumed risk that we are willing to take when planned comparisons are at stake.

Suppose we wanted to conduct $c = 5$ planned comparisons. We find from Eq. (8–6) that

$$\tilde{\alpha}_{planned} = \frac{.20}{5} = .04$$

is the adjusted significance level that we will use to evaluate the significance of *all five* planned comparisons. A quick calculation will indicate that this new rejection probability results in an *FW* rate of $(c)(\tilde{\alpha}_{planned}) = (5)(.04) = .20$, which is the *FW* rate we adopted in this example for the entire set of planned comparisons.

Table 8–1 summarizes the calculation of $\tilde{\alpha}_{planned}$ for several values of c, using $a = 5$. You will note that when $c \leq df_A$, no correction is applied and the *FW* varies with the number of comparisons. On the other hand, when $c > df_A$, the *FW* rate remains constant at $\tilde{\alpha}_{FW_{planned}} = .20$ and the significance level used to evaluate the comparisons is systematically lowered as a consequence.[5]

8.3   POST HOC COMPARISONS

Post hoc comparisons often take the form of an intensive "milking" of a set of results, in which the search for significant comparisons is dictated by the outcome

---

[5]Other strategies have been proposed for increasing the power of planned comparisons. One of these involves the use of significance levels chosen on the basis of the *importance* of each planned comparison (see Rosenthal & Rubin, 1984, and a related paper by de Cani, 1984).

of the experiment. The motivation, of course, is to extract the maximum amount of information from any given study. Another reason for conducting post hoc comparisons is that the results of such tests often lead to future experiments. An interesting comparison, significant or not, may form the basis for a new experiment. In the next study, for example, we might choose to manipulate more extensively the different treatments contributing to the comparison we have isolated.

The total number of possible single-*df* comparisons, which includes differences between pairs of means and complex comparisons between means, is staggering, even for a "modest" experimental design. Using the formula in footnote 2, we find that for $a = 3$, there are 6 such comparisons possible; for $a = 4$, there are 25; for $a = 5$, there are 90; and for $a = 6$, there are 301. You can appreciate the concern for the *FW* rate when the pool of potential comparisons is as large as these.

An early procedure introduced by Fisher (1935) is still a popular method for controlling the *FW* error (Gaito & Nobrega, 1981). The procedure is simple, consisting of two steps: the test of the omnibus *F*, followed by the unrestricted testing of comparisons among the means, provided that the overall *F* is *significant*. If the omnibus *F* is not significant, no additional tests are conducted. Fisher's procedure, which is called the **least significant difference test**, controls the *FW* error indirectly, by conditionalizing one's decision to conduct post hoc comparisons on the significance of the omnibus *F* test. That is, type I errors can be committed only when this *F* is significant; and when the overall null hypothesis is true, this will occur only a small proportion of the time, namely, the proportion specified by α. Thus, the *FW* is kept under control on the average by reducing greatly the proportion of times when a researcher conducts post hoc comparisons and the overall null hypothesis is true.

Fisher's procedure has been criticized for not providing adequate control over the *FW* error (see, for example, Hayter, 1986; Keselman, Games, & Rogan, 1980; Ramsey, 1981; Ryan, 1980). The test has been criticized on several other grounds as well (see Keppel, 1982, pp. 158–159; Zwick & Marascuilo, 1984). In view of these problems, I cannot recommend the Fisher test as a general strategy for analyzing the outcome of a complex study, as some methodologists have recommended (for example, Cohen & Cohen, 1983, pp. 172–176; Davis & Gaito, 1984).

Many other approaches are designed to deal directly with the problem of *FW* error. All such techniques employ the same basic solution we observed with the Bonferroni test, namely, a *reduction* in the size of the critical region. In fact, Games (1971b; 1978b) points out that the different procedures all involve the same underlying test statistic and differ only in the ways by which this reduction in the *PC* rate is achieved. For convenience, I will refer to procedures that employ this general method of controlling the *FW* error as **alpha-adjusted techniques**. The logic behind these techniques is straightforward: If we make it more difficult to reject the null hypothesis for each comparison tested, which must happen when the size of the rejection region is reduced, fewer type I errors will be committed and the *FW* error rate will thus be lowered. Just how much of an "adjustment" is made depends on a number of factors, such as our willingness to make type I er rors in general, the number of post hoc comparisons actually conducted, and the pool of comparisons from which comparisons are specifically chosen. As you will see when you enter the research arena, there is no general agreement among researchers or even among authors of statistical texts and articles concerning these points.

The Scheffé Test: *FW* Corrections for All Comparisons

The **Scheffé test** (Scheffé, 1953) is a technique that allows a researcher to maintain the *FW* rate at a particular value regardless of the number of comparisons actually conducted. For this reason, then, the Scheffé test is flexible in its application to the analysis of an experiment.

The Scheffé test requires no special tables since it is based on the values of the *F* statistic that appear in standard *F* tables. The procedure is simple. We calculate $F_{comp.}$ in the usual fashion but evaluate the significance of the obtained *F* with a special critical value, F_S. This quantity is defined as follows:

$$F_S = (a - 1)F(df_A, df_{S/A}) \tag{8-7}$$

where $F(df_A, df_{S/A})$ is the critical value of *F* for the *omnibus* analysis of variance and is found in Table A–1 under the desired α level. (Be sure to note that the value of $df_{num.}$ is equal to $a - 1$ and *not* to $df_{comp.}$ —a common mistake made by students in my classes.) The choice of significance level at this point sets the maximum value that familywise error α_{FW} may take regardless of the number of comparisons conducted. Thus, an *F* chosen from Table A–1 at the .05 level of significance and entered into Eq. (8–7) will create a critical value of *F* (F_S) that sets a maximum limit on the *FW* rate at .05. Using critical values of *F* at other α levels sets the limit at these probabilities correspondingly.

As an example, suppose we performed an experiment with $a = 5$ treatment conditions and $n = 9$ subjects assigned randomly to each group. We will assume that the $MS_{S/A}$, which is based on $(a)(n - 1) = 5(9 - 1) = 40$ degrees of freedom, is 13.22. The means for the treatment groups are presented in Table 8–2. Suppose we decided to compare the average of two of the groups (a_1 and a_5) with the average of the other three (a_2, a_3, and a_4). The first average is $(12.78 + 11.44)/2 = 12.11$, and the second average is $(7.89 + 7.11 + 8.78)/3 = 7.93$, indicating a sizable difference between the two means $(12.11 - 7.93 = 4.18)$. A convenient set of coefficients with which to calculate the comparison sum of squares is 3, -2, -2, -2, 3. Substituting the necessary values in Eq. (6–5), we have

$$
\begin{aligned}
SS_{A_{comp.}} &= \frac{n\,(\hat{\psi})^2}{\Sigma c_i^2} \\
&= \frac{(9)[(3)(12.78) + (-2)(7.89) + (-2)(7.11) + (-2)(8.78) + (3)(11.44)]^2}{(3)^2 + (-2)^2 + (-2)^2 + (-2)^2 + (3)^2} \\
&= 189.00
\end{aligned}
$$

The next operation is to form an *F* ratio. Since we are still contrasting only two means in this comparison, the number of *df* for the $SS_{A_{comp.}}$ is 1 and the $MS_{A_{comp.}} =$

Table 8–2   Numerical Example: Treatment Means

	a_1	a_2	a_3	a_4	a_5
			LEVELS		
Means	12.78	7.89	7.11	8.78	11.44

$189.00/1 = 189.00$. The F ratio is specified in Eq. (6–6) and consists simply of dividing the $MS_{A_{comp.}}$ by the $MS_{S/A}$. In this case,

$$F_{comp.} = \frac{189.00}{13.22} = 14.30$$

Normally, this F would be compared with the critical value of $F(1, 40)$, which at $\alpha = .05$ is 4.08. For the Scheffé test, however, we determine the critical value of F_S by substituting in Eq. (8–7), for which we will need the critical value for the omnibus F, in this case $F(4, 40) = 2.61$ at $\alpha = .05$. Substituting in Eq. (8–7), we find

$$F_S = (a - 1)F(4, 40)$$
$$= (5 - 1)(2.61) = 10.44$$

Since the obtained $F_{comp.}$ of 14.30 exceeds this critical value demanded by the Scheffé test (10.44), we can reject the null hypothesis.

Perhaps you noticed the severity of the Scheffé correction, which is reflected in the difference between the two critical values, 4.08 for an uncorrected planned comparison versus 10.44 for the Scheffé test. Translated to a PC rate, the Scheffé correction is equivalent to a significance level of about $\alpha = .0025$. This marked reduction in the PC rate (from $\alpha = .05$ to $\alpha = .0025$) is necessary to set the FW error at a value no greater than $\alpha_{FW} = .05$. When the frame of reference consists of all possible comparisons, however, the correction needs to be severe.

The Tukey Test: Comparisons Between All Pairs of Means

There are times when a researcher may be interested in evaluating the significance of all possible differences between pairs of treatment means. The total number of these pairwise comparisons may be determined by solving the following simple formula: $(a)(a - 1)/2$. Applied research is often of this type—different books are compared in a classroom to determine which book is best; a consumer testing agency evaluates a number of similar products and attempts to order and to group the products in terms of effectiveness; and so on. In these cases, the intent is clearly to compare each treatment condition—each book or product, for example—with all other treatment conditions. Presumably there would be little or no interest in more complex comparisons unless there were good reasons for combining certain conditions: for example, products from the same manufacturer or books by the same author. Theoretically motivated research, on the other hand, produces experimental designs that generate a limited number of meaningful comparisons, which generally will not include all possible pairwise comparisons but rather a smaller number of pairwise comparisons combined with a couple of complex comparisons.

Many alternative tests have been developed to control the *FW* error under the circumstances in which a researcher wishes to conduct all pairwise comparisons. The Scheffé test is not recommended for this situation since it is less powerful than most, if not all, of the techniques that have been proposed. I will discuss the **Tukey test**, which is generally recommended for most experimental situations.[6]

The Tukey test (Tukey, 1953) may be used to maintain the *FW* rate at the chosen value of α_{FW} for the entire set of pairwise comparisons. The test is performed easily by arranging the treatment means in ascending order of magnitude on the dependent variable, as illustrated in Table 8–3. Entries within the body of this table represent the differences between any two treatment means. In the first row, for example,

$$\overline{Y}_{A_2} - \overline{Y}_{A_3} = 7.89 - 7.11 = .78$$

$$\overline{Y}_{A_4} - \overline{Y}_{A_3} = 8.78 - 7.11 = 1.67$$

and so on. Differences are not entered for comparisons below the main diagonal of the table since the listing would be an exact mirror image of the differences appearing above the diagonal.

The next step is to calculate the *minimum* pairwise difference between means that must be exceeded to be significant with the Tukey test. This value $(\overline{d}_T)$ is given by the formula

$$\overline{d}_T = q_T \sqrt{\frac{MS_{S/A}}{n}} \tag{8–8}$$

where q_T = an entry in the table of the **studentized range statistic** (Table A–5)

$MS_{S/A}$ = the error term the overall analysis of variance

n = the sample size for each group

If you look at Table A–5, you will see that three quantities enter into the determination of q_T: df_{error} (the *df* associated with the $MS_{S/A}$), k (the number of treatment means—*a* in this design), and α_{FW} (the *FW* error rate chosen for the Tukey test). For this example, $df_{error} = df_{S/A} = 40$, $k = a = 5$, and $\alpha_{FW} = .05$; the value of q_T is 4.04. Substituting in Eq. (8–8), we find

$$\overline{d}_T = 4.04 \sqrt{\frac{13.22}{9}} = 4.04 \sqrt{1.469} = 4.90$$

---

[6]The Tukey test runs into problems with heterogeneous treatment variances. For alternative procedures and detailed discussions of the control of the *FW* error for pairwise comparisons, see, for example, books by Hochberg and Tamhane (1987) and Miller (1981) and reviews by Jaccard, Becker, and Wood (1984), which I recommend for its useful coverage of the topic; Ramsey (1981); Wilcox (1987a); and Zwick and Marascuilo (1984).

Table 8–3   An Example of Pairwise Comparisons

MEANS	*LEVELS* *(ORDERED BY SIZE OF TREATMENT MEANS)*				
	a_3 7.11	a_2 7.89	a_4 8.78	a_5 11.44	a_1 12.78
$\overline{Y}_{A_3} = 7.11$	—	.78	1.67	4.33	5.67
$\overline{Y}_{A_2} = 7.89$		—	.89	3.55	4.89
$\overline{Y}_{A_4} = 8.78$			—	2.66	4.00
$\overline{Y}_{A_5} = 11.44$				—	1.34
$\overline{Y}_{A_1} = 12.78$					—

An inspection of the differences in Table 8–3 reveals that only the largest difference ($\overline{Y}_{A_1} - \overline{Y}_{A_3} = 12.78 - 7.11 = 5.67$) exceeds the critical value for the Tukey test and would be declared significant.

The Tukey test can be used in conjunction with the F test, although calculating $F_{comp.}$ for each pair is not as convenient as calculating mean differences. In any case, the critical value of F (F_T) against which $F_{comp.}$ is compared is given by the following formula:

$$F_T = \frac{(q_T)^2}{2} \tag{8-9}$$

In the present case, $F_T = (4.04)^2/2 = 8.16$.

A well-known alternative to the Tukey test is the **Newman-Keuls test**, which is distinguished by the fact that significance testing follows a series of sequential tests, each with a different critical value to establish the significance between pairs of means. The computational details of this test may be found in Kirk (1982, pp. 123–125) and Winer (1971, pp. 191–196). Although popular in the past, this test is generally not recommended because of its failure to control α_{FW} under all circumstances (see Einot & Gabriel, 1975; Ramsey, 1981). I mention it now because of its widespread use in the past and its continued popularity among researchers (Gaito & Nobrega, 1981).

The Dunnett Test: Pairwise Comparisons Involving a Single Group

When we include a control (or baseline) condition in an experiment, we are often interested in a number of different comparisons. As a first step in the analysis, we might compare the control group with the average score for the combined experiment groups—a sort of overall control-experimental contrast. Additionally, we might evaluate the significance of any differences observed among the experimental groups alone—a sort of omnibus F test for the experiment groups (see Sec. 6.5). Finally, we would probably consider multiple comparisons involving a contrast of each of the experimental groups with the single control group. Because of the necessary increase in the number of comparisons when a single control group is compared with several experimental groups, we might want to exercise some control of the *FW* error rate.

The **Dunnett test** (Dunnett, 1955) is a specialized *FW* correction technique that compensates for the increased number of potential type I errors, but it is not as "corrective" as the other post hoc tests because it takes into consideration only a limited number of comparisons—the control-experimental contrasts. The simplest way to conduct the Dunnett test is to calculate the control-experimental mean differences and to compare them against a critical mean difference $(\bar{d}_D)$ that must be exceeded to be significant at the chosen *FW* level. The formula for calculating this critical difference is

$$\bar{d}_D = q_D \sqrt{\frac{2(MS_{S/A})}{n}} \tag{8-10}$$

where q_D = an entry in Table A–6 of Appendix A

$MS_{S/A}$ = the error term from the overall analysis of variance

n = the sample size for each group

The value of q_D is determined by the total number of conditions (k) involved in the analysis, the degrees of freedom associated with the error term $(df_{S/A})$, and the value chosen for *FW* error (α_{FW}). If you choose to work with the F test rather than with differences between means, you can use

$$F_D = (q_D)^2 \tag{8-11}$$

as the critical value with which to evaluate $F_{comp.}$.

As an example, I will again use the data from Table 8–2. To set the example in context, let's assume that these data were drawn from an experiment comparing the amounts of memory loss for several different experimental conditions. There are four experimental groups (a_2, a_3, a_4, a_5), each differing in the types of interfering activities they received between learning and recall. A control group (a_1) received a neutral task during the period in which the experimental subjects were experiencing interference.

Although other questions might be asked of the data (for example, questions about meaningful comparisons among the experimental groups), it is of interest to determine whether each of the experimental groups showed a significant loss relative to the control group. To calculate the critical C-E difference, we need to obtain q_D. Although the argument could be made that only differences in favor of the control group make any sense, most researchers would prefer to choose a nondirectional alternative hypothesis. What this means is that we want to be alert to positive as well as negative differences in the experiment. If we set our significance level at $\alpha_{FW} = .05$, we will set aside half of the rejection region for positive deviations from the control and the other half for negative deviations.[7]

---

[7]Such a procedure is often called a **two-tailed test**. Under certain circumstances, where there is absolutely no interest in differences occurring in one of the directions, researchers may choose a directional alternative hypothesis and use a **one-tailed test**, in which the entire rejection region is concentrated in either the positive or negative direction. We considered directional and nondirectional tests in Chap. 6 (pp. 120–123).

To find the value of q_D, we locate the part of Table A–6 labeled Two-Tailed Comparisons and look for the entry at $k = 5$, $df_{error} = df_{S/A} = 40$, and $\alpha_{FW} = .05$. (A directional test would be conducted with the values given in the part of Table A–6 labeled One-Tailed Comparisons.) For this combination, $q_D = 2.54$. Substituting in Eq. (8–10) gives us as the critical difference between the control and an experimental mean:

$$\bar{d}_D = 2.54 \sqrt{\frac{2(13.22)}{9}} = 2.54 \sqrt{2.938} = 4.35$$

This is the difference that must be exceeded to allow the rejection of the null hypothesis that the control group and a particular experimental group are equal. From Table 8–2, the observed differences are

$$\bar{Y}_{A_1} - \bar{Y}_{A_2} = 12.78 - 7.89 = 4.89 \qquad \bar{Y}_{A_1} - \bar{Y}_{A_3} = 12.78 - 7.11 = 5.67$$

$$\bar{Y}_{A_1} - \bar{Y}_{A_4} = 12.78 - 8.78 = 4.00 \qquad \bar{Y}_{A_1} - \bar{Y}_{A_5} = 12.78 - 11.44 = 1.34$$

Since the first two differences (involving a_2 and a_3) exceed the critical value of 4.35, we can conclude that the specific interfering activities represented by these two conditions produced a significant memory deficit. The other two experimental treatments (a_4 and a_5) did not result in a significant loss of memory.

8.4 RECOMMENDATIONS AND GUIDELINES

You can now appreciate the serious dilemma faced by all researchers. On the one hand, you attempt to design experiments that are analytically rich and lead to a number of interesting comparisons and analyses, whereas on the other hand, you fully realize that cumulative type I error is present whenever two or more statistical tests are performed in the analysis of a single experiment. At one extreme, you could take the position that all possible findings are important and resist either restricting the number of comparisons undertaken or using some procedure to control the increase in the *FW* error. At the other extreme, you could maintain that accidental findings are to be avoided and adopt strong corrective methods to prevent the accumulation of type I error resulting from the assessment of two or more comparisons. In the first case, you would evaluate all comparisons at the same *PC* rate (for example, $\alpha = .05$); in the second case, you would subject all comparisons to the Scheffé correction (for example, $\alpha_{FW} = .05$). The extreme positions are clear, but few researchers subscribe to either point of view. Most of us strike some balance between these two extremes in an attempt to detect the presence of the most important findings, while still maintaining a reasonable control of the *FW* error.

It is useful at this point to place the concept of familywise type I error within an experimental context. Suppose we repeated an experiment 2,000 times and each time performed the same five comparisons. In addition, suppose that the overall null hypothesis is true. From Eq. (8–2), we determine that our *FW* error is approximately $(5)(.05) = .25$ for any given experiment. This means, of course, that the probability of making at least one type I error within any given set of five comparisons is .25. Do you realize, however, that this *FW* error is produced primarily from experiments in which only *one* type I error has occurred? That is, out of the roughly 500 such experiments in which we expect to commit one or more type I errors—(.25)(2,000) = 500 experiments—nearly 90 percent of them will contain only *one* type I error (see Myers, 1979, pp. 292–293). I suspect that many researchers believe that a high *FW* error rate means a large number of type I errors within a single study, which is suggested, of course, by the definition of the *FW* error itself: the probability of one *or more* type I errors occurring in a set of statistical tests. The fact is that when the number of comparisons increases, the bulk of the increase in *FW* error consists of experiments with only one type I error, and instances of two (or more) type I errors are relatively small (and drop off fast with increasing numbers of errors).

It is also useful to realize that the *FW* error we calculated with Eq. (8–2) assumes the worst, namely, that all the population treatment means are equal. It is probably safe to say that few experiments are conducted in which the overall null hypothesis is true. What this means, therefore, is that our actual probability of committing familywise type I error is some value less than Eq. (8–2) would predict.

I intend these comments to underscore the negative aspect associated with all alpha-adjusted *FW* corrections—a necessary loss of power for detecting true differences between means when they are present in an experiment. What we are doing in effect is pitting the avoidance of what amounts to *one* type I error against our chances of detecting the real differences that may be present. Statisticians have appropriately discovered ways for us to control familywise type I error, but it is up to researchers to determine whether such procedures are appropriate or desirable. We need to be informed about the consequences of our actions when we conduct a number of comparisons, but the responsibility of deciding what to do with them is ours.

I stated at the beginning of this chapter that there is little agreement concerning what should be done about *FW* error. I will end this chapter with a number of recommendations and suggestions designed to help you chart your own course of action.

The Decision to Conduct Planned Comparisons

I recommend that we continue to give planned comparisons a privileged status in the analysis of a research project. In this regard, I am in close agreement with the position taken by Davis and Gaito (1984), who argue that an overconcern for type I error in any particular experiment may actually impede progress in that area of research. An active researcher uses an experiment to test research hypotheses and to discover new facts. Any decrease in power produced by controlling the *FW* error may discourage a researcher from following a promising lead or continuing with a potentially productive line of investigation. To avoid letting this happen to us, suppose we decided not to control the *FW* error for planned comparisons. How do we protect ourselves from the additional risk of type I errors when we test a set of planned comparisons? The answer is *replication*, either by repeating the experiment or by including the critical comparisons in a subsequent study. Since the probability of making the same type I error in two independent experiments is relatively small, a single failure to duplicate an earlier finding would immediately bring into question the earlier conclusions. Thus, type I errors will soon be discovered and removed in an active research field, without the need for elaborate alpha-adjusted techniques.

The decision to restrict the number of planned comparisons or to introduce some correction in the decision process, then, depends on our attitude concerning type I and type II errors and the sort of balance that we want to achieve between them. You must work this problem out for yourself and then deal with the additional problem of convincing others that your findings will hold up in a replication. In short, part of your planning should include a concern for planned comparisons and your attitude toward them, as well as a concern for the logic of the experimental design and a realistic estimate of the power for the experiment in general and for the planned comparisons in particular. The implicit standard adopted by most researchers of conducting up to $a - 1$ planned comparisons without special correction seems reasonable except, perhaps, when the number of treatment conditions is particularly large and the FW error for planned comparisons becomes sizable as a consequence. Planned comparisons are special and should be evaluated with a sensitive statistical test. The modified Bonferroni test offers a way to maintain this standard in situations in which the number of comparisons exceeds this assumed limit.

Choosing a Familywise Type I Error Rate

I have stressed the cost of controlling the FW error, namely, a substantial reduction in our ability to detect true differences between treatments. I already pointed out that the Scheffé correction for the numerical example with $a = 5$ conditions ($F_S = 10.44$) is equivalent to a per comparison significance level of .0025. This greatly reduced rejection region is how the Scheffé test controls FW error for all possible comparisons, but clearly, this is accomplished at a great loss of power. The other correction techniques paint a less dramatic but similar picture. The equivalent PC level for the Bonferroni test depends on the number of planned comparisons involved; with $c = 5$ comparisons, the PC rate is .05/5 = .01, and with $c = 10$, the rate is .05/10 = .005. The Tukey correction for all possible pairwise comparisons ($F_T = 8.16$) is equivalent to a PC rate of .007, and the Dunnett correction for all possible control-experimental differences ($F_D = 6.45$) is equivalent to a PC rate of .015.[8]

The concern for FW error is usually expressed without regard for any increase in type II error that may result. There is no inherent reason why this needs to be the case, as Keselman, Games, and Rogan (1980) point out. We could, for example, exert a less stringent control of the FW rate simply by choosing $\alpha_{FW} =$ .10 or .25. If we were to set $\alpha_{FW} = .25$, for instance, the Scheffé correction, which

---

[8]The critical value, F_D, is obtained from Eq. (8–11): $F_D - q_D^2 - (2.54)^2 - 6.45.$

would be based on the critical omnibus F found at $\alpha = .25$, $F(4,40) = 1.40$, becomes $F_S = (5 - 1)(1.40) = 5.60$; the corresponding PC level is .023, rather than the .0025 associated with $\alpha = .05$.[9]

If you decide to maintain reasonable control over familywise type I error, I strongly urge your imaginative use of "nontraditional" values of FW to avoid losing substantial amounts of power. You should also consider increasing your sample size as well. In fact, it makes little sense to control the FW error without assessing beforehand the effect that such a control might have on power for specific comparisons (see Davis & Gaito, 1984, p. 9), particularly when an FW procedure is applied to the analysis of planned comparisons. If you determine your original sample size by means of a power analysis—which I strongly urge you to do (see Chap. 4)—your estimates will be considerably lower if you plan to control the FW error during the statistical analysis as well.

Let's consider an example. Suppose you determined that a sample size of $n = 10$ will provide sufficient power (for example, .80) to produce significant outcomes ($\alpha = .05$), given the results you expect to find. Your analysis plan calls for $c = 5$ comparisons. If you decide to control the FW error with the Bonferroni test, your per comparison significance level will be $\alpha/c = .05/5 = .01$, which necessarily means that your power will drop. Let's assume that your smallest single-df comparison is expected to produce an effect size of $\phi = 2$ with a sample size of $n = 10$. You will now need to turn to the Pearson-Hartley power charts in Table A–2 ($df_{num.} = 1$) and locate the power functions for $\alpha = .05$, which are found on the right side of this chart. If you extend a vertical line from $\phi = 2$ until it intersects the function labeled $df_{denom.} = 60$, which we will assume is the correct degrees of freedom for the error term, you will find that power is approximately .80. Up to this point, at least, you seem to be in good shape—you have chosen a sample size that will give reasonable power to detect your smallest planned comparison.

However, your concern for FW error requires that you set $\alpha = .01$, not .05. An examination of the other set of power functions in this chart ($\alpha = .01$) indicates that power is about .57 for this particular comparison (a vertical line drawn from $\phi = 2$ intersects the power function for $df_{denom.} = 60$ at power $= .57$). What this means is that you now have about a 50–50 chance of detecting this difference, which is probably too low for research purposes. With a little arithmetic, I determined that you would need a sample size of $n = 16$ to return the power to the original value of .80—the value before we applied the FW correction. Your options at this point are several: Forget the comparison altogether; accept the low power of .57; increase your sample size from $n = 10$ to $n = 16$; or modify your concern for the FW error, either by choosing a less severe correction or even by dropping the FW correction for these comparisons.[10]

---

[9]Similar suggestions have been offered for reducing the severity of the Bonferroni test either by increasing α_{FW} for all planned comparisons (Silverstein, 1986) or by allocating the PC rates in proportion to the importance attached to individual comparisons (de Cani, 1984; Holland & Copenhaver, 1988; Rosenthal & Rubin, 1984).

[10]Hsu (1980) discusses a method for controlling power and the FW for a set of planned orthogonal comparisons.

Deciding to Suspend Judgment

The major obstacle to a general plan for dealing with multiple comparisons that will satisfy most researchers is the different attitudes toward type I and type II errors held by different investigators. This stumbling block can be circumvented rather than removed simply by adding a *third decision category* to the evaluation process when the two concerns for the problem—*FW* and power—are in conflict. This conflict occurs, of course, whenever $F_{comp.}$ is significant as a planned comparison evaluated at an uncorrected significance level (α) but is not significant when the α level is corrected to reduce familywise type I error. Instead of deciding to reject or not to reject the null hypothesis in such ambiguous cases, I propose that we recognize this ambiguity by deciding to **suspend judgment** concerning the status of the null hypothesis. By taking no formal action in this situation, we avoid committing either a type I or a type II error. As a consequence, the decision does not contribute to familywise error since the null hypothesis has not been formally rejected. Suspending judgment calls attention to a potential true difference and avoids creating the obscurity often associated with a difference that is labeled "nonsignificant." According to Davis and Gaito (1984), early methodologists implied this approach when they suggested that ". . . such a result is *suggestive* of significance, but *not definitive*" (p. 7). The use of a third decision category of suspending judgment, then, introduces flexibility and clarity into a situation in which arbitrariness and ambiguity instead have been the rule.

How might this procedure work in practice? The first step is to determine the critical value of the test statistic at the *uncorrected* level of significance (α). This value, which I will call F_α, is used to define the lower boundary of the rejection region for planned comparisons. The second step is to set a more stringent criterion for rejection that reflects one's concern for familywise type I error. This value, which I will call F_{FW}, refers to the beginning of the rejection region for the correction technique considered most appropriate for the analysis. I can now state the three decision rules as follows:

If $F_{comp.}$ **equals or exceeds F_{FW}, reject H_0.**

If $F_{comp.}$ **falls between F_α and F_{FW}, suspend judgment.**

If $F_{comp.}$ **is less than F_α, retain H_0.**

These three rules are summarized in Fig. 8–1.

As an illustration, let's return to the experiment we used as a numerical example of the Scheffé test (pp. 172–173). For that particular experiment, the critical value for the Scheffé test was $F_S = 10.44$, and the critical value for planned comparisons was $F_\alpha = 4.08$. The decision rules for this case become

If $F_{comp.}$ $\geq$ **10.44, reject H_0.**

If $F_{comp.}$ **falls between 4.08 and 10.44, suspend judgment.**

If $F_{comp.}$ < **4.08, retain H_0.**

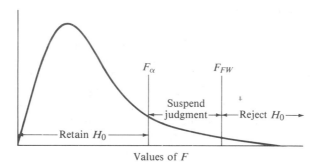

FIGURE 8–1   A summary of the three decision rules.

The value for $F_{comp.}$ in this example was 14.30, which means that we would reject H_0 since it exceeds the critical value for the Scheffé correction ($F_s = 10.44$).

The three-rule system recognizes the ambiguity that exists when a comparison is significant under one criterion (as a planned comparison) but not significant under a more severe criterion (as an alpha-corrected comparison). By suspending judgment, we avoid committing either type of error and simply conclude that the evidence is not sufficiently strong to justify either one of the usual conclusions. Since we have not formally rejected the null hypothesis, no type I error is committed, and the *FW* error is left unaffected by this decision. Since we have suspended judgment, no type II error is committed, and interesting and unexpected findings, often overlooked when a Scheffé test or other correction technique is used, can be assimilated into the interpretation of the experiment and perhaps earmarked for future replication and study.

Summary

You are now in a position to make up your own mind concerning the evaluation of analytical comparisons. The fact that there is little agreement among methodologists concerning specific courses of action to be followed with multiple comparisons simply means that the issues are complex and that no single solution can be offered to meet adequately the varied needs of researchers. Consequently, you should view the situation not with dispair and frustration but rather with a realization that you can and must work the problem out for yourself. The first step is to understand the basic issue—which is simple, really—that analytical comparisons, which are conducted in virtually every experiment we will consider in psychology, increase type I error in a predictable and inevitable fashion. Does this bother you? Your degree of concern, which is based on your attitude toward the relative importance of type I and type II errors for you and for your research field, will contribute greatly to your decision. Whatever plan you may adopt, however, you should make some attempt to estimate the degree of power under which you will be operating for comparisons of primary interest to you. I will now offer some recommendations and guidelines that may help you decide how to evaluate the analytical comparisons derived from your research.

Planned Comparisons. Planned comparisons usually represent the motivating force behind an experiment. These comparisons are targeted from the start of the investigation and reflect a researcher's interest in particular combinations of conditions. Planned comparisons are examples of what Tukey (1977, 1980) calls **confirmatory statistical analysis**, in which specific questions that can be confirmed or disconfirmed are tested in an experiment. In keeping with the special status accorded planned comparisons, I recommend using the uncorrected *PC* rate, α, to evaluate the relevant test statistics. If the number of planned comparisons exceeds the number of degrees of freedom associated with the overall treatment mean square, I suggest the use of the modified Bonferroni test (pp. 169–170) to maintain the *FW* error for planned comparisons at the level dictated by df_A, namely, $(a - 1)$ (α). Planned comparisons need not be orthogonal, although orthogonal comparisons do provide an unambiguous allocation of the treatment variation observed in an experiment.

Post Hoc Comparisons. In post hoc data analysis, the type of question asked shifts from "Is *this* difference significant?" which characterizes planned comparisons, to "*Which* differences are significant?" which characterizes post hoc comparisons. The concern is with the whole set of treatments rather than with particular combinations of conditions. The probability of finding significant differences by chance depends on the number of treatment conditions; hence, it makes sense to worry about the *FW* rate under these circumstances.

It is my opinion that post hoc comparisons should be subjected to a more stringent standard to guard against committing an unacceptably large number of type I errors. Indiscriminant testing, in which theory has little effect in defining the nature of the comparisons, utilizes the least amount of extrastatistical information and thus supports the weakest inferences. Just which correction technique you choose depends on the sorts of comparisons examined in the post hoc analysis. If the comparisons consist only of differences between a control condition and several experimental conditions, the Dunnett test (pp. 175–177) is appropriate. If the total set of pairwise comparisons are considered, the Tukey test (pp. 173–175) is recommended. Finally, if you are truly sorting through all types of comparison— pairwise and complex—the Scheffé (pp. 172–173) is the correct choice.

As a form of "safety net" to counteract any loss of power when post hoc corrections are applied, I recommend the decision to suspend judgment (pp. 181–182). By suspending judgment on post hoc differences that would be significant as planned comparisons but are not sufficiently large to be significant with a post hoc test, we can minimize the danger of missing small but interesting findings discovered during the course of systematically combing through the data. The question of power can then be dealt with later—by conducting future experiments that are specifically designed to study these post hoc findings for which judgment was suspended. In short, what Tukey (1977) calls **exploratory data analysis**, the uncarthing of interesting and unexpected findings, often generates the planned comparisons studied and examined in subsequent experiments.

8.5   EXERCISES[11]

1. Problem 1 in the exercises for Chap. 6 is an experiment investigating the effects of two drugs (a depressant and a stimulant) on the activity of rats; each drug was represented by two dosage levels (low and high). In addition, there was a control group that received no drug. There were $n = 4$ rats assigned to each of the $a = 5$ treatment conditions. The original analysis consisted of four planned comparisons (see p. 140). Suppose the experimenter decided to add to the analysis plan comparisons between the control and each of the four drug conditions, bringing the total number of planned comparisons to eight.

   a. What is the FW type I error associated with this new research plan? Use Eq. (8–2) and the 5 percent level of significance.

   b. Suppose the researcher was persuaded to use the Bonferroni (or Dunn) test to control for FW type I error and to set $\alpha_{FW} = .05$. What is the new per comparison significance level (α_B) required by this test? How does α_B translate into a critical value of F_B?

   c. Suppose, instead, that the researcher decided to use the modified Bonferroni test. What is the per comparison significance level ($\tilde{\alpha}_{planned}$) required by this test? (Use $\alpha = .05$.) How does $\tilde{\alpha}_{planned}$ translate into a critical value of $F_{planned}$?

2. Assume that we have a control group and seven experimental groups, with $n = 16$ subjects for each group. The $MS_{S/A} = 28.75$. The totals for each group are as follows:

C	E_1	E_2	E_3	E_4	E_5	E_6	E_7
289	270	241	279	191	213	205	198

   a. Is the overall F significant?

   b. Use Dunnett's test to determine which of the treatment means is significantly different from the mean of the control group. Use a two-tailed test at $\alpha = .05$.

   c. Conduct the same set of comparisons with the Scheffé procedure, $\alpha = .05$. Do your conclusions change?

3. Suppose we have an experiment with independent groups of $n = 7$ subjects randomly assigned to each of $a = 4$ treatment conditions. The error term is $MS_{S/A} = 58.65$. The treatment means are 56.86, 47.57, 62.29, and 53.29.

   a. Evaluate all pairwise differences, using no correction for FW type I error (set $\alpha = .05$).

   b. Evaluate the same pairwise differences with the Tukey test, $\alpha = .05$.

   c. How would you modify your conclusions in part b if you adopted the three-decision procedure described in Sec. 8.4?

---

[11]The answers to these problems are found in Appendix B.

PART III

FACTORIAL EXPERIMENTS
WITH TWO FACTORS

In Chapters 9 through 13, I will consider experiments in which treatment conditions are classified with respect to the levels represented on *two* independent variables. In all these discussions, I will be assuming that subjects serve in only one of the treatment conditions, that they provide only a single score or observation, and that they are randomly assigned to one of the conditions. We refer to these sorts of experiments as **completely randomized factorial designs.** I will consider other types of designs in later chapters.

The most common means by which two or more independent variables are manipulated in an experiment is a *factorial arrangement of the treatments* or, more simply, a **factorial experiment** or **design.** I will use these terms interchangeably. In a factorial design, the experiment includes every possible combination of the levels of the independent variables. Suppose, for example, that two variables are manipulated concurrently in a study—the magnitude of the food reward given to a hungry rat for completing a run through a maze and the difficulty of the maze the rat must learn. Let's assume there are three levels of food magnitude (small, medium, and large) and two levels of maze difficulty (easy and hard). The factorial arrangement of the treatment conditions is specified by the six cells in the following table. I will often call such an arrangement a **factorial matrix** or simply a matrix. The cells in the matrix represent the following treatment combinations: small-easy, small-hard, medium-easy, medium-hard, large-easy, and large-hard. Each magnitude of reward (represented by the columns) is combined with each type of maze (represented by the rows). Factorial designs are sometimes referred to as experiments in which the independent variables are completely **crossed.** We can think of the crossing in terms of a multiplication of the levels of the different independent variables. In this example, the treatment combinations may be enumerated by multiplying (small + medium + large) by (easy + hard) to produce the six treatment combinations of the design.

An Example of a Two-Variable Factorial Experiment

TYPE OF	REWARD MAGNITUDE		
MAZE	Small	Medium	Large
Easy			
Hard			

The factorial experiment is probably most effective at the reconstructive stage of science, where investigators begin to approximate the "real" world by manipulating a number of independent variables simultaneously. Of course, the type of design we choose depends on the complexity with which the phenomenon we are studying is determined. It is clear, however, that the factorial experiment has advantages of *economy, control,* and *generality.* Factorial designs are economical in the sense that they provide considerably more information than separate single-factor experiments, often at reduced cost of subjects, time, and effort. Factorial designs achieve experimental control by providing a way to remove important, but unwanted, sources of variability that otherwise would contribute to our estimates of error variance. (I will discuss this use of factorial designs in Chap. 14.) Finally, factorial designs allow us to assess the generality of a particular finding by studying the effects of one independent variable under different experimental conditions. We evaluate this generality by examining the results of a factorial experiment for *interaction.* I will discuss this new concept in detail in Chap. 9.

There are five chapters in Part III. Chapter 9 considers the important characteristics of factorial designs. In Chap. 10, I will cover the standard analysis of the two-factor experiment. Chapters 11 and 12 present analytical comparisons that are particularly useful in the detailed analysis of this type of experimental design. The final chapter in Part III, Chap. 13, considers the analysis of experiments with unequal sample sizes.

9

Introduction to the Factorial Design

A great deal of research in the behavioral sciences consists of the identification of variables contributing to a given phenomenon. Quite typically, an experiment may be designed to focus attention on a single independent variable or factor. A main characteristic of this type of investigation is that it represents an assessment of how a variable operates under "ideal" conditions—with all other important variables held constant or permitted to vary randomly across the different conditions. An alternative approach is to study the influence of one independent variable in conjunction with variations in one or more additional independent variables. Here, the primary question is whether a particular variable studied concurrently with another variable in a factorial design will show the same effect as it would when studied separately in a single-factor design.

9.1   BASIC INFORMATION AVAILABLE
FROM FACTORIAL DESIGNS

Factorial experiments are rich with information. We can study not only the effects of the two independent variables separately but also how they combine to influence the dependent variable.

Simple Effects of an Independent Variable

A factorial design actually consists of a set of *single*-factor experiments. Suppose we are putting together a reading series for elementary schools and that we have reason to believe that the format of the books will influence reading speed. Two factors we might consider are the length of the printed lines and the contrast between the printed letters and the paper. Let's assume that we chose three line lengths (3, 5, and 7 inches) and three contrasts (low, medium, and high). Suppose we created three single-factor experiments as follows: One consists of three groups of children randomly assigned to the different line conditions in which the letters for all three groups are printed with *low* contrast. This single-factor experiment studies the effects of line length on reading speed under conditions of low contrast, and if the manipulation were successful, we would attribute any significant differences to the variation of line length. Two other experiments are exact duplicates of the first except that the letters are printed with *medium* contrast for one and with *high* contrast for the other. These three experiments are depicted on the left in Table 9–1. As you can see, these experiments represent component parts of a factorial design. Each component experiment provides information about the effects of line length, but under different conditions of contrast.

As diagrammed in Table 9–2, we can also view the factorial design as a set of component single-factor experiments involving the other independent variable, contrast. The left-hand experiment at the top of the table consists of a single-factor design in which different groups of subjects receive the reading material under one of three conditions of contrast (low, medium, or high); all children read material printed in 3-inch lines. The second experiment duplicates the first exactly except

Table 9–1   Component Single-Factor Experiments Representing the Simple Effects of Line Length

Simple Effects of Line Length	Factorial Design

that the material is printed with 5-inch lines; similarly, the third duplicates the first except that the material is printed with 7-inch lines. Each component experiment provides information about the effects of contrast, but for lines of different length.

The results of these component single-factor experiments are called the **simple effects** of an independent variable.[1] Thus, the results of the first component experiment in Table 9–1 (first row) are referred to as the simple effects of line length for letters printed in low contrast, and the results of the third component experiment in Table 9–2 (third column) are called the simple effects of contrast for reading material printed in 7-inch lines.

One of the advantages of factorial designs is *economy*. If we had studied reading speed with a true single-factor design and not with a factorial, we would have created two experiments, one in which we manipulated line length alone and another in which we manipulated contrast alone, holding in both cases all factors constant (including contrast or length) or permitting them to vary randomly. In comparison, we have a total of six component single-factor experiments embedded in our factorial experiment—three involving the effects of line length and three the effects of contrast. This is a considerable gain, particularly when you consider the fact that the two single-factor experiments would require a total of six groups of subjects (3 + 3), whereas the six component experiments require only three more.

Interaction Effects

Although it may be informative to study the effects of the two independent variables separately for each component single-factor experiment, we would certainly

---

[1] They are more commonly called the **simple *main* effects** of an independent variable. I prefer to use the shorter version (*simple effects*) to distinguish these effects from another statistical concept, namely, main effects. I will consider this concept later in this chapter.

Table 9–2   Component Single-Factor Experiments Representing the Simple Effects of Contrast

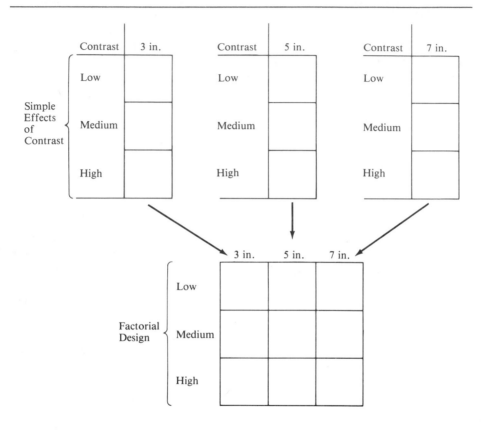

want to *compare* these results. For example, we would want to determine whether the simple effects of line length that we find with low contrast are the same as those we observe for medium contrast or for high contrast. Similarly, we would also want to know whether the simple effects of contrast that we obtain with 3-inch lines are the same as those we observe for 5- and 7-inch lines. A unique feature of the factorial design is the possibility of comparing the results of each set of three component single-factor experiments, one involving the three line-length experiments and the other involving the three contrast experiments. A comparison of this sort—a comparison among the simple effects of the component experiments— is called the analysis of **interaction**. If the outcomes of the different component experiments within either set are the same, interaction is absent; that is, if the effects of the component experiments are duplicated for each level of the other independent variable, there is no interaction. On the other hand, if the outcomes are different, interaction is present: The effects of the component experiments are not the same for all levels of the other independent variable. We will return to this important concept in Sec. 9.2.

Table 9–3   Cell Means Contributing to the Main Effects

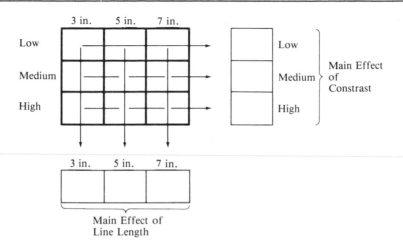

Main Effect of
Line Length

Main Effects

The **main effects** of an independent variable refer to the *average* of the component single-factor experiments making up the factorial design. The main effect of line length, for example, refers to the effects of this independent variable when the other independent variable, contrast, is ignored or disregarded. As illustrated by the arrows in Table 9–3, we obtain this main effect by combining the individual treatment means from each component experiment involving the manipulation of line length to produce new averages that reflect variations in line length alone. In a similar fashion, we obtain the main effect of the contrast variable by combining the means from each component experiment involving the manipulation of contrast. Main effects are most easily interpreted when interaction is *absent*. Under these circumstances, the effects of either independent variable—line length or contrast—do not depend on the other independent variable, implying that we can safely combine these results and study the effects of each independent variable separately, in the same way we would study the effects from two actual single-factor experiments, even though the data are combined from a factorial design.

Summary

A factorial design produces three important pieces of information. First, we have the simple effects, which refer to the results of the component single-factor experiments making up the factorial design. These effects reflect treatment effects associated with one of the independent variables, with the other one held constant. Second, we have interaction effects, which reflect a comparison of the simple effects. Interaction is present when the component single-factor experiments produce different results; interaction is absent when the results are the same. Finally, we have main effects, which essentially transform the factorial design into two single-factor experiments. Main effects are of primary interest in the absence of interaction, when it is safe to combine the data from the component experiments.

9.2   THE CONCEPT OF INTERACTION

Interaction is the one new concept introduced by the factorial experiment. Main effects have essentially the same meaning as in the single-factor analysis of variance and they are calculated in exactly the same way. Moreover, as you will see in later chapters, factorials with three or more variables involve no additional principles. Thus, it is important to understand the single-factor analysis of variance since many of the principles and procedures found in this simplest of experimental designs—such as partitioning sums of squares, the logic of hypothesis testing, and planned and post hoc comparisons—are also found in the more complicated designs. By the same token, the two-factor analysis of variance forms a building block for designs involving three or more variables, with the concept of interaction linking them all together.

An Example of No Interaction

Table 9–4 presents some hypothetical results for the experiment on reading speed I have been discussing. Assume that equal numbers of children are included in each of the nine conditions and that the values presented in the table represent the average reading scores found in the experiment. I will refer to line length as factor A and to the three line lengths defining that independent variable as levels a_1, a_2, and a_3. Correspondingly, I will refer to contrast as factor B and to the three levels of contrast as levels b_1, b_2, and b_3.

The main effect of line length (factor A) is obtained by summing (or collapsing over) the three cell means for the different contrast conditions and then averaging these sums. The last row of the table gives these means for the three length conditions. These averages are called the column **marginal means** of the matrix. Thus, the average reading speed for subjects in the 3-inch condition is found by combining the means from the three contrast conditions and calculating an average. In this case, we have

$$\bar{Y}_{A_1} = \frac{.89 + 3.89 + 4.22}{3} = \frac{9.00}{3} = 3.00$$

Table 9–4   Example of No Interaction

| CONTRAST (FACTOR B) | LINE LENGTH (FACTOR A) | | | Mean |
	3 in. (a_1)	5 in. (a_2)	7 in. (a_3)	
Low (b_1)	.89	2.22	2.89	2.00
Medium (b_2)	3.89	5.22	5.89	5.00
High (b_3)	4.22	5.55	6.22	5.33
Mean	3.00	4.33	5.00	4.11

This mean represents the average performance of *all* the subjects in the experiment who received the 3-inch lines; the specific conditions of factor *B*, namely, the three contrasts, are unimportant at this point. We can obtain similar averages for the subjects receiving the 5- and 7-inch materials. These two marginal means are given in the other two columns.

In a like fashion, the row marginal averages give us information concerning the main effect of the different contrasts. That is, the average reading speed for subjects in the low-contrast condition is given by an average of the means for the three length conditions. Thus,

$$\overline{Y}_{B_1} = \frac{.89 + 2.22 + 2.89}{3} = \frac{6.00}{3} = 2.00$$

This averaging for the other contrast conditions appears in the final column of the table. Each of these marginal means represents the average performance of all the subjects who received the specified contrast condition, disregarding the particular condition of factor *A*—that is, which line length—these subjects also received.

Let's look first at the marginal averages for line length, which are plotted on the left side in Fig. 9–1. As you can see, reading speed increases steadily as the length of the lines increases from 3 to 7 inches. You can think of this plot as a general description of the overall or main effects of factor *A*. Now, would you say that this overall relationship is *representative* of the results obtained in the component single-factor experiments found in the three rows within the body of Table 9–4? To help answer this question, I have plotted these cell means in a double-classification plot on the right side of Fig. 9–1. I accomplished this classification by marking off line length on the baseline, plotting the cell means on the graph, and connecting the means from the same component single-factor experiment. It is clear that the functions for the three component experiments are *parallel*, which means that the pattern of differences obtained with line length is exactly the same at each level of the other independent variable. There is *no interaction*.

We arrive at the same conclusion if we focus on the other independent variable, contrast. The left-hand graph in Fig. 9–2 plots the main (or average) effects

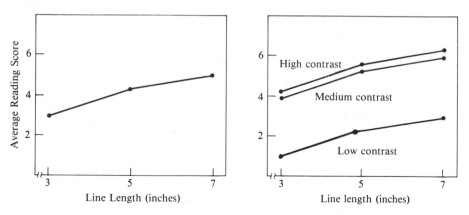

Figure 9–1 Plot of data presented in Table 9–4; an example of no interaction.

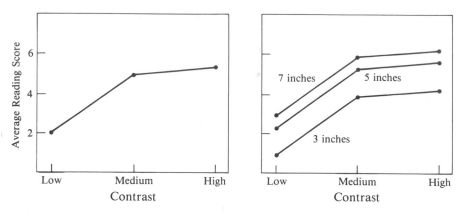

Figure 9–2   Plot of data presented in Table 9–4; an example of no interaction.

of factor B. (For the purposes of this example, I have assumed that the levels of the contrast variable are equally spaced.) Low contrast produces the lowest reading scores, and medium and high contrast produce higher but similar averages. The results of the component single-factor experiments, which we find in the three columns within the body of Table 9–4, are plotted in the right-hand graph. Again, you can see that the patterns of differences associated with the contrast variable (factor B) are the same for each of these component experiments, and there is no interaction.

In the absence of interaction, we usually focus our attention on the main effects—that is, the two sets of marginal means—rather than on the cell means. Since the effects of line length, for example, do not depend on any particular condition of contrast, we can safely combine the results from the relevant component experiments without distorting the outcome of the experiment. We can make a similar argument for the contrast variable.

An Example of Interaction

Table 9–5 presents a second set of hypothetical results using the same experimental design. Note that the same main effects are present; that is, the means in the row and column margins of Table 9–5 are identical to the corresponding means in the

Table 9–5   Example of Interaction

| CONTRAST (FACTOR B) | *LINE LENGTH (FACTOR A)* | | | |
	3 in. (a_1)	5 in. (a_2)	7 in. (a_3)	Mean
Low (b_1)	1.00	2.00	3.00	2.00
Medium (b_2)	3.00	5.00	7.00	5.00
High (b_3)	5.00	6.00	5.00	5.33
Mean	3.00	4.33	5.00	4.11

margins of Table 9–4. There is a big difference, however, when we look at the simple effects of the two independent variables. To facilitate the comparisons of the simple effects, I have plotted the data within the body of the table in Fig. 9–3. For the graph on the left, line length appears on the baseline, and for the graph on the right, contrast appears on the baseline. In either plot, you can clearly see that the patterns of differences reflected by the simple effects are *not* the same at all levels of the other independent variable—interaction is present.

To be more specific, consider the simple effects of line length at level b_1—the cell means in the first row of Table 9–5. This row is the component single-factor experiment in which all subjects are tested under conditions of low contrast. These three means are plotted in the left-hand graph of Fig. 9–3. An inspection of the figure indicates that the relationship is positive and even linear. The simple effect at level b_2 (the second row) also shows a positive linear trend for all the subjects receiving the medium materials, although it is steeper than in the low-contrast case. But see what happens to the subjects who receive the high-contrast materials. The relationship in this third component experiment is curvilinear: The reading scores first increase and then decrease with line length.

You can see an analogous deviation of the simple effects when we look at the cell means in each of the three data columns, which are plotted in the right-hand graph of Fig. 9–3. Here, we are considering the component experiments in which contrast is varied while length is held constant. For the simple effect of contrast for 3-inch lines (the first column), you can see that the relationship is linear. For the simple effect for 5-inch lines (the second column), the relationship is not as sharply defined, with the function starting to "bend over" away from the linear trend. In the third column (7-inch lines), we have an actual reversal of the trend—that is, a curvilinear relationship, maximum performance being found with a medium contrast.

With either plot of the data, then, we can determine at a glance that the particular form of the relationship between the independent variable plotted against the baseline (line length or contrast) and the scores—that is, the shape of the curve drawn between successive points on the baseline—is not the same at the three different levels of the other independent variable. A simple way to describe this situ-

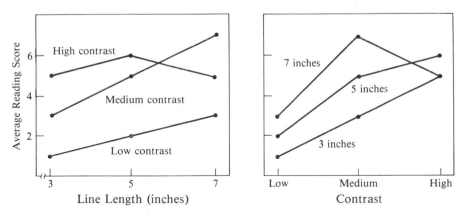

Figure 9–3 Plot of data presented in Table 9–5; an example of interaction.

ation is to say that the three curves are not parallel. When we find an interaction, it is usually a good idea to plot the results of the experiment just as I have done in Fig. 9–3. The shape or form of the interaction will become readily apparent. We do not typically plot the data both ways but rather choose for the baseline the independent variable that makes the most sense for the research hypotheses under consideration. Whichever way the data are plotted, however, an interaction will be revealed by nonparallel curves for the conditions plotted within the body of the figure.

You can now understand why we are less interested in the main effects when interaction is present than when it is absent. In either plot, you can see that the patterns of differences depicted by the simple effects are not the same as the pattern depicted by either the row or the column marginal means (the main, or average, effects). The main effects are not representative of the simple effects and, thus, provide a distorted view of the actual outcome of the single-factor experiments making up the factorial design. There was no such distortion with our first example in which interaction was absent (see Figs. 9–1 and 9–2).

Defining Interaction

The presence of interaction indicates that conclusions based on main effects alone will not fully describe the outcome of a factorial experiment. Instead, the effects of each independent variable must be interpreted with the levels of the other independent variable in mind. I will now consider several definitions that specify this important concept succinctly and precisely.

One definition is stated in terms of the two independent variables:

An interaction is present when the effects of one independent variable on behavior change at the different levels of the second independent variable.

This definition contains a critical point often missed by beginning students, namely, the focus on the *behavioral effects* of the independent variables. A common mistake is to think of two independent variables as influencing one another. One independent variable does not influence the other independent variable—this makes no sense—yet students often make this mistake on an examination. Independent variables influence the *dependent* variable, the behavior under study in an experiment.

Another way of defining interaction is to focus on the pattern of results associated with an independent variable. That is,

An interaction is present when the pattern of differences associated with an independent variable changes at the different levels of the other independent variable.

The pattern of differences refers to the analysis of the effects of a complex, multi-level factor into a number of meaningful single-df comparisons—that is, differences between means. Each component single-factor experiment, which makes up a factorial design, may be analyzed with these comparisons in mind. Suppose, for example, one of the independent variables consists of three levels, a control and two experimental treatments. We would probably consider examining a number of differences between two means, such as a comparison between the two experimental treatments, a comparison between the control and each of the experimental treatments, and a comparison between the control and the combined experimental treatments. If an interaction is present, the specific pattern of these differences will not all be the same for each of the component single-factor experiments constituting the factorial. We will consider analyses that focus on these patterns of differences in Chaps. 11 and 12.

A more formal definition of interaction is in terms of the simple effects since a simple effect is the effect of one independent variable at a specific level of the other independent variable:

> **An interaction is present when the simple effects of one independent variable are not the same at all levels of the second independent variable.**

A related definition focuses on the main, or average, effects:

> **An interaction is present when the main effect of an independent variable is not representative of the simple effects of that variable.**

Other definitions of interaction are possible. One student created a definition that attempted to avoid any reference to statistical "jargon" but focused instead on the differences observed among the cell means:

> **An interaction is present when the differences between the cell means representing the effect of factor *A* at one level of factor *B* do not equal the corresponding differences at another level of factor *B*.**

Cohen and Cohen (1983) use the term *conditionalized* to express interaction. Expressed this way, the definition becomes

> **An interaction is present when the effects of one of the independent variables are conditionally related to the levels of the other independent variable.**

Pedhazur (1982), on the other hand, expresses interaction in terms of *constant effects*. Using this phrase, we have

> **An interaction is present when one of the independent variables does not have a constant effect at all levels of the other independent variable.**

My reason for offering a number of different definitions of interaction is to broaden your understanding of the concept and to provide alternative ways of expressing it. Students have difficulty in defining interaction correctly and precisely.[2] The difficulty seems *semantic* rather than conceptual or statistical. The concept is important for your understanding of the factorial design we are considering in this chapter and of the more complex designs we will discuss in later chapters.

---

[2]Problem 1 in the exercises for this chapter duplicates some of the misdefinitions offered by graduate students on a final examination.

Implications of Interaction for Theory

The presence of an interaction often requires more complexity in our theoretical explanations of data than would be the case if no interaction were present. Consider the two different outcomes we have been discussing. Both examples indicate the importance of the two independent variables. In the first case, where there is no interaction, the effect of one of the independent variables adds to the effect of the other variable. The combination is simple. In the second case, on the other hand, the combination is complex—it will take a considerable amount of theoretical ingenuity to explain why the relationship between line length and reading speed is different for the three different levels of contrast or why the relationship between contrast and reading speed is different for the different line lengths.

This discussion has focused on the complexity of post hoc explanations of a set of data when an interaction is found. In an increasing number of experiments being reported in the literature, interactions not only are predicted but also represent the major interest of the studies. Consider, for example, research in developmental psychology. Gollin (1965) indicates that it is not particularly revealing of developmental processes simply to compare a number of different age groups on a given task. Instead, he suggests that more interesting information is obtained from the discovery of interactions involving some manipulated independent variables and the age dimension. To show that two age groups differ on one task but not on another allows us to speculate about the different developmental processes present in the two groups and required of the two tasks. To find a main effect of age or of task suggests very little about the processes involved in the phenomenon under study. As Gollin puts it, "The uncovering of both the similarity *and* the difference in performance obviously gives us an order of information about the two groups which is quite different than if we had simply demonstrated that they did or did not differ on one or the other task" (p. 166).

The discovery or the prediction of interactions may lead to a greater understanding of the behavior under study. Lashley's classic study of the effect of the amount of brain damage on maze performance by rats is an excellent example. Lashley (1929) varied the amount of cortical tissue destroyed from a small amount (1 to 10 percent) to a large amount (over 50 percent) and tested these animals on three mazes differing in difficulty. The mean numbers of errors committed by his subjects during learning are presented in Table 9–6. As you can see, Lashley found very slight differences among the operated groups on the easiest maze but ex-

Table 9–6   The Effects of Maze Difficulty and Amount of Brain Damage on Errors in Maze Learning in Rats (Lashley, 1929)

MAZE DIFFICULTY	*AMOUNT OF BRAIN DAMAGE (IN PERCENTAGES)*					
	1–10	**11–20**	**21–30**	**31–40**	**41–50**	**>50**
Easy	6.6	7.2	31.8	29.3	34.7	40.0
Moderate	15.4	40.0	43.5	63.2	52.8	66.6
Hard	33.4	266.0	396.0	485.0	580.0	1,446.0

tremely dramatic differences on the most difficult maze. If Lashley had run his animals on only one of the mazes, he would have missed this important finding: that the destruction of cortical tissue affects primarily the acquisition of complex learning tasks. That is, there is no uniform overall learning deficit; the effect of brain damage depends on the complexity of the material being acquired.

In short, then, if behavior is complexly determined, we will need factorial experiments to isolate and to tease out these complexities. The factorial design allows us to manipulate two or more independent variables concurrently and to obtain some idea of how the variables combine to produce the behavior. An assessment of the interaction provides a hint to the rules of combination.

Further Examples of Interaction and Lack of Interaction

To broaden your understanding of the two-variable or $A \times B$ interaction and to provide some practice in extracting information from double-classification tables and plots, consider the hypothetical outcomes of a factorial experiment in which both factors are represented by two levels each—called a 2×2 (read "2-by-2") factorial design. The means for each set of four treatment combinations are presented in Table 9–7.

You have seen that the means in the margins of a two-factor matrix reflect the main effects of the two independent variables and that the cell means within the body of the matrix reflect the presence or absence of an interaction. In this discussion I will assume that if any difference is present between the column marginal means or between the row marginal means, a corresponding main effect is present, and that if the effect of one independent variable changes at the two levels of the other independent variable, an interaction is present. (As you will see, the *significance* of main effects and of interaction is assessed by means of an F ratio.) We will look at eight examples, representing each of the possible combinations of the presence or absence of the two main effects and the interaction.

Table 9–7   Eight Different Outcomes of the Same Two-Factor Experiment

(1)

	a_1	a_2	Mean
b_1	5	5	5
b_2	5	5	5
Mean:	5	5	

(2)

	a_1	a_2	Mean
b_1	4	6	5
b_2	4	6	5
Mean:	4	6	

(3)

	a_1	a_2	Mean
b_1	7	7	7
b_2	3	3	3
Mean:	5	5	

(4)

	a_1	a_2	Mean
b_1	6	8	7
b_2	2	4	3
Mean:	4	6	

(5)

	a_1	a_2	Mean
b_1	6	4	5
b_2	4	6	5
Mean:	5	5	

(6)

	a_1	a_2	Mean
b_1	5	5	5
b_2	3	7	5
Mean:	4	6	

(7)

	a_1	a_2	Mean
b_1	8	6	7
b_2	2	4	3
Mean:	5	5	

(8)

	a_1	a_2	Mean
b_1	7	7	7
b_2	1	5	3
Mean:	4	6	

Before we begin, let's review some basic definitions.

A *factorial design* consists of a set of single-factor designs in which the same independent variable is manipulated but in combination with a second independent variable (see Tables 9–1 and 9–2).

The *simple effects* of an independent variable consist of the differences among the means for any one of these component experiments. That is, the differences associated with the single-factor experiment involving factor A at level b_1, for example, are called the simple effects of factor A at level b_1.

Interaction is defined in terms of a comparison among a set of simple effects. Interaction is present when we find that the simple effects associated with one independent variable are not the same at all levels of the other independent variable.

Finally, the *main effect* of an independent variable factor refers to the overall or average effects of the variable, obtained by combining the entire set of component experiments involving that factor.

We will now consider the examples.

The first four examples in Table 9–7 contain no interaction. The first example represents a completely negative study in the sense that neither the main effects nor an interaction is present. This outcome is illustrated by the identical four means in the body of the matrix. The column marginal means are equal, indicating the absence of a main effect of factor A; similarly, the equal row marginal means indicate an absence of a main effect of factor B. A plot of the cell means in panel 1 of Fig. 9–4 indicates that no $A \times B$ interaction is present in the data. The second example illustrates a case in which there is only a main effect of factor A. You can see this by inspecting the column marginal means, which are different, and the row marginal means, which are equal. There is also no $A \times B$ interaction, as you may see in panel 2 of the figure—the two curves at b_1 and b_2 are parallel. In the next example, the marginal means show that there is a main effect of factor B but no main effect of factor A. Again, no interaction is present since the two curves at b_1 and b_2 are parallel. The outcome in example 4 indicates that there is a main effect

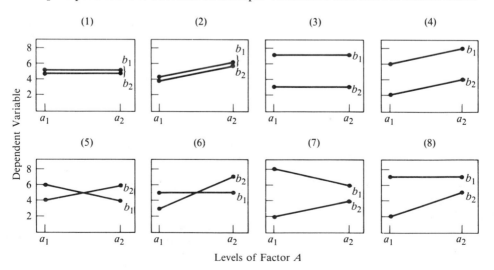

Figure 9–4   Plot of data presented in Table 9–7.

for both independent variables; this may be seen in the two sets of marginal means. The plot in Fig. 9–4 shows that the effects of factor A are the same at both levels of factor B—that is, there is no interaction.

The last four examples contain $A \times B$ interactions. Look at the marginal means for example 5. There is no difference between the two column means and no difference between the two row means; hence, there are no main effects of factors A and B, respectively. On the basis of the main effects, then, we might conclude that our manipulations were ineffective, that neither factor had an effect. But look at the cell means within the body of the matrix. The two independent variables produce quite striking effects. As you can see, a_1 is superior to a_2 when factor A is manipulated in conjunction with level b_1, but this superiority is reversed when factor A is manipulated in conjunction with level b_2. (You can see a similar reversal of the simple effects of factor B in this graph.) The $A \times B$ interaction is so severe that the simple effects of both independent variables have cancelled each other. The interaction is clear in Fig. 9–4. This example stresses the point that the main effects reflect treatment *averages* and, as such, do not necessarily reflect the true outcome of the experiment. This type of interaction is sometimes called a *complete interaction* because it shows that the effect of one independent variable depends completely on the levels of the other.

The next two examples illustrate situations in which there is an interaction and one main effect. The main effect in example 6, for instance, is revealed in the column marginal means—that is, a main effect of factor A—and the interaction is readily apparent in the plot of the cell means in panel 6 of Fig. 9–4. In this case, the effect of factor A is absent at b_1 but it is sizable at b_2. In example 7 the situation is reversed; the row marginal means indicate a main effect of factor B and the non-parallel lines in panel 7 indicate an interaction of the two independent variables. The final experiment (example 8) provides an instance in which all three effects are present. Not only is there a main effect for both of the two independent variables (see the column and row marginal means), but also the form of the function relating factor A to the dependent variable is different at the two levels of factor B, indicating the presence of an interaction.

You have seen that it is possible to obtain eight different combinations of the presence or absence of the two main effects and the interaction. Obviously, there is an infinite number of ways in which the actual means may turn out to reflect one of these combinations. The presence of main effects is revealed by the variation between the marginal means in the two-way matrix, and the presence of an $A \times B$ interaction is revealed by the appearance of nonparallel lines in a double-classification plot of the cell means. We are now ready to consider how we can turn these observations into variances, which will reflect these three effects, and how we can test their significance.

9.3   EXERCISES[3]

1. I have duplicated definitions of interaction given on an examination by students in one of my classes. Each "definition" fails to define the concept precisely. See if you can detect the "fatal" flaw in each attempt.

[3]The answers to these problems are found in Appendix B.

   a. Interaction exists when the levels of one independent variable affect the other.

   b. Interaction refers to the influence of independent variables on the dependent variable.

   c. Interaction occurs when the effects of one level of an independent variable are different at the different levels of another independent variable.

   d. Interaction occurs when the values of one independent variable are dependent on the levels of the other independent variable in a two-factor design.

2. The individual $\overline{Y}_{AB}$ cell means for a 4×2 factorial experiment are given in a set of six examples. For each example, indicate which factorial effects are present. (Assume that the means are population values and, thus, are error-free.)

(a)

	a_1	a_2	a_3	a_4
b_1	10	12	14	16
b_2	8	10	12	14

(b)

	a_1	a_2	a_3	a_4
b_1	10	14	12	16
b_2	7	11	9	13

(c)

	a_1	a_2	a_3	a_4
b_1	10	14	12	16
b_2	12	10	8	14

(d)

	a_1	a_2	a_3	a_4
b_1	10	12	14	16
b_2	14	12	10	8

(e)

	a_1	a_2	a_3	a_4
b_1	10	12	14	16
b_2	8	9	10	11

(f)

	a_1	a_2	a_3	a_4
b_1	12	12	8	8
b_2	8	8	12	12

10

Rationale and Rules for Calculating the Major Effects

You saw in Chap. 2 how the total sum of squares could be partitioned into two parts: (1) a part reflecting the deviation of the treatment groups from the overall mean (the between-groups sum of squares—SS_{bg}) and (2) a part reflecting the variability of subjects treated alike (the within-groups sum of squares—SS_{wg}). I then discussed how we could test the null hypothesis. In subsequent chapters of Part II, you saw that we could ask more refined questions of the data by dividing the SS_{bg} into component sums of squares. The analysis of the factorial experiment follows a similar pattern, except that the SS_{bg} is not of systematic interest. That is, we are primarily interested in the *further division* of the SS_{bg} into three orthogonal components: (1) a sum of squares reflecting the main effect of factor A (SS_A), (2) a sum of squares reflecting the main effect of factor B (SS_B), and (3) a sum of squares representing the $A \times B$ interaction ($SS_{A \times B}$). In this chapter, I will consider only the most common case, that having the same number of subjects in each of the treatment conditions. I will discuss the analysis of experiments with unequal sample sizes in Chap. 13.

10.1   PARTITIONING THE TOTAL SUM OF SQUARES

Before we consider the division (or partitioning) of the total sum of squares, I will expand the notational system so that I can make explicit the operations needed for the analysis of the two-way factorial design.

Design and Notation

The system I use is summarized in Table 10–1. The factorial arrangement of the two independent variables, illustrated with $a = 2$ and $b = 3$, is enumerated in the upper portion of the table. I have indicated that there is a total of $(a)(b) = (2)(3) = 6$ treatment conditions, each with a sample size of $n = 4$ different subjects, who have been randomly assigned to the different conditions.

Table 10–1 Design and Notation for the Two-Factor Design

Experimental Design

FACTOR B	FACTOR A	
	a_1	a_2
b_1	$n = 4$	$n = 4$
b_2	$n = 4$	$n = 4$
b_3	$n = 4$	$n = 4$

Data Matrix

TREATMENT COMBINATIONS

a_1b_1	a_1b_2	a_1b_3	a_2b_1	a_2b_2	a_2b_3
$Y_{1,1,1}$	$Y_{1,2,1}$	$Y_{1,3,1}$	$Y_{2,1,1}$	$Y_{2,2,1}$	$Y_{2,3,1}$
$Y_{1,1,2}$	$Y_{1,2,2}$	$Y_{1,3,2}$	$Y_{2,1,2}$	$Y_{2,2,2}$	$Y_{2,3,2}$
$Y_{1,1,3}$	$Y_{1,2,3}$	$Y_{1,3,3}$	$Y_{2,1,3}$	$Y_{2,2,3}$	$Y_{2,3,3}$
$Y_{1,1,4}$	$Y_{1,2,4}$	$Y_{1,3,4}$	$Y_{2,1,4}$	$Y_{2,2,4}$	$Y_{2,3,4}$

AB Matrix

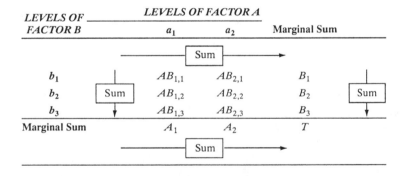

A basic observation or score in this design is denoted as Y_{ijk} to indicate that it represents the score of a single subject in a particular combination of the levels of factors A and B. These scores are arranged in the Y or **data matrix**, which appears in the middle portion of the table. If it is necessary to specify a particular score in one of the treatment conditions, I will use all three subscripts—one for the level of factor A (the i subscript), one for the level of factor B (the j subscript), and one for the score within the treatment cell (the kL subscript). As in the single-factor case, however, I will drop the subscripts whenever there is no ambiguity about what arithmetic operations are being specified.

An **AB matrix**, where the remainder of the notational system is illustrated, is presented in the bottom portion of Table 10–1. The basic entry within the body of this matrix (often called the **cells** of the matrix) is the quantity AB_{ij}. This quantity represents the sum of the Y scores at a particular combination of levels of the two factors. These are the totals that we would obtain if we summed the $n = 4$ individual scores (Y) in any one column of the data matrix. I will also refer to these sums as the **treatment sums** or **totals**. They form the basic ingredient in the determination of the sums of squares associated with different experimental treatments.

To calculate the two main effects, we will have to obtain the column and row totals shown in the margins of the AB matrix and hereafter referred to as the column and row marginal totals, respectively. As indicated in the table, column marginal totals (A_i) are formed by summing all the cell totals in each column of the matrix, row marginal totals (B_j) are formed by summing all the cell totals in each row of the matrix, and the grand total (T) is obtained by summing either set of marginal totals or summing all the Y scores in the data matrix.

For purposes of examining results and reporting data, we will want to convert the various treatment sums listed in the AB matrix into means. This is accomplished, of course, by dividing each sum by the appropriate number of observations. The basic symbol for a mean is $\overline{Y}$, with subscripts added to identify the nature of the sum involved.

$$\overline{Y}_{AB} = \frac{AB}{n} \qquad\qquad \overline{Y}_A = \frac{A}{(b)(n)}$$

$$\overline{Y}_B = \frac{B}{(a)(n)} \qquad\qquad \overline{Y}_T = \frac{T}{(a)(b)(n)}$$

Component Deviations

As a first step, it is useful to think of the six treatment means as coming from a single-factor experiment. According to the formulas given in Chap. 2, the total sum of squares can then be broken down into

$$SS_T = SS_{bg} + SS_{wg}$$

Up to this point, then, there is nothing new to the analysis. We will now refine SS_{bg}.

The SS_{bg} is based on the deviation of each individual treatment mean from the total mean—that is, $\overline{Y}_{AB_{ij}} - \overline{Y}_T$. Consider the deviation produced by a group of subjects receiving a particular treatment combination of factors A and B. This deviation can be influenced by three sources of variability: the A_i main effect, the B_j main effect, and the $A \times B$ interaction effect for this combination of treatments. Each of these effects can be expressed as a deviation involving familiar quantities:

$$\overline{Y}_{AB_{ij}} - \overline{Y}_T = (\overline{Y}_{A_i} - \overline{Y}_T) + (\overline{Y}_{B_j} - \overline{Y}_T)$$
$$+ (\overline{Y}_{AB_{ij}} - \overline{Y}_{A_i} - \overline{Y}_{B_j} + \overline{Y}_T) \qquad (10\text{–}1)$$

Suppose we try to understand Eq. (10–1) a little better. First, we can verify that the equation is correct by performing the indicated additions and subtractions. To be more specific, there is only one $\overline{Y}_{AB_{ij}}$ on the right-hand side of Eq. (10–1), and so it will stay, but $\overline{Y}_{A_i}$ and $\overline{Y}_{B_j}$ will both drop out since each appears once as a positive quantity and once as a negative quantity. The final term, $\overline{Y}_T$, appears three times on the right—twice as a positive quantity and once as a negative quantity. Thus, we are left with the same expression, $\overline{Y}_{AB_{ij}} - \overline{Y}_T$, on both sides of the equation.

The second point concerns the specification of the interaction effect. To show that the third quantity on the right of Eq. (10–1) reflects an interaction, we can redefine an interaction as a *residual* deviation. That is, the interaction effect represents whatever is left of the deviation of the individual treatment mean $(\overline{Y}_{AB_{ij}})$ from the grand mean $(\overline{Y}_T)$ that cannot be accounted for by the two relevant main effects. In symbols,

$$\text{interaction effect} = (\text{deviation from } \overline{Y}_T) - (A_i \text{ effect}) - (B_j \text{ effect})$$
$$= (\overline{Y}_{AB_{ij}} - \overline{Y}_T) - (\overline{Y}_{A_i} - \overline{Y}_T) - (\overline{Y}_{B_j} - \overline{Y}_T)$$

Performing some simple algebra, we obtain

$$\text{interaction effect} = \overline{Y}_{AB_{ij}} - \overline{Y}_T - \overline{Y}_{A_i} + \overline{Y}_T - \overline{Y}_{B_j} + \overline{Y}_T$$
$$= \overline{Y}_{AB_{ij}} - \overline{Y}_{A_i} - \overline{Y}_{B_j} + \overline{Y}_T$$

We are now ready to include the individual subjects from the different treatment groups in this specification of component deviations. We can easily expand Eq. (10–1) to accommodate the deviation of any given subject (Y_{ijk}) from the mean of all the subjects $(\overline{Y}_T)$. A complete subdivision of the total deviation $(Y_{ijk} - \overline{Y}_T)$ is given by the formula

$$
Y_{ijk} - \overline{Y}_T = (\overline{Y}_{A_i} - \overline{Y}_T) + (\overline{Y}_{B_j} - \overline{Y}_T)
$$
$$
+ (\overline{Y}_{AB_{ij}} - \overline{Y}_{A_i} - \overline{Y}_{B_j} + \overline{Y}_T) + (Y_{ijk} - \overline{Y}_{AB_{ij}})
\tag{10–2}
$$

In words, the deviation of any subject from the grand mean can be broken down into four separate components: (1) an A_i treatment effect, (2) a B_j treatment effect, (3) an $A \times B$ interaction effect, and (4) the deviation of the subject from his or her individual treatment mean.

Now that the component deviations have been enumerated for each subject, they can be squared and summed to produce the corresponding sums of squares for the analysis. Expressing these operations with symbols produces what are called *defining formulas*. Rather than looking at these defining formulas, which preserve the "meaning" of Eq. (10–2), I will move directly to the corresponding computational formulas, which are much easier to use in calculating the sums of squares.

10.2   A SYSTEM FOR GENERATING COMPUTATIONAL FORMULAS

In this section, I consider a system for generating the computational formulas for sums of squares. The system is introduced here in the context of the two-factor design, but it can be applied to a large variety of experimental designs, as you will see in later chapters. The method is based on the relationship between the *df* statement for a given source of variance and the corresponding formula for the sum of squares. The main purpose of this section is to introduce you to this useful system. In the next section, I will summarize the complete analysis and discuss in more detail the meaning behind some of the operations.

The system consists of three steps. First, we identify the sources of variance normally extracted in an analysis of variance. Second, we use the *df* statement for each of these sources to specify the basic ratios required and how they are combined to form each corresponding sum of squares. Finally, we construct the formulas for the basic ratios from a set of simple rules.

Identifying the Sources of Variance

There is a simple rule for specifying the sources of variance. I have already discussed what these sources would be in the present case, but it is useful to see how the rule applies in a situation with which we are familiar. This rule "works" with completely balanced designs of the sort covered through Chap. 14 of this book. The rule will be modified to accommodate the analysis of the more complex designs I present later.

1. List all factors, including the within-groups factor.
2. Form all possible interactions with these factors, omitting the within-groups factor.

For the two-factor design, step 1 results in a listing of

$$A, B, \text{ and } S/AB$$

The within-groups factor S/AB (read "subjects within AB") represents the variability due to subjects treated alike; that is, this source consists of the variability of subjects in each of the $(a)(b)$ groups, pooled or summed over these different groups. Step 2 results in the listing of a single interaction:

$$A \times B$$

Using the *df* Statement

I will discuss the meaning of degrees of freedom in the next section. For the present, I just consider formulas that specify the *df*'s for the different sources of variance. For the two main effects, the *df*'s are simply the number of levels for each factor minus 1:

$$df_A = a - 1 \text{ and } df_B = b - 1$$

For the $A \times B$ interaction, the degrees of freedom are the product of the *df*'s associated with factors A and B:

$$df_{A \times B} = (df_A)(df_B) = (a - 1)(b - 1) \tag{10-3}$$

The calculation of the *df* for the within-groups source S/AB is more complicated.

The variability for this source is due to a subject factor (factor S), and for this factor, $df_S = n - 1$. However, since this factor is present in each of the $(a)(b)$ treatment conditions, the df for S/AB is found by multiplying df_S by the total number of groups, $(a)(b)$:

$$df_{S/AB} = (a)(b)(df_S) = (a)(b)(n - 1)$$

Finally, the value of the df for the total sum of squares consists of the total number of observations, $(a)(b)(n)$, minus 1:

$$df_T = (a)(b)(n) - 1$$

Table 10–2 summarizes the steps followed in generating the computational formulas for the different sums of squares. The sources of variance and their corresponding df's are listed in the first two columns. In column 3, the different df's are multiplied in an expanded form, with the sets of letters arranged by decreasing numbers of letters.[1] When present, the number 1 is listed last. As you will see, the expanded df statement represents the backbone of the overall computational scheme.

Each term in these expanded df statements—single letters, combinations of letters, or 1—denotes a different *basic ratio* needed to calculate any given sum of squares. In addition, the expanded df statements themselves indicate how we combine these basic ratios to produce the different sums of squares. This point is made explicit in column 4, where each computational formula is written in terms of the basic ratios. The pair of brackets symbolizes a basic ratio; the letter or letters inside the brackets specify quantities from either the data matrix or the AB matrix that we use to calculate that particular ratio. You will note that the letter T has been substituted for the numeral 1 in the move from column 3 to column 4, but other than that, the translation from the expanded df statement to the computational formula is simple and direct. You should also note the correspondence between these formulas and the respective deviation specified in Eq. (10–2). All that remains is to summarize the operations required to define each basic ratio.

Table 10–2   Generating the Computational Formulas

(1) Source	(2) df	(3) Expanded df	(4) Computational Formula[a]
A	$a - 1$	$a - 1$	$[A] - [T]$
B	$b - 1$	$b - 1$	$[B] - [T]$
$A \times B$	$(a - 1)(b - 1)$	$(a)(b) - a - b + 1$	$[AB] - [A] - [B] + [T]$
S/AB	$(a)(b)(n - 1)$	$(a)(b)(n) - (a)(b)$	$[Y] - [AB]$
Total	$(a)(b)(n) - 1$	$(a)(b)(n) - 1$	$[Y] - [T]$

[a]Letters inside brackets represent basic ratios. See text and Table 10–3 for an explanation.

[1]You may have forgotten how to multiply the quantity $(a - 1)$ by the quantity $(b - 1)$. You start by multiplying the -1 in the second quantity times the two terms in the first quantity—that is, $(-1)(a - 1)$—which produces $-a$ and $+1$. Next you multiply the b in the second quantity times the two terms in the first quantity—that is, $(b)(a - 1)$—which gives us $(b)(a)$ and $-b$. Finally, we arrange these four products to produce $(a)(b) - a - b + 1$.

Forming the Basic Ratios

You will recall from Chap. 2 that basic ratios follow a consistent computational scheme, namely, squaring and then summing a set of quantities followed by a division specified by the following rule:

> **Whenever you square a total for the numerator, you will divide by the number of scores that went into the total.**

Table 10–3 summarizes these operations for each of the basic ratios required for the analysis of variance.

Column 1 lists the basic quantities entering into the calculations, namely, the two sets of marginal totals (A and B), the individual treatment sums from the body of the AB matrix (AB), the individual observations (Y), and the grand total (T). Column 2 indicates the squaring and summing operations performed on the entire set of relevant sums (in the case of A, B, AB, and T) or the entire set of scores (in the case of Y). The appropriate denominator for each basic ratio is specified in column 3. You should verify that each denominator represents the number of scores contributing to any one of the squared totals; that is, an A sum is based on $(b)(n)$ observations, a B sum is based on $(a)(n)$ observations, an AB sum is based on n observations, a Y score is based on 1 observation (not indicated in the table), and the grand sum T is based on $(a)(b)(n)$ observations. Finally, each basic ratio is uniquely coded to simplify computational formulas for the different sums of squares.

Summary

This system is general and may be applied to all the designs I will consider in this book. The system elaborated here ensures that you will never "forget" the compu-

Table 10–3   Development of the Basic Ratios

(1) Basic Quantity	(2) Square and Sum	(3) Complete Ratio	(4) Letter Code
A	ΣA^2	$\dfrac{\Sigma A^2}{(b)(n)}$	$[A]$
B	ΣB^2	$\dfrac{\Sigma B^2}{(a)(n)}$	$[B]$
AB	$\Sigma (AB)^2$	$\dfrac{\Sigma (AB)^2}{n}$	$[AB]$
Y	ΣY^2	ΣY^2	$[Y]$
T	T^2	$\dfrac{T^2}{(a)(b)(n)}$	$[T]$

tational formulas since you can very easily reconstruct them. Some of the steps will drop out with practice. You should not lose touch with the basic system, however, as it will prove extremely useful in generating formulas for the more complex designs we will consider later.

10.3 SUMMARY OF THE ANALYSIS OF VARIANCE

In this section, we consider the computational formulas again, but this time in conjunction with the remaining steps in the analysis of variance.

Sums of Squares

The computational formulas for the component sums of squares are presented in Table 10–4. For convenience, each term in the computational formulas is expressed in its complete form only once—when it first appears in the analysis. Thereafter, each basic ratio is designated by the letter code, in which a particular term is identified by the letter or letters appearing in the numerator. The totals required for the SS_A are the column marginal totals in the AB matrix presented in Table 10–1. The totals required for the SS_B come from the row marginal totals in the AB matrix. The totals for the first term in the computational formula for the $SS_{A \times B}$ are the individual cell totals found within the body of the AB matrix. Finally, the scores for the first term in the formula for the $SS_{S/AB}$ appear in the Y data matrix. The within-groups sum of squares ($SS_{S/AB}$) reflects the variability of subjects treated alike. That is, it consists of the variability of subjects receiving the same treatment combination, pooled over all the $(a)(b)$ treatment groups.

Table 10–4 Computational Formulas: Two-Factor Analysis of Variance

Source	Computational Formula[a]	df	MS	F
A	$\dfrac{\Sigma A^2}{(b)(n)} - \dfrac{T^2}{(a)(b)(n)}$	$a - 1$	$\dfrac{SS_A}{df_A}$	$\dfrac{MS_A}{MS_{S/AB}}$
B	$\dfrac{\Sigma B^2}{(a)(n)} - [T]$	$b - 1$	$\dfrac{SS_B}{df_B}$	$\dfrac{MS_B}{MS_{S/AB}}$
A × B	$\dfrac{\Sigma (AB)^2}{n} - [A] - [B] + [T]$	$(a - 1)(b - 1)$	$\dfrac{SS_{A \times B}}{df_{A \times B}}$	$\dfrac{MS_{A \times B}}{MS_{S/AB}}$
Within (S/AB)	$\Sigma Y^2 - [AB]$	$(a)(b)(n - 1)$	$\dfrac{SS_{S/AB}}{df_{S/AB}}$	
Total	$[Y] - [T]$	$(a)(b)(n) - 1$		

[a]Bracketed letters represent complete terms in the computational formulas; a particular term is identified by the letter(s) appearing in the numerator.

Degrees of Freedom

The *df* for any source of variance must satisfy the statement given in Eq. (3–2):

> The *df* equal the number of different observations on which each sum of squares is based minus the number of constraints operating on these observations.

For the two main effects, the observations involved are the marginal sums (or means) for the rows and columns. For the SS_A, the number of such observations is a; since the column marginal totals (the A sums) must sum to the grand sum T, there is one constraint. Thus,

$$df_A = a - 1$$

This constraint is symbolized in Table 10–5 by an X placed in the margin at a_4. (This level was picked arbitrarily; any of the a levels would do.) For the SS_B, the number of observations is b; since the marginal row totals (the B sums) must also sum to T, one constraint is placed on the independence of these observations. Thus,

$$df_B = b - 1$$

This constraint is symbolized by an X placed in the margin at b_3.

The *df* for the $SS_{A \times B}$ are obtained from Eq. (10–3):

$$df_{A \times B} = (a - 1)(b - 1)$$

the product of the *df* associated with the two main effects. You can understand this formula by considering the cells within the AB matrix in Table 10–5. The question basically is how many of the AB sums are free to vary once certain restrictions of the matrix are met. You have already seen that the marginal sums for the columns and rows must satisfy the requirement that

$$\Sigma A = T \text{ and } \Sigma B = T$$

What about the AB sums within the body of the matrix? For any one of the columns, the sum of the cell totals must equal the corresponding marginal total. This places one restriction on each of the columns; these restrictions are represented by X's in the row at level b_3. (This row was again picked arbitrarily.) A similar restriction is placed on the rows: The sum of the cell totals in any one of the rows must equal the corresponding marginal totals. These restrictions are indicated by X's in

Table 10–5   Representation of *df* Associated with the SS_A, SS_B, and $SS_{A \times B}$

	FACTOR A				
FACTOR B	a_1	a_2	a_3	a_4	Sum
b_1				X	B_1
b_2				X	B_2
b_3	X	X	X	X	X
Sum	A_1	A_2	A_3	X	T

the column at level a_4. The unmarked cells, then, represent the df for the $A \times B$ interaction. This rectangle is bounded on one side by $a - 1$ columns and on the other side by $b - 1$ rows, and the total of "free" cells without X's is the quantity $(a - 1)(b - 1)$.

The df for the within-groups sum of squares $SS_{S/AB}$ follow the same general rule for the determination of the number of df. Since this sum of squares consists of a within-group sum of squares that is pooled over the $(a)(b)$ groups, we can start by finding the df for each individual cell in the matrix:

$$SS_{S/AB_{ij}} = n - 1$$

One df is lost because of the restriction that the n different Y scores must sum to the cell total AB_{ij}. Now, if we sum the df's over the $(a)(b)$ cells, we obtain

$$df_{S/AB} = \Sigma df_{S/AB_{ij}} = (a)(b)(n - 1)$$

Mean Squares and F Ratios

The mean squares are found by dividing each sum of squares by its corresponding df:

$$MS = \frac{SS}{df}$$

These are enumerated in the fourth column of Table 10–4. The F ratios are formed in each case by dividing the mean squares by the $MS_{S/AB}$:

$$F_A = \frac{MS_A}{MS_{S/AB}}$$

$$F_B = \frac{MS_B}{MS_{S/AB}}$$

$$F_{A \times B} = \frac{MS_{A \times B}}{MS_{S/AB}}$$

These F ratios are evaluated in the F table under the appropriate numerator and denominator df's. The logic behind the construction of these ratios is the same as that offered in the single-factor case. We will review this argument in Sec. 10.5.

Orthogonality of the Two-Way Analysis

It is possible to show that the SS_A, SS_B, and $SS_{A \times B}$ are mutually orthogonal—that is, that they provide independent information about the outcome of the experiment.[2] The three sources of variance extracted in the analysis I have been discussing represent an efficient way of dividing up the df associated with the total

[2]See Keppel (1982, pp. 625–628) for a proof of this statement.

between-groups sum of squares. It would certainly be possible to divide this sum of squares into a different set of orthogonal comparisons. Nevertheless, investigators present most factorial experiments in a way that makes obvious their intention to extract and to evaluate the sources of variance listed in Table 10–4. In actuality, then, we can think of the analysis of a two-way factorial experiment as consisting of a set of *planned orthogonal comparisons*. But we are not restricted to these comparisons alone. Often we will want to isolate the locus of a significant main effect or of an interaction. Procedures for accomplishing these comparisons will be discussed in Chaps. 11 and 12.

10.4   A NUMERICAL EXAMPLE

We are now ready for a numerical example showing all the steps required for the analysis of a two-way factorial experiment. The example consists of a hypothetical investigation of the role of drive level and certain drugs on the learning performance of monkeys. The animals are given a series of 20 "oddity" problems. In this task, three objects (two the same, one different) are presented to the monkeys, and the subject's task is to learn to select the nonduplicated, or "odd," object. A food reward is placed in a well underneath the correct object. A trial consists of the presentation of the three objects and the monkey's selection of one of them. The response measure (Y) is the number of errors in the 20 training trials. One of the independent variables (factor A) consists of a control and two drug conditions, and the other variable (factor B) is the drive level of the animals, either 1 hour of food deprivation or 24 hours of food deprivation. Four monkeys are randomly assigned to each treatment combination. Thus, the design is a 3 × 2 factorial with a cell sample size of $n = 4$. The error scores for the individual animals appear in Table 10–6.

Table 10–6   Numerical Example: Preliminary Analysis

	Control, 1 hr.	Drug X, 1 hr.	Drug Y, 1 hr.	Control, 24 hr.	Drug X, 24 hr.	Drug Y, 24 hr.
	a_1b_1	a_2b_1	a_3b_1	a_1b_2	a_2b_2	a_3b_2
	1	13	9	15	6	14
	4	5	16	6	18	7
	0	7	18	10	9	6
	7	15	13	13	15	13
AB_{ij}:	12	40	56	44	48	40
ΣY^2:	66	468	830	530	666	450
$\overline{Y}_{A_iB_j}$	3.00	10.00	14.00	11.00	12.00	10.00
s_{ij}:	3.16	4.76	3.92	3.92	5.48	4.08

Preliminary Analysis

The first step in any analysis is to perform some initial calculations on the Y scores to facilitate the later calculations and to provide a first glimpse at the results. For each treatment combination, we obtain the sum of the scores and the sum of the squared scores. For the group at $a_1 b_1$,

$$AB_{1,1} = \Sigma Y_{1,1,k} = 1 + 4 + 0 + 7 = 12$$

$$\Sigma Y^2_{1,1,k} = (1)^2 + (4)^2 + (0)^2 + (7)^2 = 66$$

From these sums, we can calculate the treatment means $\overline{Y}_{A_{ij}}$ and the standard deviation s_{ij}. For the same group,

$$\overline{Y}_{A_1 B_1} = \frac{AB_{1,1}}{n} = \frac{12}{4} = 3.00$$

$$s_{1,1} = \sqrt{\frac{\Sigma(Y_{1,1,k} - \overline{Y}_{A_1 B_1})^2}{n - 1}}$$

$$= \sqrt{\frac{(1 - 3)^2 + (4 - 3)^2 + (0 - 3)^3 + (7 - 3)^2}{4 - 1}}$$

$$= \sqrt{\frac{30}{3}} = 3.16$$

Rather than using deviations, we can calculate the standard deviation with a computational formula based on the Y scores and the group sum AB:

$$s_{1,1} = \sqrt{\frac{\Sigma Y^2_{1,1,k} - (AB_{1,1})^2 / n}{n - 1}}$$

$$= \sqrt{\frac{66 - (12)^2 / 4}{4 - 1}}$$

$$= \sqrt{\frac{66 - 36}{3}} = \sqrt{\frac{30}{3}} = 3.16$$

The means and standard deviations for all of the treatment groups are presented in the last two rows of Table 10–6.

It is usually a good idea to plot the treatment means so that you can see more readily whether an interaction is present. This has been done in Fig. 10–1. The figure shows an interaction of the two independent variables. It appears that the manipulation of drugs (factor A) had little effect on errors committed by the hungry monkeys and had a marked effect on errors with the less hungry monkeys. More specifically, hungry animals are not affected by the two drugs, whereas less hungry animals are. Now that we have a "feel" for the way the experiment came out (and what the analysis should reveal), we can proceed with the calculations.

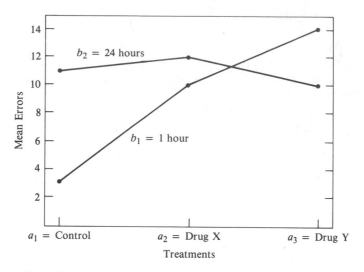

Figure 10–1   Plot of the data presented in Table 10–6.

Analysis of Variance

The first step is to arrange the AB sums from Table 10–6 in an AB matrix to facilitate the calculations of the different sums of squares. This has been done in Table 10–7. To avoid time-consuming errors, it is a good idea to verify that the sum of the row marginal totals equals the sum of the column marginal totals. Next, we substitute the information available in the AB and the Y data matrices into the computational formulas for the sums of squares given in Table 10–4. We perform these operations in two steps: (1) the calculation of the basic ratios and (2) the addition and subtraction of these terms in the actual determination of the various sums of squares. We will now solve for these basic quantities and identify each by means of the letter code. Working first with the AB matrix, we obtain

$$[T] = \frac{T^2}{(a)(b)(n)} = \frac{(240)^2}{(3)(2)(4)} = \frac{57,600}{24} = 2,400.00$$

$$[A] = \frac{\Sigma A^2}{(b)(n)} = \frac{(56)^2 + (88)^2 + (96)^2}{(2)(4)} = \frac{20,096}{8} = 2,512.00$$

$$[B] = \frac{\Sigma B^2}{(a)(n)} = \frac{(108)^2 + (132)^2}{(3)(4)} = \frac{29,088}{12} = 2,424.00$$

Table 10–7   *AB* Matrix

| DRIVE (FACTOR B) | TREATMENTS (FACTOR A) | | | |
	Control (a_1)	Drug X (a_2)	Drug Y (a_3)	Sum
1 hr. (b_1)	12	40	56	108
24 hr. (b_2)	44	48	40	132
Sum	56	88	96	240

$$[AB] = \frac{\Sigma(AB)^2}{n} = \frac{(12)^2 + (44)^2 + \ldots + (56)^2 + (40)^2}{4}$$

$$= \frac{10,720}{4} = 2,680.00$$

The final calculation requires the subtotals presented in the data matrix:

$$[Y] = \Sigma Y^2 = 66 + 468 + 830 + 530 + 666 + 450 = 3,010$$

We can now obtain the sums of squares by combining the quantities we have just calculated in the patterns specified in Table 10–4:

$$SS_A = [A] - [T] = 2,512.00 - 2,400.00 = 112.00$$

$$SS_B = [B] - [T] = 2,424.00 - 2,400.00 = 24.00$$

$$SS_{A \times B} = [AB] - [A] - [B] + [T]$$

$$= 2,680.00 - 2,512.00 - 2,424.00 + 2,400.00 = 144.00$$

$$SS_{S/AB} = [Y] - [AB] = 3,010 - 2,680.00 = 330.00$$

$$SS_T = [Y] - [T] = 3,010 - 2,400.00 = 610.00$$

These sums of squares have been entered in Table 10–8 as an example of a standard summary table for an analysis of variance. We should check for computational errors in our calculations by summing the component sums of squares to verify that the total equals the SS_T.

The numerical values of the degrees of freedom are found by simple substitution in the formulas appearing in Table 10–4:

$$df_A = a - 1 = 3 - 1 = 2$$
$$df_B = b - 1 = 2 - 1 = 1$$

$$df_{A \times B} = (a - 1)(b - 1) = (3 - 1)(2 - 1) = 2$$

$$df_{S/AB} = (a)(b)(n - 1) = (3)(2)(4 - 1) = 18$$

$$df_T = (a)(b)(n) - 1 = (3)(2)(4) - 1 = 24 - 1 = 23$$

Table 10–8   Summary of the Analysis

Source	SS	df	MS	F
A	112.00	2	56.00	3.06
B	24.00	1	24.00	1.31
$A \times B$	144.00	2	72.00	3.93*
S/AB	330.00	18	18.33	
Total	610.00	23		

*$p < .05$.

As a check, we should verify that the sum of the component degrees of freedom equals df_T.

The mean squares are obtained by dividing each sum of squares by the appropriate df. Finally, each mean square reflecting in part the contribution of a different component of interest is tested against the mean square representing error variance—that is, the within-groups mean square $MS_{S/AB}$.[3] The obtained F ratios are compared with the critical values of F in Table A–1. In this example, only the interaction source of variance reaches an acceptable level of significance.

10.5   THE STATISTICAL MODEL

As with the single-factor design, the statistical analyses we have just covered are based on a particular statistical model. We will consider this model first and then the consequences of violating the assumptions associated with it.

The Linear Model

The linear model underlying the present analysis begins with a statement of the components contributing to any score in the experiment (Y_{ijk}):

$$Y_{ijk} = \mu_T + \alpha_i + \beta_j + (\alpha\beta)_{ij} + \epsilon_{ijk}$$

where μ_T = the overall mean of the population
   α_i = the average treatment effect at level a_i ($\alpha_i = \mu_i - \mu_T$)
   β_j = the average treatment effect at level b_j ($\beta_j = \mu_j - \mu_T$)
   $(\alpha\beta)_{ij}$ = the interaction effect at cell $a_i b_j$ ($(\alpha\beta)_{ij} = \mu_{ij} - \mu_i - \mu_j + \mu_T$)
   ϵ_{ijk} = experimental error associated with each score ($\epsilon_{ijk} = Y_{ijk} - \mu_{ij}$)

The statistical hypotheses for the main effects and the interaction can be stated in terms of these parameters.

$$A \text{ main effect: } H_0\text{: All } \alpha_i = 0$$
$$H_1\text{: Not all } \alpha_i = 0$$

$$B \text{ main effect: } H_0\text{: All } \beta_j = 0$$
$$H_1\text{: Not all } \beta_j = 0$$

$$A \times B \text{ interaction: } H_0\text{: All } (\alpha\beta)_{ij} = 0$$
$$H_1\text{: Not all } (\alpha\beta)_{ij} = 0$$

---

[3] The $MS_{S/AB}$ is literally an average of the separate group variances. To illustrate, we can use the standard deviations in Table 10–6 to calculate $MS_{S/AB}$:

$$MS_{S/AB} = \frac{\Sigma s_{ij}^2}{(a)(b)} = \frac{(3.16)^2 + (4.76)^2 + (3.92)^2 + (3.92)^2 + (5.48)^2 + (4.08)^2}{(3)(2)}$$

$$= \frac{110.05}{6} = 18.34$$

which is identical to the value in Table 10–8 except for rounding error.

The expected values of the mean squares that we calculate in the analysis of variance, $E(MS)$, refer to the factors contributing to the average value of each mean square obtained with repeated samplings from a given set of populations. For the present design,

$$E(MS_A) = \sigma^2_{error} + (b)(n)(\theta^2_A)$$

$$E(MS_B) = \sigma^2_{error} + (a)(n)(\theta^2_B)$$

$$E(MS_{A \times B}) = \sigma^2_{error} + (n)(\theta^2_{A \times B})$$

In the fixed-effects model, which is the model treated here and which is appropriate for most research applications, the three values of θ^2 are defined as follows:[4]

$$\theta^2_A = \frac{\Sigma \alpha^2_i}{a - 1}$$

$$\theta^2_B = \frac{\Sigma \beta^2_j}{b - 1}$$

$$\theta^2_{A \times B} = \frac{\Sigma (\alpha\beta^2_{ij})}{(a - 1)(b - 1)}$$

To round the picture

$$E(MS_{S/AB}) = \sigma^2_{error}$$

The essential logic behind the analysis of variance lies in the construction of ratios that have the form

$$\frac{MS_{effect}}{MS_{error}}$$

where the expected value of MS_{error} matches the expected value of the MS_{effect} in all respects except for the variance component reflecting the effect. Symbolically,

$$E(MS_{effect}) = error + effect$$

$$E(MS_{error}) = error$$

Under the null hypothesis, the variance component reflecting the effect will be zero, the null-hypothesis component ("effect") drops out, and

$$E(MS_{effect}) = E(MS_{error})$$

Under these circumstances, then, the ratio

$$\frac{MS_{effect}}{MS_{error}}$$

---

[4]The fixed-effects statistical model is discussed in Chap. 22.

will be distributed as $F(df_{effect}, df_{error})$, provided the usual assumptions of normality, homogeneity of variance, and independence are satisfied (see pp. 96–99). (We will consider the issue of violating these assumptions in a moment.) We can then relate the observed ratio to the tabled values of F and assess its significance by applying the usual decision rules.

For this design, I have already noted that

$$E(MS_{S/AB}) = \sigma^2_{error}$$

Consequently, this mean square is the appropriate error term for all three mean squares reflecting factorial effects—because in each case, when H_0 is true, the null-hypothesis component drops out and we are dividing one estimate of error variance by another, independent estimate of error variance.

Violating the Assumptions

Although not investigated in as much detail, the consequences of violating the assumptions underlying the analysis of the completely randomized, two-factor design are generally the same as those discussed for the single-factor design in Chap. 5. The independence assumption is fundamental to the analysis and is usually guaranteed by randomly assigning subjects to the treatment conditions and testing subjects individually. Of the two assumptions concerning the distribution of scores within the treatment populations—normality and variance homogeneity—the latter has been more widely studied and the consequences of violating the assumption presumably are more important.

We can test for heterogeneity of the within-group variances with the Brown-Forsythe (1974b) test, which is based on the deviations of the Y scores from the median of the relevant treatment group. We can adapt the test to the factorial simply by treating the $(a)(b)$ treatment groups as coming from a single-factor design and proceeding with the test as described in Chap. 5 (see pp. 102–104). In evaluating the homogeneity assumption, we should probably set $\alpha = .10$ (or higher) to increase the power of the test. A significant F indicates that the critical values of F in Table A–1 are not correct and that our actual significance level may be several percentage points higher than our nominal significance level of $\alpha = .05$. Instead of conducting the Brown-Forsythe test, we can calculate $F_{max.}$, which consists of the largest within-group variance divided by the smallest within-group variance. We would become concerned if $F_{max.}$ is appreciably greater than 3, which is roughly the point beyond which heterogeneity of variance begins to inflate the actual α level beyond acceptable limits. Using the data from Table 10–6, we find

$$F_{max.} = \frac{s^2_{largest}}{s^2_{smallest}} = \frac{(5.48)^2}{(3.16)^2} = \frac{30.03}{9.99} = 3.01$$

indicating that the data are approaching the point beyond which we should become concerned about heterogeneity.

What if $F_{max.}$ is greater than 3? As indicated in Chap. 5, variance heterogeneity leads to an increase in type I error (see Table 5–2, p. 107). We can "correct" for this inflation simply by lowering our significance level from $\alpha = .05$ to $\alpha = .025$, which should restore our actual significance level to $\alpha = .05$. I recommend this particular strategy until we know more about the effects of variance heterogeneity in the factorial design.

10.6 ESTIMATING POPULATION TREATMENT MEANS

Confidence-bounded intervals can be constructed for the population treatment means μ_{ij} and the population means defining main effects (μ_i = the average of the μ_{ij}'s at a particular level of factor A; μ_j = the average of the μ_{ij}'s at a particular level of factor B). A general formula specifying the upper and lower limits of confidence intervals is

$$\text{(population estimate)} \pm t(\hat{\sigma}_M) \tag{10-4}$$

where the population estimate = the appropriate observed mean
$$(\overline{Y}_{AB}, \overline{Y}_A, \text{ or } \overline{Y}_B)$$
t = a value obtained from Table A–3 (at $df = df_{S/AB}$ and the chosen level of α)
$\hat{\sigma}_M$ = the estimate of the appropriate standard error of the mean

A general formula for this last quantity is as follows:

$$\hat{\sigma}_M = \sqrt{\frac{MS_{S/AB}}{\text{(number of observations)}}} \tag{10-5}$$

where $MS_{S/AB}$ is the error term from the factorial analysis and the number of observations refers to the number of scores contributing to the mean upon which the population estimate is based—n for $\overline{Y}_{AB}$, $(b)(n)$ for $\overline{Y}_A$, and $(a)(n)$ for $\overline{Y}_B$. (See problem 1 in the exercises for an illustration of these calculations.)

10.7 ESTIMATING TREATMENT MAGNITUDE (OMEGA SQUARED)

In addition to the statistical evaluation of the main effects and interaction, we should also calculate and report estimates of their magnitude. (I discussed the usefulness of such measures in Sec. 4.1.) The measure favored by experimenters is estimated omega squared ($\hat{\omega}^2$). When applied to the single-factor design, this measure may be defined as

$$\hat{\omega}_A^2 = \frac{\hat{\sigma}_A^2}{\hat{\sigma}_A^2 + \hat{\sigma}_{S/A}^2} \tag{10-6}$$

where $\hat{\sigma}_A^2$ is an estimate of the variance among the population treatment means and $\hat{\sigma}_{S/A}^2$ is an estimate of the variability within the treatment populations. Although the computational formulas I provided in Chap. 4 were written in terms of sums of squares, mean squares, and F, their meaning reduces to Eq. (10–6).

Standard Omega Squared

Two ways of defining estimated omega squared have been proposed for the factorial design. One definition relates the variance estimate of the treatment effect to a variance estimate of *all sources* in an experiment. I will refer to this estimate of relative treatment magnitude as the **standard omega squared**. The standard estimated omega squared for the main effect of factor A, for example, is given by

$$\hat{\omega}_A^2 = \frac{\hat{\sigma}_A^2}{\hat{\sigma}_T^2} \qquad (10\text{–}7)$$

where $\hat{\sigma}_T^2$ in this case is the sum of the estimated variance components for all sources normally extracted in the analysis:

$$\hat{\sigma}_T^2 = \hat{\sigma}_A^2 + \hat{\sigma}_B^2 + \hat{\sigma}_{A \times B}^2 + \hat{\sigma}_{S/AB}^2$$

A general formula for estimating the standard omega squared for the three factorial treatment effects is

$$\hat{\omega}_{effect}^2 = \frac{\hat{\sigma}_{effect}^2}{\hat{\sigma}_T^2} \qquad (10\text{–}8)$$

Formulas for estimating the different variance components are presented in column 1 of Table 10–9. Since $\hat{\sigma}_T^2$ includes all the variance components, we will need to calculate each one to estimate standard omega squared for any of the three treatment effects. This step has been accomplished in column 2 of the table, using the data from Table 10–8. Substituting Eq. (10–8) to estimate $\hat{\omega}_{A \times B}^2$, for example, we have

$$\hat{\omega}_{A \times B}^2 = \frac{\hat{\sigma}_{A \times B}}{\hat{\sigma}_T^2}$$

Table 10–9   Formulas for Estimating Variance Components

Variance Component	(1) Formula	(2) Calculations
$\hat{\sigma}_A^2$	$\dfrac{df_A\,(MS_A - MS_{S/AB})}{(a)(b)(n)}$	$\dfrac{(2)(56.00 - 18.33)}{(3)(2)(4)} = 3.14$
$\hat{\sigma}_B^2$	$\dfrac{df_B\,(MS_B - MS_{S/AB})}{(a)(b)(n)}$	$\dfrac{(1)(24.00 - 18.33)}{(3)(2)(4)} = .24$
$\hat{\sigma}_{A \times B}^2$	$\dfrac{df_{A \times B}\,(MS_{A \times B} - MS_{S/AB})}{(a)(b)(n)}$	$\dfrac{(2)(72.00 - 18.33)}{(3)(2)(4)} = 4.47$
$\hat{\sigma}_{S/AB}^2$	$MS_{S/AB}$	18.33

$$= \frac{4.47}{3.14 + .24 + 4.47 + 18.33} = \frac{4.47}{26.18} = .171$$

In this example, the interaction accounts for 17.1 percent of the total variance.[5]

Partial Omega Squared

A serious objection has been raised concerning the appropriateness of this general approach (see Cohen, 1973; Keppel, 1973, p. 553). As I have indicated, this definition relates the estimate of the population treatment component to the sum of all the components specified under the model. Thus, a particular estimated omega squared, say $\hat{\omega}_A^2$, will be defined differently for each type of experimental design. For instance,

$$\hat{\omega}_A^2 = \frac{\hat{\sigma}_A^2}{\hat{\sigma}_A^2 + \hat{\sigma}_{S/A}^2}$$

for the single-factor design, and

$$\hat{\omega}_A^2 = \frac{\hat{\sigma}_A^2}{\hat{\sigma}_A^2 + \hat{\sigma}_B^2 + \hat{\sigma}_{A \times B}^2 + \hat{\sigma}_{S/AB}^2}$$

for the two-factor design. Depending on the nature of the design, therefore, the same manipulation (factor A) will result in different estimated omega squares, even when the variance component estimated for that manipulation is identical in these designs.

A reasonable solution to this problem, which I recommend for most experimental situations, consists of using a different definition for estimating omega squared, one that relates the treatment component to the sum of only *two* components, the treatment component and the error component. In symbols,

$$\hat{\omega}_{effect}^2 = \frac{\hat{\sigma}_{effect}^2}{\hat{\sigma}_{effect}^2 + \hat{\sigma}_{error}^2} \tag{10–9}$$

This revised definition has been called **partial omega squared** (see Keren & Lewis, 1979).[6] Adapting Eq. (10–9) to estimate $\hat{\omega}_{A \times B}^2$, for example, we have

$$\hat{\omega}_{A \times B}^2 = \frac{\hat{\sigma}_{A \times B}^2}{\hat{\sigma}_{A \times B}^2 + \hat{\sigma}_{S/AB}^2}$$

$$= \frac{4.47}{4.47 + 18.33} = \frac{4.47}{22.80} = .196$$

The value we obtained with Eq. (10–8) was .171. Because the denominator for

---

[5]Occasionally you will want to estimate relative treatment magnitude from a published research report, which usually will not include the information required by the computational formulas in Table 10–9. Fortunately, we can obtain these estimates by using formulas developed by Charter (1982), which involve information that is generally available in most research reports.

[6]The term *partial* comes from correlational statistics and emphasizes the fact that the formula estimates treatment magnitude in such a way that the estimate is not affected by other effects in the design.

partial omega squared is necessarily smaller than the one for Eq. (10–8), the partial omega squared will be larger.

Comparing the Sizes of Omega Squared

Researchers are frequently interested in comparing the sizes of estimated omega squared within the same factorial experiment. In these cases, they might ask if the main effect for factor A is larger than the main effect for factor B or for the interaction. Although it is tempting to compare these $\hat{\omega}^2_{effect}$'s directly, any conclusion about differences must be based on appropriate statistical tests. It is not sufficient to conclude that the estimates of omega squared for two sources are different when one source is significant and the other is not (Rosenthal & Rubin, 1982). Ronis (1981) introduced a statistical procedure for comparing treatment magnitudes, but it can be applied only to designs in which all factors consist of only two levels. Fowler (1987) provides a more general method, which corrects this limitation, but it does so with a procedure that most researchers will find difficult to apply.

Even if we were able to compare two estimates of treatment magnitude statistically, however, we still must take care in how we interpret any significant difference we may find. As Ronis (1981) puts it, ''to draw clear conclusions about the relative impact of two independent variables, we must have some assurance that the manipulations of the two variables are of comparable magnitudes'' (p. 998). Applying this caution to our numerical example, we could ask how meaningful a comparison is between the treatment magnitudes of a main effect based on different drugs (factor A) and one based on two levels of food deprivation (factor B). Ronis discusses several ways in which a researcher might select comparable manipulations for the two independent variables, but these are often difficult to achieve in practice.

In short, as tempting as such comparisons may be, we should keep in mind that comparisons of treatment magnitude within an experiment must be coupled with an appropriate statistical test and that they will be difficult to interpret unambiguously unless we can show that the two independent variables represent comparable manipulations.

10.8   DETERMINING SAMPLE SIZE

We considered power and design sensitivity in Chap. 4, where you were shown how we can use power determinations to choose an adequate sample size. (See pp. 76–80 for a review of these procedures.) We can use power estimates to serve the same important function in factorial designs as well.[7]

Using Population Deviations

To estimate sample size, we have to specify the nature of the population treatment effects we are interested in detecting and to guess at the magnitude of the error

---

[7]An extension of power estimates to factorial designs is given comprehensive treatment by Cohen (1977, Chap. 8; see especially pp. 376–379 and 400–403 for application to the two-factor design).

variance we expect to find in the experiment. These and other values, including a trial sample size (n'), are entered in a formula that provides a value for ϕ^2_{effect}; we then refer the square root of this value, ϕ_{effect}, to appropriate power charts to estimate the power associated under these circumstances. If the power is inadequate, a new trial sample size is used to calculate ϕ^2_{effect} again and to determine the level of power achieved by this increase in sample size. We repeat this trial-and-error procedure until we achieve the level of power we want.

A general formula for ϕ^2_{effect} is given by

$$\phi^2_{effect} = \frac{(\text{no. obsn})[\Sigma (\text{dev.})^2]}{(df_{effect} + 1)(\sigma^2_{error})} \tag{10-10}$$

where (no. obsn) = the number of observations that will contribute to each basic deviation

$\Sigma (\text{dev.})^2$ = the basic population deviations constituting the treatment effects in question

df_{effect} = the df associated with the treatment effects, calculated in the usual fashion

σ^2_{error} = the population error variance

Table 10–10 illustrates how Eq. (10–10) is adapted for the $A \times B$ factorial design. The basic deviations for each factorial effect are listed in column 1 of the table. These deviations come from the formal statement of the structural model (see Sec. 10.5). The numbers of observations on which estimates of these deviations would be based in an actual experiment appear in column 2. For the main effect of factor A, $(b)(n')$ observations are available to estimate the deviation for any given mean; for the main effect of factor B, $(a)(n')$ are available; and for the interaction, n' observations are available. (You will recall that n' represents the trial sample size we systematically adjust when using the power charts to estimate the sample size required to achieve certain power with a new experiment.) The formulas for ϕ^2_{effect}, which result from substituting relevant values into Eq. (10–10), are presented in column 3 of the table.

Consider these three formulas. In determining the sample size to be used in

Table 10–10 Formulas for ϕ^2_{effect} in the $A \times B$ Design

Source	(1) Deviation	(2) Number of Observations	(3) ϕ^2_{effect}
A	$\alpha_i = \mu_i - \mu_T$	$(b)(n')$	$\dfrac{(b)(n')[\Sigma (\alpha_i)^2]}{(a)(\sigma^2_{S/AB})}$
B	$\beta_j = \mu_j - \mu_T$	$(a)(n')$	$\dfrac{(a)(n')[\Sigma (\beta_j)^2]}{(b)(\sigma^2_{S/AB})}$
$A \times B$	$(\alpha\beta)_{ij} = \mu_{ij} - \mu_i - \mu_j + \mu_T$	n'	$\dfrac{n'[\Sigma (\alpha\beta_{ij})^2]}{[(a-1)(b-1) + 1](\sigma^2_{S/AB})}$

any given experiment, we will vary n' since the levels of factors A and B (a and b, respectively) are determined by the nature of the experimental questions we want to ask and thus are presumably fixed at this stage of the planning. If we are interested in achieving a certain power for all three factorial effects, the final sample size will be determined by the *largest* estimate of n'. Generally, the largest estimate will come from the interaction because power is in part a function of the actual number of observations contributing to the different means; due to the nature of the factorial design, fewer observations contribute to the cell means (that is, interaction) than to either set of marginal means (that is, the main effects). Thus, if we are interested primarily in interaction, which often will be the case with a factorial design, we only need to work with the corresponding relevant formula in estimating sample size.

An Example. Let's consider an example based on an actual experiment.[8] A researcher was interested in the possibility that a certain drug administered after learning would enhance memory for the task 24 hours later. On Day 1, laboratory rats were placed in an apparatus, in which they were administered an electric shock if they failed to enter a distinctive adjoining chamber within 30 seconds; each rat was given 2 chances to avoid the shock. Immediately following training, one group was administered a drug (the experimental condition) and another some inert substance (the control condition). On Day 2, all animals were tested 8 more times in the avoidance apparatus; the dependent variable consisted of the number of times each animal avoided the shock over the 8 trials. After successfully replicating the facilitating property of the drug in a number of related experiments, the researcher planned a more elaborate series of experiments designed to pinpoint the locus of the effect of the drug in the brain. This would be accomplished by introducing a second independent variable (operation) in which animals either had a particular area of the brain removed surgically or were given a control or sham operation. The basic design is a factorial in which factor A consists of two levels (control and drug) and factor B consists of two levels (sham and actual operation).

The earlier research provided the experimenter with stable estimates of the sorts of drug effects he could expect in this experimental setting and of error variance. He predicted the following idealized outcome:

	No Drug (a_1)	Drug (a_2)	Mean
Sham operation (b_1)	4.2	5.8	5.0
Actual operation (b_2)	3.0	3.0	3.0
Mean	3.6	4.4	4.0

His estimate of error variance was $\sigma^2_{S/AB} = 2.5$. As you can see from the predicted means, the researcher expected to obtain the usual enhancement of performance

[8]I wish to thank Dr. Joe Martinez and Patricia Janak for providing me with this illustration.

by the drug for the animals receiving the sham operation (4.2 versus 5.8   avoidances) and to eliminate the effect completely for the animals receiving the actual operation (3.0 versus 3.0)—an interaction; he also expected a depression in performance for both groups of animals receiving the operation—a main effect.

We begin by calculating the deviations representing the interaction effect. Using the cell and marginal means from the factorial matrix, we find

$$(\alpha\beta)_{1,1} = \mu_{A_1B_1} - \mu_{A_1} - \mu_{B_1} + \mu_T = 4.2 - 3.6 - 5.0 + 4.0 = -.4$$
$$(\alpha\beta)_{2,1} = \mu_{A_2B_1} - \mu_{A_2} - \mu_{B_1} + \mu_T = 5.8 - 4.4 - 5.0 + 4.0 = .4$$
$$(\alpha\beta)_{1,2} = \mu_{A_1B_2} - \mu_{A_1} - \mu_{B_2} + \mu_T = 3.0 - 3.6 - 3.0 + 4.0 = .4$$
$$(\alpha\beta)_{2,2} = \mu_{A_2B_2} - \mu_{A_2} - \mu_{B_2} + \mu_T = 3.0 - 4.4 - 3.0 + 4.0 = -.4$$

Next, we sum the squared deviations:

$$\Sigma(\alpha\beta_{ij})^2 = (-.4)^2 + (.4)^2 + (.4)^2 + (-.4)^2 = .64$$

Substituting in the formula for $\phi^2_{A \times B}$ in Table 10–10, we have

$$\phi^2_{A \times B} - \frac{n'(.64)}{[(2-1)(2-1)+1](2.5)} = \frac{n'(.64)}{2(2.5)} = .128\,n' \qquad (10\text{–}11)$$

To use the power charts, we need the square root of ϕ^2:

$$\phi_{A \times B} = \sqrt{.128}\,n' = .358\,\sqrt{n'}$$

We are now in a position to use the Pearson-Hartley power charts in Table A–2. Since the $df_{num.} = 1$, we will use the first power chart. We now begin the process of trying different sample sizes until we find one that produces reasonable power (.80). Suppose we try $n' = 31$ as our trial sample size.[9] Then,

$$\phi_{A \times B} = .358\sqrt{31} = (.358)(5.57) = 1.99$$

This calculation establishes a location on the baseline of the power chart ($\alpha = .05$) of $\phi = 1.99$. We now need to determine which power function is appropriate:

$$df_{denom.} = (a)(b)(n-1) = (2)(2)(31-1) = 120$$

Using the curve for $df_{denom.} = \infty$, we find power to be slightly greater than our targeted value of .80. It appears, therefore, that a sample size of about $n = 30$, to pick a round number, will provide reasonable power to detect this interaction effect. If the resulting power were appreciably lower (or higher) than .80, we would have to raise (or lower) the trial sample size and assess the consequences of this change. We would continue this process until the desired level of power was achieved.

---

[9]A strategy for selecting the initial trial sample size was introduced in Chap. 4 (p. 79). Briefly, we begin with Eq. (10–11) and solve for n'; that is, $n' = \phi^2_{A \times B}/.128$. We now find the value for ϕ associated with power .80; using the curve at $df_{denom.} = 60$ from the first power chart, we find $\phi = 2.0$. Finally, we substitute this value in the equation we just obtained and solve for n'. This gives us $n' = (2.0)^2/.128 = 31.25$. I used $n' - 31$ as the trial sample size.

Determining Sample Size for an Exact Replication

Researchers often wish to repeat an experiment exactly but with a sample size that will assure significance when it is conducted a second time. The first experiment may have been a pilot study, or the results may have been unexpected but interesting and worthy of replication. Although it is usually not appropriate to base a power analysis on sample data, which reflect to some extent error variability, we can use a procedure that circumvents this problem by using the F ratios obtained in the original study.[10] (An F ratio, in which MS_{effect} is divided by MS_{error}, adjusts treatment effects for error variability.)

Let's assume that our interest centers primarily on the $A \times B$ interaction, which is a reasonable assumption given the nature of the design. In the specific case, in which an exact replication is being attempted, differing only in the number of subjects that are run, we can use the following formula to estimate the ϕ^2 for the interaction:

$$\phi^2_{A \times B} = \left\{\frac{n'}{n_{old}}\right\}\left\{\frac{(a-1)(b-1)}{(a-1)(b-1)+1}\right\}\left\{F_{A \times B} - 1\right\} \tag{10-12}$$

where n' is the trial sample size for the *new* experiment and n_{old} is the actual sample size for the original experiment. An example of this general procedure is given in problem 4 in the exercises.

Reemphasizing the Need to Control Power

Conducting a power analysis can be a sobering experience, particularly when you discover that you will need an unacceptably large sample size to obtain reasonable assurance (that is, power = .80) that you will be able to detect the differences you have hypothesized. On the other hand, what is the sense of conducting the experiment if the power is low? Low power means that you have a poor chance of detecting these differences when they are real, that is, actually present in the treatment populations. There are other ways to increase power, which we discussed in Chap. 4 (pp. 80–82). One of these, which deserves thoughtful consideration, is adopting a more flexible significance level ($\alpha = .10$, for example). An increase in the rejection region produces an increase in power.

Any relaxation of our protection against type I error will need to be defended, of course. The argument is greatly strengthened, in my opinion, when theory predicts certain specific outcomes. In the example we have been considering in this section, the researcher predicted a particular pattern of results. He was not interested in a significant interaction in general but one in which the drug effect is eliminated by the removal of specific brain tissue. Any other sort of interaction would work against his theory. I believe that explicit planned outcomes such as this one are ideal candidates for more flexible significance levels, but only when the significance level is selected in conjunction with a power analysis conducted during the planning stages of an experiment.

[10]I am indebted to Dr. Thomas D. Wickens, who called my attention to this procedure.

Behavioral scientists are generally not familiar with this quite sensible option. By ignoring power when we design experiments, we have no real choice except to focus on the control of type I error—we choose a reasonable and affordable sample size and set the significance level (usually α = .05). Power (and type II error) is virtually uncontrolled. Numerous reviews by methodologists (for example, Cohen, 1962; Sedlmeier & Gigerenzer, 1989) reveal that our experiments are substantially underpowered. On the other hand, this is exactly what can happen when we conduct experiments with no information about power. In contrast, choosing to set power in advance represents a responsible way of achieving a rational balance between type I and type II errors. If the results are not significant or if we fail to obtain the predicted pattern of results, we at least know what the risks were of committing a type II error. We are in a much stronger position to accept a negative outcome under these circumstances than if we made no attempt to control power.

10.9 EXERCISES[11]

1. A two-variable factorial experiment is designed in which factor A consists of a = 5 equally spaced levels of shock intensity and factor B consists of b 3 discrimination tasks of different difficulty (b_1 = easy, b_2 = medium, and b_3 = hard). There are n = 5 rats assigned to each of the $(a)(b)$ = (5)(3) = 15 treatment conditions. The animals are to learn to avoid the shock by solving the discrimination task within a 10-second period. The response measure consists of the number of learning trials needed to reach the criterion of an avoidance of the shock on three consecutive trials. The data are given in the following data matrix.

a_1 b_1	a_1 b_2	a_1 b_3	a_2 b_1	a_2 b_2	a_2 b_3	a_3 b_1	a_3 b_2	a_3 b_3	a_4 b_1	a_4 b_2	a_4 b_3	a_5 b_1	a_5 b_2	a_5 b_3
6	14	15	5	12	14	8	11	16	13	14	16	15	15	17
7	18	18	11	10	17	11	10	20	12	19	18	19	12	15
3	12	14	6	15	15	13	15	17	10	17	19	13	16	19
4	13	13	5	14	11	9	17	13	14	12	11	17	18	14
9	11	15	7	11	14	7	12	16	9	13	14	12	13	16

   a. Conduct an analysis of variance on these data. Reserve your calculations for problem 4 in the exercises for Chap. 11.
   b. Construct a 95 percent confidence interval based on the following means: one of the cell means ($\overline{Y}_{A_1B_1}$) and two of the marginal means, one contributing to the main effect of factor A ($\overline{Y}_{A_2}$) and the other to the main effect of factor B ($\overline{Y}_{B_3}$).
   c. Estimate standard omega squared for each of the factorial effects.
   d. Estimate partial omega squared for each of the factorial effects.
2. Consider the factorial design displayed in the following data matrix and the scores produced by the n = 3 subjects in each of the treatment conditions.

[11]The answers to these problems are found in Appendix B.

a_1	a_1	a_1	a_2	a_2	a_2	a_3	a_3	a_3
b_1	b_2	b_3	b_1	b_2	b_3	b_1	b_2	b_3
10	11	9	18	15	19	8	12	11
9	8	7	16	12	16	11	9	7
7	8	9	13	16	20	10	8	7

a. Conduct an analysis of variance on these data. Reserve your calculations for problem 2 in the exercises for Chap. 11.

b. Estimate standard and partial omega squared for each of the factorial effects.

3. To conserve space, most psychology journals do not publish analysis-of-variance summary tables, except when the analysis is complicated and there are many significant sources of variance. Thus, the most that we can expect to find is a table of means and a report of the obtained values of F. At times, however, we will wish that the researcher had extracted certain comparisons that are of particular interest to us. We can perform these analyses ourselves even though the researcher has not provided a detailed summary of the analysis. Suppose we had been given the following table of means:

	a_1	a_2	a_3
b_1	11	12	10
b_2	3	10	14

and we have been told that only the $A \times B$ interaction is significant, $F = 3.93, p <$ .05. Assuming that there are $n = 4$ subjects in each treatment condition, reconstruct the entire summary table, the SS's, the df's, and the F's.

4. The AB matrix of cell totals from a 3 × 2 factorial experiment with $n = 5$ subjects follows:

	a_1	a_2	a_3
b_1	11	30	36
b_2	22	15	30

a. Perform an analysis of variance. (Assume $MS_{S/AB} = 14.66$.)

b. Although none of the sources of variance is significant, you are still interested in interaction, particularly since it reflects the pattern of means predicted by your theory. Encouraged by these results, you plan to conduct an exact replication of the experiment. What sample size would you need to achieve a significant interaction, setting $\alpha = .05$ and power $= .80$?

11

Detailed Analyses
of Main Effects
and Simple Effects

Not only does the factorial design represent an efficient way of studying the separate and joint effects of two or more independent variables on behavior, but the design is also a rich source of analytical comparisons that can be used to pinpoint the specific treatment conditions responsible for a significant main effect or a significant interaction. A test for interaction usually represents a logical first step in the analysis of a two-factor experiment in the sense that the outcome of this test generally will influence the nature of the analyses that follow. That is, if the interaction is significant, less attention will be paid to the two main effects, and the analysis will tend to focus on a search for the specific conditions contributing to the significant interaction. On the other hand, if the interaction is not significant, attention is generally directed to the detailed analysis of the two main effects. Thus, the analysis of interaction concentrates on the individual *cell means* and the joint variation of the two independent variables, whereas the analysis of the main effects concentrates on the *marginal means* and the variation of each independent variable averaged over the levels of the other.

A significant interaction does not mean that we lose all interest in the main effects. The presence of interaction usually means that we must *qualify* any interpretation of the effects of one of the independent variables, by taking into consideration how they are influenced by the other independent variable. However, if a main effect is strong enough to show up in spite of the interaction, its presence must enter our theoretical interpretations, not be disregarded. Estimates of relative treatment magnitude are useful in these situations. A large main effect, relative to an interaction, indicates that we should consider both the main effect and interaction when we describe or interpret our data.

When we considered the analysis of the single-factor design, I discussed and illustrated the varieties of analytical comparisons we might choose to make either in lieu of the overall F test (that is, planned comparisons) or following a significant overall F. All the procedures we considered in these earlier chapters are applicable and easily adapted to factorial experiments. Since the basic ideas are the same, I will not pursue these procedures as deeply as I did in Chaps. 6 through 8. This chapter deals with the analysis of *individual* independent variables, either as main effects, when the other independent variable is *disregarded*, or as simple effects, when the other independent variable is *held constant*. In either case, the analyses are functionally identical to the analysis of a single-factor design, except that they are set within the context of the factorial, of course. As you will see, the computations are nearly the same. The analyses we will consider in Chap. 12, on the other hand, are unique to the factorial design and will require special techniques. We will begin this chapter with the analysis of main effects, in which the parallel with the single-factor experiments will be obvious.

11.1   COMPARING THE MARGINAL MEANS

The marginal means for any one variable are obtained by averaging over or, in essence, eliminating the classification of the other independent variable. We have two sets of marginal means, one for each of the two factors in the design. You can actually think of each set of means as coming from two single-factor designs. As you will see, the only change in the computational formulas is an adjustment for the number of observations contributing to each set of marginal means.

The significance of comparisons is evaluated with the error term from the overall analysis, namely, $MS_{S/AB}$. At first glance, you might have thought that an estimate more analogous to the single-factor analysis would be one based on subjects receiving the same level of factor A, level a_1 for example, forgetting about the B classification. Such a variance would not represent an estimate of "pure" error variance, however, since the subjects at level a_1 differ systematically with regard to factor B—some received a_1 in conjunction with b_1, some in conjunction with b_2, and so on. Only the error term from the two-factor analysis provides the sort of estimate we need, that is, one that reflects the true variability of subjects treated alike.

Computational Formulas

A general formula for calculating the sum of squares for a single-df comparison is given by

$$SS_{\hat{\psi}} = \frac{(\text{no. obsn. per mean})(\hat{\psi})^2}{\Sigma c^2} \tag{11–1}$$

where (no. obsn. per mean) = the number of observations contributing to
$\qquad\qquad\qquad\qquad\qquad$ the means involved in the comparison
$\qquad\qquad\qquad\quad \hat{\psi}$ = the comparison between two means;
$\qquad\qquad\qquad\quad \Sigma c^2$ = the sum of the squared coefficients
$\qquad\qquad\qquad\qquad\qquad$ reflecting the comparison

Adapted to a comparison involving the $\overline{Y}_{A_i}$ means, Eq. (11–1) becomes

$$SS_{A_{comp.}} = \frac{(b)(n)(\hat{\psi}_A)^2}{\Sigma c_i^2} \tag{11–2}$$

where $(b)(n)$ is the number of observations contributing to each mean and $\hat{\psi}_A$ represents the comparison between the $\overline{Y}_{A_i}$ means, which is expressed by

$$\hat{\psi}_A = \Sigma (c_i)(\overline{Y}_{Ai}) \tag{11–3}$$

It is not really necessary to present the formula in terms of the other factor as well since the identification of a particular factor as A or B is purely arbitrary. I will consider the corresponding formula in this initial discussion, however. If we are comparing the $\overline{Y}_{B_j}$ means, the number of observations is $(a)(n)$—n observations in each cell of the AB matrix and a levels of factor A over which the averaging takes place. The formula becomes

$$SS_{B_{comp.}} = \frac{(a)(n)(\hat{\psi}_B)^2}{\Sigma c_j^2} \tag{11–4}$$

In terms of the marginal means $\overline{Y}_{B_j}$

$$\hat{\psi}_B = \Sigma \, (c_j)(\overline{Y}_{B_j}) \tag{11-5}$$

After this point, the procedure is identical to that outlined for the single-factor case. The F ratios for comparisons of either type are

$$F_{A_{comp.}} = \frac{MS_{A_{comp.}}}{MS_{S/AB}}$$

$$F_{B_{comp.}} = \frac{MS_{B_{comp.}}}{MS_{S/AB}}$$

where the denominator is the estimate of error variability calculated for two-factor analysis of variance—that is, the pooled within-group variance.[1] The df for the numerator and denominator for both F ratios are $df_{num.} = 1$ and $df_{denom.} = df_{S/AB}$ $= (a)(b)(n - 1)$.

A Numerical Example

As an example, consider the data in Table 10–6 (p. 214) and suppose that we wanted to compare two means, $\overline{Y}_{A_1}$ and $\overline{Y}_{A_3}$ (control versus drug Y). For this comparison, the coefficients would be 1, 0, and -1 for levels a_1, a_2, and a_3, respectively. For this comparison, then, we have the following:

	a_1	a_2	a_3
Coefficients (c_i):	1	0	-1
Marginal means $(\overline{Y}_{A_i})$:	7.00	11.00	12.00

We then substitute in Eq. (11–3) to calculate the mean difference,

$$\hat{\psi}_A = \Sigma \, (c_i)(\overline{Y}_{A_i}) = (1)(7.00) + (0)(11.00) + (-1)(12.00) = -5.00$$

and then in Eq. (11–2) to calculate the comparison sum of squares,

$$SS_{A_{comp.}} = \frac{(b)(n)(\hat{\psi}_A)^2}{\Sigma c_i^2} = \frac{(2)(4)(-5.00)^2}{(1)^2 + (0)^2 + (-1)^2} = \frac{200.00}{2} = 100.00$$

The mean square and the F ratio are as follows:

$$MS_{A_{comp.}} = \frac{100.00}{1} = 100.00 \text{ and } F = \frac{100.00}{18.33} = 5.46$$

(The value for the $MS_{S/AB}$, 18.33, was taken from Table 10–8.) Since the critical value of $F(1, 18) = 4.41$ at $\alpha = .05$, the null hypothesis is rejected, and we can conclude that drug Y produces significantly more errors on the discrimination task than found with the control condition.

---

[1] You may recall that heterogeneity of variance presents some special problems in the analysis of single-df comparisons in the single-factor design (see Chap. 6, pp. 123–128). Presumably there are similar problems for corresponding analyses involving marginal means, but these conditions have not been studied sufficiently for me to offer an informed recommendation.

Interpreting Main Effects

In general, the interpretation of any main effect depends on the presence or absence of significant interaction effects. If there is no interaction or if the interaction is significant but trivial, the outcome of the F tests involving the main effects can be interpreted without caution. With a sizable and significant interaction, on the other hand, the meaning of these F tests must be carefully contemplated.

To illustrate, consider the example presented in Fig. 11–1. On the left, the two curves do not cross within the limits of the factor A selected for the experiment. In spite of the interaction showing that the largest difference between b_1 and b_2 is found at a_2, it is also true that b_1 is *consistently* above b_2. This is an example of an **ordinal interaction**, where the relative ranking of the levels of factor B in this case does not change at the different levels of factor A. In this situation, it would be appropriate to conclude that in general the treatment represented by level b_1 results in performance that is higher than the treatment at level b_2. If we replot (on the right), with factor B on the baseline, we see what is called a **disordinal interaction**. In this view of the experiment, the rank order of the levels of factor A changes at the different levels of factor B. No general conclusion may be reached concerning the influence of factor A.

The example shows that before significant main effects are interpreted and an interaction is present, it is wise to plot the data both ways (or to look at the values within the AB matrix with regard to both the rows and the columns) to see whether ordinality exists. If it does, the main effect may be interpreted as a main effect. If it does not, the main effect cannot be interpreted independently of the interaction.

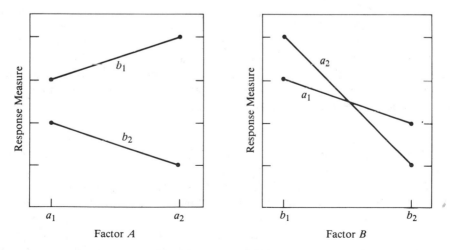

Figure 11–1 Example of an ordinal interaction (left panel) and of a disordinal interaction (right panel).

Table 11–1   The Analysis of Interaction

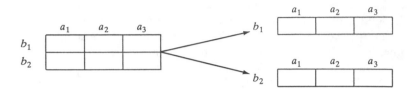

Analysis of the Simple Effects of Factor *A*

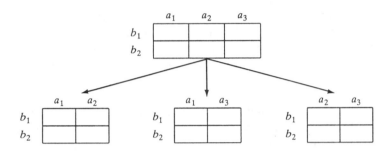

Analysis of Interaction Comparisons

11.2   TWO STRATEGIES FOR ANALYZING INTERACTION

As with a significant omnibus F test in a single-factor design, a significant interaction in a two-factor design is not very informative by itself. The presence of an interaction merely indicates that the main effects of the two factors do not perfectly predict the individual cell means—that some variability among the cell means is not fully attributable to the main effects of the two independent variables. Although an interaction may take many forms, generally only a few of these will be tolerable to the researcher. Most investigators do not wish just for an interaction—any interaction—when they design a factorial experiment. Instead, they are expecting a certain pattern of results. In a real sense, many comparisons that they conduct involving the cell means represent an attempt to assess the veracity of their predictions.

Interaction can be analyzed by means of two useful procedures. As illustrated in the upper portion of Table 11–1, the first divides the factorial design into a set of component single-factor experiments, which collectively make up the design. Each row of the factorial design, then, represents a single-factor experiment in which factor *A* has been manipulated and can be analyzed in any meaningful fashion to reveal the nature of the results. Each of these component experiments differs with regard to the specific *B* treatment held constant for any given row. This approach to examining interaction is called an **analysis of the simple effects of factor *A***. In Chap. 9, I indicated that interaction may be defined in terms of the *differences* among the simple effects; the analysis of simple effects is designed to establish the differential patterns of these single-factor outcomes. The simple effects of either factor A or factor B, or even both factors, can be examined in an analysis. Only the simple effects of factor A have been shown in Table 11–1, to simplify the exposition.

The second general method of analyzing interaction transforms the factorial design into a set of smaller factorials, as illustrated in the lower portion of Table 11–1. The first design on the left, for example, consists of a factorial experiment in which factor A consists of two levels rather than three, namely, a_1 and a_2. The second design involves levels a_1 and a_3, and the third design involves levels a_2 and a_3. Tests for interaction in these and other "miniature" factorial designs created from the original factorial manipulation also help to isolate the particular features of the two independent variables responsible for the overall interaction. I will call this second approach the **analysis of interaction comparisons**.

Both types of analyses decompose the factorial design into smaller, more analytical components. The analysis of simple effects concentrates on the component *single*-factor experiments constituting the factorial design, whereas the analysis of interaction comparisons concentrates on the smaller component *factorial* experiments that collectively make up the larger factorial design. I will consider the analysis of simple effects next and the analysis of interaction comparisons in Chap. 12.

11.3 ANALYZING THE SIMPLE EFFECTS

The analyses of main effects and of simple effects are related in the sense that they both involve the analysis of the effects of a *single* independent variable. That is, main effects are based on the differences among the *marginal means* and reflect variations of only one of the independent variables; the process of calculating the marginal means eliminates the other independent variable from consideration. Simple effects are based on the differences among the *cell means* within a particular row or column of the matrix of means; isolating a set of cell means in a particular row or column also eliminates the other independent variable by holding it constant at that level.

An analysis of simple effects, then, turns to the data found in the body of the AB matrix and examines the outcome of the experiment row by row or column by column (or, at times, both ways). A significant interaction means quite literally that the simple effects of either independent variable are not the same. An examination of the simple effects is undertaken to establish statistically the nature of these different patterns of results. Consider the data from the numerical example in the last chapter, which are presented again in Fig. 11–2. We know that the interaction is significant, and our eyes tell us that the interaction is due to large differences in mean errors between the two drug conditions and the control condition (factor A) for the animals that are only slightly hungry ($b_1 = 1$ hour without food) and the absence of differences among the three conditions when the animals are quite hungry ($b_2 = 24$ hours without food). An analysis of the simple effects of factor could provide statistical evidence in support of this observation. As you

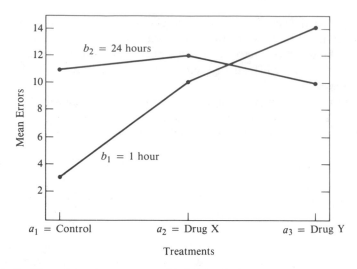

Figure 11–2   Plot of the data presented in Table 10–6.

will see in a moment, the analysis concentrates on one of the sets of three groups—the animals tested after 1 hour or those tested after 24 hours—and treats the data as if they had come from a single-factor experiment conducted at that particular level of factor B. Each set is analyzed separately and yields the sort of information available from any single-factor design. In this example, we would expect to find a significant simple effect for the 1-hour groups and no significant simple effect for the 24-hour groups.

The same sorts of questions can be asked of the other independent variable, the amount of food deprivation (factor B). An examination of Fig. 11–2 suggests that the interaction can also be described as resulting from a sizable increase in errors by the hungrier animals in the control condition and a relative absence of differences between the two drive levels for animals in the two drug conditions. An analysis of the simple effects would test the difference between the two drive conditions separately for the control, drug X, and drug Y conditions and provide statistical evidence for this particular observation.

Selecting a Set of Simple Effects for Analysis

Because they represent partially redundant information, we normally do not analyze both sets of simple effects, although there is no compelling reason against such a procedure. Usually, we will choose to analyze the set of simple effects that is the most "natural," useful, or potentially revealing—the manipulation that will be the easiest to explain. There are other factors that might influence our selection if we are unable to decide on the basis of potential explanatory power. For example, if one of the independent variables represents a quantitative manipulation and the other a qualitative manipulation, we should probably choose to analyze the simple effects of the quantitative factor, which would allow us to compare the *trends* exhibited at the different levels of the qualitative factor. Another possibility is to select the set of simple effects that reflects the larger estimates of treatment magnitude; analyses performed on this set may provide more information about the factors contributing to a significant interaction than the set with the smaller estimates. Finally, we might choose to analyze the simple effects of the independent variable with the greater number of levels; this strategy has the practical advantage of resulting in the smallest number of simple effects to examine.

Computational Formulas

Table 11–2 makes explicit the relationship between the simple effects of factor A and the main effect of factor A. The main effect is based on the deviation of the marginal means ($\overline{Y}_{A_1}$, $\overline{Y}_{A_2}$, and $\overline{Y}_{A_3}$) from the grand mean ($\overline{Y}_T$). The simple effects of factor A are based on analogous deviations, except that the individual means are the cell means in a particular row of the AB matrix and the grand mean is the average of those particular means. Consider the simple effect of factor A at level b_1, which represents the variability of the three cell means at a_1, a_2, and a_3 about the overall marginal mean $\overline{Y}_{B_1}$. Table 11–2 illustrates the nature of this source of variance.

The simplest way to view this analysis is to convert each row of the AB matrix into a single-factor design and then obtain the desired sums of squares by means of the computational formulas appropriate for an actual single-factor design. To assist in this translation, we can change the notation system from the factorial representation to one appropriate for a single-factor experiment. Continuing with this example, we isolate the relevant row in the AB matrix of sums, upon which the analysis will be conducted, and transform the notation in the following manner:

	a_1	a_2	a_3	Sum
Factorial symbols	$AB_{1,1}$	$AB_{2,1}$	$AB_{3,1}$	B_1
Single-factor symbols	"A_1"	"A_2"	"A_3"	"T"

(The quotation marks around the single-factor symbols are intended to remind

Table 11–2 Means Involved in the Simple Effects of Factor A

FACTOR B	FACTOR A a_1	a_2	a_3	Marginal Mean	Effect
b_1	$\overline{Y}_{A_1B_1}$	$\overline{Y}_{A_2B_1}$	$\overline{Y}_{A_3B_1}$	$\overline{Y}_{B_1}$	$\longrightarrow$ A at b_1
b_2	$\overline{Y}_{A_1B_2}$	$\overline{Y}_{A_2B_2}$	$\overline{Y}_{A_3B_2}$	$\overline{Y}_{B_2}$ $\longrightarrow$ A at b_2
Marginal Mean	$\overline{Y}_{A_1}$	$\overline{Y}_{A_2}$	$\overline{Y}_{A_3}$	$\overline{Y}_T$ $\longrightarrow$ A Main Effect

you that these are special symbols designed for this analysis.) The necessary formulas for the sum of squares, which we will refer to as "A at b_1," can now be written as follows:

$$SS_{A \text{ at } b_1} = \frac{\Sigma (\text{"}A\text{"})^2}{n} - \frac{(\text{"}T\text{"})^2}{(a)(n)} \tag{11-6}$$

You can see, then, that a simple effect is quite literally the between-groups variation of a single-factor experiment extracted from the larger factorial design. Translated back to the factorial notation, Eq. (11-6) becomes

$$SS_{A \text{ at } b_1} = \frac{\Sigma (AB_{i1})^2}{n} - \frac{B_1^2}{(a)(n)} \tag{11-7}$$

The degrees of freedom for each simple effect equal 1 less than the number of cell sums:

$$df_{A \text{ at } b_j} = a - 1 \tag{11-8}$$

The mean squares for simple effects are obtained as usual, by dividing each sum of squares by the appropriate df. The error term for each of these mean squares is the within-groups mean square from the original analysis, $MS_{S/AB}$. That is,

$$F = \frac{MS_{A \text{ at } b_j}}{MS_{S/AB}} \tag{11-9}$$

unless there is heterogeneity of within-group variances. If there is heterogeneity, one solution is to conduct the analysis as a series of *actual* single-factor experiments and to base the error term on the within-group variability of only those observations involved in each single-factor experiment. The result is simply a one-way analysis of variance, with both the effect and error terms calculated on the scores at level b_j.[2]

An analogous analysis can be conducted on the simple effects of factor B—that is, the effect of the B manipulation at the different levels of factor A. Although I do not present the analysis here, because of space limitations, you should have no difficulty extending the analysis of the simple effects of factor A to the other independent variable. An example of this analysis is given in problem 3 of the exercises.

A Numerical Example

I will illustrate the analysis of simple effects with the data summarized in Fig. 11-2. The AB matrix for this example is presented again in Table 11-3. I will calculate the simple effects of the control-drug variable (factor A) at the two levels of drive (1 hour and 24 hours). The effects of control-drug treatments with nearly satiated animals are reflected by the cell sums in the first row of the AB matrix. Applying Eq. (11-7) to these data, we find

---

[2]At this point you would follow the procedures outlined in Chap. 5 (see pp. 102–108).

Table 11–3 *AB* Matrix from Chapter 10

DRIVE (FACTOR B)	TREATMENTS (FACTOR A)			Sum
	Control (a_1)	Drug X (a_2)	Drug Y (a_3)	
1 hr. (b_1)	12	40	56	108
24 hr. (b_2)	44	48	40	132
Sum	56	88	96	240

$$SS_{A \text{ at } b_1} = \frac{\Sigma (AB_{i1})^2}{n} - \frac{B_1^2}{(a)(n)}$$

$$= \frac{(12)^2 + (40)^2 + (56)^2}{4} - \frac{(108)^2}{(3)(4)}$$

$$= 248.00$$

The effects of the same manipulation with hungry animals (simple effect of A at level b_2) are reflected by the cell sums appearing in the second row of the AB matrix. Substituting in Eq. (11–7), we have

$$SS_{A \text{ at } b_2} = \frac{\Sigma (AB_{i2})^2}{n} - \frac{B_2^2}{(a)(n)}$$

$$= \frac{(44)^2 + (48)^2 + (40)^2}{4} - \frac{(132)^2}{(3)(4)}$$

$$= 8.00$$

These two sums of squares are entered in Table 11–4.

The remainder of the analysis is summarized in Table 11–4. The df's, mean squares, and F ratios are obtained through straightforward substitution in the relevant formulas. The resulting F's substantiate statistically what we observed in our earlier examination of Fig. 11–2, namely, that the drug manipulation is effective only when the animals are relatively satiated.

Relationship Between Simple Effects and the $A \times B$ Interaction

It may not be evident, but each simple effect contains *two* treatment effects: (1) a portion of the $A \times B$ interaction and (2) a portion of the main effect of the factor under examination. More specifically, whereas the $SS_{A \times B}$ is independent of (that

Table 11–4 Analysis of the Simple Effects of Factor A

Source	SS	df	MS	F
A at b_1	248.00	2	124.00	6.76*
A at b_2	8.00	2	4.00	.22
S/AB		18	18.33	

*$p < .05$.

is, orthogonal to) the SS_A, the simple effects of factor A are not orthogonal to either SS_A or $SS_{A \times B}$. What this means, then, is that a significant simple effect does not represent significant interaction effects at the particular level of the other independent variable but, rather, the variability of the interaction and main effects *combined*. We may see this by summing the complete set of simple effects and finding that

$$\Sigma\, SS_{A \text{ at } b_j} = SS_{A \times B} + SS_A \tag{11-10}$$

In words, the sum of the simple effects of factor A equals the total of the sums of squares associated with factor A and the $A \times B$ interaction. What Eq. (11–10) tells us is that an analysis of simple effects is not a breakdown of the $SS_{A \times B}$ into a complete set of orthogonal comparisons.[3]

One useful application of Eq. (11–10) is to provide a check on our arithmetic. That is, if the sum of the simple effects does not equal the sum of the $SS_{A \times B}$ and the SS_A, we know that we have made an error in our calculations. From the original analysis (Table 10–8, p. 217), $SS_{A \times B} = 144.00$ and $SS_A = 112.00$. Substituting these values and the information from the analysis of the simple effects of factor A (Table 11–4) in Eq. (11–10), we find

$$248.00 + 8.00 \overset{?}{=} 144.00 + 112.00$$

$$256.00 = 256.00$$

An analogous relationship exists for the other set of simple effects. In this case, the sum of the simple effects equals the sum of the sums of squares associated with factor B and the $A \times B$ interaction. In symbols,

$$\Sigma\, SS_{B \text{ at } a_i} = SS_{A \times B} + SS_B \tag{11-11}$$

(You can verify this relationship by completing problem 3 at the end of this chapter, where the data of Table 11–3 are used to illustrate the calculation of the simple effects of factor B.)

Interpreting Simple Effects

The analysis of simple effects is especially useful when theory predicts the nature of the interaction. Testing the significance of simple effects under these circumstances often helps us establish the details of the theoretical prediction. The interaction test tells us whether the simple effects may be considered the same (no interaction) or different (interaction). An analysis of simple effects probes more deeply into the interaction to determine the specific portions of the original AB matrix that are largely responsible for its statistical significance.

As an example, consider the following four groups:

---

[3]Marascuilo and Levin (1970) make this point quite clearly and offer a procedure by which the significance of interaction effects alone may be evaluated. These and related issues are discussed in detail by Rosenthal and Rosnow (1984) and Rosnow and Rosenthal (1989a).

Group 1: Learn A, Learn B, Test A
Group 2: Learn A,– – – – –, Test A
Group 3: Learn A, Learn B,– –, Test A
Group 4: Learn A,– –, Test A

All groups learn task A and are later tested on task A. The difference between the first two groups is that group 1 learns task B before the test, whereas group 2 is given a rest activity instead (represented by the dashes). Groups 3 and 4 match groups 1 and 2, respectively, except for the delay of the final test.

This experiment is a 2 × 2 factorial in which one of the independent variables consists of the presence or absence of a second task (task B) and the other consists of the time of the test, either after a short interval ("immediate") or delayed. More specifically, the design may be diagrammed as follows:

	Presence of a Second Task?	
Time of test	Yes	No
Immediate	Group 1	Group 2
Delayed	Group 3	Group 4

There is reason to believe that group 1 will do more poorly on the test than will group 2; this outcome has been called *extinction*. Several theories postulate that extinguished material can "recover" with time. Thus, groups 3 and 4 should show less of a difference on the test than groups 1 and 2—that is, that extinction has dissipated. In terms of the 2 × 2 factorial, there should be an interaction of the two independent variables. However, certain theories also predict what is termed an *absolute* recovery, an actual improvement in performance by group 3 relative to group 1. To assess the significance of such a finding, we will need to analyze the simple effects. Two possible outcomes of this experiment are presented in Fig. 11–3. Both graphs show an interaction and both show a smaller effect of having learned task B when the test is given after a delay than immediately afterward. On the other hand, only the one on the right shows absolute recovery.

This example shows how a test of the simple effects can resolve differences between different theories. Most of the time, however, researchers analyze simple effects with the hope that additional information concerning the nature of the interaction may be revealed

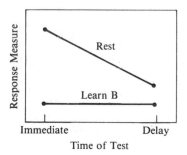 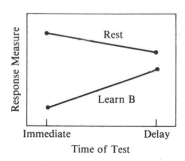

Figure 11–3 Two possible outcomes of the same 2 × 2 factorial experiment.

Occasionally you will see simple effects tested with no mention of the statistical test of interaction. The typical pattern of results will consist of two simple effects—one that is significant and one that is not—and the researcher concludes that interaction is present. The trouble with this argument is that the formal test of interaction assesses the *differences* in simple effects. An inference of interaction that is based on the test of simple effects alone does not provide this necessary information. Consider the following matrix of cell means:

	a_1	a_2
b_1	12	2
b_2	5	1

The difference between the two levels of factor A at level b_1 is $12 - 2 = 10$, and the corresponding difference at level b_2 is $5 - 1 = 4$. Let's assume that $n = 10$ and $MS_{S/AB} = 60$. The AB matrix of sums corresponding to these means is presented on the left in Table 11–5. On the right, you will find the calculations for the analysis of the simple effects of factor A. As you can see, the difference at b_1 is significant, whereas the one at b_2 is not. Given this particular statistical outcome, many researchers would be tempted to conclude that the $A \times B$ interaction is significant. Suppose we find out. Using the basic ratios at the bottom of Table 11–5, we find

$$SS_{A \times B} = [AB] - [A] - [B] + [T] = 90$$

Since $df_{A \times B} = 1, MS_{A \times B} = 90$. The $F = MS_{A \times B}/MS_{S/AB} = 90/60 = 1.50$ is not significant.

Table 11–5   An Example of Interpreting Simple Effects

	AB Matrix			Analysis of Simple Effects of Factor A

	a_1	a_2	Sum	
b_1	120	20	140	$SS_{A \text{ at } b_1} = \dfrac{(120)^2 + (20)^2}{10} - \dfrac{(140)^2}{(2)(10)} = 500; F = \dfrac{500}{60} = 8.33*$
b_2	50	10	60	$SS_{A \text{ at } b_2} = \dfrac{(50)^2 + (10)^2}{10} - \dfrac{(60)^2}{(2)(10)} = 80; F = \dfrac{80}{60} = 1.33$
Sum	170	30	200	

Basic Ratios

$$[AB] = \frac{(120)^2 + (20)^2 + (50)^2 + (10)^2}{10} = 1,740 \qquad [A] = \frac{(170)^2 + (30)^2}{(2)(10)} = 1,490$$

$$[B] = \frac{(140)^2 + (60)^2}{(2)(10)} = 1,160 \qquad [T] = \frac{(200)^2}{(2)(2)(10)} = 1,000$$

*$p < .05$.

Do you understand how this result occurred? A simple effect of factor A does not reflect "pure" interaction but is also influenced by the average or main effect of the factor, as you saw with Eq. (11–10). In this case, a sizable main effect contributed to the outcome of the analysis. If we are interested in comparing the simple effects, we must turn to an analysis that specifically assesses these differences. This is the formal test for interaction, which in this case compares the difference at b_1 (a difference of 10) with the corresponding difference at b_2 (a difference of 4); we saw that the interaction—the difference between the two simple effects—is not significant. Thus, testing the simple effects alone does not provide an unambiguous picture of interaction.

11.4 ANALYZING SIMPLE COMPARISONS

Given the analogy between the analysis of simple effects and the analysis of a corresponding single-factor design, you would certainly expect to conduct additional comparisons involving a set of means producing significant overall F's. The reason is the same, of course; we cannot establish the locus of a significant simple effect if more than two treatment conditions are involved. In general, whenever any effect has more than 1 df, the effect can be viewed as a composite of component effects, where the composite is frequently global and unanalytical and the component effects are focused and analytical. The strategy we use in analyzing simple effects follows the same general principle: If the $df > 1$, we conduct a number of single-df comparisons, chosen to shed light on the reason or reasons for the significant simple effect. I will call such analyses **simple comparisons**—*comparisons* to be continuous with the single-factor design and *simple* to indicate that the comparisons represent a detailed analysis of simple effects.

A Numerical Example

Given the analogy between the analysis of simple effects and single-factor designs, we can easily evaluate simple comparisons by viewing a set of row or column means as the product of a single-factor experiment and then apply the computational formulas of Chap. 6 to obtain the desired sums of squares. For example, suppose we wanted to compare the control condition (a_1) with drug X (a_2) for the satiated animals (level b_1). The relevant data and coefficients are as follows:

	a_1	a_2	a_3
Cell means	3.00	10.00	14.00
Coefficients	1	-1	0

The formula for a single-df comparison conducted with data from an actual single-factor design is given by Eq. (6–5); that is,

$$SS_{A_{comp.}} = \frac{n\,(\hat{\psi}\,)^2}{\sum c_i^2}$$

Simply substituting the $\overline{Y}_{A_i B_j}$ cell means for the $\overline{Y}_{A_i}$ treatment means in the single-factor design, we obtain

$$SS_{A_{comp} \text{.at } b_1} = \frac{n\,(\hat{\psi}_{A \text{ at } b_1})^2}{\Sigma c_i^2} \tag{11-12}$$

where $\hat{\psi}_{A \text{ at } b_1}$ refers to the difference between the two means specified by this comparison. That is,

$$\hat{\psi}_{A \text{ at } b_1} = \Sigma\,(c_i)(\overline{Y}_{A_i B_1}) \tag{11-13}$$

Entering the relevant quantities in these two equations, we find

$$\hat{\psi}_{A \text{ at } b_1} = (1)(3.00) + (-1)(10.00) + (0)(14.00) = -7.00$$

$$SS_{A \text{ at } b_1} = \frac{4(-7.00)^2}{(1)^2 + (-1)^2 + (0)^2} = \frac{196.00}{2} = 98.00$$

The number of df for this comparison is 1. The F ratio is formed by dividing the mean square for the comparison by the overall error term from the original analysis, $MS_{S/AB}$. We calculate

$$F_{A \text{ at } b_1} = \frac{98.00}{18.33} = 5.35$$

which is significant at $p < .05$ ($df_{num.} = 1$ and $df_{denom.} = 18$).

The corresponding comparison for the hungry animals (b_2) reveals the following:

$$\hat{\psi}_{A \text{ at } b_2} = (1)(11.00) + (-1)(12.00) + (0)(10.00) = -1.00$$

$$SS_{A \text{ at } b_2} = \frac{4(-1.00)^2}{(1)^2 + (-1)^2 + (0)^2} = \frac{4.00}{2} = 2.00$$

$$F_{A \text{ at } b_2} = \frac{2.00}{18.33} = .11$$

This difference is not significant.

Simple comparisons are amazingly versatile. Any meaningful comparison involving one of the independent variables with the other independent variable held constant can be conducted. These comparisons might include pairwise comparisons such as the ones I just conducted, more complex comparisons that involve the averaging of conditions, and trend analysis. In all these cases, the focus is on the means in a particular row or column of the matrix of cell means, which as you have seen, can be transformed into an equivalent single-factor design to facilitate the specific calculations.

Interpreting Simple Comparisons

Once you have completed your analyses of the simple effects—the effects themselves and any follow-up simple comparisons—you usually need to conduct an analysis that focuses on interaction again. Consider the analysis from the last section, where we found that the difference between the control condition and drug X was significant for satiated animals (b_1) but not significant for hungry animals (b_2). Can we conclude that the difference between the control condition and drug X for the satiated animals ($3 - 10 = -7$) is *greater* than the corresponding difference for the hungry animals ($11 - 12 = -1$)? Certainly, the pattern of outcomes supports this conclusion. Unfortunately, however, we have not explicitly tested whether the difference of -7 for the satiated animals is statistically different from the difference of -1 for the hungry animals. Until we do, we can say nothing definitive about any difference in the outcome of these two comparisons. We will discuss exactly this sort of analysis in Chap. 12.

11.5 CONTROLLING FAMILYWISE TYPE I ERROR

Familywise type I error becomes relevant the instant we conduct more than one statistical test in the analysis of an experiment. Familywise error (FW), you will recall from Chap. 8, refers to the probability of making at least one type I error in a set of statistical tests. Any increase in the number of statistical tests conducted, therefore, potentially results in an increase in FW error as well. Familywise error is the inevitable penalty associated with conducting additional comparisons. On the other hand, inhibiting this exploration of a set of data, or making it more difficult to reject the null hypothesis, incurs a different sort of penalty, namely, an increase in type II error. Any solution to this problem requires finding some way to come to terms with the two types of statistical error.

Planned comparisons of some sort are usually found in the analysis of factorial experiments. Certainly the tests of the standard factorial effects—the two main effects and the interaction—qualify as planned comparisons. That is, the very nature of the design implies that these three tests were planned before the data were collected. It is common practice in psychology to disregard the increase in FW error associated with these three tests.

What about the analyses we considered in this chapter: the analysis of simple effects and simple comparisons, when the interaction is significant, and the analysis of comparisons involving the marginal means, when it is not? There is a fortuitous quality to these analyses in the sense that they are undertaken generally only when an overall F has been conducted and is significant. More explicitly, we examine simple effects only when the $A \times B$ interaction is significant, simple comparisons only when a simple effect is significant, and main comparisons only when a main effect is significant. In the absence of any planned comparisons, this is a reasonable strategy. But how should we deal with the increase in FW error that results from this approach?

One possibility is to do nothing. Some form of control operates when we restrict ourselves to the further analysis of only significant effects. Another form of control is exerted when we add the requirement that the comparisons make theoretical sense. We are not going to make all possible comparisons between cell means. We are going to restrict ourselves to meaningful comparisons within a row or within a column, and not cross row or column boundaries, since such comparisons are generally uninterpretable because of the simultaneous change of the levels of *both* independent variables. Moreover, type I errors may be readily discovered as researchers attempt to replicate significant and interesting findings of their own and of others.

Methodologists have introduced a wide variety of adjustment techniques, but none of these has captured the attention of researchers except, perhaps, a Bonferroni adjustment for simple effects. This correction usually consists of controlling FW error for the entire set of simple effects, which is accomplished by using $\alpha = .05/b$ as the significance level for evaluating the simple effects of factor A and $\alpha = .05/a$ for the simple effects of factor B. In our numerical example, we would use $\alpha = .05/2 = .025$ for the simple effects of factor A and $\alpha = .05/3 = .017$ for the simple effects of factor B. These corrections would guarantee that α_{FW} will be no greater than .05 for each set of tests.

You are certainly more on your own when the topic of familywise error is raised during the planning and analysis of a factorial experiment than was the case with the single-factor experiment. In either situation, you will have to set your own criteria and worry about the consequences stemming from your decision. But there has been considerably less discussion of the problem with the factorial design.[4] Current practice in psychological research favors analyses without correction for FW rate. Certainly, more discussion of the problem of FW error is needed so that researchers can see clearly the issue at stake and the long-term consequences of alternative solutions to the problem.

11.6   SUMMARY OF THE DIFFERENT ANALYSES

This chapter has focused on one strategy for undertaking the detailed analysis of a factorial experiment: We begin with a test of the $A \times B$ interaction and then, depending on the outcome of this test, systematically examine the influence of one of the independent variables, either as simple effects, where the other independent variable is held constant, or as main effects, where it is ignored. The steps in the analysis are summarized in Fig. 11–4.

At the top of the decision tree I have listed the first step in the analysis, the evaluation of the $A \times B$ interaction. The decision tree branches at this point depending on the outcome of this statistical test. If the interaction is significant, we can conclude that the simple effects of either factor are not the same at all levels of the other factor. We proceed, therefore, to test each simple effect for significance and follow each significant test with a number of meaningful comparisons, in an attempt to discover how these simple effects are different. The analysis at this point flows directly from the original rationale for a factorial experiment, namely, an extension of an independent variable studied in a single-factor design to a factorial design, in which the variable is manipulated in conjunction with a second independent variable. The final step in the analysis of simple effects and simple

---

[4]See Boik (1979) for an interesting illustration of how one might control FW type I error in a factorial experiment.

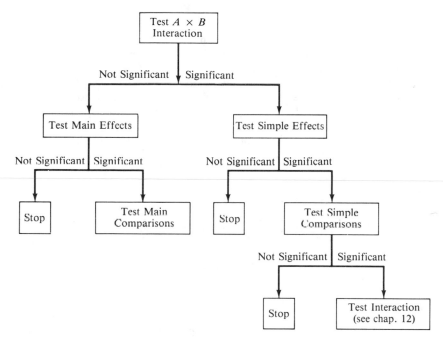

Figure 11–4 *Summary of the analysis of simple effects.*

comparisons is to determine whether a significant comparison at one level of the other factor is statistically different from the outcome observed with the same comparison at the other levels of the factor as well. We will consider this special analysis in Chap. 12.

Returning to the top of Fig. 11–4, we can review the steps we follow when the interaction is not significant, namely, an analysis of the two main effects. We evaluate the significance of each main effect and follow a significant outcome with meaningful "main" comparisons involving the relevant marginal means. Because the effects of the two independent variables do not depend on the other factor, we can concentrate our energies in understanding and interpreting the meaning of these overall effects.

This analysis strategy is widely followed in the behavioral sciences, in part because it provides a useful approach for interpreting a significant interaction and because it corresponds to the way in which many researchers think about the factorial experiments they design. My summary of this approach is not intended to imply that the analysis of a factorial experiment is characterized by the mechanical application of these steps to the results of an experiment. I consider a research plan theoretically motivated and inspired when a researcher attempts to follow up significant findings in an illuminating manner. It takes practice to use these analyses productively, but the time spent mastering these basic analyses will greatly increase the usefulness of the factorial design as a device for discovering new relationships between independent variables and behavior.

11.7 EXERCISES[5]

1. Suppose an experiment is conducted in which three strains of rats are to be compared. One strain was obtained by selectively breeding rats that performed exceptionally well in a maze-learning task (the "bright" rats); a second strain was obtained by selectively breeding rats that performed quite poorly in the same task (the "dull" rats); and a third strain consisted of rats that were bred without regard for maze-learning performance (the "mixed" rats). One group from each strain was raised under "enriched" environmental conditions, and a second group was raised under "impoverished" conditions. Following six months of exposure to one of the two environments, all the rats were tested in a standard laboratory maze. There were eight rats, randomly assigned to each of the environments from each of the three strains. The response measure consisted of the trials needed to perform the maze without error. The following treatment means were obtained:

ENVIRONMENT (Factor B)	STRAIN (Factor A)		
	Bright	Mixed	Dull
Enriched	3.50	4.00	7.50
Impoverished	3.75	7.75	11.00

Assume that the statistical analysis indicates that the interaction is significant, leading us to concentrate on the individual treatment means rather than on the marginal means. For each of the following questions, identify the specific means to be compared in the analysis and calculate the mean square for that effect:
   a. What are the effects of the two environments on each of the three strains of rats?
   b. Do the three groups of rats differ in learning performance when they have been reared in the enriched environment?
   c. Do the bright and mixed strains reared in the enriched environment differ in learning performance?
2. Problem 2 in the exercises for Chap. 10 revealed only a significant main effect of factor A. Conduct the following single-df comparisons involving the marginal means $(\overline{Y}_A)$:
   a. Test the pairwise difference between $\overline{Y}_{A_1}$ and $\overline{Y}_{A_3}$.
   b. Test the complex comparison involving the difference between $\overline{Y}_{A_2}$ and the average of the other two marginal means $(\overline{Y}_{A_1}$ and $\overline{Y}_{A_3})$.
3. From the data appearing in Table 11–3 (p. 241),
   a. Test the significance of the simple effects of factor B.
   b. Show that the total sum of squares associated with the three simple effects equals the sum of SS_B and $SS_{A \times B}$.
4. Problem 1 in the exercises for Chap. 10 revealed a significant $A \times B$ interaction, setting the stage for an analysis of simple effects of either factor (or both factors).
   a. As an example, test the significance of the simple effects of factor A at level b_1.
   b. Since the simple effect is significant, you would probably be interested in examining a number of meaningful single-df comparisons, which in the context of this analysis, are simple comparisons. Test the pairwise difference between the means at levels a_1 and a_5.
   c. You may have noticed that factor A is a quantitative independent variable

[5]The answers to these problems are found in Appendix B.

(equally spaced levels of shock intensity), so that the simple comparison in part b consists of a comparison between the two extreme intensities. A more appropriate approach would be to examine the trend components, rather than search for pairwise differences. As an example, test the significance of the linear component of this simple effect.

5. This problem illustrates a common misconception that the discovery of one simple effect that is significant and one that is not necessarily significant implies that the interaction is significant. Following are the treatment means for a 2 × 2 factorial design:

	a_1	a_2
b_1	3	8
b_2	2	5

a. Test the significance of the two simple effects of factor A. (Assume that $n = 6$ and $MS_{S/AB} = 9.00$.)

b. Now test the significance of the interaction.

12

The Analysis of Interaction Comparisons

Interaction comparisons represent a different approach to the analysis of interaction than does an analysis of simple effects, although they do have certain features in common. Let's return to Table 11–1 (p. 236) for a moment. The lower display illustrated the basic nature of interaction comparisons, namely, a focus on a meaningful component of the original factorial design. Suppose a_1 represents a control condition, and a_2 and a_3 represent two drug conditions, as in the numerical example we have analyzed in the last two chapters. A component factorial formed by isolating levels a_1 and a_2 provides information about the interaction of *these two treatment conditions* with the other independent variable (hours of food deprivation, or hunger drive). More specifically, this component factorial allows us to assess a more specific interaction, namely, the influence of drive (factor B) on the difference between the control condition and drug X. A significant interaction would mean that this particular difference depends on the level of the hunger drive manipulated in this experiment. You should note that the overall $A \times B$ interaction does not provide this specific information because in essence it is a *composite* of other interaction comparisons, including this one. This composite nature of the $A \times B$ interaction is present whenever either independent variable consists of more than two levels or, necessarily, when the degrees of freedom associated with the $A \times B$ interaction are greater than 1.

Interaction comparisons are created whenever particular levels of an independent variable are singled out for analysis. The interaction comparisons pictured in Table 11–1 consist of pairwise comparisons between two levels of factor A. Interaction comparisons can also be formed by combining levels. Continuing with our example, we might be interested in comparing the control condition a_1 with the combined drug conditions $a_2 + a_3$ to see whether this comparison—that is, the difference between the control and the average of the two drug conditions—interacts with the other independent variable (drive).

It may have occurred to you that either independent variable can supply the comparison examined in an interaction comparison. In our numerical example, factor B consisted of only two levels, which means that the only analytical comparison involving this factor is the difference between b_1 and b_2; but with additional levels of factor B, interaction comparisons involving this independent variable are now possible. Table 12–1 illustrates this possibility schematically with a 3 × 3 design.

At the top left side of the table, you will find the original factorial design. The X's appearing in each of the cells of the AB matrix indicate that the entire set of cell means is under examination, as would be the case for testing the significance of the overall $A \times B$ interaction. Rather than working with the total matrix, however, let's conceive of the design as a series of smaller, more analytically focused factorial experiments. A particularly meaningful single-*df* comparison involving either (or both) of the independent variables guides us to a new, smaller factorial created by the comparison (or comparisons). If the interaction comparison is created by transforming factor A into a pairwise comparison involving levels a_1 and a_2, for example, we create the 2 × 3 represented by the matrix immediately below the original design, where the X's designate the cells relevant for this analysis. This interaction comparison provides information about the interaction of $A_{comp.}$ and

Table 12–1   Schematic Diagram of Interaction Comparisons

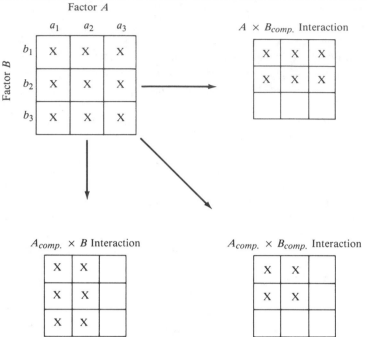

factor B and tells us whether the size of this comparison depends on the levels of factor B.

An analogous arrangement is created by transforming factor B into a pairwise comparison involving levels b_1 and b_2, which is depicted in the matrix to the right of the original design; in this case, the interaction comparison tells us about the interaction of factor A with $B_{comp.}$. Finally, on the diagonal extending from the original matrix, we have the most refined interaction comparison of all, one that is formed by crossing a comparison involving factor A (a_1 versus a_2) with a comparison involving factor B (b_1 versus b_2).

I will designate interaction comparisons by the following notation:

$A_{comp.} \times B$ refers to an interaction comparison in which factor A supplies the comparison, while the levels of factor B remain intact.

$A \times B_{comp.}$ refers to an interaction comparison in which factor B supplies the comparison, while the levels of factor A remain intact.

$A_{comp.} \times B_{comp.}$ refers to an interaction comparison in which both factors supply the comparisons.

The first two interaction comparisons are conceptually the same, of course: They both consist of a single-df comparison crossed with an intact factor. Boik (1979) refers to the interaction obtained from this type of interaction comparison as a **partial interaction**; others use the term **treatment-contrast interaction** (Kirk, 1982).

The other type of interaction comparison, which is formed by applying single-*df* comparisons to both independent variables simultaneously, is commonly called an **interaction contrast**, or alternatively, **interacting contrasts**. I will consider the analysis of interaction contrasts first, followed by the analysis of partial interactions.

12.1 INTERACTION CONTRASTS

Interaction contrasts are the most common type of interaction comparison in the behavioral sciences. One reason is their analytical power in helping us to understand and to interpret interaction. Because interaction contrasts have only 1 *df*, they represent components of a composite interaction that can be refined or reduced no further. Another reason is the fact that many factorial designs contain a factor with only two levels, which automatically creates interaction contrasts when the other factor is refined by the use of single-*df* comparisons. We will consider two examples of interaction contrasts in which factor *B* has only two levels, one contrast based on a pairwise comparison and the other based on a complex comparison. We will use our continuing numerical example to illustrate the two analyses, in which factor *B* (drive) consists of only two levels, which produces the functional equivalence of a single-*df* comparison. We will consider interaction contrasts extracted from a larger experiment in Sec. 12.2.

Pairwise Interaction Contrasts

One interesting comparison is between the two drug conditions (a_2 and a_3). The cell means from the original *AB* matrix are presented on the left side of Table 12–2. On the right, I have illustrated the nature of this contrast, a 2×2 matrix formed by crossing $A_{comp.}$ (a_2 versus a_3) with $B_{comp.}$ (b_1 versus b_2), which is how I will refer to factor *B* in this context. A comparison of the differences between the two drugs, listed to the far right of the matrix, gives us a convenient way to examine the interaction.[1] That is, these differences are *simple comparisons* of factor *A*—the simple comparison involving the two drug conditions at b_1 and at b_2—and interaction is defined in terms of the difference between these simple comparisons. More explicitly, the simple comparison for the satiated animals (b_1) is -4.00 and for the hungry animals (b_2) 2.00. Do these two simple comparisons differ significantly? A test of the interaction contained in this 2×2 matrix provides an answer to this question.

Table 12–2 An Example of a Pairwise Interaction Contrast

	Original *AB* Matrix of Means				Interaction Contrast and Simple Comparisons		
	a_1	a_2	a_3		Drug X (a_2)	Drug Y (a_3)	$\hat{\psi}_{A \text{ at } b_j}$
b_1	3.00	10.00	14.00	1 hr. (b_1)	10.00	14.00	-4.00
b_2	11.00	12.00	10.00	24 hr. (b_2)	12.00	10.00	2.00

[1]You might find it useful to plot the data from the matrix and examine the interaction visually.

Computational Formulas. Translating an interaction contrast into a sum of squares is a surprisingly simple matter. The key to the calculations is an estimate of the interaction effect under consideration, which I will designate $\hat{\psi}_{A \times B}$. One way to obtain this estimate is from the means in the 2 × 2 matrix directly—taking the two simple comparisons we have already calculated and subtracting one from the other. Using the information from Table 12–2, we find

$$\hat{\psi}_{A \times B} = \hat{\psi}_{A \text{ at } b_1} - \hat{\psi}_{A \text{ at } b_2} \tag{12-1}$$

$$= (-4.00) - (2.00) = -6.00$$

This estimated interaction effect is then entered into the following formula to obtain the desired sums of squares:

$$SS_{A_{comp.} \times B_{comp.}} = \frac{n (\hat{\psi}_{A \times B})^2}{(\Sigma c_i^2)(\Sigma c_j^2)} \tag{12-2}$$

where c_i = the coefficients defining $A_{comp.}$ (c_i: 0, 1, −1)
c_j = the coefficients defining $B_{comp.}$ (c_j: 1, −1)

For this example, then, $\Sigma c_i^2 = (0)^2 + (1)^2 + (-1)^2 = 2$, and $\Sigma c_j^2 = (1)^2 + (-1)^2 = 2$. Substituting in Eq. (12–2) gives us

$$SS_{A_{comp.} \times B_{comp.}} = \frac{4(-6.00)^2}{(2)(2)} = \frac{144.00}{4} = 36.00$$

A frequently used equivalent method defines the interaction effect as a sum of the weighted cell means, rather than in terms of simple comparisons. We start by calculating the special interaction coefficients that we will use to weight the cell means. An easy way to determine these coefficients is to list the two sets of coefficients defining the interaction contrast along the appropriate sides of an AB matrix, as illustrated in Table 12–3. The interaction coefficients, which I will denote d_{ij}, are simply the *products* of the pairs of coefficients—one from $A_{comp.}$ and the other from $B_{comp.}$—associated with each cell of the matrix. The coefficient for $a_1 b_1$ ($d_{1,1}$), for example, is found by multiplying the coefficient at level a_1 (0) by the coefficient at level b_1 (1); that is, $d_{1,1} = (0)(1) = 0$. The coefficient for $a_3 b_2$ ($d_{3,2}$) is found by multiplying the coefficient at level a_3 (−1) by the coefficient at level b_2 (−1); that is, $d_{3,2} = (-1)(-1) = 1$. The d_{ij}'s for the interaction contrast are enumerated within the body of the AB matrix.

The interaction effect is calculated by weighting (or multiplying) each cell mean by the appropriate d_{ij} and then summing them:

$$\hat{\psi}_{A \times B} = \Sigma (d_{ij})(\overline{Y}_{A_i B_j}) \tag{12-3}$$

Table 12-3 Coefficients for the Interaction Contrast

	c_j	c_i:	(a_1) 0	(a_2) 1	(a_3) −1
(b_1)	1		0	1	−1
(b_2)	−1		0	−1	1

If you will refer back to the AB matrix of cell means in Table 12–2, the interaction effect becomes

$$\hat{\psi}_{A \times B} = (0)(3.00) + (1)(10.00) + (-1)(14.00)$$
$$+ (0)(11.00) + (-1)(12.00) + (1)(10.00) = -6.00$$

which is identical to the one we obtained with the other method.

The sum of squares may be calculated either with Eq. (12–2) or an equivalent formula that includes the specialized coefficients:

$$SS_{A_{comp.} \times B_{comp.}} = \frac{n(\hat{\psi}_{A \times B})^2}{\Sigma d_{ij}^2} \tag{12–4}$$

From Table 12–3, we find

$$\Sigma d_{ij}^2 = (0)^2 + (1)^2 + (-1)^2 + (0)^2 + (-1)^2 + (1)^2 = 4$$

Substituting in Eq. (12–4),

$$SS_{A_{comp.} \times B_{comp.}} = \frac{4(-6.00)^2}{4} = 36.00$$

which is identical to the value we found with Eq. (12–2).

Each method serves a function in the analysis of interaction contrasts. The method dealing with the 2×2 matrix directly (Table 12–2) has the advantage of making the nature of the interaction explicit. The method that uses special coefficients and the total AB matrix of cell means (Table 12–3) is a step removed from the 2×2 matrix but represents an efficient way of calculating the interaction effect when a large number of interaction contrasts is involved. The method also has the advantage of providing a functional link in applying correlational statistics, such as multiple regression and correlation (MRC), to the analysis of experimental designs (see Keppel & Zedeck, 1989). Whichever method you use, however, you should make a practice of examining the 2×2 matrix or a graph of these data, especially when an interaction contrast is significant. It is this display of means, defined entirely in terms of two single-df comparisons, that must be interpreted when significant interaction is obtained.

Evaluating Interaction Contrasts.   Each interaction contrast is associated with 1 df and so, $MS_{A_{comp.} \times B_{comp.}} = SS_{A_{comp.} \times B_{comp.}}$. The F ratio is formed by dividing the mean square for the contrast by the error term from the overall analysis of variance. That is,

$$F = \frac{MS_{A_{comp.} \times B_{comp.}}}{MS_{S/AB}} \tag{12–5}$$

which is evaluated against a critical value of F with $df_{num.} = 1$ and $df_{denom.} = df_{S/AB}$. Using the error term from the overall analysis ($MS_{S/AB} = 18.33$), we find

$$F = \frac{36.00}{18.33} = 1.96$$

which is not significant.

Simple Comparisons.   The interaction contrast was not significant, suggesting that the difference between the two drugs does not depend on the other factor (drive). If the interaction contrast had been significant, however, we would probably have continued with the analysis by testing the two simple comparisons—that is, the difference between the two drugs for the satiated animals (-4.00) and the difference between the two drugs for the hungry animals (2.00). It is at this point that the analysis of an interaction contrast converges with the analysis of simple effects, which we considered in Chap. 11 (pp. 237–245). To elaborate, a significant interaction implies that the simple effects of a factor are not the same at all levels of the other factor. In the case of an interaction contrast, in which each factor is a single-df comparison, the analysis would involve an evaluation of $A_{comp.}$ at the two levels of the other comparison.

The computational formula for the sums of squares involves familiar operations:

$$SS_{A_{comp.} \text{ at } b_1} = \frac{n(\hat{\psi}_{A \text{ at } b_1})^2}{\Sigma d^2 \text{ at } b_1} \tag{12–6}$$

$$SS_{A_{comp.} \text{ at } b_2} = \frac{n(\hat{\psi}_{A \text{ at } b_2})^2}{\Sigma d^2 \text{ at } b_2} \tag{12–7}$$

You should note that the denominator in both cases consists of the sum of the squared interaction coefficients (d_{ij}) obtained separately for the two levels of $B_{comp.}$ (b_1 and b_2). We can obtain this information from Table 12–3. To illustrate,

$$SS_{A_{comp.} \text{ at } b_1} = \frac{4(-4.00)^2}{(0)^2 + (1)^2 + (-1)^2} = \frac{64.00}{2} = 32.00$$

$$SS_{A_{comp.} \text{ at } b_2} = \frac{4(-2.00)^2}{(0)^2 + (-1)^2 + (1)^2} = \frac{16.00}{2} = 8.00$$

Both simple comparisons are based on 1 df. The error term would again come from the overall analysis ($MS_{S/AB}$).

Complex Interaction Contrasts

A complex interaction contrast is created when one (or both) of the single-df comparisons is a complex contrast—that is, a comparison in which at least one level of the comparison results from averaging two or more conditions. An obvious complex comparison from the numerical example is a contrast between the control (a_1) and the combined drug conditions (a_2 and a_3). The resulting interaction contrast is presented on the left side of Table 12–4, which indicates that the combined drug

Table 12–4   An Example of a Complex Interaction Contrast

	Control	Combined Drugs	$\hat{\psi}_{A \text{ at } b_j}$	c_j	c_i :	(a_1) 1	(a_2) $-\frac{1}{2}$	(a_3) $-\frac{1}{2}$
1 hr. (b_1)	3.00	12.00	-9.00	(b_1) 1		1	$-\frac{1}{2}$	$-\frac{1}{2}$
24 hr. (b_2)	11.00	11.00	0.00	(b_2) -1		-1	$\frac{1}{2}$	$\frac{1}{2}$

conditions showed an increase in errors over the control condition for the satiated animals (b_1) but no difference between them for the hungry animals (b_2). Using Eq. (12–1), we can find the estimated interaction effect:

$$\hat{\psi}_{A \times B} = \hat{\psi}_{A \text{ at } b_1} - \hat{\psi}_{A \text{ at } b_2}$$
$$= (-9.00) - (0.00) = -9.00$$

Alternatively, we can calculate the same quantity with the special interaction coefficients (d_{ij}), which are presented on the right side of Table 12–4 and are formed by cross-multiplying the coefficients for $A_{comp.}$ $(1, -\frac{1}{2}, -\frac{1}{2})$ with the coefficients for $B_{comp.}$ $(1, -1)$. Using Eq. (12–3), we find

$$\hat{\psi}_{A \times B} = (1)(3.00) + (-\tfrac{1}{2})(10.00) + (-\tfrac{1}{2})(14.00)$$
$$+ (-1)(11.00) + (\tfrac{1}{2})(12.00) + (\tfrac{1}{2})(10.00) = -9.00$$

We also find that

$$\Sigma\, d_{ij}^2 = (1)^2 + (-\tfrac{1}{2})^2 + (-\tfrac{1}{2})^2 + (-1)^2 + (\tfrac{1}{2})^2 + (\tfrac{1}{2})^2 = 3$$

Substituting these quantities in Eq. (12–4), we find

$$SS_{A_{comp.} \times B_{comp.}} = \frac{n(\hat{\psi}_{A \times B})^2}{\Sigma d_{ij}^2} = \frac{4(-9.00)^2}{3} = \frac{324.00}{3} = 108.00$$

This comparison is based on 1 df, and

$$F = \frac{MS_{A_{comp.} \times B_{comp.}}}{MS_{S/AB}} = \frac{108.00}{18.33} = 5.89$$

which is significant.

Given a significant interaction contrast, we will usually want to test the two simple comparisons for significance. The difference between the control and combined drug conditions is $\hat{\psi}_{A \text{ at } b_1} = -9.00$ for the satiated animals. Turning to Eq. (12–6), we obtain

$$SS_{A_{comp. \text{ at }} b_1} = \frac{n(\hat{\psi}_{A \text{ at } b_1})^2}{\Sigma\, d^2 \text{ at } b_1}$$

$$= \frac{4(-9.00)^2}{(1)^2 + (-\tfrac{1}{2})^2 + (-\tfrac{1}{2})^2} = \frac{324.00}{1.5} = 216.00$$

Finally, we calculate $F = 216.00/18.33 = 11.78$, which is significant. It is pointless to test the other simple comparison because the difference is zero.

In sum, this analysis has identified an important component of the $A \times B$ interaction, namely, a general increase in errors when the drugs are administered to satiated animals, and no effect when the drugs are administered to hungry animals. The original analysis (Table 10–8) revealed that $SS_{A \times B} = 144.00$. We have found that a substantial proportion of the variability, $108.00/144.00 = .75$ (or 75 percent), is associated with this particular interaction comparison.

Orthogonality of Interaction Contrasts

It is interesting to note that when a set of orthogonal comparisons involving one factor is used to create a corresponding set of interaction contrasts, the interaction contrasts are orthogonal as well. You may recall that one property of a complete set of orthogonal comparisons is that the corresponding sums of squares will sum to the overall sum of squares. The same relationship holds for a complete orthogonal set of interaction contrasts. We have considered two interaction contrasts, one consisting of a pairwise comparison between the two drug conditions and the other a complex comparison between the control and the combined drug conditions. These two comparisons are orthogonal, which we can verify by multiplying corresponding coefficients and summing them:

$$\Sigma\,(c_i)(c_i') \;=\; (0)(1) + (1)(-\tfrac{1}{2}) + (-1)(-\tfrac{1}{2}) \;=\; 0$$

where c_i refers to the coefficients for the first comparison $(0, 1, -1)$ and c_i' refers to the coefficients for the second comparison $(1, -\tfrac{1}{2}, -\tfrac{1}{2})$. The sum of squares was 36.00 for the first interaction contrast and 108.00 for the second. The sum of these two values, $36.00 + 108.00 = 144.00$, exactly equals the sum of squares for the overall $A \times B$ interaction.

    This property of orthogonal comparisons suggests that a tidy way to conceptualize the $A \times B$ interaction is in terms of a set of orthogonal interaction contrasts, as I have demonstrated with our example. On the other hand, orthogonality is not the only criterion to consider when we plan an analysis, as I stressed in Chap. 6; the meaning of the different comparisons in a set is of greater importance.

12.2   INTERACTION CONTRASTS FROM LARGE FACTORIAL DESIGNS

I introduced interaction contrasts with an example in which only factor A supplied the single-df comparisons because factor B contained only two levels and, thus, represented a single-df comparison by default. In this section, we will consider an example in which an interaction contrast is created from a 3×3 factorial design.

An Example of an Analytical Set of Interaction Contrasts

Suppose we are interested in the effects of positive and negative feedback given during the learning of different types of material in the laboratory. Factor A consists of three conditions, namely, a control (a_1) which receives no verbal feedback during learning and two groups that do, one that receives positive comments following each training trial (a_2) and the other that receives negative comments following each trial (a_3). After mastering the material, the subjects—fifth-grade school children—are tested for recall one week later. The question of interest is whether memory for this material will be influenced by the nature of the feedback they received during training. Since the effects of this independent variable may vary, depending on the nature of the learning material, it makes sense to include several types of learning material as a second independent variable (factor B). Three types of learning material were prepared for the children:

b_1 = low-frequency words with low emotional content
b_2 = high-frequency words with low emotional content
b_3 = high-frequency words with high emotional content[2]

Without seeing the data, you should be able to devise a number of meaningful single-df comparisons for both independent variables. Factor A suggests three pairwise comparisons: one between positive and negative feedback and two involving the control condition (no verbal feedback) and the two feedback conditions separately, as well as one complex comparison, namely, the control versus the combined feedback conditions. Factor B suggests two pairwise comparisons: one comparing the memory for low- and high-frequency words (b_1 versus b_2), where the degree of emotionality (low) is the same for both sets of words, and the other comparing memory for words of low and high emotional content (b_2 versus b_3), where word frequency (high) is the same for both sets of words. These two sets of single-df comparisons can be used to construct a total of eight interaction contrasts, simply by crossing each of the four comparisons we created for factor A with the two comparisons we created for factor B. These eight interaction contrasts are presented as 2×2 designs below the overall 3×3 design in Table 12–5.

Each of these miniature factorials isolates a different aspect of the overall $A \times B$ interaction. The four designs on the left all involve a comparison between words of low and high frequency (b_1 versus b_2), but in conjunction with different $A_{comp.}$'s, thus yielding four different interaction contrasts. Let's consider what basic questions each one addresses, starting from the top:

Is the difference between positive and negative feedback (a_2 versus a_3) the same for low- and high-frequency words?
Is the difference between the control and the combined feedback conditions (a_1 versus $a_2 + a_3$) the same for low- and high-frequency words?
Is the difference between the control and positive feedback (a_1 versus a_2) the same for low- and high-frequency words?
Is the difference between the control and negative feedback (a_1 versus a_3) the same for low- and high-frequency words?

The four designs on the right all involve a comparison between words of low and high emotional content (b_2 versus b_3), again in conjunction with the four different $A_{comp.}$'s. In this case, the same basic questions addressed by the four $A_{comp.}$'s are now asked in conjunction with the emotionality factor. The questions then become

Is the difference between positive and negative feedback the same for words of low and high emotionality?
Is the difference between the control and the combined feedback conditions the same for words of low and high emotionality?

---

[2]This design is purposely unbalanced. Most researchers would have included a fourth condition, low-frequency words with high emotional content, to balance the study properly.

Table 12–5   Examples of Interaction Contrasts

	Control	Positive	Negative
Low Freq., Low Emot.			
High Freq., Low Emot.			
High Freq., High Emot.			

	Positive	Negative
Low Freq.		
High Freq.		

	Positive	Negative
Low Emot.		
High Emot.		

	Control	Combined Feedback
Low Freq.		
High Freq.		

	Control	Combined Feedback
Low Emot.		
High Emot.		

	Control	Positive
Low Freq.		
High Freq.		

	Control	Positive
Low Emot.		
High Emot.		

	Control	Negative
Low Freq.		
High Freq.		

	Control	.Negative
Low Emot.		
High Emot.		

Is the difference between the control and positive feedback the same for words of low and high emotionality?

Is the difference between the control and negative feedback the same for words of low and high emotionality?

Each of the eight interaction contrasts addresses a different and quite specific question, questions that are certainly not addressed explicitly by the overall $A \times B$ interaction. Moreover, you can also see that interaction contrasts usually represent *planned comparisons* since they flow directly from the specific comparisons devised for both independent variables in the planning stages of an experiment.

A Numerical Example

Let's consider a numerical example based on this new factorial design. The individual cell means, each of which are based on $n = 5$ children, are presented in Table 12–6. I will illustrate the computational procedures for one of the eight in-

Table 12–6 Numerical Example

Factor B	Factor A		
	Control (a_1)	Positive (a_2)	Negative (a_3)
Low freq., Low emot. (b_1)	8.4	7.8	8.0
High freq., Low emot. (b_2)	8.8	8.0	7.6
High freq., High emot. (b_3)	8.0	4.4	3.8

teraction contrasts presented in Table 12–5, namely, the contrast formed by crossing the $A_{comp.}$ involving a comparison of the control and combined feedback conditions (a_1 versus an average of a_2 and a_3) with the $B_{comp.}$ involving a comparison between the words of low and high emotional content (b_2 versus b_3).

Calculating the Interaction Contrast.   We begin by forming the 2×2 matrix for this interaction contrast, which you will find in Table 12–7. The values for the combined feedback conditions are simply averages of the relevant cell means for the positive and negative feedback conditions. The average is $(8.0 + 7.6)/2 = 7.8$ for the low condition (b_2) and $(4.4 + 3.8)/2 = 4.1$ for the high condition (b_3). As you can see, there appears to be an interaction in that the difference between the control and the combined feedback conditions is smaller for the subjects learning the words of low emotionality ($8.8 - 7.8 = 1.0$) than for the subjects learning the words of high emotionality ($8.0 - 4.1 = 3.9$). Stated another way, an interaction is present because the simple comparison involving $A_{comp.}$ (control versus combined feedback conditions) is not the same at both levels of $B_{comp.}$ (low versus high emotional content).

Calculating the Sum of Squares.   The estimated interaction effect is obtained by entering the information from Table 12–7 in Eq. (12–1):

$$\hat{\psi}_{A \times B} = \hat{\psi}_{A \text{ at } b_2} - \hat{\psi}_{A \text{ at } b_3}$$

$$= (1.0) - (3.9) = -2.9$$

We will use Eq. (12–2) to calculate the sum of squares for this interaction effect:

$$SS_{A_{comp.} \times B_{comp.}} = \frac{n\,(\hat{\psi}_{A \times B})^2}{(\Sigma\, c_i^2)(\Sigma\, c_j^2)}$$

Table 12–7 An Example of a Complex Interaction Contrast

	Control Condition	Combined Feedback	$\hat{\psi}_{A \text{ at } b_j}$
Low emot.	8.8	7.8	1.0
High emot.	8.0	4.1	3.9

where c_i = the coefficients defining $A_{comp.}$ $(c_i: 1, -\frac{1}{2}, -\frac{1}{2})$

c_j = the coefficients defining $B_{comp.}(c_j: 0, 1, -1)$

For this example, then, $\Sigma c_i^2 = (1)^2 + (-\frac{1}{2})^2 + (-\frac{1}{2})^2 = 1.5$, and $\Sigma c_j^2 = (0)^2 + (1)^2 + (-1)^2 = 2$. Substituting in Eq. (12–2) gives us

$$SS_{A_{comp.} \times B_{comp.}} = \frac{5(-2.9)^2}{(1.5)(2)} = \frac{42.05}{3} = 14.02$$

You will recall that I introduced an equivalent method for defining the estimated interaction effect, which relied on special interaction coefficients (see pp. 256–257). These coefficients (d_{ij}) are formed by cross-multiplying corresponding coefficients from the relevant $A_{comp.}$ and $B_{comp.}$. The coefficients for this example are presented in Table 12–8. We can now calculate the interaction effect by multiplying each coefficient times the appropriate cell mean in Table 12–6 and summing these products.

$$\hat{\psi}_{A \times B} = \Sigma(d_{ij})(\overline{Y}_{A_i B_j})$$

$$= (0)(8.4) + (0)(7.8) + (0)(8.0)$$
$$+ (1)(8.8) + (-\frac{1}{2})(8.0) + (-\frac{1}{2})(7.6)$$
$$+ (-1)(8.0) + (\frac{1}{2})(4.4) + (\frac{1}{2})(3.8) = -2.9$$

which is identical to the value we calculated previously. To calculate the sum of squares, we need to square and then sum the special coefficients:

$$\Sigma d_{ij}^2 = (0)^2 + (0)^2 + \ldots + (\frac{1}{2})^2 + (\frac{1}{2})^2 = 3$$

Substituting this information in Eq. (12–4), we find

$$SS_{A_{comp.} \times B_{comp.}} = \frac{n(\hat{\psi}_{A \times B})^2}{\Sigma d_{ij}^2} = \frac{5(-2.9)^2}{3} = \frac{42.05}{3} = 14.02$$

which is identical to the value we obtained with Eq. (12–2).

Evaluating the Interaction Contrast. The interaction is evaluated in the usual fashion, dividing the $MS_{A_{comp.} \times B_{comp.}}$ by the error term from the overall analysis, which in this case we assume is $MS_{S/AB} = 1.75$. The $df_{num.} = 1$, of course, and $df_{denom.} = df_{S/AB} = (a)(b)(n - 1) = (3)(3)(5 - 1) = 36$. The resulting F,

Table 12–8   Coefficients for the Interaction Contrast

	c_j	c_i:	(a_1) 1	(a_2) $-\frac{1}{2}$	(a_3) $-\frac{1}{2}$
(b_1)	0		0	0	0
(b_2)	1		1	$-\frac{1}{2}$	$-\frac{1}{2}$
(b_3)	-1		-1	$\frac{1}{2}$	$\frac{1}{2}$

$$F = \frac{MS_{A_{comp.} \times B_{comp.}}}{MS_{S/AB}} = \frac{14.02}{1.75} = 8.01$$

is significant.

Analyzing Simple Comparisons. As outlined in Chap. 11, we generally follow a significant interaction with an analysis of simple effects. Although a significant interaction indicates that the simple effects are not the same, we still need to examine the simple effects themselves to determine which are significant and which are not. In the present case, the simple effects are actually simple comparisons. We considered the analysis of simple comparisons in Sec. 12.1 (p. 258). Now I will test the simple effects of $A_{comp.}$ (the comparison between the control and combined feedback conditions). The formula for simple comparisons is given by

$$SS_{A_{comp.} \text{ at } bj} = \frac{n(\hat{\psi}_{A \text{ at } b_j})^2}{\Sigma d^2 \text{ at } b_j} \tag{12-8}$$

where the subscript j refers to the two levels of $B_{comp.}$. I will use plus $(+)$ as the subscript for the level of the comparison associated with positive coefficients and minus $(-)$ as the subscript for the level of the comparison associated with negative coefficients. This notation facilitates the designation of the levels of a complex comparison, where several levels are combined. In the present example, then, $(+)$ refers to the low emotionality condition (b_2) and $(-)$ refers to the high emotionality condition (b_3). You should also note that the denominator term in Eq. (12-8) consists of the squared interaction coefficients summed over the coefficients contributing to this particular simple effect. Let's see how this works.

From Table 12-7, we find that the difference between the control and combined feedback conditions is 1.0 for words of low emotional content. For the relevant interaction coefficients, we turn to the second row of Table 12-8 and then calculate

$$\Sigma d^2 \text{ at } b_{(+)} = (1)^2 + (-\tfrac{1}{2})^2 + (-\tfrac{1}{2})^2 = 1.5$$

Substituting this information in Eq. (12-8), we have

$$SS_{A_{comp.} \text{ at } b(+)} = \frac{5(1.0)^2}{1.5} = \frac{5.0}{1.5} = 3.33$$

The comparison is not significant ($F = 3.33/1.75 = 1.90$). For the corresponding analysis for words of high emotional content, the difference between the control and combined feedback conditions is 3.9, and the sum of the squared coefficients comes from the third row of Table 12-8; that is,

$$\Sigma d^2 \text{ at } b_{(-)} = (-1)^2 + (\tfrac{1}{2})^2 + (\tfrac{1}{2})^2 = 1.5$$

The sum of squares for this simple comparison,

$$SS_{A_{comp.} \text{ at } b(-)} = \frac{5(3.9)^2}{1.5} = \frac{76.05}{1.5} = 50.70$$

is significant ($F = 50.70/1.75 = 28.97$).

Summary of the Analysis.   This analysis indicates that differences in memory due to the introduction of verbal feedback during learning (control versus combined feedback conditions) depends on the emotional quality of the words learned by the subjects, which is shown by the significant interaction contrast involving these two comparisons. Moreover, the analysis of simple comparisons reveals that this interaction is due to a small and nonsignificant effect for the words of low emotional content and a large, significant effect for the words of high emotional content.

12.3   TREND ANALYSIS APPLIED TO INTERACTION CONTRASTS

When the levels of one of the independent variables of a factorial experiment represent points along a quantitative dimension or scale, it is usually fruitful to examine trend components in some systematic fashion. Functionally, there is no difference between a complex comparison and a trend component. Although a complex comparison groups certain conditions according to some logical plan, a trend component groups them in a manner specified by that component. In Chap. 7, you saw how linear and higher-order trend components can be extracted from a single-factor experiment. What does it mean to conduct a similar analysis within the context of a factorial design? The general purpose of trend analysis is to search for underlying trends that are relatively simple in form—that is, functions that contain trends no more complicated than quadratic or cubic. When applied to main effects, trend analysis is essentially identical to the single-factor case. When applied to interaction, trend analysis uses the same computational formulas required for interaction comparisons but attempts to describe interaction in terms of relatively simple trend components.

A Linear Interaction Contrast

Suppose we performed a 5×2 factorial experiment where the $a = 5$ levels are equally spaced on some quantitative scale. Two possible outcomes of this experiment are presented in Fig. 12–1. If we consider the functions at each level of factor B, they are both primarily linear in shape; that is, a straight line drawn through each set of five means would provide a relatively accurate description of the relationship between the dependent variable and factor A (the quantitative independent variable). The graph on the left depicts a case in which the slopes of the two curves at b_1 and b_2 are approximately *equal*; the graph on the right depicts a case in which the slopes of the two curves are *different*. The first case is an example in which an overall linear trend is present, but the slopes of the two straight lines do not depend on the levels of factor B. On the other hand, the second case also shows that linear trend is present but that the slopes of the two straight lines depend on the levels of factor B—that is, the slope at level b_1 is considerably steeper than the slope at level b_2. This is an example of an interaction involving the linear component.

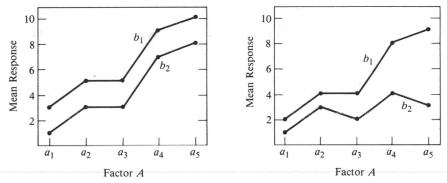

Figure 12–1 Example of the absence (left panel) and the presence (right panel) of a linear interaction component.

A linear interaction is present whenever the slopes of the best-fitting straight lines drawn through the cell means at each level of the other independent variable (factor *B* here) are statistically different. In many respects, an interaction of this sort is no different from any other interaction involving a single-*df* comparison that we considered in Secs. 12.1 and 12.2, except that instead of referring to "slope," as we do in a trend analysis, we refer instead to the differences between the two levels of the comparison associated with a qualitative independent variable.

Another way of thinking about trend analysis and interaction is in terms of the relationship that describes what happens to the differences between the levels of factor *B* (b_1 and b_2 in this example) as the levels of the quantitative factor (factor *A*) increase. Table 12–9 gives the cell means for the two hypothetical experiments plotted in Fig. 12–1. At the bottom of each *AB* matrix I have entered the difference between b_1 and b_2. You will note that these differences remain constant for the first example and increase steadily for the second example. In this example, then, the presence of a linear component of the interaction means that the simple effects of factor *B* (the difference between b_1 and b_2) increase in a linear fashion as a function of the quantitative independent variable, factor *A*.

To say that the linear component of the interaction is significant, then, is to indicate that the slope of the best-fitting *linear* function for factor *A* is not the same for the different levels of factor *B*. Said another way, the simple linear com-

Table 12–9 Two Examples of Linear Trend

	Interaction Absent						Interaction Present				
	a_1	a_2	a_3	a_4	a_5		a_1	a_2	a_3	a_4	a_5
b_1	3	5	5	9	10	b_1	2	4	4	8	9
b_2	1	3	3	7	8	b_2	1	3	2	4	3
Diff.	2	2	2	2	2	**Diff.**	1	1	2	4	6

ponents—the particular set of comparisons that focus on linear trend—are not the same. If we find that the $SS_{A \times B}$ is due largely to the interaction of these linear functions—that is, to the differences in slope—we will have pinpointed the source of the interaction to a particular mathematical component of the function relating variations in the independent variable (factor A in this case) to the behavior under study. However one views it, the linear component of this particular interaction provides a succinct and accurate summary of the overall $A \times B$ interaction depicted in Fig. 12–1.

A Quadratic Interaction Contrast

Consider next the example presented in Fig. 12–2, in which factor A again is a quantitative independent variable, this time with $a = 4$ equally spaced intervals on some quantitative dimension. Clearly, an interaction is present. Let's try to describe it in terms of trend components. At level b_1, the means rise and fall as factor A increases, describing an obvious quadratic trend. A quadratic trend is also present at level b_2, but it is roughly of opposite curvature. What we see, then, is a rather sizable interaction involving the quadratic component. We can interpret this interaction another way by considering the differences between b_1 and b_2 for each level of factor A. As you can see, this difference is small at a_1, increases in size at a_2 and a_3, and then becomes small again at a_4. What this means, then, is that with the presence of a quadratic component of an interaction, the effects of the other independent variable (factor B) may be described by a quadratic function—in this case, an inverted U, which increases and then decreases. Whether anything can be made out of this particular finding, of course, depends on existing theory and the ingenuity of the investigator.

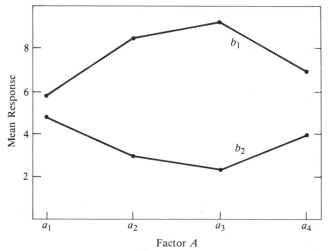

Figure 12–2   *An example of an interaction involving the quadratic component.*

A Numerical Example

I will use the data from our original numerical example in Chap. 10 to illustrate the calculations for testing the significance of a linear interaction contrast. To do so, let's assume that factor A now consists of three equally spaced dosage levels of a particular drug, rather than a control and two drug conditions. Since the linear component is a single-df comparison and factor B contains two levels in this example, the analysis qualifies as an interaction contrast—an interaction effect associated with 1 df. We start by calculating the special interaction coefficients d_{ij}, which are obtained by cross-multiplying the linear coefficients for factor A by the coefficients representing the two levels of factor B. (The coefficients for linear trend come from Table A–4.) The results of this operation are presented in the left-hand matrix of Table 12–10. The next step is to use these coefficients to weight the cell means, the results of which are found in the right-hand matrix of the table. The cell means were taken from Table 12–2 (p. 255). To illustrate, the weighted cell mean at a_1b_1 is found by multiplying the interaction coefficient for this cell by the corresponding cell mean: $(d_{1,1})(\overline{Y}_{A_1B_1}) = (-1)(3.00) = -3.00$.

The sum of squares for this linear interaction contrast is calculated by substituting in Eq. (12–4):

$$SS_{A_{linear} \times B_{comp.}} = \frac{n(\hat{\psi}_{A \times B})^2}{\Sigma d_{ij}^2}$$

To complete the specified calculations, we need the sample size $n = 4$, the estimate of the interaction effect ($\hat{\psi}_{A \times B}$), and the sum of the squared interaction coefficients. The estimate of the interaction effect is found by summing the entire set of weighted cell means. From Table 12–10, we find

$$\hat{\psi}_{A \times B} = \Sigma (d_{ij})(\overline{Y}_{A_iB_j}) = -3.00 + 0.00 + \ldots + 0.00 + (-10.00) = 12.00$$

Also from Table 12–10, we can calculate the sum of the squared interaction coefficients:

$$\Sigma d_{ij}^2 = (-1)^2 + (0)^2 + \ldots + (0)^2 + (-1)^2 = 4$$

We are now able to calculate the sum of squares:

$$SS_{A_{linear} \times B_{comp.}} = \frac{4(12.00)^2}{4} = \frac{576.00}{4} = 144.00$$

The linear component of an interaction contrast has 1 df; the error term comes

Table 12–10 Example of a Linear Trend Analysis

			Interaction Coefficients				Weighted Cell Means		
			(a_1)	(a_2)	(a_3)				
	c_j	c_i:	-1	0	1		a_1	a_2	a_3
(b_1)	1		-1	0	1	b_1	-3.00	0.00	14.00
(b_2)	-1		1	0	-1	b_2	11.00	0.00	-10.00

from the overall analysis ($MS_{S/AB} = 18.33$). The $F = 144.00/18.33 = 7.86$ is significant.

You can see this interaction by referring to Fig. 11–2 and visualizing the "linear trend" at the two levels of factor B. The slope of the best-fitting straight line drawn through the cell means at b_1 suggests a strong linear function, whereas the one at b_2 is virtually nonexistent. These judgments can be subjected to statistical test by examining the simple trend components at b_1 and b_2. The computational formula for simple comparisons was given by Eq. (12–8); rewritten for the linear trend analysis it becomes

$$SS_{A_{linear} \text{ at } b_j} = \frac{n(\hat{\psi}_{linear \text{ at } b_j})^2}{\Sigma \, d^2 \text{ at } b_j} \tag{12–9}$$

We can obtain the information we need from Table 12–10. For level b_1, we use the values found in the first row of both matrices:

$$\hat{\psi}_{linear \text{ at } b_1} = -3.00 + 0.00 + 14.00 = 11.00$$

$$\Sigma \, d^2 \text{ at } b_1 = (-1)^2 + (0)^2 + (1)^2 = 2$$

Substituting in Eq. (12–9), we obtain

$$SS_{A_{linear} \text{ at } b_1} = \frac{4(11.00)^2}{2} = \frac{484.00}{2} = 242.00$$

With 1 df, $F = 242.00/18.33 = 13.20$. This test indicates that the linear trend at level b_1 is significant. Performing the same test at level b_2, we find

$$SS_{A_{linear} \text{ at } b_2} = \frac{4(1.00)^2}{2} = \frac{4.00}{2} = 2.00$$

The $F = 2.00/18.33 = .11$ is not significant.

Since $df_{A \times B} = 2$, we could extract a quadratic trend component from this analysis, but this would be pointless because the linear component fully accounts for the interaction; that is, $SS_{A \times B} = 144.00$, and we found that $SS_{A_{linear} \times B_{comp.}} = 144.00$. If this were not the case and there was either a theoretical reason or significant residual variation remaining when we subtract the linear component from $SS_{A \times B}$, we would probably examine the quadratic component of the interaction. The computational procedure is exactly the same; the only difference is that we must substitute the appropriate quadratic coefficients for the linear coefficients.

12.4   ANALYZING PARTIAL INTERACTIONS

A partial interaction is derived from a factorial design for which the numbers of levels of *both* factors are greater than 2; a 3 × 3 is the "smallest" factorial design that can yield partial interactions. As defined at the beginning of this chapter, a partial interaction consists of a single-*df* comparison crossed with an *intact* factor. Let's return to our example of the effects on memory from the verbal feedback given during learning, where factor A consists of a control and two feedback conditions (positive feedback and negative feedback) and factor B consists of three types of learning materials (see Table 12–6). Although the specific types of materials were of interest in Sec. 12.2, when we used this example to illustrate interaction contrasts, they remain essentially undifferentiated in the present context. For our purposes in this section, we will simply consider factor B as consisting of three levels and not pay attention to the nature of any differences between them.

Given the nature of this experimental design, most researchers would not be interested in testing the overall $A \times B$ interaction since it does not bear directly on the interesting research questions examined by this experiment. Two of these research questions are expressed as partial factorials in Table 12–11. The partial factorial on the left focuses on the two feedback conditions a_2 and a_3; the control condition a_1 has been omitted entirely. The result is a 2×3 factorial design in which factor A has become a single-df comparison. The interest in this analysis is the possibility of an interaction between this comparison (the difference between positive and negative feedback) and factor B (the three types of learning material). The question asked is this: Does the difference between positive and negative feedback depend on the type of material being learned by the subjects?

The partial factorial on the right compares the control condition a_1 with an average of the two feedback conditions. As you can see, the design again becomes a 2×3 factorial in which the two levels of $A_{comp.}$ cross with the three levels of factor B. The partial interaction in this case will answer this question: Does the difference between the control and the combined feedback conditions vary with the type of material learned? Both partial interactions ask meaningful questions of the data, although they are not as specific as the questions asked when interaction contrasts are formed with the same experimental design. Table 12–5 (p. 262) illustrates this difference. The partial interaction pays no direct attention to the questions embedded within the manipulation of the other independent variable (factor B in this example); the interaction contrast subdivides the other factor into exactly these questions, giving greater specificity to the analysis of interaction.

A Numerical Example

Arranging the Data for Analysis.   We can calculate a partial interaction by working with the cell means and transforming them into single-df comparisons,

Table 12–11   Examples of Two Partial Factorials

	Positive a_2	Negative a_3		Control Condition a_1	Combined Feedback $a_2 + a_3$
b_1			b_1		
b_2			b_2		
b_3			b_3		

from which point we can then obtain the necessary interaction sum of squares. The hypothetical data for this example, which originally appeared in Table 12–6, are presented again on the left side of Table 12–12. I will now calculate one of the partial interactions diagrammed in Table 12–11, namely, the interaction between the control and the combined feedback conditions and factor B. Coefficients for this comparison are the set 1, $-\frac{1}{2}$, $-\frac{1}{2}$. The particular set of means reflecting this comparison at each level of factor B, which is derived from the original matrix of cell means, is presented in the center of Table 12–12. At b_1, for example, the control mean comes directly from the matrix, and we obtain the combined feedback mean by averaging the cell means for the two feedback conditions, that is, $(7.8 + 8.0)/2 = 7.9$. The simple comparisons $\psi_{A \, at \, b_j}$, expressed as differences between the control and the combined means, are presented on the right side of Table 12–12. Each of the three differences, .5, 1.0, and 3.9, is a simple comparison involving factor A differing with regard to the level of factor B involved. Interaction is present if the simple effects (or simple comparisons in this case) are not the same at all levels of the other independent variable. The test for the partial or contrast $\times$ treatment interaction consists of an assessment of the differences among these three simple comparisons. If the null hypothesis that these simple comparisons are the same is rejected, we can conclude that a partial interaction is present. An inspection of the simple comparisons in Table 12–12 suggests the possibility that this partial interaction may be significant.

Computational Formulas.   A relatively easy way to calculate the sum of squares for a partial interaction is to take advantage of the general relationship between the simple effects of a factor, on the one hand, and the main effect of that factor and the interaction, on the other. We discussed this relationship in Sec. 11.3 (pp. 241–242). In terms of factor A, this relationship is expressed as follows:

$$\Sigma \, SS_{A \, at \, b_j} = SS_{A \times B} + SS_A$$

That is, the sum of the sums of squares associated with the simple effects of factor A equals the sum of the sums of squares associated with the $A \times B$ interaction and the main effect of factor A. We can extend this relationship to simple comparisons by changing the subscripts appropriately:

$$\Sigma \, SS_{A_{comp.} \, at \, b_j} = SS_{A_{comp.} \times B} + SS_{A_{comp.}}$$

Table 12–12   A Numerical Example of a Partial Interaction

	Original $A \times B$ Design				Partial Factorial			Simple Comparisons
	Control a_1	Positive a_2	Negative a_3		Control Condition	Combined Feedback		$\hat{\psi}_{A \, at \, b_j}$
b_1	8.4	7.8	8.0	b_1	8.4	7.9	b_1	.5
b_2	8.8	8.0	7.6	b_2	8.8	7.8	b_2	1.0
b_3	8.0	4.4	3.8	b_3	8.0	4.1	b_3	3.9
Mean	8.40	6.73	6.47	**Mean**	8.4	6.6		

Since you already know how to calculate sums of squares for simple comparisons (the quantities on the left of the equal sign) and comparison main effects (one of the quantities on the right of the equal sign), we can obtain the third quantity—the sum of squares for the partial interaction—by *subtraction*. To be more explicit,

$$SS_{A_{comp.} \times B} = \Sigma SS_{A_{comp.} \text{ at } b_j} - SS_{A_{comp.}} \tag{12-10}$$

Conducting the Analysis.   As a first step, we will calculate the simple comparisons with the formula

$$SS_{A_{comp.} \text{ at } b_j} = \frac{n(\hat{\psi}_{A \text{ at } b_j})^2}{\Sigma c_i^2} \tag{12-11}$$

Calculating first

$$\Sigma c_i^2 = (1)^2 + (-\tfrac{1}{2})^2 + (-\tfrac{1}{2})^2 = 1.5$$

and substituting in Eq. (12–11), remembering that $n = 5$, we find

$$SS_{A_{comp.} \text{ at } b_1} = \frac{5(.5)^2}{1.5} = \frac{1.25}{1.5} = .83$$

$$SS_{A_{comp.} \text{ at } b_2} = \frac{5(1.0)^2}{1.5} = \frac{5}{1.5} = 3.33$$

$$SS_{A_{comp.} \text{ at } b_3} = \frac{5(3.9)^2}{1.5} = \frac{76.05}{1.5} = 50.70$$

The sum of these sums of squares gives us the first quantity required by Eq. (12–10),

$$\Sigma SS_{A_{comp.} \text{ at } b_j} = .83 + 3.33 + 50.70 = 54.86$$

Next, we calculate the comparison main effect. From Eq. (11–3), we can calculate $\hat{\psi}_A$ by using the marginal means $\overline{Y}_{A_i}$ provided in the left-hand matrix of Table 12–12:

$$\hat{\psi}_A = \Sigma (c_i)(\overline{Y}_{A_i}) = (1)(8.40) + (-\tfrac{1}{2})(6.73) + (-\tfrac{1}{2})(6.47) = 1.80$$

Substituting in Eq. (11–2), we find

$$SS_{A_{comp.}} = \frac{(b)(n)(\hat{\psi}_A)^2}{\Sigma c_i^2} = \frac{(3)(5)(1.80)^2}{1.5} = \frac{48.60}{1.5} = 32.40$$

Finally, we calculate the sum of squares for the partial interaction by using Eq. (12–10) and obtain

$$SS_{A_{comp.} \times B} = \Sigma SS_{A_{comp.} \text{ at } b_j} - SS_{A_{comp.}}$$
$$= 54.86 - 32.40 = 22.46$$

The number of degrees of freedom for a partial interaction is given by the formula

$$df_{A_{comp.} \times B} = (df_{A_{comp.}})(df_B)$$ (12–12)

In this example, $df_{A_{comp.} \times B} = (1)(3 - 1) = 2$. The mean square is obtained by dividing the sum of squares by the degrees of freedom:

$$MS_{A_{comp} \times B} = \frac{22.46}{2} = 11.23$$

The F ratio is formed by dividing this mean square by the within-groups mean square from the overall analysis of variance ($MS_{S/AB}$):

$$F = \frac{MS_{A_{comp.} \times B}}{MS_{S/AB}}$$ (12–13)

If we assume that $MS_{S/AB} = 1.75$, $F = 11.23/1.75 = 6.42$, which is significant. (The critical value of F is found in the F table at $df_{num.} = 2$ and $df_{denom.} = 36$.)

Simple Comparisons

Since the partial interaction is significant, we would usually determine which of the simple comparisons are significant and which are not. This is an easy task because we calculated the relevant sums of squares during the course of evaluating the interaction. From these earlier calculations, we found the comparison sums of squares to be .83, 3.33, and 50.70 for levels b_1 through b_3, respectively. Each sum of squares is associated with 1 df, of course. The only significant simple comparison is the one at b_3:

$$F = \frac{MS_{A_{comp.} \text{ at } b_3}}{MS_{S/AB}} = \frac{50.70}{1.75} = 28.97$$

Comment

This analysis certainly provides more information about the interaction of factors A and B than is provided by the omnibus $A \times B$ interaction, which tells us only that there is an interaction somewhere in the matrix of cell means. The analysis of the partial interaction gave us more precise information about the nature of the interaction, namely, that the size of the negative effect of verbal feedback on memory (control versus combined feedback) depends on the nature of the learning materials (factor B) and that although all three types of material exhibit a negative effect of feedback, only the difference for material represented by level b_3 is significant.

This analysis is most appropriate when we have no interest in the specific levels constituting factor B or have no basis for arranging them into meaningful comparisons. However, this example is really not of this sort, as you saw in Sec. 12.2, when we analyzed interaction contrasts derived from the same set of data. Table 12–5 (p. 262) and the discussion associated with it illustrate how interaction contrasts can provide a much more focused description of the interaction. For the present example, we know only that the difference between the control and the combined feedback conditions depends on the type of learning material. The analysis of interaction contrasts summarized in Sec. 12.2 indicates that this interaction is due primarily to a difference in the emotional content of the words. Moreover, an analysis of the simple comparisons revealed that only the words with high emotional content exhibited a significant effect. The conclusion offered by the analysis of interaction contrasts is considerably more specific and focused in comparison with the omnibus $A \times B$ interaction and even with the partial interaction we just considered.

12.5 SUMMARY OF THE DIFFERENT ANALYSES

It should be clear to you by now that a factorial experiment provides a wealth of information beyond that found with the overall analysis of variance. Not all analyses are relevant to all factorial designs since the nature of the experimental design and your research questions will lead you to a particular collection of tests. It is important that you maintain a general understanding of the analyses—what they measure and what information they yield—so that you can incorporate them into your thinking as you plan an experiment.

The approaches described in this chapter and in Chap. 11 are interrelated in the sense that once an interaction has been specified—whether an omnibus interaction, a partial one, or an interaction contrast—the analysis branches to a consideration of simple effects when the interaction is significant and main effects when it is not. The analysis of simple effects described in the last chapter proceeds methodically, assessing each simple effect separately and, usually following a significant F, with one or more single-df comparisons; the analysis ends by determining whether the significant comparisons themselves interact with the other independent variable. At this point, the analysis of simple effects moves to an analysis of interaction comparisons (see pp. 248–249).

The fundamental differences in the two strategies revolve around statistical power and analytical elegance. Analyses based on interaction comparisons are the *planned comparisons* of the factorial design. Because they are not dependent on the outcome of an *omnibus F* test, they are more powerful than the corresponding analyses extracted from the analysis of simple effects. It is entirely possible, for example, that a significant and theoretically important interaction contrast will not be discovered because it has been averaged with other nonsignificant interaction effects in the omnibus test. An example of this situation is found in problem 5 in the exercises.

Interaction comparisons derive naturally from single-factor designs. If an independent variable can be profitably viewed as a set of single-df comparisons, these same comparisons can usually play a central role in the analysis of a factorial design involving that or a related independent variable. You have seen how easily this took place with the numerical example involving the negative effects on memory produced by the verbal feedback (in comparison with a control condition) on three different types of learning material. The feedback manipulation (factor A) was easily transformed into four meaningful single-df comparisons (see Table

12–5). The other manipulation (factor B = three types of learning material) was similarly transformed into two meaningful comparisons. It would make perfectly good sense to study either set of comparisons in a single-factor experiment. If we conceptualize a particular independent variable in terms of these analytical comparisons, we can usually extend exactly the same analysis to the factorial, with all the benefits that such an extension would have. In short, this analytical approach to the design and analysis of factorial experiments represents a flexible and powerful way to study the factors that affect how two independent variables combine to influence behavior.

12.6 EXERCISES[3]

1. An experimenter is interested in the effects of alcohol on aggressive behavior in fish. There are to be four treatment conditions: no alcohol, laboratory alcohol, and two commercial brands of whiskey known to contain large amounts of various impurities valued for their distinctive contribution to the taste and smell of the two whiskeys. A fish is placed in a tank containing the appropriate substance and after a period of time is exposed to another fish introduced into the tank in a clear plastic tube. Aggression is measured by the number of bites directed toward the other fish during a 5-minute testing period. A second independent variable, the length of exposure to the water in the testing tank, is combined factorially with the alcohol variable. This variable will consist of two levels, namely, 2 and 10 minutes before the second fish is introduced into the tank.
   a. What meaningful questions can the experimenter consider in analyzing the main effects of the alcohol variable?
   b. How can these questions be extended to the analysis of the interaction of the two independent variables? What will each analysis tell you?
2. Problem 1 in the exercises for Chap. 11 (p. 250) involved an experiment on the effects of selective breeding in which one of the independent variables (factor A) consisted of three strains of rats (bright, mixed, and dull) and the other (factor B) consisted of two different environments in which the rats were raised (enriched and impoverished). Factor A lends itself to a number of meaningful single-df comparisons. For example, a comparison between the bright and dull rats reflects both the positive and the negative effects of the selective breeding; in contrast, a comparison between bright and mixed focuses on the positive effects, and a comparison between dull and mixed focuses on the negative effects. Each of these single-df comparisons defines a different interaction contrast. For each one,
   a. Form the relevant 2 × 2 matrix of means.
   b. Calculate the sum of squares for the interaction contrast.
   c. State in your own words the nature of the interaction.
3. Suppose we were interested in the effects of different incentives on the solving of problems by fifth-grade students. (We considered a related experiment in Sec. 6.5.) Factor A consists of three levels (verbal praise, monetary reward, and no specific incentive). A second independent variable consists of two levels of problem complexity (simple and complex). There are n = 5 children randomly assigned to the six treat-

---

[3]The answers to these problems are found in Appendix B.

ment conditions. The response measure is the number of problems solved in 20 minutes. The means for the different treatment groups are as follows:

TASK (B)	INCENTIVE CONDITIONS (A)		
	Verbal	Monetary	None
Simple	14.40	13.20	14.00
Complex	9.60	10.80	6.40

For this example, $MS_{S/AB} = 3.09$.

a. Given the nature of this experimental design, it is unlikely that a researcher would be interested in the standard analysis of variance. Instead, certain interaction comparisons would be more desirable alternatives. An obvious analysis is to examine the interaction contrast formed by crossing the two incentive conditions (verbal versus monetary) with the two levels of the task variable (simple versus complex). Test the significance of this interaction. What does this test reveal?

b. Given the outcome of the test you conducted in part a, it is probably safe to combine the two incentive conditions (verbal and monetary) and to form an interaction contrast comparing the difference between the combined incentive conditions and the control condition (none) at the two levels of the task variable. What does this test reveal?

c. Since the interaction contrast is significant, you would probably be interested in assessing the significance of the simple comparisons. As an example, determine whether the difference between the combined incentive condition and the control condition is significant for the simple task and for the complex task.

4. Consider an experiment in which performance on a task is studied as a function of pretraining experience. One independent variable is the amount of pretraining—3, 6, 9, and 12 trials (factor A)—and the other variable is the nature of the pretraining— facilitating or interfering (factor B). The outcome of this experiment was presented in Fig. 12–2 (p. 268). The treatment sums and the AB matrix follow:

	a_1	a_2	a_3	a_4	Sum
b_1	29	42	46	35	152
b_2	24	15	12	20	71
Sum	53	57	58	55	223

Assume there were $n = 5$ subjects assigned to each treatment condition and that $MS_{S/AB} = 4.84$.

a. Conduct an overall analysis of variance.

b. Since the $A \times B$ interaction is significant and factor A represents a quantitative manipulation, it is a natural next step to examine the trend components of the interaction. What does this analysis reveal?

c. In part b, you discovered that the quadratic component of the interaction is significant. An inspection of Fig. 12–2 suggests that this interaction results from the presence of a concave-downward trend (an inverted U) at b_1 and a concave-upward trend (a U) at b_2. Are either of these simple quadratic trends significant?

5. This problem demonstrates that it is possible for a significant interaction contrast to be "hidden" in the test of the omnibus $A \times B$ interaction, which in fact is based on an average of several interaction contrasts. An experimenter is studying the effects of administering a certain drug on reducing the activity of hyperactive boys. Two groups

of boys are identified, one consisting of hyperactive boys and the other consisting of "normal" boys who are matched on a number of variables known to be related to activity. Each group is randomly assigned to one of three conditions: two groups that receive either a low or a high dosage of the drug and a placebo or control condition that receives an inert substance. The children are participants in a summer program for fourth-grade children. The boys receive pills containing either the drug or the placebo for two weeks preceding the test. On the test day, they are observed in a play situation by trained observers, who rate their levels of activity on a specially devised scale. The six fictitious cell sums, which are each based on $n = 5$ subjects, follow.

Type of	Drug Conditions		
Children	Placebo	Low	High
Hyperactive	40	9	11
Normal	20	6	5

a. Conduct an overall analysis of variance. (Assume $MS_{S/AB} = 2.75$.)

b. You will note that the $A \times B$ interaction is not significant. A more appropriate analysis, given the nature of the design, is to evaluate a number of interaction contrasts. One of these involves the two drug conditions (low and high dosage). Test the significance of this interaction.

c. Given the outcome of the analysis in part b, we can combine the two drug conditions and form an interaction contrast involving the placebo and the combined drug conditions. Test the significance of this interaction.

13

Analysis of Experiments with Unequal Sample Sizes

Most experiments contain an equal number of subjects in each of the treatment conditions, most obviously to give equal weight to all the conditions in the statistical analysis. Additionally, using equal sample sizes minimizes the effects of violating the distributional assumptions of the analysis of variance—that is, normality and homogeneity of variance. Finally, unequal sample sizes require different computational formulas for the sums of squares in the analysis of variance and can cause serious complications when they appear in factorial designs. We will first consider the primary reason for unequal sample sizes, namely, the inadvertant loss of subjects, and the threat that such losses make to the integrity of an experiment. We will then consider the specialized techniques that have been developed to analyze the data from experiments with unequal sample sizes.

13.1   LOSS OF SUBJECTS

In most cases, unequal sample sizes are not planned but are forced on us by the accidental loss of subjects during the course of the experiment. Why should subjects fail to complete an experiment? In animal studies, for example, subjects are frequently lost through death and sickness. In human studies, in which testing is to continue over several days, subjects are discarded when they fail to complete the experimental sequence. In a memory study, for instance, some subjects may fail to return for their final retention test a week later, perhaps because of illness or a conflicting appointment. Subjects also may be lost when studies require them to reach a performance criterion, such as a certain level of mastery; those who fail to do so are eliminated from the experiment. A third class of situations occurs when some subjects fail to produce responses that meet the criteria established for the response measure. Suppose we are interested in the speed with which correct responses are made. If subjects fail to give a correct response, they cannot contribute to the analysis. Or suppose we want to analyze the percentage of times errors produced on some task are of a particular type. If subjects fail to make any errors, they cannot contribute to the analysis. In such situations, subjects are eliminated because they fail to give scorable responses.

It is of critical importance to determine the *implication* of these losses. That is, we have assigned our subjects to the treatment conditions in such a way that any differences among the groups at the start of the experiment will be attributed to chance factors. It is this fundamental assumption that allows us to test the null hypothesis. We are not concerned with the loss of subjects per se but with this question: Has the loss of subjects—for whatever reason—resulted in a loss of *randomness*? If it has, we must either find a way to restore randomness or simply junk the experiment. No form of statistical juggling will rectify this situation. If randomness may still be safely assumed or has been restored, we can proceed with the statistical analysis of the data.

In each situation, we have to determine whether the reason for the loss of subjects is in any way associated with particular experimental treatments. In animal research, for instance, certain experimental conditions (such as operations, drugs, high levels of food or water deprivation, or exhausting training procedures) may actually be responsible for the loss. If this were the case, only the strongest and healthiest animals would survive, and the result would be an obvious confounding of subject differences and treatment conditions: The difficult conditions would contain a larger proportion of healthy animals than the less trying conditions. Replacing the lost subjects with new animals drawn from the same population will not provide an adequate solution since the replacement subjects will not "match" the ones who were lost. If it can be shown that the loss of subjects was approximately the same from all the conditions or that the loss was not related to the experimental treatments, we may be able to continue with the analysis.

The same considerations are relevant when human subjects fail to complete the experiment. In the memory study I mentioned, it is likely that more subjects will be lost with the longer retention intervals, where the subjects have a greater "opportunity" to get sick. It is not known whether the loss of these subjects affects randomness. A researcher could attempt to see if the subjects who were lost and the subjects who were retained were equivalent in learning, although equality at this point in the experiment does not necessarily mean that the two sets of subjects would have been equivalent at recall. In some experiments, an attempt is made to impose the same subject loss on *all* conditions. For example, suppose we require all subjects to return for the later retention test and we follow the rule of discarding any subject who fails to return. The subject who is tested at the long interval and does not return is dropped from the experiment by default. But so is the subject who is tested at a shorter interval and fails to return for the later appointment.

The loss of subjects through failure to reach a criterion of mastery poses similar problems. Clearly, subjects who fail to learn are by definition poorer learners. If one group suffers a greater loss, which may very well occur if the conditions differ in difficulty, the subjects completing the training in the difficult condition represent a greater proportion of fast learners than those completing it in the easier conditions. The replacement of subjects lost in the difficult condition would not solve this problem since the replacement subjects would not match in ability the subjects who were discarded. One possibility is to compare the different groups at a lower criterion—one that will allow all the subjects to be included. In this way, no subjects will be lost. Such a solution will be adequate if the smaller sample of behavior provides sufficient information to suit the needs of the researcher.

Some experimenters solve this problem by artificially imposing a subject selection on the groups that suffer fewer or no losses. Thus, if it can be assumed that only the poorer subjects were dropped from the more difficult conditions for failure to reach the performance criterion, it might be possible to drop an equal number of the *poorest* subjects from *all* the treatment conditions. A similar procedure is sometimes followed when subjects fail to give scorable responses. Suppose, for example, that an investigator is studying the speed of correct responses under a number of different treatment conditions. As I have pointed out, subjects may fail to give a correct response and thus not provide a speed score. Some researchers attempt to resolve this difficulty by excluding subjects with the poorest record from the other conditions in an attempt to "restore" equivalence of the groups. In all these situations, however, it is assumed that the subjects whose data are discarded in the manner described are subjects who would have failed to reach the criterion or to have any correct responses *if they had been in the condition produc- ing the failures*. This is often a questionable assumption, but it must be made be- fore any meaningful inferences can be drawn from the data adjusted in this manner.

Clearly, then, the loss of subjects is of paramount concern to the experi- menter. You have seen that if the loss of subjects is related to the phenomenon under study, randomness is destroyed and a systematic bias may be added to the differences among the means, which cannot be disentangled from the influence of the treatment effects. This is a problem of experimental design that must be solved by the researcher. If the researcher can be convinced (and can convince others) that the subject loss could not have resulted in a bias, there are statistical proce- dures available that will allow his or her results to be analyzed. We will consider these methods next.

13.2   ANALYZING EXPERIMENTS WITH UNEQUAL SAMPLE SIZES

Most experiments are conducted with equal numbers of subjects assigned to each basic treatment condition. Fundamentally, this is the wisest way to proceed: Equal sample sizes guarantee that each treatment condition contributes equally to the analysis of a study, which the logic of our experimental designs presumably re- quires. Moreover, equal sample sizes reduce any problems associated with viola- tions of the assumptions underlying the analysis of variance, which can be consid- erable with unequal sample sizes (see Glass, Peckham, & Sanders, 1972; Milligan, Wong, & Thompson, 1987), and they are most efficient from the standpoint of power. Unfortunately, even the most careful researchers have unequal sample sizes thrust on them through the loss of subjects.

Problems with Unequal Sample Sizes

There are really two problems associated with the analysis of the data from exper- iments with unequal sample sizes. The first is of utmost importance: The unequal sample sizes must *not* have resulted from the systematic operation of psychological sources. In other words, the reason for the differential numbers of subjects must be *unrelated* to the experimental treatments. Otherwise, the benefit derived from the random assignment of subjects to conditions—a "guarantee" of equivalent groups of subjects in each treatment conditions—is lost. If this in fact occurs, the scientific value of the experimental results is greatly reduced unless some proce- dure is found that will restore the equivalency. In the discussion that follows, we will assume that the unequal sample sizes have occurred for reasons independent of the experimental conditions.

The second problem is practical: How do we analyze the data? One method for dealing with unequal sample sizes is to randomly discard data so that the same number of subjects is represented in each of the treatment conditions. In a 2 × 2 design, for example, suppose one subject was lost from one condition and two from another because of equipment failure; equal sample sizes would be restored by randomly discarding one subject from the first condition, none from the second, and two from the remaining two. Given the alternatives, this is a reasonable course of action, particularly if only a small number of subjects is involved and you have provided for this contingency by including a few more subjects per condition than you normally would need to achieve the power you desired had the loss of subjects not occurred. All other methods are flawed in one way or another (see Milligan, Wong & Thompson, 1987).[1] We will discuss next special problems associated with violations of the statistical assumptions. Following this discussion, we will consider the most popular methods for coping with unequal sample sizes, first for the single-factor design and then for the factorial design.

Violating Statistical Assumptions

Violating the statistical assumptions of normality and homogeneity of variance seriously affects our interpretation of analyses conducted on experiments with unequal sample sizes. In Chap. 5, I indicated that the F test is relatively uninfluenced by even substantial deviations from normality. Heterogeneity among the group variances, on the other hand, produces a demonstrable increase in type I error, which begins to become a problem when the ratio of the largest to the smallest variance ($F_{max.}$) is larger than 3. Under most experimental situations, we can correct for this positive bias by adopting a more stringent significance level, such as $\alpha = .025$.

When unequal sample sizes are present, however, the consequences of violating both assumptions increases substantially. Moreover, with heterogeneous variances, the nature of the effect depends on whether the larger variances are associated with the groups with the smallest sample sizes or with the largest sample sizes (see, for example, Glass, Peckham, & Sanders, 1972; Wilcox, 1987a). These consequences have been reported for single-factor and two-factor designs. Milligan, Wong, and Thompson (1987), for example, studied various patterns of sample sizes and heterogeneity in a Monte Carlo investigation with a 2 × 2 factorial design; they clearly show substantial variations in the actual α levels, which, again, depend on the way in which the variances are paired with the sample sizes. Although many of their simulations were carried out with variations in sample sizes that would never be tolerated in actual experiments, they did find that a small variation in sample sizes ($n_{ij} = 4, 5, 5, 6$) produced actual rejection rates of $\alpha = .10$ when the nominal rejection rate was $\alpha = .05$.

Unfortunately, there are no useful rules of thumb that specify the point at which unequal sample sizes and variance heterogeneity become a serious problem. Milligan, Wong, and Thompson (1987) discuss several possible alternative courses of action, but none is as effective as avoiding unequal sample sizes in the first place. In any case, you must interpret carefully any analyses conducted with data

---

[1] Herr (1986) provides an interesting history of the development of statistical solutions to the problem of unequal sample sizes and factorial designs.

from experiments with unequal sample sizes, particularly when there are even mild deviations from the assumptions of normality and homogeneity of variance.

13.3 UNEQUAL SAMPLE SIZES AND THE SINGLE-FACTOR DESIGN

Two specialized analyses are commonly used to deal with unequal sample sizes in the completely randomized, single-factor design. One of these, **the method of unweighted means,** handles the problem by treating each mean *equally*, which is accomplished by substituting an average sample size for the actual sample sizes associated with the different groups. The other approach, **the method of weighted means,** weights each mean *differentially* according to the actual sample sizes. We will consider the analysis of unweighted means first.

Analysis of Unweighted Means

The Overall Analysis.   The defining formula for SS_A with equal sample size n is expressed as follows:

$$SS_A = n[\Sigma (\overline{Y}_A - \overline{Y}_T)^2] \tag{13-1}$$

The corresponding defining formula for the method of unweighted means is quite similar, except for two changes. First, we calculate the grand mean simply by averaging the a treatment means:

$$\overline{Y}_T^* = \frac{\Sigma \overline{Y}_A}{a} \tag{13-2}$$

I use the asterisk to distinguish this grand mean—an *unweighted* average of the treatment means—from the grand mean we use in the analysis of weighted means. This latter mean, $\overline{Y}_T$, takes into consideration the numbers of subjects in each of the groups. With equal sample sizes, $\overline{Y}_T^* = \overline{Y}_T$. Second, we substitute an *average* sample size, n_h, for n in the defining formula. This average is called the **harmonic mean,** a special average obtained by dividing the number of groups by the sum of the reciprocals of the group sample sizes. In the context of the single-factor design,

$$n_h = \frac{a}{1/n_1 + 1/n_2 + 1/n_3 + \dots} = \frac{a}{\Sigma (1/n_i)} \tag{13-3}$$

With these two changes, the defining formula for SS_A based on unweighted means becomes

$$SS_A = n_h[\Sigma (\overline{Y}_A - \overline{Y}_T^*)^2] \tag{13-4}$$

For a numerical example, consider the data presented in Table 13-1, in which the last score in level a_3 has been deleted. (These data originally appeared in Table 2-1.) We will assume that an error by the experimenter, which was not discovered

Table 13–1   Numerical Example: Unequal Sample Sizes

	a_1	a_2	a_3
	16	4	2
	18	6	10
	10	8	9
	12	10	13
	19	2	—
Sum:	75	30	34
Sample Size:	5	5	4
Mean:	15.0	6.0	8.5
ΣY^2:	1,185	220	354
Sum of Squares:	60.0	40.0	65.0

until after the study had been completed, rendered the original score ($Y_{3,5} = 11$) useless. The information we need for the analysis is provided in Table 13–1. We begin by calculating the average of the treatment means:

$$\bar{Y}_T^* = \frac{15.0 + 6.0 + 8.5}{3} = 9.83$$

Next, we obtain the harmonic mean of the sample sizes; substituting in Eq. (13–3), we find

$$n_h = \frac{3}{1/5 + 1/5 + 1/4} = \frac{3}{.20 + .20 + .25} = \frac{3}{.65} = 4.62$$

We can now calculate the treatment sum of squares by entering the relevant values into Eq. (13–4).

$$SS_A = (4.62)[(15.0 - 9.83)^2 + (6.0 - 9.83)^2 + (8.5 - 9.83)^2]$$

$$= (4.62)[(5.17)^2 + (-3.83)^2 + (-1.33)^2]$$

$$= (4.62)(43.17) = 199.45$$

The treatment mean square is obtained in the usual manner:

$$MS_A = \frac{SS_A}{df_A} = \frac{199.45}{3 - 1} = 99.73$$

The final step in the analysis of unweighted means is the calculation of the error term, $MS_{S/A}$, which consists of the pooled within-groups sum of squares divided by the pooled within-groups degrees of freedom:

$$MS_{S/A} = \frac{\Sigma SS_{S/A_i}}{\Sigma df_{S/A_i}} \tag{13–5}$$

With equal sample sizes, Eq. (13–5) produces the same value for the $MS_{S/A}$ that we find with the more familiar computational formulas. The within-group sums of squares are presented in the last row of Table 13–1. Completing the calculations specified in Eq. (13–5), we find

$$MS_{S/A} = \frac{60.0 + 40.0 + 65.0}{4 + 4 + 3} = \frac{165.0}{11} = 15.00$$

We can now calculate the F ratio:

$$F = \frac{MS_A}{MS_{S/A}} = \frac{99.73}{15.00} = 6.65$$

which, with $df_{num.} = 2$ and $df_{denom.} = 11$, is significant. The original example with all the data included gave us $MS_A = 105.00$, $MS_{S/A} = 14.17$, $F = 7.41$ ($df_{num.} = 2$ and $df_{denom.} = 12$).

Estimating Treatment Magnitude (Omega Squared).   The formulas for estimating omega squared have been shown to be incorrect for experiments in which equal sample sizes were planned but for which differential subject loss produced unequal sample sizes. Wang (1982) discusses the problem of estimating omega squared under these circumstances and provides a numerical example of one solution.

Single-df Comparisons.   The computational formula for single-df comparisons is identical to the one we use with equal sample sizes, except that n_h is substituted for n:

$$SS_{A_{comp.}} = \frac{n_h(\hat{\psi})^2}{\Sigma \, c_i^2} \qquad (13-6)$$

where $\hat{\psi}$ is the difference between the two means involved in the comparison. We work directly with the means, and the differences in sample sizes do not enter into the calculations. Suppose wanted to compare a_1 and a_3. With the appropriate coefficients $(1, 0, -1)$, we calculate

$$\hat{\psi} = (1)(15.0) + (0)(6.0) + (-1)(8.5) = 6.5$$

Substituting in Eq. (13–6), we obtain

$$SS_{A_{comp.}} = \frac{(4.62)(6.5)^2}{(1)^2 + (0)^2 + (-1)^2} = \frac{195.20}{2} = 97.60$$

The F is formed in the usual fashion, $F = 97.60/15.00 = 6.51$; in this case, $df_{num.} = 1$ and $df_{denom.} = 11$ and the F is significant.

Analysis of Weighted Means

The Overall Analysis.   An alternative approach to the problem of unequal sample sizes is a technique that weights each mean in proportion to its sample size, which as you have seen, is exactly the opposite of the approach we have just considered. The defining formula for the analysis of weighted means is as follows:

$$SS_A = \Sigma [(n_i)(\bar{Y}_A - \bar{Y}_T)^2]$$ (13–7)

The critical feature of this formula is that the deviation of each group mean $\bar{Y}_A$ from the grand mean $\bar{Y}_T$ is weighted (that is, multiplied) by the group sample size n_i. The grand mean in this case is the grand mean of all the Y scores, which is defined as

$$\bar{Y}_T = \frac{\Sigma Y}{N}$$ (13–8)

where N is the total number of observations in the experiment. In our example,

$$\bar{Y}_T = \frac{16 + 18 + \ldots + 9 + 13}{5 + 5 + 4} = \frac{139}{14} = 9.93$$

Substituting in Eq. (13–7), we obtain

$$SS_A = (5)(15.0 - 9.93)^2 + (5)(6.0 - 9.93)^2 + (4)(8.5 - 9.93)^2$$

$$- 5(5.07)^2 + 5(-3.93)^2 + 4(-1.43)^2$$

$$= 128.52 + 77.22 + 8.18 = 213.92$$

The corresponding sum of squares from the unweighted analysis was 199.45. The error term is identical to the one we found for the unweighted analysis. From this point on, then, the two analyses follow the same operations. That is, $MS_A = 213.92/2 = 106.96$, and $F = MS_A/MS_{S/A} = 106.96/15.00 = 7.13$. With $df_{num.} = 2$ and $df_{denom.} = 11$, the F is significant.

Single-df Comparisons.   The differential weighting of means is carried over to analyses between means:

$$SS_{A_{comp.}} = \frac{(\hat{\psi})^2}{\Sigma \dfrac{c_i^2}{n_i}}$$ (13–9)

With equal sample sizes, Eq. (13–9) is equivalent to the usual computational formula.[2] Using the same comparison between a_1 and a_3 ($\hat{\psi} = 6.5$),

$$SS_{A_{comp.}} = \frac{(6.5)^2}{\dfrac{(1)^2}{5} + \dfrac{(0)^2}{5} + \dfrac{(-1)^2}{4}}$$

$$= \frac{42.25}{.20 + .00 + .25} = \frac{42.25}{.45} = 93.89$$

The value we obtained with unweighted means was $SS_{A_{comp.}} = 97.60$.

---

[2]You can prove this assertion for yourself either by substituting n for n_i and performing some algebraic manipulations or by calculating a numerical example with Eq. (13–9) and the standard formula, $SS_{A_{comp}} = (n)(\hat{\psi})^2/(\Sigma c_i^2)$.

Comment

Intuitively, the analysis of unweighted means closely resembles the standard analysis procedures: The analysis is based on the treatment means and weights them equally. The analysis of weighted means is also based on the treatment means, but in this case they contribute in direct proportion to their sample sizes. The two different approaches produce roughly equivalent results. This will generally be the case when the differences in sample size are slight—as they should be in a well-controlled experiment.

From a statistical point of view, the analysis of unweighted means produces an F ratio that is not distributed precisely according to the sampling distribution of F; the F is slightly biased in the positive direction, which means that the critical values of F obtained from Table A–1 are slightly smaller than the values should be (Gosslee & Lucas, 1965). More specifically, the tabled values of F for the 5 percent level of significance may reflect the 6 or 7 percent level when the analysis of unweighted means is used. We can easily correct for this bias by setting $\alpha = .025$ when operating at the 5 percent level of significance or by adjusting the $df_{denom.}$ used to enter the F table (see Gosslee & Lucas, 1965).

In short, there is little difference in the outcomes of these two approaches to the analysis of single-factor experiments with unequal sample sizes. We will begin to see discrepancies between the two approaches when the differences in sample sizes are substantial. On the other hand, we might question the appropriateness of any statistical analysis under these circumstances. More important, we might even question the validity of any experimental procedure that permits this sort of subject loss to occur.

13.4   UNEQUAL SAMPLE SIZES
AND THE TWO-FACTOR DESIGN

Subject loss in the two-factor design plays havoc with the standard statistical analysis. The property of orthogonality, which normally extends to the main effects and interaction in the factorial design with equal sample sizes, generally does not hold with unequal sample sizes, which usually renders the analysis of weighted means inappropriate.[3] Such designs are often called **unbalanced** or **nonorthogonal factorial designs**. We will consider two approaches to the analysis of nonorthogonal designs, one analysis based on unweighted means and one that requires special procedures.

---

[3]Occasionally, you will see factorial designs in which unequal sample sizes are an integral part of the design. This frequently occurs when one of the independent variables consists of a classification of subjects—for example, socioeconomic status—and a researcher wants the levels of this variable to reflect the distribution of the groups in the population. Designs of this sort are called **proportional factorial designs** because the same relative proportions in the population are maintained at all levels of the other independent variable. See Kirk (1982, pp. 407–411) for a detailed description of this type of design.

Analysis of Unweighted Means

The Overall Analysis. We can easily adapt the analysis of unweighted means to cope with unequal sample sizes in the factorial design. I will present a procedure that takes advantage of the standard computational formulas for the sums of squares used in Chap. 10. We begin by calculating the average sample size n_h, which again is the harmonic mean of the sample sizes. For the two-way factorial,

$$n_h = \frac{(a)(b)}{1/n_{1,1} + 1/n_{1,2} + \ldots} = \frac{(a)(b)}{\Sigma\,(1/n_{ij})} \tag{13-10}$$

That is, we divide the total number of treatment cells, $(a)(b)$, by the sum of the reciprocals of the cell sample sizes, n_{ij}. We next calculate unweighted *AB sums*, which I will denote AB^*, simply by multiplying each cell mean by n_h:

$$AB^* = n_h(\overline{Y}_{AB}) \tag{13-11}$$

These unweighted AB sums are then entered into a standard AB matrix (an AB^* matrix, to be consistent), and we continue with the analysis as we would normally with equal sample sizes. The only change in the formulas for the sums of squares is that we substitute n_h for n in the computational formulas.

The numerical example is based on the data from Table 10–6; the experiment is a 3×2 factorial, in which factor A consists of a control and two drug conditions and factor B consists of two levels of food deprivation. Table 13–2 presents these same data except for the last Y score for the subject in cell a_3b_2. We begin by calculating the harmonic mean of the sample sizes. Using Eq. (13–10), we find

$$n_h = \frac{(3)(2)}{1/4 + 1/4 + 1/4 + 1/4 + 1/4 + 1/3}$$

$$= \frac{6}{.25 + .25 + .25 + .25 + .25 + .33} = \frac{6}{1.58} = 3.80$$

Next, we multiply each cell mean by $n_h = 3.80$ to produce the adjusted cell sums

Table 13–2 Numerical Example of a Nonorthogonal Design

	a_1b_1	a_2b_1	a_3b_1	a_1b_2	a_2b_2	a_3b_2
	1	13	9	15	6	14
	4	5	16	6	18	7
	0	7	18	10	9	6
	7	15	13	13	15	—
Sum:	12	40	56	44	48	27
Sample Size:	4	4	4	4	4	3
Mean:	3.0	10.0	14.0	11.0	12.0	9.0
ΣY^2:	66	468	830	530	666	281
Sum of Squares:	30.0	68.0	46.0	46.0	90.0	38.0

AB^*, with which we will calculate the basic ratios required for the sums of squares.[4] The adjusted cell mean for a_1b_1, for example, is

$$AB_{1,1}^* = n_h(\overline{Y}_{A_1B_1}) = (3.80)(3.0) = 11.4$$

The adjusted cell sums for the six treatment conditions are presented in Table 13–3.

We now use the standard computational formulas for the basic ratios, remembering to substitute $n_h = 3.80$ for n. With the adjusted sums in Table 13–3, we find

$$[T^*] = \frac{(T^*)^2}{(a)(b)(n_h)} = \frac{(224.2)^2}{(3)(2)(3.80)} = 2{,}204.63$$

$$[A^*] = \frac{\Sigma (A^*)^2}{(b)(n_h)} = \frac{(53.2)^2 + (83.6)^2 + (87.4)^2}{(2)(3.80)} = 2{,}297.10$$

$$[B^*] = \frac{\Sigma (B^*)^2}{(a)(n_h)} = \frac{(102.6)^2 + (121.6)^2}{(3)(3.80)} = 2{,}220.47$$

$$[AB^*] = \frac{\Sigma (AB^*)^2}{n_h} = \frac{(11.4)^2 + (38.0)^2 + \ldots + (45.6)^2 + (34.2)^2}{3.80}$$

$$= 2{,}473.80$$

The arithmetical operations required to transform the basic ratios into sums of squares are listed in Table 13–4.

The error term for this analysis is calculated in the same way as in the analysis of the single-factor design; more specifically, $MS_{S/AB}$ consists of the pooled within-groups sum of squares divided by the pooled within-groups degrees of freedom. In symbols,

$$MS_{S/AB} = \frac{\Sigma \, SS_{S/AB_j}}{\Sigma \, df_{S/AB_j}} \tag{13–12}$$

Substituting the information from Table 13–2 into Eq. (13–12), we find

$$MS_{S/AB} = \frac{30.0 + 68.0 + 46.0 + 46.0 + 90.0 + 38.0}{3 + 3 + 3 + 3 + 3 + 2} = \frac{318.0}{17} = 18.71$$

The final analysis reveals only a significant $A \times B$ interaction.

Table 13–3   Adjusted AB^* Matrix

	a_1	a_2	a_3	Sum
b_1	11.4	38.0	53.2	102.6
b_2	41.8	45.6	34.2	121.6
Sum	53.2	83.6	87.4	224.2

[4]If you are concerned about rounding error, you could carry all calculations to three places and round to two places for the final F.

Table 13–4   Summary of the Analysis of Unweighted Means

Source	Sum of Squares	df	MS	F
A	$[A^*] - [T^*] \; = \; 92.47$	2	46.24	2.47
B	$[B^*] - [T^*] \; = \; 15.84$	1	15.84	.85
$A \times B$	$[AB^*] - [A^*] - [B^*] + [T^*] \; = \; 160.86$	2	80.43	4.30*
S/AB	318.00	17	18.71	

*$p < .05$.

Additional Analyses.   Any of the additional analyses discussed for the two-way factorial design in Chaps. 11 and 12 may be conducted with the analysis of unweighted means. The formulas for the simple effects of the two independent variables, which were written in terms of treatment *sums*, will use the adjusted information found in the AB^* matrix. The formulas for single-*df* comparisons and for interaction comparisons, which were written in terms of treatment *means*, will use the means directly.[5] The only change that must be made is to substitute n_h for n whenever the latter quantity appears in a computational formula. Otherwise, the methods and procedures are identical to those outlined for equal sample sizes. Examples of these analyses may be found in problem 3 in the exercises.

Comment.   This analysis can be easily extended to higher-order factorial designs. By basing the main effects and interaction on the cell means and weighting them equally in any calculations, we produce sums of squares that are orthogonal. The nonorthogonality is still present within the total data set, however, which you would discover if you added up all the component sums of squares—which would not equal SS_T, as is the case in the balanced factorial.

The appeal of the analysis of unweighted means is its direct translation of the relevant sums of squares from the matrix of treatment means. There still remains the slight bias associated with these tests, however, that I mentioned earlier in this chapter. This problem can be easily dealt with by working at a slightly more stringent significance level—for example, setting $\alpha = .025$ when you are operating at the 5 percent level of significance.

Analysis of Unique Sources

The analysis of weighted means does not translate to the unbalanced factorial design. In its place, applied statisticians recommend a technique that produces sums of squares that uniquely reflect the intended source of variability. I will call this procedure the **analysis of unique sources**. The rational for this analysis derives from multiple correlation and generally requires a computer program to perform the complicated computations. Without going into detail, let's examine the rationale behind this approach.

---

[5]The means used to extract single-*df* comparisons involving main effects are obtained by averaging the appropriate cell means ($\overline{Y}_{AB}$). For example, the overall mean for level a_1 is $(3.0 + 11.0)/2 = 7.0$, and for level b_1 is $(3.0 + 10.0 + 14.0)/3 = 9.0$.

The Overall Analysis.   We will begin with a sum of squares that reflects the total amount of systematic variation attributed to the treatment manipulations. In a balanced factorial, this would be the between-groups sum of squares, of course, which contains variation due to the two main effects and the interaction; that is, $SS_{bg} = SS_A + SS_B + SS_{A \times B}$. Unfortunately, this useful relationship does not hold in an unbalanced factorial. In its place, suppose we use the procedures of multiple correlation to produce a related sum of squares, which reflects the combined influence of the two main effects and the interaction as a *composite* and not in a form that may be subdivided into a number of orthogonal components. I will use a special notation to designate this sum of squares, namely, $SS_{A, B, A \times B}$. Although this composite sum of squares cannot be subdivided in the normal manner into the three factorial treatment components, it does in fact reflect the total amount of systematic variation attributable to the treatment manipulations and, as such, can serve as a reference against which other composite sums of squares may be compared.

To elaborate, suppose we created three additional composite sums of squares, each reflecting the collective influence of a different combination of *two* of the sources of variability we normally extract in the overall analysis of the factorial. This set would contain the following composite sums of squares:

$$SS_{A, B} = \text{a composite of the two main effects}$$
$$SS_{A, A \times B} = \text{a composite of the } A \text{ main effect and the } A \times B \text{ interaction}$$
$$SS_{B, A \times B} = \text{a composite of the } B \text{ main effect and the } A \times B \text{ interaction}[6]$$

Let's see how we can use the information provided by $SS_{A,B,A \times B}$ and these three composite sums of squares to determine the amount of variation attributed to a given source alone, with no influence from the other sources.

Suppose we now subtract any one of the three sums of squares, which reflect the composite influence of two factors, from $SS_{A,B, A \times B}$—that is, the sum of squares reflecting the composite influence of *all three factors*. The difference between these two composite sums of squares will create a new sum of squares, which now reflects the *unique* influence of the remaining factor. Thus,

$$SS_{A, B, A \times B} - SS_{B, A \times B} = SS_{A(unique)} \qquad (13\text{--}13)$$

$$SS_{A, B, A \times B} - SS_{A, A \times B} = SS_{B(unique)} \qquad (13\text{--}14)$$

$$SS_{A, B, A \times B} - SS_{A, B} = SS_{A \times B(unique)} \qquad (13\text{--}15)$$

Each of these new sums of squares reflects only that variability that is uniquely associated with a particular main effect or interaction. This property of uniqueness is present in *balanced* factorials but is absent to some degree in unbalanced (or nonorthogonal) designs. The remainder of the analysis parallels the procedures I outlined for the analysis of unweighted means, including the definition of the error term.

The results of such an analysis, which was carried out by a specialized computer program, are presented in Table 13–5. If you compare these sums of squares

---

[6]Each of these unique sums of squares is a special quantity obtained within the context of multiple correlation. They cannot be obtained by analysis of variance. The composite sum of squares containing all three effects, $SS_{A, B, A \times B}$, is equal to SS_{bg}, which in the context of the unbalanced, is defined as
$$SS_{bg} = \Sigma n_{ij}(\overline{Y}_{A_iB_j} - \overline{Y}_T)^2$$

Table 13–5 Summary of the Analysis of Unique Sources

Source	SS	df	MS	F
A	94.00	2	47.00	2.51
B	15.79	1	15.79	.84
A × B	156.00	2	78.00	4.17*
S/AB	318.00	17	18.71	

*$p < .05$.

with those we obtained with the analysis of unweighted means (Table 13–4), you will find they are quite close. In general, when the subject loss is slight, the two procedures give comparable results.

Additional Analyses. Applied statisticians often recommend that additional analyses such as the analysis of simple effects, simple comparisons, and single-*df* comparisons involving the main effects — are best subjected to a one-way analysis of weighted means, using the error term from the overall analysis. Thus, you would extract the relevant means and then calculate the sums of squares following the procedures outlined earlier in this chapter.

Comment. A major problem with this approach to the analysis of unbalanced designs is that many experimenters are unfamiliar with it. Since researchers are unable to calculate these unique sums of squares from within the context of analysis of variance, they must turn to somewhat mysterious and certainly "foreign" methods and procedures.[7] The analyses do not represent direct translations of the variations observed among the treatment means, but a sort of statistical abstraction; many researchers will feel uncomfortable, if not suspicious, with this approach. Many will prefer to discard data randomly to achieve equal sample sizes, provided the additional loss of subjects does not adversely affect power. Alternatively, some might conduct their analyses with unweighted means and simply adopt a slightly more stringent significance level to compensate for any positive bias that may be associated with the *F* tests.

13.5 EXERCISES[8]

1. The following data were originally presented in Table 2–3 as an example of a single-factor experiment with equal sample sizes. I have randomly deleted three scores, indicated by dashes, to produce an experiment with unequal sample sizes.

a_1	a_2	a_3
16	4	—
18	6	10
—	8	9
—	10	13
19	2	11

[7]See Keppel and Zedeck (1989, pp. 541–546) for a discussion of how these analyses are accomplished within the framework of multiple correlation.
[8]The answers to these problems are found in Appendix B.

    a. Conduct two analyses of variance, one with the method of unweighted means and the other with the method of weighted means.

    b. Using both methods, conduct the following single-*df* comparisons:

        (1) A comparison between the first group and an average of the other two groups

        (2) A comparison between the second and third group

2. The following data were originally presented in Table 10–6 as an example of a two-factor experiment with equal sample sizes. In this example, factor A consisted of a control and two drug conditions (drug X and drug Y) and factor B consisted of two levels of food deprivation (1 hr. and 24 hr.) I have randomly deleted 4 scores, indicated by dashes, to produce an experiment with unequal sample sizes.

a_1b_1	a_2b_1	a_3b_1	a_1b_2	a_2b_2	a_3b_2
1	13	9	15	6	14
4	—	16	6	—	7
0	7	18	10	9	6
7	15	—	13	—	13

Perform an overall analysis, using the method of unweighted means.

3. In this problem, you will be conducting various detailed analyses on the data set in problem 2. Although not explicitly discussed in this chapter, you simply conduct the analysis on the means (and AB^* sums based on these means), using the formulas from Chaps. 11 and 12. When necessary, substitute the harmonic mean of the sample sizes (n_h) for n.

    a. As an example of the detailed analysis of a main effect, test the significance of the control and drug Y (these two marginal means are based on an average of the relevant means at b_1 and b_2).

    b. Analyze the simple effects of factor A at both levels of factor B.

    c. Test the significance of the simple comparison between the control and drug X for the animals under 1 hr. food deprivation (b_1).

    d. Test the significance of the interaction contrast involving the two drug conditions (drug X versus drug Y) and the two drive conditions (1 hr. versus 24 hr.).

PART IV

DESIGNS WITH A CONTROL OR CONCOMITANT VARIABLE

Completely randomized designs share a common problem: They are relatively deficient in power. We usually attempt to solve this problem by attempting to hold various nuisance factors constant and by choosing a sample size that will produce an appropriate degree of power. Fortunately, there are other ways to increase the sensitivity of an experiment. The most common method of increasing sensitivity (or statistical power) in psychology is to administer all the treatment conditions to the same group of subjects. We will consider this approach to the problem in Part V. But there are many situations in which it is not advisable nor feasible to test subjects more than once. For these, the procedures I will describe in Part IV are quite reasonable alternatives.

Both procedures we will consider depend on information that is usually available or collected before the start of the experiment. This information, which we will call a **control variable** or a **concomitant variable**, measures some characteristic of individuals that is reasonably correlated with the dependent variable. We can find examples of such characteristics in most areas of the behavioral sciences. In problem-solving experiments or experiments on learning, for instance, we might turn to scores on intelligence tests or to grade-point averages. In perceptual or psychophysical experiments, differences in sensory acuity might be considered an important concomitant variable. In educational research, differences in socioeconomic status are a possibility, and in social psychology, differences in certain attitudes may be used by the investigator. The difference between the two procedures I will discuss is *when* and *how* this information is incorporated into the experimental design and the statistical analysis.

One procedure uses this information to assign subjects to the experimental conditions. Subjects are segregated into homogeneous *blocks*, based on their scores on the concomitant variable. If the variable is grade-point average (GPA), there will be blocks of subjects with high GPAs, moderate GPAs, low GPAs—the exact definition depending on the number of subjects available, the number of treatment conditions, and the relationship between the concomitant variable and the dependent variable. The finer the grouping, the more closely matched will be the subjects within a block. Once the blocks are formed, subjects within any given block are randomly assigned to the treatment conditions. As a consequence of these procedures, the design becomes a *factorial design*, in which one factor is the manipulated variable and the other is blocks. For these reasons, then, the design is variously referred to as a **blocking design,** a **treatments × blocks design,** or a **randomized block design;** I prefer to use the term *blocking design*. The increased sensitivity usually associated with this design is achieved by basing the error term on subsets of data that are *more homogeneous* (and less variable) than the undifferentiated groups created by randomly assigning subjects to treatments without regard for the concomitant variable. The final result of this procedure generally is a smaller error term and an increase in power over the single-factor alternative.

The other procedure achieves its increased sensitivity by *statistical* means rather than by transforming the experiment from a single-factor to a two-factor design. Although measures on the concomitant variable are obtained before the start of the experiment, they are *not* used in the assignment of subjects to the treatment conditions, as they are in the blocking design. Subjects are simply randomly assigned to the treatment groups in the usual manner, and the experiment remains a completely randomized single-factor design. The statistical analysis does change, however. More specifically, we use information about the relationship between the concomitant variable and the dependent variable to adjust for chance differences among the treatment groups and to refine our estimate of error variance. The result of these operations, known as the **analysis of covariance,** is a smaller error term and a more sensitive and powerful experiment. The main disadvantage of the analysis of covariance is its computational complexity, which with the increased availability of statistical software programs that will perform the analysis, is no longer a serious problem.

We will discuss both procedures in Chap. 14. In earlier editions of *Design and Analysis*, I presented the analysis of covariance toward the end of the book. I have moved the discussion of this technique forward in this edition and combined it with the blocking design; collectively, the two procedures form a natural bridge or transition between the completely randomized designs, in which unsystematic variability is largely left unchecked, and the *within-subjects* or *repeated measures designs*, which achieve marked reductions in unsystematic variability by using the same subjects in all or a subset of the treatment conditions. We will consider within-subjects designs in Part V.

14

Designs with Randomized Blocks and the Analysis of Covariance

---

For the designs we have discussed so far, individual differences are essentially allowed to remain unchecked. We assign subjects to the experimental treatments in a random fashion, so that a "good" subject is just as likely to be assigned to a particular condition as is a "poor" one. Obviously, we do not expect groups of subjects assigned in this way to be equivalent on all critical subject characteristics. Some groups will be favored with the better subjects; some will not. There is no *bias*, however, because each treatment condition has an equal probability of being assigned high- and low-ability subjects.

One way to help the system "work" is to select subjects from the most *homogeneous* population possible. If, in a hypothetical situation, we were able to obtain a pool of perfectly matched subjects and then assigned them randomly to the different conditions, we would feel quite confident that the groups were nearly equivalent at the outset. (There are still other factors that would be responsible for variability in the scores of subjects treated alike, such as variations in the testing environment, in the actual treatments, in the subjects themselves, and so on.) If we could assign subjects to the treatments from a homogeneous pool, there would be another related benefit: a marked reduction in the within-groups mean square. I will pursue this point in some detail since the latter possibility holds great interest for the researcher.

The first step in accomplishing a reduction in error variance is to find some basis for selecting the subjects for our experiment. That is, we must identify those characteristics of subjects that are known to influence the behavior of interest and that may be measured *before* the start of the experiment. If we are able to do so, we can select a homogeneous group of subjects to serve in the study. We would randomly assign these selected subjects to the different treatment conditions. This type of procedure would reduce the within-groups variance by restricting the variation due to a particular subject characteristic that otherwise would be left unchecked in an experiment.

We must be concerned, of course, about the potentially limited generalizability such a set of results would offer. That is, the treatment effects obtained with subjects of "average" intelligence or with subjects from middle-income families might not be representative of the effects that would be obtained with subjects from other portions of the general population. To be more specific, there might be an *interaction* between the treatments and the subject characteristic that formed the basis for the selection. Fortunately, it is possible to avoid this difficulty and at the same time maintain the advantage of homogeneous groupings of subjects.

14.1 THE BLOCKING DESIGN

The blocking design provides a solution to this problem of generalization by including more than one block of homogeneous subjects in the experiment. Rather than drawing a single group of subjects from one ability level, the blocking design includes groups of homogeneous subjects drawn from two or more ability levels.

The Design and Analysis

Suppose we had a pool of 60 subjects available for an experiment and that there are $a = 4$ levels of the treatment factor (factor A). If we were conducting a completely randomized single-factor experiment, we would randomly assign $n = 15$ subjects to each of the four treatment conditions. On the basis of information available to us before the start of the experiment, let's assume that we can classify the 60 subjects into three blocks, each containing 20 subjects who are relatively homogeneous on the classification factor. The blocking design is formed by assigning the subjects within each block to the four experimental conditions, as diagrammed in the upper portion of Table 14–1. (The blocking design appears on the right, and the corresponding single-factor design appears on the left.)

Table 14–1 Comparison of Blocked and Unblocked Designs

Completely Randomized Design					Treatments × Blocks Design			
LEVELS OF FACTOR A						*LEVELS OF FACTOR A*		
a_1	a_2	a_3	a_4	**BLOCKS**	a_1	a_2	a_3	a_4
$n = 15$	$n = 15$	$n = 15$	$n = 15$	b_1	$n = 5$	$n = 5$	$n = 5$	$n = 5$
				b_2	$n = 5$	$n = 5$	$n = 5$	$n = 5$
				b_3	$n = 5$	$n = 5$	$n = 5$	$n = 5$

Sources of Variance and Degrees of Freedom			
Source	*df*	Source	*df*
A	$a - 1 = 3$	A	$a - 1 = 3$
S/A	$(a)(n - 1) = 56$	B	$b - 1 = 2$
Total	$(a)(n) - 1 = 59$	$A \times B$	$(a - 1)(b - 1) = 6$
		S/AB	$(a)(b)(n - 1) = 48$
		Total	$(a)(b)(n) - 1 = 59$

We can view the blocking design as consisting of three independent experiments, one containing subjects of high ability, say, a second containing subjects of medium ability, and a third containing subjects of low ability. In each case, the subjects within each of these blocks are randomly assigned to the four treatment conditions. Note that the design was constructed in two steps: first an initial grouping of subjects into blocks and then the random assignment of subjects within each block to the different conditions. In essence, the original single-factor experiment has become a two-factor design, with factor A completely crossing with the blocking factor (factor B in this example).

The sources of variance and corresponding df's for the two designs are given in the lower portion of the table. As you can see, the analysis of this design requires no new computational procedures. We simply apply the formulas for the analysis of the completely randomized two-factor experiment. The sums of squares are extracted in the usual way, and the error term is based on a pooling of subjects within specific treatment-block combinations. This general type of design, in which blocking is introduced as an independent variable, may be extended to multifactor designs. All that the presence of "blocks" does is to increase by 1 the number of factors represented in the experiment.

The use of a blocking factor often results in an experiment that is more sensitive than the corresponding experiment without blocks. The error term in the completely randomized experiment of Table 14–1, $MS_{S/A}$, reflects the variability of subjects from populations in which the blocking factor was allowed to vary without control. In contrast, the error term for the blocking design, $MS_{S/AB}$, reflects the variability of subjects from populations in which variation within the blocking factor was greatly restricted. Additionally, any treatments × blocks interaction, which remains undetected in the completely randomized experiment, is isolated and removed from the error term in the blocking design.[1] An example of a blocking design may be found in problem 1 in the exercises.

If you decide to introduce a blocking factor into an experiment, you should be aware that there is an optimal number of blocks, which depends on the correlation between the concomitant variable and the dependent variable, the total number of subjects available to you, and the number of treatment conditions in your study. Feldt (1958) has provided a table that can help you choose the optimal number of blocks that will achieve maximum precision with the blocking design.[2]

Comments

The advantages of the blocking design are considerable. Blocking helps to equate the treatment groups before the start of the experiment more effectively than is accomplished in the completely randomized design. Moreover, the power is greater because of the smaller error term usually associated with the blocking design. Additionally, the design allows an assessment of possible interactions be-

---

[1] A sizable treatments × blocks interaction would reveal itself as differences among the within-group variances in the single-factor study.

[2] I considered the factors involved in designing a study with a blocking factor, including a portion of Feldt's table, in the second edition of this book (pp. 250–252).

tween treatment effects and blocks. If such an interaction is significant, we will know that the effects of the treatments do not generalize across the abilities or classification of subjects represented in the experiment. If these interactions are not significant, we have achieved a certain degree of generalizability of the results.[3]

I must also mention certain disadvantages of this type of design. First, there is the cost of introducing the blocking factor. Second, it may be difficult to find blocking factors that are highly correlated with the dependent variable used in the experiment. Finally, we must be concerned with the possible loss of power when the blocking factor is poorly correlated with the dependent variable. Suppose, for example, that there is no correlation between the concomitant variable and the dependent variable. Under these circumstances, the error term will be based on sets of scores that are just as variable as those in a completely randomized experiment without blocking, and we will suffer a loss in power because there are fewer *df* associated with the error term in the blocking design than in the one without block ing. This discrepancy in the *df*'s of error terms increases with the number of blocks, the number of treatment levels, and the number of treatment factors. In this regard, Feldt (1958) concludes that it is more efficient to use the unblocked design when the correlation between the blocking factor and the dependent variable is less than .2. Again, if the assessment of treatments × blocks interactions is the primary purpose of the study, a low correlation will not affect the decision to use randomized blocks in an experiment.

14.2   ANALYSIS OF COVARIANCE: AN OVERVIEW

The primary function of an experimental design is to create a setting in which observations can be related to variations in treatments in an unambiguous and unequivocal manner. The major problem, of course, is the unavoidable presence of error variance, which introduces uncertainty into the outcome of any experiment. The completely randomized design minimizes systematic bias through the random assignment of subjects to treatments, but it does so at the expense of a relatively insensitive experiment—that is, a large error term. The blocking design also relies on random assignment to minimize systematic bias, but it introduces the blocking factor, which permits a reduction in the size of the error term and an increase in the sensitivity of the experiment.

The analysis of covariance reduces experimental error by statistical, rather than by experimental, means. Subjects are first measured on the concomitant variable, usually called the **covariate** in the context of the analysis of covariance, which consists of some relevant ability or characteristic. Subjects are then randomly assigned to the treatment groups without regard for their scores on the covariate. Only at the time of the statistical analysis does this information come into play, when it is used to accomplish two important adjustments: (1) to refine esti-

---

[3]In certain fields, the interaction is of primary interest. An important area in educational research, for example, is concerned with the interaction of aptitudes and treatments. To illustrate, a researcher may be interested in whether the abilities of children interact with the type of instructional method used. Cronbach and Snow (1977) provide a detailed discussion of this type of design.

mates of experimental error and (2) to adjust treatment effects for any differences between the treatment groups that existed before the experimental treatments were administered. Because subjects were randomly assigned to the treatment conditions, we would expect to find relatively small differences among the treatments on the covariate and considerably larger differences on the covariate among the subjects within the different treatment conditions. Thus, the analysis of covariance is expected to achieve its greatest benefits by reducing the size of the *error term*; any correction for preexisting differences produced through random assignment will be small by comparison.

14.3   THE BASIS FOR STATISTICAL CONTROL: LINEAR REGRESSION

Linear regression consists of a statistical technique for establishing a linear function—a straight line—relating two variables. Let's see how the linear function is established for a single set of scores—for example, the scores of subjects in one of the treatment conditions of an experiment—and then how it is used to reduce the variability of the subjects on the dependent variable.

The Linear Regression Equation

Suppose we let X be a score on the covariate and Y the corresponding score on the dependent variable. We can write the formula for a straight line relating the dependent variable (Y) to the covariate (X) as

$$Y = a + (b)(X)$$

where a = a constant called the **Y intercept** and consists of the value
of Y when $X = 0$
b = a constant called the **slope** or tilt and reflects the change in Y
associated with a given change in X

The sign of the slope indicates the direction of the linear relationship. A positive slope means that the two variables change in the *same* direction—Y increases as X increases or Y decreases as X decreases—whereas a negative slope means that the two variables change in *opposite* directions—Y increases as X decreases or Y decreases as X increases.

The Linear Regression Line.   The two constants required to specify a straight line, the slope and the intercept, must be estimated from a set of data consisting of a pair of scores for each subject—that is, an X score and a corresponding Y score. In the context of the analysis of covariance, the X scores will be obtained before the experimental treatments are introduced and the Y scores will be the responses observed after the treatments are administered. The procedures we follow in estimating these two constants produce an equation for the line that keeps the sum of the squared discrepancies of the actual data from the line at a minimum value. This is called a **regression line** and is often described as the best-fitting straight line obtained by applying the **criterion of least squares**.

Estimating Slope. The slope of a line can be defined as follows:

$$\text{slope } (b) = \frac{\text{change in } Y}{\text{change in } X}$$

With data that describe a straight line perfectly—for example, the same temperatures measured on the Celsius and Fahrenheit scales—slope can be determined by choosing any two pairs of scores. With behavioral data, however, linear relationships will not be perfect, which means that no two sets of X, Y pairs can be guaranteed to give the slope of the regression line. What is needed, then, is a formula that takes all the data into consideration in estimating the best-fitting straight line. Such a formula is the following:

$$\text{slope } (b) = \frac{\Sigma (X_i - \bar{X})(Y_i - \bar{Y})}{\Sigma (X_i - \bar{X})^2} \tag{14-1}$$

The denominator of Eq. (14–1) is a familiar quantity, namely, a sum of squares involving the X scores (SS_X), which, of course, is based on the deviation of the X scores from their mean. The numerator is based on *pairs* of deviations, one involving the deviation of the X score from $\bar{X}$ and the other involving the deviation of the corresponding Y score from $\bar{Y}$; as you can see, the two members of each pair of deviations are multiplied and the resulting products are then summed over the total sample of subjects. I will refer to this quantity as the **sum of products**, abbreviated SP_{XY}. We can now express the formula for the slope—known as the **linear regression coefficient**—more simply as follows:

$$b = \frac{SP_{XY}}{SS_X} \tag{14-2}$$

Before we continue, I need to say a few words about the sum of products. A useful property of SP_{XY} is that it is influenced by the degree to which the X and Y variables vary together, or *covary*.[4] This is easily illustrated by considering the formula for the product-moment correlation (r_{XY}), written in terms of SP_{XY} and sums of squares on the two variables (SS_X and SS_Y):

$$r_{XY} = \frac{SP_{XY}}{\sqrt{(SS_X)(SS_Y)}} \tag{14-3}$$

The product-moment correlation reflects, of course, the degree to which the X and Y variables are linearly related. Since the two sums of squares reflect the variability of the X and Y scores considered separately, the sum of products must carry the information about the linear relationship between the two variables.

[4]When the sum of products is divided by the appropriate degrees of freedom, the quantity produced is called **covariance**; that is,

$$\text{covariance } (X, Y) = \frac{SP_{XY}}{df}$$

I will illustrate the process of estimating the slope of the linear regression line with the set of paired scores presented in Table 14–2, where an X score and a Y score are listed for each of $n = 8$ subjects. To use Eq. (14–1) to estimate the slope, we need two deviations for each subject, $X - \overline{X}$ and $Y - \overline{Y}$, which you will find in columns 4 and 5, respectively; the products formed by multiplying each member of the pair is presented in column 6. We can now calculate SS_X and SP_{XY}:

$$SS_X = \Sigma (X - \overline{X})^2$$

$$= (2.12)^2 + (-1.88)^2 + \ldots + (1.12)^2 + (4.12)^2 = 50.88$$

$$SP_{XY} = \Sigma (X_i - \overline{X})(Y_i - \overline{Y})$$

$$= 16.96 + 11.28 + \ldots + 0.00 + 24.72 = 92.00$$

We can now calculate the slope by substituting these quantities in Eq. (14–2); that is,

$$b = \frac{SP_{XY}}{SS_X} = \frac{92.00}{50.88} = 1.81$$

This value of slope means that if the covariate (X) changes by one unit, the linear regression line predicts a change in the same direction of 1.81 units on the dependent variable (Y).

Estimating the Intercept.   The Y intercept, a, is obtained quite easily by substituting in the formula:

$$a = \overline{Y} - (b)(\overline{X}) \tag{14–4}$$

Entering the relevant data from Table 14–2 and the value of $b = 1.81$, we compute

$$a = 7.00 - (1.81)(7.88) = 7.00 - 14.26 = -7.26$$

This value of a indicates that the linear regression line predicts a value of $Y =$

Table 14–2   Pairs of Scores for Eight Subjects

(1) Subject	(2) X	(3) Y	(4) $X - \overline{X}$	(5) $Y - \overline{Y}$	(6) $(X-\overline{X})(Y-\overline{Y})$
1	10	15	2.12	8.00	16.96
2	6	1	-1.88	-6.00	11.28
3	5	4	-2.88	-3.00	8.64
4	8	6	.12	-1.00	$-.12$
5	9	10	1.12	3.00	3.36
6	4	0	-3.88	-7.00	27.16
7	9	7	1.12	0.00	0.00
8	12	13	4.12	6.00	24.72
Mean	**7.88**	**7.00**			

−7.26 when $X = 0$, a value that may not make sense logically but is necessary to specify this particular line of best fit.

The Regression Equation.   We are now able to write the equation for the regression line by substituting the estimates of slope and the Y intercept in the equation for a straight line as follows:

$$Y' = a + (b)(X) = -7.26 + (1.81)(X)$$

where Y' refers to the value of Y predicted by the regression line for any given value of X. What I will now do with the regression equation is to show how a knowledge of the linear relationship between the covariate and the dependent variable can be used to reduce the estimate of uncontrolled variability of the Y scores.

Uncontrolled (or Residual) Variation

I have plotted the pairs of X and Y scores from Table 14–2 in Fig. 14–1. The horizontal line on the graph represents the value of the mean of the Y scores, $\overline{Y} = 7.00$. The deviation of each data point from this line is also indicated. These deviations, when squared and summed, produce SS_Y, of course. This sum of squares reflects the variability of the set of Y scores in the absence of information about the co-

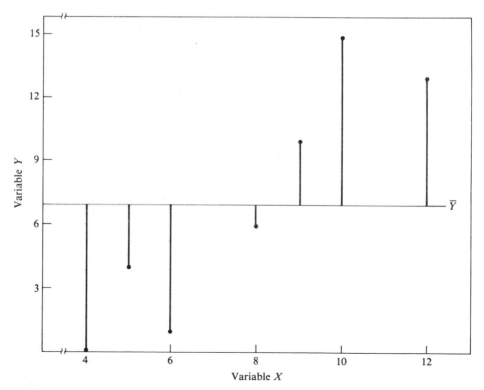

Figure 14–1   Deviation of Y scores from $\overline{Y}$.

variate (X) and its relationship to the dependent variable (Y); this absence of information is implied by the fact that the horizontal line drawn from $\overline{Y}$ is a line with *zero slope*, which only happens when there is no linear relationship between X and Y. Using the deviations in column 5 of Table 14–2, we find

$$SS_Y = \Sigma (Y - \overline{Y})^2$$

$$= (8.00)^2 + (-6.00)^2 + \ldots + (0.00)^2 + (6.00)^2 = 204.00$$

Let's see what happens to the sum of squares when we take into consideration the linear relationship between the X and Y variables. Suppose we use the regression equation to estimate a value of Y for each subject (Y_i'), which is based on information available before the start of the experiment, namely, each subject's score on the covariate (X_i). This has been done in column 4 of Table 14–3. To illustrate the calculations for the first subject,

$$Y_1' = -7.26 + (1.81)(X_1)$$

$$= -7.26 + (1.81)(10) = -7.26 + 18.10 = 10.84$$

The regression line, which can be drawn once two values of Y' have been calculated, is presented in Fig. 14–2, together with the original eight data points.

Consider the regression line for a moment. Notice how much more closely it approaches the data points than did the horizontal line in Fig. 14–1. Suppose we use these deviations from the regression line to calculate a new sum of squares — one reflecting the variability remaining after we take into consideration the linear relationship between the two variables. This discrepancy between an actual Y score and the score predicted by linear regression $(Y - Y')$ is presented in column 5 of Table 14–3 for each of the eight subjects. Again, for the first subject, this discrepancy is

$$Y_1 - Y_1' = 15 - 10.84 = 4.16$$

Squaring and summing these differences gives us

$$SS_{Y(adj.)} = \Sigma (Y_i - Y_i')^2$$

$$= (4.16)^2 + (-2.60)^2 + \ldots + (-2.03)^2 + (-1.46)^2 = 37.63$$

These calculations verify what our eyes could see in Fig. 14–1 and Fig. 14–2,

Table 14–3   Analysis of Predicted Y Scores (Y′)

(1) Subject	(2) X	(3) Y	(4) Y′	(5) Y − Y′
1	10	15	10.84	4.16
2	6	1	3.60	−2.60
3	5	4	1.79	2.21
4	8	6	7.22	−1.22
5	9	10	9.03	.97
6	4	0	−.02	.02
7	9	7	9.03	−2.03
8	12	13	14.46	−1.46

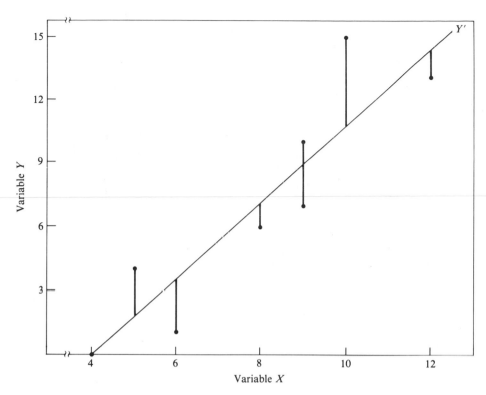

Figure 14–2   Deviation of Y scores from the regression line.

namely, that the variability is much smaller when the deviations are based on the regression line ($SS_{Y(adj.)}$ = 37.63) than when they are based on the mean of the Y scores (SS_Y = 204.00).

You have seen how we can use information obtained before the start of an experiment to reduce the variability among a set of Y scores. As you will shortly discover, the analysis of covariance produces a similar type of adjusted sum of squares, which is then used to calculate the error term. Depending on the strength of the relationship between the covariate and the dependent variable, the gain in *sensitivity*, or *power*, which is reflected by the smaller error term resulting from an analysis of covariance, can be considerable.

Estimating Treatment Effects

The other purpose of the analysis of covariance is to obtain a more precise estimate of the treatment effects. As you know, a major source of error in estimating treatment effects occurs as a result of assigning subjects randomly to conditions, which inevitably produces treatment groups that are imperfectly matched at the outset. When covariate scores are available, however, we have information about differences between treatment groups that existed before the experiment was performed.

As you will see, the analysis of covariance again uses linear regression to produce an adjusted treatment mean square that takes these chance differences into consideration.

It is important to note that this adjustment for group differences can either increase or decrease the size of the treatment mean square. To illustrate, let's assume that the mean on the dependent variable is 10 for one group and 15 for another group. Suppose the means on the covariate are the same for the two groups. Under these circumstances, of course, we would expect no adjustment of the two Y's because the groups are equal at the start of the experiment. But suppose that the two means on the covariate are 7 and 5, respectively, and that there is a positive linear relationship between the X and Y variables. Because of the slight advantage of the first group over the second, any adjustment for this difference on the *dependent variable* would lower the mean for the group with this advantage (group 1) and raise the mean for the group with this disadvantage (group 2), which effectively increases the treatment effect. That is, the adjusted mean for group 1 will be less than 10 and the adjusted mean for group 2 will be greater than 15, creating a larger difference than was observed originally. On the other hand, suppose the situation is reversed and that the means on the covariate are 5 and 7, respectively. Under these circumstances, the adjustment would raise the mean for group 1 to some value greater than 10 and lower the mean for group 2 to some value less than 15, which now decreases the original treatment effect.

Since any differences among the groups on the covariate must be due to chance factors, we would expect the adjustment to increase the size of the treatment effects in half of our experiments and to decrease the size of the treatment effects in the other half.[5] Whatever the case, the adjustment should be minor in comparison with the reduction in the size of the error term normally associated with an analysis of covariance.

14.4   THE COMPLETELY RANDOMIZED SINGLE-FACTOR EXPERIMENT

The analysis of covariance applied to the completely randomized single-factor experiment has many elements of similarity with an ordinary analysis of variance. In fact, the first step actually consists of calculating three familiar sums of squares— SS_A, $SS_{S/A}$, and SS_T—in the usual manner twice, once using the scores obtained on the covariate and once using the scores obtained on the dependent variable. Moreover, the corresponding sums of products—SP_A, $SP_{S/A}$, and SP_T—are calculated from analogous computational formulas. The second step consists of the adjustment of the treatment and within-groups sums of squares for differences observed on the covariate. Finally, we obtain the adjusted estimates of the treatment populations means, which can then be used for conducting analytical comparisons among the treatment conditions.

---

[5]Huitema (1980, pp. 31–38) provides an excellent discussion of the effects of adjusting the treatment effects for chance differences on the covariate.

The Covariate (X)

The main criterion for a covariate is a substantial linear correlation with the dependent variable (Y). In most cases, the scores on the covariate are obtained *before* the initiation of the experimental treatment. There may be a formal pretest of some sort administered to all potential participants in the experiment, or the scores may be available from records of the subjects. Achievement scores, IQ determinations, and grade-point averages are common examples. Occasionally, the scores are gathered *after* the experiment is completed. Such a procedure is defensible only when it is certain that the experimental treatment did *not* influence the covariate. For relatively "permanent" characteristics of subjects (for example, intelligence, reading ability, sensory acuity, and so on), this may be a reasonable assumption, but for labile tendencies (for example, anxiety, ego involvement, motivation, and so on) it may be an untenable position to take. The analysis of covariance is predicated on the assumption that the covariate is *independent* of the experimental treatments. Therefore, we should carefully scrutinize any covariate that is obtained following the end of the experiment.

Calculating the Sums of Squares and the Sums of Products

In this design, we are assuming that there are *a* treatment conditions and that *n* subjects have been randomly assigned to each. Each of the subjects provides two scores, one from the covariate (X), which is obtained before the experiment begins, and the other from the dependent variable (Y).

The first step in the analysis of covariance is the calculation of the sums of squares and the sums of products. We begin with the basic ratios, which are specified in Table 14–4. The basic ratios for the covariate and the dependent variable are identical to those introduced in Chap. 2 for a single-factor analysis of variance. The only change in these formulas is the addition of the subscripts X and Y to designate the source of the scores.

The formulas for the basic ratios involving products may take a while to comprehend, until you discover the underlying pattern. Consider the numerators

Table 14–4   Basic Ratios for Calculating Sums of Squares and Sums of Products

Covariate (X)	Products of X and Y	Dependent Variable (Y)
$[T_X] = \dfrac{T_X^2}{(a)(n)}$	$[T_{XY}] = \dfrac{(T_X)(T_Y)}{(a)(n)}$	$[T_Y] = \dfrac{T_Y^2}{(a)(n)}$
$[A_X] = \dfrac{\Sigma A_X^2}{n}$	$[A_{XY}] = \dfrac{\Sigma (A_X)(A_Y)}{n}$	$[A_Y] = \dfrac{\Sigma A_Y^2}{n}$
$[X] = \Sigma X^2$	$[XY] = \Sigma (X)(Y)$	$[Y] = \Sigma Y^2$

for each of the three basic ratios. As you can see, the numerators consist of products obtained from the same quantities we square in the usual formulas.[6]

> We have the product of T_X and T_Y—that is, $(T_X)(T_Y)$—instead of the square of these two quantities.
> We have the products of A_X and A_Y—that is, $(A_X)(A_Y)$—instead of the squares of these two quantities.
> We have the products of X and Y—that is, $(X)(Y)$—instead of the squares of these two quantities.

The other parts of the formulas are the same as the other basic ratios.

As a numerical example, assume that we have three levels of factor A, with $n = 8$ subjects in each condition. Further, let's assume that the subjects were given a pretest before the start of the experiment and were assigned randomly to the three treatment conditions without regard for their scores. The pairs of X and Y scores are presented in Table 14–5.

An inspection of the data suggests a positive correlation between the two sets of scores within each of the treatment conditions—that is, the larger the score on the covariate, the larger the score on the dependent variable. The presence of any within-group correlation usually implies that the adjusted error term will be smaller than the unadjusted one. The means on the dependent variable indicate a numerical difference among the conditions and the means on the covariate suggest that the groups were relatively comparable at the start of the experiment.

Working first with the scores on the covariate, we find

$$[T_X] = \frac{(180)^2}{(3)(8)} = 1,350.00$$

Table 14–5   Numerical Example

	a_1			a_2			a_3	
	X	Y		X	Y		X	Y
	10	15		4	6		7	14
	6	1		8	13		8	9
	5	4		8	5		7	16
	8	6		8	18		3	7
	9	10		6	9		6	13
	4	0		11	7		8	18
	9	7		10	15		6	13
	12	13		9	15		8	6
Sum:	63	56		64	88		53	96
Mean:	7.88	7.00		8.00	11.00		6.63	12.00
ΣX^2 or ΣY^2:	547	596		546	1,134		371	1,280
$\Sigma (X)(Y)$:	533			728			651	

$$T_X = 63 + 64 + 53 = 180$$
$$T_Y = 56 + 88 + 96 = 240$$

[6] I have omitted the subscripts i and j to simplify the formulas. It should be understood that the products refer to quantities obtained from corresponding groups or subjects.

$$[A_X] = \frac{(63)^2 + (64)^2 + (53)^2}{8} = 1,359.25$$

$$[X] = (10)^2 + (6)^2 + \ldots + (6)^2 + (8)^2 = 1,464$$

Identical operations on the scores on the dependent variable produce

$$[T_Y] = \frac{(240)^2}{(3)(8)} = 2,400.00$$

$$[A_Y] = \frac{(56)^2 + (88)^2 + (96)^2}{8} = 2,512.00$$

$$[Y] = (15)^2 + (1)^2 + \ldots + (13)^2 + (6)^2 = 3,010$$

Finally, we perform the analogous calculations with the products:

$$[T_{XY}] = \frac{(180)(240)}{(3)(8)} = 1,800.00$$

$$[A_{XY}] = \frac{(63)(56) + (64)(88) + (53)(96)}{8} = 1,781.00$$

$$[XY] = (10)(15) + (6)(1) + \ldots + (6)(13) + (8)(6) = 1,912$$

The final part of this step in the analysis of covariance is to calculate the sums of squares and the sums of products that we will need to complete the analysis. These calculations are completed in Table 14–6. As you can see, the same familiar patterns of combining the basic ratios, which we first used in Chap. 2, are duplicated in these calculations.

Calculating the Adjusted Sums of Squares

The second and final step in the overall analysis of covariance is to bring together the appropriate quantities to provide an adjustment of the sums of squares, based on the dependent variable, for the linear effect of the covariate. Let's start with the total sum of squares. The computational formula for the adjusted total sum of squares involves quantities we have already calculated:

$$SS_{T(adj.)} = SS_{T(Y)} - \frac{(SP_{T(XY)})^2}{SS_{T(X)}} \tag{14–5}$$

Substituting the values from Table 14–6 in Eq. (14–5), we find

Table 14–6   Sums of Squares and Sums of Products

Source	Covariate (X)	Dependent Variable (Y)	Products $(X)(Y)$
A	$[A_X] - [T_X] = 9.25$	$[A_Y] - [T_Y] = 112.00$	$[A_{XY}] - [T_{XY}] = -19.00$
S/A	$[X] - [A_X] = 104.75$	$[Y] - [A_Y] = 498.00$	$[XY] - [A_{XY}] = 131.00$
Total	$[X] - [T_X] = 114.00$	$[Y] - [T_Y] = 610.00$	$[XY] - [T_{XY}] = 112.00$

$$SS_{T(adj.)} = 610.00 - \frac{(112.00)^2}{114.00} = 610.00 - 110.04 = 499.96$$

The formula for adjusting the within-groups sum of squares is identical to Eq. (14–5) except for the quantities involved; that is,

$$SS_{S/A(adj.)} = SS_{S/A(Y)} - \frac{(SP_{S/A(XY)})^2}{SS_{S/A(X)}} \tag{14–6}$$

Substituting the relevant quantities into Eq. (14–6), we have

$$SS_{S/A(adj.)} = 498.00 - \frac{(131.00)^2}{104.75} = 498.00 - 163.83 = 334.17$$

We obtain the adjusted treatment sum of squares in a different manner, namely, by subtracting the adjusted within-groups sum of squares from the adjusted total sum of squares:[7]

$$SS_{A(adj.)} = SS_{T(adj.)} - SS_{S/A(adj.)} \tag{14–7}$$

Substituting the two quantities we just calculated into Eq. (14–7), we find

$$SS_{A(adj.)} = 499.96 - 334.17 = 165.79$$

The three adjusted sums of squares are entered in Table 14–7 for the completion of the analysis of covariance.

The Analysis of Covariance

The degrees of freedom for the adjusted treatment source are unchanged in the analysis of covariance. The df for the error term, on the other hand, is 1 less than the degrees of freedom usually associated with the $MS_{S/A}$. That is, rather than the usual $df_{S/A} = (a)(n - 1) = (3)(8 - 1) = 21$, the degrees of freedom become

$$df_{S/A(adj.)} = (a)(n - 1) - 1 \tag{14–8}$$

or, $df_{S/A(adj.)} = 20$. The loss of 1 df is due to the estimation of the population slope in the calculation of the adjusted within-groups sum of squares. The degrees of freedom associated with the adjusted treatment sum of squares are unaffected in the analysis of covariance because a regression line was not used in the computation of this sum of squares.

Table 14–7   Summary of the Analysis of Covariance

Source	$SS_{(adj.)}$	df	$MS_{(adj.)}$	F
A	165.79	2	82.90	4.96*
S/A	334.17	20	16.71	

*$p < .05$.

[7]You might wonder why the treatment sum of squares is not adjusted in the same way as the other two sums of squares. The reason usually given is that this "indirect" method guarantees that the treatment effects do not enter into the adjustment process (see Kirk, 1982, p. 727).

The remaining steps in the analysis involve the calculation of the adjusted mean squares and the F ratio. As indicated in Table 14–7, the resulting

$$F = \frac{MS_{A(adj.)}}{MS_{S/A(adj.)}} = \frac{82.90}{16.71} = 4.96$$

is significant, when evaluated against the tabled value of $F(2, 20)$.

It is instructive to see what this analysis of covariance has accomplished. If we calculate the F on the unadjusted Y scores, we find that the differences among the three means are not significant. Using the information in Table 14–6, we find

$$F = \frac{SS_{A(Y)}/df_A}{SS_{S/A(Y)}/df_{S/A}}$$

$$= \frac{112.00/2}{498.00/21} = \frac{56.00}{23.71} = 2.36$$

a value that lies between the 10 and 25 percent levels of significance. The larger F from the analysis of covariance was the result of *two* changes: (1) a *decrease* in the size of the within-groups mean square, which we expected from the correlation between the two sets of scores (16.71 versus 23.71), and (2) an *increase* in the size of the effect of factor A (82.90 versus 56.00). This latter adjustment "corrects" for chance differences between the groups on the covariate. (See p. 308 for an explanation.)

Adjusting the Treatment Means

One of the consequences of the analysis of covariance is a correction of the treatment effects for chance differences on the covariate. This correction should now be extended to the means themselves. It is the adjusted means that you would report in any summary of your work. In addition, the adjusted means are the ones you will use to conduct any comparisons between specific treatment groups.

The adjustments are performed by substituting the means from the X and Y variables in an equation that relates the predicted (or adjusted) means to differences among the means on the covariate. This relationship is given by the formula

$$\bar{Y}'_{A_i} = \bar{Y}_{A_i} - b_{S/A}(\bar{X}_{A_i} - \bar{X}_T) \tag{14–9}$$

where $\bar{Y}'_{A_i}$ = the adjusted treatment mean for level a_i
  $\bar{Y}_{A_i}$ = the unadjusted treatment mean for level a_i
  $b_{S/A}$ = the average within-groups regression coefficient.
  $\bar{X}_{A_i}$ = the group mean on the covariate for level a_i
  $\bar{X}_T$ = the grand mean on the covariate

The within-groups regression coefficient, $b_{S/A}$, is easily calculated by substituting calculations we have already performed into the formula:[8]

---

[8]Actually, $b_{S/A}$ is an average that weights each group coefficient by the variability of the groups on the covariate. I will demonstrate this fact when I consider the regression assumptions—see pp. 316–321.

$$b_{S/A} = \frac{SP_{S/A}}{SS_{S/A(X)}} \tag{14-10}$$

Using the relevant numbers from Table 14–6, we have

$$b_{S/A} = \frac{131.00}{104.75} = 1.25$$

If you look closely at Eq. (14–9), you will see that the adjusted mean of a treatment group, $\overline{Y}_{A_1}'$, is found by subtracting from the observed mean $\overline{Y}_{A_i}$ a value that takes into consideration the deviation of the group from the overall mean on the covariate—that is, $(b_{S/A})(\overline{X}_{A_i} - \overline{X}_T)$.

We are now able to calculate the adjustment means. The group means on the covariate and the dependent variable may be found in Table 14–5. The overall mean on the covariate is simply the average of the three group means, $\overline{X}_T = 7.50$. We obtain the adjusted treatment means by substituting the relevant information into Eq. (14–9) as follows:

$$\overline{Y}_{A_1}' = 7.00 - (1.25)(7.88 - 7.50) = 7.00 - .48 = 6.52$$

$$\overline{Y}_{A_2}' = 11.00 - (1.25)(8.00 - 7.50) = 11.00 - .63 = 10.37$$

$$\overline{Y}_{A_3}' = 12.00 - (1.25)(6.63 - 7.50) = 12.00 + 1.09 = 13.09$$

You can see that the adjustments for the linear effect of the covariate have spread out the treatment means, which explains why the adjusted treatment mean square $(MS_{A(adj.)} = 82.90)$ calculated previously was larger than the unadjusted mean square $(MS_A = 56.00)$. Whether the adjustment will increase or decrease the differences among the treatment means is a matter of chance, as I noted earlier. In the present case, the random assignment of subjects produced a situation that, in a sense, worked *against* the observed outcome of the experiment. Thus, any correction for this particular inequality of the groups would tend to increase the differences, which is what happened in this example. If the inequality had been reversed, with random assignment working in favor of the outcome, the correction would serve to decrease the differences.

Conducting Comparisons Among the Adjusted Means

We may perform any of the comparisons on the adjusted means that we would consider with unadjusted data from a single-factor experiment. These techniques were discussed in detail in Chaps. 6 and 7. In all these single-df comparisons, we calculate the sum of squares for the particular comparison in exactly the same fashion as we would for the analysis of variance, except that we substitute the adjusted treatment means for the unadjusted ones. More explicitly, the general formula for a single-df comparison is translated as

$$SS_{A_{comp.(adj.)}} = \frac{n(\hat{\psi}')^2}{\Sigma c_i^2} \tag{14-11}$$

where $\hat{\psi}'$ is the comparison based on the adjusted means; that is,

$$\hat{\psi}' = \Sigma (c_i)(\overline{Y}'_{A_i}) \tag{14-12}$$

As an example, let's compare the adjusted mean at level a_1 with the combined adjusted means at levels a_2 and a_3. The coefficients for this comparison and the adjusted means follow:

	a_1	a_2	a_3
c_i:	1	$-\frac{1}{2}$	$-\frac{1}{2}$
$\overline{Y}'_{A_i}$:	6.52	10.37	13.09

The difference between the two means becomes

$$\hat{\psi}' = (1)(6.52) + (-\tfrac{1}{2})(10.37) + (-\tfrac{1}{2})(13.09) = 6.52 - 11.73 = -5.21$$

Substituting this information in Eq. (14–11), we find

$$SS_{A_{comp.(adj.)}} = \frac{8(-5.21)^2}{(1)^2 + (-\tfrac{1}{2})^2 + (-\tfrac{1}{2})^2} = \frac{217.15}{1.5} = 144.77$$

The main change in the analysis is in the calculation of the error term. In the one-factor analysis of variance, we would use the $MS_{S/A}$. A natural extension to the analysis of covariance would suggest that we use $MS_{S/A(adj.)}$. For certain theoretical reasons, however, which need not concern us here, we must perform an additional operation on the adjusted error term before we can evaluate adjusted comparisons. I will refer to this mean square as the MS'_{error}, which is calculated as follows:[9]

$$MS'_{error} = MS_{S/A(adj.)} + \left(MS_{S/A(adj.)}\right)\left(\frac{MS_{A(X)}}{SS_{S/A(X)}}\right) \tag{14-13}$$

where $MS_{S/A(adj.)}$ = the adjusted error term from the analysis of covariance
$MS_{A(X)}$ = the between-groups mean square based on the covariate X
$SS_{S/A(X)}$ = the within-groups sum of squares also based on the covariate

An inspection of Eq. (14–13) reveals that the MS'_{error} will equal the $MS_{S/A(adj.)}$ only when $MS_{A(X)} = 0$, which will rarely happen, of course, and that the size of the adjustment called for is directly related to the differences among the treatment conditions on the covariate. The degrees of freedom for this error term are the same as those associated with $df_{S/A(adj.)}$.

The only new quantity we need to calculate before we can obtain MS'_{error} is the mean square for the treatment groups on the covariate ($MS_{A(X)}$). Using the infor-

---

[9] An alternative formula for MS'_{error}, proposed for *planned comparisons* (see Winer, 1971, p. 779), produces a different error term for each comparison. Apparently, this specialized formula is needed only when $df_{S/A(adj.)} < 20$ and when the differences among the treatment groups on the covariate are significant (see Snedecor, 1956, pp. 401–402). This extra step is generally not necessary in most practical applications.

mation in Table 14–6, we find $MS_{A(X)} = SS_{A(X)}/df_A = 9.25/2 = 4.63$. We can now substitute this quantity together with other quantities from Tables 14–6 and 14–7 in Eq. (14–13) to calculate MS'_{error}:

$$MS'_{error} = 16.71 + \left(16.71\right)\left(\frac{4.63}{104.75}\right)$$

$$= 16.71 + (16.71)(.04) = 16.71 + .67 = 17.38$$

The F ratio for the comparison calculated previously becomes

$$F = \frac{MS_{A_{comp.(adj.)}}}{MS'_{error}} \tag{14–14}$$

$$= \frac{144.77}{17.38} = 8.33$$

This F is evaluated with $df_{num.} = 1$ and $df_{denom.} = df_{S/A(adj.)}$, which in this example is 20. This comparison is significant.

Assumptions Underlying the Analysis of Covariance

The assumptions underlying the analysis of variance continue to apply in the corresponding analysis of covariance. Several additional assumptions, which apply to the analysis of covariance in particular, are concerned with the nature of the regression between the covariate and the dependent variable.[10]

The Assumption of Linear Regression.   One of the assumptions associated with the analysis of covariance is that of **linear regression**. The assumption is that the deviations from regression—that is, the residual scores—are normally and independently distributed in the population, with means of zero and homogeneous variances. Since these assumptions concerning the distribution of the residuals will generally not hold if the true regression is not linear, many refer to them as an assumption of linear regression. What this means is that if linear regression is used in the analysis, whereas the true regression is of another form (for example, curvilinear), adjustments will not be of great benefit. More important, however, we could question the meaning of the adjusted treatment means, which are also adjusted on the assumption of linear regression.[11]

The Assumption of Homogeneous Group Regression Coefficients.   The other assumption specifies **homogeneity of regression coefficients** for the different treatment populations. Although not obvious from the general formulas, the within-groups regression coefficient ($b_{S/A}$), which is central to the analysis of covariance, is actually an *average* of the regression coefficients for each treatment

---

[10]Useful discussions are found in Elashoff (1969); Glass, Peckham, and Sanders (1972); and Huitema (1980, Chap. 6).

[11]Discussions of the statistical test of this assumption can be found in Kirk (1982, pp. 733–734) and Winer (pp. 774–775).

group. The current wisdom concerning this assumption suggests that the analysis of covariance is robust with regard to the homogeneity issue. On the basis of available Monte Carlo studies, Glass, Peckham, and Sanders (1972), for example, concluded that differences in group regression coefficients have little effect on the distribution of the F statistic, provided that the group sample sizes are equal. Although some of these findings have not gone unchallenged (Rogosa, 1980), later work corroborates this conclusion (see, for example, Dretzke, Levin, & Serlin, 1982; Levy, 1980).

On the other hand, significant differences among the group regression coefficients mean that the effects of the independent variable must be interpreted with caution. More specifically, what these differences mean is that an interaction is present between the subject characteristic chosen for the covariate and factor A and that we should determine how the magnitude of the effects of factor A depends on the different "levels" of this subject characteristic. It is important to note that this same interaction would be revealed in a corresponding blocking design by the treatments × blocks interaction. If that interaction were significant, we would probably concentrate our efforts on analyzing the simple effects of the independent variable for the different levels of the blocking factor. Exactly the same strategy is recommended for the analysis of covariance, when the differences among the group regression coefficients are significant, except that the statistical procedure is different and complicated. This procedure, which is known as the Johnson-Neyman technique (Johnson & Neyman, 1936), can become quite complex when more than two groups are involved. Huitema (1980, Chap. 13) provides an excellent discussion of this and related analyses.

My recommendation, then, is to test for group differences in the regression coefficients. If they are not significant, you can turn to the analysis of covariance with renewed confidence concerning the interpretability of your results. If the differences are significant, you may find it difficult to interpret your results and may need statistical advice on how best to proceed.

Testing for Homogeneity of Group Regression Coefficients

The adjustment for the linear effect of the covariate involves the average within-groups regression coefficient, namely, $b_{S/A}$. As I have noted, an important assumption of the analysis of covariance is that regression coefficients based only on the data from each treatment group (b_{S/A_i}) are the same, that is, homogeneous. This assumption is tested by contrasting two sources of variance: (1) a source reflecting the deviation of the group regression coefficients from the average regression coefficient, and (2) a source reflecting the deviation of individual subjects from their own group regression lines. The first source is actually a sort of *between-groups* source of variance, but one involving group regression coefficients rather than group means. I will refer to the sum of squares associated with this source as the **between-groups regression sum of squares** ($SS_{bet.\ regr.}$). The second source is a sort of *within-groups* source of variance, but one involving the deviation of subjects from their group regression lines rather than from their group means. I will refer to the sum of squares associated with this source as the **within-groups regression sum of squares** ($SS_{w.\ regr.}$).

We start with the following relationship:

$$SS_{S/A(adj.)} = SS_{bet.\ regr.} + SS_{w.\ regr.} \tag{14–15}$$

Since we have already obtained the adjusted within-groups sum of squares $SS_{S/A(adj.)}$ in the overall analysis of covariance, we need to calculate only one additional sum of squares to be able to complete the analysis. I will focus on the calculation of the second component, $SS_{w.\ regr.}$, and obtain the other sum of squares, $SS_{bet.\ regr.}$, by subtraction.

Understanding the Basic Calculations.   To understand the calculations for $SS_{w.\ regr.}$, let's return to an earlier analysis in which we examined the linear regression line for a *single* group. Consider first the regression line and the data points plotted in Fig. 14–2 (p. 307). The deviations of the individual Y scores from this line represent the variation that is not associated with the linear relationship between the X and Y variables. If we square and then sum these deviations, we obtain the $SS_{w.\ regr.}$ for this particular group of scores, which, coincidentally, happens to be group a_1 from our numerical example, which you can verify by turning to Table 14–5. Within the context of the numerical example, then, this sum of squares is one of the quantities we need to complete the analysis of the group regression coefficients:

$$SS_{w.\ regr.} = SS_{w.\ regr.(a_1)} + SS_{w.\ regr.(a_2)} + SS_{w.\ regr.(a_3)}$$

I obtained the residual sum of squares for group a_1 in a laborious manner, namely, by calculating the deviation of each Y score from the regression line, which is documented in Table 14–3 (p. 306). We can obtain the same information with considerably less effort by using computational formulas. I will illustrate the procedure with the data from group a_1 and then extend the process to all three groups. As a reminder, the residual sum of squares for this group was defined in the earlier analysis as follows:

$$SS_{w.\ regr.(a_1)} = \Sigma\,(Y_i - Y_i')^2$$

where Y_i = a score on the dependent variable for one of the subjects in this group

Y_i' = the Y score predicted for this subject on the basis of the linear regression equation

Using the deviations from column 5 of Table 14–3, we found

$$SS_{w.\ regr.(a_1)} = (4.16)^2 + (-2.60)^2 + \ldots + (-2.03)^2 + (-1.46)^2 = 37.63$$

We can obtain the same sum of squares by using familiar operations, which I will illustrate with the relevant information for this same group as it appears in Table 14–5:

$$SS_{w.\ regr.\,(a_1)} = SS_Y - SS_{lin.\ regr.}$$

$$= SS_Y - \frac{(SP_{XY})^2}{SS_X} \tag{14-16}$$

where $SS_Y = \Sigma Y^2 - \frac{(\Sigma Y)^2}{n} = 596 - \frac{(56)^2}{8} = 204.00$

$SP_{XY} = \Sigma (X)(Y) - \frac{(\Sigma X)(\Sigma Y)}{n} = 533 - \frac{(63)(56)}{8} = 92.00$ *(handwritten: doesn't match formulas in 14-4, 14-6)*

$SS_X = \Sigma X^2 - \frac{(\Sigma X)^2}{n} = 547 - \frac{(63)^2}{8} = 50.88$

Completing the operations specified in Eq. (14–16), we find

$$SS_{w.\,regr.\,(a_1)} = 204.00 - \frac{(92.00)^2}{50.88} = 204.00 - 166.35 = 37.65$$

Except for rounding error, the two sums of squares are equal (37.63 versus 37.65).

Conducting the Analysis.   We can now begin the analysis. We will calculate first the residual sums of squares separately for each treatment group and then combine them to produce $SS_{w.\,regr.}$. The basic information we need to calculate the necessary sums of squares and sums of products is found in Table 14–5. The steps I illustrated in the last paragraph for group a_1 are recorded in the first row of Table 14–8. The same steps, performed on the two sets of corresponding information for groups a_2 and a_3, are presented in the next two rows of the table. We calculate the $SS_{w.\,regr.}$ simply by pooling the three residual sums of squares:

$$SS_{w.\,regr.} = 37.65 + 149.06 + 116.68 = 303.39$$

In a moment, we will use this pooled residual sum of squares to calculate the error term we will use to test the homogeneity assumption.

The other sum of squares we need for this analysis reflects the variability among the regression coefficients for the three individual groups. As indicated earlier, we can obtain this sum of squares, $SS_{bet.\,regr.}$, by subtraction. More specifically, you will recall from Eq. (14–15) that

$$SS_{S/A(adj.)} = SS_{bet.\,regr.} + SS_{w.\,regr.}$$

By rearranging this formula appropriately, we find

$$SS_{bet.\,regr.} = SS_{S/A(adj.)} - SS_{w.\,regr.} \tag{14-17}$$

Table 14–8   Calculating the Sum of the Squared Deviations from the Individual Group Regression Lines

	SS_Y	SS_X	SP_{XY}	$SS_{lin.\,regr.}$	$SS_{w.\,regr.}$
a_1	204.00	50.88	$533 - \frac{(63)(56)}{8} = 92.00$	$\frac{(92.00)^2}{50.88} = 166.35$	$204.00 - 166.35 = 37.65$
a_2	166.00	34.00	$728 - \frac{(64)(88)}{8} = 24.00$	$\frac{(24.00)^2}{34.00} = 16.94$	$166.00 - 16.94 = 149.06$
a_3	128.00	19.88	$651 - \frac{(53)(96)}{8} = 15.00$	$\frac{(15.00)^2}{19.88} = 11.32$	$128.00 - 11.32 = 116.68$

We can obtain $SS_{S/A(adj.)}$ from the overall analysis of covariance (Table 14–7) and $SS_{w. regr.}$ from the last paragraph. Substituting these values in Eq. (14–17),

$$SS_{bet. regr.} = 334.17 - 303.39 = 30.78$$

The remainder of the analysis is summarized in Table 14–9, where I have entered the relevant sums of squares. The df for the deviation among the group regression coefficients are 1 less than the number of group coefficients:

$$df_{bet. regr.} = a - 1 = 3 - 1 = 2 \tag{14–18}$$

The df for the deviation of the Y scores from the group regression lines equals the number of subjects (n) minus 2, summed over the a treatment groups:

$$df_{w. regr.} = (a)(n - 2) = (3)(8 - 2) = 18 \tag{14–19}$$

The additional df is lost by estimating a different regression coefficient for each group. The mean squares are calculated by dividing each sum of squares by the relevant df.

The test of the hypothesis that the group regression coefficients are equal is simply

$$F = \frac{MS_{bet. regr.}}{MS_{w. regr.}} \tag{14–20}$$

The numerator reflects the degree to which the group regression coefficients deviate from each other. The denominator reflects the degree to which the separate coefficients fail to predict the actual scores on the dependent variable. The result of the F test, which is summarized in the table, indicates that the hypothesis of homogeneous group regression coefficients is tenable.

Calculating Group Regression Coefficients.   We can easily calculate the regression coefficient for each separate group. The formula is given by

$$b_{S/A_i} = \frac{SP_{S/A_i}}{SS_{S/A_i (X)}} \tag{14–21}$$

Substituting values from Table 14–8 in Eq. (14–21), we have

$$b_{S/A_1} = \frac{92.00}{50.88} = 1.81$$

$$b_{S/A_2} = \frac{24.00}{34.00} = .71$$

Table 14–9   Summary of the Analysis

Source	SS	df	MS	F
Between regression	30.78	2	15.39	.91
Within regression	303.39	18	16.86	
$S/A_{(adj.)}$	334.17	20		

$$b_{S/A_3} = \frac{15.00}{19.88} = .75$$

(The hypothesis we have just tested is that these three regression coefficients are equal.) The average within-groups coefficient, which formed the basis for adjusting the mean of the treatment groups, was found to be $b_{S/A} = 1.25$. I mentioned earlier that this within-groups regression coefficient is actually a weighted average of the individual group coefficients:

$$b_{S/A} = \frac{\Sigma (SS_{S/A_i(X)})(b_{S/A_i})}{\Sigma SS_{S/A_i(X)}} \tag{14–22}$$

In words, the group coefficients are weighted (multiplied by) the corresponding within-group sum of squares on the covariate, summed, and divided by the sum of the weights. Substituting in Eq. (14–22) the values we calculated in the last para graph and in Table 14–8, we find the average within-groups regression coefficient to be

$$b_{S/A} = \frac{(50.88)(1.81) + (34.00)(.71) + (19.88)(.75)}{50.88 + 34.00 + 19.88}$$

$$= \frac{131.14}{104.76} = 1.25$$

which is equal to the value we calculated previously.

While I am on the subject, another useful index of the relationship between the covariate and the dependent variable is the **within-groups correlation coefficient**. This index is obtained by combining quantities with which we are already familiar:

$$r_{S/A} = \frac{SP_{S/A}}{\sqrt{(SS_{S/A(X)})(SS_{S/A(Y)})}} \tag{14–23}$$

From Table 14–6 (p. 311),

$$r_{S/A} = \frac{131.00}{\sqrt{(104.75)(498.00)}} = \frac{131.00}{228.40} = .57$$

The precision afforded by the analysis of covariance is directly related to the magnitude of the within-groups correlation.

Estimating Treatment Magnitude

We first considered estimates of treatment magnitude in Chap. 4 (pp. 63–68), where you saw how such estimates can help us to interpret significance tests. Any application of these measures to the results of an experiment subjected to an analysis of covariance should take into consideration the *adjusted* values of the estimates of variability that are central to the analysis. One measure of treatment magnitude is the squared multiple correlation (R^2), for example, which in the context of a single-factor design, is defined as the proportion of total variability associated with the treatment manipulations:

$$R^2_A = \frac{SS_A}{SS_T} \qquad (14\text{-}24)$$

A straightforward adaptation of this formula to the present context simply substitutes the adjusted sums of squares from the analysis of covariance for the unadjusted ones specified in Eq. (14–24):

$$R^2_{A(adj.)} = \frac{SS_{A(adj.)}}{SS_{T(adj.)}} \qquad (14\text{-}25)$$

which Huitema (1980, p. 43) refers to as the "proportion of adjusted variability." Let's apply Eq. (14–25) to our example. From Table 14–7, we find $SS_{A(adj.)} = 165.79$ and $SS_{T(adj.)} = SS_{A(adj.)} + SS_{S/A(adj.)} = 165.79 + 334.17 = 499.96$, which gives us

$$R^2_{A(adj.)} = \frac{165.79}{499.96} = .332$$

This means that approximately 33 percent of the adjusted variation on the dependent variable is associated with the experimental manipulations. It is instructive to compare this value with the one we would have obtained from an analysis of variance performed on the same data. Substituting the data from Table 14–6 into Eq. (14–24), we find

$$R^2_A = \frac{112.00}{610.00} = .184$$

The difference between the two values is considerable.

We can also adapt omega squared, an estimate of treatment magnitude more commonly used with experiments, for use with the analysis of covariance. This measure ($\hat{\omega}^2_A$) consists of the ratio of estimated variance components; more specifically,[12]

$$\hat{\omega}^2_A = \frac{\hat{\sigma}^2_A}{\hat{\sigma}^2_A + \hat{\sigma}^2_{S/A}} = \frac{\hat{\sigma}^2_A}{\hat{\sigma}^2_T} \qquad (14\text{-}26)$$

where $\hat{\sigma}^2_A$ = the estimated treatment component
$\hat{\sigma}^2_{S/A}$ = the estimated error component

Formulas for these two estimates are based on information available from the summary of the analysis of variance:

$$\hat{\sigma}^2_A = \frac{df_A(MS_A - MS_{S/A})}{(a)(n)} \qquad (14\text{-}27)$$

---

[12]The formula I am presenting here as Eq. (14–26) is algebraically equivalent to the formula I presented in Chap. 4 as Eq. (4–1). I have chosen this particular formula since it better displays the logic behind this index of treatment magnitude.

$$\hat{\sigma}^2_{S/A} = MS_{S/A} \tag{14-28}$$

All we need to adapt these formulas for the analysis of covariance is to substitute adjusted mean squares for the unadjusted mean squares. This gives us

$$\hat{\omega}^2_{A(adj.)} = \frac{\hat{\sigma}^2_{A(adj.)}}{\hat{\sigma}^2_{A(adj.)} + \hat{\sigma}^2_{S/A(adj.)}} \tag{14-29}$$

$$\hat{\sigma}^2_{A(adj.)} = \frac{df_A(MS_{A(adj.)} - MS_{S/A(adj.)})}{(a)(n)} \tag{14-30}$$

$$\hat{\sigma}^2_{S/A(adj.)} = MS_{S/A(adj.)} \tag{14-31}$$

I will now calculate estimated omega squared for the numerical example. The relevant data are found in Table 14–7. Substituting in the last three equations, we find

$$\hat{\sigma}^2_{A(adj.)} = \frac{2(82.90 - 16.71)}{(3)(8)} = \frac{132.38}{24} = 5.52$$

$$\hat{\sigma}^2_{S/A(adj.)} = 16.71$$

$$\hat{\omega}^2_{A(adj.)} = \frac{5.52}{5.52 + 16.71} = \frac{5.52}{22.23} = .248$$

With this index, then, almost 25 percent of the total variance is explained by the experimental treatments.[13] To compare this estimated omega squared with the one based on the unadjusted analysis of variance, we can use the information in Table 14–6, where we determine that $MS_A = 112.00/2 = 56.00$ and $MS_{S/A} = 498.00/(3)(8 - 1) = 23.71$. Substituting in Eqs. (14–27) and (14–28) for the two variance components and in Eq. (14–26) for estimated omega squared, we find

$$\hat{\sigma}^2_A = \frac{2(56.00 - 23.71)}{(3)(8)} = \frac{64.58}{24} = 2.69$$

$$\hat{\sigma}^2_{S/A} = 23.71$$

$$\hat{\omega}^2_A = \frac{2.69}{2.69 + 23.71} = \frac{2.69}{26.40} = .102$$

Again, we see the same striking difference between the estimate of omega squared based on the analysis of covariance and one based on the analysis of variance.

Estimating Power

A primary reason why most researchers turn to the analysis of covariance is to increase the sensitivity of their experiments. Researchers usually take this step, however, without formally considering the power that might be achieved by adopt-

---

[13]Because of the way the two indices are defined, R^2 will always be larger than the corresponding omega squared (see p. 66).

ing this analysis. In many cases, the gain in sensitivity provided by the analysis of covariance will not be sufficient to make up for a small sample size. You saw in Chap. 4 how we can use power estimates to make a rational decision concerning our choice of sample size. The obvious next step is to extend this procedure to the analysis of covariance.

There is no change in the basic procedures I outlined in Chap. 4 for the single-factor design. As a reminder, we used Eq. (4–4) to estimate a statistic,

$$\phi_A^2 = n' \frac{\Sigma (\mu_i - \mu_T)^2/a}{\sigma_{S/A}^2}$$

where n' = the trial sample size
μ_i = the population treatment means
μ_T = the mean of the population treatment means
a = the number of treatment means
$\sigma_{S/A}^2$ = the average variance in the treatment populations

Then, in conjunction with the Pearson and Hartley power charts, we used ϕ_A^2 to discover the value of n' that will produce the power we wish to achieve. The only modification we need to adapt this formula for the analysis of covariance is to substitute an estimate of the population *residual* variance ($\sigma_{S/A(adj.)}^2$) for the unadjusted within-groups variance ($\sigma_{S/A}^2$) in Eq. (4–4). From this point on, the procedure is the same.

How do we estimate the population residual variance? If we happened to have data from a related study in which a covariate was introduced, we could base our estimate of $\sigma_{S/A(adj.)}^2$ on the $MS_{S/A(adj.)}$ obtained from that experiment. In most cases, however, such information will not be available. A more likely possibility is to combine two estimates: the correlation between the covariate and the dependent variable for one study and the within-groups variance from another. We can then use this information to estimate the population residual variance as follows:

$$\sigma_{S/A(adj.)}^2 = (1 - r_{XY}^2)(\sigma_{S/A}^2) \tag{14-32}$$

where r_{XY}^2 = the correlation between the covariate (X) and the dependent variable (Y)
$\sigma_{S/A}^2$ = the pooled within-group variance

Cohen (1977, pp. 379–380) briefly considers the use of power analyses within the context of the analysis of covariance, and Rogers and Hopkins (1988) offer a more comprehensive discussion of the procedure.

Testing for Group Differences on the Covariate

Because of random assignment, we do not expect to find significant differences among the treatment groups on the covariate—except for those cases that must occur by chance 5 percent of the time. We should perform this test nevertheless since it provides a check on our randomization procedures. If the F is significant, we should examine these methods carefully before concluding that the test reflects only the vagaries of chance and not some unforeseen bias that may have contaminated our results. Assuming that we find no problem with our assignment methods, we simply accept the finding as a type I error and be thankful that we can turn to the analysis of covariance to remove this particular bias, which if left uncorrected would have given us a false picture of the effects of our treatments. On the other hand, you should realize that many researchers will be suspicious of the results from such analyses, or at least of the group or groups that apparently are the "deviant" ones. The analysis of covariance is a technique designed to adjust for chance differences among the groups, but for many, the adjustment of significant differences is still a cause for concern.

What should we do if the F is not significant? This does not prove that our groups were matched before the experiment began, of course, but the nonsignificant F does increase our confidence in the integrity of our experimental design and of our results. Some researchers question whether they should exert the extra computational effort demanded by the analysis of covariance under these circumstances, that is, when the groups do not differ significantly on the covariate. (This additional effort is considerably reduced, of course, if you are using a statistical software program for the analysis of your data.) In any case, you should not forget that the primary benefit of the analysis of covariance is *precision* and that the gain in power you achieve by using the adjusted error term may be substantial.

Multiple Covariates

Occasionally, even greater precision may result if we include additional covariates in the analysis. There is often little gain in precision with the addition of three or more covariates, however, provided that the first two are reasonably correlated with the dependent variable and uncorrelated with each other.

The adjustment made with two covariates essentially involves the separate adjustments of the $SS_{A(Y)}$ and $SS_{S/A(Y)}$ for the linear effects of the two covariates. Winer (1971, pp. 809–812) discusses the analysis with a number of covariates, and Kirk (1982, pp. 737–740) provides a worked example of a one-factor analysis of covariance with two covariates. At this point you will probably not be interested in hand calculation and will turn to the computer to process the analysis.

14.5   EXTENDING THE ANALYSIS OF COVARIANCE TO THE TWO-FACTOR DESIGN

The analysis of covariance is easily extended to the two-factor design. The adjustment of the error term again involves subtracting variation that is predictable from a covariate. The adjustment of treatment effects, although somewhat different from the procedure I presented for the single-factor design, still uses the average within-groups regression coefficient and discrepancies among the relevant treatment means on the covariate to make corrections for chance differences between groups produced by the random assignment of subjects to conditions.

Unfortunately, space limitations do not allow a comprehensive coverage of this analysis of covariance. The analysis is discussed in a number of applied statistics books, however, including Keppel (1982, pp. 509–511), Kirk (1982, pp. 743–747), Myers (1979, pp. 422–424), and Winer (1971, pp. 788–792), who also presents a worked numerical example. You might also consult the detailed and useful book by Huitema (1980), which is devoted to the analysis of covariance and related procedures.

14.6   CHOOSING BETWEEN BLOCKING AND THE ANALYSIS OF COVARIANCE

I began this chapter by drawing a distinction between two general methods for increasing the precision of an experiment, namely, direct (or experimental) methods and purely statistical procedures. As a reminder, the direct method achieves control of error variance by isolating sources normally included in the error term of the completely randomized design and removing them in the statistical analysis. In the blocking design, we introduce a blocking factor into an experiment—for example, IQ, reading-proficiency scores, socioeconomic status, and gender—and its inclusion permits us to remove from the error term the effects of the blocking factor and its interaction with the treatment variables. Statistical control, as exemplified by the analysis of covariance, uses *regression analysis* to achieve the increase in precision. Both procedures begin at the same point, namely, with measures on the covariate, but they differ on how this information is utilized in designing the experiment and then analyzing it.

What can we say about these two options? The blocking design is simpler conceptually and requires fewer assumptions. On the other hand, the analysis of covariance is easier to administer because the total pool of subjects does not need to be identified and measured on the X variable before the study can begin. This possibility may prove to be a major consideration for many researchers who schedule their subjects for individual sessions and cannot measure them on the X variable until they appear in the laboratory to serve in the experiment; for these researchers, then, the blocking design is simply not feasible. Both methods increase precision and sensitivity, although they achieve this desirable goal differently. In addition, both provide information on the interaction of the subject characteristic used as the X variable. This information is obtained directly from the analysis of the blocking design in the form of a treatments × blocks interaction. The analogous information in the analysis of covariance is reflected in a comparison of the slopes of the individual regression lines obtained separately for each group (see pp. 316–317).

Suppose your main interest in using either approach is to increase the sensitivity of your experiment and that you can use either method to accomplish this goal. An early study by Feldt (1958) suggested that the size of the correlation between the X and Y variables was the critical factor. In a later investigation, Maxwell, Delaney, and Dill (1984) argue that what is most crucial is the *form* of the relationship between the two variables. If the regression is not linear, blocking is the preferable procedure. In most other cases, analysis of covariance is the method of choice.

14.7 EXERCISES[14]

1. As an example of a blocking design, consider the data presented in problem 1 of the exercises for Chap. 2, in which there were $a = 5$ treatment conditions and $n = 10$ subjects randomly assigned to each condition. Suppose that 5 assistants had collected these data, each running a total of 10 subjects, 2 per condition. Experimenters can be treated as "blocks" and the data analyzed as a blocking design. The data, arranged by the $b = 5$ blocks, are presented in the following table:

EXPERIMENTERS (B) (BLOCKS)	TREATMENTS (A)				
	a_1	a_2	a_3	a_4	a_5
b_1	13	7	12	10	13
	9	4	11	12	6
b_2	8	4	4	9	14
	7	1	9	7	12
b_3	8	10	5	15	13
	6	7	10	14	10
b_4	6	5	2	10	8
	7	9	8	17	4
b_5	6	5	3	14	9
	10	8	6	12	11

   a. Analyze the data as a blocking design.
   b. Compare the results of this analysis with the single-factor analysis you completed in problem 3 of the exercises for Chap. 3 (p. 61). What have you gained from this new analysis? What have you lost?
2. The subjects for this experiment were assigned randomly to the $a = 3$ different levels of the independent variable. The covariate scores were obtained before the administration of the experimental treatments. The data matrix follows.

a_1		a_2		a_3	
X	Y	X	Y	X	Y
2	11	5	15	2	12
1	8	3	12	2	9
4	8	1	16	5	8
1	9	3	19	1	11
3	7	3	16	3	7
5	9	5	20	1	7

   a. Perform an analysis of covariance on these data.
   b. Disregard the covariate information and perform a corresponding analysis of variance. Do you feel that the experimenter benefited from the introduction of the covariate into the statistical analysis? Be specific. (Hint: Calculate the within-groups correlation coefficient, $r_{S/A}$.)
3. Consider another single-factor design and the scores produced by the $n = 4$ subjects

---

[14]The answers to these problems are found in Appendix B.

in each of the $a = 4$ treatment conditions. The covariate scores were obtained before the start of the experiment, and the subjects were assigned randomly to the conditions without knowledge of these scores.

a_1		a_2		a_3		a_4	
X	Y	X	Y	X	Y	X	Y
2	11	5	9	2	12	4	15
1	8	5	7	3	7	5	12
5	8	1	9	4	6	3	16
4	7	3	10	1	11	4	14

a. Perform an analysis of covariance on these data.
b. Calculate the adjusted treatment means.
c. Evaluate the following single-*df* comparisons:
  (1) A pairwise comparison between the first two groups
  (2) A complex comparison between the fourth group and an average of the other three groups

PART V

WITHIN-SUBJECTS DESIGNS

All the experimental designs I have considered in the preceding chapters have been based on the assumption that subjects are assigned randomly to the different conditions in the experiment and are given only one of the treatments. I have referred to such experiments as completely randomized designs. They are also known as **between-subjects designs** because all the sources of variability extracted in the analysis of variance represent differences between subjects. In contrast, it is possible to represent each of these designs in a different arrangement, in which subjects serve in all or in a particular subset of the treatment conditions. Under these circumstances, some of the sources of variance isolated in the analysis will reflect differences within each subject, and for this reason, such designs are called **within-subjects designs**. Another common way to describe within-subjects designs is to refer to them as designs with repeated measures. Both terms—*within subjects* and *repeated measures*—stress the nature of this type of design, namely, that repeated measurements are taken and treatment effects are associated with differences observed within subjects.

Within-subjects designs constitute a considerably large proportion of the experiments conducted in the behavioral sciences. On the one hand, within-subjects designs are the obvious choice to study such behavioral changes as learning, transfer of training, forgetting, attitude change, and so on; on the other hand, they are particularly efficient and sensitive, especially in comparison with an equivalent between-subjects design. In this part of the text, I will examine in detail the most common examples of within-subjects designs. What you will find is that the computational formulas for the sources of variation due to the experimental factors—that is, the main effects and interactions—remain unchanged. The only new procedures introduced by within-subjects designs involve the selection and calculation of the appropriate error term for a particular source of variance or comparison.

Essentially any between-subjects design can be converted into a within-subjects design, but this conversion requires the implementation of a number of special procedures that attempt to eliminate potential problems associated with this type of design. Chapter 15 will consider these problems and their solution. Chapters 16 through 18 will be concerned with the more specific details of the statistical analysis of the most common within-subjects designs found in the behavioral sciences. More specifically, Chap. 16 will present the analysis of the single-factor within subjects design. Chapters 17 and 18 consider the complications that arise when a within-subjects factor is combined with a between-subjects factor in what is called a **mixed within-subjects design**. We will return to more complicated within-subjects designs in Part VI. Chapter 21, for example, will deal with the analysis of a two-factor design in which both independent variables involve repeated measures, and Chap. 22 will consider the analysis of more complicated within-subjects designs.

15

Introduction to Within-Subjects Designs

The number of possible ways in which within-subjects designs can be constructed increases greatly with the number of independent variables included in an experiment. I will begin our discussion with the possibilities available with the two-factor design. The remainder of the chapter will be concerned with the special problems created when we introduce a within-subjects manipulation into an experimental design and the usual ways in which these problems are solved.

15.1 EXAMPLES OF WITHIN-SUBJECTS DESIGNS

The simplest form of within-subjects design is considered in Chap. 16 and involves a single independent variable, all levels of which are administered to the same subjects. When two independent variables are combined factorially, two types of within-subjects designs are possible. The design either will be entirely a "pure" within-subjects design, with all subjects serving in all $(a)(b)$ treatment combinations, or will involve repeated measures for one factor and independent measures (that is, independent groups) for the other. This latter design is frequently referred to by psychologists as a **mixed design** and by statisticians as a **split-plot design**. The term *mixed* is particularly apt in that there are sources of variance that are produced by between-subjects differences and by within-subjects differences; both types of differences contribute to the statistical analysis.

   In within-subjects designs, "subjects" become an important basis for classification and analysis, and we will find it convenient to refer to subjects as a *factor*. To recognize this role of subjects in within-subjects designs and to anticipate future analyses and explanations, I will use S to refer to "factor S"—the subjects factor—in the designation of the different within-subjects designs. With this in mind, I will distinguish between various within-subjects designs by placing a within-subject's (or repeated) factor within parentheses. Thus, I will designate the "pure" within-subjects case as the $(A \times B \times S)$ design and the mixed case as the $A \times (B \times S)$ design. In the first design, the parentheses surround both independent variables, indicating that this two-factor design is a "pure" within-subjects experiment; in the second design, the parentheses surround only factor B, indicating that this experiment is a mixed design and that factor B is the repeated factor. To round out the picture, the completely randomized two-factor design is designated as usual without the parentheses and without the specification of S; that is, it is designated $A \times B$.

   The distinction between the three types of designs may be readily seen in Table 15–1. For this display, the same 2×3 design, each containing a total of $(a)(b)(n) = 18$ observations, is presented in the table. The upper display indicates that each of the $n = 3$ subjects serves in all six of the treatment combinations. The middle display depicts the $A \times (B \times S)$ design. Here the same six treatment combinations are present, but any given subject serves in only three of them. Moreover, the particular set of three is explicitly specified, namely, that the same set of subjects $(s_1, s_2, $ and $s_3)$ serves in all three levels of factor B, but only in combination with the a_1 level of factor A, whereas a different set of subjects $(s_4, s_5, $ and $s_6)$ receives the three levels of factor B in combination with the a_2 of factor A. In the

Table 15–1 Comparison of Two-Factor Designs

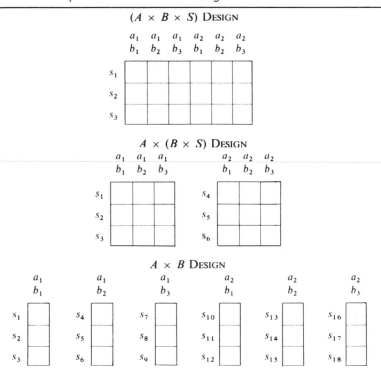

bottom panel of Table 15–1, the $A \times B$ design is depicted. In this case there are $n = 3$ different subjects in each of the six treatment combinations; no subject serves in more than one condition of the experiment.

The complexity of higher-order within-subjects designs increases dramatically with the number of independent variables. As you will see in Chap. 22, however, a fairly simple rule can be stated to guide us through the appropriate statistical analysis. Again, the primary complication is not in the calculation of the factorial effects but in the error terms with which they are evaluated statistically.

Advantages of Within-Subjects Designs

The main advantage of within-subjects designs is the control of subject variability—that is, individual differences. Take as an example a single-factor experiment. When we form independent groups of subjects in a between-subjects design, we do not expect them to be equivalent in ability or on any other factor, for that matter. We realize that these between-group differences, which are the natural outcome of randomly assigning subjects to conditions, will be superimposed over whatever treatment effects we may have been fortunate enough to produce by our experimental manipulations. But suppose we select only one group of subjects and have them serve in all the treatment conditions. On the face of it, such a procedure seems to guarantee that any differences we observe among the treatment conditions will reflect the effects of the treatment alone.

A moment's reflection, however, will indicate that this is an oversimplification. For this ideal outcome to take place, a subject would have to remain *constant* during the course of the experiment so that we can attribute any changes in behavior to the effects of the independent variable. Such an expectation is unrealistic, of course. Individuals will respond differently on each test for a host of reasons: changes in attention and motivation, learning about the task, and so on. Not only is a subject not the "same" individual on successive tasks, but we also expect other uncontrolled sources of variability, such as variations in the physical environment or in the testing apparatus, to show themselves by producing differences between the treatment means. In short, then, the variance attributed to factor A will still contain an error component even when the same subjects are tested in all the treatment conditions.

On the other hand, these sorts of changes will probably not be as great as the differences produced through the random assignment of subjects to the different experimental conditions. The error component associated with factor A, therefore, should be *smaller* in the case of repeated measures than that expected in an experiment with independent groups of subjects. This reduction in error variance represents a direct increase in economy and statistical power. There are also other ways in which the within-subjects design is economical. The running time per observation, for example, may be cut drastically by the omission of detailed instructions that overlap with the different treatment conditions. With animals as subjects, a great deal of time can be saved in the pretraining needed to "prepare" the animals for the experimental treatments.

In addition to an increase in efficiency, the repeated-measures design has become the most common experimental design with which to study such phenomena as learning, transfer, and practice effects of all sorts. In these research areas, the interest is in the changes in performance that result from successive experience with a task. In a learning experiment, for example, the experience consists of repeated exposures of the same learning task—number of trials becomes the independent variable. In a transfer experiment, the interest may be in the development of learning skills through experience with other tasks and materials. In these studies, each subject receives each level of the independent variable, which in this case, consists of the various numbers of previous trials or tasks.

Disadvantages of Within-Subjects Designs

Several major disadvantages are associated with repeated-measures designs, and they are all interrelated. One concerns the fact that subjects will change systematically during the course of multiple testing. I will refer to any such overall change as a **practice effect**. Subjects may show a general improvement during the course of testing, in which case, the practice effect is positive; alternatively, fatigue or boredom may build up on the successive tests to produce a negative practice effect. In some research areas, we can effectively disregard these positive practice effects when we have reason to believe that performance has effectively reached an asymptote, so that additional practice on the task does not produce any further improvement. For instance, if we are studying sensory functioning or performance on motor tasks that require a lot of learning, we ordinarily assume that a general practice effect is no longer present. On the other hand, if fatigue or boredom is the major source of change in performance with multiple testing, it may be possible to eliminate these factors by introducing a rest of sufficient length between successive tasks or by using highly motivating instructions and incentives. In most cases, however, researchers generally assume that practice effects will be present and that they cannot be eliminated completely.

Since practice effects are a real possibility, it follows that the current performance of a subject will reflect in part the effect of the particular treatment being administered—the direct effect of the treatment—as well as any practice effect that may also be present—indirect effects from prior experience in the experiment. Only the treatment administered *first* is immune to the effects of practice. A problem arises if we use the same order in administering the treatments to all subjects since we will be unable to disentangle the contribution of the treatment effect from the contribution of the practice effect. In this case, then, practice effects and treatment effects are confounded. A common solution to this problem is to employ enough testing orders to ensure the equal occurrence of each experimental treatment at each stage of practice in the experiment. This is usually accomplished through **counterbalancing**, which we will consider in the next section.

A second difficulty with within-subjects designs is the possibility of **differential carryover effects**, which counterbalancing will not control. In contrast with general practice effects, which affect all treatment conditions equally, differential carryover effects are quite specific, the earlier administration of one treatment affecting a subject's performance on a later condition one way and on a different condition another way. Consider, for example, an experiment with $a = 3$ conditions. Will two of the conditions—a_1 and a_2—equally affect the subsequent administration of the third, a_3? Suppose the three treatment conditions differ greatly in difficulty. Will subjects receiving the most difficult condition first behave exactly the same way under the conditions of medium difficulty, say, as subjects receiving the easiest condition first? Or will subjects receiving a control condition first display the same level of performance on one experimental treatment as do subjects receiving instead another experimental treatment first? In either case, if the answer is no, we have an instance of differential carryover effects. I will discuss this problem in Sec. 15.3.

A third problem of the repeated measures is statistical. The statistical model justifying the analyses is highly restrictive in the sense that the individual scores are supposed to exhibit certain mathematical properties. I will consider these assumptions in Chap. 16. For the moment, however, it is sufficient to observe that even when carryover effects can be shown to be symmetrical and to have caused no distortion of the effects of the independent variable, the data still may not fit the assumptions of the model, producing complications in the statistical analyses.

A final problem concerns the generalizability of results. Most researchers choose a within-subjects design for its *sensitivity* and assume that any differences they may find are "design independent" —that is, these results would be duplicated with a completely randomized design as well. Unfortunately, this assumption does not always hold, as you will see when we discuss this problem in Sec. 15.4.

15.2   CONTROLLING PRACTICE EFFECTS

Practice effects are usually always present in psychology experiments, which means we must take steps to avoid confounding them with treatment effects. Although this potential confounding could be eliminated by using a different random ordering of the treatment conditions for each subject, most researchers use some form of systematic counterbalancing instead.

Counterbalancing

Counterbalancing refers to a technique of ordering sequences of conditions so that each treatment is administered first, second, third, and so on an equal number of times. Consider the counterbalancing arrangement in the upper portion of Table 15–2, which is often called a **Latin square**. There are $a = 4$ treatment conditions and each subject receives each condition once. The order in which the conditions are presented is represented by the columns of the square (called *testing positions*), and the particular sequence of treatments is indicated by the entries in the rows of the square. To balance practice effects, we need four sequences. In the first sequence, for example, the subject (s_1) receives the treatments in the order a_1, a_2, a_3,

Table 15–2 . An Example of Counterbalancing

SUBJECT (OR SEQUENCE)	TESTING POSITION (P)			
	P_1	P_2	P_3	P_4
s_1	a_1 1	a_2 8	a_3 13	a_4 15
s_2	a_3 6	a_1 5	a_4 14	a_2 12
s_3	a_2 4	a_4 11	a_1 8	a_3 14
s_4	a_4 7	a_3 10	a_2 11	a_1 9

SUBJECT (OR SEQUENCE)	TREATMENT CONDITION (A)			
	a_1	a_2	a_3	a_4
s_1	1	8	13	15
s_2	5	12	6	14
s_3	8	4	14	11
s_4	9	11	10	7
Sum	23	35	43	47
Mean	5.75	8.75	10.75	11.75

a_4, whereas in the other three sequences, the subjects (s_2, s_3, and s_4) receive the different treatments in the orders specified in the table. In an actual experiment, a sequence will commonly represent a group of subjects who receive the same sequence; in these cases, equal numbers of subjects are assigned to each of the four sequences.

If you examine the entries in the first column of the table, you will note that each level of factor A is presented once as the first task that different subjects receive. Moving to the second column, you can see that each condition is again presented once as the second task different subjects receive. The same property holds true for the remaining columns in the table. The purpose of this arrangement is to spread any practice effects over the four treatment conditions equally. No matter what form the practice effects may take, their influence is the same for each of the treatments.

Examining Practice Effects.   Consider the data presented in the body of this counterbalancing matrix. I have rearranged these scores according to the relevant treatment conditions in the lower matrix of Table 15–2. The column marginal means for this data matrix reflect the treatment effects we found in the example. Suppose, for a moment, that we had presented the four conditions in only one of these orders, the fourth sequence, say. As you can see, we would have observed a different pattern of differences than the one we found when we averaged the scores over the four sequences. When we consider the column averages, a_4, for example, is the best of the four conditions, but when we consider the same condition in the fourth sequence, it is the *worst*. You will see other discrepancies as well. In fact, if you examine the patterns of results obtained with each of the four sequences, you will discover that each pattern is different. These differences in outcome have occurred because each score reflects the combined effects of the treatment received and of practice. It is only when we bring together the data from the different counterbalancing sequences that the treatment effects are revealed, without contamination by the effects of practice.

To show you how this occurs, I have plotted the scores in Fig. 15–1 as a function of condition and of testing position. I accomplished this by examining the treatment conditions separately and extracting the relevant data from the upper matrix as a function of testing position. Consider, for example, the scores for level a_2. Table 15–2 shows that this condition was presented first for s_3, second for s_1, third for s_4, and fourth for s_2. I then plotted the four scores associated with the different testing positions—4, 8, 11, and 12—on the graph according to the position of testing. I followed this same procedure for all four conditions. An inspection of the figure reveals a marked practice effect, but one that is the same for each treatment condition. That is, there is *no interaction* between testing position and treatments; the same treatment effects are found at each of the testing positions.

The absence of interaction between position and treatments is critical in a within-subjects design. Let's see why. Consider the interaction depicted in Fig. 15–2. You can see that differences among the treatment conditions tend to diminish during the course of testing. When the four tasks are given as first tasks in the four different sequences, the differences among the treatments are at a maximum. In

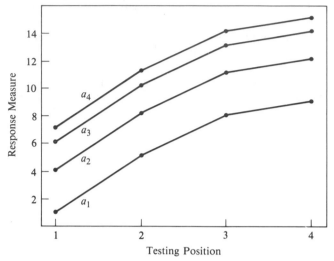

Figure 15–1   Plot of the data in Table 15–2.

contrast, when the four tasks are given as the last tasks in the different sequences, the differences among them very nearly disappear. Given this particular outcome, we still might be willing to generalize these findings in spite of the interaction, because the results are *consistent*. If the interaction had exhibited *reversals*, where the ordering of the conditions changed from test to test, however, an overall F test of the main effect of treatments would be relatively meaningless.[1]

It is always possible to analyze the data from the first testing session separately from those of the other sessions. Performance at this point is completely

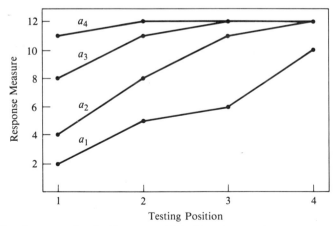

Figure 15–2   An example of a Treatment X Position interaction.

[1]A consistent ordering of the treatments is called an **ordinal interaction** and an inconsistent order is called a **disordinal interaction**. I discussed these two types of interaction in Chap. 11 (p. 235).

uncontaminated by the effects of prior testing. Of course, such an analysis involves a retreat to a single-factor design with independent groups of subjects, and we lose the advantages of the within-subjects design. We will also be left with a relatively impoverished experiment—that is, small numbers of subjects in each treatment condition—and quite low power. It might be possible to use portions of the data matrix in which the interaction is absent. In this example, we might base an analysis on the first two testing sessions, changing the design from the original within-subjects design in which each subject receives all treatments to one in which subjects receive only two.[2]

Constructing Counterbalanced Sequences

You should give special attention to the construction of counterbalanced arrangements of the treatment conditions. The least desirable arrangement, and one that many researchers still employ, is a *cyclic* one, in which the basic sequence remains the same but is shifted one position to the left (or right) for each subsequent sequence. Set in the context of our present example, where sequence 1 consists of the order 1–2–3–4, a cyclic arrangement is formed when sequence 2 consists of the order 2–3–4–1, sequence 3 consists of the order 3–4–1–2, and sequence 4 consists of the order 4–1–2–3. The order of the conditions is counterbalanced, but the basic sequence has not been varied—a_1 always follows a_4, a_2 always follows a_1, and so on.

A far better arrangement is one in which each condition precedes and follows all other conditions once, an arrangement that is said to be **digram-balanced**. The arrangement shown in Table 15–2 is an example. An inspection of this arrangement will verify that each condition immediately precedes and follows the other three conditions once. Wagenaar (1969) discusses digram-balanced arrangements and a method for constructing them. Namboodiri (1972, pp. 56–57) describes an alternative method. The main problem is that digram-balanced arrangements are only possible with experiments having an even number of treatment conditions. With odd numbers of levels, digram balancing requires the use of two separate arrangements. For $a = 3$, a total of six sequences are needed; for $a = 5$, ten sequences are needed; and so on. Namboodiri indicates how to create these special sets of sequences.

If digram balancing is not important, you should use some random method for selecting your sequencing of treatments.[3] For any counterbalancing arrangement, however, the actual treatment conditions should be assigned randomly to the designations specifying the treatments, and subjects should be randomly assigned in equal numbers to the different sequences you create.

---

[2] This modified design is called an **incomplete block design**, where a block refers to a subject or group of subjects receiving a particular sequence. Kirk (1968, Chap. 11) provides a comprehensive discussion of this sort of design.

[3] Details concerning the construction of counterbalancing arrangements can be found in Kirk (1982, pp. 309–312), Myers (1979, pp. 252–255), and Winer (1971, pp. 685–691).

15.3   DIFFERENTIAL CARRYOVER EFFECTS

The treatment × position interaction depicted in Fig. 15–2 is an example of **differential carryover effects**. Generally, these effects refer to situations in which earlier treatments continue to have an influence after a test is complete and thus affect the treatment conditions that follow: A drug administered earlier has not completely cleared the system, or a special instruction given previously is still remembered by a subject.

The most common way of reducing differential carryover effects is to provide sufficient time between sessions to allow the complete dissipation of the preceding treatment condition. Methodological work is usually required to determine how effective the time separation really is. In research with drugs, it may be necessary to distinguish between the physiological reaction to the presence of drugs in the subject's system and the subject's psychological state following a drug session. Will a subject be affected by the experience of a drug in an earlier session even though the drug itself is completely purged from the body?

A similar problem must be considered when attempts are made to change a subject's perception of a task through the use of differential instructions—a common procedure used in psychological experimentation. Let's consider some examples. If subjects are told that performance on a given task is a measure of intelligence (as a way of increasing one's anxiety or drive level), how will they view any future tasks presented to them when the "set" is changed? If subjects are told to learn a set of material by the use of one sort of strategy, will they be able to drop that method and adopt a new one when the conditions are switched? If subjects are led to believe that one thing will occur but are given another set of treatments—a technique used in so-called deception experiments—will they believe what the experimenter says under a subsequent treatment condition? If some of the experimental conditions are frightening or distasteful, how will subjects react when they are told that they will not be given a similar treatment in a subsequent condition? If they have been given an electric shock for making incorrect responses in a task, for example, will they be unaffected by this experience when they are told they will not be shocked in another condition? These are all examples of situations that should not be studied in within-subjects designs. Greenwald (1976) refers to such possibilities as "context effects" and provides a useful discussion of these sorts of problems.[4]

In many cases, the presence of treatment × position interactions simply rules out the within-subjects design for the study of a particular phenomenon. In other cases, however, these interactions have become the object of study, with experiments designed to shed light on the reasons for their occurrence. As an example, consider the early studies of short-term memory in which subjects were asked to recall nonsense syllables after varying amounts of time ranging from 3 to 18 seconds. The amazing finding was an extremely rapid drop in recall from 90 percent

---

[4]Poulton and his associates (for example, Poulton, 1973, 1975; Poulton & Freeman, 1966) have amassed considerable data concerning differential carryover effects in within-subjects designs. Dawes (1969) discusses additional difficulties encountered when these effects are present. For an objection to the points raised by Poulton in these discussions, see Rothstein (1974) and Poulton's reply (1974).

after 3 seconds to 10 percent after 18 seconds. Keppel and Underwood (1962) showed that differential carryover effects were operating in this sort of experiment, the short intervals showing very little change as a function of testing position and the long retention intervals showing a dramatic drop in performance. An example of this finding is presented in Fig. 15–3, which charts performance for subjects tested after 3 seconds and 18 seconds as a function of when in a sequence of tests they were tested. Clearly an interaction is present: Forgetting is not observed between 3 seconds and 18 seconds on the very first test, but it appears on the second test and continues to increase on later tests. The effect seems to stabilize toward the end of testing.

Empirical and theoretical interest in this particular treatment × position interaction has been immense. The increase in forgetting has been attributed to a process known as *proactive inhibition* specifically produced by the previous tests. Subsequent research has focused on the nature of proactive inhibition: Under what other circumstances does it occur? What factors influence its size? Are there situations where it can be eliminated? What began as a questioning of research methodology introduced a new phenomenon that itself became the object of study and speculation.

15.4   OTHER CONSIDERATIONS

By now you should be convinced that the design of an experiment with repeated measures requires a great deal of care and attention to detail. If practice effects are

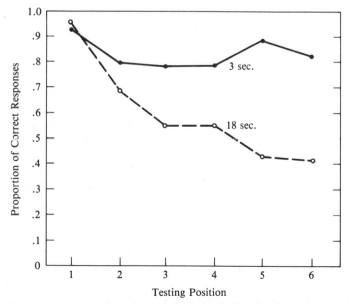

Figure 15–3   Retention as a function of testing position and length of retention interval. (From Keppel, G. and Underwood, B. J. Proactive inhibition in short-term retention of single items. *Journal of Verbal Learning and Verbal Behavior,* 1962, *1,* 153–161. Copyright 1962 by Academic Press, Inc. Reprinted by permission.)

not balanced between treatment conditions or if serious differential carryover effects are present, the within-subjects design simply will not provide data that are interpretable in any useful manner. In this section, I will examine a number of additional points that should be considered in the design and analysis of an experiment with repeated measures.

Simultaneous Within-Subjects Designs

The within-subjects designs we have discussed so far have consisted of the successive administration of the different treatment conditions to the same subject. Because of the possibility of practice effects, we have to vary the order in which the treatments are presented in such a way that practice effects and treatment effects are not confounded. As you have seen, counterbalancing solves this problem. Suppose we try something different and present the different conditions to the subjects more or less simultaneously. A simple example will illustrate the distinction. Suppose a language teacher is interested in the relative difficulty of learning equivalent English and Italian words in the English-Italian order versus the Italian-English order. The question might be studied in a within-subjects design, with half of the subjects learning a set of words in the English-Italian order followed by a different set of words in the Italian order, and the other half of the subjects learning the two sets in the reverse order, Italian-English followed by English-Italian. The same experiment can be conducted in a simultaneous design in which both sets of words are presented randomly as a single list to learn rather than as two temporally separated lists of material.

The clear advantage of this latter arrangement is the elimination of practice effects because both types of pairs in effect are learned "simultaneously." But there remains a problem, unfortunately: the possibility of **contrast effects**. As an example, consider an experiment reported by Grice and Hunter (1964) in which the effect of the loudness of a conditioned stimulus in a classical-conditioning study was investigated under two experimental situations, one a between-subjects design in which one group of subjects received the soft conditioned stimulus and another group received the loud stimulus, and the other a simultaneous within-subjects design in which the soft and loud stimuli were intermixed during learning. The simultaneous design revealed a dramatic difference in the learning produced by the two stimuli, whereas the between-subjects design produced a marked reduction in the effect. Postman and Riley (1957) contrasted the learning of pairs of similar or dissimilar elements in a between-subjects design in which one group of subjects learned a list of similar pairs and another a list of dissimilar pairs, with a simultaneous within-subjects design in which both types of pairs were combined into a single list. They found no difference in the speed of learning of the two types of pairs when they were studied in a between-subjects design and a striking difference when they were studied in a simultaneous within-subjects design.

The Statistical Comparison of Experimental Designs

It is fairly simple to compare the findings of a successive within-subjects design with the findings of a simultaneous within-subjects design. All that is necessary is to arrange the data in a factorial matrix, one factor representing the actual manipulation, for example, the order of the English-Italian pairs, and the other factor the type of design. The former would involve repeated measurements and the latter independent groups of subjects serving in the two different designs. The analysis would be patterned after the standard "mixed" analysis of variance (Chap. 17), and the focus of attention would be the interaction between the two factors.

A comparison of either type of within-subjects design, in which subjects receive all the treatment conditions, with a between-subjects manipulation, in which subjects receive only one of the treatment conditions, also involves a factorial design, but the analysis is considerably more complicated. Erlbacher (1977) presents a worked example of how this type of analysis may be conducted. The general logic of the analysis can be extended to even more complex types of comparisons.

Within-Subjects Designs for Which $n = 1$

In certain areas of research, we occasionally see the ultimate in within-subjects designs—studies in which *one* subject serves many times in all the treatment conditions. Designs of this sort are sometimes called "$n = 1$" research. Consider, for example, a study reported by Ericsson and Polson (1988), who discovered an individual with unique memory skills and set about subjecting him to intense experimentation. Their design consisted of a 4×3 factorial experiment, which was administered several times to the same gifted subject. The rationale for this type of design is to study intensely the behavior of a unique and rare individual under the controlled situations an experiment affords.

Another example is the pioneering research on learning and memory by Hermann Ebbinghaus (1885), who conducted numerous experiments on himself. Although some have wondered whether his results were colored by the fact that he was both subject and experimenter, the amazing point is that many of his fundamental findings have stood the crucial test of replications by others, with more traditional designs.

A more common example of research of this sort are experiments in which a series of $n = 1$ studies is conducted. Each study is complete within itself, including several replications of the treatment conditions. The interest is to see whether the treatment effects observed with one subject are reasonably duplicated with two or more subjects. We see designs of this sort when a great deal of investment is required to train subjects or to create certain experimental preparations. In many cases, this type of research can be analyzed with the procedures considered in this section of the book.

16

The Single-Factor Within-Subjects Design

This chapter covers the analysis of the simplest design in which repeated measures may be used, the single-factor experiment. In this case, the easiest way to think of the design is as a *factorial* experiment in which subjects (factor S) are treated as a second factor. In this arrangement, then, both the independent variable (factor A) and subjects (factor S) are completely crossed; that is, each subject receives each of the a treatments.

16.1 DESIGN AND NOTATION

The single-factor design and the scores and totals that we will find necessary for the analysis are presented in Table 16–1. It is convenient and accurate to refer to this as an $(A \times S)$ design. The parentheses indicate that factor A is a within-subjects manipulation. Each subject provides a different Y scores, one from each of the treatments of factor A he or she receives. The data are entered into a matrix that has the levels of factor A listed along the columns and the levels of factor S—that is, the individual subjects—listed along the rows.

The notational system is identical to the one used for the single-factor experiment with independent groups of subjects. That is, the scores in the data matrix are symbolized as Y_{ij}, where the subscript i denotes the particular level of factor A and the subscript j denotes one of the n different subjects (factor S). The marginal totals needed for the analysis are also presented in the table. It is here, however, that the notation for the $(A \times S)$ design differs from that for independent groups. Specifically, in addition to the usual column marginal totals or treatment sums (A_i), *row* marginal totals S_j are also calculated. The S_j terms consist of the overall totals for each subject—the sum of the Y scores produced at each level of factor A. (Such a quantity was not possible in the completely randomized design, of course,

Table 16–1 Notational System: $(A \times S)$ Design

SUBJECTS	LEVELS OF FACTOR A			Sum
	a_1	a_2	a_3	
s_1	$Y_{1,1}$	$Y_{2,1}$	$Y_{3,1}$	S_1
s_2	$Y_{1,2}$	$Y_{2,2}$	$Y_{3,2}$	S_2
s_3	$Y_{1,3}$	$Y_{2,3}$	$Y_{3,3}$	S_3
Sum	A_1	A_2	A_3	T

because different subjects were represented in each cell of the data matrix.) The symbol T continues to signify the grand total of all individual Y_{ij} scores.

16.2   COMPUTATIONAL FORMULAS

I have already indicated that the $(A \times S)$ design represents a complete crossing of factors A and S. Therefore, the calculations required of this type of design follow those enumerated for the two-way design in Chap. 10. The only exception is that there is no within-groups factor in the $(A \times S)$ design—there is only *one* score in each cell of the AS matrix, and consequently, there can be no within-cell variability. I will now consider the overall analysis of variance.[1]

The Overall Analysis

From our knowledge of the two-way factorial, we would expect to extract from the total sum of squares SS_T the following: two main effects, SS_A and SS_S, and the interaction $SS_{A \times S}$. These sources are presented in Table 16–2. Each sum of squares is calculated from basic ratios, symbolized as brackets around capital letters. Each letter designation refers to a score, in the case of $[Y]$, or to a sum, in the case of $[A]$, $[S]$, and $[T]$; each ratio is formed by squaring and then summing all designated quantities in the AS matrix and dividing by the number of observations contributing to any one of the quantities. For T, this number is $(a)(n)$; for A, this number is n; for S, this number is a; and for Y, this number is 1 and is usually not shown in the formula. These operations are specified in the second column of the table for the first term in each formula, except in the case of the last row, where the formula for the second term, $[T]$, is presented. The df's listed in the third column

Table 16–2   Computational Formulas for the $(A \times S)$ Design

Source	Basic Ratio[a]	df	SS	MS	F
A	$[A] = \dfrac{\Sigma A^2}{n}$	$a - 1$	$[A] - [T]$	$\dfrac{SS_A}{df_A}$	$\dfrac{MS_A}{MS_{A \times S}}$
S	$[S] = \dfrac{\Sigma S^2}{a}$	$n - 1$	$[S] - [T]$	$\dfrac{SS_S}{df_S}$	
$A \times S$	$[Y] = \Sigma Y^2$	$(a - 1)(n - 1)$	$[Y] - [A] - [S] + [T]$	$\dfrac{SS_{A \times S}}{df_{A \times S}}$	
Total	$[T] = \dfrac{T^2}{(a)(n)}$	$(a)(n) - 1$	$[Y] - [T]$		

[a]Bracketed letters represent terms in computational formulas; a particular term is identified by the letter appearing in the numerator.

[1]I will discuss an alternative analysis in Sec. 16.7, which is more appropriate when significant practice effects are present.

for each source of variance are obtained by following the usual rules. As you have seen previously, the expanded version of each *df* statement can be used to specify the patterns in which the basic ratios are combined. The computational formulas for the sums of squares are presented in the fourth column of the table. The mean squares are constructed by dividing sums of squares by corresponding *df*'s. The only new operation specified in Table 16–2 is the selection of the error term for the MS_A. In the table, I have indicated that the interaction mean square $MS_{A \times S}$ serves this function, but the justification of this choice will require some discussion.

One way to explain this choice of error term is to turn for a moment to the completely randomized design. In this design, the total sum of squares consists entirely of between-subject differences—each observation is obtained from a different subject and each observation is independent of the others. As you saw in Chap. 2, SS_T can be divided into two parts, SS_A and $SS_{S/A}$. The first part represents variation associated with the treatment conditions and reflects treatment effects and experimental error. The second part represents the variation associated with subjects treated alike, a "pure" reflection of experimental error—that is, individual differences and other uncontrolled sources of variation. Returning to the within-subjects design, you can see that a different sort of uncontrolled variation is operating to produce chance differences among the treatment conditions. This variation cannot be due to differences between subjects, as it is in the completely randomized design, since each subject serves in all the conditions. Rather, it is due to the *inconsistency* with which the same subjects perform under the different treatments. This inconsistency is reflected by the treatment × subject interaction. Typically, this source of variability is considerably smaller than the one that is based on uncontrolled differences between subjects.

The isolation of uncontrolled variation in the within-subjects design can be illustrated quite simply by considering the sums of squares we normally extract in the two types of designs. Both analyses isolate the treatment sum of squares from the total sum of squares. In the completely randomized design, the remaining variation,

$$SS_{S/A} = SS_T - SS_A$$

is used to estimate error variance. In the within-subjects design, however, this variation is refined further by subtracting a sum of squares that represents the average differences between subjects, SS_S, which reflects the stable and consistent behavior of subjects observed in the context of the overall experiment. This residual, namely,

$$SS_{residual} = SS_{S/A} - SS_S$$

is actually the treatment × subject sum of squares. Using the basic ratios to define $SS_{S/A}$ and SS_S and a little algebra, we have

$$SS_{residual} = ([Y] - [A]) - ([S] - [T])$$
$$= [Y] - [A] - [S] + [T] = SS_{A \times S}$$

The increased sensitivity of the within-subjects design, then, comes from the removal of between-subject differences from the within-groups estimate of unsystematic variation operating in an experiment. In most cases, this gain is considerable.

16.3   A NUMERICAL EXAMPLE

As a numerical example, consider the data presented in Table 16–3. The design consists of $a = 3$ levels of the treatment factor and $n = 6$ subjects. Each subject received a different order of the three conditions, as indicated on the left side of the AS matrix, which spreads the effects of practice equally across three levels of factor A.[2]

As a first step, I will calculate the basic ratios for the overall analysis. Using the formulas specified in Table 16–2 and the data from the AS matrix, we find

$$[T] = \frac{T^2}{(a)(n)} = \frac{(204)^2}{(3)(6)} = 2,312.00$$

$$[A] = \frac{\Sigma A^2}{n} = \frac{(48)^2 + (90)^2 + (66)^2}{6} = 2,460.00$$

$$[S] = \frac{\Sigma S^2}{a} = \frac{(29)^2 + (35)^2 + \ldots + (46)^2 + (34)^2}{3} = 2,379.33$$

$$[Y] = \Sigma Y^2 = (8)^2 + (8)^2 + \ldots + (18)^2 + (7)^2 = 2,684$$

These numbers are combined in the pattern indicated in Table 16–4 to produce the appropriate sums of the squares. The remainder of the analysis follows directly from the formulas given in Table 16–2 and thus requires no comment. The main effect of factor A is significant.

Table 16–3   Numerical Example: AS Matrix

ORDER OF TREATMENTS		TREATMENTS			
		a_1	a_2	a_3	Sum
(a_1, a_2, a_3)	s_1	8	12	9	29
(a_2, a_3, a_1)	s_2	8	13	14	35
(a_3, a_1, a_2)	s_3	9	15	6	30
(a_1, a_3, a_2)	s_4	0	18	12	30
(a_2, a_1, a_3)	s_5	13	15	18	46
(a_3, a_2, a_1)	s_6	10	17	7	34
	Sum	48	90	66	204

[2] Alternatively, we could have balanced practice effects by using only the first three sequences (or the second three sequences) twice, with s_1 and s_2 receiving one of the three sequences, s_3 and s_4 receiving another, and s_5 and s_6 receiving the third. The advantage of using the complete set of sequences in this case is that the arrangement is *digram-balanced* (see p. 339). Neither of the two subsets alone has this property.

Table 16–4 Summary of the Analysis

Source	Sum of Squares	df	MS	F
A	$[A] - [T]$ = 148.00	2	74.00	4.72*
S	$[S] - [T]$ = 67.33	5	13.47	
A × S	$[Y] - [A] - [S] + [T]$ = 156.67	10	15.67	
Total	$[Y] - [T]$ = 372.00	17		

*$p < .05$.

Comment

I indicated in the last chapter that the within-subjects design is generally more sensitive in detecting differences among means than is a companion experiment with independent groups. Let's assume that the data we have just analyzed were produced with a completely randomized design in which three different groups of subjects were tested at a_1, a_2, and a_3, instead of the same six subjects being tested on all three conditions. We can conduct this analysis with the information we have already calculated. The sum of squares for the main effect of factor A remains the same, of course; that is,

$$SS_A = [A] - [T] = 2,460.00 - 2,312.00 = 148.00$$

The sum of squares for the within-groups source is

$$SS_{S/A} = [Y] - [A] = 2,684 - 2,460.00 = 224.00$$

The df associated with the $SS_{S/A}$ are found with the usual formula:

$$df_{S/A} = (a)(n - 1) = 3(6 - 1) = 15$$

The $MS_{S/A}$ is obtained by dividing the $SS_{S/A}$ by the relevant df:

$$MS_{S/A} = \frac{224.00}{15} = 14.93$$

The resulting F ratio for the main effect of factor A now becomes

$$F = \frac{MS_A}{MS_{S/A}} = \frac{74.00}{14.93} = 4.96$$

and is also significant.

A rough index of the relative efficiency of the two designs can be obtained by forming a ratio of the two error terms and multiplying by 100.[3] For the comparison between the independent groups and the standard within-subjects design,

$$\text{relative efficiency} = \frac{MS_{S/A}}{MS_{A \times S}} \times 100$$

[3]Kirk (1982) offers a general discussion of efficiency (p. 7). He also presents a formula for relative efficiency that corrects for the differences in the df's associated with the two error terms (pp. 271–272).

$$= \frac{14.93}{15.67} \times 100 = 95.3 \text{ percent}$$

A value greater than 100 percent would indicate greater efficiency with the within-subjects design. The value of 95.3 percent is not what we would expect since a value of less than 100 percent implies that the within-subjects design is less efficient than the between-subjects design.

What happened in this example? The data for this numerical example were created to demonstrate that the sensitivity of a within-subjects design may be masked by the presence of sizable *practice effects*. I will discuss this problem in Sec. 16.7 and show how the sensitivity may be restored by a simple, supplementary analysis. For the time being, I will concentrate on the standard analysis and return to this complication in Sec. 16.7.

16.4   STATISTICAL MODEL AND ASSUMPTIONS

In this section, we will consider the statistical model and special assumptions that underlie the analysis of the single-factor within-subjects design. As you will see, even small deviations from these assumptions complicate the interpretation of the overall F test. I will describe the statistical model first.

Linear Model

The linear model underlying the analysis of variance is usually specified by expressing the basic score Y_{ij} as a sum of a number of quantities:

$$Y_{ij} = \mu_T + \alpha_i + \pi_j + (\alpha\pi)_{ij} + \epsilon_{ij}$$

where μ_T = the overall mean of the population
α_i = the treatment effect at level a_i $(\mu_i - \mu_T)$
π_j = the subject effect for the jth subject $(\mu_j - \mu_T)$
$(\alpha\pi)_{ij}$ = the interaction of treatment and subject at $a_i s_j$
    $(\mu_{ij} - \mu_i - \mu_j + \mu_T)$
ϵ_{ij} = experimental error

From this basic statement, expected values of the mean squares for the sources we normally extract in the analysis are written in terms of population variance components. The error term for evaluating the main effect of factor A is found by locating a mean square the expectation of which matches the expected value of the main effect (except for the population treatment component, of course). More specifically, the expected values for these two mean squares are

$$E(MS_A) = \sigma_{error}^2 + \sigma_{A \times s}^2 + n(\theta_A^2)$$

$$E(MS_{A \times s}) = \sigma_{error}^2 + \sigma_{A \times s}^2$$

You will note that the expected value of the interaction mean square contains two quantities, σ^2_{error} and $\sigma^2_{A \times S}$, the first of which refers to uncontrolled sources of variability—for example, variations in the testing conditions or measurement error—and the second of which refers to differential reactions of subjects to the treatment conditions (interaction). Although we can distinguish between these two sources of variability theoretically, we cannot disentangle their separate contributions in this particular design.[4]

The Homogeneity Assumptions

The statistical analysis of within-subjects designs operates under the same distribution assumptions required of completely randomized designs, namely, normality, homogeneity of within-treatment variances, and independence. In addition, however, certain assumptions are made concerning the correlations between the multiple measures obtained from the same subjects. I will describe these new assumptions first and then indicate the consequences when they are violated, as they often are in the behavioral sciences. Finally, I will discuss various ways to deal with these problems.

The Assumptions.   Suppose we arrange the data from the $(A \times S)$ design into a set of smaller AS matrices formed by isolating pairs of treatment conditions. There would be three such matrices for our numerical example, one consisting of levels a_1 and a_2, another of levels a_1 and a_3, and a third of levels a_2 and a_3. For each pair of treatments, suppose we subtract the two scores for each of the subjects and then calculate the variances based on these three sets of difference scores. The assumption is that these three variances of differences are equal in the population. This assumption is more formally stated in terms of population within-treatment variances and of correlations between pairs of treatments and is referred to as the **sphericity assumption.**[5]

Tests of the sphericity assumption are described by Huynh and Feldt (1970), Huynh and Mandeville (1979), and Rouanet and Lépine (1970), but they are complicated and beyond the scope of this book. Some statistical computer programs provide tests of this assumption, but most of the tests have been questioned because of assumptions of their own that complicate any interpretation of their outcome (see, for example, Keselman, Rogan, Mendoza, & Breen, 1980). The safest course of action is to assume that the sphericity assumption does not hold for most experiments in the behavioral sciences and to direct your efforts instead to dealing directly with the problems resulting from these violations.

---

[4]The linear model underlying the analysis we have just completed is sometimes called the **nonadditive model,** which emphasizes the fact that the treatment × subject interaction is included in the equation. The **additive model,** in which this interaction is absent, is not a reasonable model for within-subjects designs in the behavioral sciences. Comprehensive presentations of the linear models normally adopted with repeated-measures designs can be found in Kirk (1982), Myers (1979), and Winer (1971).

[5]The sphericity assumption, which is also called the **circularity assumption,** has a more formal definition, which is slightly less restrictive than the one I have given. Kirk (1982, pp. 253–266) and Myers (1979, pp. 163–174) provide useful discussions of the statistical model and its underlying assumptions.

Implications of Violating the Sphericity Assumption. Violating the assumption of homogeneity of within-group variances in the completely randomized designs does not affect our evaluation of F tests unless the ratio of the largest to the smallest variance is greater than 3. Variance heterogeneity becomes more of a problem, however, with unequal sample sizes or when single-df comparisons are involved. We discussed problems of variance heterogeneity for experiments with equal sample sizes in Chap. 5 (pp. 98–99), for experiments with unequal sample sizes in Chap. 13 (pp. 283–284) and for single-df comparisons in Chap. 6 (pp. 123–128).

In contrast, even minor violations of the sphericity assumption in repeated-measures designs can seriously affect our interpretation of F ratios (see, for example, Boik, 1981). More specifically, these violations produce sampling distributions of the F ratio that are not distributed as F when the null hypothesis is true, which means that the standard F tables cannot be directly used to judge the significance of an observed F. Since it is known that when violations are present the actual sampling distribution shifts to the *right* of the central F distribution, the critical values of F obtained from Table A–1 are *too small*. That is, the actual critical values we should be using are larger than those listed in the F table.

Under these circumstances, the F test is said to be biased in a *positive* direction. It could be the case, for example, that the tabled value of F at $\alpha = .05$ actually represents a significance level that is greater than .05—for example, $\alpha = .10$. If we do not make an adjustment in our rejection procedure, we will in effect be operating at a more "lenient" significance level than we had set originally. As a consequence, we will reject the null hypothesis falsely a greater percentage of the time than our statements of significance would imply.

Correcting the Positive Bias. Several ways of solving the problem of positive bias have been proposed in the literature. One solution is to perform the usual analysis of variance but to evaluate the observed F ratios against a new critical value that for statistical convenience assumes the presence of *maximal heterogeneity*. In practice, this is accomplished easily by evaluating the F in this design with $df_{num.} = 1$ and $df_{denom.} = n - 1$, instead of $df_{num.} = a - 1$ and $df_{num.} = (a - 1)(n - 1)$. Applied to our numerical example, in which $a = 3$ and $n = 6$, we would use $F(1, 5) = 6.61$ as our critical value, rather than $F(2, 10) = 4.10$. Since the observed value of F was 4.72, we would not have declared the overall F significant if we had performed this corrective test.

This procedure is known as the **Geisser-Greenhouse correction** (Geisser & Greenhouse, 1958). It is important to note that the mean squares obtained from the analysis are still calculated with the usual df's and not on these corrected ones. The corrected df's are used only when we turn to the F table to find the critical value.

The main difficulty with the Geisser-Greenhouse correction is that it tends to overcorrect, reducing the type I error below the desired level. That is, the significance level may actually be $\alpha = .02$ rather than the value planned ($\alpha = .05$). Only if the heterogeneity is at its theoretical maximum will the new statistical test reflect the correct significance level. In other words, the F ratios are now biased in a *negative* direction. Thus, if we proceed in the normal fashion and use an uncorrected value of F when there is heterogeneity, the test is positively biased; if we use the correction, the test is probably negatively biased.

The Box Correction.   Box (1954b) introduced a method for adjusting numerator and denominator df's by a factor that reflects the degree of heterogeneity actually present in an experiment. This factor, $\hat{\varepsilon}$, is estimated from the data. Examples of the calculations required to obtain the adjustment factor $\hat{\varepsilon}$, which are complex but manageable, can be found in Kirk (1982, p. 262), who calls the factor $\hat{\theta}$; Myers (1978, pp. 173–174); and Winer (1971, pp. 523–524). Huynh and Feldt (1976) introduced a related correction factor, $\tilde{\varepsilon}$, which they recommend should be used when $\hat{\varepsilon}$ is greater than .75 (see pp. 75–76 of their article for the formulas; see also Kirk, 1982, p. 262). In either case, the procedure is the same, the $df_{num.}$ is found by multiplying df_A by one of the correction factors—that is, either $\hat{\varepsilon}$ or $\tilde{\varepsilon}$; the $df_{denom.}$ is found by multiplying $df_{A \times S}$ the same way. The resulting corrections, reflected by the new degrees of freedom, will not be as great as those imposed by the Geisser-Greenhouse procedure, unless maximal heterogeneity is present.

A number of methodologists recommend using a testing strategy advocated by Greenhouse and Geisser (1959), which was designed to avoid calculating $\hat{\varepsilon}$ except when logically necessary:

Evaluate F at $df_{num.} = a - 1$ and $df_{denom.} = (a - 1)(n - 1)$. If the F is not significant, we retain the null hypothesis; if it is significant, we turn to the next step.

Apply the Geisser-Greenhouse correction and evaluate F at $df_{num.} = 1$ and $df_{denom.} = n - 1$. If the F is significant under this overly stringent criterion, we reject the null hypothesis; if it is not significant, we turn to the next step.

Calculate $\hat{\varepsilon}$ and apply the Box correction. If the F is significant, we reject the null hypothesis; if it is not, we retain the null hypothesis.

You can also avoid these complicated calculations by using a computer. The Box correction factor $\hat{\varepsilon}$ is available from a number of comprehensive statistical packages, including SPSSX, Version 4, and BMDP4V.

Missing Data

Occasionally there will be missing data; one or more Y scores sometimes will be missing for a subject (or some subjects). The least ambiguous course of action is to replace such subjects entirely and to duplicate the testing conditions for the new subject(s). But perhaps this is not feasible. Procedures are available by which missing data can be estimated from the data available in the AS matrix. These require the assumption that the data loss is unrelated to the differences in the treatment conditions. Kirk (1982, pp. 268–270) and Myers (1979, pp. 177–178) discuss methods for estimating missing data under these circumstances.

16.5   EFFECT SIZE AND POWER

In my discussions of the completely randomized designs, I stressed the value of estimating treatment effects and of using power estimates to help us choose an appropriate sample size to use in a proposed experiment. The arguments hold true for within-subjects designs as well, but certain complications arise. I will consider the problems associated with estimating effect size first.

Estimating Treatment Effects (Omega Squared)

There are two major problems in estimating omega squared in the within-subjects design. First, there is the definition itself. The standard treatments of the concept define omega squared as

$$\omega_A^2 = \frac{\sigma_A^2}{\sigma_T^2}$$

where σ_T^2 is the sum of the relevant variance components. The problem lies in defining these relevant components. In the completely randomized single-factor design, there were two components, σ_A^2 and σ_{error}^2 and no ambiguity. In the completely randomized factorial design, however, there were two possibilities for defining σ_T^2, namely, $\sigma_A^2 + \sigma_{error}^2$ or $\sigma_A^2 + \sigma_{error}^2$ plus the variance components associated with all other main effects and interactions. I argued in favor of the first definition, which defines a *partial* omega squared, because it gives the same meaning to the concept regardless of the nature of the design (see pp. 223–224). Because the $(A \times S)$ is a factorial design with respect to subjects, there are again two ways of defining σ_T^2, specifically,

$$\sigma_T^2 = \sigma_A^2 + \sigma_{error}^2 \text{ and } \sigma_T^2 = \sigma_A^2 + \sigma_S^2 + \sigma_{error}^2$$

The two definitions will give different values for ω_A^2.

The second problem concerns estimating the different variance components from an experiment. Vaughan and Corballis (1969), for example, give a formula that admittedly overestimates σ_T^2 and, consequently, underestimates ω_A^2. Myers (1979, pp. 178–179) offers two estimates of omega squared, which together set a range of values within which the "actual" ω_A^2 will fall.

I have argued that estimates of relative treatment provide useful information that supplements the actual significance test. But because of these two theoretical uncertainties, however—the definition of σ_T^2 and the estimates of the components themselves—any recommendation must be provisional. Until there is more work on these problems and methodologists develop a consensus concerning the definition of a more useful index, I offer a definition that is continuous with the concept of partial omega squared:

$$\hat{\sigma}_A^2 = \frac{df_A(MS_A - MS_{A \times S})}{(a)(n)} \tag{16-1}$$

$$\hat{\sigma}_{error}^2 = MS_{A \times S} \tag{16-2}$$

$$\hat{\omega}_A^2 = \frac{\hat{\sigma}_A^2}{\hat{\sigma}_A^2 + \hat{\sigma}_{error}^2} \tag{16-3}$$

Using Power Estimates to Choose Sample Size

In previous chapters, you have seen why power estimates are vital in the realistic planning of completely randomized designs. The same arguments hold for the within-subjects designs as well. Again you will need to estimate the minimum treatment effects you wish to detect and the error variance you expect to be present. You then combine these estimates with other information about your experiment to calculate the statistic ϕ_A^2, which is then translated into an estimate of power. For the $(A \times S)$ design,

$$\phi_A^2 = n' \frac{\Sigma \,(\text{dev.})^2}{(a)(\sigma_{error}^2)} \tag{16–4}$$

where n' = the trial sample size
$\Sigma \,(\text{dev.})^2$ = the basic population deviations $(\mu_i - \mu_j)$
a = the number of treatment conditions
σ_{error}^2 = the relevant population error variance

The last quantity, σ_{error}^2, may be estimated from a pilot study or from previous research you have conducted or has been reported in the literature.

At this point, you turn to the Pearson-Hartley power charts (Table A–2) and fiddle with different trial sample sizes (n') until you achieve the power you want for your proposed study. If you need to counterbalance the orders of the treatments, you would select a sample size that is some multiple of the number of treatment conditions (a). For our numerical example, in which $a = 3$, our sample size would be some multiple of 3—that is, 3, 6, 9, and so on. A nonmultiple will not permit the counterbalancing procedure to work properly.

Violating Homogeneity Assumptions. The procedures I have outlined for estimating power and setting sample size assume that the sphericity assumption, which we discussed in Sec. 16.4, is upheld. In most cases, the data will depart from the form specified by the assumptions underlying the statistical model, which will have a direct consequence on power, particularly if we will apply some sort of correction to reduce the positive bias associated with the standard F test. This correction is achieved by making it more difficult to reject the null hypothesis, which is what is intended when the focus is type I error but which has an opposite effect when the focus is type II error. That is, power will be reduced when any of these correction techniques is applied. Possible solutions to this problem are only beginning to be proposed (see, for example, Muller & Barton, 1989), leaving us in an ambiguous position with regard to planning sample size.

What we need is a convenient and realistic way to estimate the sample size necessary for a within-subjects experiment that will not satisfy the sphericity assumption. I propose we use the Geisser-Greenhouse correction in the power determinations. The only change necessary is in the selection of power charts and the specific power function. Assuming perfect sphericity, we would use the chart for $df_{num.} = a - 1$ and $df_{denom.} = (a - 1)(n - 1)$; this is the procedure I outlined previously. If it seems likely that the sphericity assumption will not be met and that we will probably use the Geisser-Greenhouse correction in analyzing the data, the chart we should now use is one that takes that correction into account, namely, $df_{num.} = 1$ and $df_{denom.} = n - 1$. If we have any way of obtaining a realistic estimate of $\hat{\epsilon}$, which seems unlikely in most practical situations, we would use the power chart appropriate to that new combination of df's.

16.6   COMPARISONS INVOLVING THE TREATMENT MEANS

All of the types of comparisons discussed in Part II for the completely randomized single-factor design are available for the corresponding within-subjects design. There is one important difference, however, and this again lies in the selection of the error term.

Error Terms for Comparisons

You have seen that the mean square used to test the main effect of factor A, $MS_{A \times S}$, is influenced by two components: experimental error and the treatment $\times$ subject interaction. In our evaluation of the overall treatment effect, in which all treatment means are compared, it makes intuitive sense to use an error term based on all the scores in the experiment. However, this overall interaction mean square is generally *not* appropriate for evaluating the significance of individual comparisons. The $MS_{A \times S}$ is an *average* of a set of individual *comparison* $\times$ subject interactions and, as such, may not provide an appropriate estimate of the specific interaction reflecting itself in the particular set of treatment means we are considering. Let's consider an example from an actual experiment, consisting of $a = 6$ treatments and $n = 8$ subjects.[6] The overall error term was $MS_{A \times S} = 2.79$, and the separate error terms for five single-df comparisons were 1.48, 3.90, 1.03, 2.51, and 5.05—a range of nearly 5 to 1. If the overall error term had been used to evaluate these comparisons, the resultant F's would have been too small for comparisons 1 and 3, too large for comparisons 2 and 5, and about right for comparison 4.

Research has shown that even minor violations of the sphericity assumption can produce sizable differences among separate error terms (see, for example, Keselman, Rogan, & Games, 1981). The safest strategy is to construct separate error terms for *all* comparisons. The computational procedures we will follow in this section have been specifically devised to facilitate the calculation of the individual error terms needed for within-subjects designs. Consequently, the analysis differs considerably from that presented in Chap. 6 for the completely randomized design, which worked directly with the treatment means. The approach taken here conducts what amounts to a within-subjects analysis on the information relevant for the single-df comparison; we will work with scores and sums in a specialized

[6]Keppel, Postman, and Zavortink (1968).

matrix I will call an *AS* **comparison matrix.** We can then with minor modifications employ the formulas for the overall within-subjects analysis.

Forming the *AS* Comparison Matrix

The key to the analysis is the *AS* comparison matrix, which captures the information relevant to the specific comparison under consideration. For a pairwise comparison, the procedure is simple: We extract the two relevant scores for each subject and place them directly in the new matrix. For a complex comparison, the procedure involves an intermediate step in which each Y score is weighted by the relevant coefficient before being placed in the comparison matrix. This procedure is best illustrated with an example, which we will base on the data from the earlier numerical example.

Suppose we wanted to compare the mean at level a_2 with the mean of the other two levels combined (a_1 and a_3). The coefficients I will use are the set c_i: $\frac{1}{2}$, -1, $\frac{1}{2}$, although any appropriate set will do (the set 1, -2, 1, for example, will avoid decimal numbers). The matrix on the left side of Table 16–5 contains the Y scores weighted by the appropriate coefficients. To illustrate the procedure for the first subject, we take the three original Y scores for this subject, which were 8, 12, and 9 (see Table 16–3, p. 348); when weighted by the coefficients, the three scores become $(+\frac{1}{2})(8) = +4.0$; $(-1)(12) = -12$; and $(+\frac{1}{2})(9) = +4.5$, respectively. The scores for the other subjects are constructed in the same way. We now begin to construct the *AS* comparison matrix by adding together for each subject the scores weighted by a *positive* coefficient and entering them in column 1 of the comparison matrix, which appears on the right side of Table 16–5; for s_1, we would place 8.5 (4.0 + 4.5) in the first column. The weighted sums in this column represent the "positive" part of the single-*df* comparison, which I have labeled $a_{(+)}$. The sums of the scores weighted by a *negative* coefficient are next entered in column 2 of the comparison matrix. (We delete the negative signs at this point as they are not relevant for the rest of the analysis.) Since there is only one negative coefficient for this comparison, the "sum" for s_1 is 12. The sums appearing in this column are labeled $a_{(-)}$.

From this point on, we treat this comparison matrix exactly as if it were an

Table 16–5   *Constructing an AS Comparison Matrix*

| | Weighted Y Scores | | | | *AS* Comparison Matrix | | |
	a_1	a_2	a_3		$a_{(+)}$	$a_{(-)}$	Sum
s_1	+4.0	−12	+4.5	s_1	8.5	12.0	20.5
s_2	+4.0	−13	+7.0	s_2	11.0	13.0	24.0
s_3	+4.5	−15	+3.0	s_3	7.5	15.0	22.5
s_4	+0.0	−18	+6.0	s_4	6.0	18.0	24.0
s_5	+6.5	−15	+9.0	s_5	15.5	15.0	30.5
s_6	+5.0	−17	+3.5	s_6	8.5	17.0	25.5
				Sum	57.0	90.0	147.0

actual $(A \times S)$ design with *two* levels of factor A . In this case, however, "factor A " is actually the single-df comparison reflected by the choice of coefficients. The presence of a true difference between the two means specified by this comparison is reflected in the difference between the mean at $a_{(+)}$ and the one at $a_{(-)}$. The logic behind the analysis parallels the arguments we considered for evaluating the overall effect of factor A . The effect of "factor A" —that is, the single-df comparison—reflects the effect itself plus experimental error and any interaction between the comparison and subjects. The interaction mean square, on the other hand, reflects only experimental error and the interaction, and thus provides an appropriate error term for the F test. The interaction mean square from the overall analysis, $MS_{A \times S}$, is not an appropriate error term because it reflects an average interaction, which usually is not relevant for a specific analytical comparison. We are now ready to perform a statistical analysis on the data in this new AS matrix.

Completing the Analysis

The first step is to calculate the basic ratios, remembering that the number of treatment levels is two in this analysis, not three. I will use a prime to refer to the levels associated with $A_{comp.}$; thus $a' = 2$. From the formulas in Table 16–2 (p. 346), we have

$$[T] = \frac{T^2}{(a')(n)} = \frac{(147.0)^2}{(2)(6)} = 1{,}800.75$$

$$[A] = \frac{\Sigma A^2}{n} = \frac{(57.0)^2 + (90.0)^2}{6} = 1{,}891.50$$

$$[S] = \frac{\Sigma S^2}{a'} = \frac{(20.5)^2 + (24.0)^2 + \ldots + (30.5)^2 + (25.5)^2}{2} = 1{,}829.50$$

$$[Y] = \Sigma Y^2 = (8.5)^2 + (11.0)^2 + \ldots + (15.0)^2 + (17.0)^2 = 1{,}974.00$$

The remainder of the analysis is summarized in Table 16–6. The error term is an interaction of this particular comparison—a_2 versus a_1 and a_3 combined—with subjects and, as such, it provides the appropriate baseline against which this comparison is evaluated. The resulting F ratio, formed by dividing the comparison mean square by the special error term, is significant.

Table 16–6   Summary of the Analysis of a Comparison

Source	Sum of Squares		df	MS	F
$A_{comp.}$	$[A] - [T]$ =	90.75	1	90.75	8.44*
S	$[S] - [T]$ =	28.75	5	5.75	
$A_{comp.} \times S$	$[Y] - [A] - [S] + [T]$ =	53.75	5	10.75	
Total	$[Y] - [T]$ =	173.25	11		

*$p < .05$.

Comments on Using Comparison Matrices

The advantage of this way of analyzing single-*df* comparisons is that it retains the logic of the overall analysis of variance. Once the comparison matrix is formed, the analysis parallels the standard analysis. This approach is most easily understood with pairwise comparisons, where you simply extract the two relevant sets of data without going through the procedure of weighting the scores and combining them to form the comparison matrix.

Forming a Comparison Matrix for a Trend Component.   Students have reported difficulties in applying this method to the analysis of trend, where the coefficients are more complicated than those we usually encounter in the analysis of qualitative independent variables. Problem 2 in the Exercises provides you with an example of trend analysis. Let's see how we would construct the comparison matrix for this problem. Factor A consisted of $a = 6$ equally spaced intervals. The coefficients for linear trend, which we obtain from Appendix A–4, are -5, -3, -1, 1, 3, 5. I will illustrate the process with the data from the first subject. In the following table, I have listed the linear coefficients and the six Y scores for s_1 in the first two rows and the weighted Y scores—the products obtained by multiplying each score by the corresponding linear coefficient—in the last row:

c_i:	-5	-3	-1	$+1$	$+3$	$+5$
Y_{i1}:	7	3	2	2	1	1
$(c_i)(Y_{i1})$:	-35	-9	-2	$+2$	$+3$	$+5$

We would then combine the three scores weighted by positive coefficients ($+2$, $+3$, and $+5$) and enter their sum (10) in the column labeled $a_{(+)}$; similarly, we would combine the Y scores with negative weights (-35, -9, and -2) and enter their sum (46) in the column labeled $a_{(-)}$. We would repeat these operations for each of the remaining subjects in order to complete the comparison matrix. After this point, the analysis continues as illustrated earlier.

Standardizing the Comparison Sums of Squares.   In all previous analyses involving coefficients, we did not worry about the actual values of the coefficients just as long as they were some multiple of the coefficients for the basic comparison. In comparing the mean for a_2 with the mean for a_1 and a_3 combined, for example, we used the basic set $\frac{1}{2}$, -1, $\frac{1}{2}$, but we could have used 1, -2, 1 or -1, 2, -1 or even 22, -44, 22 and obtained the same sum of square for the comparison. The reason for this convenient outcome is that the computational formulas compensated for the different multipliers used to create related sets of coefficients— for example, the $+2$ that we use to transform the set $\frac{1}{2}$, -1, $\frac{1}{2}$ into a computationally more convenient set (1, -2, 1).

The computational procedure presented for the $(A \times S)$ design does not have this compensating quality at the level of the sums of squares. That is, the standard analysis, which we applied to a comparison matrix and sums of weighted Y scores, assumes the use of actual Y scores, not weighted ones. Only when the analysis involves a pairwise comparison, where the coefficients have the form 1, -1, 0, 0, and so on, will the sums of squares be unaffected by this computational procedure. I did not mention this complication when I presented the analysis because the final F ratio is correct. This occurs because both the numerator mean square ($MS_{A_{comp.}}$) and the denominator mean square ($MS_{A_{comp.} \times s}$) are based on the weighted Y scores and the influence of the different multipliers on these two quantities is perfectly balanced when the F ratio is calculated. That is, the F's will be identical for any set of coefficients representing the same basic comparison, even though the sums of squares (and corresponding mean squares) are not.

It is a simple matter to adjust or standardize the sums of squares so that they are independent of the particular coefficients used to represent the comparison. All we need to do is to divide each sum of squares of interest by an adjustment factor that is based on the particular coefficients entering in the calculations:

$$\text{adjustment factor} = \frac{\Sigma c_i^2}{2} \tag{16-5}$$

In our numerical example, where the coefficients were $\frac{1}{2}$, -1, $\frac{1}{2}$, the adjustment factor is

$$\frac{(\frac{1}{2})^2 + (-1)^2 + (\frac{1}{2})^2}{2} = \frac{.25 + 1 + .25}{2} = .75$$

Applying this correction to the two unadjusted sums of squares from Table 16-6 that are critical for this analysis, we find

$$SS_{A_{comp.}} = \frac{90.75}{.75} = 121.00 \quad \text{and} \quad SS_{A_{comp.} \times s} = \frac{53.75}{.75} = 71.67$$

The mean squares are obtained in the normal fashion; that is,

$$MS_{A_{comp.}} = \frac{121.00}{1} = 121.00 \quad \text{and} \quad MS_{A_{comp.} \times s} = \frac{71.67}{5} = 14.33$$

and the F ratio becomes $121.00/14.33 = 8.44$, which is identical to the F in Table 16-6, as promised.

Again I stress that the adjustments are not needed if your only interest is in the outcome of the F test: The F based on unadjusted and adjusted sums of squares are identical. The adjustment *is* necessary, however, if you are interested in subtracting sums of squares found by different single-df comparisons from the overall SS_A or in combining them.[7] The adjustment is also necessary in the analysis of

---

[7]This can happen when you are working with a complete set of *orthogonal* comparisons and you either want to show that the sum of the individual sums of squares equals the overall sum of squares or to obtain the last sum of squares by subtraction. Suppose, for example, that we wanted to compare the two levels we combined (a_1 and a_3) in the numerical example. Since the original comparison ($\frac{1}{2}$, -1, $\frac{1}{2}$) and this one (1, 0, -1) are orthogonal, we could obtain

$$SS_{A_{comp.\ 2}} = SS_A - SS_{A_{comp.\ 1}}$$

$$SS_{A_{comp.\ 2} \times s} = SS_A \times s - SS_{A_{comp.\ 1} \times s}$$

rather than forming a comparison matrix and calculating the two sums of squares directly. This alternative procedure will only work with adjusted sums of squares.

within-subjects designs that include between-subjects factors, which we will consider in Chaps. 18 and 19. Generally, I recommend that you make a habit of adjusting sums of squares whenever the analysis is based on weighted Y scores so that you will not make a serious mistake when this adjustment is vital.

16.7 REMOVING PRACTICE EFFECTS FROM THE ERROR TERM

It is not generally appreciated that practice effects can reduce the sensitivity of a within-subjects design. Let's consider a simple example. Suppose we have $a = 3$ conditions and $n = 3$ subjects who receive all three conditions in three different sequences. Let's assume that the only factor influencing the Y scores is a practice effect. I have depicted such a situation in the matrix on the left in Table 16–7, where the data are arranged according to the order of the test. All subjects have a score of 0 on the first test, a score of 1 on the second test, and a score of 2 on the third test, regardless of which condition they received on any given test. The data have been rearranged according to treatment condition in the right-hand matrix. A quick calculation, using the basic ratios at the bottom of the table, reveals

$$SS_A = [A] - [T] = 9 - 9 = 0$$

$$SS_S = [S] - [T] = 9 - 9 = 0$$

$$SS_{A \times S} = [Y] - [A] - [S] + [T] = 15 - 9 - 9 + 9 = 6$$

Because of the way I created the scores, you are probably not surprised that the sums of scores for treatments and for subjects are zero. But the value of 6 for $SS_{A \times S}$ is a different matter. In general, counterbalancing schemes will spread the effects of practice over the treatment conditions equally, but they will deposit these practice effects in the $SS_{A \times S}$. This means, therefore, that the sensitivity of a within-subjects design will be reduced to the extent that practice effects are present.

Table 16–7 An Illustration of a Practice Effect and Its Influence on $SS_{A \times S}$

Sequence		p_1	p_2	p_3		a_1	a_2	a_3	Sum
(a_1, a_2, a_3)	s_1	0	1	2	s_1	0	1	2	3
(a_2, a_3, a_1)	s_2	0	1	2	s_2	2	0	1	3
(a_3, a_1, a_2)	s_3	0	1	2	s_3	1	2	0	3
					Sum	3	3	3	9

$$[T] = \frac{(9)^2}{(3)(3)} = 9$$

$$[A] = \frac{(3)^2 + (3)^2 + (3)^2}{3} = 9$$

$$[S] = \frac{(3)^2 + (3)^2 + (3)^2}{3} = 9$$

$$[Y] = (0)^2 + (2)^2 + \ldots + (1)^2 + (0)^2 = 15$$

Fortunately, we can easily remove practice effects from the error term with some simple calculations. Suppose we let P_1 refer to the sum of all the observations on the first test, P_2 the sum of all the observations on the second test, and so on. We can then calculate a sum of squares for "practice" as follows:

$$SS_P = \frac{\Sigma P^2}{n} - \frac{T^2}{(a)(n)} \qquad (16\text{-}6)$$

The df for this source is $p - 1$, where p is the number of tests each subject receives. All we need to do now is to subtract the sum of squares for practice from the interaction sum of squares to obtain a "practice-free" sum of squares, which I will call $SS_{A \times S \,(residual)}$. These operations are summarized in Table 16–8. This residual sum of squares, divided by the appropriate number of degrees of freedom—calculated by subtracting df_P from $df_{A \times S}$—is the error term with which the overall treatment effects are evaluated.

Let's return to the example in Table 16–7. From the matrix on the left, we find that the "practice" subtotals are

$$P_1 = 0 + 0 + 0 = 0$$
$$P_2 = 1 + 1 + 1 = 3$$
$$P_3 = 2 + 2 + 2 = 6$$

Substituting in Eq. (16–6), we find

$$SS_P = \frac{(0)^2 + (3)^2 + (6)^2}{3} - \frac{(9)^2}{(3)(3)} = 15 - 9 = 6$$

Subtracting this sum of squares from $SS_{A \times S}$, we have

$$SS_{A \times S \,(residual)} = SS_{A \times S} - SS_P = 6 - 6 = 0$$

which illustrates that this operation in fact does remove the practice effects from the error term.

Suppose we apply this analysis to the data appearing in Table 16–3 (p. 348). To calculate SS_P, we need to arrange the Y scores according to testing order, which I have done in Table 16–9. From Table 16–3, we see that the fourth subject, for example, received the three conditions in the order a_1, a_3, a_2 and produced scores of 0, 18, and 12, respectively; rearranging these scores in the order they were collected, we have 0, 12, and 18, which is how they were entered in Table 16–9. From the information in the table, we obtain

Table 16–8   Removing Practice Effects from the $SS_{A \times S}$

Source	Sum of Squares	df
$A \times S$	$[Y] - [A] - [S] + [T]$	$(a - 1)(n - 1)$
Position (P)	$\dfrac{\Sigma P^2}{n} - [T]$	$p - 1$
$A \times S$ (residual)	$SS_{A \times S} - SS_P$	$df_{A \times S} - df_P$

Table 16–9 Analysis of the Practice Effect

	ORDINAL POSITION OF TREATMENTS			Sum
	P_1	P_2	P_3	
s_1	8	12	9	29
s_2	13	14	8	35
s_3	6	9	15	30
s_4	0	12	18	30
s_5	15	13	18	46
s_6	7	17	10	34
Sum	49	77	78	204

$$SS_P = \frac{(49)^2 + (77)^2 + (78)^2}{6} - \frac{(204)^2}{(3)(6)} = 2{,}402.33 - 2{,}312.00 = 90.33$$

We can now calculate the refined error term by subtraction:

$$SS_{A \times S \, (residual)} = SS_{A \times S} - SS_P = 156.67 - 90.33 = 66.34$$

The remainder of the analysis is summarized in Table 16–10. The F for the overall treatment effects is significant and, more important, is considerably larger than the one we obtained with the standard analysis in which practice effects were ignored ($F = 4.72$). You will note that I have also evaluated the significance of the practice effect ($F = MS_P/MS_{A \times S \, (residual)} = 5.45$), which is significant.

Earlier in this chapter, I noted that the sensitivity of the within-subjects design may be clouded by practice effects. This particular numerical example was designed to demonstrate this possibility. You may recall that in Sec. 16.3 (pp. 349–350) we determined that the within-subjects design was slightly less efficient than a corresponding between-subjects design. That is, we found

$$\text{relative efficiency} = \frac{MS_{S/A}}{MS_{A \times S}} \times 100 = \frac{14.93}{15.67} \times 100 = 95.3 \text{ percent}$$

If we measure relative efficiency with respect to the error term with the practice effect removed ($MS_{A \times S \, (residual)} = 8.29$), we now see the expected difference between the two types of design:

Table 16–10 Summary of the Revised Analysis

Source	SS	df	MS	F
A	148.00	2	74.00	8.93*
S	67.33	5	13.47	
P	90.33	2	45.17	5.45*
$A \times S_{(residual)}$	66.34	8	8.29	
Total	372.00	17		

*$p < .05$.

$$\text{relative efficiency} = \frac{MS_{S/A}}{MS_{A \times S(residual)}} \times 100$$

$$= \frac{14.93}{8.29} \times 100 = 180.1 \text{ percent}$$

As indicated, the data were created to show the benefits of removing practice effects from the standard analysis. With actual data, we would see a considerable gain in efficiency when we compare the standard analysis with the completely randomized design; but if there are any practice effects at all, the smaller error term from the analysis we have just considered will increase the attractiveness of using repeated measures to study a given phenomenon.[8]

Comment

Any gain in sensitivity we might obtain by removing practice effects from the error term should be extended to the evaluation of single-*df* comparisons. Unfortunately, the relatively simple analysis we have just considered does not lend itself to the calculation of separate error terms often required for comparisons. In the second edition of *Design and Analysis*, I presented a method that accomplishes this goal by removing the practice effects from the individual *Y* scores, rather than from the overall error term. This procedure is more complicated than the one we just considered but has the distinct advantage of increasing the sensitivity of the analysis of single-*df* comparisons. I suggest that you conduct a preliminary analysis first in which you test the significance of the overall practice effects, using a more liberal significance level than usual (for example, $\alpha = .25$). If the *F* is significant and you plan to evaluate single-*df* comparisons with separate error terms, you should undertake the analysis described in the second edition (Keppel, 1982, pp. 399–404). On the other hand, if the *F* is not significant, you can proceed with the analysis without worrying about the effects of practice on the analysis of your experiment.

A second point concerns the need to check on the possibility of an interaction between treatments and testing position. As you saw in Chap. 15, this can be accomplished graphically by plotting the data as a function of testing position and examining the trends for each level of factor *A* . Any suspicious departure from parallel functions—that is, any interaction—should be assessed statistically by means of a fairly complicated statistical analysis, which I will not consider.[9] A sizable treatment × position interaction should lead to a questioning of the wisdom of using a within-subjects design to study this particular phenomenon.

16.8 EXERCISES[10]

1. Desert iguanas are thought to use their tongues to obtain information about their environment by sampling odors that may be important for their survival and repro-

---

[8]This is often called a **Latin square analysis**. The name is derived from the counterbalancing arrangements used to balance practice effects.
[9]Myers (1979, pp. 274–278) describes and illustrates this analysis in some detail.
[10]The answers to these problems are found in Appendix B.

ductive success. Pedersen (1988) studied the rates of tongue extrusions in desert iguanas who were exposed to sands collected from $a = 5$ different environments. These consisted of a_1 = clean sand, a_2 = sand from an iguana's home cage, a_3 = sand from cages housing other iguanas, a_4 = sand from cages housing western whiptail lizards, and a_5 = sand from cages housing desert kangaroo rats. (The latter two species are frequently seen in close contact with desert iguanas in their natural habitat.) A total of $n = 10$ iguanas served in the experiment. Each was tested in each condition on successive days; the order of testing was randomly determined for each animal. The iguanas were videotaped during each 30-minute test session; the response measure was the number of tongue extrusions observed during each test session. The data follow.[11]

Subject	Clean Sand a_1	Home Cage a_2	Iguanas a_3	Lizards a_4	K. Rats a_5
1	24	15	41	30	50
2	6	6	0	6	13
3	4	0	5	4	9
4	11	9	10	14	18
5	0	0	0	0	0
6	8	15	10	15	38
7	8	5	2	6	15
8	0	0	0	11	54
9	0	3	2	1	11
10	7	7	4	7	23

a. Perform an analysis of variance on these data.

b. A rich variety of meaningful questions can be examined with this experiment. For example, a_1 (clean sand) provides information about the rate at which each iguana extrudes its tongue in the absence of any special odors; thus, it is of interest to compare each of the other four conditions with this reference condition. Of perhaps greater interest are comparisons between conditions representing different odors—for example, home cage versus other iguanas, other iguanas versus lizards and kangaroo rats, lizards versus kangaroo rats, and so on. Certain complex comparisons may also be interesting: clean sand versus all other conditions combined, home cage and other iguanas combined versus lizard and kangaroo rat combined, and so on. From among this large set of meaningful questions, conduct the following single-*df* comparisons:

   (1) Clean sand versus home cage

   (2) Other iguanas versus home cage

   (3) Kangaroo rats versus lizards and other iguanas combined

2. Subjects in an actual experiment (Keppel, Postman, & Zavortink, 1968) learned a list of 10 pairs of words on one day and recalled the pairs two days later. Following recall, the subjects learned a second list of pairs, and these were also recalled after a delay of two days. This cycle of learning-recall-learning-recall was continued for six lists. The independent variable was the *ordinal position* of a particular list, that is, whether the list was learned and recalled first or second . . . or sixth in the sequence. There were $n = 8$ subjects in the experiment. Their recall data for the $a = 6$ lists are presented in the following table:

[11]These data were generously provided by Dr. Joanne Pedersen.

| | Ordinal Position of the Lists (A) | | | | | |
Subjects (S)	a_1	a_2	a_3	a_4	a_5	a_6
1	7	3	2	2	1	1
2	4	8	3	8	1	2
3	7	6	3	1	5	4
4	8	6	1	0	2	0
5	7	2	3	0	1	3
6	6	3	3	1	1	1
7	4	2	0	0	0	0
8	6	7	5	1	3	2

a. Perform an analysis of variance on these data.

b. Plot the means on a graph. You will note two striking trends, namely, a general downward slope to the curve (a linear trend) and a concave-upward curvature (a quadratic trend). Is there any statistical support for these observations?

3. An experiment is conducted in which four different drugs (a_2, a_3, a_4, and a_5) and a placebo (a_1) are administered to each of $n = 5$ different animals. The response measure consists of the number of discrimination problems solved within a given time limit. The data follow.

	a_1	a_2	a_3	a_4	a_5
s_1	p_3	p_2	p_1	p_4	p_5
	11	11	9	6	7
s_2	p_4	p_1	p_5	p_2	p_3
	8	13	2	10	5
s_3	p_1	p_3	p_4	p_5	p_2
	13	9	3	4	6
s_4	p_2	p_5	p_3	p_1	p_4
	12	3	6	13	6
s_5	p_5	p_4	p_2	p_3	p_1
	7	8	8	9	13

You will note that each Y score appears below a "position number" (p), which indicates where in the testing sequence that particular condition was administered. For the first subject, for example, a_1 was the third condition that subject received (p_3), a_2 was the second condition (p_2), a_3 was the first condition (p_1), a_4 was the fourth condition (p_4), and a_5 was the last condition (p_5).

a. Conduct a standard analysis of variance on these data.

b. Is there a significant practice effect?

c. Use the residual error term to test the significance of the treatment effect in this example.

17

The Mixed Two-Factor Within-Subjects Design

The Overall Analysis and the Analysis of Main Effects and Simple Effects

Within-subjects factorial designs are extremely popular in the behavioral sciences, and for good reason: They examine the effects of several independent variables manipulated simultaneously and offer greater sensitivity than a completely randomized, between-subjects counterpart. As indicated in Chap. 15 (see Table 15–1, p. 333), two types of within-subjects designs are possible when two independent variables are manipulated factorially, namely, a design in which subjects receive all the treatment combinations, which we will consider in Chap. 21, and a design in which subjects receive only a subset of the total, the $A \times (B \times S)$ design. In this latter case, the subset consists of all combinations of one factor—the within-subjects factor—in conjunction with only *one level* of the other factor—the between-subjects factor. This blending of within-subjects and between-subjects factors is often called a **mixed within-subjects factorial design**. Mixed factorial designs are more common than "pure" within-subjects factorial designs. This chapter and the next will cover in detail the analysis of the mixed two-factor design.

The mixed design represents a combination of the two generic types of designs considered previously: independent groups, constituting the levels of one factor (factor A), and repeated measures, constituting the levels of the other factor (factor B). As you will see, the analysis of the mixed design contains features of the one-factor design with independent groups and features of the one-factor design with repeated measures. Consequently, because of this blending of the two types of design, the analysis will not be simple.

The most common example of this type of design is one in which the repeated factor represents *trials* or *successive tasks* in a learning experiment. Rarely will we be interested in an $(A \times S)$ experiment in which trials make up the independent variable. The reason for this is, of course, that all we can hope to show with this type of experiment is that learning does or does not occur and, if so, what the shape of the function is over trials (that is, the levels of the independent variable). More typically, we will want to compare the learning curves for different treatment groups. Under these circumstances, the various treatments (factor A) will be administered to independent groups of subjects and all subjects will receive a certain number of learning trials (factor B). Thus, the experiment becomes an $A \times (B \times S)$ design. With this particular design, we can still compare the different treatment groups on performance averaged over all the learning trials (the main effect of factor A). In addition to this information, however, we can compare the shapes of the learning curves for the different treatment groups. To be more specific, we can ask whether the effects of practice (trials) are the same for the different levels of factor A—that is, whether there is an $A \times B$ interaction (an interaction of treatments and trials).

17.1   THE OVERALL ANALYSIS OF VARIANCE

The $A \times (B \times S)$ design represents a combination of two single-factor experiments, one with independent groups (factor A) and the other with repeated measures (factor B). This description is not completely accurate, however, since the two-factor design contains an $A \times B$ interaction, which obviously cannot be present in either of the single-factor experiments. Nevertheless, the analogy is sufficiently close to give us a feel for the composite nature of the mixed design. Table 17–1 makes this point explicit. The component sources of variance for a completely randomized single-factor experiment are listed in the first column. The component sources for a single-factor experiment with repeated measures are listed in the third column.[1] The component sources of variance for the $A \times (B \times S)$ design are listed in the middle column of the table.

An inspection of the table reveals that the completely randomized design is perfectly duplicated in the mixed design. The same could be said of the $(B \times S)$ design except that the designations of subjects is different. In the mixed design, factor S is designated S/A to reflect the fact that there is a different group of subjects at each level of the between-subjects factor, factor A. This difference should become clearer when we consider the details of the analysis.

Design and Notation

The notational system for the mixed design is presented in Table 17–2. The ABS matrix contains the individual observations (Y) recorded in the experiment. The

Table 17–1   A Comparison of the Sources of Variance in Two Single-Factor Experiments with Those in the $A \times (B \times S)$ Design

Completely Randomized Design	$A \times (B \times S)$ Design	$(B \times S)$ Design
A	A	
S/A	S/A	S
	B	B
	$B \times S/A$	$B \times S$
	$A \times B$	

[1] I will refer to this independent variable as factor B and to the experiment as a $(B \times S)$ design to facilitate the comparison of the designs.

Table 17–2   Notational System: $A \times (B \times S)$ Design

ABS Matrix

SUBJECT	a_1			SUBJECT	a_2		
	b_1	b_2	b_3		b_1	b_2	b_3
s_1	$Y_{1,1,1}$	$Y_{1,2,1}$	$Y_{1,3,1}$	s_4	$Y_{2,1,4}$	$Y_{2,2,4}$	$Y_{2,3,4}$
s_2	$Y_{1,1,2}$	$Y_{1,2,2}$	$Y_{1,3,2}$	s_5	$Y_{2,1,5}$	$Y_{2,2,5}$	$Y_{2,3,5}$
s_3	$Y_{1,1,3}$	$Y_{1,2,3}$	$Y_{1,3,3}$	s_6	$Y_{2,1,6}$	$Y_{2,2,6}$	$Y_{2,3,6}$

AS Matrix

	a_1		a_2
s_1	$AS_{1,1}$	s_4	$AS_{2,4}$
s_2	$AS_{1,2}$	s_5	$AS_{2,5}$
s_3	$AS_{1,3}$	s_6	$AS_{2,6}$
Sum	A_1	Sum	A_2

AB Matrix

	b_1	b_2	b_3	Sum
a_1	$AB_{1,1}$	$AB_{1,2}$	$AB_{1,3}$	A_1
a_2	$AB_{2,1}$	$AB_{2,2}$	$AB_{2,3}$	A_2
Sum	B_1	B_2	B_3	T

information listed in the *ABS* matrix is used to create two additional matrices. The first is the *AB* matrix, which is identical to the *AB* matrix formed in the analysis of any two-factor design and is created by summing the individual scores obtained in each of the $(a)(b)$ treatment conditions. As usual, the various totals provided by this matrix permit the calculation of the two main effects and the $A \times B$ interaction. One more matrix is required for the analysis of the $A \times (B \times S)$ design, namely, the *AS* matrix, which lists the *total score* for each subject obtained when the set of observations produced by each subject is summed. The subtotal for each subject is designated AS_{ik} to indicate that it is the sum of all the scores for a particular subject, s_k, in a particular A treatment group, a_i. The *AS* and *ABS* matrices provide the information needed to calculate the two error terms that will be required for the statistical analysis.

Sums of Squares and Degrees of Freedom

In Chap. 10 you saw how the computational formula for sums of squares can be constructed from *df* statements (see pp. 208–209). To find the *df* for any source of variance, we apply the following rule:

Multiply (1) the products of the *df* 's of factors to the left of the diagonal by (2) the product of the levels of factors to the right of the diagonal.

To see how to apply this rule, consider the sources of variation normally extracted in the mixed design, as presented in column 1 of Table 17–3. For the two main effects of A and B, the *df* 's are simply $a - 1$ and $b - 1$, respectively. The degrees of freedom for the $A \times B$ interaction are obtained by multiplying df_A by df_B. (Since no diagonal is present, only the first part of the rule applies.) The degrees of freedom for the S/A source is found by multiplying the *df* on the left of the diagonal ($df_S = n - 1$) by the number of levels of factor A:

Table 17–3 Computational Formulas

(1) Source	(2) Basic Ratio	(3) df	(4) Sum of Squares	(5) MS	(6) F
A	$[A] = \dfrac{\Sigma\, A^2}{(b)(n)}$	$a - 1$	$[A] - [T]$	$\dfrac{SS_A}{df_A}$	$\dfrac{MS_A}{MS_{S/A}}$
S/A	$[AS] = \dfrac{\Sigma\, (AS)^2}{b}$	$(a)(n - 1)$	$[AS] - [A]$	$\dfrac{SS_{S/A}}{df_{S/A}}$	
B	$[B] = \dfrac{\Sigma\, B^2}{(a)(n)}$	$b - 1$	$[B] - [T]$	$\dfrac{SS_B}{df_B}$	$\dfrac{MS_B}{MS_{B \times S/A}}$
$A \times B$	$[AB] = \dfrac{\Sigma\, (AB)^2}{n}$	$(a - 1)(b - 1)$	$[AB] - [A] - [B] + [T]$	$\dfrac{SS_{A \times B}}{df_{A \times B}}$	$\dfrac{MS_{A \times B}}{MS_{B \times S/A}}$
$B \times S/A$	$[Y] = \Sigma\, Y^2$	$(a)(b - 1)(n - 1)$	$[Y] - [AB] - [AS] + [A]$	$\dfrac{SS_{B \times S/A}}{df_{B \times S/A}}$	
Total	$[T] = \dfrac{T^2}{(a)(b)(n)}$	$(a)(b)(n)\ \ 1$	$[Y] - [T]$		

$$df_{S/A} = (df_S)(a) = (n - 1)(a)$$

A rearranged equivalent of this *df* statement, $(a)(n - 1)$, is presented in column 3 of the table. The degrees of freedom for the $B \times S/A$ source is obtained by multiplying the product, $(df_B)(df_S)$, by the number of levels of factor $A(a)$. In symbols,

$$df_{B \times S/A} = (df_B)(df_S)(a)$$
$$= (b - 1)(n - 1)(a)$$

The rearranged version of this formula is presented in the table. The *df* statement for the total variation is simply 1 less than the total number of observations $(a)(b)(n)$, namely, $(a)(b)(n) - 1$.

The *df* statements, when expanded, indicate which basic ratios are required for calculating the corresponding sums of squares and how they are combined. The formulas for the main effects, interaction, and total are presented in column 4 of Table 17–3. Since they are identical to those presented in Chap. 10, they should require no explanation. I will work through the steps for the two new sources of variance, S/A and $B \times S/A$. For the first, the expanded *df* statement,

$$df_{S/A} = (a)(n - 1) = (a)(n) - a$$

indicates that two basic ratios are involved, $[AS]$ and $[A]$. These ratios are calculated by performing the familiar operations of (1) squaring, (2) summing, and (3) dividing by the number of observations contributing to any one of the squared numbers. In the case of $[AS]$, this number is b since each AS sum is obtained by adding up the individual observations for any given subject, and there are b of them. In the case of [A], this number is $(b)(n)$ since each A total is obtained by adding together a total of $(b)(n)$ scores. For the other new source of variance, the expanded df statement,

$$df_{B \times S/A} = (a)(b - 1)(n - 1) = (a)(b)(n) - (a)(b) - (a)(n) + a$$

indicates four basic ratios, namely, [Y], which is based on the individual Y scores; [AB]; [AS]; and [A]. The formulas for these basic ratios are presented in column 2 of Table 17–3.

Mean Squares and F Ratios

The mean squares are calculated by dividing each sum of squares by the appropriate number of degrees of freedom, as shown in column 5 of the table. The formation of the three F ratios, which is indicated in column 6, does follow a logical pattern. More specifically, you will note that the error term for a factorial treatment effect that is not based on repeated measures (the MS_A in this design) is the within-groups mean square, $MS_{S/A}$, whereas the error term for the two factorial effects that are based on repeated measures (MS_B and $MS_{A \times B}$) is the mean square reflecting an interaction of the repeated factor (B) with factor S ($MS_{B \times S/A}$). Table 17–4 highlights this division of the analysis schematically. The part of the data isolated on the left side of the table consists of the within-subjects portion of the analysis, and the part on the right consists of the between-subjects portion of the analysis.

The use of $MS_{S/A}$ to evaluate the significance of the A main effect is easy to understand when I point out that we could take the AS sums; disregard the fact that they were obtained from a mixed factorial design; and analyze them as if they were data generated from a completely randomized, single-factor design. The F ratios in the two analyses would be identical.[2] The justification of the other error term is a bit more complicated. Consider the data in the ABS matrix at one of the levels of factor A, say, a_1. This portion of the ABS matrix can be thought of as a single-factor within-subjects design involving factor B and n subjects. The error term for evaluating the differences among the treatment means in this submatrix would be the $B \times S$ interaction. The same argument holds for each $B \times S$ matrix at each level of factor A. When these data are brought together in the factorial analysis, the variation among the B means at each level of factor A is reflected in the B main effect and the $A \times B$ interaction. The error term for these two factorial treatment effects, $MS_{B \times S/A}$, is actually an average of the separate $B \times S$ interactions, each of which is the appropriate error term for its portion of the data. The use of an average of these individual error terms is justified if we can assume that they are roughly the same, that is, homogeneous.

A Numerical Example

The numerical example consists of a fictitious experiment in which subjects are given a digit-cancelation task under three conditions of motivation. The subjects

---

[2]The sums of squares would be different, however, since the denominators for the basic ratios all include b in the mixed design, which is not present, of course, in the single-factor design. The b factors cancel when the F ratio is formed, which accounts for the identical answers from the two analyses.

Table 17–4   Schematic Representation of the Analysis

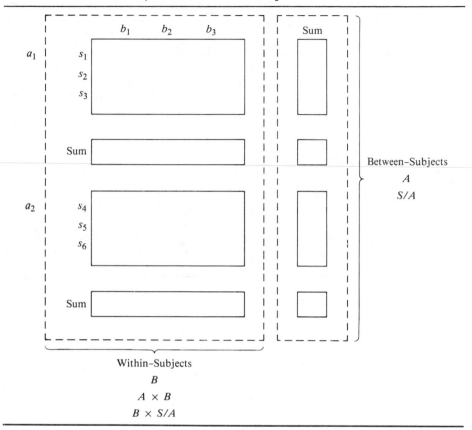

in a_1 are simply asked to do their "best." Subjects in a_2, on the other hand, are given highly motivating instructions, and subjects in a_3 are offered \$5 if they perform at some predetermined level. Each subject (there are n = 4 subjects per treatment group) is given four 30-second trials (factor B), in which they cancel certain specified digits from a long series of digits in a test booklet. The response measure consists of the number of digits canceled within the time period. The mixed factorial was chosen instead of a "pure" within-subjects design because it was considered unlikely that subjects could switch from one condition of motivation to another without being influenced by the preceding conditions they had received. The design, then, is a 3 × 4 mixed factorial design, with n = 4 subjects randomly assigned to each of the three levels of factor A. The total number of subjects in this example is $(a)(n)$ = (3)(4) = 12, and the total number of observations is $(a)(b)(n)$ = (3)(4)(4) = 48. The data are presented in Table 17–5.

I will begin the analysis by calculating the basic ratios specified in Table 17–3. From the AS matrix in Table 17–5,

$$[A] = \frac{\Sigma A^2}{(b)(n)} = \frac{(230)^2 + (283)^2 + (345)^2}{(4)(4)} = 15{,}750.88$$

Table 17–5   Numerical Example: $A \times (B \times S)$ Design

ABS Matrix

	a_1					a_2					a_3			
	b_1	b_2	b_3	b_4		b_1	b_2	b_3	b_4		b_1	b_2	b_3	b_4
s_1	13	14	17	20	s_5	5	10	17	21	s_9	13	24	28	30
s_2	10	11	15	14	s_6	8	15	22	24	s_{10}	9	22	22	24
s_3	13	19	18	21	s_7	14	16	23	23	s_{11}	14	22	28	28
s_4	4	12	14	15	s_8	12	21	26	26	s_{12}	8	18	27	28

AS Matrix

	a_1		a_2		a_3
s_1	64	s_5	53	s_9	95
s_2	50	s_6	69	s_{10}	77
s_3	71	s_7	76	s_{11}	92
s_4	45	s_8	85	s_{12}	81
Sum	230	**Sum**	283	**Sum**	345

AB Matrix

	b_1	b_2	b_3	b_4	Sum
a_1	40	56	64	70	230
a_2	39	62	88	94	283
a_3	44	86	105	110	345
Sum	123	204	257	274	858

$$[AS] = \frac{\Sigma\,(AS)^2}{b} = \frac{(64)^2 + (50)^2 + \ldots + (92)^2 + (81)^2}{4} = 16{,}053.00$$

From the AB matrix,

$$[T] = \frac{T^2}{(a)(b)(n)} = \frac{(858)^2}{(3)(4)(4)} = 15{,}336.75$$

$$[B] = \frac{\Sigma\,B^2}{(a)(n)} = \frac{(123)^2 + (204)^2 + (257)^2 + (274)^2}{(3)(4)} = 16{,}489.17$$

$$[AB] = \frac{\Sigma\,(AB)^2}{n} = \frac{(40)^2 + (39)^2 + \ldots + (94)^2 + (110)^2}{4} = 17{,}033.50$$

Finally, from the ABS matrix,

$$[Y] = \Sigma\,Y^2 = (13)^2 + (10)^2 + \ldots + (28)^2 + (28)^2 = 17{,}426$$

The remainder of the analysis is summarized in Table 17–6. The analysis reveals that all factorial treatment effects are significant.

It is instructive to compare the two error terms obtained in this analysis. As you can see, the error term for the between-subjects portion of the analysis, $MS_{S/A}$ = 33.57, is considerably larger than the error term for the within-subjects portion, $MS_{B \times S/A} = 3.35$. The difference in the sizes of the error terms reflects the increased sensitivity of the repeated-measures portion of the mixed design in detecting the influence of independent variables. Although these data are artificial, the tenfold difference created for this example is not uncommon in the literature.

Table 17–6   Summary of the Analysis

Source	Sum of Squares	df	MS	F
A	$15{,}750.88 - 15{,}336.75 = \quad 414.13$	2	207.07	6.17*
S/A	$16{,}053.00 - [A] = \quad 302.12$	9	33.57	
B	$16{,}489.17 - [T] = 1{,}152.42$	3	384.14	114.67*
A × B	$17{,}033.50 - [A] - [B] + [T] = \quad 130.20$	6	21.70	6.48*
B × S/A	$17{,}426 - [AB] - [AS] + [A] = \quad 90.38$	27	3.35	
Total	$[Y] - [T] = 2{,}089.25$	47		

*$p < .05$.

The Composite Nature of the Error Terms

Both error terms are averages based on pooled sources of variability. The within-groups term, $MS_{S/A}$, is an average of the within-group variances reflecting the deviation of a subject's average score from the overall mean for that subject's group. To illustrate, I will calculate the three within-group variances—at levels a_1, a_2, and a_3—and average them. For the three sums of squares, we use the AS totals listed in the AS matrix of Table 17–5 as follows:

$$SS_{S/A_1} = \frac{(64)^2 + (50)^2 + (71)^2 + (45)^2}{4} - \frac{(230)^2}{(4)(4)}$$

$$= 3{,}415.50 - 3{,}306.25 = 109.25$$

$$SS_{S/A_2} = \frac{(53)^2 + (69)^2 + (76)^2 + (85)^2}{4} - \frac{(283)^2}{(4)(4)}$$

$$= 5{,}142.75 - 5{,}005.56 = 137.19$$

$$SS_{S/A_3} = \frac{(95)^2 + (77)^2 + (92)^2 + (81)^2}{4} - \frac{(345)^2}{(4)(4)}$$

$$= 7{,}494.75 - 7{,}439.06 = 55.69$$

The three mean squares are obtained by dividing each sum of squares by the appropriate number of degrees of freedom, $n - 1$:

$$MS_{S/A_1} = \frac{109.25}{4 - 1} = 36.42$$

$$MS_{S/A_2} = \frac{137.19}{4 - 1} = 45.73$$

$$MS_{S/A_3} = \frac{55.69}{4 - 1} = 18.56$$

The average of these three mean squares is

$$\frac{36.42 + 45.73 + 18.56}{3} = 33.57$$

which is equal to the $MS_{S/A}$ listed in Table 17–6.

The repeated-measures error term ($MS_{B \times S/A}$) is an average of the separate $B \times S$ interactions at the different levels of factor A. To show this, I will calculate the three component sums of squares for the $B \times S$ interaction, using the data from the ABS matrix in Table 17–5. To simplify the calculations, I have arranged the data in Table 17–7 as three separate within-subjects designs; you can actually use the computational formulas for the single-factor within-subjects design to calculate sums of squares for the three $B \times S$ interactions:

$$SS_{B \times S/A_1} = (13)^2 + (10)^2 + \ldots + (21)^2 + (15)^2$$

$$- \frac{(40)^2 + (56)^2 + (64)^2 + (70)^2}{4}$$

$$- \frac{(64)^2 + (50)^2 + (71)^2 + (45)^2}{4} + \frac{(230)^2}{(4)(4)}$$

$$= 3,572 - 3,433.00 - 3,415.50 + 3,306.25 = 29.75$$

$$SS_{B \times S/A_2} = (5)^2 + (8)^2 + \ldots + (23)^2 + (26)^2$$

$$- \frac{(39)^2 + (62)^2 + (88)^2 + (94)^2}{4}$$

$$- \frac{(53)^2 + (69)^2 + (76)^2 + (85)^2}{4} + \frac{(283)^2}{(4)(4)}$$

$$= 5,651 - 5,486.25 - 5,142.75 + 5,005.56 = 27.56$$

$$SS_{B \times S/A_3} = (13)^2 + (9)^2 + \ldots + (28)^2 + (28)^2$$

Table 17–7   Separate $B \times S$ Matrices

	b_1	b_2	b_3	b_4	Sum
				***ABS* Matrix at a_1**	
s_1	13	14	17	20	64
s_2	10	11	15	14	50
s_3	13	19	18	21	71
s_4	4	12	14	15	45
Sum	40	56	64	70	230

	b_1	b_2	b_3	b_4	Sum
				***ABS* Matrix at a_2**	
s_5	5	10	17	21	53
s_6	8	15	22	24	69
s_7	14	16	23	23	76
s_8	12	21	26	26	85
Sum	39	62	88	94	283

	b_1	b_2	b_3	b_4	Sum
			***ABS* Matrix at a_3**		
s_9	13	24	28	30	95
s_{10}	9	22	22	24	77
s_{11}	14	22	28	28	92
s_{12}	8	18	27	28	81
Sum	44	86	105	110	345

$$- \frac{(44)^2 + (86)^2 + (105)^2 + (110)^2}{4}$$

$$- \frac{(95)^2 + (77)^2 + (92)^2 + (81)^2}{4} + \frac{(345)^2}{(4)(4)}$$

$$= 8{,}203 - 8{,}114.25 - 7{,}494.75 + 7{,}439.06 = 33.06$$

The number of df for each interaction is $(b - 1)(n - 1) = (4 - 1)(4 - 1) = 9$, and the mean squares are

$$MS_{B \times S/A_1} = \frac{29.75}{9} = 3.31$$

$$MS_{B \times S/A_2} = \frac{27.56}{9} = 3.06$$

$$MS_{B \times S/A_3} = \frac{33.06}{9} = 3.67$$

The average of these three mean squares is

$$\frac{3.31 + 3.06 + 3.67}{3} = 3.35$$

which is equal to the $MS_{B \times S/A}$ in Table 17–6.

17.2 STATISTICAL MODEL AND ASSUMPTIONS

The analysis of the mixed two-factor within-subjects design is based on a particular statistical model and a number of assumptions. We will consider the statistical model first.

Linear Model

The linear model on which the analysis is based can be written as follows:

$$Y_{ijk} = \mu_T + \alpha_i + \pi_k + \beta_j + (\alpha\beta)_{ij} + (\beta\pi)_{jk} + \epsilon_{ijk}$$

Several new quantities should be identified. Specifically, π_k represents the average effect for each subject, $(\beta\pi)_{jk}$ designates the interaction effect associated with the B treatments and subjects, and ϵ_{ijk} refers to uncontrolled sources of variability. These three components are usually assumed to be random factors. On the basis of the linear model and certain other assumptions, the expected values for the various sources of variance normally extracted in the analysis can be derived.

Assumptions

As I have mentioned before, the assumptions under which the F ratios obtained from the analysis of designs with repeated measures are distributed according to the F distribution are more restrictive than with completely randomized designs. In addition, violations of these assumptions are more serious. One of these assumptions, the **sphericity assumption**, requires the homogeneity of variances within treatment conditions and the homogeneity of correlations between pairs of treatment conditions; we considered this assumption in Chap. 16 (see pp. 351–352). With the mixed factorial design, we have the additional assumption that the nature of the variances and correlations are the same across the levels of the nonrepeated factor.[3]

The consequence of violating the homogeneity assumptions is to increase type I error. Collier, Baker, Mandeville, and Hayes (1967), for example, used the computer and Monte Carlo procedures to provide an estimate of the magnitude of the bias in the standard analysis of an $A \times (B \times S)$ design. They included 15 different conditions of heterogeneity in their study. The results of these determinations showed no bias on the test of the A main effect—the *nonrepeated* factor— but sizable positive biases on the tests involving *repeated measures*, namely, the B main effect and the $A \times B$ interaction. Similar findings have been reported by others (see, for example, Keselman & Keselman, 1988; Milligan, Wong, & Thompson, 1987).

Although a variety of methods have been devised to correct this positive bias (Rasmussen, Heumann, Heumann, & Botzum, 1989), the simplest strategy is to apply the Geisser-Greenhouse correction, which I introduced in Chap. 16 (pp. 352–353). As applied to mixed factorial design, there are two corrections, one for the B main effect and the other for the $A \times B$ interaction; no correction is necessary for the main effect of A because no repeated factors are involved. For the B main effect, the correction is achieved by looking up the critical F with

$$df_{num.} = 1 \text{ and } df_{denom.} = (a)(n - 1)$$

For the numerical example, then, we would use $F(1, 9) = 5.12$ as the critical value rather than $F(3, 27) = 2.98$; since $F = 114.67$, we would conclude that trials produced an effect in any case. For the $A \times B$ interaction, the Geisser-Greenhouse correction specifies

$$df_{num.} = a - 1 \text{ and } df_{denom.} = (a)(n - 1)$$

Applied to the numerical example, we would use $F(2, 9) = 4.26$, rather than $F(6, 27) = 2.47$. Since the obtained $F = 6.48$, we would reject the null hypothesis with either criterion.

The Geisser-Greenhouse test is strictly applicable only when maximum heterogeneity is present; for less severe violations, the test tends to overcorrect. Procedures are available for applying a correction that is appropriate for any given condition of heterogeneity (see p. 353).

Missing Data and Unequal Sample Sizes

The analyses in this chapter assume equal sample sizes and a complete set of test scores from each subject. Occasionally, problems arise in an experiment—for ex-

---

[3]This assumption has been called the **multisample sphericity assumption** (Huynh, 1978).

ample, equipment failure, an experimenter error, or an unexpected disturbance—
that result in the loss of an observation for a particular subject. In some cases, the
simplest solution is to replace the subject for whom data are missing with a new
subject tested under the same circumstances as the discarded subject. In other
cases, replacement subjects may not be available or may be too costly to run
through the complete set of conditions. In this situation, a researcher can choose
to use special procedures designed to provide estimates of the missing data or to
discard all subjects with missing observations and analyze the data with unequal
sample sizes. However one decides to deal with these problems, the overriding concern is whether the loss of data or of subjects is related to the treatment conditions.
If this possibility cannot be reasonably dismissed, the validity of the experiment
will probably be brought into question.

Assuming that the reason(s) for the data loss can be attributed to chance factors alone, there are ways to analyze partially missing data (see Kirk, 1982, pp.
268–270). The loss of an entire subject or the presence of unequal sample sizes in
general may be handled by the procedures considered in Chap. 13 (pp. 280–282),
but it frequently will cause serious problems of interpretation, particularly if the
homogeneity assumptions are violated (Milligan, Wong, & Thompson, 1987). My
advice is to avoid unequal sample sizes, by discarding subjects if necessary, and if
this is not feasible, to enlist the help of a statistical consultant who can deal specifically with your particular problem and experimental situation.

Removing Practice Effects

Practice effects are always a problem in a within-subjects design, unless, as in the
present example, they are the object of study. First, we need to neutralize the effects of practice, which is generally accomplished by some form of counterbalancing (see pp. 336–337). However, as I showed in Chap. 16, the presence of practice
effects can reduce the sensitivity of a single-factor within-subjects design unless
steps are taken to remove its influence (see pp. 361–363). The same sort of problem
exists in the mixed factorial design. In this case, the repeated-measures error term,
$MS_{B \times S/A}$, will be directly influenced by any practice effects that may be present.
We can remove practice effects from the error term, either by subtracting the effects of practice from the error term or from the Y scores directly. This latter procedure is particularly useful when more theoretically focused analyses are conducted. Unfortunately, space limitations do not permit me to present these
procedures here, but they are discussed in detail in the second edition of this book
(see pp. 420–428, 430–431, 434–437).

17.3   ANALYZING MAIN EFFECTS

In the absence of a significant $A \times B$ interaction, we usually direct our attention
to the detailed analysis of the main effects, which in most cases consists of single-
df or main comparisons. The computational procedures depend on whether the

comparisons involve the nonrepeated factor (factor A) or the repeated factor (factor B). We will consider the nonrepeated factor first.

Analyses Involving the Nonrepeated Factor

If a main comparison involves factor A, the nonrepeated factor, the computational procedures for the sum of squares $(SS_{A_{comp.}})$ are identical to those presented in Chap. 11 for the completely randomized factorial design (see pp. 233–234). Most typically, we would conduct the analysis on the marginal treatment means. We would then determine the difference between the two means involved in the comparison $(\hat{\psi}_A)$ and complete the following calculations:

$$SS_{A_{comp.}} = \frac{(b)(n)(\hat{\psi}_A)^2}{\Sigma \, c_i^2} \tag{17–1}$$

The error term for this analysis is $MS_{S/A}$, the within-groups mean square from the between-subjects portion of the overall analysis.

To illustrate the procedure with the numerical example, even though we might not be interested in main comparisons because of the significant $A \times B$ interaction, let's compare the group receiving highly motivating instructions (a_2) with the group offered a monetary incentive (a_3). We can obtain the marginal means by dividing the A marginal sums from the AB matrix in Table 17–5 ($A_1 = 230, A_2 = 283$, and $A_3 = 345$) by the number of observations, $(b)(n) = (4)(4) = 16$; the three means are 14.38, 17.69, and 21.56, respectively. The coefficients for this comparison are $0, 1, -, 1$ and the difference is

$$\hat{\psi}_A = (0)(14.38) + (1)(17.69) + (-1)(21.56) = -3.87$$

Substituting in Eq. (17–1), we find

$$SS_{A_{comp.}} = \frac{(4)(4)(-3.87)^2}{(0)^2 + (1)^2 + (-1)^2} = \frac{239.63}{2} = 119.82$$

Since $df_{A_{comp.}} = 1, MS_{A_{comp.}} = 119.82$, and the F becomes

$$F = \frac{MS_{A_{comp.}}}{MS_{S/A}} = \frac{119.82}{33.57} = 3.57$$

which is not significant.

Analyses Involving the Repeated Factor

If a comparison involves factor B, the repeated factor, separate error terms are usually required and a specialized analysis is needed. The analysis is similar to the procedure we followed when we analyzed single-df comparisons in the $(A \times S)$ design. This consisted of weighting the Y scores for each subject, forming a specialized matrix, and then performing a standard analysis on the transformed data set. Let's apply this procedure to the mixed factorial design.

The first step is to weight the individual Y scores in the ABS matrix by the coefficients for the single-*df* comparison being conducted on the repeated factor. In the second step, we combine the positive scores for each subject and place them in the first column of an *ABS comparison matrix*; similarly, we combine the negative scores and place them in the second column of the new matrix, dropping the sign in the process. Finally, we conduct an ordinary analysis of variance on the transformed data. Let's see how this is accomplished.

Since factor B is a quantitative independent variable (trials), the most obvious analytical approach would be an analysis of trend. I will examine instead a related comparison between trial 1 and trial 4 and illustrate trend analysis when we consider interaction comparisons in Chap. 18. Constructing an *ABS* comparison matrix is easy for a pairwise comparison $(1, 0, 0, -1)$: We simply take the Y scores from level b_1 (the level with the positive coefficient) and place them in the column labeled $b_{(+)}$ and take the scores from level b_4 (the level with the negative coefficient) and place them in the column labeled $b_{(-)}$. The resulting *ABS* comparison matrix appears in Table 17–8, along with the other two comparison matrices needed for the analysis. We can now follow the procedures for the overall analysis of the $A \times (B \times S)$ design, remembering that b has become $b' = 2$ in this specialized arrangement of the data.

The basic ratios are calculated from the information provided in Table 17–8.

$$[T] = \frac{T^2}{(a)(b')(n)} = \frac{(397)^2}{(3)(2)(4)} = 6{,}567.04$$

$$[A] = \frac{\Sigma A^2}{(b')(n)} = \frac{(110)^2 + (133)^2 + (154)^2}{(2)(4)} = 6{,}688.13$$

Table 17–8 Constructing Comparison Matrices for a Comparison Involving Factor B

ABS Comparison Matrix

	a_1			a_2			a_3	
	$b_{(+)}$	$b_{(-)}$		$b_{(+)}$	$b_{(-)}$		$b_{(+)}$	$b_{(-)}$
s_1	13	20	s_5	5	21	s_9	13	30
s_2	10	14	s_6	8	24	s_{10}	9	24
s_3	13	21	s_7	14	23	s_{11}	14	28
s_4	4	15	s_8	12	26	s_{12}	8	28

AS Comparison Matrix

	a_1		a_2		a_3
s_1	33	s_5	26	s_9	43
s_2	24	s_6	32	s_{10}	33
s_3	34	s_7	37	s_{11}	42
s_4	19	s_8	38	s_{12}	36
Sum	110	Sum	133	Sum	154

AB Comparison Matrix

	$b_{(+)}$	$b_{(-)}$	Sum
a_1	40	70	110
a_2	39	94	133
a_3	44	110	154
Sum	123	274	397

$$[B] = \frac{\Sigma B^2}{(a)(n)} = \frac{(123)^2 + (274)^2}{(3)(4)} = 7{,}517.08$$

$$[AB] = \frac{\Sigma (AB)^2}{n} = \frac{(40)^2 + (39)^2 + \ldots + (94)^2 + (110)^2}{4} = 7{,}723.25$$

$$[AS] = \frac{\Sigma (AS)^2}{b'} = \frac{(33)^2 + (24)^2 + \ldots + (42)^2 + (36)^2}{2} = 6{,}846.50$$

$$[Y] = \Sigma Y^2 = (13)^2 + (10)^2 + \ldots + (28)^2 + (28)^2 = 7{,}921$$

These quantities are combined in Table 17–9 to produce the various sums of squares normally obtained with this analysis.

Our interest in this analysis is the evaluation of the main comparison, $B_{comp.}$, and not the evaluation of the other two factorial treatment effects extracted in this analysis, namely, A and $A \times B_{comp.}$. I have included all sources in this analysis, however, to illustrate the parallel with the overall analysis of the $A \times (B \times S)$ design and to avoid any confusion that an abbreviated analysis might produce.[4] As you have seen in earlier chapters, the error term for a comparison involving a within-subjects factor is an interaction of the comparison with subjects. In the context of this experiment, the interaction is between $B_{comp.}$ and S. Since there is a different $B_{comp.} \times S$ interaction for each level of factor A, which are pooled or averaged together for the final analysis, we will refer to it as $B_{comp.} \times S/A$. As you can see, the main comparison is significant (that is, $F = MS_{B_{comp.}}/MS_{B_{comp.} \times S/A} = 950.04/4.38 = 216.90$).

You will recall that we adjusted the analysis of single-df comparisons in the $(A \times S)$ design for the fact that we used weighted Y scores instead of unweighted ones in the calculations. The corresponding correction for the present design is essentially the same as that conducted in Chap. 16. That is, we apply the correction by dividing each sum of squares in Table 17–9 by

Table 17–9 Summary of the Analysis of a Main Comparison

Source	Sum of Squares		df	MS	F
A	$[A] - [T] =$	121.09	2	60.55	3.44[a]
S/A	$[AS] - [A] =$	158.37	9	17.60	
$B_{comp.}$	$[B] - [T] =$	950.04	1	950.04	216.90*
$A \times B_{comp.}$	$[AB] - [A] - [B] + [T] =$	85.08	2	42.54	9.71[a]
$B_{comp.} \times S/A$	$[Y] - [AB] - [AS] + [A] =$	39.38	9	4.38	
Total	$[Y] - [T] =$	1,353.96	23		

*$p < .05$.
[a]This F is not relevant to this analysis.

[4]This analysis is actually an analysis of a *partial interaction* in which one of the factors is transformed into a single-df comparison (factor B in this case), while the other factor remains intact. I will discuss this analysis in Sec. 18.1.

$$\text{adjustment factor} \ = \ \frac{\Sigma \ c_j^2}{2} \tag{17-2}$$

In the present example, where $\Sigma \ c_j^2 \ = \ 2$, the adjustment factor is $2/2 = 1$, and no correction is necessary.

17.4   ANALYZING SIMPLE EFFECTS: AN OVERVIEW

A significant interaction can be subjected to two different forms of analysis: an analysis of simple effects, which I will consider in this chapter, and an analysis of interaction comparisons, which I will consider in Chap. 18. Both sets of procedures attempt to discover the particular treatment combinations responsible for a significant $A \times B$ interaction.

The analysis of simple effects involves examining the data in the AB matrix row by row or column by column and looking for significance attributable to the variation of one of the independent variables while the other factor is held constant. (See Chap. 11 for a detailed discussion of the meaning and use of an analysis of simple effects.) I will consider the analysis of the simple effects involving the repeated factor (B at a_i) in Sec. 17.5 and the corresponding analysis involving the nonrepeated factor (A at b_j) in Sec. 17.6. The error terms for the two analyses are different and require different approaches.

The Issue of Pooling Error Terms

The $A \times (B \times S)$ design is made up of a set of $(B \times S)$ designs, one at each level of factor A. The two error terms in the overall analysis represent *pooled* sources of variability. The $MS_{S/A}$ is based on mean squares reflecting the variability of subjects within each of the independent groups (MS_{S/A_1}, MS_{S/A_2}, MS_{S/A_3}, and so on), which are averaged (or pooled) to form the error term. Similarly, the $MS_{B \times S/A}$ is based on mean squares reflecting the interactions of factor B and subjects for each of the independent groups ($MS_{B \times S/A_1}$, $MS_{B \times S/A_2}$, $MS_{B \times S/A_3}$, and so on), which also are pooled to form the error term. The issue surrounding the analysis of simple effects is whether we should extend this type of pooling in the calculation of the error terms used to evaluate their significance.

Let me illustrate. Perhaps the most straightforward way of conducting an analysis of the simple effects of factor B is to divide the data into a set of single-factor within-subjects designs and to treat the data exactly as if they had been produced by an actual ($B \times S$) design. This approach will produce a different error term to assess the significance of each simple effect. That is, the $B \times S$ interaction for group a_1 will be used to evaluate the simple effects of B at a_1; the $B \times S$ interaction for group a_2 will be used to evaluate the simple effects of B at a_2; and so on. The other approach assumes that the $B \times S$ interactions are homogeneous and uses their average, which of course, is the repeated-measures error term from the overall analysis— $B \times S/A$ —as the error term to evaluate *all* the simple effects.

The second approach of pooling has two distinct advantages. First, the analysis is computationally simpler. That is, the overall analysis provides all the information we need to form error terms for the analysis of simple effects. In contrast, the first approach requires considerable additional calculations to extract the individual error terms from the relevant subsets of data. The second advantage is the increase in power achieved by pooling the df's from the separate error terms. This is no small consideration, particularly when sample size is relatively small. In our numerical example, where $n = 4$, the df for a single $B \times S$ interaction is $(b - 1)(n - 1) = (4 - 1)(4 - 1) = 9$, and the df for the pooled error term is $df_{B \times S/A} = 27$.

The reason for separate error terms is to provide error terms that are appropriate for the simple effects under consideration. Suppose the $B \times S$ interaction for group a_1 is twice as large as that for group a_2. If we used the average of these two error terms to evaluate the simple effects of factor B for *both* groups, we would overestimate the significance of the simple effect for the first group and underestimate its significance for the second group.

I recommend against pooling in the mixed factorial design. This procedure has the advantage of providing the appropriate error terms regardless of whether it is safe to pool the data from all groups or not. In my opinion, the issue of bias is more important than either the computational simplicity or the increased power associated with pooled error terms. If you are concerned about power, you would be better advised to increase sample size slightly rather than to depend on the pooled degrees of freedom. The procedures I will illustrate follow the principle of basing error terms only on the data relevant to the particular analysis.

17.5   SIMPLE EFFECTS INVOLVING THE REPEATED FACTOR

The analysis of the simple effects of factor B, the repeated factor, isolates the data for a single group and proceeds as if the data represented an actual single-factor within-subjects design.

Analyzing the Simple Effects

Let's return to our numerical example and suppose we were interested in conducting an analysis of the simple effects of factor B at level a_3—the effects of trials for the group of subjects receiving the monetary incentive. We begin by isolating the ABS matrix for this group of subjects and then analyzing these data as if they were obtained from an actual single-factor within-subjects design. The relevant data matrix, which already appears in Table 17–7, is presented again in the upper portion of Table 17–10. For convenience, I will use Y to refer to scores within the body of the matrix, B for the sums at each level of factor B, S for the sums for each subject, and T for the grand sum of the matrix. Using the information from Table 17–10, we obtain

$$[T] = \frac{T^2}{(b)(n)} = \frac{(345)^2}{(4)(4)} = 7,439.06$$

$$[B] = \frac{\Sigma B^2}{n} = \frac{(44)^2 + (86)^2 + (105)^2 + (110)^2}{4} = 8{,}114.25$$

$$[S] = \frac{\Sigma S^2}{b} = \frac{(95)^2 + (77)^2 + (92)^2 + (81)^2}{4} = 7{,}494.75$$

$$[Y] = \Sigma Y^2 = (13)^2 + (9)^2 + \ldots + (28)^2 + (28)^2 = 8{,}203$$

The analysis is completed in the lower portion of Table 17–10. As you can see, the simple effect is significant (that is, $F = MS_{B \text{ at } a_3}/MS_{B \times S \text{ at } a_3} = 225.06/3.67 = 61.32$).[5]

Analyzing Simple Comparisons

A significant simple effect should usually be followed by a number of single-df comparisons designed to identify the factors contributing to the significant simple effect. With trials as the significant factor, we would probably want to examine any trends associated with this effect. The steady increase in performance from trial 1 to trial 4 suggests the presence of a linear trend—that is, the increase over trials may be described by a straight line. Instead of the trend analysis, I will illustrate the procedures by conducting an analysis that compares the first and fourth trials (b_1 and b_4).

Again, the analysis is equivalent to the analysis of a single-df comparison in

Table 17–10   Analysis of the Simple Effects of the Repeated Factor

	b_1	b_2	b_3	b_4	Sum
	ABS Matrix for Level a_3				
S_9	13	24	28	30	95
S_{10}	9	22	22	24	77
S_{11}	14	22	28	28	92
S_{12}	8	18	27	28	81
Sum	44	86	105	110	345

Summary of the Analysis

Source	Sum of Squares	df	MS	F
B at a_3	$[B] - [T] = 675.19$	3	225.06	61.32*
S	$[S] - [T] = 55.69$	3	18.56	
$B \times S$ at a_3	$[Y] - [B] - [S] + [T] = 33.06$	9	3.67	
Total	$[Y] - [T] = 763.94$	15		

*$p < .05$.

[5]If you decided that it was safe to use the pooled error term from the overall analysis ($MS_{B \times S/A} = 3.35$), the F would also be significant; that is, $F - 225.06/3.35 = 67.18$.

a single-factor within-subjects design. We start by arranging the data from Table 17–10 into an appropriate comparison matrix. Usually we would weight the Y scores with coefficients reflecting the comparison and then use the weighted scores to form the matrix. Because a pairwise comparison is involved $(1, 0, 0, -1)$, however, we may skip the weighting process and simply place the Y scores associated with the positive coefficient (b_1) in the column labeled $b_{(+)}$ and the Y scores associated with the negative coefficient (b_4) in the column labeled $b_{(-)}$. This comparison matrix is presented in the upper portion of Table 17–11. The analysis at this point corresponds to one appropriate for an actual single-factor within-subjects design with $b' = 2$ groups. Using the information in the comparison matrix, we find

$$[T] = \frac{T^2}{(b')(n)} = \frac{(154)^2}{(2)(4)} = 2{,}964.50$$

$$[B] = \frac{\Sigma B^2}{n} = \frac{(44)^2 + (110)^2}{4} = 3{,}509.00$$

$$[S] = \frac{\Sigma S^2}{b'} = \frac{(43)^2 + (33)^2 + (42)^2 + (36)^2}{2} = 2{,}999.00$$

$$[Y] = \Sigma Y^2 = (13)^2 + (9)^2 + \ldots + (28)^2 + (28)^2 = 3{,}554$$

The analysis is completed in the lower portion of Table 17–11. We do not have to adjust the sums of squares for this analysis because a pairwise is involved; that is, the adjustment factor $= 1$. With a complex comparison, we would divide each

Table 17–11   Analysis of the Simple Comparison Involving the Repeated Factor

Comparison Matrix

	$b_{(+)}$	$b_{(-)}$	Sum
s_9	13	30	43
s_{10}	9	24	33
s_{11}	14	28	42
s_{12}	8	28	36
Sum	44	110	154

Summary of the Analysis

Source	Sum of Squares	df	MS	F
B comp. at a_3	$[B] - [T] = 544.50$	1	544.50	155.57*
S	$[S] - [T] = 34.50$	3	11.50	
B comp. $\times$ S at a_3	$[Y] - [B] - [S] + [T] = 10.50$	3	3.50	
Total	$[Y] - [T] = 589.50$	7		

*$p < .05$.

sum of squares by the correction factor specified by Eq. (17–2). The difference between trial 1 and trial 4 is significant for this group of subjects.[6]

17.6   SIMPLE EFFECTS INVOLVING THE NONREPEATED FACTOR

The simple effects of factor A , the nonrepeated factor, are based on what we can view as individual, completely randomized single-factor experiments at the different levels of the repeated factor (factor B). I will illustrate the analysis procedures with a numerical example.

Analyzing the Simple Effects

There are four sets of simple effects for the nonrepeated factor, one for each level of factor B: the simple effects of A on the first trial (b_1), on the second trial (b_2), and so on. I will analyze the simple effects of factor A on the last trial (level b_4). I have extracted these data from the original ABS matrix in Table 17–5 and placed them in the upper portion of Table 17–12. You can easily see that arranged this way, the data correspond to a completely randomized single-factor design consisting of three independent groups of $n = 4$ subjects, the first receiving no special instructions, the second receiving highly motivating instructions, and the third receiving a monetary incentive. The error term for this type of design is a within-groups mean square, which is based on the pooled variability of subjects treated alike.

If we treat these data as if they were the results of an actual, completely randomized single-factor design, we would obtain the following basic ratios:

$$[T] = \frac{T^2}{(a)(n)} = \frac{(70 + 94 + 110)^2}{(3)(4)} = 6{,}256.33$$

$$[A] = \frac{\Sigma A^2}{n} = \frac{(70)^2 + (94)^2 + (110)^2}{4} = 6{,}459.00$$

$$[Y] = \Sigma Y^2 = (20)^2 + (14)^2 + \ldots + (28)^2 + (28)^2 = 6{,}528$$

The analysis is completed in the bottom portion of Table 17–12. The F is significant.[7]

---

[6]The error term for the alternative analysis would be based on the same $B_{comp.} \times S$ interaction pooled over the three independent groups. We happened to calculate this quantity in Sec. 17.3 in the context of another analysis. From Table 17–9, $MS_{B_{comp.} \times S/A} = 4.38$, and the $F = 544.50/4.38 = 124.32$ is also significant.

[7]Some authors recommend a special type of pooling in which we average the four error terms from the entire set of simple effects. This pooled error term is usually called the **within-cell mean square**. I recommend against this procedure because we usually find that the error terms are not homogeneous with this sort of design. For a discussion of the within-cell mean square, see Kirk (1982, pp. 509–510) and Winer (1971, pp. 529–532).

Table 17–12   Simple Effects of Factor A at Level b_4

<table>
<tr><td colspan="7" align="center">Data Matrix</td></tr>
<tr><td colspan="2" align="center">a_1</td><td colspan="2" align="center">a_2</td><td colspan="2" align="center">a_3</td></tr>
<tr><td>s_1</td><td>20</td><td>s_5</td><td>21</td><td>s_9</td><td>30</td></tr>
<tr><td>s_2</td><td>14</td><td>s_6</td><td>24</td><td>s_{10}</td><td>24</td></tr>
<tr><td>s_3</td><td>21</td><td>s_7</td><td>23</td><td>s_{11}</td><td>28</td></tr>
<tr><td>s_4</td><td>15</td><td>s_8</td><td>26</td><td>s_{12}</td><td>28</td></tr>
<tr><td>Sum</td><td>70</td><td>Sum</td><td>94</td><td>Sum</td><td>110</td></tr>
</table>

<table>
<tr><td colspan="5" align="center">Summary of the Analysis</td></tr>
<tr><th>Source</th><th>Sum of Squares</th><th>df</th><th>MS</th><th>F</th></tr>
<tr><td>A at b_4</td><td>$[A] - [T] = 202.67$</td><td>2</td><td>101.34</td><td>13.21*</td></tr>
<tr><td>S/A at b_4</td><td>$[Y] - [A] = 69.00$</td><td>9</td><td>7.67</td><td></td></tr>
<tr><td>Total</td><td>$[Y] - [T] = 271.67$</td><td>11</td><td></td><td></td></tr>
</table>

*$p < .05$.

Analyzing Simple Comparisons

When a simple effect is significant, we would probably want to test a number of simple comparisons. The procedure is identical to that for an actual, completely randomized single-factor experiment, which I discussed in Chap. 6. The analysis is usually conducted on the group means, which in this example are 17.50, 23.50, and 27.50 for groups a_1, a_2, and a_3, respectively. The sum of squares for the simple comparison is easily obtained by using the general formula from Chap. 6 for the sum of squares for a single-df comparison, which is based on the difference between the two means ($\hat{\psi}$). Suppose we wanted to compare a_1 with the combined scores from the other two groups. Using the coefficients 2, -1, -1, we find

$$\hat{\psi}_{A_{comp.} \text{ at } b_4} = (2)(17.50) + (-1)(23.50) + (-1)(27.50) = -16.00$$

Substituting in the equivalent of Eq. (6–5), we find

$$SS_{A_{comp.} \text{ at } b_4} = \frac{n \,(\hat{\psi}_{A \text{ at } b_4})^2}{\Sigma\, c_i^2} = \frac{4(-16.00)^2}{6} = 170.67$$

Since this is a single-df comparison, $MS_{A_{comp.} \text{ at } b_4} = 170.67$.[8] The error term for this simple comparison comes from the analysis of the relevant simple effects, which is summarized in Table 17–12. The final calculations reveal

$$F = \frac{MS_{A_{comp.} \text{ at } b_4}}{MS_{S/A \text{ at } b_4}} = \frac{170.67}{7.67} = 22.25$$

which, with $df_{num.} = 1$ and $df_{num.} = 9$, is significant.

---

[8]There is no need to adjust the sum of squares from this analysis because Eq. (6–5) automatically corrects for your choice of specific coefficients for any given comparison.

17.7 EXERCISES[9]

1. Consider a mixed two-factor within-subjects design in which factor A (the between-subjects factor) consists of $a = 2$ levels and factor B (the within-subjects factor) consists of $b = 4$ levels. The data for a hypothetical experiment follow. There are $n = 4$ subjects assigned randomly to each of the two levels of factor A; the order of the b treatments is appropriately counterbalanced.

		a_1					a_2		
	b_1	b_2	b_3	b_4		b_1	b_2	b_3	b_4
s_1	3	4	7	3	s_5	5	6	11	7
s_2	6	8	12	9	s_6	10	12	18	15
s_3	7	13	11	11	s_7	10	15	15	14
s_4	0	3	6	6	s_8	5	7	11	9

   a. Conduct a standard analysis of variance with these data.
   b. Calculate the sum of squares for the $B \times S$ interaction at level a_1 and the corresponding sum of squares at level a_2. Show that the sum of these two interaction sums of squares equals $SS_{B \times S/A}$.
   c. Since the $A \times B$ interaction is not significant, the main effects may be interpreted unambiguously. Perform the following single-df comparisons on the main effect of the within-subjects factor (factor B):
      (1) A pairwise comparison between levels b_1 and b_2
      (2) A complex comparison between level b_3 and an average of levels b_1 and b_2
2. Subjects are given a vigilance task in which they detect targets on a simulated radar screen during a 40-minute test session. Factor A consists of three types of displays: black targets on a white background (a_1), white targets on a black background (a_2) and amber targets on a black background (a_3). Each subject (there are $n = 4$ subjects per display group) is given three 40-minute test sessions, one per day (factor B). The response measure consists of the number of targets detected during the test session. The data from this experiment follow.

		a_1				a_2				a_3	
	b_1	b_2	b_3		b_1	b_2	b_3		b_1	b_2	b_3
s_1	23	24	27	s_5	15	20	27	s_9	23	34	38
s_2	20	21	25	s_6	18	25	32	s_{10}	19	32	32
s_3	23	29	28	s_7	24	26	33	s_{11}	24	32	38
s_4	14	22	24	s_8	22	31	36	s_{12}	18	28	37

   Perform a standard analysis of variance with these data. Save your calculations for problem 5 in the exercises for Chap. 18.
3. The $A \times B$ interaction in the last problem was significant. One useful way to study a significant interaction is by means of simple effects. There are two sets of simple effects, of course, one examining the effects of the different radar displays (simple effects of factor A) and the other examining the effects of test session (simple effects of factor B). Both sets of simple effects might be of interest in this study. This problem

[9]The answers to these problems are found in Appendix B.

will be concerned with the analysis of the nonrepeated factor (factor A) and problem 4 will be concerned with the analysis of the repeated factor (factor B).

  a. Analyze the simple effects of the three radar displays for each of the $b = 3$ test sessions.

  b. The analysis in part a indicates that the three displays do not differ on the first test session but do so on subsequent sessions. A researcher would probably be interested in analyzing the significant simple effects further by conducting a number of simple comparisons involving the three displays. As an example, use the data from the third session (level b_3) to test the pairwise comparison between a_1 and a_2.

4. This problem provides an example of the analysis of the simple effects of factor B, which consists of $b = 3$ test sessions.

  a. Analyze the simple effects of trials for each of the $a = 3$ radar displays.

  b. It may have occurred to you that the outcome of this analysis is not particularly helpful in identifying the locus of the significant $A \times B$ interaction since all we have discovered is that each simple effect of factor B (test sessions) is significant. A more useful outcome is one in which some simple effects are significant and some are not or one in which the simple effects represent variation in opposite directions. Neither situation is present with these data. Nevertheless, we still need an illustration of an analysis that follows a significant simple effect. As an example, conduct the following simple comparisons, using the data from the group detecting targets on the amber radar screen (level a_3):

  (1) A pairwise comparison between the first and third test sessions

  (2) A complex comparison between the first test session and the last two

18

The Mixed Two-Factor Within-Subjects Design

Analysis of Interaction Comparisons

Interaction comparisons consist of miniature factorial arrangements created from a larger, multilevel factorial design. Analytical questions, usually in the form of single-*df* comparisons, are applied to either independent variable separately to allow us to study **partial interactions** or are applied to both simultaneously to form **interaction contrasts**. I introduced the analysis of interaction comparisons in Chap. 12. Although the meaning of these analyses is the same when they are extended to the mixed factorial design, the analyses themselves are more complicated because of the need for different types of error terms—one for the between-subjects portion and the other for the within-subjects portion. I will consider the analysis of partial interactions first because we can understand the complications more easily when only one of the factors is transformed into a single-*df* comparison. I will consider the analysis of interaction contrasts in Sec. 18.3.

18.1   PARTIAL INTERACTIONS INVOLVING THE REPEATED FACTOR ($B_{comp.}$)

A common example of a partial interaction involving the repeated factor is a trend analysis conducted within the context of an experiment on learning, in which the repeated factor consists of a series of trials, practice sessions, or related tasks.[1] The numerical example from Chap. 17 is a case in point—the effects of three types of motivating conditions (factor *A*) is studied over a series of four trials. The results of the experiment are plotted in Fig. 18–1. As you can see, all three groups show marked improvement over the four test trials (that is, learning clearly took place).

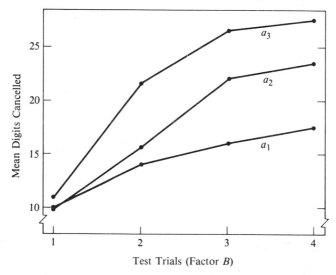

Figure 18–1   A plot of the data from the numerical example.

---

[1] We first considered trend analysis in Chap. 7 and discussed its application to the factorial design in Chap. 12 (see pp. 266–270).

A trend analysis would attempt to describe this improvement in terms of idealized mathematical components. Because of its relative simplicity, most trend analyses begin with linear trend. Try drawing a straight line through the four means for each group of subjects. Although the "fit" is not perfect—all three curves have a tendency to "bend over" —the three straight lines do a fairly good job of capturing the outcome of the study.

The Overall Analysis

I will demonstrate trend analysis with the linear component. It is a relatively easy matter to extend the analysis to more complex trend components (for example, the quadratic component); all you need to do is to substitute the new set of coefficients in the various formulas and repeat the calculations. The analysis of linear trend compares the three best-fitting straight lines drawn through the data for the three groups. If the slopes are different, as they appear to be in Fig. 18–1, the interaction of the trend component with factor A—the $A \times B_{linear}$ interaction—will be significant. In essence, the analysis compares the slopes of these best-fitting straight lines. We will consider the analysis in two major steps: calculating the error terms and calculating the partial interaction itself.

Step 1: Calculating the Error Terms.   The first step consists of calculating the error terms for the analysis. We begin by transforming the data from the ABS matrix into an ABS comparison matrix. The coefficients for linear trend are found in Table A–4 and consist of the set -3, -1, 1, 3. The four individual Y scores for each subject, which are found in Table 17–5 (p. 374), are then weighted by these coefficients. Let's consider the four Y scores for the second subject at level a_1, which follow with the coefficients and the weighted scores:

	b_1	b_2	b_3	b_4
Coefficients:	-3	-1	$+1$	$+3$
Y scores:	10	11	15	14
Weighted scores:	-30	-11	$+15$	$+42$

The weighted scores for all the subjects in this example are presented in the upper portion of Table 18–1.

The next step is to add separately for each subject the two positive and two negative weighted scores and to place the two sums in an ABS comparison matrix. Again for this subject, the sum of the two positive scores is $15 + 42 = 57$, and the sum of the two negative scores is $-30 + (-11) = -41$. The positive sum is placed in the ABS comparison matrix under level $b_{(+)}$, and the negative sum (sign deleted) is placed in the matrix under level $b_{(-)}$. This comparison matrix is presented in the middle portion of Table 18–1. You will note that the marginal sums have also been calculated in this matrix, which will facilitate computing the basic ratios we will need for the two error terms.

For the purposes of these calculations, we will use Y to designate the entries

Table 18–1   Calculating the Error Terms for a Partial Interaction Involving the Repeated Factor

Weighted Y Scores

	a_1					a_2					a_3			
	b_1	b_2	b_3	b_4		b_1	b_2	b_3	b_4		b_1	b_2	b_3	b_4
s_1	-39	-14	$+17$	$+60$	s_5	-15	-10	$+17$	$+63$	s_9	-39	-24	$+28$	$+90$
s_2	-30	-11	$+15$	$+42$	s_6	-24	-15	$+22$	$+72$	s_{10}	-27	-22	$+22$	$+72$
s_3	-39	-19	$+18$	$+63$	s_7	-42	-16	$+23$	$+69$	s_{11}	-42	-22	$+28$	$+84$
s_4	-12	-12	$+14$	$+45$	s_8	-36	-21	$+26$	$+78$	s_{12}	-24	-18	$+27$	$+84$

ABS Comparison Matrix

	a_1					a_2					a_3		
	$b_{(+)}$	$b_{(-)}$	Sum		$b_{(+)}$	$b_{(-)}$	Sum		$b_{(+)}$	$b_{(-)}$	Sum
s_1	77	53	130	s_5	80	25	105	s_9	118	63	181
s_2	57	41	98	s_6	94	39	133	s_{10}	94	49	143
s_3	81	58	139	s_7	92	58	150	s_{11}	112	64	176
s_4	59	24	83	s_8	104	57	161	s_{12}	111	42	153
Sum	274	176	450	Sum	370	179	549	Sum	435	218	653

Calculating the Error Terms

Source	Unadjusted Sum of Squares		$SS_{adj.}$	df	MS
S/A	$[AS] - [A]$ =	2,433.25	243.33	9	27.04
$B_{linear} \times S/A$	$[Y] - [AB] - [AS] + [A]$ =	411.25	41.13	9	4.57

in the body of the three comparison matrices, AB to designate the column marginal sums, AS to designate the row marginal sums, and A to designate the sum of all the Y scores in any given matrix; remember also, that the number of levels associated with factor B, which has been transformed into B_{linear}, is $b' = 2$. The basic ratios we need are calculated as follows:

$$[A] = \frac{\Sigma A^2}{(b')(n)} = \frac{(450)^2 + (549)^2 + (653)^2}{(2)(4)} = 116,288.75$$

$$[AB] = \frac{\Sigma (AB)^2}{n} = \frac{(274)^2 + (176)^2 + \ldots + (435)^2 + (218)^2}{4} = 127,935.50$$

$$[AS] = \frac{\Sigma (AS)^2}{b'} = \frac{(130)^2 + (98)^2 + \ldots + (176)^2 + (153)^2}{2} = 118,722.00$$

$$[Y] = \Sigma Y^2 = (77)^2 + (57)^2 + \ldots + (64)^2 + (42)^2 = 130,780$$

We now combine these quantities in the patterns specified for the two error terms in the overall analysis (see Table 17–3, p. 371), which has been accomplished in the bottom portion of Table 18–1.

Because we used weighted Y scores in these calculations, we will need to adjust the two sums of squares before they may be used as error terms in the final analysis.[2] We correct both SS's by dividing the unadjusted quantity by the following adjustment factor:

$$\text{adjustment factor} = \frac{\Sigma\, c_j^2}{2} \tag{18-1}$$

where the numerator is the sum of the squared coefficients used to weight the Y scores for the analysis. For this analysis, then,

$$\text{adjustment factor} = \frac{(-3)^2 + (-1)^2 + (1)^2 + (3)^2}{2} = \frac{20}{2} = 10$$

The results of dividing each unadjusted sum of squares by 10 are given in the third column. The df's and MS's are calculated in the usual manner.

Step 2: Calculating the Comparison Effects.   The sums of squares for the treatment or comparison effects are easily obtained with basic ratios based on information contained in an AB comparison matrix, which is presented in the upper portion of Table 18–2; the AB sums are the column totals from the ABS compari-

Table 18–2   Completing the Analysis of a Partial Interaction Involving the Repeated Factor

AB Comparison Matrix

	$b_{(+)}$	$b_{(-)}$	Sum
a_1	274	176	450
a_2	370	179	549
a_3	435	218	653
Sum	1,079	573	1,652

Summary of the Analysis

Source	$SS_{adj.}$	df	MS	F
A	257.61	2	128.81	4.76*
S/A	243.33	9	27.04	
B_{linear}	1,066.82	1	1,066.82	233.44*
$A \times B_{linear}$	97.86	2	48.93	10.71*
$B_{linear} \times S/A$	41.13	9	4.57	

*$p < .05$.

[2] Whether an adjustment is necessary depends on the particular analysis involved. To avoid confusion, I suggest adjusting all sums of squares when you are using a special comparison matrix in your calculations.

son matrix in Table 18–1. I will use A to designate the row marginal totals, B to designate the column marginal totals, and T to designate the grand total of the matrix. Calculating the basic ratios, we find[3]

$$[T] = \frac{T^2}{(a)(b')(n)} = \frac{(1,652)^2}{(3)(2)(4)} = 113,712.67$$

$$[A] = \frac{\Sigma A^2}{(b')(n)} = \frac{(450)^2 + (549)^2 + (653)^2}{(2)(4)} = 116,288.75$$

$$[B] = \frac{\Sigma B^2}{(a)(n)} = \frac{(1,079)^2 + (573)^2}{(3)(4)} = 124,380.83$$

$$[AB] = \frac{\Sigma (AB)^2}{n} = \frac{(274)^2 + (370)^2 + \ldots + (179)^2 + (218)^2}{4} = 127,935.50$$

The unadjusted sums of squares become

$$SS_A = [A] - [T] = 2,576.08$$

$$SS_{B_{linear}} = [B] - [T] = 10,668.16$$

$$SS_{A \times B_{linear}} = [AB] - [A] - [B] + [T] = 978.59$$

Again, we need to divide each sum of squares by the correction factor for this comparison (10) to take into account the use of weighted Y scores in the analysis. I have entered the adjusted sums of squares in the lower portion of Table 18–2, along with the adjusted sums of squares for the two error terms from Table 18–1. The analysis is completed in Table 18–2. Both F's are significant for the two sources involving the linear trend (B_{linear} and $A \times B_{linear}$); that is,

$$F = \frac{MS_{B_{linear}}}{MS_{B_{linear} \times S/A}} = \frac{1,066.82}{4.57} = 233.44$$

$$F = \frac{MS_{A \times B_{linear}}}{MS_{B_{linear} \times S/A}} = \frac{48.93}{4.57} = 10.71$$

The main effect of factor A is of little interest to us in this analysis.

How do we interpret these results? Our main focus is the partial interaction. The fact that it is significant means that the linear function relating the dependent variable and practice trials (factor B) is not the same for all three groups. We can understand what is happening by examining the difference between the sums at $b_{(+)}$ and $b_{(-)}$ for each level of factor A in the upper portion of Table 18–2. As you can see, the difference found with group a_1 $(274 - 176 = 98)$ is about half the size of the difference found with group a_2 $(370 - 179 = 191)$ and with group a_3 $(435 - 218 = 217)$. (A difference of zero would signify the absence of linear trend.) The

---

[3] I calculated two of the basic ratios, $[A]$ and $[AB]$, in the first step. I am calculating them twice to avoid confusion.

two main effects in this analysis are of lesser interest, given the significant partial interaction.

Analyzing Simple Comparisons

Given the significant interaction, we would probably want to determine whether the linear trend is significant for each of the groups. I will illustrate the procedure with the subjects given the instruction "do your best" (level a_1). The most straight-forward way of testing this simple comparison is to extract the subset of data for this group from the ABS comparison matrix in Table 18–1, which I have done in the upper portion of Table 18–3. As you can see, this matrix is equivalent to a single-factor within-subjects design, where $b' = 2$ and $n = 4$. If we let Y refer to the weighted sums within the matrix, B refer to the column marginal sums, S refer to the row marginal sums, and T refer to the grand sum of the matrix, we find the following basic ratios:

$$[T] = \frac{T^2}{(b')(n)} = \frac{(450)^2}{(2)(4)} = 25{,}312.50$$

$$[B] = \frac{\Sigma B^2}{n} = \frac{(274)^2 + (176)^2}{4} = 26{,}513.00$$

$$[S] = \frac{\Sigma S^2}{b'} = \frac{(130)^2 + (98)^2 + (139)^2 + (83)^2}{2} = 26{,}357.00$$

Table 18–3 Analysis of a Simple Comparison Following a Significant Partial Interaction

Simple Comparison Matrix at Level a_1

	$b_{(+)}$	$b_{(-)}$	Sum
s_1	77	53	130
s_2	57	41	98
s_3	81	58	139
s_4	59	24	83
Sum	274	176	450

Summary of the Analysis

Source	Unadjusted Sum of Squares		$SS_{adj.}$[a]	df	MS	F
B_{linear} at a_1	$[B] - [T]$ =	1,200.50	120.05	1	120.05	38.98*
S	$[S] - [T]$ =	1,044.50	104.45	3	34.82	
$B_{linear} \times S$ at a_1	$[Y] - [B] - [S] + [T]$ =	92.50	9.25	3	3.08	
Total	$[Y] - [T]$ =	2,337.50	233.75	7		

*$p < .05$.
[a]Adjustment factor = 10.

$$[Y] = \Sigma Y^2 = (77)^2 + (57)^2 + \ldots + (58)^2 + (24)^2 = 27,650$$

The analysis is completed in the lower portion of Table 18–3. The linear trend is significant for this group; that is, $F = 120.05/3.08 = 38.98$.[4]

Summary

The analysis of the $A \times B_{comp.}$ interaction is summarized in Table 18–4. A 3×3 mixed factorial design with $n = 2$ subjects is represented at the top. An $A \times B_{comp.}$ partial factorial, created by superimposing a comparison between levels b_1 and b_2, is presented in the middle. From this representation, you can easily see that the data still describe a mixed factorial design except that $B_{comp.}$ has replaced the original factor B. The error term for the partial interaction is a $B_{comp.} \times S$ interaction pooled over the three independent groups. The final representation depicts the data arrangement for a simple comparison involving factor B ($B_{comp.}$) at a particular level of factor A (a_1). The design at this point is a single-factor within-subjects design in which the independent variable (factor B) has been transformed into the two levels reflecting $B_{comp.}$, which in this case is b_1 versus b_2. The analysis is functionally equivalent to a corresponding analysis in an actual single-factor within-

Table 18–4   Schematic Representation of the Analysis of an $A \times B_{comp.}$ Partial Interaction

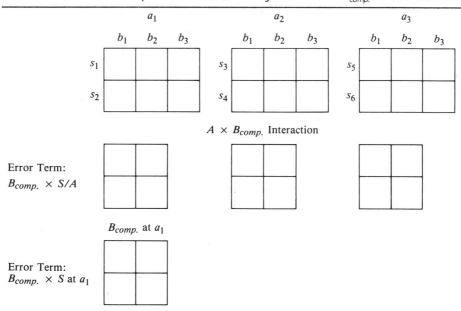

$A \times B_{comp.}$ Interaction

Error Term:
$B_{comp.} \times S/A$

$B_{comp.}$ at a_1

Error Term:
$B_{comp.} \times S$ at a_1

---

[4] As I indicated in Sec. 17.4 (pp. 383–384), there may be some circumstances in which you feel it is safe to pool the error term from all three groups of subjects rather than use the error terms calculated separately for each group. If so, you can use the error term from the analysis of the partial interaction summarized in Table 18–2 ($MS_{B_{linear} \times S/A} = 4.57$) to evaluate the simple comparisons for each of the independent groups instead of the separate ones. For this example, the F(1, 9) = 120.05/4.57 = 26.27 is also significant.

subjects design. The error term is an interaction of $B_{comp.}$ and the subjects at this particular level of factor A.

18.2   PARTIAL INTERACTIONS INVOLVING THE NONREPEATED FACTOR ($A_{comp.}$)

The nonrepeated factor in this example lends itself to a number of potentially useful single-*df* comparisons. For example, we might consider two comparisons, one between the two groups receiving relatively strong motivation (a_2 = highly motivating instructions and a_3 = monetary incentive) and the other between the "control" group (a_1 = "do your best") and the other two groups combined. In the first case, we are asking whether the difference between a_2 and a_3 remains constant over the four test trials. An inspection of Fig. 18–1 indicates that it may, which suggests that the partial interaction, $A_{comp.} \times B$, would not be significant. In the second case, we are asking whether the comparison between "weak" and "strong" motivation varies as a function of test trials. Turning again to Fig. 18–1, we see that this difference is quite small on the first test but increases substantially over the other three trials. With this comparison, then, we might expect to find a significant $A_{comp.} \times B$ interaction.

The main complication with the analysis of a partial interaction involving the nonrepeated factor concerns a decision of whether to use the data from all three groups to calculate the error terms or to use only the data from the groups actually contributing to the comparison itself. In the second comparison, where we are comparing a_1 versus the other two groups combined, there is no ambiguity since the comparison involves all three groups. But what about the first comparison, where we are comparing the group receiving highly motivating instructions (a_2) with the group receiving the monetary incentive (a_3)? Should the error terms be based only on the data from these two groups or should they all be pooled, regardless of the nature of the comparison?

Little work has been done on this problem with mixed factorial designs. The procedure I recommend is to pool data only from groups that are relevant to the $A_{comp.}$ under investigation. This procedure has the advantage of providing appropriate error terms regardless of whether it is safe to pool the data from all groups or not. I will illustrate the process by analyzing the comparison between the two groups receiving the "strong" motivation (a_2 versus a_3).

The Overall Analysis

Again, it is convenient to divide the analysis of the partial interaction into two major computational steps, one involving the error terms and the other involving the comparison effects.

Step 1: Calculating the Error Terms.   For this step, we simply isolate the data from those groups relevant to the partial interaction and then calculate the two error terms from this new data set. This has been done in the upper portion of Table 18–5, with the $B \times S$ matrix for group a_2 on the left and the $B \times S$ matrix for group a_3 on the right. I will use Y to designate the entries in the body of these two matrices, AB to designate the column marginal sums, AS to designate the row marginal sums, and A to designate the sum of all the Y scores in any given matrix. The basic ratios we need are calculated as follows:

$$[A] = \frac{\Sigma A^2}{(b)(n)} = \frac{(283)^2 + (345)^2}{(4)(4)} = 12{,}444.63$$

$$[AB] = \frac{\Sigma (AB)^2}{n} = \frac{(39)^2 + (62)^2 + \ldots + (105)^2 + (110)^2}{4} = 13{,}600.50$$

$$[AS] = \frac{\Sigma (AS)^2}{b} = \frac{(53)^2 + (69)^2 + \ldots + (92)^2 + (81)^2}{4} = 12{,}637.50$$

$$[Y] = \Sigma Y^2 = (5)^2 + (8)^2 + \ldots + (28)^2 + (28)^2 = 13{,}854$$

We now combine these quantities in the patterns specified for the two error terms in the overall analysis, which has been accomplished in the lower portion of Table 18–5. You will note that in identifying these sources I have used *comp.* as a subscript to distinguish the error terms obtained from the groups relevant to this particular $A_{comp.}$ from the corresponding error term from the overall analysis for which all groups are included. The two sums of squares we calculate do not need to be adjusted at this point since they were based on the unweighted Y scores; all we did was to select the groups to be included in the analysis, not transform or weight the Y scores.

Table 18–5   Calculating the Error Terms for a Partial Interaction Involving the Nonrepeated Factor

ABS **Comparison Matrix**

	b_1	b_2	b_3	b_4	Sum		b_1	b_2	b_3	b_4	Sum
			a_2						a_3		
s_5	5	10	17	21	53	s_9	13	24	28	30	95
s_6	8	15	22	24	69	s_{10}	9	22	22	24	77
s_7	14	16	23	23	76	s_{11}	14	22	28	28	92
s_8	12	21	26	26	85	s_{12}	8	18	27	28	81
Sum	39	62	88	94	283	Sum	44	86	105	110	345

Calculating the Error Terms

Source	Sum of Squares	df	MS
$S/A_{comp.}$	$[AS] - [A] \;=\; 192.87$	6	32.15
$B \times S/A_{comp.}$	$[Y] - [AB] - [AS] + [A] \;=\; 60.63$	18	3.37

Step 2: Calculating the Comparison Effects.   In this step, we need to form an AB comparison matrix, which is presented in the upper portion of Table 18–6. I created this matrix by taking the AB sums for a_2 from Table 18–5 and placing them in the row labeled $a_{(+)}$ and taking the corresponding sums for a_3 and placing them in the row labeled $a_{(-)}$. I will use A to designate the row marginal totals, B to designate the column marginal totals, and T to designate the grand total of the matrix. Remember that the number of levels associated with $A_{comp.}$ is $a' = 2$. Calculating the basic ratios, we find

$$[T] = \frac{T^2}{(a')(b)(n)} = \frac{(628)^2}{(2)(4)(4)} = 12{,}324.50$$

$$[A] = \frac{\Sigma A^2}{(b)(n)} = \frac{(283)^2 + (345)^2}{(4)(4)} = 12{,}444.63$$

$$[B] = \frac{\Sigma B^2}{(a')(n)} = \frac{(83)^2 + (148)^2 + (193)^2 + (204)^2}{(2)(4)} = 13{,}457.25$$

$$[AB] = \frac{\Sigma (AB)^2}{n} = \frac{(39)^2 + (44)^2 + \ldots + (94)^2 + (110)^2}{4} - 13{,}600.50$$

The remainder of the analysis is summarized in the bottom portion of Table 18–6. It was not necessary to adjust the sums of squares calculated from this AB comparison matrix because $A_{comp.}$ was a pairwise comparison $(0, 1, -1)$. If a complex comparison were involved, we would divide each sum of squares by the

$$\text{adjustment factor} = \frac{\Sigma c_i^2}{2} \tag{18–2}$$

Table 18–6   Completing the Analysis of a Partial Interaction Involving the Nonrepeated Factor

AB Comparison Matrix					
	b_1	b_2	b_3	b_4	Sum
$a_{(+)}$	39	62	88	94	283
$a_{(-)}$	44	86	105	110	345
Sum	83	148	193	204	628

Summary of the Analysis				
Source	Sum of Squares	df	MS	F
$A_{comp.}$	$[A] - [T] = \quad 120.13$	1	120.13	3.74
$S/A_{comp.}$	(from Table 18–5) $\quad 192.87$	6	32.15	
B	$[B] - [T] = \quad 1{,}132.75$	3	377.58	112.04*
$A_{comp.} \times B$	$[AB] - [A] - [B] + [T] = \quad 23.12$	3	7.71	2.29
$B \times S/A_{comp.}$	(from Table 18–5) $\quad 60.63$	18	3.37	

*$p < .05$.

The F for neither the partial interaction ($F = MS_{A_{comp.} \times B}/MS_{B \times S/A_{comp.}} = 7.71/3.37 = 2.29$) nor the main comparison ($F = MS_{A_{comp.}}/MS_{S/A_{comp.}} = 120.13/32.15 = 3.74$) is significant.[5]

Analyzing Simple Comparisons

We will usually want to follow a significant interaction with an analysis of simple comparisons. If the interaction had been significant, we would probably want to determine the trials on which the difference between the two groups was significant and the ones on which it was not. Following the principle that we base the analysis on those data contributing to an effect, we would isolate the individual Y scores for the appropriate level of factor B (trial) and perform the analysis on that data set. I will illustrate the process by testing the simple comparison for the first trial (b_1). The relevant data are presented in the upper portion of Table 18–7, which I extracted from the appropriate columns in the upper portion of Table 18–5. You can see that the data correspond to a completely randomized single-factor design, which means we can conduct the analysis accordingly. If we let Y refer to the individual data values, A refer to the treatment sums, and T refer to the grand total, we have the following basic ratios:

$$[T] = \frac{T^2}{(a')(n)} = \frac{(83)^2}{(2)(4)} = 861.13$$

Table 18–7   Analysis of a Simple Comparison Involving the Nonrepeated Analysis

Relevant Data

	$a_{(+)}$		$a_{(-)}$	
s_5	5	s_9	13	
s_6	8	s_{10}	9	
s_7	14	s_{11}	14	
s_8	12	s_{12}	8	
Sum	39	Sum	44	$T = 39 + 44 = 83$

Summary of the Analysis

Source	Sum of Squares	df	MS	F
$A_{comp.}$ at b_1	$[A] - [T] = 3.12$	1	3.12	.25
$S/A_{comp.}$ at b_1	$[Y] - [A] = 74.75$	6	12.46	
Total	$[Y] - [T] = 77.87$	7		

[5]These outcomes are not changed if we pool the data from all three groups. These error terms would come from the overall analysis (see Table 17–6, p. 375). That is, the error term for the partial interaction would be $MS_{B \times S/A} = 3.35$, and the error term for the main comparison would be $MS_{S/A} = 33.57$.

$$[A] = \frac{\Sigma A^2}{n} = \frac{(39)^2 + (44)^2}{4} = 864.25$$

$$[Y] = \Sigma Y^2 = (5)^2 + (8)^2 + \ldots + (14)^2 + (8)^2 = 939$$

The analysis is completed in the lower portion of the table. The difference between the two conditions on the first test is not significant.[6]

Analyzing a Complex Partial Interaction

We would follow the same basic procedures if the partial interaction were based on a complex comparison, such as a comparison between a_1 and the other two groups combined (a_2 and a_3). I will briefly illustrate the process with this complex comparison because certain aspects of this analysis must be pointed out.

    The Overall Analysis. The first step involves calculating the error terms, which we derive from an *ABS* comparison matrix that includes the $B \times S$ arrangements for each of the three groups since all these groups are involved in this comparison. The two submatrices for a_2 and a_3 may be found in Table 18–5, and the one for a_1 appears in the upper portion of Table 18–8. Coordinating our efforts between these two tables, we can calculate the necessary basic ratios. Again I will use Y to designate the entries in the body of the three comparison matrices, AB to designate the column marginal sums, AS to designate the row marginal sums, and

Table 18–8   Calculating the Error Terms for a Complex Partial Interaction Involving the Nonrepeated Factor

***ABS* Comparison Matrix**[a]

	b_1	b_2	b_3	b_4	Sum
s_1	13	14	17	20	64
s_2	10	11	15	14	50
s_3	13	19	18	21	71
s_4	4	12	14	15	45
Sum	40	56	64	70	230

(column span header: a_1)

Calculating the Error Terms

Source	Sum of Squares	df	MS
$S/A_{comp.}$	$[AS] - [A] = 302.12$	9	33.57
$B \times S/A_{comp.}$	$[Y] - [AB] - [AS] + [A] = 90.38$	27	3.35

[a] See Table 18–5 for a_2 and a_3

[6] If you feel that pooling is justified, the error term you would use ($MS_{S/A \text{ at } b_1}$) would come from an analysis of the simple effects of factor A at level b_1.

A to designate the sum of all the Y scores in any given matrix. The basic ratios we need are calculated as follows:

$$[A] = \frac{\Sigma A^2}{(b)(n)} = \frac{(230)^2 + (283)^2 + (345)^2}{(4)(4)} = 15,750.88$$

$$[AB] = \frac{\Sigma (AB)^2}{n} = \frac{(40)^2 + (56)^2 + \ldots + (105)^2 + (110)^2}{4} = 17,033.50$$

$$[AS] = \frac{\Sigma (AS)^2}{b} = \frac{(64)^2 + (50)^2 + \ldots + (92)^2 + (81)^2}{4} = 16,053.00$$

$$[Y] = \Sigma Y^2 = (13)^2 + (10)^2 + \ldots + (28)^2 + (28)^2 = 17,426$$

The calculations of the error terms are completed in the lower portion of Table 18–8.[7]

The sums of squares for the treatment effects are now calculated from a specialized AB comparison matrix in which the AB sums are weighted by the appropriate coefficients for $A_{comp.}$ and combined according to the sign of the coefficients. We begin with the AB matrix, which is found in Table 17–5 (p. 374), and weight each sum by multiplying the sum by the appropriate coefficient. The coefficients for the three levels of factor A are 2, -1, -1. To illustrate, the AB sums at level a_1 are 40, 56, 64, and 70 for levels b_1 through b_4, respectively. The weighted AB sums for this group, then, are obtained by multiplying each sum by 2; the results of this multiplication are presented on the left in the upper portion of Table 18–9. The weighted sums for the other two groups (a_2 and a_3) are all found

Table 18–9 Completing the Analysis of a Complex Partial Interaction Involving the Nonrepeated Factor

Weighted AB Sums						AB Comparison Matrix				
		b_1	b_2	b_3	b_4		b_1	b_2	b_3	b_4	Sum
a_1	(+2)	+80	+112	+128	+140	$a_{(+)}$	80	112	128	140	460
a_2	(−1)	−39	−62	−88	−94	$a_{(-)}$	83	148	193	204	628
a_3	(−1)	−44	−86	−105	−110	Sum	163	260	321	344	1,088

Summary of the Analysis					
Source	Unadjusted Sum of Squares		$SS_{adj.}$	df	MS	F
$A_{comp.}$	$[A] - [T] =$	882.00	294.00	1	294.00	8.76*
$S/A_{comp.}$	(from Table 18–8)		302.12	9	33.57	
B	$[B] - [T] =$	2,451.25	817.08	3	272.36	81.30*
$A_{comp.} \times B$	$[AB] - [A] - [B] + [T] =$	321.25	107.08	3	35.69	10.65*
$B \times S/A_{comp.}$	(from Table 18–8)		90.38	27	3.35	

*$p < .05$.

---

[7]The two error terms are identical to the two from the overall analysis (see Table 17–6, p. 375), which will occur whenever a complex comparison involves all the independent groups of subjects, as is the case in this particular example.

by multiplying each sum by -1. These weighted sums are also presented in the table. We now form the *AB* comparison matrix based on these weights. First, we place each of the positive weighted sums in the row labeled $a_{(+)}$. Second, we combine each set of two negative sums and place them in the row labeled $a_{(-)}$. We can now use the sums in this *AB* comparison matrix to calculate the treatment effects. I will again use *A* to designate the row marginal totals, *B* to designate the column marginal totals, and *T* to designate the grand total of the matrix. In addition, you should remember that $a' = 2$ for this matrix. Calculating the basic ratios, we find

$$[T] = \frac{T^2}{(a')(b)(n)} = \frac{(1,088)^2}{(2)(4)(4)} = 36,992.00$$

$$[A] = \frac{\Sigma A^2}{(b)(n)} = \frac{(460)^2 + (628)^2}{(4)(4)} = 37,874.00$$

$$[B] = \frac{\Sigma B^2}{(a')(n)} = \frac{(163)^2 + (260)^2 + (321)^2 + (344)^2}{(2)(4)} = 39,443.25$$

$$[AB] = \frac{\Sigma (AB)^2}{n} = \frac{(80)^2 + (83)^2 + \ldots + (140)^2 + (204)^2}{4} = 40,646.50$$

The remainder of the analysis is summarized in the bottom portion of Table 18–9. Since these calculations were based on *AB* sums weighted by a complex comparison $(2, -1, -1)$, we will need to adjust the sums of squares. (The sums of squares for the two error terms were based on unweighted *Y* scores and do not need to be adjusted.) From Eq. (18–2), we find

$$\text{adjustment factor} = \frac{\Sigma c_i^2}{2} = \frac{(2)^2 + (-1)^2 + (-1)^2}{2} = \frac{6}{2} = 3$$

The adjusted sums of squares, which we obtain by dividing each unadjusted sum of squares by 3, are presented in the third column of the analysis summary. The partial interaction is significant, substantiating our observation that the effect of weak and strong motivation ($a_{(+)}$ versus $a_{(-)}$) increases over the four test periods.

Analyzing a Simple Comparison.   Because of the significant partial interaction, we would probably be interested in testing the simple comparisons to see which of the comparisons between weak and strong motivation observed over the four test trials is significant. Let's look at the simple comparison at level b_1 (the first test trial). We begin by extracting the relevant data from the original *ABS* matrix (Table 17–5), where we find the individual *Y* scores for all three groups. These data are presented in the upper portion of Table 18–10. As you can see, the data arrangement corresponds to a completely randomized single-factor design with $a = 3$ conditions (a_1, a_2, and a_3). The most convenient way to obtain the error term is with an overall analysis of variance and then a calculation of the sum of squares for the simple comparison from the treatment means.

If we let Y refer to the individual data values and A to the treatment sums, we can specify the sum of squares for the error term as follows:

$$SS_{S/A \text{ at } b_1} = \Sigma Y^2 - \frac{\Sigma A^2}{n}$$

Using the data in Table 18–10, we find

$$SS_{S/A \text{ at } b_1} = [(13)^3 + (10)^2 + \ldots + (14)^2 + (8)^2] - \frac{(40)^2 + (39)^2 + (44)^2}{4}$$

$$= 1,393 - 1,264.25 = 128.75$$

This quantity is entered in the bottom portion of Table 18–10. The degrees of freedom for this sum of squares are found by pooling the df's for the individual groups. The df for any one group $= 4 - 1 = 3$, and there are 3 groups; thus, $df_{S/A \text{ at } b_1} = (3)(3) = 9$.

The sum of squares for the simple comparison is easily obtained by using the general formula from Chap. 6 for the sum of squares for a single-df comparison, which is based on the difference between the two means ($\hat{\psi}$). For this example,

$$\hat{\psi}_{A \text{ at } b_1} = (2)(10.00) + (-1)(9.75) + (-1)(11.00) = -.75$$

Substituting in Eq. (6–5), we find

$$SS_{A_{comp.} \text{ at } b_1} = \frac{n(\hat{\psi}_{A \text{ at } b_i})^2}{\Sigma c_i^2} = \frac{4(-.75)^2}{6} = .38$$

Table 18–10   Analysis of a Simple Comparison Following a Significant Complex Partial Interaction

Relevant Data							
	a_1			a_2			a_3
s_1	13	s_5	5		s_9	13	
s_2	10	s_6	8		s_{10}	9	
s_3	13	s_7	14		s_{11}	14	
s_4	4	s_8	12		s_{12}	8	
Sum	40	Sum	39		Sum	44	
Mean	10.00	Mean	9.75		Mean	11.00	

Summary of the Analysis				
Source	SS	df	MS	F
$A_{comp.}$ at b_1	.38	1	.38	.03
$S/A_{comp.}$ at b_1	128.75	9	14.31	

The remainder of the analysis is summarized in Table 18–10.[8] The simple comparison is not significant.

Summary

The analysis of the $A_{comp.} \times B$ interaction is summarized in Table 18–11, where a partial factorial is created by selecting the data from two of the levels of factor A. You can see clearly that the error term for the interaction is an interaction of factor B and subjects, pooled over the two groups contributing to this particular analysis. The simple comparison derived from this partial factorial, depicted at the bottom of the table, represents the functional equivalent of a completely randomized single-factor design. Viewed in this way, the error term is based on the variability of subjects within each of the independent groups at this particular level of factor B (b_1), pooled over those groups relevant to this comparison (groups a_1 and a_2).

18.3 ANALYZING INTERACTION CONTRASTS

Interaction is most precisely pinpointed by the use of interaction contrasts. You will recall from Chap. 12 (pp. 253–255) that an interaction contrast is an interac-

Table 18–11 Schematic Representation of the Analysis of an $A_{comp.} \times B$ Partial Interaction

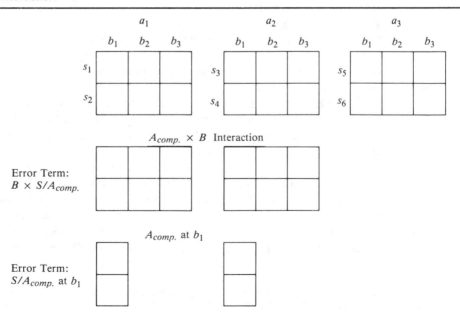

----

[8]We did not have to adjust the sums of squares for this analysis. The error term was based on the unweighted Y scores, and the standard formula for the comparison sum of squares, Eq. (6–5), already takes into consideration our choice of coefficients.

tion comparison formed when *both* independent variables are transformed into single-*df* comparisons to create what amounts to a 2 × 2 factorial design and which produces a highly specific $A_{comp.} \times B_{comp.}$ interaction. The focus of such an analysis is the interaction. If the interaction is not significant, we would probably examine the comparison main effects within the context of the overall analysis.

Calculating the Error Term for an Interaction Contrast

The analysis of interaction contrasts is more complicated than those we have considered previously because of the mixed nature of the design and the need for specialized error terms. For convenience and for the sake of clarity, I will describe this analysis in terms of two major steps: calculating the error terms and calculating the comparison effects.

An Overview of the Process. We have been basing our selection of error terms for the analysis of partial interactions on the principle that the error terms must be calculated only from the data that are relevant to the comparison effects under consideration. When the partial interaction involved the repeated factor, we based the error terms on weighted *Y* scores and segregated them accordingly; when the partial interaction involved the nonrepeated factor, we based the error terms on the *Y* scores associated with the levels of factor *A* that were contributing to the comparison. As you will see, the error terms for an interaction contrast, which involves single-*df* comparisons on both factors, will be based on *Y* scores weighted by the coefficients for $B_{comp.}$ and on the data from the groups specified by the coefficients for $A_{comp.}$. Let's consider the application of this principle of data selection in detail.

With regard to $A_{comp.}$, we will include only those groups actually involved in the comparison. If $A_{comp.}$ is a pairwise comparison between a_1 and a_2, for example, we will use only the *Y* scores produced by subjects assigned to these two groups. If $A_{comp.}$ is a complex comparison, we will use only the *Y* scores produced by the subjects assigned to the groups relevant to the complex comparison. Suppose that $a = 4$ and that we wanted to compare a_1 versus groups a_2 and a_3 combined. We would use the *Y* scores for these three groups, but not those for group a_4, because this latter group is not relevant for this particular analysis. If we wanted to examine a comparison that involved all four groups, such as a comparison between group a_1 and the other three groups or a trend component, we would use the *Y* scores for all four groups because all groups are relevant for the analysis. What about the comparison involving the repeated factor ($B_{comp.}$)? Here, we will continue with the procedure I introduced in Chap. 16 of weighting the *Y* scores by the relevant coefficients for $B_{comp.}$ and combining them to create an *ABS* comparison matrix.[9]

---

[9]Most methodologists agree with the second part of my recommendation, namely, that we should use special error terms when repeated factors are involved, but disagree with the first. That is, they generally recommend that we calculate the special error terms from all independent groups, not just those that are relevant to a comparison. My approach represents the safest strategy, however, because it produces error terms that are "correct" regardless of whether the group estimates are homogeneous or not.

A Numerical Example. I will illustrate the process with the data from the 3 × 4 mixed factorial design we have been analyzing in this chapter. You will recall that factor A, the between-subjects factor, consists of three conditions of motivation, namely, a group of subjects asked to "do their best" (a_1), a group receiving highly motivating instructions (a_2), and a group receiving an attractive monetary incentive (a_3). In Sec. 18.2, we considered two single-df comparisons derived from factor A, a comparison between the two groups receiving conditions designed to produce "strong" motivation (a_2 and a_3) and a comparison between the group assumed to be performing under relatively "weak" motivation (a_1) and an average of the two groups assumed to be performing under "strong" motivation ($a_2 + a_3$). I will use the first comparison for the $A_{comp.}$ in this example. Factor B, the within-subjects factor, consists of four successive trials on which subjects canceled as many digits as they could within a 30-second period. In Sec. 18.1, we examined the linear trend component; for a change, I will use a comparison between b_1 and b_4 as the $B_{comp.}$ in this example. The original data appear in Table 17-5 (p. 374).

I have indicated that each of the two comparisons contributes to the selection of the data relevant to the calculation of the error term. As a reminder, the role of $A_{comp.}$ is to identify which of the independent groups are relevant to the analysis. Since this comparison involves only two of the three groups in this design, we will include only these data in the calculation of the error term. We now turn to the comparison involving the repeated factor, which exerts its influence by weighting the individual Y scores included in the analysis. The weights for this analysis are the coefficients 1, 0, 0, -1, which exclude the data from levels b_2 and b_3. We can easily form the ABS comparison matrix by placing the Y scores from level b_1 under $b_{(+)}$ and those from level b_4 under $b_{(-)}$. The results of this procedure are presented in Table 18–12. You will note that the table contains comparison matrices for only those groups involved in $A_{comp.}$ (groups a_2 and a_3).

The error term we are seeking is a $B_{comp.} \times S$ interaction, pooled over the relevant levels of factor A, which, in this case, are a_2 and a_3. To illustrate the pooling process, I will calculate the sum of squares for each interaction separately and then combine them. For level a_2,

$$SS_{B_{comp.} \times S/A_2} = [(5)^2 + (8)^2 + \ldots + (23)^2 + (26)^2] - \frac{(39)^2 + (94)^2}{4}$$

Table 18–12 Data for Calculating the Error Term for an Interaction Contrast

	a_2				a_3		
	$b_{(+)}$	$b_{(-)}$	Sum		$b_{(+)}$	$b_{(-)}$	Sum
s_5	5	21	26	s_9	13	30	43
s_6	8	24	32	s_{10}	9	24	33
s_7	14	23	37	s_{11}	14	28	42
s_8	12	26	38	s_{12}	8	28	36
Sum	39	94	133	Sum	44	110	154

$$- \frac{(26)^2 + (32)^2 + (37)^2 + (38)^2}{2} + \frac{(133)^2}{(2)(4)}$$

$$= 2{,}651 - 2{,}589.25 - 2{,}256.50 + 2{,}211.13 = 16.38$$

and for level a_3,

$$SS_{B_{comp.} \times S/A_3} = [(13)^2 + (9)^2 + \ldots + (28)^2 + (28)^2] - \frac{(44)^2 + (110)^2}{4}$$

$$- \frac{(43)^2 + (33)^2 + (42)^2 + (36)^2}{2} + \frac{(154)^2}{(2)(4)}$$

$$= 3{,}554 - 3{,}509.00 - 2{,}999.00 + 2{,}964.50 = 10.50$$

The pooled sum of squares for the error term becomes

$$SS_{B_{comp.} \times S/A_{comp.}} = 16.38 + 10.50 = 26.88$$

Since $B_{comp.}$ is a pairwise comparison $(1, 0, 0, -1)$, the adjustment factor is 1 and no correction is necessary, as it is when complex comparisons are involved. The degrees of freedom are also obtained by pooling. That is, the *df* for the interaction of $B_{comp.}$ and S for either group is $(b' - 1)(n - 1) = (2 - 1)(4 - 1) = 3$; and the *df* for the two groups combined is $3 + 3 = 6$. The mean square for the error term is

$$MS_{B_{comp.} \times S/A_{comp.}} = \frac{26.88}{6} = 4.48$$

Calculating the Interaction Contrast

There are various ways to calculate an interaction contrast. One way to define it is to compare the difference between the means on the first and fourth test for group a_2 with the corresponding difference for group a_3. The relevant means are

	b_1	b_4
a_2	9.75	23.50
a_3	11.00	27.50

and the interaction contrast is

$$\hat{\psi}_{A \times B} = (9.75 - 23.50) - (11.00 - 27.50) = 2.75$$

Although it is easy to obtain the interaction contrast when both $A_{comp.}$ and $B_{comp.}$ are pairwise comparisons, as in the present case, I prefer to use a procedure that will work properly for any interaction contrast. The key to the calculation is the formation of a set of special *interaction coefficients*, which we obtain by cross-multiplying the coefficients for the two comparisons defining the interaction contrast. Such an arrangement is presented on the left in Table 18–13. The matrix lists the coefficients for $A_{comp.}$ in the left-hand margin and the coefficients for $B_{comp.}$ in the upper margin; the interaction coefficients d_{ij}, which are formed by multiplying each $A_{comp.}$ coefficient by each $B_{comp.}$ coefficient, are presented in the body of the

Table 18–13 Calculating an Interaction Contrast

	c_i	c_j:	(b_1) +1	(b_2) 0	(b_3) 0	(b_4) −1
(a_1)	0		0	0	0	0
(a_2)	+1		+1	0	0	−1
(a_3)	−1		−1	0	0	+1

Interaction Coefficients (left matrix above)

Treatment Means

	b_1	b_2	b_3	b_4
a_1	10.00	14.00	16.00	17.50
a_2	9.75	15.50	22.00	23.50
a_3	11.00	21.50	26.25	27.50

Weighted Treatment Means

	b_1	b_2	b_3	b_4
a_1	0.00	0.00	0.00	0.00
a_2	+9.75	0.00	0.00	−23.50
a_3	−11.00	0.00	0.00	+27.50

matrix. On the right, you will find a matrix containing the treatment means $(\overline{Y}_{A_iB_j})$, calculated from the data presented in Table 17–5. The results of multiplying each of these means by the corresponding interaction coefficients are presented in the bottom matrix. The weighted mean at level a_1b_1, for example, is obtained by multiplying the mean (10.00) by the interaction coefficient (0). We will use these weighted means to calculate the SS for the interaction contrast:

$$\hat{\psi}_{A \times B} = \Sigma (d_{ij})(\overline{Y}_{A_iB_j}) \tag{18-3}$$

$$= 0.00 + 9.75 + \ldots - 23.50 + 27.50 = 2.75$$

We calculate the sum of squares for the interaction contrast by substituting in the following formula:

$$SS_{A_{comp.} \times B_{comp.}} = \frac{(n)(\hat{\psi}_{A \times B})^2}{\Sigma d_{ij}^2} \tag{18-4}$$

$$= \frac{4(2.75)^2}{(0)^2 + (1)^2 + \ldots + (-1)^2 + (1)^2} = \frac{30.25}{4} = 7.56$$

This sum of squares is associated with 1 df, and so, $MS_{A_{comp.} \times B_{comp.}} = 7.56$. The F for the interaction contrast,

$$F = \frac{MS_{A_{comp.} \times B_{comp.}}}{MS_{B_{comp.} \times S/A_{comp.}}}$$

$$= \frac{7.56}{4.48} = 1.69$$

is not significant.[10]

[10]The conclusion is unchanged if we use the error term based on all three groups. More specifically, the SS for the $B_{comp.} \times S$ interaction for group a_1 is 12.50, which when combined with the corresponding SS's for groups a_2 and a_3 (16.38 and 10.50), gives us $SS_{B_{comp.} \times S/A} = 12.50 + 16.38 + 10.50 = 39.38$; the pooled degrees of freedom become $df_{B_{comp.} \times S/A} = 3 + 3 + 3 = 9$; and the resulting mean square is 39.38/9 = 4.38. The F for the interaction contrast, $F = 7.56/4.38 = 1.73$, is also not significant.

Analyzing Simple Comparisons

If this interaction contrast had been significant, we might have been interested in examining one or both sets of simple comparisons. In terms of $A_{comp.}$, one set would consist of assessing the significance of the difference between the highly motivating instructions and the monetary incentive (a_2 versus a_3) on the first test trial (b_1) and on the fourth test trial (b_4). In terms of $B_{comp.}$, on the other hand, the set would consist of comparing the difference between the first and fourth trials for the group with highly motivating instructions and for the group receiving monetary incentive. We can easily calculate the sums of squares for these two sets of simple comparisons by using the general formula for a single-df comparison. I will illustrate this procedure first and then discuss the calculation of the error terms.

Calculating Simple Comparisons. As with the interaction contrasts, the key to the analysis is in the construction of the appropriate set of coefficients. Suppose we want to determine whether the gain from the first test trial to the fourth test trial is significant for the subjects receiving the highly motivating instructions, which I will call level $a_{(+)}$ to signify that this condition was associated with the positive coefficient used to define $A_{comp.}$.[11] We return to the 3 × 4 matrix containing the interaction coefficients and highlight only those coefficients associated with level $a_{(+)}$, which is level a_2 in this case. Only the highlighted coefficients are relevant for this particular simple comparison.

To illustrate, consider the matrix of interaction coefficients on the left in Table 18–14. These are the same coefficients we used to calculate the interaction contrast. You will notice that I have highlighted the coefficients in the second row, which identifies the relevant coefficients for this particular analysis. We now use the highlighted coefficients to weight the corresponding treatment means and then substitute this information into a general formula for single-df comparisons:

$$\hat{\psi}_{B \, at \, a_{(+)}} = (1)(9.75) + (0)(15.50) + (0)(22.00) + (-1)(23.50) = -13.75$$

$$\Sigma \, d^2 \, at \, a_{(+)} = (1)^2 + (0)^2 + (0)^2 + (-1)^2 = 2$$

$$SS_{B_{comp.} \, at \, a_{(+)}} = \frac{4(-13.75)^2}{2} = 378.13$$

Table 18–14   Analyzing the Simple Comparison of $B_{comp.}$

		Interaction Coefficients					Treatment Means			
		(b_1)	(b_2)	(b_3)	(b_4)					
	c_i	c_j: +1	0	0	−1		b_1	b_2	b_3	b_4
(a_1)	0	0	0	0	0	a_1	10.00	14.00	16.00	17.50
(a_2)	+1	+1	0	0	−1	a_2	9.75	15.50	22.00	23.50
(a_3)	−1	−1	0	0	+1	a_3	11.00	21.50	26.25	27.50

[11]Although I do not need the subscripts " + " and " − " here to distinguish between the levels of a comparison—the level designation would suffice—I do need them for complex comparisons in which two or more levels are combined to form a level in a comparison.

Table 18–15 Analyzing the Simple Comparison of $A_{comp.}$

			Interaction Coefficients						Treatment Means		
	c_i	c_j:	(b_1) +1	(b_2) 0	(b_3) 0	(b_4) −1		b_1	b_2	b_3	b_4
(a_1)	0		0	0	0	0	a_1	10.00	14.00	16.00	17.50
(a_2)	+1		+1	0	0	−1	a_2	9.75	15.50	22.00	23.50
(a_3)	−1		−1	0	0	+1	a_3	11.00	21.50	26.25	27.50

The corresponding simple comparison at level $a_{(-)}$ (level a_3) is obtained by highlighting the coefficients and treatment means at level $a_{(-)}$ and following through the same calculations.

The simple comparisons of $A_{comp.}$ are obtained in a similar fashion. Suppose we wanted to compare the two groups on the first trial $(b_{(+)})$. To illustrate, the interaction coefficients and the matrix of treatment means are presented again in Table 18–15, but this time I have highlighted the first column in both matrices—the column relevant to this particular simple comparison. We now calculate

$$\hat{\psi}_{A \text{ at } b_{(+)}} = (0)(10.00) + (1)(9.75) + (-1)(11.00) = -1.25$$

$$\Sigma\, d^2 \text{ at } b_{(+)} = (0)^2 + (1)^2 + (-1)^2 = 2$$

$$SS_{A_{comp.} \text{ at } b_{(+)}} = \frac{4(-1.25)^2}{2} = 3.13$$

Calculating the Error Terms. The error terms are based on the data contributing to the simple comparison under consideration. We considered first the comparison involving the within-subjects factor, namely, the difference between the first and fourth test trials for the subjects receiving the highly motivating instructions. The relevant data matrix may be found in Table 18–12, on the left (the matrix associated with level a_2). This matrix corresponds to a single-factor within-subjects design, with $b' = 2$ levels and $n = 4$ subjects, and the error term would be the $B_{comp.} \times S$ interaction for this data matrix.[12] That is,

$$SS_{B_{comp.} \times S/A_{(+)}} = [(5)^2 + (8)^2 + \ldots + (23)^2 + (26)^2] - \frac{(39)^2 + (94)^2}{4}$$

$$- \frac{(26)^2 + (32)^2 + (37)^2 + (38)^2}{2} + \frac{(133)^2}{(2)(4)}$$

$$= 2{,}651 - 2{,}589.25 - 2{,}256.50 + 2{,}211.13 = 16.38$$

This sum of squares is associated with $(b' - 1)(n - 1) = (2 - 1)(4 - 1) = 3\, df$. The F, which becomes

---

[12]If more than one group were involved, which will happen with complex comparisons, we would calculate the $B_{comp.} \times S$ interactions for each group and pool them. If you feel that it is safe to pool the interaction sums of squares, you would use the error term I described in footnote 10.

$$F = \frac{378.13/1}{16.38/3} = \frac{378.13}{5.46} = 69.25$$

is significant.

The error term for the simple comparison involving the between-subjects factor is also based on the data contributing to this comparison. The simple comparison involves the two sets of scores on the first trial $(b_{(+)})$, one from group a_2 $(a_{(+)})$ and the other from group a_3 $(a_{(-)})$. The relevant data are presented in Table 18–16. As you can see, the data correspond to a completely randomized single-factor experiment with $a' = 2$ levels and $n = 4$ subjects per condition.[13] From these data, we find

$$SS_{S/A_{comp.} \text{ at } b_{(+)}} = [(5)^2 + (8)^2 + \ldots + (14)^2 + (8)^2] - \frac{(39)^2 + (44)^2}{4}$$

$$= 939 - 864.25 = 74.75$$

This sum of squares is associated with $(2)(4 - 1) = 6\ df$. The F,

$$F = \frac{3.13/1}{74.75/6} = \frac{3.13}{12.46} = .25$$

is not significant.

Summary

Table 18–17 summarizes the analysis of an interaction contrast. The relationship between the overall mixed factorial design and the portion extracted for an interaction contrast is illustrated in the second row of the table. The $A_{comp.}$ selects the groups that are relevant (a_1 and a_2 in this example), and $B_{comp.}$ selects the Y scores that are relevant (b_1 and b_2). The error term for evaluating the interaction contrast is, therefore, the $B_{comp.} \times S/A_{comp.}$—the interaction between $B_{comp.}$ and subjects, pooled over the groups relevant to $A_{comp.}$. Two types of simple comparisons are possible following a significant interaction contrast, one involving $A_{comp.}$ at the two "levels" of $B_{comp.}$ and the other involving $B_{comp.}$ at the two "levels" of $A_{comp.}$.

Table 18–16   Data for Calculating the Error Term for the Simple Comparison of $A_{comp.}$

	a_2		a_3
s_5	5	s_9	13
s_6	8	s_{10}	9
s_7	14	s_{11}	14
s_8	12	s_{12}	8
Sum	39	Sum	44

[13]If more than two groups were involved in this comparison, which would occur with a complex comparison, we would still have a completely randomized experiment but with more than two independent groups; the error term would consist of a pooling of the individual within-group sums of squares for the relevant groups.

Table 18–17 Schematic Representation of the Analysis of an Interaction Contrast

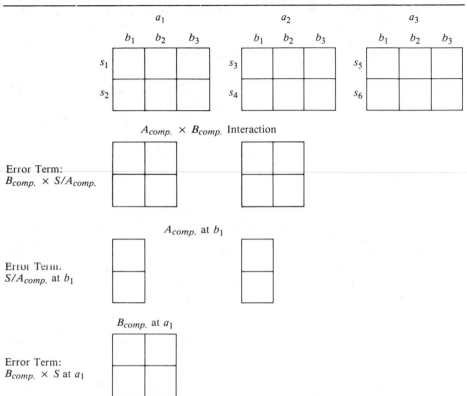

Table 18–17 indicates the data relevant to each type of comparison and thus reveals the nature of the error term that is used to evaluate these comparisons. In the case of the simple comparison involving $A_{comp.}$, the design reduces to a completely randomized single-factor design, which means that the error term is based on the variability of subjects at this particular "level" of $B_{comp.}$, pooled over the "levels" of $A_{comp.}$. For the simple comparison involving $B_{comp.}$, the design becomes a single-factor within-subjects design, which means that the error term is an interaction between $B_{comp.}$ and the subjects at this "level" of $A_{comp.}$.

18.4 EXERCISES[14]

1. In this experiment, 12 subjects (small nonhuman mammals) were randomly assigned to one of three treatment groups. Condition a_1 was a control group that was prepared for surgery and given anesthetic but not operated on. Condition a_2 consisted of a group of subjects that were operated on and had an area of the brain critical to the interest of the researcher removed. Condition a_3 consisted of a group of subjects that was also operated on but had an area of the brain removed that was thought to be

---

[14]The answers to these problems are found in Appendix B.

unrelated to the behavior under study. The second factor in the experiment was a battery of four different tests. We will not be concerned with the exact nature of the tests except to note that they were relevant to the research. Each of the subjects was tested on the four tests; the order in which the tests were administered was appropriately counterbalanced. The following data were obtained:

	a_1 (Control)					a_2 (Critical Area)					a_3 (Noncritical Area)			
	b_1	b_2	b_3	b_4		b_1	b_2	b_3	b_4		b_1	b_2	b_3	b_4
s_1	4	6	11	8	s_5	5	6	5	2	s_9	9	6	10	10
s_2	8	10	14	10	s_6	7	12	9	5	s_{10}	10	10	13	13
s_3	11	16	16	16	s_7	13	15	14	11	s_{11}	13	10	14	15
s_4	11	14	19	16	s_8	12	14	12	8	s_{12}	6	10	11	14

Perform a standard analysis of variance with these data.

2. Factor A in the preceding problem suggests a number of single-df comparisons, which may be used to create partial factorial designs. (Factor B consists of $b = 4$ unspecified tests; no information was provided to permit meaningful comparisons to be specified for the analysis of this independent variable.) For example, we could compare the control group (a_1) with the group having a noncritical area of the brain removed (a_3), which would focus on the effects of removing brain tissue (a_1 versus a_3), and more important, we could compare the two groups having the operation, which would focus on the critical location of the brain tissue removed.

   a. Assess the significance of the partial interaction involving factor B and the comparison between the two operated groups.

   b. In words, describe the nature of this interaction.

   c. A natural next step is to determine on which of the tests the difference between the two groups is significant. As an example, test the significance of the difference on the fourth test (level b_4).

3. For the purpose of illustration, let's form a partial factorial based on the repeated factor (factor B), even though we have no theoretical basis for doing so. Let's assume that an interesting comparison involves the first and fourth test and that factor A will be analyzed intact.

   a. Assess the significance of the partial interaction involving factor A and the comparison between the first and fourth tests.

   b. In words, describe the nature of this interaction.

   c. As an example of a simple comparison, test the significance of the difference between the two tests for the control group (level a_1).

4. Suppose we had good theoretical reasons for comparing the results obtained with the last two tests (b_3 and b_4). We are now able to create an interaction contrast by combining this comparison with a meaningful single-df comparison involving factor A .

   a. As an example, test the significance of an interaction contrast involving the comparison between the last two tests and the comparison between the two operated groups (levels a_2 and a_3).

   b. What can you conclude from this analysis?

5. Problem 2 in the exercises for Chap. 17 involves an experiment in which groups detecting targets on three different radar displays (factor A) were compared over three test periods (factor B). Many researchers would consider examining trend compo-

nents in the detailed analysis of this sort of experiment. Let's concentrate on the linear trend component.

a. As a first step, we will look at the partial interaction formed by crossing the linear component of factor B with all three levels of factor A . Test the significance of this partial interaction.

b. Let's now look at the interaction contrast formed by crossing the linear component with the comparison between the two groups detecting targets on a black background (levels a_2 and a_3). Test the significance of this interaction contrast.

c. As another example, test the significance of the interaction contrast formed by crossing the linear component with a comparison between the group detecting targets on a white background (level a_1) with the combined data from the two groups detecting targets on a black background (levels a_2 and a_3).

PART VI

HIGHER-ORDER FACTORIAL EXPERIMENTS

The analysis of experiments involving three or more independent variables introduces no new concepts or procedures. Our task in Part VI is to see how the basic analyses of one- and two-factor experiments are extended to these multifactor designs. We will begin by examining the design and analysis of factorial experiments with three independent variables. We will then turn our attention to more complicated within-subjects designs than those already considered.

As I indicated, we will begin with a discussion of the analysis of the relatively common three-factor design in which three independent variables are arranged in a completely crossed fashion. As before, this means that each possible combination of the levels associated with each independent variable is represented in the design. A two-way factorial was represented by a rectangle, the levels of factor A defining one dimension and the levels of factor B defining the other dimension. Continuing with this geometrical representation, we can picture the three way factorial as a rectangular solid, in which the levels of factors A and B mark off the width and the height, respectively, and the levels of the third factor, C, mark off the depth. This may be seen in the figure appearing on p. 420, where each of the separate blocks making up the display represents a different combination of the levels of the three factors.

Chapter 19 presents an overview of the three-way design and the standard analysis that is normally applied to it. Chapter 20 is concerned with the detailed analysis of the three-factor design—that is, the use of simple effects and of interaction comparisons to provide an analytical picture of the results of this type of factorial experiment. The development of the statistical analyses in these two chapters will provide an illustration of how the basic procedures developed for the two-factor design—the simplest form of factorial experiment—can be extended and

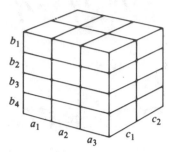

generalized to the meaningful analysis of the three-factor design. In the final two chapters, we will be concerned with the analysis of higher-order factorial designs, which include repeated measures. In Chap. 21, for example, we will consider a two-factor within-subjects design in which both independent variables involve repeated measurements on a single group of subjects. We conclude in Chap. 22 with a general discussion of higher-order factorial designs in which a set of rules will be presented that will facilitate the analysis of factorial designs with any number of independent variables and consisting of any combination of between-subjects and within-subjects factors.

At some point you will begin using statistical software programs to perform the operations presented in these chapters. There are two reasons why you should have some idea of these computational procedures nevertheless. First, knowing what to expect from an analysis will help you recognize when the program gives you incorrect information, either because you have made a mistake of some sort—for example, entering the wrong data, incorrectly coding your conditions for the program, or specifying the wrong design in your instructions to the program—or because there is a "bug" in the program. Second, there will be times when you will want to conduct additional tests and the procedures for these cannot be easily obtained with the program. When this happens, you will have to rely on your understanding of the statistical procedures and watch the output of the program carefully as it works through the tests or, alternatively, perform the calculations yourself.

19

The Three-Factor Design

The Basic Analysis

This chapter examines closely the single new statistical quantity introduced by adding a third independent variable to a factorial design—the three-way interaction. Following this discussion, I will turn to the computational formulas for the standard analysis of variance of data obtained from a three-factor experiment and end the chapter with a numerical example. Chapter 20 illustrates the rich detail of information that can be extracted from this design in addition to the usual main effects and interactions.

19.1   FACTORIAL COMPONENTS
OF THE THREE-WAY DESIGN

It is instructive to think about the ingredients that go into a three-factor design. Consider the display presented in Table 19–1. In the top section of the table, each of the independent variables is represented in a different single-factor experiment. You have seen in Chap. 9 that the two-way factorial is in essence constructed from two single-factor experiments. Three such two-way factorials are possible with three independent variables: a crossing of factors A and B, a crossing of factors A and C, and a crossing of factors B and C. These experiments are enumerated in the middle section of the table. Finally, a three-way factorial can be viewed as a *two-way* factorial design crossed with a third factor. Three such crossings are possible, and they are listed in the bottom section of the table. Because the same three factors are incorporated, each of these instances of a three-way factorial specifies the same set of treatment combinations.

Any one of the three ways of displaying a three-factor design can be used to organize the data from an experiment. I will refer to these displays as ABC **matrices**. At a glance, you can see that all possible $(a)(b)(c) = (3)(4)(2) = 24$ combinations of the three independent variables are enumerated as individual cells in the ABC matrix. This particular design would be referred to as a $3 \times 4 \times 2$ factorial.

Suppose we consider Table 19–1 in reverse. We start with the three-way factorials at the bottom. By collapsing across any of the three independent variables and combining the scores contained therein, we will obtain a two-dimensional data matrix: an AB matrix when we collapse across the levels of factor C, an AC matrix when we collapse across the levels of factor B, and a BC matrix when we collapse

Table 19–1 Relationship Between the Three-Way Factorial and Lower-Order Designs

SINGLE-FACTOR EXPERIMENTS

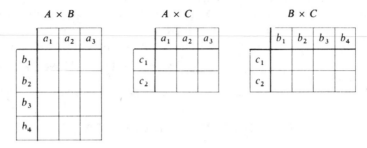

TWO-WAY FACTORIALS

THREE-WAY FACTORIALS

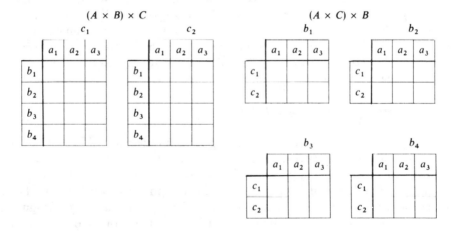

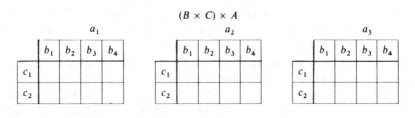

across the levels of factor A. From these three matrices, we can obtain information concerning the respective two-way interactions, which represent interactions averaged over the levels of the remaining independent variable. Because of the collapsing, these interactions will not necessarily be the same as those obtained from a standard two-way factorial.[1]

From the two-way matrices, we can obtain information concerning respective main effects for each of the three independent variables. These main effects are estimates of the effects of one of the independent variables averaged over the levels of the other two independent variables. In addition to the three main effects and the three two-way interactions, which may be investigated with appropriate two-way factorial experiments, we obtain from the ABC matrix information that is unique to this design, namely, how the three variables combine to affect the behavior we are studying. That is, we are able to determine the presence or absence of a *three-way* interaction.

19.2   THREE-WAY INTERACTION

The three-way interaction is called by a number of names, such as the **three-way**, the **second-order**, the **triple**, or the $A \times B \times C$ **interaction.** I will use these labels interchangeably. One way to understand the meaning of this higher-order interaction is to look at a concrete example. This illustration comes from an experiment reported by Wallace and Underwood (1964), in which the main purpose was an assessment of the triple interaction. To understand why this was the case, we must consider some of the reasoning behind the experiment.

An Example of a Three-Way Interaction

Briefly, Wallace and Underwood (1964) began with the assumption that the presentation of a common word will elicit from the subject an implicit associative response; for example, a subject may think of the word *table* upon the presentation of the word *chair* or of *apple* upon the presentation of the word *orange*. These associations are thought to be the result of experience with a language. Linguistic associations are assumed to facilitate learning when they correspond to the requirements of the learning task and to interfere with learning when they do not. One implication of this theory was tested in the experiment by including as two of the independent variables the strength of the linguistic associations and the type of learning task.

The degree of strength (factor A) was varied by constructing learning materials from two pools of words. One pool contained groups of words from the same conceptual class, such as *fruits*: *apple, peach, pear*; *colors*: *green, blue, red*; or *parts of the body*: *leg, head, arm*. The other pool contained no words from the same conceptual class—for example, *fly, saw, snow, car, sun*, and so on. It was

---

[1]These interactions will be identical only when there is no three-way interaction, a concept I will discuss in Sec. 19.2.

assumed that words from the same category are highly associated, whereas words from different categories are not. Two types of learning tasks (factor B) were compared: a free-recall task in which subjects could recall a series of words in any order they wished, and a paired-word task in which they were required to learn specific word pairs. A crossing of these two factors resulted in two free-recall lists and two paired-word lists. In each case, one of the lists contained words of a low degree of association and another contained words of a high degree of association. The free-recall lists were constructed by randomly ordering the words from a given pool, and the lists of paired words were constructed by randomly forming pairs of words from the appropriate pool.

It was predicted that there would be an interaction between these two independent variables. More specifically, Wallace and Underwood anticipated that strong associations between words would facilitate free-recall learning in that the high interconnections among the words within a group would facilitate the recall of the separate words. Thus, the high list would be learned more quickly than the low list. In direct contrast, they predicted that strong interword associations would retard the learning of the word pairs since the interconnections among the words would be in conflict with the arbitrary pairs that the subjects were required to learn. Thus, the high list would be learned more slowly than the low list. In short, then, they predicted an interaction between the two factors—namely, that associative strength (factor A) would have opposite effects on the two learning tasks (factor B).

For the third independent variable, Wallace and Underwood compared the learning of these tasks and materials by college students and by mental retardates. This final variable was introduced with the thought that the degree of linguistic development was being "manipulated" by studying these two groups of individuals. It was assumed that college students have stronger and more extensive linguistic habits than do mental retardates. Therefore, the researchers predicted that associative strength would have less effect on the performance of retarded subjects than it would on the performance of college students. That is, the negative and positive effects of associative strength (the $A \times B$ interaction), which I described in the last paragraph, should be found with college students but should be greatly diminished or even absent with retardates.

The complete design is specified in Table 19–2. Each of the three independent variables (strength, task, and type of subject) is represented by two levels. Thus, there are $(a)(b)(c) = (2)(2)(2) = 8$ treatment combinations in the experiment. The results of the study are reproduced in Fig. 19–1. It will be noted that the expected strength × task ($A \times B$) interaction was obtained with the college stu-

Table 19–2 Experimental Design of Wallace and Underwood (1964)

College Students			Mental Retardates		
	Degree of Association			Degree of Association	
Task	Low	High	Task	Low	High
Free Recall			Free Recall		
Paired Associate			Paired Associate		

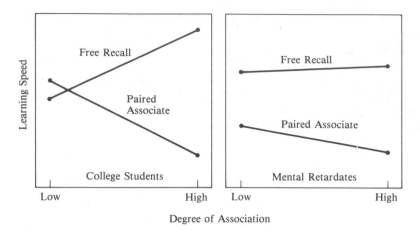

Figure 19–1   From Wallace, W. P., and Underwood, B. J. Speed of learning as a function of learning task, degree of association, and type of subject. *Journal of Educational Psychology*, 1964, *55*, 362–370. Copyright 1964 by the American Psychological Association. Reprinted by permission.

dents but was virtually nonexistent with the mental retardates. This pattern of results represents an interaction of *three* independent variables. For Wallace and Underwood, the outcome provided strong support for their theoretical speculations. That is, they found that assumed linguistic associations could facilitate as well as interfere with learning and that the magnitude of these opposed effects seemed to depend on the degree of linguistic development of the subjects.

Defining the Three-Way Interaction

In developing a definition of the three-way interaction, let's return to Chap. 9 and the definitions of the *two*-way interaction. In that context, I defined an interaction as a situation in which the effects of one of the independent variables are not the same at all levels of the second independent variable. We can define a three-way interaction by modifying this relatively simple definition to accommodate the increased complexity of the higher-order interaction. More specifically, we say that

> **Three variables interact when the *interaction* of two of the variables is not the same at all levels of the *third* variable.**

You can see that this definition is satisfied by the data summarized in Fig. 19–1. That is, the two-way interaction of strength and task is not the same for college students (one level of the third variable) as it is for mental retardates (the other level of the third variable).

When considering interactions, many students have difficulty making the transition from two to three independent variables. Suppose we go back to an interaction of two variables. Recall from the discussion in Chap. 9 that a two-way interaction is present when the simple effects of one of the variables are not the same at the different levels of the other variable. By analogy,

A three-way interaction is present when the *simple interaction* effects of two variables are not the same at different levels of the third variable.

A **simple interaction** in this context is an interaction between two independent variables with a third independent variable held constant. Three sets of simple interactions are possible in this type of design:

The $A \times B$ interaction effects at the different levels of factor C ($A \times B$ interaction at c_k);

The $A \times C$ interaction effects at the different levels of factor B ($A \times C$ interaction at b_j)

The $B \times C$ interaction effects at the different levels of factor A ($B \times C$ interaction at a_i)

When there is a three-way interaction, the simple interaction effects for any one of the sets will not be the same at all levels of the corresponding third variable.

It is important to note that the simple interaction effects merely need to be *different*; they do not need to represent significant two-way interactions themselves. This is why Fig. 19–1 is such a good example. If we had conducted the experiment only with retardates as subjects, we would not have observed the two-way interaction; under these circumstances, we would have concluded that associative strength produces no effect with either type of learning task. However, if we had conducted this experiment only with college students, we would have concluded that there is a severe interaction of the two variables. In short, when you consider the results of these separate "two-factor" experiments brought together in a three-factor design, you can see that no one summary statement is possible; we must indicate that the two independent variables, associative strength and learning task, produce a different pattern of results with the two types of subjects. Said another way, the presence of an $A \times B \times C$ interaction signals the fact that the interpretation of the two-way interactions, which we obtain by collapsing across the levels of one of the variables, must be made with caution, just as an $A \times B$ interaction in the two-factor case means that the interpretation of the main effects must be made with caution. Translated to our example, you can see that a general statement describing the interaction of associative strength and learning task cannot be made without a specification of the type of subject being tested.

It is much easier to grasp the meaning of a three-way interaction when the experiment is your own and you have gone through the agonizing steps in planning it than when it is simply an example in a statistics book, where the independent variables are represented by theoretically neutral letters. A researcher does not turn to a three-way factorial unless he or she has thought about the real possibilities of the higher-order interaction—of what it will mean if it does materialize as predicted and what it will mean if it does not. Wallace and Underwood (1964), for example, already knew that associative strength would show opposite results with the free-recall and word-pair tasks. Their intent was to test their theoretical interpretation of this interaction by manipulating a third independent variable that would reduce or eliminate the interaction. This variable, represented by a contrast of college students and mental retardates, was assumed to be a way of reducing the strength of linguistic associations without changing the nature of the materials. Their prediction of a three-way interaction followed directly from their original theoretical explanation and their assumptions of the effects of comparing college students and mental retardates.

The point is that we usually progress to a three-way interaction by following the logic of our own research program. You should understand precisely what a higher-order interaction means, so that you will know when you are predicting its occurrence or nonoccurrence in a three-way factorial.

19.3   COMPUTATIONAL FORMULAS
AND ANALYSIS SUMMARY

Before turning to the actual analysis, I will discuss the notation needed to specify the various calculations involved in the analysis of a three-way factorial design.

Design and Notation

The notational system is illustrated in Table 19–3. Inspection of the ABC matrix at the top of the table indicates that the design is a $3 \times 2 \times 2$ factorial, with factor A represented with $a = 3$ levels, factor B with $b = 2$ levels, and factor C with $c = 2$ levels. Let's assume that $n = 3$ subjects were randomly assigned to each of the $(a)(b)(c) = (3)(2)(2) = 12$ treatment combinations.

A basic score or individual observation is again Y in the notational system for the three-factor design. When it is necessary to specify a particular observation in one of the cells in the ABC matrix, I will do so by using four subscripts, namely,

Table 19–3   Summary Matrices for the Three-Factor Design

ABC Matrix

	c_1			c_2		
	a_1	a_2	a_3	a_1	a_2	a_3
b_1	$ABC_{1,1,1}$	$ABC_{2,1,1}$	$ABC_{3,1,1}$	$ABC_{1,1,2}$	$ABC_{2,1,2}$	$ABC_{3,1,2}$
b_2	$ABC_{1,2,1}$	$ABC_{2,2,1}$	$ABC_{3,2,1}$	$ABC_{1,2,2}$	$ABC_{2,2,2}$	$ABC_{3,2,2}$

AB Matrix					**AC Matrix**				
	a_1	a_2	a_3	**Sum**		a_1	a_2	a_3	**Sum**
b_1	$AB_{1,1}$	$AB_{2,1}$	$AB_{3,1}$	B_1	c_1	$AC_{1,1}$	$AC_{2,1}$	$AC_{3,1}$	C_1
b_2	$AB_{1,2}$	$AB_{2,2}$	$AB_{3,2}$	B_2	c_2	$AC_{1,2}$	$AC_{2,2}$	$AC_{3,2}$	C_2
Sum	A_1	A_2	A_3	T	**Sum**	A_1	A_2	A_3	T

BC Matrix

	c_1	c_2	**Sum**
b_1	$BC_{1,1}$	$BC_{1,2}$	B_1
b_2	$BC_{2,1}$	$BC_{2,2}$	B_2
Sum	C_1	C_2	T

i to refer to the level of factor A, j to refer to the level of factor B, k to refer to the level of factor C, and l to refer to the specific subject in the ijkth cell. I will use notational subscripts only when necessary to avoid ambiguity in the calculations.

Table 19–3 presents the four matrices from which we will calculate the different factorial treatment effects. The first is the *ABC* **matrix**. This matrix contains the totals for each of the $(a)(b)(c)$ treatment combinations; they are denoted ABC_{ijk}. The *ABC* sums are obtained by adding up the relevant Y scores in each of the $(a)(b)(c)$ cells or groups.

The other three matrices presented in the table are two-factor matrices formed when the levels of a third factor are disregarded—that is, summed across or collapsed over. Thus, the *AB* **matrix** superimposes the left-hand and right-hand portions of the *ABC* matrix, eliminating the C classification. Any sum listed within the body of the *AB* matrix is obtained by combining corresponding treatment sums from the different levels of factor C. For example,

$$AB_{1,1} = ABC_{1,1,1} + ABC_{1,1,2} \quad \text{and} \quad AB_{3,2} = ABC_{3,2,1} + ABC_{3,2,2}$$

The marginal totals in the *AB* matrix should represent familiar ground: The column marginal totals are the A_i sums, the row marginal totals are the B_j totals, and the sum of either the row marginal totals or the column marginal totals is the grand sum T.

The *AC* and *BC* matrices are formed in a similar way. The totals within the body of the *AC* **matrix** are obtained by summing corresponding totals from the different levels of factor B. For example,

$$AC_{2,2} = ABC_{2,1,2} + ABC_{2,2,2} \quad \text{and} \quad AC_{3,1} = ABC_{3,1,1} + ABC_{3,2,1}$$

The marginal totals of the *AC* matrix provide the A_i sums (column marginal totals), the C_k sums (row marginal totals), and T (the sum of either the row or column marginal totals).

Turning finally to the *BC* **matrix**, we see that the totals within the body of this matrix are found by collapsing across the levels of factor A. For the sum at level b_1c_2, for example,

$$BC_{1,2} - ABC_{1,1,2} + ABC_{2,1,2} + ABC_{3,1,2}$$

You may have noticed that marginal totals in any two-way matrix (AB, AC, or BC) are duplicated in the other matrices. This redundancy is useful in an actual analysis as a check on one's accuracy in forming a two-way matrix from the *ABC*, or three-way, matrix.

The symbols for the means based on the different sums specified in Table 19–3 consist of $\overline{Y}$ combined with appropriate subscripts:

$\overline{Y}_{A_iB_jC_k}$ = a cell mean obtained by dividing the appropriate *ABC* subtotal by n

$\overline{Y}_{A_iB_j}$ = a marginal mean obtained by dividing the appropriate *AB* subtotal by $(c)(n)$

$\overline{Y}_{A_iC_k}$ = a marginal mean obtained by dividing the appropriate *AC*

$\overline{Y}_{B_j C_k}$ = a marginal mean obtained by dividing the appropriate BC subtotal by $(b)(n)$

$\overline{Y}_{A_i}$ = a marginal mean obtained by dividing the appropriate A subtotal by $(b)(c)(n)$

$\overline{Y}_{B_j}$ = a marginal mean obtained by dividing the appropriate B subtotal by $(a)(c)(n)$

$\overline{Y}_{C_k}$ = a marginal mean obtained by dividing the appropriate C subtotal by $(a)(b)(n)$

$\overline{Y}_T$ = the grand mean obtained by dividing T by $(a)(b)(c)(n)$

Partitioning the Total Sum of Squares

In this representation of a three-way factorial, I assumed that there are $n = 3$ subjects in each cell of the ABC matrix, and thus there are $(a)(b)(c)(n) = 36$ subjects in the entire experiment. As with any completely randomized experiment, the variability of the individual scores from the grand mean (the SS_T) can be partitioned into a between-groups sum of squares (SS_{bg} = the variability of the cell means $\overline{Y}_{A_i B_j C_k}$ from $\overline{Y}_T$) and a within-groups sum of squares (SS_{wg} = the variability of subjects treated alike, pooled over the specific treatment conditions). As with the two-factor analysis described in Chap. 10, we can subdivide the SS_{bg} into a set of useful components.

I have already hinted at the nature of these sources of variance. That is, the SS_{bg} can be partitioned into a set of three main effects (one for each independent variable), a set of three two-way interactions ($A \times B$, $A \times C$, and $B \times C$), and the three-way interaction. In symbols

$$SS_{bg} = SS_A + SS_B + SS_C + SS_{A \times B} + SS_{A \times C} + SS_{B \times C} + SS_{A \times B \times C}$$

$$(19\text{--}1)$$

It is a simple step to include in Eq. (19–1) the variability of the individual subjects:

$$\begin{aligned} SS_T &= SS_{bg} + SS_{wg} \\ &= SS_A + SS_B + SS_C + SS_{A \times B} + SS_{A \times C} + SS_{B \times C} \\ &\quad + SS_{A \times B \times C} + SS_{S/ABC} \end{aligned} \quad (19\text{--}2)$$

The last source of variance, the $SS_{S/ABC}$, is the within-groups sum of squares and refers to the pooled sums of squares of subjects within each of the different $(a)(b)(c)$ treatment cells. I will now construct the computational formulas for these component sums of squares.

Generating the Computational Formulas

In Chap. 10, I presented a procedure by which the computational formulas for the sums of squares are constructed from the corresponding df statements. I will apply the same set of rules to the present analysis. The development of the formulas takes place in three basic steps, through which I will work quickly. If you require further guidance, please refer to the earlier discussion (pp. 207–211).

Identifying the Sources of Variance. This step has been completed by Eq. (19–2), but I will still apply the rules given in Chap. 10 as an additional demonstration of how they work:

1. List factors: A, B, C, and S/ABC
2. Form interactions: $A \times B$, $A \times C, B \times C$, and $A \times B \times C$

These sources of variance are presented in column 1 of Table 19–4.

Using the df Statements. The degrees of freedom associated with each source of variance are listed in column 2 of Table 19–4. The df's for the main effects equal the number of treatment levels minus 1. The df's for the interaction sums of squares are found by multiplying the df's associated with the factors specified by the interaction:

$$df_{A \times B} = (df_A)(df_B) = (a - 1)(b - 1)$$
$$df_{A \times C} = (df_A)(df_C) = (a - 1)(c - 1)$$
$$df_{B \times C} = (df_B)(df_C) = (b - 1)(c - 1)$$
$$df_{A \times B \times C} = (df_A)(df_B)(df_C) = (a - 1)(b - 1)(c - 1)$$

In each case, the df's reflect the number of cells in the corresponding data matrices that are free to vary (see pp. 212–213).

The degrees of freedom for the $SS_{S/ABC}$ are calculated by pooling the df associated with factor S, that is, $n - 1$, over the $(a)(b)(c)$ treatment cells:

$$df_{S/ABC} = (a)(b)(c)(df_S) = (a)(b)(c)(n - 1)$$

The degrees of freedom for the SS_T are 1 less than the total number of observations in the experiment:

$$df_T = (a)(b)(c)(n) - 1$$

Column 3 of Table 19–4 lists the different sets of df statements in expanded form.[2] This arrangement constitutes the backbone of the generating system. The individual terms in these expressions—the letters and combinations of letters—indicate the nature of the basic ratios, which I will consider next, and the specific way in which these ratios are combined to form the various sums of squares required for the analysis of variance.

Forming the Basic Ratios. The construction of basic ratios, you will recall, follows a consistent pattern of operations—that is, the squaring and then summing of a set of quantities (scores or sums of scores) followed by a division specified by the number of observations contributing to any of the quantities in the set. Column 4 of Table 19–4 lists the basic ratio for the first term in each formula except

---

[2]See footnote 1 in Chap. 10 (p. 209) for a discussion how to perform these multiplications.

Table 19–4 Constructing the Computational Formulas from the Expanded df Statements

(1) Source	(2) df	(3) df Expanded	(4) Basic Ratio	(5) Sum of Squares	(6) MS	(7) F
A	$a-1$	$a-1$	$[A] = \dfrac{\Sigma A^2}{(b)(c)(n)}$	$[A] - [T]$	$\dfrac{SS_A}{df_A}$	$\dfrac{MS_A}{MS_{S/ABC}}$
B	$b-1$	$b-1$	$[B] = \dfrac{\Sigma B^2}{(a)(c)(n)}$	$[B] - [T]$	$\dfrac{SS_B}{df_B}$	$\dfrac{MS_B}{MS_{S/ABC}}$
C	$c-1$	$c-1$	$[C] = \dfrac{\Sigma C^2}{(a)(b)(n)}$	$[C] - [T]$	$\dfrac{SS_C}{df_C}$	$\dfrac{MS_C}{MS_{S/ABC}}$
$A \times B$	$(a-1)(b-1)$	$ab - a - b + 1$	$[AB] = \dfrac{\Sigma (AB)^2}{(c)(n)}$	$[AB] - [A] - [B] + [T]$	$\dfrac{SS_{A \times B}}{df_{A \times B}}$	$\dfrac{MS_{A \times B}}{MS_{S/ABC}}$
$A \times C$	$(a-1)(c-1)$	$ac - a - c + 1$	$[AC] = \dfrac{\Sigma (AC)^2}{(b)(n)}$	$[AC] - [A] - [C] + [T]$	$\dfrac{SS_{A \times C}}{df_{A \times C}}$	$\dfrac{MS_{A \times C}}{MS_{S/ABC}}$
$B \times C$	$(b-1)(c-1)$	$bc - b - c + 1$	$[BC] = \dfrac{\Sigma (BC)^2}{(a)(n)}$	$[BC] - [B] - [C] + [T]$	$\dfrac{SS_{B \times C}}{df_{B \times C}}$	$\dfrac{MS_{B \times C}}{MS_{S/ABC}}$
$A \times B \times C$	$(a-1)(b-1)(c-1)$	$abc - ab - ac - bc$ $+ a + b + c - 1$	$[ABC] = \dfrac{\Sigma (ABC)^2}{n}$	$[ABC] - [AB] - [AC] -$ $[BC] + [A] + [B] + [C] - [T]$	$\dfrac{SS_{A \times B \times C}}{df_{A \times B \times C}}$	$\dfrac{MS_{A \times B \times C}}{MS_{S/ABC}}$
S / ABC	$(a)(b)(c)(n-1)$	$abcn - abc$	$[Y] = \Sigma Y^2$	$[Y] - [ABC]$	$\dfrac{SS_{S/ABC}}{df_{S/ABC}}$	
Total	$(a)(b)(c)(n) - 1$	$abcn - 1$	$[T] = \dfrac{T^2}{(a)(b)(c)(n)}$	$[Y] - [T]$		

in the last row, where the basic ratio associated with the numeral 1 in the expanded *df* statements, [*T*], is listed to complete the enumeration. You should verify for yourself the systematic way each basic ratio is constructed.

Summary of the Analysis of Variance

Sums of Squares and Degrees of Freedom. The formulas for the sums of squares and the respective degrees of freedom are presented in Table 19–4 in columns 5 and 2, respectively.

Mean Squares and F Ratios. The mean squares are obtained by dividing each component sum of squares by its corresponding *df*, as indicated in Table 19–4, column 6. Each of these mean squares, except the $MS_{S/ABC}$, provides an estimate of the population treatment effects (main effects or interaction) plus error variance. The $MS_{S/ABC}$ provides an independent estimate of error variance alone and is used as the error term for assessing the statistical significance of each source of systematic variability.

Statistical Model and Assumptions

The linear model for the three-factor design contains a listing of the different population effects potentially contributing to a single observation in the experiment:

$$Y_{ijkl} = \mu_T + \alpha_i + \beta_j + \gamma_k + (\alpha\beta)_{ij} + (\alpha\gamma)_{ik} + (\beta\gamma)_{jk} + (\alpha\beta\gamma)_{ijk} + \epsilon_{ijkl}$$

where μ_T = the overall mean of the population

α_i, β_j, and γ_k = the average treatment effects at levels a_i, b_j, and c_k, respectively

$(\alpha\beta)_{ij}, (\alpha\gamma)_{ik},$ and $(\beta\gamma)_{jk}$ = the average interaction effects at $a_i b_j$, $a_i c_k$ and $b_j c_k$, respectively

$(\alpha\beta\gamma)_{ijk}$ = the three-way interaction effect at cell $a_i b_j c_k$

ϵ_{ijkl} = experimental error unique to subject "*l*" in group $a_i b_j c_k$

From this model and the assumptions concerning the underlying treatment populations—normality, homogeneity of variance, and independence—expected mean squares can be formed that specify the factor (or factors) contributing to each mean square entering into the formation of the *F* ratios.[3] The null hypothesis in each case specifies the absence of population treatment effects, whereas the alternative hypothesis specifies their presence. When the null hypothesis is true, ratios formed by dividing these mean squares by the $MS_{S/ABC}$ are distributed as *F* (with appropriate numerator and denominator *df*'s). Obtained *F* ratios that exceed theoretical values at some significance level (α) lead to the rejection of the null hypothesis and the acceptance of the alternative hypothesis.[4]

---

[3] See the discussion of the effects of heterogeneity of variance in the analysis of the completely randomized two-way factorial design in Chap. 10 (pp. 220–221).

[4] This statement is correct only for the fixed-effects model, which is appropriate for most research applications. See Chap. 22 (pp. 485–487) for a discussion of the different models.

19.4   A NUMERICAL EXAMPLE

The numerical example, based on the experiment first considered in Chap. 12, is concerned with the effects of verbal feedback given during the acquisition of different types of learning material on memory tested one week later.

The Design

The design is a $3 \times 2 \times 2$ factorial, in which factor A consists of the feedback manipulation: a control condition that receives no verbal feedback and two treatment conditions that receive either positive or negative feedback during the learning portion of the experiment. Factor B consists of two types of learning material, one made up of words of low emotional content and the other words of high emotional content. The dependent variable is the number words subjects recall one week after learning. At this point, the design resembles the example considered in Chap. 12, except that one level of factor B has been dropped to simplify the design. To create a three-way factorial design, suppose I introduce a developmental factor into the example; factor C consists of two age groups, children in the fifth grade (c_1) and seniors in high school (c_2). You may recall that the original study was conducted with fifth-grade children. The question we are examining with this design, then, is whether we will obtain the same sorts of findings with seniors as well.

The factorial design is summarized by the matrix of group means in Table 19–5. The means on the left are for the fifth-grade children and were taken from the earlier example in Chap. 12; the means on the right are for the seniors in high school. These means have been plotted in Fig. 19–2. The left-hand display exhibits a clear interaction between the feedback variable (factor A) and the emotionality of the words (factor B). It appears that both types of verbal feedback—positive and negative—administered during learning have a negative effect on the memory for words of high emotional content and virtually no effect on the memory for words of low emotional content. (We studied this particular interaction in detail in Chap. 12.) What about the right-hand display, where the means for the seniors appear? It appears that feedback has only a small effect on memory for these subjects and that the interaction that figured so prominently for the younger subjects is virtually absent. The data exhibit a three-way interaction because the interaction of two independent variables (factors A and B) is not the same at both levels of the third variable (factor C).

We will assume that each of the group means is based on $n = 5$ subjects. The ABC cell totals associated with the cell means are presented in Table 19–6. You

Table 19–5   Cell Means for the Numerical Example

	Fifth Grade (c_1)				Seniors (c_2)		
	Control (a_1)	Positive (a_2)	Negative (a_3)		Control (a_1)	Positive (a_2)	Negative (a_3)
Low (b_1)	8.8	8.0	7.6	Low (b_1)	9.0	8.4	8.0
High (b_2)	8.0	4.4	3.8	High (b_2)	7.8	7.4	7.2

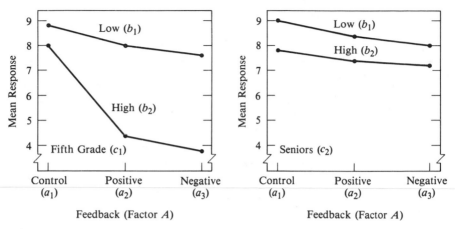

Figure 19–2   Plot of the cell means.

may have noticed that the individual Y scores are missing, which I have omitted to conserve space. I have provided sufficient information, however, to complete the statistical analysis—more specifically, the values of the cell sums (ABC_{ijk}) and the sum of the squared Y scores for the entire set of observations. The cell totals are entered in the ABC matrix, and the sum of the squared Y scores is given at the bottom of the table.

The Analysis

We begin by preparing the necessary two-way matrices; these are presented in Table 19–7. The marginal totals of the two-way matrices provide the sums needed to calculate the three main effects. The totals within the body of the matrices provide the additional sums needed to calculate the three two-way interactions. The cell totals in the ABC matrix are used in the calculation of the three-way interaction and the within-groups sums of squares. To guard against computational errors in the formation of these matrices, it is a good idea to verify for each two-way matrix that the sum of the row and column marginal totals equal the grand sum, T.

We are now ready to calculate the basic terms entering into the computational formulas for the sums of squares. From any of the two-way matrices,

Table 19–6   The *ABC* Matrix of Cell Sums

	Fifth Grade (c_1)				Seniors (c_2)		
	Control (a_1)	Positive (a_2)	Negative (a_3)		Control (a_1)	Positive (a_2)	Negative (a_3)
Low (b_1)	44	40	38	**Low (b_1)**	45	42	40
High (b_2)	40	22	19	**High (b_2)**	39	37	36

$$\Sigma Y^2 = 3{,}484$$

Table 19–7   Two-Way Matrices

<table>
<tr><td colspan="5" align="center">AB Matrix</td><td colspan="5" align="center">AC Matrix</td></tr>
<tr><td></td><td>a_1</td><td>a_2</td><td>a_3</td><td>Sum</td><td></td><td>a_1</td><td>a_2</td><td>a_3</td><td>Sum</td></tr>
<tr><td>b_1</td><td>89</td><td>82</td><td>78</td><td>249</td><td>c_1</td><td>84</td><td>62</td><td>57</td><td>203</td></tr>
<tr><td>b_2</td><td>79</td><td>59</td><td>55</td><td>193</td><td>c_2</td><td>84</td><td>79</td><td>76</td><td>239</td></tr>
<tr><td>Sum</td><td>168</td><td>141</td><td>133</td><td>442</td><td>Sum</td><td>168</td><td>141</td><td>133</td><td>442</td></tr>
</table>

<table>
<tr><td colspan="4" align="center">BC Matrix</td></tr>
<tr><td></td><td>c_1</td><td>c_2</td><td>Sum</td></tr>
<tr><td>b_1</td><td>122</td><td>127</td><td>249</td></tr>
<tr><td>b_2</td><td>81</td><td>112</td><td>193</td></tr>
<tr><td>Sum</td><td>203</td><td>239</td><td>442</td></tr>
</table>

$$[T] = \frac{T^2}{(a)(b)(c)(n)} = \frac{(442)^2}{(3)(2)(2)(5)} = 3{,}256.07$$

From the margins of either the AB or the AC matrix,

$$[A] = \frac{\Sigma A^2}{(b)(c)(n)} = \frac{(168)^2 + (141)^2 + (133)^2}{(2)(2)(5)} = 3{,}289.70$$

From either the AB or BC matrix,

$$[B] = \frac{\Sigma B^2}{(a)(c)(n)} = \frac{(249)^2 + (193)^2}{(3)(2)(5)} = 3{,}308.33$$

and from either the AC or BC matrix,

$$[C] = \frac{\Sigma C^2}{(a)(b)(n)} = \frac{(203)^2 + (239)^2}{(3)(2)(5)} = 3{,}277.67$$

Our next task is the computation of the first terms entering into the determination of the SS's for the two-way interactions. From the AB matrix,

$$[AB] = \frac{\Sigma (AB)^2}{(c)(n)} = \frac{(89)^2 + (82)^2 + \ldots + (59)^2 + (55)^2}{(2)(5)} = 3{,}347.60$$

from the AC matrix,

$$[AC] = \frac{\Sigma (AC)^2}{(b)(n)} = \frac{(84)^2 + (62)^2 + \ldots + (79)^2 + (76)^2}{(2)(5)} = 3{,}322.20$$

and from the BC matrix,

$$[BC] = \frac{\Sigma (BC)^2}{(a)(n)} = \frac{(122)^2 + (127)^2 + (81)^2 + (112)^2}{(3)(5)} = 3{,}341.20$$

We next obtain the first term of the $SS_{A \times B \times C}$. The totals needed for this sum of squares are found in the ABC matrix (Table 19–6):

$$[ABC] = \frac{\Sigma (ABC)^2}{(n)} = \frac{(44)^2 + (40)^2 + \ldots + (37)^2 + (36)^2}{(5)} = 3,400.00$$

The final quantity needed for the $SS_{S/ABC}$ and the SS_T is the sum of the squared scores, which is found at the bottom of Table 19–6:

$$[Y] = \Sigma Y^2 = 3,484$$

These basic quantities and the patterns in which we combine them to calculate the sums of squares are entered in the second column of Table 19–8. The final steps in the analysis are summarized in the remaining columns of the table. The results of the F tests are given in the final column of the table. The important challenge now is to be able to assess the "meaning" of these various statistical comparisons.

Interpreting the Results

How do we interpret these results? Exactly how we proceed at this point depends on the logic of our design, the analyses we plan to evaluate, and the outcome of the statistical tests. The logic of our experimental design suggests certain ways to examine the data. The standard analysis we have just completed is usually only a preliminary step in the process. In the complete absence of theoretical anticipations, we would turn first to the test of the three-way interaction. If the $A \times B \times C$ in- teraction were significant, we would then consider analyses designed to illuminate the nature of this effect; if the interaction were not significant, we most likely would then consider the *two*-way interactions, which effectively removes one of the independent variables from consideration. We discuss this approach in Chap. 20.

The three-way interaction was not significant in our numerical example, but we did have some explicit expectations concerning its nature. That is, we were interested in whether a particular interaction found with the fifth-grade children — an interaction showing a significantly larger difference between the control and combined feedback conditions for the words of high emotional content than for the words of low emotional content — would be duplicated with high school seniors. The test of the $A \times B \times C$ interaction in this analysis was an *omnibus* test and, thus, did not focus on this particular aspect of the three-way interaction. We will consider a more appropriate analysis in Chap. 20.

19.5 ESTIMATING TREATMENT MAGNITUDE (OMEGA SQUARED)

We can easily adapt for the three-factor design the formulas in Chap. 10 for estimating relative treatment magnitude. Estimates of relative treatment magnitude, most typically omega squared, can help us interpret nonsignificant results.

Table 19-8 Summary of the Analysis

Source	Basic Ratio[a]	Sums of Squares	df	MS	F
Feedback (A)	[A] = 3,289.70	[A] − [T] = 33.63	2	16.82	9.61*
Emotionality (B)	[B] = 3,308.33	[B] − [T] = 52.26	1	52.26	29.86*
Grade (C)	[C] = 3,277.67	[C] − [T] = 21.60	1	21.60	12.34*
A × B	[AB] = 3,347.60	[AB] − [A] − [B] + [T] = 5.64	2	2.82	1.61
A × C	[AC] = 3,322.20	[AC] − [A] − [C] + [T] = 10.90	2	5.45	3.11
B × C	[BC] = 3,341.20	[BC] − [B] − [C] + [T] = 11.27	1	11.27	6.44*
A × B × C	[ABC] = 3,400.00	[ABC] − [AB] − [AC] − [BC] + [A] + [B] + [C] − [T] = 8.63	2	4.32	2.47
S/ABC	[Y] = 3,484	[Y] − [ABC] = 84.00	48	1.75	
Total	[T] = 3,256.07	[Y] − [T] = 227.93	59		

[a]Bracketed letters represent complete terms in computational formulas; a particular term is identified by the letter(s) appearing in the numerator.

*p < .05.

438

Standard Omega Squared

We distinguished between two ways of defining omega squared for a factorial design. The standard definition consists of an estimated variance component for the effect ($\hat{\sigma}^2_{effect}$) divided by the sum of the estimated variance components for all sources normally extracted in the analysis ($\hat{\sigma}^2_T$). That is,

$$\hat{\omega}^2_{effect} = \frac{\hat{\sigma}^2_{effect}}{\hat{\sigma}^2_T} \tag{19-4}$$

where, in the case of the three-factor design,

$$\hat{\sigma}^2_T = \hat{\sigma}^2_A + \hat{\sigma}^2_B + \hat{\sigma}^2_C + \hat{\sigma}_{A \times B} + \hat{\sigma}_{A \times C} + \hat{\sigma}_{B \times C} + \hat{\sigma}_{A \times B \times C} + \hat{\sigma}_{S/ABC} \tag{19-5}$$

Formulas for estimating variance components for treatment effects have the form

$$\hat{\sigma}^2_{effect} = \frac{df_{effect}(MS_{effect} - MS_{S/ABC})}{(a)(b)(c)(n)} \tag{19-6}$$

and the corresponding estimate for the error component is

$$\hat{\sigma}_{S/ABC} = MS_{S/ABC} \tag{19-7}$$

Partial Omega Squared

An alternative definition of estimated omega squared consists of a ratio that relates the variance component of the effect to a different denominator made up of the variance component of the effect and error. In symbols,

$$\hat{\omega}^2_{effect} = \frac{\hat{\sigma}^2_{effect}}{\hat{\sigma}^2_{effect} + \hat{\sigma}^2_{error}} \tag{19-8}$$

This estimate of relative treatment magnitude, called **partial omega squared**, has the advantage of not being directly influenced by the presence of other factorial effects. Everything else being equal, an estimated partial omega squared for the overall effect of factor A, for example, will be defined equivalently regardless of the number of factors with which it is manipulated. Substituting in Eq. (19–8), then, the partial omega squared for this effect ($\hat{\omega}^2_A$) is estimated by the following:

$$\frac{\hat{\sigma}^2_A}{\hat{\sigma}^2_A + \hat{\sigma}^2_{S/A}}, \quad \frac{\hat{\sigma}^2_A}{\hat{\sigma}^2_A + \hat{\sigma}^2_{S/AB}}, \quad \text{and} \quad \frac{\hat{\sigma}^2_A}{\hat{\sigma}^2_A + \hat{\sigma}^2_{S/ABC}},$$

for the one-, two-, and three-way factorial designs, respectively. Because of this property of consistency across designs, I prefer this measure to the standard estimated omega squared.

We were primarily interested in the three-way interaction, which was not significant in the overall analysis of variance. Nevertheless, we should still estimate partial omega squared since power may have been low in this example. Using Eq. (19–6), we find

$$\hat{\sigma}^2_{A \times B \times C} = \frac{df_{A \times B \times C} (MS_{A \times B \times C} - MS_{S/ABC})}{(a)(b)(c)(n)}$$

$$= \frac{2(4.32 - 1.75)}{(3)(2)(2)(5)} = \frac{5.14}{60} = .0857$$

and from Eq. (19–7) we have

$$\hat{\sigma}^2_{S/ABC} = MS_{S/ABC} = 1.75$$

Substituting in Eq. (19–8), we obtain

$$\hat{\omega}^2_{A \times B \times C} = \frac{\hat{\sigma}^2_{A \times B \times C}}{\hat{\sigma}^2_{A \times B \times C} + \hat{\sigma}^2_{S/ABC}} = \frac{.0857}{.0857 + 1.75} = .0467$$

This means that the three-way interaction produces an effect somewhere between "small" ($\hat{\omega}^2_{effect} = .01$) and "medium" ($\hat{\omega}^2_{effect} = .06$) and suggests that a three-way interaction may be present and that our experiment simply had insufficient power to detect it.[5]

19.6   USING POWER TO DETERMINE SAMPLE SIZE

Power determinations, as you will recall, provide a rational way of setting sample size (n). We considered procedures for determining sample size in Chap. 4 (pp. 76–80) for the single-factor design and in Chap. 10 (pp. 224–229) for the two-way factorial. These procedures may be adapted for the three-factor design. We will consider three possible approaches.

Using Population Deviations

The first procedure works with population means and deviations derived from them, which we will then use to estimate ϕ. We then use this quantity, you may recall, to determine power from the power charts for different trial values for sample size, which I call n'. The general formula for this estimate is given by

$$\phi^2_{effect} = \frac{(\text{no. obsn.})[\Sigma (\text{dev.})^2]}{(df_{effect} + 1)(\sigma^2_{error})} \tag{19–9}$$

where (no. obsn.) = the number of observations that will contribute to each basic deviation

Σ (dev.)^2 = the basic population deviations constituting the treatment effect in question

---

[5]The standard estimated omega squared is .0224, less than half the size of the value we obtained with the formula for partial estimated omega squared.

$$df_{effect} = \text{the } df \text{ associated with the treatment effects,}$$
$$\text{calculated in the usual fashion}$$
$$\sigma^2_{error} = \text{the population error variance}$$

The biggest stumbling block, of course, will be estimating the relevant population means from which the deviations are derived. If you are able to make realistic guesses for the population means and can estimate the population error variance, you can calculate the relevant deviations from formulas presented in Winer (1971, pp. 335–340).[6] I illustrated this procedure for the two-way interaction in Chap. 10 (pp. 226–227). After this point, you simply follow the trial-and-error procedure described in the earlier chapters for determining sample size.

Using a Pilot Study

A realistic alternative is to base your estimate of sample size on a pilot study that you wish to replicate. We can base our estimate on a formula presented in Chap. 10 (p. 228). With the three-way interaction in mind,

$$\phi^2_{A \times B \times C} = \left(\frac{n'}{n_{old}}\right)\left(\frac{df_{A \times B \times C}}{df_{A \times B \times C} + 1}\right)(F_{A \times B \times C} - 1) \tag{19-10}$$

where n' = the trial sample size
n_{old} = the sample size from the pilot study
$df_{A \times B \times C}$ = the df associated with the three-way interaction
$F_{A \times B \times C}$ = the F associated with that effect in the pilot study

Since we were particularly interested in the three-way interaction, which was present but not significant in the overall analysis, we might consider repeating the experiment with a new set of subjects. We can use the information from our first study to help us to determine an appropriate sample size for this replication.

To illustrate, we can use the information in Table 19–8 to calculate $\phi^2_{A \times B \times C}$. Substituting in Eq. (19–10), we find

$$\phi^2_{A \times B \times C} = \left(\frac{n'}{5}\right)\left(\frac{2}{2 + 1}\right)(2.47 - 1) = \frac{(n')(2.94)}{15} = .1960\, n' \tag{19-11}$$

Suppose we want to set power at .80. To start the process with a reasonable trial sample size, we can rearrange Eq. (19–11) in terms of n'; that is,

$$n' = \frac{\phi^2_{A \times B \times C}}{.1960} \tag{19-12}$$

[6]The deviation for the three-way interaction, for example, is given by

$$(\alpha\beta\gamma)_{ijk} = \mu_{ijk} - \mu_{ij} - \mu_{ik} - \mu_{jk} + \mu_i + \mu_j + \mu_k - \mu_T$$

where μ_{ijk} = a given cell mean
$\mu_{ij}, \mu_{ik},$ and μ_{jk} = the relevant marginal means from the two-way matrices
$\mu_i, \mu_j,$ and μ_k = the relevant means reflecting the main effects
μ_T = the grand mean

and then use the Pearson-Hartley power charts to determine a reasonable value for ϕ. We obtain our first trial sample size by substituting this ϕ into Eq. (19–12) and solving for n'.

Let's see how this is done. We turn to the second power chart in Table A–4 ($df_{num.}$ = 2) and find the ϕ associated with a = .05, power = .80, and $df_{denom.}$ = 60. This value is ϕ = 1.82. Entering this value in Eq. (19–12), we find

$$n' = \frac{(1.82)^2}{.1960} = 16.9$$

We will use 17 for our first trial sample size. Substituting this value into Eq. (19–11), we find

$$\phi^2_{A \times B \times C} = (.1960)(17) = 3.332$$

$$\phi_{A \times B \times C} = \sqrt{3.332} = 1.825$$

We now need to determine the power associated with $\phi = 1.825$. Returning to the power chart, but using the power function at dfdenom. = ∞ because the df for this sample size would be $df_{S/ABC}$ = 192, we find power slightly higher than .80. A sample size of n = 16 should be about right.

Using Partial Omega Squared

Cohen (1977) presents a method for determining sample size that is based on some estimate of relative treatment magnitude (pp. 396–400). Suppose we wanted to detect a three-way interaction in this example that has a partial omega squared of at least ω^2 = .06 ("medium"). In order to use Cohen's special tables we need to calculate f, where

$$f^2 = \frac{\omega^2}{1 - \omega^2} = \frac{.06}{1 - .06} = .0638$$

$$f = \sqrt{.0638} = .253$$

With this information and Cohen's tables, I find n = 13.75, or 14.

19.7   EXERCISES[7]

1. Following are the outcomes of 10 three-way factorial experiments. The design in each example is the same—a 2 × 2 × 2 factorial. The main intent of this problem is to test your ability to identify three-way interactions in a set of data. Indicate the presence or absence of a triple interaction for each example. (Please assume for this problem that the means are "error-free.") When the three-way interaction is not present, indicate which, if any, of the two-way interactions are present. Finally, are there any main effects that may be interpreted unambiguously in any of these examples?

[7]The answers to these problems are found in Appendix B.

	TREATMENT CONDITIONS							
	a_1 b_1 c_1	a_1 b_1 c_2	a_1 b_2 c_1	a_1 b_2 c_2	a_2 b_1 c_1	a_2 b_1 c_2	a_2 b_2 c_1	a_2 b_2 c_2
EXAMPLES								
1	1	1	1	1	3	3	3	3
2	2	2	1	1	3	3	2	2
3	3	2	2	1	4	3	3	2
4	1	1	3	3	3	3	1	1
5	1	2	2	3	2	3	1	2
6	2	0	1	1	4	2	3	3
7	2	4	1	3	0	3	1	4
8	2	3	1	4	0	4	1	3
9	2	2	1	1	4	4	3	4
10	1	0	2	3	2	3	1	0

2. Consider the following results of a $3 \times 3 \times 2$ factorial experiment in which $n = 4$ subjects are randomly assigned to each of the treatment conditions:

TREATMENT CONDITIONS																	
a_1 b_1 c_1	a_1 b_1 c_2	a_1 b_2 c_1	a_1 b_2 c_2	a_1 b_3 c_1	a_1 b_3 c_2	a_2 b_1 c_1	a_2 b_1 c_2	a_2 b_2 c_1	a_2 b_2 c_2	a_2 b_3 c_1	a_2 b_3 c_2	a_3 b_1 c_1	a_3 b_1 c_2	a_3 b_2 c_1	a_3 b_2 c_2	a_3 b_3 c_1	a_3 b_3 c_2
7	7	2	2	4	1	10	6	4	1	7	1	13	12	9	7	8	7
4	5	4	3	3	3	7	5	6	3	4	3	10	13	8	6	5	7
5	5	3	4	0	2	6	5	3	4	5	3	13	11	9	7	6	4
6	6	3	1	3	2	8	6	5	5	5	0	8	12	10	6	6	6

   a. Conduct an analysis of variance on these data. Save your calculations for problem 1 of the exercises for Chap. 20.
   b. Given the outcome of the analysis, to what sources of variance would you now give close attention?

3. Suppose a $4 \times 3 \times 2$ factorial experiment is conducted. The sums for the treatment conditions, which are based on $n = 5$ subjects, follow.

	c_1					c_2			
	a_1	a_2	a_3	a_4		a_1	a_2	a_3	a_4
b_1	35	46	49	55	b_1	37	49	56	65
b_2	42	51	55	62	b_2	40	38	44	42
b_3	29	40	45	49	b_3	27	23	19	14

   a. Conduct an analysis of variance on these data. (Assume $MS_{S/ABC} = 1.86$.) Save your calculations for problem 2 of the exercises for Chap. 20.
   b. Given the outcome of the analysis, to what sources of variance would you now give close attention?

20

The Three-Factor Design

Simple Effects and Interaction Comparisons

Further Analyses
Extending the Analysis to Lower-Order Effects

Because of the factorial arrangement of three independent variables, the detailed analysis of the three-factor design can be quite complex. We will consider two approaches or strategies for asking analytical questions of our data. The first approach, the *analysis of simple effects*, attempts to isolate the source or sources of a higher-order interaction in terms of simple effects. The second approach, the *analysis of interaction comparisons*, accomplishes this same goal by assessing the contribution of specific single-df comparisons to interactions observed with the three-factor design.

20.1   ANALYZING SIMPLE EFFECTS: AN OVERVIEW

You will recall that a significant interaction in a two-factor design means that the simple effects of either independent variable are not the same at all levels of the other independent variable. For that reason, the statistical assessment of simple effects, which will indicate which of these simple effects are significant and which are not, represents an important analytical tool for examining the nature of the $A \times B$ interaction. The analysis of simple effects serves the same function in the three-factor design, except that more analytical questions are possible because of the complexity of the three-way interaction and because there are three two-way interactions that may also enter the picture.

The Critical Nature of the Three-Way Interaction

Although there will always be exceptions, all analyses begin with the three-way interaction. This will be true whether we plan to keep our independent variables intact, at least initially, or to focus on specific interaction comparisons instead. In either case, the general strategy is to test the three-way interaction and to move to additional analyses depending on the outcome of this test. You should be familiar with the pattern by now:

> If the interaction is significant, proceed with an analysis of the simple effects contributing to the effect.
> If the interaction is not significant, collapse the data over one of the factors and examine the significance of the next lower factorial treatment effect.

Table 20–1   Representation of the Analysis of the Simple Effects of the $A \times B \times C$ Interaction

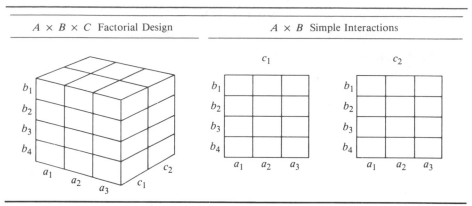

| $A \times B \times C$ Factorial Design | $A \times B$ Simple Interactions |

Let's see how this would apply to a $3 \times 4 \times 2$ factorial design. The design is diagrammed on the left of Table 20–1 as a rectangular solid in which each cube represents one of 24 treatment combinations created by this design. A significant interaction means that the simple effects contributing to it are not all the same. The next step consists of assessing the interactions between any two of the independent variables (I selected factors A and B) separately at each level of the third independent variable (factor C). The result is the arrangement diagrammed on the right—two separate $A \times B$ designs, one at level c_1 and the other at level c_2. At this point, the analysis parallels the one for an actual two-factor design, even though the analysis is set within the context of a three-factor design.

The interaction itself is called a **simple interaction** to distinguish it from an actual two-way interaction in a two-way design. More formally, we will refer to the simple interaction on the left as the "simple $A \times B$ interaction at level c_1," and the one on the right as the "simple $A \times B$ interaction at level c_2." In short, an analysis of a significant three-way interaction consists of a set of two-way analyses in which the independent variable not involved (factor C in this example) is held constant. A significant simple interaction will often be analyzed further, as you will see when we discuss the procedure in more detail.

A Nonsignificant Three-Way Interaction

The lack of a significant three-way interaction means that the results of the experiment can be safely interpreted by considering the three independent variables two at a time, rather than all three simultaneously. In a sense, the three-way design is collapsed into less complex two-way designs for analysis and interpretive purposes, in the same way we focused on main effects in the two-factor design when the $A \times B$ interaction was not significant. I will refer to a two-factor design created by disregarding one of the factors in a three-way design as an *average* two-way design to distinguish the information produced from it by an *actual* two-factor design, such as those we considered in earlier chapters.

Once we have reached this point in the analysis, we apply the same logic that would be appropriate for an actual two-factor design. More specifically, we assess the average two-way interaction, and if significant, we proceed to examine the simple effects of one of the factors, with the other held constant, and if not, we examine the main effects of the two independent variables.

Comment

I do not intend to imply that this overall strategy represents a general blueprint or obligatory plan for the analysis of three-factor experiments. On the contrary, statistical analyses are the servants of the researcher and should be based on the analyses that are relevant to the research questions developed in the initial planning stages of an experiment. I will now consider how these different analyses are actually conducted.

20.2   ANALYZING SIMPLE INTERACTIONS

As I have noted already, analyses of simple interactions are undertaken when the three-way interaction is significant. The analysis is nothing more than an analysis of the interaction of two of the independent variables at each of the levels of the third. There are three ways we can perform this analysis:

The simple $A \times B$ interactions at the separate levels of factor C
The simple $A \times C$ interactions at the separate levels of factor B
The simple $B \times C$ interactions at the separate levels of factor A

The particular breakdown you choose for the analysis depends on the most meaningful way for you to think about the three-way interaction.

The Analysis

I will discuss the analysis with the data from Chap. 19 in which factor A had three feedback conditions (none, positive, and negative), factor B had two types of learning materials (low and high emotionality), and factor C had two grade levels (fifth-grade children and high-school seniors). For the purposes of this discussion, let's assume that the three-way interaction had been significant, even though it was not (see Table 19–8, p. 438). We will examine the simple interaction involving feedback and emotionality for the fifth-grade children. The individual cell sums, which are based on $n = 5$ subjects, are presented in Table 20–2.

The analysis of this simple interaction quite literally consists of a two-way analysis of variance conducted on the data obtained with the fifth-grade children only. To emphasize this point, I will use the formulas from Chap. 10 to calculate the sums of squares, using quotation marks to distinguish the sums from this part of the ABC matrix from the one used in an actual $A \times B$ design:

Table 20–2   Matrix of Sums for the Analysis of the Simple $A \times B$ at c_1

	Control (a_1)	Positive (a_2)	Negative (a_3)	Sum
Low (b_1)	44	40	38	122
High (b_2)	40	22	19	81
Sum	84	62	57	203

$$SS_{A \times B \, at \, c_1} = \frac{\Sigma \, (\text{``}AB\text{''})^2}{n} - \frac{\Sigma \, (\text{``}A\text{''})^2}{(b)(n)} - \frac{\Sigma \, (\text{``}B\text{''})^2}{(a)(n)} + \frac{(\text{``}T\text{''})^2}{(a)(b)(n)} \quad (20\text{–}1)$$

Except for the quotation marks, Eq. (20–1) is identical to the formula for $SS_{A \times B}$ in Table 10–4 (p. 211). Substituting the sums from Table 20–2 in Eq. (20–1), we find

$$SS_{A \times B \, at \, c_1} = \frac{(44)^2 + (40)^2 + \ldots + (22)^2 + (19)^2}{5} - \frac{(84)^2 + (62)^2 + (57)^2}{(2)(5)}$$

$$- \frac{(122)^2 + (81)^2}{(3)(5)} + \frac{(203)^2}{(3)(2)(5)}$$

$$= 1{,}485.00 - 1{,}414.90 - 1{,}429.67 + 1{,}373.63 = 14.06$$

The degrees of freedom for this sum of squares are the same as they would be in an actual two-factor design, namely,

$$df_{A \times B \, at \, c_1} = (a - 1)(b - 1) \quad (20\text{–}2)$$

$$= (3 - 1)(2 - 1) = 2$$

The mean square is obtained by dividing the sum of squares by the appropriate number of degrees of freedom:

$$MS_{A \times B \, at \, c_1} = \frac{SS_{A \times B \, at \, c_1}}{df_{A \times B \, at \, c_1}} \quad (20\text{–}3)$$

$$= \frac{14.06}{2} = 7.03$$

The F ratio is given by the formula

$$F = \frac{MS_{A \times B \, at \, c_1}}{MS_{S/ABC}} \quad (20\text{–}4)$$

unless there is heterogeneity of within-groups variance.[1] The $MS_{S/ABC}$ from this example was 1.75. The F becomes

---

[1]Under these circumstances, separate error terms based on the pooled within-group mean squares should be calculated for each of the AB matrices at the different levels of factor C. In this case, the analysis is exactly a two-way analysis, including the error term. See also the relevant discussion in Chap. 10 (pp. 220–221).

$$F = \frac{7.03}{1.75} = 4.02$$

With $df_{num.} = 2$ and $df_{denom.} = 48$, this F is significant.

Further Analyses

A significant simple interaction suggests the same sort of analysis that would follow a significant $A \times B$ interaction in a two-factor design, namely, the analysis of the simple effects of one of the independent variables conducted separately at the different levels of the other independent variable. At this point, then, we are going over familiar ground. It does not matter that the data come from a three-factor design; as we have seen with the simple $A \times B$ interaction, the formulas correspond to those appropriate for an actual two-factor design.

To illustrate, let's consider the effects of feedback (factor A) for the list of words with high emotional content (b_2). The treatment sums for this analysis are now equivalent to a *single* factor design. Isolating the second row from Table 20–2, we obtain

a_1	a_2	a_3	Sum
40	22	19	81

Treating this matrix as a single-factor design gives us

$$SS_{A \text{ at } b_2c_1} = \frac{\Sigma \, (\text{``}A\text{''})^2}{n} - \frac{(\text{``}T\text{''})^2}{(a)(n)} \tag{20-5}$$

$$= \frac{(40)^2 + (22)^2 + (19)^2}{5} - \frac{(81)^2}{(3)(5)}$$

$$= 489.00 - 437.40 = 51.60$$

The degrees of freedom are

$$df_{A \text{ at } b_2c_1} = a - 1 \tag{20-6}$$

$$= 3 - 1 = 2$$

The mean square becomes $MS_{A \text{ at } b_2c_1} = 51.60/2 = 25.80$, and the resulting F is

$$F = \frac{25.80}{1.75} = 14.74$$

which is significant ($df_{num.} = 2$, $df_{denom.} = 48$).

As you saw in the context of a two-factor design, the discovery of a significant simple effect will often initiate a search for meaningful comparisons that are responsible for the significant F. It is an easy matter to extend the analysis to a three-factor design. Several single-df comparisons suggest themselves: positive versus negative feedback, control versus combined feedback, control versus positive feedback, and control versus negative feedback. I will look at the comparison between the control and combined feedback conditions. The means associated with these conditions are 8.0 for the control, 4.4 for the positive feedback condition, and 3.8 for the negative feedback conditions. The difference between the control and combined feedback conditions is

$$\hat{\psi}_{A \text{ at } b_2 c_1} = (1)(8.0) + (-\tfrac{1}{2})(4.4) + (-\tfrac{1}{2})(3.8) = 3.9$$

We can calculate the sum of squares for this comparison by substituting into an adaptation of Eq. (11–12):

$$SS_{A_{comp} \text{ at } b_2 c_1} = \frac{n(\hat{\psi}_{A \text{ at } b_2 c_1})^2}{\Sigma \, c_i^2} \tag{20–7}$$

$$= \frac{5(3.9)^2}{(1)^2 + (-\tfrac{1}{2})^2 + (-\tfrac{1}{2})^2} = \frac{76.05}{1.5} = 50.70$$

This comparison has 1 df. The F,

$$F = \frac{MS_{A_{comp. \text{ at } b_2 c_1}}}{MS_{S/ABC}} = \frac{50.70}{1.75} = 28.97$$

is significant.

Summary

Although the analysis I have just illustrated was not justified because of the non-significant $A \times B \times C$ interaction, you can still appreciate the systematic way in which this strategy approaches the analysis of a significant three-way interaction. If the three-way interaction is significant, we know that the simple two-way interactions are not equal. To identify the reasons for this significance, we then proceed to determine which of these interactions are significant and which are not. Usually, we will continue this process of further analysis when we discover a significant effect. In the example, we found a significant, simple two-way interaction between feedback and emotionality for the fifth-grade children ($A \times B$ at level c_1), which suggests that the effects of feedback in this particular analysis are not the same for words of low and high emotional content. Further analysis of the simple effects of the feedback variable in this subset of the data helps to identify the factors responsible for the interaction effects.

20.3   ANALYSES FOLLOWING A NONSIGNIFICANT THREE-WAY INTERACTION

The three two-way interactions in an $A \times B \times C$ design are average interactions, in the same way that the main effects represent the average effects of the independent variable. With a significant triple interaction, anything we may say about the two-way interactions and the main effects will be colored by the presence of the higher-order interaction. On the other hand, if the $A \times B \times C$ interaction is not significant, we can consider the two-way interactions directly, without ambiguity.

Analyzing the Two-Way Interactions

With a nonsignificant three-way interaction, the design—for all practical purposes—becomes three two-factor designs. Again, we are on familiar territory. We may now analyze each two-way arrangement of the data in exactly the same way we would analyze these arrangements if they had been produced by an actual two-way experiment.

Analyzing Simple Effects. To illustrate, let's look at the average $A \times B$ interaction, which again is not statistically justified because it was not significant in the overall analysis conducted in Chap. 19 (see Table 19–8, p. 438). A significant two-way interaction would mean that the simple effects of one of the factors would depend on the levels of the other factor. Thus, if the interaction had been significant, we would probably evaluate the significance of these simple effects. The computational formula for the simple effect of factor A at level b_1, for example, took the following form in Chap. 11:

$$SS_{A \text{ at } b_1} = \frac{\Sigma (AB_{i1})^2}{n} - \frac{B_1^2}{(a)(n)}$$

The only change needed to adapt this formula to the three-way factorial is in the denominators, to accommodate the fact that each AB sum contains $(c)(n)$ observations—instead of n—and the B_1 sum contains $(a)(c)(n)$ observations—instead of $(a)(n)$:

$$SS_{A \text{ at } b_1} = \frac{\Sigma (AB_{i1})^2}{(c)(n)} - \frac{B_1^2}{(a)(c)(n)} \tag{20-8}$$

The new denominators, of course, reflect the operation of a familiar rule: We divide by the number of observations contributing to the basic total. Substituting the relevant sums from the first row of the AB matrix in Table 19–7 (p. 436), we find

$$SS_{A \text{ at } b_1} = \frac{(89)^2 + (82)^2 + (78)^2}{(2)(5)} - \frac{(249)^2}{(3)(2)(5)}$$

$$= 2,072.90 - 2,066.70 = 6.20$$

This sum of squares is associated with $a - 1 = 2$ *df.* Thus,

$$MS_{A \text{ at } b_1} = \frac{6.20}{2} = 3.10$$

The error term for this analysis comes from overall analysis ($MS_{S/ABC} = 1.75$). The $F = 3.10/1.75 = 1.77$ is not significant.

Analyzing Simple Comparisons. If the feedback variable (factor A) had been significant, we probably would have examined various simple comparisons relevant to this manipulation. The procedures outlined in Chap. 11 would be followed here and the formulas adapted in the same manner to reflect the actual number of observations contributing to the means being compared.

Analyzing Main Effects

Our interest in the main effects depends on the status of the interactions. If the three-way interaction were significant, we would have less interest in the lower-order effects. If this interaction were not significant, our interest would shift to the average two-way interactions; again, our interest in the main effects depends on the status of *these* interactions as well. If none of the average two-way interactions is significant either, we will be vitally interested in the outcome of all three main effects. If one of the average two-way interactions is significant, we may have difficulty interpreting either main effect of the two interacting factors, but we can analyze and safely interpret the *noninteracting* main effect. If two of these interactions are significant, we may have little systematic interest in any of the three main effects since any interpretation of each one must be qualified in view of the significant interactions. Our numerical example showed only the $B \times C$ interaction to be significant (see Table 19–8). This would suggest that the main effect of the feedback variable could be interpreted unambiguously.

20.4   INTERACTION COMPARISONS: AN OVERVIEW

The analyses we have considered so far begin with the overall factorial design and systematically examine the results from the most complex level (the three-way interaction) to the least (the main effects). Single-df comparisons come into play only when significant variation is discovered. An alternative approach views the analysis differently: Theoretical or other considerations suggest a number of smaller, more focused three-way designs that I will collectively refer to as **interaction comparisons**. Your first introduction to interaction comparisons occurred in Chap. 12, in the context of the two-factor design. The potential for interaction comparisons in the three-factor design is considerably greater than in the two-factor case, as you will see in a moment.

A Classification of Interaction Comparisons

Consider the three-factor design depicted in Table 20–3 — a $3 \times 3 \times 3$ factorial. At the top of the table, I have placed X's in all the cells of the ABC matrix to emphasize the fact that all treatment conditions contribute to the overall three-way interaction extracted by the standard analysis of variance and to the undifferentiated character of this interaction.

The first level at which the triple interaction is refined occurs when one of the independent variables is viewed in terms of one or more single-df comparisons. I have chosen factor A and a comparison between levels a_1 and a_2 to illustrate this case. Under these circumstances, level a_3 is entirely disregarded in the calculation of the resulting $A_{comp.} \times B \times C$ interaction, with the result that an ABC matrix is produced in which only part of the information available for the three-way interaction is relevant. This situation is illustrated by the absence of X's in the cells associated with level a_3 in the second ABC matrix in Table 20–3. In this case, a

Table 20–3   Systematic Representation of Interaction Comparisons

	c_1			c_2			c_3		
	a_1	a_2	a_3	a_1	a_2	a_3	a_1	a_2	a_3
$A \times B \times C$ Interaction — b_1	X	X	X	X	X	X	X	X	X
b_2	X	X	X	X	X	X	X	X	X
b_3	X	X	X	X	X	X	X	X	X

	1	−1	0	1	−1	0	1	−1	0
$A_{comp.} \times B \times C$ Interaction	X	X		X	X		X	X	
	X	X		X	X		X	X	
	X	X		X	X		X	X	

		1	−1	0	1	−1	0	1	−1	0
$A_{comp.} \times B_{comp.} \times C$ Interaction	0									
	1	X	X		X	X		X	X	
	−1	X	X		X	X		X	X	

		1			0			−1		
		1	−1	0	1	−1	0	1	−1	0
$A_{comp.} \times B_{comp.} \times C_{comp.}$ Interaction — 0										
1		X	X					X	X	
−1		X	X					X	X	

significant three-way interaction will reflect the interaction of $A_{comp.}$ with the other two independent variables—a more focused picture of the interaction of the three factors than that provided by the overall $A \times B \times C$ interaction.

The next level of refinement occurs when two of the independent variables are simultaneously viewed as single-*df* comparisons, a situation illustrated in the third ABC matrix in the table. In this case, factor B is represented by a comparison between levels b_2 and b_3, and factor A continues to be represented by the original comparison (a_1 versus a_2). The cells involved in this comparison are again indicated by X's. This level of interaction comparison produces an $A_{comp.} \times B_{comp.} \times C$ interaction.

The highest level of refinement occurs when all three factors are expressed as comparisons to produce an $A_{comp.} \times B_{comp.} \times C_{comp.}$ interaction, which is reflected in the last ABC matrix in the table. Here, factor C is represented by a comparison between levels c_1 and c_3, and the other two comparisons remain as before. The focus of this interaction is maximal, the three-way interaction being expressed in its simplest, most analytical state, as shown by the eight X's, namely, a $2 \times 2 \times 2$ factorial design. This fundamental component of the three-way interaction will be called an **interaction contrast** of the three-way interaction and given a special symbol, $\hat{\psi}_{A \times B \times C}$. This symbol emphasizes the fact that an interaction contrast can be expressed numerically as the difference between pairs of means—which you will see in the next section—and as such, represents a facet or component of interaction that can be subdivided no further, since the *df* for an interaction contrast is 1.

Comment

We will focus on the interaction contrast for two reasons: One is its special analytical properties; the other is that it is probably the most common type of interaction comparison in the behavioral sciences. The reason is simple: Most three-factor designs are designed with only one of the independent variables represented by more than two levels. This means that all interaction comparisons must be interaction contrasts. A $4 \times 2 \times 2$ design, for example, can yield only interaction contrasts— factor *A* supplies the single-*df* comparisons and the other two factors are already single-*df* comparisons by default. Our numerical example, which is a design of this sort, will illustrate how this occurs.

20.5   ANALYZING INTERACTION CONTRASTS

The analytical quality of an interaction contrast lies in its conceptualization, which produces a representation of interaction that can be reduced no further. Once conceptualized, however, the $2 \times 2 \times 2$ factorial is analyzed in the same way as the overall $A \times B \times C$ design. That is, we will examine the three-way interaction first and conduct additional *F* tests depending on the outcome of this test. The procedure exactly parallels the one considered in Secs. 20.1 through 20.3.[2]

Evaluating the Three-Way Interaction Contrast

Let's return to our numerical example. In this design, only factor *A* can generate actual single-*df* comparisons (that is, $a = 3$) since the other two factors are single-*df* comparisons by default ($b = c = 2$). At the outset, we could consider a total of four interaction contrasts:

> A comparison between the positive and negative feedback conditions
> A comparison between the control condition and the combined feedback conditions
> A comparison between the control and the positive feedback conditions
> A comparison between the control and the negative feedback conditions

Each comparison forms the basis for a different interaction contrast. We will examine a comparison between the control and combined feedback conditions.

The nature of this interaction contrast is illustrated in Table 20–4. The ma-

---

[2]For a different approach to these calculations, see Keppel (1982, pp. 320–323).

Table 20–4   Analysis of an Interaction Contrast

| | Fifth Grade | | | | Seniors | | |
	Control	Combined Feedback	Diff		Control	Combined Feedback	Diff
Low Emot.	8.8	7.8	1.0	**Low Emot.**	9.0	8.2	.8
High Emot.	8.0	4.1	3.9	**High Emot.**	7.8	7.3	.5

$$\hat{\psi}_{A \times B \text{ at } c_1} = 1.0 - 3.9 = -2.9 \qquad\qquad \hat{\psi}_{A \times B \text{ at } c_2} = .8 - .5 = .3$$

$$\hat{\psi}_{A \times B \times C} = -2.9 - .3 = -3.2$$

trix on the left permits us to examine the interaction between the control and combined feedback conditions ($A_{comp.}$) and the emotional content of the words ($B_{comp.}$ = low versus high) for the fifth-grade children. You can see that there is an interaction because the difference between the control and the combined feedback appears to be appreciably smaller for words of low emotional content ($8.8 - 7.8 = 1.0$) than for words of high emotional content ($8.0 - 4.1 = 3.9$). The interaction effect for this matrix is $\hat{\psi}_{A \times B \text{ at } c_1} = 1.0 - 3.9 = -2.9$. What about the matrix on the right, where we can examine the corresponding interaction for the high school seniors? In this case, the interaction is smaller and in opposite direction; that is, $\hat{\psi}_{A \times B \text{ at } c_2} = .8 - .5 = .3$.

A three-way interaction means that the simple interactions of two of the factors are not the same at all levels of the third. In this case, we are comparing the simple interaction for the fifth-grade children (-2.9) against the simple interaction for high school seniors ($.3$):

$$\hat{\psi}_{A \times B \times C} = \hat{\psi}_{A \times B \text{ at } c_1} - \hat{\psi}_{A \times B \text{ at } c_2} \tag{20–9}$$
$$= -2.9 - .3 = -3.2$$

We translate this interaction effect into a sum of squares by using a familiar set of operations, namely,

$$SS_{A_{comp.} \times B_{comp.} \times C_{comp.}} = \frac{n(\hat{\psi}_{A \times B \times C})^2}{(\Sigma\, c_i^2)(\Sigma\, c_j^2)(\Sigma\, c_k^2)} \tag{20–10}$$

where $\Sigma\, c_i^2 = (1)^2 + (-\frac{1}{2})^2 + (-\frac{1}{2})^2 = 1.5$
$\qquad\quad\, \Sigma\, c_j^2 = (1)^2 + (-1)^2 = 2$
$\qquad\quad\, \Sigma\, c_k^2 = (1)^2 + (-1)^2 = 2$

For this example,

$$SS_{A_{comp.} \times B_{comp.} \times C_{comp.}} = \frac{5(-3.2)^2}{(1.5)(2)(2)} = \frac{51.20}{6} = 8.53$$

You may recall that we can calculate an interaction contrast by using special interaction coefficients. In the present context, these coefficients (d_{ijk}) are obtained by calculating the triple products of appropriate coefficients from the three comparisons for each cell in the original ABC matrix. The interaction coefficients for this interaction contrast are presented in Table 20–5. The interaction coefficient

Table 20–5   Coefficients for the Interaction Contrast

			(c_1)						(c_2)	
c_k:			1						-1	
	c_j	c_i:	(a_1) 1	(a_2) $-\frac{1}{2}$	(a_3) $-\frac{1}{2}$	c_j	c_i:	(a_1) 1	(a_2) $-\frac{1}{2}$	(a_3) $-\frac{1}{2}$
(b_1)	1		1	$-\frac{1}{2}$	$-\frac{1}{2}$	(b_1)	1	-1	$\frac{1}{2}$	$\frac{1}{2}$
(b_2)	-1		-1	$\frac{1}{2}$	$\frac{1}{2}$	(b_2)	-1	1	$-\frac{1}{2}$	$-\frac{1}{2}$

for cell $a_3b_1c_2$, for example, is found by multiplying the coefficient associated with level a_3 $(-\frac{1}{2})$ by the coefficients associated with level b_1 (1) and level c_2 (-1); that is, $d_{3,1,2} = (-\frac{1}{2})(1)(-1) = \frac{1}{2}$. The interaction effect is the sum of the treatment means weighted by the interaction coefficients:

$$\hat{\psi}_{A \times B \times C} = \Sigma (d_{ijk})(\overline{Y}_{A_i B_j C_k}) \tag{20–11}$$

Substituting the values for the interaction coefficients (d_{ijk}) from Table 20–5 and the corresponding values for the cell means $(\overline{Y}_{A_i B_j C_k})$ from Table 19–5 (p. 434), we have

$$\begin{aligned}
\hat{\psi}_{A \times B \times C} = {}& (1)(8.8) + (-\tfrac{1}{2})(8.0) + (-\tfrac{1}{2})(7.6) + (-1)(8.0) + (\tfrac{1}{2})(4.4) \\
& + (\tfrac{1}{2})(3.8) + (-1)(9.0) + (\tfrac{1}{2})(8.4) + (\tfrac{1}{2})(8.0) + (1)(7.8) \\
& + (-\tfrac{1}{2})(7.4) + (-\tfrac{1}{2})(7.2) \\
= {}& -3.2
\end{aligned}$$

which is identical to the one we calculated with Eq. (20–9). The sum of squares for this interaction contrast becomes

$$\begin{aligned}
SS_{A_{comp.} \times B_{comp.} \times C_{comp.}} &= \frac{n(\hat{\psi}_{A \times B \times C})^2}{\Sigma d_{ijk}^2} \tag{20–12} \\
&= \frac{5(-3.2)^2}{(1)^2 + (-\tfrac{1}{2})^2 + \ldots + (-\tfrac{1}{2})^2 + (-\tfrac{1}{2})^2} \\
&= \frac{51.20}{6} = 8.53
\end{aligned}$$

which is identical to the value obtained with Eq. (20–10).

This interaction contrast has 1 df and the error term is $MS_{S/ABC} = 1.75$. Thus,

$$\begin{aligned}
F &= \frac{MS_{A_{comp.} \times B_{comp.} \times C_{comp.}}}{MS_{S/ABC}} \tag{20–13} \\
&= \frac{8.53}{1.75} = 4.87
\end{aligned}$$

which is significant.

Please note what has happened. The standard analysis of variance conducted in Chap. 19 produced a nonsignificant three-way interaction (see p. 438), whereas the present analysis reveals a *significant interaction contrast*. This demonstration illustrates the value of interaction comparisons: A significant interaction contrast may be masked by the averaging that takes place when we test an *omnibus* effect. This interaction contrast was an obvious candidate for analysis, given the basic logic underlying the decision to include a control and two feedback conditions in the choice of levels to constitute factor A. Why would we include this particular arrangement of conditions if we were not interested in comparisons such as this one? The interaction contrast focuses directly on the interaction of this comparison with the other two represented in this design.

Further Analyses

A significant three-way interaction means that the simple two-way interactions are different. As an example of the next step, then, we will evaluate the significance of the interactions between $A_{comp.}$ (control versus combined feedback) and $B_{comp.}$ (low versus high emotionality) separately at each level of $C_{comp.}$ —once at c_1 (fifth-grade children) and once at c_2 (high school seniors). An inspection of Table 20–4 suggests that the simple interaction will be significant for the fifth-grade children but not for the seniors.

We can conduct this analysis easily with the information we already have at hand. Table 20–4, for example, gives the two simple interaction effects, and Table 20–5 provides the appropriate coefficients. To illustrate with the data from the fifth-grade children (c_1), we have

$$SS_{A_{comp.} \times B_{comp.} \text{ at } c_1} = \frac{n(\hat{\psi}_{A \times B \text{ at } c_1})^2}{\Sigma \, d^2 \text{ at } c_1} \tag{20–14}$$

$$= \frac{5(-2.9)^2}{(1)^2 + (-\frac{1}{2})^2 + (-\frac{1}{2})^2 + (-1)^2 + (\frac{1}{2})^2 + (\frac{1}{2})^2}$$

$$= \frac{42.05}{3} = 14.02$$

This interaction is significant ($F = 14.02/1.75 = 8.01$). Without showing the calculations, the corresponding simple interaction for the seniors is not significant ($F = .15/1.75 = .09$).

This analysis indicates that the significant interaction contrast has resulted from a significant simple interaction between $A_{comp.}$ and $B_{comp.}$ for the fifth-grade children and a nonsignificant corresponding interaction for the seniors. The final step is to analyze the significant simple interaction more closely for details of its nature. An inspection of Table 20–4 suggests that the simple $A_{comp.}$ for the words of low emotional content (1.0) will not be significant, whereas the simple $A_{comp.}$ for the words of high emotional content (3.9) will be significant. Again, the analysis is easily accomplished with the information in Tables 20–4 and 20–5. I will illustrate the calculations with the data from b_2 (high emotionality):

$$SS_{A_{comp.} \text{ at } b_2 c_1} = \frac{n(\hat{\psi}_{A \text{ at } b_2 c_1})^2}{\Sigma \, d^2 \text{ at } b_2 c_1} \tag{20–15}$$

$$= \frac{5\,(3.9)^2}{(-1)^2 + (\frac{1}{2})^2 + (\frac{1}{2})^2} = \frac{76.05}{1.5} = 50.70$$

This difference is significant ($F = 50.70/1.75 = 28.97$); the corresponding difference for the words of low emotional content is not significant ($F = 3.33/1.75 = 1.90$).

Extending the Analysis to Lower-Order Effects

The general strategy we have been following in this chapter has been to follow a *nonsignificant* three-way interaction with an analysis of the average two-way interactions and of the main effects. We certainly can extend this approach to the analysis of interaction comparisons. All you need to do is to work with the two-way matrix of means and adapt the formulas from Chap. 12 and the two-factor design to the analysis of data from a three-factor design. All this process requires is to adjust for the appropriate numbers of observations (illustrated in Sec. 20.3).

In most cases, however, you will have little interest in these analyses. One reason is that your focus is on the three-way interaction contrast, which is how you planned your analysis; the significance of this interaction and the pattern of simple effects contributing to its significance are the important outcomes of this analysis. Another reason concerns the meaning of two-way interactions and main effects that involve only a portion of the data. The situation is complex, however, and you will want to give considerable thought to the usefulness of these analyses under these circumstances.

20.6   ANALYZING PARTIAL FACTORIALS

Although I have focused on the analysis of interaction contrasts, there will be times when not all of your independent variables will lend themselves to single-df comparisons, at least as planned comparisons. Under these circumstances, you may wish to assess the significance of several partial interactions instead of interaction contrasts. I will not discuss these analyses in this book. If the partial interactions you contemplate involve pairwise comparisons—such as those illustrated by the two middle examples in Table 20–4 (p. 453), you can simply isolate the relevant cells from the *ABC* matrix and analyze the selected data set, using the formulas for the standard analyses. Consider the first partial factorial in Table 20–4 (an $A_{comp.} \times B \times C$ partial factorial), where $A_{comp.}$ is a pairwise comparison. If you redefine this analysis as a $2 \times 3 \times 3$ design, you can proceed with the analysis by using the formulas from Chap. 19 and from Secs. 20.2 and 20.3. If complex comparisons are involved, you can use the method outlined and illustrated in Keppel (1982, pp. 320–331).

20.7   SUMMARY AND COMMENTS

Factorial designs contain a great deal of information, but it is up to you to take full advantage of this valuable research tool. To be able to manipulate several independent variables simultaneously and to determine how they jointly influence behavior expands our ability to examine phenomena more realistically and more comprehensively. But mastering the skills necessary to conduct an ordinary analysis of variance or even just learning to read and to comprehend an analysis-of-variance summary table is only a first step in the total process. Far more challenging and far more critical is learning to utilize the factorial design to its maximum potential and to design experiments that capitalize on the analytical methods and techniques available to the sophisticated research analyst.

You should pay special attention to Chaps. 11 and 12, which first introduced these analytical techniques—the analysis of simple effects and the analysis of interaction comparisons—in the context of the two-factor design. Make certain that you understand what the analysis of simple effects can tell you about the nature of interaction and how partial factorials and interaction contrasts can provide an analytical way to view the manipulation of complex independent variables. Simple effects are central to the definition of interaction. A significant two-way interaction means that the simple effects of one factor are not the same at all levels of the other factor, and an analysis of these simple effects provides a useful and logical method for determining the ways in which these simple effects are different.

This chapter provides your first glimpse at generalizing these techniques to higher-order factorial designs. You should expect to move back and forth between this chapter and Chaps. 11 and 12, however, since the more complex analyses presented in this chapter are critically dependent on a mastery and understanding of the simpler analyses presented in Part III. Both ways of assessing interaction find relevant application in most factorial experiments. If single-df comparisons are not planned or obvious, analyses of simple effects will dominate the data analysis. On the other hand, if these comparisons provide useful ways of thinking about the manipulated variables, the analysis of interaction comparisons will receive more emphasis in your design and analysis of factorial experiments.

20.8   EXERCISES[3]

1. The analysis of problem 2 in the exercises for Chap. 19 revealed that the three way interaction was not significant. This would mean, of course, that we would probably look next at the two-way interactions rather than at simple effects. In this problem, the $A \times C$ interaction is the only significant two-way interaction in the analysis.
   a. To identify the locus of this interaction, test the significance of the simple effects of factor C at the different levels of factor A.
   b. You will note that all three main effects are significant. Two of the main effects (A and C) are probably not of much interest because any interpretation will have to be tempered with a consideration of the interaction of these two independent variables. The one main effect that we might consider giving further attention to is the main effect of factor B. This independent variable does not enter into any interactions with the other factors. Let's assume that you are interested in making the following orthogonal comparisons involving the $\overline{Y}_{B_j}$ means:

[3]The answers to these problems are found in Appendix B.

(1) The pairwise comparison between level b_1 and level b_3

(2) The complex comparison between level b_2 and the combined results of the other two conditions

2. The analysis of problem 3 in the exercises for Chap. 19 produced a significant three-way interaction. Any interpretation of two-way interactions as well as of main effects must be made in light of the way in which the three independent variables interact to produce the significant triple interaction. An inspection of the sums in the ABC matrix suggests that one way of describing the interaction is to focus on the simple $A \times B$ interactions at the two levels of factor C. (We could have just as well looked at the other two sets of simple interaction effects—the simple $A \times C$ interactions at the different levels of factor B and the simple $B \times C$ interactions at the different levels of factor A. Which set we consider in an actual experiment depends on the independent variables we have manipulated and any hypotheses we may have about the outcome.) For this problem, then, test the significance of the simple $A \times B$ interaction effects.

3. Earlier in the chapter, we considered four interaction contrasts that might be of interest in analyzing the numerical example, based on the data appearing in Table 19–5 (p. 434). I illustrated the calculations with a comparison between the control and the combined feedback conditions (see pp. 454–456). Let's complete the analysis by testing the following interaction contrasts:

   a. An interaction contrast created by a comparison between the positive and negative feedback conditions.

   b. An interaction contrast created by a comparison between the control and the positive feedback conditions.

   c. An interaction contrast created by a comparison between the control and the negative feedback conditions.

21

The Two-Factor Within-Subjects Design

We considered two types of within-subjects designs with one repeated factor in Part V. The first was the "pure" single-factor within-subjects design, $(A \times S)$, in which a single group of subjects receives all levels of a single independent variable (Chap. 16). The second was the mixed two-factor within-subjects design, $A \times (B \times S)$, in which different groups of subjects receive all levels of one independent variable but in conjunction with different levels of the other independent variable (Chaps. 17 and 18). This chapter will consider the complications that arise when one group of subjects receives all $(a)(b)$ treatment conditions in a two-factor design—that is, a "pure" two-factor within-subjects design, $(A \times B \times S)$. In Chap. 22, we will extend the analysis of variance to even more complicated within-subjects designs.

21.1   THE OVERALL ANALYSIS

The overall analysis of the $(A \times B \times S)$ design combines elements of two analyses we have considered already, namely, the completely randomized $A \times B$ design and the $(A \times S)$ design. The factorial treatment effects—the main effects of factor A and factor B and the $A \times B$ interaction—are calculated with the same computational formulas used with the $A \times B$ design. The error terms, and there will be three, are calculated with computational formulas that are similar to those used with the $(A \times S)$ design.

Design and Notation

The design and notational system are indicated in Table 21–1. Each letter or combination of letters refers to a unique quantity calculated from the data. The ABS matrix is the data matrix in which the individual Y scores are recorded. Each of $n = 3$ subjects contributes a total of $(a)(b) = (2)(3) = 6$ scores, one under each of the treatment conditions in the experiment. Three two-way matrices are required. The AB matrix is formed in the usual manner by summing the Y scores in each treatment combination; the sums in this matrix provide the information necessary for calculating SS's for the factorial treatment effects.

    The other two matrices are used to calculate various sums of squares associated with factor S, which as you will see, become the error terms for evaluating the factorial effects. The AS matrix contains sums obtained by collapsing over the b treatments. For example, $AS_{1,1}$ represents the sum of the three Y scores for s_1 obtained under level a_1; and $AS_{2,3}$ represents the sum of the three Y scores for s_3 obtained under level a_2. Except for the fact that the AS matrix contains AS sums, based on b observations, the matrix is identical to that formed with the $(A \times S)$ design. The BS matrix contains sums obtained by collapsing over the a treatments. As an example, $BS_{2,3}$ refers to the sum of the two Y scores for s_3 obtained under level b_2. This matrix can be viewed as a single-factor design also, with factor B representing the within-subjects factor; in this case, the matrix contains BS sums based on a observations.

Table 21–1   Notation for the $(A \times B \times S)$ Design

	ABS Matrix						
	a_1				a_2		
SUBJECT	b_1	b_2	b_3		b_1	b_2	b_3
s_1	$Y_{1,1,1}$	$Y_{1,2,1}$	$Y_{1,3,1}$		$Y_{2,1,1}$	$Y_{2,2,1}$	$Y_{2,3,1}$
s_2	$Y_{1,1,2}$	$Y_{1,2,2}$	$Y_{1,3,2}$		$Y_{2,1,2}$	$Y_{2,2,2}$	$Y_{2,3,2}$
s_3	$Y_{1,1,3}$	$Y_{1,2,3}$	$Y_{1,3,3}$		$Y_{2,1,3}$	$Y_{2,2,3}$	$Y_{2,3,3}$

	AS Matrix		
	a_1	a_2	Sum
s_1	$AS_{1,1}$	$AS_{2,1}$	S_1
s_2	$AS_{1,2}$	$AS_{2,2}$	S_2
s_3	$AS_{1,3}$	$AS_{2,3}$	S_3
Sum	A_1	A_2	T

	BS Matrix			
	b_1	b_2	b_3	Sum
s_1	$BS_{1,1}$	$BS_{2,1}$	$BS_{3,1}$	S_1
s_2	$BS_{1,2}$	$BS_{2,2}$	$BS_{3,2}$	S_2
s_3	$BS_{1,3}$	$BS_{2,3}$	$BS_{3,3}$	S_3
Sum	B_1	B_2	B_3	T

	AB Matrix			
	b_1	b_2	b_3	Sum
a_1	$AB_{1,1}$	$AB_{1,2}$	$AB_{1,3}$	A_1
a_2	$AB_{2,1}$	$AB_{2,2}$	$AB_{2,3}$	A_2
Sum	B_1	B_2	B_3	T

Basic Ratios and Sums of Squares

Basic ratios are formed by squaring and then summing members of a set of quantities having the same letter designation and dividing by the number of observations contributing to any one of the members in the set. These operations are specified for each source in column 2 of Table 21–2 for the first term listed in column 3, except for the last source, which indicates the basic ratio based on the grand total T. Column 3 specifies the pattern of combination required to calculate each sum of squares; as you know by now, this pattern corresponds to the pattern of letters produced when you expand the *df* statements in column 4.

Selecting Error Terms

Mean squares are calculated by dividing each sum of squares by the appropriate number of degrees of freedom, as indicated in column 5. You will recall from our discussion of the $(A \times S)$ design that we usually suspect the presence of a treatment $\times$ subject interaction in most behavioral studies, which means that the MS_A contains this interaction and error variance, in addition to any treatment effects that may be present. This posed no problem for the evaluation of the significance of factor A, however, since the interaction mean square $MS_{A \times S}$, contains the interaction and error variance.

Table 21-2   Computational Formulas for the $(A \times B \times S)$ Design

(1) Source	(2) Basic Ratio	(3) Sum of Squares	(4) df	(5) MS	(6) F
A	$[A] = \dfrac{\Sigma A^2}{(b)(n)}$	$[A] - [T]$	$a - 1$	$\dfrac{SS_A}{df_A}$	$\dfrac{MS_A}{MS_{A \times S}}$
B	$[B] = \dfrac{\Sigma B^2}{(a)(n)}$	$[B] - [T]$	$b - 1$	$\dfrac{SS_B}{df_B}$	$\dfrac{MS_B}{MS_{B \times S}}$
$A \times B$	$[AB] = \dfrac{\Sigma (AB)^2}{n}$	$[AB] - [A] - [B] + [T]$	$(a - 1)(b - 1)$	$\dfrac{SS_{A \times B}}{df_{A \times B}}$	$\dfrac{MS_{A \times B}}{MS_{A \times B \times S}}$
S	$[S] = \dfrac{\Sigma S^2}{(a)(b)}$	$[S] - [T]$	$n - 1$	$\dfrac{SS_S}{df_S}$	
$A \times S$	$[AS] = \dfrac{\Sigma (AS)^2}{b}$	$[AS] - [A] - [S] + [T]$	$(a - 1)(n - 1)$	$\dfrac{SS_{A \times S}}{df_{A \times S}}$	
$B \times S$	$[BS] = \dfrac{\Sigma (BS)^2}{a}$	$[BS] - [B] - [S] + [T]$	$(b - 1)(n - 1)$	$\dfrac{SS_{B \times S}}{df_{B \times S}}$	
$A \times B \times S$	$[Y] = \Sigma Y^2$	$[Y] - [AB] - [AS] - [BS]$ $+ [A] + [B] + [S] - [T]$	$(a - 1)(b - 1)$ $(n - 1)$	$\dfrac{SS_{A \times B \times S}}{df_{A \times B \times S}}$	
Total	$[T] = \dfrac{T^2}{(a)(b)(n)}$	$[Y] - [T]$	$(a)(b)(n) - 1$		

The same argument applies to the present situation. Consider the AS matrix in Table 21–1. This matrix displays the results of what we may view as an $(A \times S)$ experiment, that is, a single-factor within-subjects design involving factor A (with factor B disregarded). Viewed this way, then, the main effect of factor A contains a treatment × subject interaction, error variance, and potential treatment effects. Thus, the error term for evaluating the main effect of factor A in the $(A \times B \times S)$ design is the same quantity used in the $(A \times S)$ design—$MS_{A \times S}$—because it also reflects the $A \times S$ interaction and error variance.

Similarly, the BS matrix may also be viewed as a $(B \times S)$ design—a single-factor within-subjects design involving factor B (this time with factor A disregarded). By the same logic offered to justify the use of $MS_{A \times S}$ as the error term for the MS_A in the $(A \times S)$ portion of the analysis, the main effect of factor B contains a $B \times S$ interaction, error variance, and potential treatment effects. Thus, the appropriate error term for the MS_B is the $MS_{B \times S}$, which is assumed to reflect the relevant interaction and error variance.

Finally, we have the $MS_{A \times B}$, which can also be thought to contain three components, a possible $A \times B$ interaction, an $A \times B \times$ Subjects interaction, and error variance. The mean square for the $A \times B \times S$ interaction contains the last two components—the $A \times B \times$ Subjects interaction and error variance—and thus is an appropriate error term with which to test the significance of the $A \times B$ interaction. You can see a pattern emerging, of course:

The error term for "pure" within-subjects designs will always be an interaction of the factorial treatment effect (main effect or interaction) with subjects.

Homogeneity Assumptions

As indicated in Chap. 16, the special assumptions underlying the analysis of within-subjects designs are frequently violated in psychological research and the most reasonable strategy is to take steps to deal with the consequences of these violations. In general, you can expect that your F test is positively biased, which means that you may actually be working at the 10 percent level of significance, for example, rather than at the desired 5 percent level. An easy way to compensate for this bias is to employ the Geisser-Greenhouse correction, which we first discussed in Chap. 16 (pp. 352–353). To apply this correction, we replace the usual numerator and denominator degrees of freedom with a new pair of values, which we then use to find the critical value of F in Table A–1. This new combination of df's define a sampling distribution of F that is appropriate when the sphericity or homogeneity assumption is maximally violated.

As applied to the ($A \times B \times S$) design, the correction requires the use of a single pair of values for determining the critical values for all F's, namely, $df_{num.} = 1$ and $df_{denom.} = n - 1$.[1] As indicated in Chap. 16, the Geisser-Greenhouse correction tends to overcorrect the positive bias when the actual violation is less than the maximal amount. More accurate adjustments are available (see p. 353), but they are complicated and are best conducted with a computer. Alternatively, you could adopt the strategy presented in Sec. 16.4, which may be summarized as follows:

If $F_{observed} \geq F(1, n - 1)$, reject H_0 (the Geisser-Greenhouse correction).

If $F_{observed} < F(df_{effect}, df_{error})$, retain H_0 (the usual criterion).

If $F_{observed}$ falls between these two values, use a more accurate correction.

I will illustrate the use of this strategy in the next section.

21.2   A NUMERICAL EXAMPLE

The data for a hypothetical experiment are presented in Table 21–3. For the experimental factors, the design is a 2×4 factorial design with repeated measures on both factors. Let's assume that factor A consists of two lists of 30 English words, one of low-frequency words (a_1) and the other of high-frequency words (a_2), and

---

[1] The corrected df's for all "pure" within-subjects designs are $df_{num.} = 1$ and $df_{denom.} = n - 1$. The correction for mixed within-subjects designs may be determined by the following rule:

Divide the original numerator and denominator df's by a number equal to the df associated with the repeated factor (or factors).

In symbols, the two corrected df's are

$$df_{num.} = \frac{df_{effect}}{df_{repeated factors}} \text{ and } df_{denom.} = \frac{df_{error term}}{df_{repeated factors}}$$

Table 21–3   Numerical Example: $(A \times B \times S)$ Design

ABS Matrix

	a_1				a_2			
	b_1	b_2	b_3	b_4	b_1	b_2	b_3	b_4
s_1	3	4	3	7	5	6	7	11
s_2	6	8	9	12	10	12	15	18
s_3	7	13	11	11	10	15	14	15
s_4	0	3	6	6	5	7	9	11

AS Matrix

	a_1	a_2	Sum
s_1	17	29	46
s_2	35	55	90
s_3	42	54	96
s_4	15	32	47
Sum	109	170	279

BS Matrix

	b_1	b_2	b_3	b_4	Sum
s_1	8	10	10	18	46
s_2	16	20	24	30	90
s_3	17	28	25	26	96
s_4	5	10	15	17	47
Sum	46	68	74	91	279

AB Matrix

	b_1	b_2	b_3	b_4	Sum
a_1	16	28	29	36	109
a_2	30	40	45	55	170
Sum	46	68	74	91	279

that factor B consists of four trials in which subjects first study the words and then recall them during a two-minute testing period. The words are presented in a different random order on each trial. There are $n = 4$ subjects, half of whom receive the list of low-frequency words first, followed by the list of high-frequency words, and the other half receives them in the reverse order. The Y scores are the words recalled on each test trial.

We begin the analysis by calculating the basic ratios specified in column 2 of Table 21–2. Working with the AB matrix first, we have

$$[T] = \frac{T^2}{(a)(b)(n)} = \frac{(279)^2}{(2)(4)(4)} = 2{,}432.53$$

$$[A] = \frac{\sum A^2}{(b)(n)} = \frac{(109)^2 + (170)^2}{(4)(4)} = 2{,}548.81$$

$$[B] = \frac{\sum B^2}{(a)(n)} = \frac{(46)^2 + (68)^2 + (74)^2 + (91)^2}{(2)(4)} = 2{,}562.13$$

$$[AB] = \frac{\sum (AB)^2}{n} = \frac{(16)^2 + (28)^2 + \ldots + (45)^2 + (55)^2}{4} = 2{,}681.75$$

With these basic ratios, we can calculate the sums of squares for the three factorial treatment effects; these computations are completed in Table 21–4. Turning next to the AS matrix, we find

$$[S] = \frac{\Sigma\, S^2}{(a)(b)} = \frac{(46)^2 + (90)^2 + (96)^2 + (47)^2}{(2)(4)} = 2,705.13$$

$$[AS] = \frac{\Sigma\, (AS)^2}{b} = \frac{(17)^2 + (35)^2 + \ldots + (54)^2 + (32)^2}{4} = 2,827.25$$

Combined with the basic ratios we have already obtained, we can now calculate the main effect of factor S and the $A \times S$ interaction. From the BS matrix, we obtain

$$[BS] = \frac{\Sigma\, (BS)^2}{(a)} = \frac{(8)^2 + (16)^2 + \ldots + (26)^2 + (17)^2}{2} = 2,866.50$$

It is now possible to calculate the sum of squares for the $B \times S$ interaction. Finally, we have to use the ABS data matrix to calculate the sum of squares for the $A \times B \times S$ interaction and the total sum of squares:

$$[Y] = \Sigma\, Y^2 = (3)^2 + (6)^2 + \ldots + (15)^2 + (11)^2 = 2,995$$

The remainder of the analysis is summarized in Table 21–4. As you can see, the two main effects are significant, whereas the interaction is not. This conclusion does not change if we apply the Geisser-Greenhouse correction to these F tests. Under this procedure, we would find the critical value of F with $df_{num.} = 1$ and $df_{denom.} = n - 1 = 4 - 1 = 3$, which is $F(1, 3) = 10.1$. In spite of this more stringent requirement, however, the two main effects are still significant. For comparison purposes, the uncorrected critical value for the main effect of B and the $A \times B$ interaction is $F(3, 9) = 3.86$. [The critical value for the main effect of A is not affected because $df_A = 1$ and the critical F's are the same corrected or uncorrected, namely, $F(1, 3) = 10.1$.] This is a large difference, which is due in large part to the relatively small number of subjects used for this example. If sample size had been

Table 21–4 Summary of the Analysis

Source	Sum of Squares		df	MS	F
A	$2,548.81 - 2,432.53 =$	116.28	1	116.28	59.63*
B	$2,562.13 - [T] =$	129.60	3	43.20	12.24*
$A \times B$	$2,681.75 - [A] - [B] + [T] =$	3.34	3	1.11	3.26
S	$2,705.13 - [T] =$	272.60	3	90.87	
$A \times S$	$2,827.25 - [A] - [S] + [T] =$	5.84	3	1.95	
$B \times S$	$2,866.50 - [B] - [S] + [T] =$	31.77	9	3.53	
$A \times B \times S$	$2,995 - [AB] - [AS] - [BS]$ $+ [A] + [B] + [S] - [T] =$	3.04	9	.34	
Total	$[Y] - [T] =$	562.47	31		

*$p < .05$.

$n = 11$, say, the uncorrected critical value would be $F(3, 30) = 2.92$, and the corrected value would be $F(1, 10) = 4.96$.

21.3   ANALYZING MAIN EFFECTS

If the $A \times B$ interaction is not significant, or if significant, the interaction is small or trivial, we would pay special attention to the analysis of the two main effects. Our example reveals only significant main effects. The main effect of factor A shows that overall performance was significantly better on the list of high-frequency words ($\overline{Y}_{A_2} = 170/(4)(4) = 10.63$) than on the list of low-frequency words ($\overline{Y}_{A_1} = 109/(4)(4) = 6.81$); with only two levels, we can refine this finding no further. The significant main effect of factor B shows that performance climbed steadily from the first trial ($\overline{Y}_{B_1} = 46/(2)(4) = 5.75$) to the fourth trial ($\overline{Y}_{B_4} = 91/(2)(4) = 11.38$).

Factor B, consisting of four learning trials, is a quantitative variable for which the levels are equally spaced (1, 2, 3, 4). An obvious analytical approach to these data is to perform a trend analysis, to see whether we can describe the changes over trials in a relatively simple mathematical way. Many researchers would consider assessing the linear and quadratic trends for data of this sort. I will illustrate the procedure with the linear trend. Please note that once the coefficients have been selected, the procedures I will outline are identical to those we would follow if factor B had been a qualitative, rather than a quantitative, independent variable.

The analysis focuses on the BS matrix, which for analysis purposes is equivalent to a single-factor within-subjects design (except that each "score" is the sum of two Y scores, one from a_1 and the other from a_2). We obtain the coefficients for the linear trend from Table A–4; they are -3, -1, 1, 3. You will recall from Chap. 16 that we need to calculate a special error term for this analysis—one that is based on the interaction of this single-df comparison and subjects (see pp. 356–357). We begin by constructing a comparison matrix in which two values are computed for each subject, one based on the sum of the scores weighted by the positive coefficients and the other based on the sum of the scores weighted by the negative coefficients. Table 21–5 illustrates the process. The matrix on the left displays the weighted BS sums obtained by multiplying each sum in the BS matrix (Table 21–3) by the appropriate linear coefficient. To illustrate, I have listed the linear coefficients (c_j), the BS sums for the first subject, and the corresponding products (the weighted sums) in the following table:

c_j	-3	-1	$+1$	$+3$
BS_{j1}	8	10	10	18
$(c_j)(BS_{j1})$	-24	-10	$+10$	$+54$

We now combine for each subject the two BS sums weighted by positive coefficients and place this sum in the column labeled $b_{(+)}$ in the BS comparison matrix

Table 21–5   Constructing a Comparison Matrix for Linear Trend

| | Weighted BS Sums | | | | | BS Comparison Matrix | | |
	b_1	b_2	b_3	b_4		$b_{(+)}$	$b_{(-)}$	Sum
s_1	-24	-10	$+10$	$+54$	s_1	64	34	98
s_2	-48	-20	$+24$	$+90$	s_2	114	68	182
s_3	-51	-28	$+25$	$+78$	s_3	103	79	182
s_4	-15	-10	$+15$	$+51$	s_4	66	25	91
					Sum	347	206	553

on the right side of Table 21–5. We perform the same operations for the BS sums weighted by negative coefficients and place these sums, disregarding the minus signs, in the column labeled $b_{(-)}$. For s_1, then, we place 64 (10 + 54) in the first column and 34 ($-24 + -10$) in the second column.

We now treat the sums in the BS comparison matrix as if they were obtained from a single-factor within-subjects design with two levels. In viewing the analysis in this way, we must keep in mind two minor complications. First, the "levels" of factor B in this analysis are not the same as the actual levels (I will let $b' = 2$ represent the levels of $B_{comp.}$ in this specialized analysis); and second, this "single-factor" design is actually derived from a two-factor within-subjects design, which means we will need to include a in the denominator of all basic ratios. The calculations are as follows:

$$[T] = \frac{T^2}{(a)(b')(n)} = \frac{(553)^2}{(2)(2)(4)} = 19{,}113.06$$

$$[B] = \frac{\Sigma\, B^2}{(a)(n)} = \frac{(347)^2 + (206)^2}{(2)(4)} = 20{,}355.63$$

$$[S] = \frac{\Sigma\, S^2}{(a)(b')} = \frac{(98)^2 + (182)^2 + (182)^2 + (91)^2}{(2)(2)} = 21{,}033.25$$

$$[BS] = \frac{\Sigma\, (BS)^2}{(a)} = \frac{(64)^2 + (114)^2 + \ldots + (79)^2 + (25)^2}{2} = 22{,}351.50$$

The sums of squares, which are presented in Table 21–6, are based on weighted BS sums, and thus should be adjusted so that the values for the various SS's correspond to the SS's from the overall analysis, which are based on unweighted values.

Table 21–6   Summary of the Analysis of a Main Comparison

Source	Unadjusted SS		$SS_{adj.}$	df	MS	F
B_{linear}	$[B] - [T] =$	$1{,}242.57$	124.257	1	124.257	49.25*
S	$[S] - [T] =$	$1{,}920.19$	192.019	3	64.006	
$B_{linear} \times S$	$[BS] - [B] - [S] + [T] =$	75.68	7.568	3	2.523	
Total	$[BS] - [T] =$	$3{,}238.44$	323.844	7		

*$p < .05$.

The conversion is accomplished easily by dividing each sum of squares by an adjustment factor:

$$\text{adjustment factor} \; = \; \frac{\text{sum of the squared coefficients}}{2} \qquad (21\text{--}1)$$

In the present case, the factor is

$$\text{adjustment factor} \; = \; \frac{\Sigma \, c_j^2}{2} \; = \; \frac{(-3)^2 + (-1)^2 + (1)^2 + (3)^2}{2} \; = \; 10$$

Each sum of squares is divided by 10 to obtain the adjusted sums of squares, which are listed in the third column of Table 21–6.[2] The remainder of the analysis is straightforward. The F is obtained by dividing $MS_{B_{linear}}$ by the specialized error term, $MS_{B_{linear} \times S}$. The linear trend is significant.

I noted in Chap. 16 that it is not absolutely necessary to adjust the sums of squares if all we want is the value of F. To illustrate, the F based on the unadjusted SS's,

$$F \; = \; \frac{1,242.57/1}{75.68/3} \; = \; \frac{1,242.57}{25.23} \; = \; 49.25$$

is identical to the F in Table 21–6. Still, I do recommend that you always adjust the sums of squares to avoid errors of interpretation (see pp. 360–361). The unadjusted sum of squares we calculated for the linear component of the B main effect is a case in point. The unadjusted sum of squares is $SS_{B_{linear}} = 1,242.57$, whereas the sum of squares for the main effect from the overall analysis (see Table 21–4) is $SS_B = 129.60$. Mathematically, it is not possible for a component of an effect to be greater than the effect itself. The adjusted sum of squares, $SS_{B_{linear}} = 124.257$, brings the analysis into proper perspective.

21.4   ANALYZING SIMPLE EFFECTS

Generally, if an $A \times B$ interaction is not significant, we will probably concentrate our efforts on an analysis of the main effects. The analysis we conducted in the last section is an example of this approach. On the other hand, if an interaction is significant, we would probably consider an analysis of the simple effects of the interaction. We would undertake such an analysis in the hope that we will be able to identify the primary factors contributing to the significant interaction. (We considered the analysis of simple effects in Chap. 11.)

I will illustrate the procedures by analyzing the simple effects of factor B (trials) for the high-frequency list (a_2). (This analysis is not justified statistically, of course, because the interaction was not significant.) We begin by isolating the portion of the data we wish to analyze, which I have done in the upper portion of Table 21–7. The values within the body of this matrix are the four learning scores for each subject on the high-frequency list. Please note carefully that the matrix

---

[2]I have carried these calculations to three places to avoid rounding errors.

Table 21–7 Analysis of the Simple Effects of Factor B at Level a_2

Data Matrix

	b_1	b_2	b_3	b_4	Sum
s_1	5	6	7	11	29
s_2	10	12	15	18	55
s_3	10	15	14	15	54
s_4	5	7	9	11	32
Sum	30	40	45	55	170

Summary of the Analysis

Source	Sum of the Squares	df	MS	F
B at a_2	$[B] - [T] = 81.25$	3	27.08	18.42*
S	$[S] - [T] = 145.25$	3	48.42	
$B \times S$ at a_2	$[Y] - [B] - [S] + [T] = 13.25$	9	1.47	
Total	$[Y] - [T] = 239.75$	15		

*$p < .05$.

represents a single-factor within-subjects design involving trials as the independent variable. The analysis we perform duplicates the procedures covered in Chap. 16 (see Sec. 16.2).

First, we calculate the necessary basic ratios. For convenience, I will use Y to refer to the scores within the body of the matrix, B for the sums at each level of factor B, S for the sums for each subject, and T for the grand sum of the matrix. Using the information from Table 21–7, we find

$$[T] = \frac{T^2}{(b)(n)} = \frac{(170)^2}{(4)(4)} = 1,806.25$$

$$[B] = \frac{\Sigma B^2}{n} = \frac{(30)^2 + (40)^2 + (45)^2 + (55)^2}{4} = 1,887.50$$

$$[S] = \frac{\Sigma S^2}{b} = \frac{(29)^2 + (55)^2 + (54)^2 + (32)^2}{4} = 1,951.50$$

$$[Y] = \Sigma Y^2 = (5)^2 + (10)^2 + \ldots + (15)^2 + (11)^2 = 2,046$$

The analysis is completed in the lower portion of Table 21–7. The effect of trials is significant. The analysis is also significant with the Geisser-Greenhouse correction, for which the critical $F(1, 3) = 10.1$.

Analyzing Simple Comparisons

We usually follow a significant simple effect with a number of analytical comparisons, called *simple comparisons*. In the present example, factor B is a quantitative independent variable and a trend analysis would be appropriate. Instead, I will illustrate the procedure with a pairwise comparison involving the mean on the first trial ($30/4 = 7.50$) and the mean on the fourth trial ($55/4 = 13.75$). Again, the analysis follows the steps described in Chap. 16. The necessary comparison matrix, which is presented in the upper portion of Table 21–8, is easily constructed by placing the data from level b_1 in the column labeled $b_{(+)}$ and the data from level b_4 in the column labeled $b_{(-)}$.

I will continue to use the notation from the analysis on which this illustration is based. Remember that the two "levels" of the comparison are represented by b'. The basic ratios are found as follows:

$$[T] = \frac{T^2}{(b')(n)} = \frac{(85)^2}{(2)(4)} = 903.13$$

$$[B] = \frac{\Sigma B^2}{n} = \frac{(30)^2 + (55)^2}{4} = 981.25$$

$$[S] = \frac{\Sigma S^2}{b'} = \frac{(16)^2 + (28)^2 + (25)^2 + (16)^2}{2} = 960.50$$

$$[Y] = \Sigma Y^2 = (5)^2 + (10)^2 + \ldots + (15)^2 + (11)^2 = 1{,}041$$

The rest of the analysis is summarized in the bottom portion of Table 21–8. The difference between the two means is significant.

You should note that I did not mention the adjustment factor in this particular analysis. The reason is that no correction is necessary with a pairwise comparison. That is, since the coefficients for any pairwise comparison have the form 1,

Table 21–8   Analysis of a Simple Comparison

	Comparison Matrix		
	$b_{(+)}$	$b_{(-)}$	Sum
s_1	5	11	16
s_2	10	18	28
s_3	10	15	25
s_4	5	11	16
Sum	30	55	85

	Summary of the Analysis			
Source	Sum of the Squares	df	MS	F
$B_{comp.}$ at a_2	$[B] - [T] = 78.12$	1	78.12	98.89*
S	$[S] - [T] = 57.37$	3	19.12	
$B_{comp.} \times S$ at a_2	$[Y] - [B] - [S] + [T] = 2.38$	3	.79	
Total	$[Y] - [T] = 137.87$	7		

*$p < .05$.

−1, 0, 0, and so on, the sum of the squared coefficients will always equal 2, and the adjustment factor will be $\Sigma c^2/2 = 2/2 = 1$.

21.5 ANALYZING INTERACTION COMPARISONS

The other major way of analyzing interaction is with interaction comparisons (see Chap. 12). The most precise way to represent interaction is with a 2 × 2 arrangement of the two independent variables. Such an arrangement is called an **interaction contrast**—a single-*df* representation of interaction. If an experiment is already a 2 × 2 design, the interaction is an interaction contrast by default and will probably be analyzed as an ordinary ($A \times B \times S$) design, without resort to the special procedures I will discuss in this section. A great many experiments, like the numerical example, consist of multiple levels for one of the independent variables and two levels for the other. In these cases, conceptualizing the multiple levels in terms of single-*df* comparisons immediately creates a set of interaction contrasts in which a 2 × 2 design is formed by the two "levels" representing the single-*df* comparison and two levels from the other independent variable. Experiments in which both factors are represented by more than two levels may be analyzed in one of two ways, either as an interaction contrast formed by transforming both independent variables into single-*df* comparisons or as a **partial interaction** formed by transforming only one of the independent variables into a single-*df* comparison. I will consider the analysis of an interaction contrast first.

Analyzing Interaction Contrasts

This analysis requires a special error term that reflects the specific $A_{comp.} \times B_{comp.}$ interaction with subjects, which is associated with this interaction contrast. The key to the analysis is the creation of an ABS comparison matrix reflecting the effect. I will illustrate the process with the numerical example we have been considering in this chapter. Suppose we want to see whether the difference between the first trial and the fourth trial (b_1 versus b_4) depends on the frequency of the words making up the lists (a_1 versus a_2). The coefficients for the single-*df* comparison between the two trials are 1, 0, 0, −1. Factor A is already a single-*df* comparison, which we can represent by 1, −1. Given the nature of this analysis, we can form the ABS comparison matrix simply by extracting the appropriate columns of data from the original ABS matrix in Table 21–3 (p. 466). The result of this extraction is found in Table 21–9, where the levels of $A_{comp.}$ are designated $a_{(+)}$ (low frequency) and $a_{(-)}$ (high frequency) and the levels of $B_{comp.}$ are designated $b_{(1)}$ (first trial) and $b_{(-)}$ (fourth trial). The three two-way comparison matrices (AS, BS, and AB), which are obtained by combining values in the ABS comparison matrix, are also given in Table 21–9.

  The analysis now proceeds as if the design were a 2 × 2 within-subjects factorial design, where $a' = 2$, $b' = 2$, and $n = 4$. I will now calculate the basic ratios without comment:

Table 21–9   Interaction Comparison Matrices

<table>
<thead>
<tr><th></th><th colspan="2">$a_{(+)}$</th><th colspan="2">$a_{(-)}$</th></tr>
<tr><th></th><th>$b_{(+)}$</th><th>$b_{(-)}$</th><th>$b_{(+)}$</th><th>$b_{(-)}$</th></tr>
</thead>
<tbody>
<tr><td>s_1</td><td>3</td><td>7</td><td>5</td><td>11</td></tr>
<tr><td>s_2</td><td>6</td><td>12</td><td>10</td><td>18</td></tr>
<tr><td>s_3</td><td>7</td><td>11</td><td>10</td><td>15</td></tr>
<tr><td>s_4</td><td>0</td><td>6</td><td>5</td><td>11</td></tr>
</tbody>
</table>

ABS **Comparison Matrix**

AS **Comparison Matrix**

	$a_{(+)}$	$a_{(-)}$	Sum
s_1	10	16	26
s_2	18	28	46
s_3	18	25	43
s_4	6	16	22
Sum	52	85	137

BS **Comparison Matrix**

	$b_{(+)}$	$b_{(-)}$	Sum
s_1	8	18	26
s_2	16	30	46
s_3	17	26	43
s_4	5	17	22
Sum	46	91	137

AB **Comparison Matrix**

	$b_{(+)}$	$b_{(-)}$	Sum
$a_{(+)}$	16	36	52
$a_{(-)}$	30	55	85
Sum	46	91	137

$$[T] = \frac{T^2}{(a')(b')(n)} = \frac{(137)^2}{(2)(2)(4)} = 1{,}173.06$$

$$[A] = \frac{\Sigma A^2}{(b')(n)} = \frac{(52)^2 + (85)^2}{(2)(4)} = 1{,}241.13$$

$$[B] = \frac{\Sigma B^2}{(a')(n)} = \frac{(46)^2 + (91)^2}{(2)(4)} = 1{,}299.63$$

$$[AB] = \frac{\Sigma (AB)^2}{n} = \frac{(16)^2 + (30)^2 + (36)^2 + (55)^2}{4} = 1{,}369.25$$

$$[S] = \frac{\Sigma S^2}{(a')(b')} = \frac{(26)^2 + (46)^2 + (43)^2 + (22)^2}{(2)(2)} = 1{,}281.25$$

$$[AS] = \frac{\Sigma (AS)^2}{(b')} = \frac{(10)^2 + (18)^2 + \ldots + (25)^2 + (16)^2}{2} = 1{,}352.50$$

$$[BS] = \frac{\Sigma (BS)^2}{(a')} = \frac{(8)^2 + (16)^2 + \ldots + (26)^2 + (17)^2}{2} = 1{,}411.50$$

$$[Y] = \Sigma Y^2 = (3)^2 + (6)^2 + \ldots + (15)^2 + (11)^2 = 1{,}485$$

The analysis is summarized in Table 21–10. The only significant effects are the two main comparisons. You may wonder why the interaction contrast is not significant since the $F = 6.74$. The reason is that the critical value for this comparison is $F(1, 3) = 10.1$ and the obtained F falls short of this criterion. This outcome stresses the fact that a concern for power does not disappear when you select a more sensitive within-subjects design. In this case, the sample size is alarmingly small and should be increased to $n = 8$ or higher to provide sufficient power to detect this interaction, assuming, of course, that it is present.

Again I made no mention of adjusting the sums of squares in this analysis. Generally, no adjustment is necessary in designs containing only within-subjects factors if your only interest is in the values of F, because all sums of squares are affected to the same extent by the use of weighted Y scores in this analysis. Moreover, no adjustment is necessary when the two comparisons are themselves pairwise comparisons. If one or both are complex comparisons, we should adjust all sums of squares to avoid errors of interpretation. For an $A_{comp.} \times B_{comp.}$ interaction contrast, the adjusted sums of squares are obtained by dividing the unadjusted values by

$$\text{adjustment factor} = \left(\frac{\Sigma\ c_i^2}{2}\right)\left(\frac{\Sigma\ c_j^2}{2}\right) \tag{21–2}$$

where $\Sigma\ c_i^2$ is the sum of the squared coefficients for factor A and $\Sigma\ c_j^2$ is the sum of the squared coefficients for factor B. You can see now that an interaction contrast formed by crossing two pairwise comparisons, for which $\Sigma\ c_i^2 = 2$ and $\Sigma\ c_j^2 = 2$, gives an adjustment factor of $\left(\frac{2}{2}\right)\left(\frac{2}{2}\right) = 1$.

Analyzing Simple Comparisons

You will recall from Chap. 12 that a significant interaction contrast is usually followed by a test of simple comparisons. The interaction was not significant in our example, which means that we should direct our attention instead to the two main effects rather than to the interaction. If the interaction had been significant we would then be interested in the statistical status of the simple comparisons. For

Table 21–10   Summary of the Analysis of an Interaction Contrast

Source	Sum of Squares	df	MS	F
$A_{comp.}$	$[A] - [T] = 68.07$	1	68.07	64.22*
$B_{comp.}$	$[B] - [T] = 126.57$	1	126.57	102.90*
$A_{comp.} \times B_{comp.}$	$[AB] - [A] - [B] + [T] = 1.55$	1	1.55	6.74
S	$[S] - [T] = 108.19$	3	36.06	
$A_{comp.} \times S$	$[AS] - [A] - [S] + [T] = 3.18$	3	1.06	
$B_{comp.} \times S$	$[BS] - [B] - [S] + [T] = 3.68$	3	1.23	
$A_{comp.} \times B_{comp.} \times S$	$[Y] - [AB] - [AS] - [BS]$ $+ [A] + [B] + [S] - [T] = .70$	3	.23	
Total	$[Y] - [T] = 311.94$	15		

*$p < .05$.

example, we might want to determine if performance improved between trial 1 and trial 4 for both the low- and high-frequency lists—that is, test the simple effects of $B_{comp.}$ at the two levels of the other comparison. These tests would help us to interpret the significant interaction, which only tells us that the changes associated with trials are not the same for the two lists. Alternatively, we might determine whether the difference between the low and high lists is significant on trial 1 and on trial 4—the simple effects of $A_{comp.}$ at the two levels of the other comparison. Again, a significant interaction only indicates that differences between the lists are not the same on the two trials.

The analysis of a simple comparison also requires a special error term—one that is based only on the data involved in the comparison. Suppose we wanted to determine whether the two lists differ on the first trial. We would return to the *ABS* comparison matrix in Table 21–9 and isolate the relevant data, namely, the scores at level $a_{(+)}b_{(+)}$ (low list, first trial) and at level $a_{(-)}b_{(+)}$ (high list, first trial). The resulting matrix is given in the upper portion of Table 21–11. Consider this matrix carefully. What we have is the equivalent of a single-factor within-subjects design, in which "factor A" ($A_{comp.}$) has $a' = 2$ levels and there are $n = 4$ subjects. All other data have been disregarded for this analysis.

The analysis of these data corresponds to the analysis of an actual $(A \times S)$ design. I will designate the individual scores as Y, the column marginal totals as A, the row marginal totals as S, and the grand total as T. The basic ratios are

$$[T] = \frac{T^2}{(a')(n)} = \frac{(46)^2}{(2)(4)} = 264.50$$

Table 21–11   *Analysis of the Simple Comparison Involving $A_{comp.}$ on the First Trial $(b_{(+)})$*

Comparison Matrix			
	$a_{(+)}b_{(+)}$ **Low Frequency** **Trial 1**	$a_{(-)}b_{(+)}$ **High Frequency** **Trial 1**	**Sum**
s_1	3	5	8
s_2	6	10	16
s_3	7	10	17
s_4	0	5	5
Sum	16	30	46

Summary of the Analysis				
Source	**Sum of Squares**	**df**	**MS**	**F**
$A_{comp.}$ at $b_{(+)}$	$[A] - [T] = 24.50$	1	24.50	29.52*
S	$[S] - [T] = 52.50$	3	17.50	
$A_{comp.} \times S$ at $b_{(+)}$	$[Y] - [A] - [S] + [T] = 2.50$	3	.83	
Total	$[Y] - [T] = 79.50$	7		

*$p < .05$.

$$[A] = \frac{\Sigma A^2}{n} = \frac{(16)^2 + (30)^2}{4} = 289.00$$

$$[S] = \frac{\Sigma S^2}{a'} = \frac{(8)^2 + (16)^2 + (17)^2 + (5)^2}{2} = 317.00$$

$$[Y] = \Sigma Y^2 = (3)^2 + (6)^2 + \ldots + (10)^2 + (5)^2 = 344$$

The analysis is completed in the bottom portion of Table 21–11. The significant F indicates that subjects recall significantly more high-frequency words than low-frequency words on the first learning trial. The adjustment factor for this analysis is the same as the one used for an actual $(A \times S)$ design:

$$\text{adjustment factor} = \frac{\Sigma c_i^2}{2}$$

Since $A_{comp.}$ is a pairwise comparison $(1, -1)$, the adjustment factor is 1 and there is no correction.

Analyzing Partial Interactions

Partial interactions are created when we transform one of the independent variables into a single-df comparison and leave the other one intact. The analysis follows the procedure considered earlier in this section. The key to the analysis is the creation of an ABS comparison matrix, which is accomplished in the same manner as for the analysis of an interaction contrast, except that the weights are supplied by one of the factors. The result will be an ABS matrix that consists of either two levels of factor A ($a_{(+)}$ and $a_{(-)}$) and all levels of factor B, if the partial interaction involves $A_{comp.}$, or two levels of factor B ($b_{(+)}$ and $b_{(-)}$) and all levels of factor A, if the partial interaction involves $B_{comp.}$. Except for this difference, the analysis duplicates the analysis of the interaction contrast.

21.6   SUMMARY

You have seen how the analysis of the two-factor within-subjects design builds on designs we have considered previously. The overall analysis of the $(A \times B \times S)$ design, for example, parallels the analysis of the $A \times B$ design, except, of course, for the difference in error terms. That is, the analysis of the $(A \times B \times S)$ design extracts the same factorial treatment effects from the data—two main effects and the $A \times B$ interaction—and we obtain them with the same computational formulas appropriate for the completely randomized design. Moreover, the analytical analyses we associate with a two-factor design, which include the detailed analysis of significant main effects, the systematic analysis of simple effects, and the analysis of interaction comparisons, are available with the $(A \times B \times S)$ design as well.

The only new feature introduced with this design is the nature of the error terms, and here, too, the error terms represent an extension of the logic introduced for the $(A \times S)$ design. The following principle is emerging:

The error term for a "pure" within-subjects design consists of an interaction of subjects with the treatment effect under consideration.

In the single-factor within-subjects design, for example, the error term for the overall effect of factor A is based on the $A \times S$ interaction—the interaction of the overall effect with subjects. Extending this principle to the $(A \times B \times S)$ design, we now have three error terms to evaluate the overall factorial treatment effects: The error term for the main effect of factor A is the $A \times S$ interaction, the error term for the main effect of factor B is the $B \times S$ interaction, and the error term for the $A \times B$ interaction is the $A \times B \times S$ interaction.

The principle also applies to all analyses designed to illuminate the outcome of a factorial experiment. The detailed analysis of main effects, for example, reduces to analyses appropriate for single-factor within-subjects designs: The error term is the $A_{comp.} \times S$ interaction for the main comparison $A_{comp.}$ and the $B_{comp.} \times S$ interaction for the main comparison $B_{comp.}$. Similarly, the analysis of simple effects also reduces to the analysis of single-factor within-subjects designs. For example, the analysis of the simple effect of factor A at b_1 reduces quite literally to the analysis of an $(A \times S)$ design created by isolating this particular data set from the ABS matrix; treated in this way, the error term for this simple effect is the $A \times S$ interaction at b_1. The error term for a simple comparison based on this analysis is the $A_{comp.} \times S$ interaction at b_1. Finally, the analysis of interaction comparisons follows the same principle, except as miniature $(A \times B \times S)$ designs, in which one or both independent variables become single-df comparisons.

21.7   EXERCISES[3]

1. The data for a hypothetical experiment are presented in the following data matrix. For the experimental factors, the design is a 2×4 factorial with repeated measures on both factors. There are $n = 5$ subjects, each of whom served in all of the $(a)(b) = (2)(4) = 8$ treatment conditions. Conduct an analysis of variance on these data.

	a_1				a_2			
	b_1	b_2	b_3	b_4	b_1	b_2	b_3	b_4
s_1	3	5	9	6	4	5	12	8
s_2	7	11	12	11	11	12	18	14
s_3	9	13	14	12	10	16	14	13
s_4	4	8	11	7	6	9	13	9
s_5	1	3	5	4	3	5	9	7

[3]The answers to these problems are found in Appendix B.

2. The analysis reveals significant main effects but a nonsignificant $A \times B$ interaction, indicating that we would now focus our attention on the analysis and interpretation of the marginal means. Since factor A is represented by two levels, only factor B is available for further analysis. Evaluate the following single-df comparisons involving the $\overline{Y}_{B_j}$ marginal means:

   a. A pairwise comparison between level b_1 and level b_4.

   b. A complex comparison between the combined data from levels b_1 and b_4 and the combined data from levels b_2 and b_3.

3. Although not justified by the overall analysis, conduct the following analyses:

   a. A test of the significance of the simple effect of factor B at level a_1.

   b. A test of the significance of the simple comparison of b_1 versus b_3 at level a_1.

22

Other Higher-Order Designs

Completing the Analysis
Comment

22.5   CONCLUDING REMARKS (p. 498)

22.6   EXERCISES (p. 499)

I have discussed in detail the analysis of the most common experimental designs that we find in psychology and related sciences. In this last chapter, I will show you how to extend these analyses to more complicated designs. We will begin by considering again and in more detail the uses of multifactor experiments in the behavioral sciences. Next, I will show you what sorts of information you can expect to harvest from multifactor experiments. Finally, I will outline the general structure of the statistical analysis, giving special attention to the identification of error terms for higher-order within-subjects designs.

22.1   USE OF MULTIFACTOR EXPERIMENTS IN THE BEHAVIORAL SCIENCES

I mentioned briefly in Chap. 9 the advantages of the two-factor design. Although these are even more compelling for the higher-order factorials, there are some disadvantages as well.

Advantages of Higher-Order Designs

Perhaps the most important advantage of multifactor experiments is the degree to which they begin to approximate the actual setting in which a given behavioral phenomenon naturally occurs. In this sense, then, we tend to increase our understanding of behavior as we add more relevant independent variables to our experiments. Presumably our theoretical explanations will keep abreast of the elaboration of our designs, and they will begin to take on the flavor of a comprehensive, general theory of behavior. At the present time, factorials with more than three independent variables of experimental interest are still rarely found in the literature, a fact that probably reflects the level of development in the behavioral sciences. However, we can say that when a theoretical explanation is "ready" for predictions involving a number of independent variables, the factorial experiment provides an analytical and useful tool for testing these predictions.

I should also mention other advantages of the higher-order factorials. They are efficient, providing information about the influence of an increased number of independent variables at very little increase in cost (that is, subjects, time, and energy). Further, the multifactor experiment allows us to determine the way in which the different variables combine to influence behavior. I am referring, of course, to the *assessment of interactions*. The three-way factorial, for example, produces 4 interactions, the four-way factorial contains 11 interactions, and the five-way factorial contains 26. The point is that higher-order factorials are satisfyingly rich with analytical information.

Disadvantages of Higher-Order Designs

We pay a price for this "luxury," however, and this is the possibility of too much complexity. This may sound like a direct contradiction of the preceding paragraphs, and in a sense it is. The inclusion of a large number of independent variables in an experiment carries with it the potential of a significant higher-order interaction involving all the manipulated variables. Such an interaction would require an extremely complicated statement just to describe the outcome. With the two-way factorial, an interaction indicates that any description of the influence of one of the factors demands a consideration of the specific levels represented by the other factor. With a three-way factorial, a significant higher-order interaction implies that any description of one of the two-way interactions must be made with reference to the specific levels selected for a third factor. Interactions involving four or more variables require even more complicated descriptions. Now, if it is difficult merely to summarize the pattern of a particular interaction, imagine the problem we will have in explaining these results. Obviously, if a significant higher-order interaction exerts an important influence on a phenomenon we are studying, we cannot ignore its presence. On the other hand, we might make faster progress by attempting to understand the results of the simpler designs before attempting to tackle the more complex. I will return to this issue shortly.

Another point concerns economy. As we add variables to a factorial, the number of different treatment groups expands greatly. A 3×3 design requires a total of 9 treatment combinations, a $3 \times 3 \times 3$ needs 27, and a $3 \times 3 \times 3 \times 3$ needs 81. If we hold the total number of subjects we will use in the experiment constant, the number of subjects in each specific treatment group, n, must become smaller and smaller as we increase the number of treatment groups. Suppose we had available a pool of 200 subjects (picking a large round number). With this pool of subjects, we could include as the maximum number of subjects in each treatment condition, and still maintain equal sample size, $n = 22$ subjects in the 3×3 design, $n = 7$ subjects in the $3 \times 3 \times 3$ design, and $n = 2$ subjects in the $3 \times 3 \times 3 \times 3$ design. The gain in economy breaks down at some point since we are also concerned about the *reliability* associated with each of the basic treatment means.[1] Moreover, a reduced sample size will adversely affect the power for detecting the presence of higher-order interactions.

---

[1]This number depends on the size of the within-groups variance. The larger the variability of subjects treated alike, the more subjects that will be required to reach a given criterion of stability. Stability generally refers to the size of the *confidence interval* drawn around the sample means. The size of this interval depends on the α level acceptable to an experimenter, the sample size (n), and the size of the within-groups mean square. For any given α level, a constant interval may be achieved by applying the following formula: $MS_{wg}/\sqrt{n}$. Any increase in MS_{wg} requires a corresponding increase in the sample size to ensure the maintenance of a constant confidence interval.

This important concern for the reliability or stability of the individual treatment means clearly reduces some of the apparent efficiency of the factorial experiment. Additionally, an ambitious factorial experiment, when adjusted to a reasonable sample size, may require many more subjects than are available.

There are several solutions to this problem. One that we often see is the selection of a "minimal" factorial design, each independent variable being represented by only two levels—a 2^v design, where v equals the number of independent variables. The drawback to this procedure is that we may lose important information by not including more levels for one or more of the factors. The selection of levels for each variable is arbitrary, but if it is done in some realistic fashion, the chance of missing some important behavioral change associated with any variable is reduced as the number of levels is increased. A second solution is to use a **confounded factorial design** or a **Latin square design**, which achieves a reduction in the number of subjects but with the loss of unambiguous information about higher-order interactions.[2] Third, we could use a **repeated-measures design**, in which subjects receive some or even all of the treatment conditions, considerably reducing the total number of subjects needed for an experiment. Finally, if we are able to obtain additional information about the subjects before the start of the experiment, it may be possible to use a **blocking design** or the **analysis of covariance**, both of which require fewer subjects to achieve a given degree of precision. I discussed these procedures in Chap. 14.

Predicting Higher-Order Interactions

Complex designs allow the analytical study of behavior under conditions approximating the functional stimulating environment. A question often asked, however, concerns the *interpretation* of significant higher-order interactions when and if they appear. Can you conceive of a four-way factorial in which a significant four-way interaction is predicted? Not too long ago, the same question was asked about three-way designs, and probably before that about two-way designs; yet these latter types of designs are now relatively commonplace in certain areas of the behavioral sciences.

The answer to this very reasonable question is that complex factorial experiments seem to *evolve* from less complex ones. That is, if a particular two-way interaction has cropped up in a number of different experiments, the effect will be "accepted" by the scientific community as a "fact." Eventually, theories will be developed to attempt to explain it. At this point, it is usually not too difficult to think of a third independent variable that will interact with the other two. By the same token, as we begin to assimilate the meaning of a particular three-way interaction, we will be able to think of a fourth independent variable whose interaction with the other three variables provides an interesting test of the current theoretical interpretations of the earlier findings.

I have been arguing for an analytical evolution of factorial experiments. We

[2]For a thorough discussion of these designs, see Kirk (1982, pp. 570–658) and Winer (1971, pp. 604–684).

should know how a variable "reacts" in relative isolation, and often this requires an extensive analysis of the relationship between variations in the independent variable and behavior. Armed with this knowledge and perhaps an idea concerning the processes that may be responsible for this relationship, we can then increase the complexity of our design. The factorial experiment is not adapted to the "shot-gun" approach, which is simply looking for relevant independent variables. The results of such an attempt are likely to be wholly uninterpretable. It is, rather, a device for advancing a field that has reached an appropriate stage of theoretical development.

Internal Validity and Experimental Control

In the design of any experiment, we attempt to hold constant as many factors as we can that may influence the behavior we are studying. We test all animals in the same apparatus, perhaps with the same experimenter, and often under a high degree of control of the experimental environment (temperature, illumination, background noise, and so on). Ideally, we would like to be able to hold physically constant all important variables except the ones under systematic study. Factors that we are unable to control in this fashion, or which are not sufficiently important to control, we allow to vary randomly across the treatment conditions. Thus, randomization of these so-called nuisance factors is the major way in which we obtain **internal validity**—that is, the elimination of biases that, if present, might invalidate any conclusions we draw concerning the manipulations in the experiment.

Randomization spreads the influence of uncontrolled variables over the treatment groups equally. These variables do not systematically affect the treatment means, and so any bias is avoided. They do, however, influence the *sensitivity* of the experiment because any variability due to nuisance variables becomes "deposited" in the error term—that is, results in an increase in the variability of subjects treated alike. With a larger error term, our ability to detect the presence of real treatment effects is reduced.

External Validity and Multifactor Designs

You have seen that to achieve an acceptable degree of internal validity, we must greatly restrict the conditions under which we study a given phenomenon. This implies, then, that most of our research is of limited generality (see, for example, Greenwald, Pratkanis, Leippe, and Baumgardner, 1986). The degree to which we can generalize our findings beyond the present conditions of testing has been called the **external validity** of an experiment. Frequently, a researcher will introduce a factor into an experiment solely in the hope of increasing external validity. Where one set of stimulus materials is sufficient, two or three will be used; where one experimenter could conduct the experiment, several are employed; where one arrangement of a list of words will suffice, a number of orderings is constructed. In most cases, these factors can be thought of as independent variables added to the main experimental design; thus, they effectively transform a two-factor or a three-factor experiment into an experiment of greater complexity.

These factors are certainly not introduced into an experiment because of their inherent interest. Moreover, it is clear that the resultant increase in external validity is really not very great in any far-reaching sense. In spite of these qualifications, control factors still serve an important function in establishing the generalizability of a phenomenon. To be more specific, suppose we are interested in the effect of different stimulants on reading comprehension. Since different groups of subjects receive different stimulants, we could test all the subjects on the same passage of prose material. There is no compelling reason to include two or more passages, as there can be no confounding of the passage with the stimulants. Most experimenters, however, would feel more comfortable with the experiment if additional passages were introduced. The reason is the possibility that the outcome of the experiment may be due to some unknown peculiarity of the single passage used in the experiment. For an unknown reason, drug X produces better performance than drug Y, but only with a particular passage. This may sound farfetched to the beginning student, but it is observed all too frequently in actual research.

Now that you have seen why we introduce control factors into an experiment, either for the sake of internal validity or for an increase in external validity, the question is this: What do we do about it? Some researchers ignore the control factors altogether in any statistical treatment of the data, and thus fail to take advantage of the potentially useful information about the interaction of control factors and independent variables of experimental interest or of the possible refinement of the error term resulting from the removal of sources of variability associated with the control factors from the estimate of experimental error. The statistical analysis, on the other hand, is sometimes difficult, especially when a control factor is viewed as a random-effects variable, a topic we consider next.[3]

22.2   RANDOM-EFFECTS FACTORS

In this section, we will consider a methodological procedure that may be used to increase the generalizability of the results of an experiment.

Distinguishing Between Fixed and Random Factors

An uncommon, but increasingly popular, way of increasing the external validity of results is the use of **random-effects factors** and statistical theory to generalize the findings of an experiment. A random-effects factor is an independent variable for which the levels are selected either *randomly* or *unsystematically* from a larger pool of possible levels and are assumed to represent a *random sample* obtained from this larger population of treatment conditions. A random factor is also defined as a factor for which the specific levels may be changed in a replication without changing the fundamental nature of an experiment.[4] In contrast, most independent variables represent **fixed effects**, where the levels are selected *arbitrarily*

---

[3]The statistical analysis under these circumstances can be quite complicated (see, for example, Keppel, 1982, pp. 525–537).

[4]The subject "factor" in all experiments (the S in the designation of sources) is a random factor by this definition since the specific "levels" of this factor—that is, the individual subjects—will be different in any replication of a study.

and *systematically* and are assumed to represent the entire population of treatment conditions in which a researcher has a theoretical interest. For this reason, the specific levels chosen for an experiment are an integral part of the study and may not be changed in a replication. Generalizations based on fixed effects are restricted to the specific levels or conditions actually included in the experiment. On the other hand, generalizations based on random effects may be extended beyond those levels included in the experiment to the population or pool of levels from which they were randomly selected.

In spite of this apparently important difference in the generalizability of results, most independent variables manipulated in the behavioral sciences are treated as *fixed* by researchers in the statistical analyses reported in the journals. Any extension of findings to conditions not included in an experiment is based on nonstatistical rather than on statistical considerations and arguments, for two major reasons: First, for many independent variables, the levels included in an experiment effectively exhaust the pool of possible levels. There may be only two or three drugs that produce a particular effect or only a handful of teaching methods that can be considered realistic alternatives in a classroom. Under these circumstances, there is no need to generalize since as far as the researcher is concerned, all the levels of the factor in fact are included in the experiment.

A second and related point is that a researcher usually chooses the levels to be representative of the independent variable. Suppose we are varying the intensity of background noise in a psychophysical investigation and we decide to include four levels of this variable in our experiment. If we consider the potential levels of the variable that we could use in our experiment, the number is exceedingly large. Even so, most researchers would not select the four levels randomly from this pool of potential levels. Instead, they would be influenced by some or all the following considerations: (1) whether to represent the full extent of the effective stimulus dimension in the experiment, (2) whether to choose levels that are expected to produce a reasonably large difference between adjacent levels, and (3) whether to attempt to "hit" points of inflection—points where there might be a change in the direction of the function relating the independent and dependent variables. These are the overriding considerations in the selection of the four levels, and they certainly are not met by a random procedure, which selects unsystematically from all possible levels of the variable. With random selection, there is no guarantee that the important points along the dimension will be represented in the experiment.

Random factors are created by unsystematic sampling of the levels of the independent variable, and the interest, generally, centers around statistical generalization. For instance, an educator who wants to try out a number of methods of teaching reading (a fixed factor) in the third grade may choose as a second independent variable schools within a particular city or state. Although not all third-graders in question can be included in the experiment, the researcher clearly wants to extend any conclusions to the total population of students. Thus, the factor schools becomes a random factor. Other examples of random factors might include (1) a sampling of personalities of different experimenters, (2) the order of presenting a large set of material, (3) hospitals in a particular locality, and (4) raters and ratees from different political parties.

It is important to point out that we do not have fixed or random factors in the world but rather different structural models we impose on the world when we design an experiment. Thus, the independent variable schools becomes a fixed or a random factor only in the context of an actual experiment, in which decisions are made to include all or only a portion of the potential levels in the study. In addition, you should keep in mind that the structural model adopted for an experiment usually only approximates the formal statistical model on which it is based. It will frequently be the case that even when the levels of an independent variable are not chosen randomly, the factor may still be viewed as random by a researcher since the experimental situation does represent a reasonably close approximation of the random model and the researcher wishes to generalize his or her results to the levels of the factor not included in the study.

The Effect of Random Factors on the Analysis

Most examples of random factors in psychology consist of *control factors*—factors that are not of inherent interest in themselves but are introduced to achieve some form of generality. One of our numerical examples in earlier chapters was an experiment in which subjects learned a list containing words of either low emotional content or high emotional content. One problem with this independent variable is that there are only two lists, "low" and "high." It is entirely possible that the two lists of words differ with regard to other important characteristics as well—such as frequency with which they occur in English, their length, the number of syllables, and so on—which means that the outcome of the study may have been due to these differences rather than specifically to their emotional content.

A common solution to this problem is to include several lists of each type of word, with the hope that these other characteristics will be reasonably balanced between the two emotion conditions. This introduces another independent variable into the experiment, namely, lists. Suppose we decide to have $b = 5$ lists of each type of word prepared and used with equal frequency in the study. Factor B (lists) is usually viewed as a random factor, formed by creating two sets of five different lists from a relatively large pool of potential lists.

The analysis of experiments that include a random control factor of this sort is complicated. I consider the problems created by the introduction of random factors in Appendix C.

22.3   TREATMENT EFFECTS IN HIGHER-ORDER FACTORIAL DESIGNS

You have seen that adding independent variables to an experimental design dramatically increases the amount and nature of the information we are able to identify and study. With each factor we add to a design, we retain all the information we would have been able to extract from the lower-order design and we gain new information that was simply not available from that design. The two-factor design, for example, provides information about the effects of the two independent variables, which would have been observed in two corresponding single-factor designs, in the form of main or average effects, and information about how they combine to influence behavior—namely, interaction. The three-factor design, still provides information available from three corresponding two-factor designs, in the form of main effects and two-way interactions, and information about the three-way interaction.

The Standard Yield of a Factorial Design

What about factorial designs we have not formally covered in this book? Because of the way in which additional independent variables are combined in a higher-order factorial design, they yield a consistent pattern of treatment effects, which may be described by a simple rule:

> **List the independent variables and all possible interactions (or combinations) of these factors.**

The four-factor design consists of four independent variables, A, B, C, and D. An application of this rule gives us the following:

> Four main effects—A, B, C, and D—which are defined as the average effects of the independent variables considered singly, when the data are collapsed or averaged over the levels of the three remaining factors
>
> Six two-way interactions—$A \times B$, $A \times C$, $A \times D$, $B \times C$, $B \times D$, and $C \times D$—which are produced when the data are averaged over the levels of the two remaining factors
>
> Four three-way interactions—$A \times B \times C$, $A \times B \times D$, $A \times C \times D$, and $B \times C \times D$—which are produced when the data are averaged over the levels of the one remaining factor
>
> One four-way interaction—$A \times B \times C \times D$—which reflects the outcome of the experiment at the level of the individual treatment condition

Defining Higher-Order Interactions

An interaction is defined in terms of the simple effects at the next lower level. Let me illustrate with two familiar interactions. We say a two-way interaction is present, for example, when the simple effects of one of the independent variables are not the same at all levels of the other independent variable. Similarly, we say a three-way interaction is present when the simple interaction effects of two of the independent variables are not the same at all levels of the third variable. We can extend this definition to a four-way interaction as follows:

> **A four-way interaction is present when the simple interaction effects of three of the independent variables are not the same at all levels of the fourth variable.**

That is, an $A \times B \times C \times D$ is present, for example, when the $A \times B \times C$ interaction effects are not the same at all levels of factor D. To make any sense of this definition, of course, you have to understand the meaning of a three-way interaction, but presumably you have arrived at this stage by considering a three-way interaction and wondering how that particular interaction would be affected or modified by the addition of a fourth independent variable.

Computational Formulas

Once we have listed the sources of treatment effects that we can extract from a particular factorial design, we can easily construct the computational formulas for the corresponding sums of squares simply by writing the *df* statement for each source, expanding the *df* statement, and using this information to define the relevant basic ratios and the pattern in which they are combined. To write a *df* statement for any treatment source in a factorial design, we simply multiply the *df*'s associated with the different factors listed in the source. The *df* for the $A \times B \times C \times D$ interaction consists of

$$df_{A \times B \times C \times D} = (df_A)(df_B)(df_C)(df_D)$$
$$= (a - 1)(b - 1)(c - 1)(d - 1)$$

Multiplying these quantities may be something of a mystery for some readers, but all should be able to recognize the systematic pattern that emerges:

$$(a)(b)(c)(d) - (a)(b)(c) - (a)(b)(d) - (a)(c)(d) - (b)(c)(d)$$
$$+ (a)(b) + (a)(c) + (a)(d) + (b)(c) + (b)(d) + (c)(d)$$
$$- (a) - (b) - (c) - (d) + 1$$

That is, we start with the single four-letter combination, subtract all three-letter combinations, add all two-letter combinations, subtract all single letters, and add 1.

Each letter combination refers to what I have called a basic ratio, which consists of a systematic series of arithmetical operations applied to a sum identified by the combination of letters. The general formula for any basic ratio is

$$\frac{\Sigma \ (\text{relevant sum})^2}{(\text{appropriate divisor})} \tag{22-1}$$

That is, we identify the relevant sum, square it, combine all the quantities in the particular set of squares, and divide this total by the number of observations contributing to any of the relevant sums. We then calculate the different sums of squares by adding and subtracting basic ratios in accordance with the pattern specified by the expanded *df* statement. You should by now be familiar with this process.

The Remaining Steps

The sums of squares are converted into mean squares by dividing each *SS* by the appropriate *df*. The *F* ratios are formed by dividing the mean square for a factorial treatment effect by an appropriate error term. As you have seen, an error term depends on whether the relevant independent variable or variables represent between-subjects manipulations or within-subjects manipulations. We will consider the designation of error terms next.

22.4   DESIGNATING ERROR TERMS IN HIGHER-ORDER FACTORIAL DESIGNS

Specifying the appropriate error term for a completely randomized factorial is easy—a within-groups mean square, which is based on the variability of subjects receiving the same treatment condition and averaged over all independent groups. The designation of appropriate error terms for designs with repeated measures, however, is considerably more complicated. Fortunately, there is a general rule that will help you complete your analyses if you are conducting them by hand or assist you in comprehending the computer printout if you are taking advantage of a statistical software program. In either case, you certainly must know what you (or the computer) are doing.

Factorial Design Families

The key to understanding the identification of error terms is the concept of a **factorial design family**, in which all members of the same design family share similar error terms. Thus, if you can specify the error terms associated with a particular design family, you can designate the error terms appropriate for all members of the family.

A design family is defined by the *number of within-subjects factors* included in the factorial. Let's consider first the design family in which there are *no* within-subjects factors—the completely randomized designs. As I have indicated, the error term for all completely randomized designs is a pooled, within-groups mean square, MS_{wg}. We designate such error terms with a special subscript consisting of a "slash" or diagonal, which is read "within," followed by one or more capital letters, which indicate the nature of the independent groups created by the factorial design. Thus, the within-groups error term for a completely randomized three-factor design, $MS_{S/ABC}$, clearly specifies that the mean square is based on the variability of subjects within each of the treatment groups formed by crossing three independent variables in a factorial design.

Next, let's consider the error terms for the other design families that contain one or more within-subjects factors. The nature of the error terms appropriate for any given family is most easily understood by examining "pure" within-subjects designs—that is, designs with no between-subjects factors. We considered two such design families: the $(A \times S)$ design and the $(A \times B \times S)$ design. Out of these discussions, a consistent pattern has emerged:

> **The error term for any treatment source is an interaction between subjects and the factor (or factors) contained in that source.**

Let me apply this rule to a design we have not discussed, namely, the $(A \times$

$B \times C \times S$) design, a "pure" within-subjects factorial design with three factors. Since this design is a three-way factorial, we would expect to obtain seven treatment sources in the standard analysis:

Three main effects (A, B, and C)
Three two-way interactions ($A \times B$, $A \times C$, and $B \times C$)
The $A \times B \times C$, or three-way interaction

With this rule, we can easily determine the appropriate error term for each of these treatment sources. Table 22–1 summarizes this operation, which as you can see, produces a different error term for evaluating each factorial treatment effect. More specifically, the error term for each of the main effects consists of an interaction between subjects and the relevant factor, and the error term for each of the interactions also consists of an interaction between subjects and the relevant factors.

Mixed Within-Subjects Designs

The treatment sources available from any factorial experiment are determined by the total number of independent variables included in the design. Thus, a three-factor design will always yield the same sorts of treatment effects regardless of the status of the three independent variables included in the design. A mixed factorial design will always have at least two error terms. One of these will be a within-groups mean square, which we use to evaluate any treatment source not based on repeated measures. You will recall from Chap. 17, where we considered the analysis of $A \times (B \times S)$ mixed factorial design, that the main effect of the between-subjects factor (A) was evaluated by the within-groups mean square, $MS_{S/A}$. This part of the analysis corresponds to the analysis of a completely randomized single-factor design, which may be accomplished by collapsing the data over the repeated factor (B) for each of the subjects.

The nature of the remaining error term (or terms) is determined by the number of within-subjects factors represented in the design. This is where family membership comes into play. Continuing with the example of the $A \times (B \times S)$ mixed factorial design, we see that the two factorial treatment sources that are based on factor B (the repeated factor)—the B main effect and the $A \times B$ interaction—are evaluated with an error term that resembles the error term appropriate for a single-

Table 22–1   Error Terms for the $(A \times B \times C \times S)$ Factorial Design

Treatment Source	Error Term
A	$A \times S$
B	$B \times S$
C	$C \times S$
$A \times B$	$A \times B \times S$
$A \times C$	$A \times C \times S$
$B \times C$	$B \times C \times S$
$A \times B \times C$	$A \times B \times C \times S$

factor within-subjects design, namely, an interaction of subjects with the repeated factor. In short, the family membership of the design determines the error term for treatment effects based on the repeated factor (or factors).

The error terms for a variety of factorial designs are presented in Table 22–2. Consider the first row in this table. Here I have listed three completely randomized designs—designs with one, two, or three independent variables. The row is labeled "None" to indicate that no within-subjects factors are contained in these designs. The three designs and the error terms are listed in the columns labeled according to the number of independent variables involved. As you can see, the error term for each design is a within-groups mean square. That is, the error term for the single-factor design is S/A; for the $A \times B$ design, S/AB; and for the $A \times B \times C$ design, S/ABC.

Now let's consider the column labeled "None." As you move down the column, you encounter "pure" within-subjects designs with increasing numbers of independent variables. To avoid confusion, I have designated the first independent variable as factor U, the second as factor V, and the third as factor W. Except for the strangeness of these new designations, you should be able to recognize the familiar pattern of the error terms for these three designs. For the single-factor design, there is a single error term, an interaction of subjects with the repeated factor; for the two-factor design, there are three error terms, all consisting of interactions of subjects with one or two repeated factors; and for the three-factor design, there are seven error terms, again all consisting of interactions of subjects with one, two, or three repeated factors.

Taken together, then, the four rows of this table define four distinct design families—that is, families that are distinguished by the number of within-subjects factors, ranging from none (the completely randomized design) to a factorial design with three repeated factors. Of interest to us now are the mixed factorial designs, which are defined within the remainder of the table. Let's begin with the row containing designs with one within-subjects factor. The first mixed design is an $A \times (U \times S)$ design, which corresponds to the $A \times (B \times S)$ mixed design discussed previously. As indicated in the table, there are two error terms, one for the main effect of the between-subjects factor (the main effect of factor A) and the other for the two sources based on the within-subjects factor (the main effect of U and the $A \times U$ interaction). Consider the next design in this row, an $A \times B \times (U \times S)$ design in which two between-subjects factors (factors A and B) are combined with one within-subjects factor (factor U). Again there are two error terms, a within-groups error term (S/AB), which will be used to evaluate the three sources of variance based exclusively on between-subjects factors $(A, B,$ and $A \times B)$, and a within-subjects error term consisting of an interaction of subjects with the repeated factor (factor U) pooled over the independent groups created by the two between-subjects factors; this error term will be used to evaluate all sources of variability involving the repeated factor. The last design in this family included in Table 22–2 is a mixed four-factor design, with three between-subjects factors $(A, B,$ and $C)$ and one within-subjects factor (U). As before, there are two error terms, a within-groups error term (S/ABC) and a within-subjects error term consisting of an interaction of subjects with the repeated factor pooled over the independent

Table 22–2   Error Terms for Various Types of Experimental Designs

WITHIN-SUBJECTS FACTORS			BETWEEN-SUBJECTS FACTORS			
			None	1 Factor (A)	2 Factors (A,B)	3 Factors (A,B,C)
None		Design:	—	A	A × B	A × B × C
		Error (Btn):	—	S/A	S/AB	S/ABC
1 Factor (U)		Design:	(U × S)	A × (U × S)	A × B × (U × S)	A × B × C × (U × S)
		Error (Btn):	—	S/A	S/AB	S/ABC
		Error (W/in):	U × S	U × S/A	U × S/AB	U × S/ABC
2 Factors (U, V)		Design:	(U × V × S)	A × (U × V × S)	A × B × (U × V × S)	A × B × C × (U × V × S)
		Error (Btn):	—	S/A	S/AB	S/ABC
		Error (W/in):	U × S	U × S/A	U × S/AB	U × S/ABC
			V × S	V × S/A	V × S/AB	V × S/ABC
			U × V × S	U × V × S/A	U × V × S/AB	U × V × S/ABC
3 Factors (U, V,W)		Design:	(U × V × W × S)	A × (U × V × W × S)	A × B × (U × V × W × S)	A × B × C × (U × V × W × S)
		Error (Btn):	—	S/A	S/AB	S/ABC
		Error (W/in):	U × S	U × S/A	U × S/AB	U × S/ABC
			V × S	V × S/A	V × S/AB	V × S/ABC
			W × S	W × S/A	W × S/AB	W × S/ABC
			U × V × S	U × V × S/A	U × V × S/AB	U × V × S/ABC
			U × W × S	U × W × S/A	U × W × S/AB	U × W × S/ABC
			V × W × S	V × W × S/A	V × W × S/AB	V × W × S/ABC
			U × V × W × S	U × V × W × S/A	U × V × W × S/AB	U × V × W × S/ABC

493

groups in this design. All members of this family, then, share a common repeated-measures error term that is based on the $U \times S$ interaction.

The next row contains members of the design family with two within-subjects factors. The "pure" within-subjects design determines the nature of the within-subjects error terms. As you can see, the three mixed designs in this row exhibit their family "resemblance" of three within-subjects error terms, all consisting of the same three interactions but differing in the nature of the independent groups over which these interactions are pooled. The final row in the table contains designs with three within-subjects factors. Again, the "pure" within-subjects design specifies the nature of the error terms, which is maintained by the three mixed designs in this family also listed in this row.

Selecting Error Terms

Although Table 22–2 gives an overview of the analysis of within-subjects designs, we still must determine the error term for each of the sources of variance we normally extract from a factorial design. We can accomplish this task by applying the following principle:[5]

> **If a source contains no repeated factors, the error term is the within-groups mean square.**
>
> **If a source contains a repeated factor or factors, the error term is an interaction of subjects with the repeated factor or factors pooled over the independent groups.**

I will now apply this principle to two of the more common factorial designs we have not examined in detail.

> *Mixed Three-Way Factorial: One Within-Subjects Factor.*   Let's consider a three-factor design with one within-subjects factor—the $A \times B \times (C \times S)$ design. As a preliminary step, I suggest arranging the factorial treatment effects according to the repeated factor (or factors) included in the design. The normal yield from a three-way factorial, of course, is three main effects, three two-way interactions, and one three-way interaction. We begin by listing the treatment effects containing no repeated factors, namely, A, B, and $A \times B$; the first part of the rule indicates that the within-groups source in this design, $MS_{S/AB}$, is the error term for each of them. Next, we segregate the factorial treatment effects according to the repeated factor (or factors) contained in the source. In this design, there is only one repeated factor (factor C), so that the remaining factorial treatment effects, which all involve factor C, are C, $A \times C$, $B \times C$, and $A \times B \times C$. Applying the second part of the rule to these sources indicates that the error term is the interaction of subjects with the repeated factor, pooled over the independent groups, namely, $MS_{C \times S/AB}$. These two steps are summarized in Table 22–3. Worked ex-

---

[5]These rules assume the fixed-effects model, which is the model appropriate for most experiments in the behavioral sciences. If random effects are present, you may want to consult an advanced treatment of this topic.

Table 22–3   Error Terms for the $A \times B \times (C \times S)$ Mixed Factorial Design

TREATMENT SOURCE	ERROR TERM
Between-Subjects Factors	
A	S/AB
B	S/AB
$A \times B$	S/AB
Within-Subjects Factor	
C	$C \times S/AB$
$A \times C$	$C \times S/AB$
$B \times C$	$C \times S/AB$
$A \times B \times C$	$C \times S/AB$

amples of this mixed design are found in a number of different references, including Keppel (1982, pp. 475, 606), Kirk (1982, pp. 523–528), Myers (1979, pp. 214–217), and Winer (1971, pp. 563–567).

Mixed Three Way Factorial: Two Within-Subjects Factors.   Let's extend the rule to another relatively common within-subjects design—a three-factor design containing one nonrepeated factor and two repeated factors, the $A \times (B \times C \times S)$ design. Again, we list the factorial treatment effects involving no repeated factors, which in this case is the A main effect; the error term is the within-groups mean square, $MS_{S/A}$. We list next the four sources of variance that involve one repeated factor. This gives us B and $A \times B$, which involve factor B, and C and $A \times C$, which involve factor C. The error term for the first two factorial sources is the interaction of the repeated factor (B) and subjects pooled over the independent groups, $MS_{B \times S/A}$; the error term for the second two factorial sources is the interaction of the other repeated factor (C) and subjects pooled over the independent groups, $MS_{C \times S/A}$. Finally, there are the two factorial treatment effects that contain both repeated factors, $B \times C$ and $A \times B \times C$. In this case, the error term is the interaction of the two repeated factors and subjects pooled over the independent groups, that is, $MS_{B \times C \times S/A}$. These steps are summarized in the second column of Table 22–4. You can find worked illustrations of this design in the

Table 22–4   Error Terms for the $A \times (B \times C \times S)$ Mixed Factorial Design

TREATMENT SOURCE	ERROR TERM
Between-Subjects Factor	
A	S/A
Within-Subjects Factors	
B	$B \times S/A$
$A \times B$	$B \times S/A$
C	$C \times S/A$
$A \times C$	$C \times S/A$
$B \times C$	$B \times C \times S/A$
$A \times B \times C$	$B \times C \times S/A$

following references: Keppel (1982, pp. 476–477, 606–607), Kirk (1982, pp. 535–540), Myers (1979, pp. 220–226), and Winer (1971, pp. 546–550).

Completing the Analysis

To complete the analysis, we will need to calculate the sums of squares, degrees of freedom, and mean squares. Central to these calculations is the df statement for each source of variance required for the analysis. The df statement for any source of variance is obtained by applying a rule that is based on the letters designating a given source. If the source contains no "slash," or diagonal, the rule states

Multiply the df 's associated with the factors listed in the source.

For the $A \times B \times C$ interaction, for example, the df statement consists of the product formed by multiplying the df's for all three factors:

$$(df_A)(df_B)(df_C) = (a - 1)(b - 1)(c - 1)$$

If the source contains a diagonal, the rule distinguishes between letters appearing to the left of the diagonal and letters appearing to the right. More specifically, the rule states

Multiply (1) the product of the df's of factors listed to the left of the diagonal by (2) the product of the levels of factors listed to the right of the diagonal.

As an example, consider the repeated-measures error term for the $A \times B \times (C \times S)$ factorial, $MS_{C \times S/AB}$. On the basis of the letters used to identify this source, the rule specifies that we multiply df_C and df_S (the df's of the factors listed to the left of the diagonal) by $(a)(b)$, the product of the levels of the factors listed to the right of the diagonal:

$$df_{C \times S/AB} = (df_C)(df_S)(a)(b) = (c - 1)(n - 1)(a)(b)$$

Once you have obtained the expanded df statements, you can easily transform them into computational formulas for the corresponding sums of squares. I explained these steps in detail in Chap. 10 (pp. 207–210) and have illustrated them on numerous occasions throughout this book. You should have relatively little difficulty calculating the basic ratios and combining them to produce the SS's required for the analysis.

Comment

We have now completed our formal discussion of factorial designs, but we have only scratched the surface of the possibilities. As we increase the number of independent variables in our experiments, we increase even more the number of within-subjects designs that may be created. You have already seen that the two-factor design yields three types of designs depending on the number of within-subjects factors,

$$A \times B, \ A \times (B \times S), \ \text{and} \ (A \times B \times S)$$

and that the three-factor design yields four types of designs,

$$A \times B \times C, A \times B \times (C \times S), A \times (B \times C \times S), \text{ and } (A \times B \times C \times S)$$

With higher-order designs, the situation becomes even more complicated. At the two extremes, of course, we still have the completely randomized design and the "pure" or "complete" within-subjects design, whereas in between we have even more mixed factorial designs, the number depending on the nature of the higher-order design.

Designs of this sort are becoming increasingly common in psychology. An experiment by Slobin (1966), for example, consists of a four-factor mixed factorial design in which three of the independent variables are within-subjects factors—an $A \times (B \times C \times D \times S)$ design.[6] Along with the desire to include three or more independent variables in a systematic study of behavior, researchers also realize that within-subjects designs represent an economical solution to the substantial demands for subjects that would be required with a completely randomized alternative. More specifically, higher-order factorial designs require more subjects by virtue of the fact that they produce large numbers of treatment combinations, which when multiplied by the sample size n, result in substantial total requirements for subjects; a within-subjects design reduces this total commitment. In Slobin's experiment, for example, there were five independent groups of $n = 16$ subjects each, requiring a total of $(5)(16) = 80$ subjects. The factorial combination of the three within-subjects factors produced 16 different treatment conditions. A completely randomized version of Slobin's study would require $(16)(80) = 1,280$ subjects. This total number would be even greater if we tried to equate the sensitivity associated with his within-subjects factors with corresponding between-subjects manipulations.

My point is that it is highly likely you will turn to within-subjects designs in your future research. The preceding chapters have given you an idea about how to design and analyze experiments with one, two, or even three factors. My purpose in this section was to illustrate how we can extend these methods and techniques to even more complex designs. By categorizing designs by family, I was able to show the principle behind the selection of error terms in factorial designs, which can be applied to designs of any complexity. Your knowledge of lower-level designs will continually be useful when you attempt to understand and to analyze higher-order interactions. Suppose, for example, you design a factorial experiment with four independent variables and find that the $A \times B \times C \times D$ interaction is significant. An obvious way to proceed with the analysis at this point is to examine individually the simple effects of this interaction, which take the form of three-factor designs in which the levels of one of the independent variables is held constant—for example, an $A \times B \times C$ design at level d_1, an $A \times B \times C$ design at level d_2, and so on. You should note that these analyses are functionally equivalent to the analysis of an actual three-factor design, which we have considered in detail in Chaps. 19 and 20. Thus, once you have mastered the material in these chapters, you are in

[6]Slobin's experiment is presented in more detail in problem 3 of the Exercises

a position to analyze a higher-order interaction. But what if the four-way interaction is not significant? Under these circumstances, you are still on familiar ground since the analysis reverts to simpler factorial designs created by collapsing the data over one or more independent variables.

Whether you can interpret a higher-order interaction theoretically is a different matter, of course. The statistical tools are available for analyzing the results of complex experimental designs, but the usefulness of your findings depends on your success as a theorist.

22.5   CONCLUDING REMARKS

You will undoubtedly find it necessary to consult a number of statistics books when you come across a problem that demands special treatment. When relevant, I have provided specific page numbers to the primary statistical source books written for psychologists, Kirk (1982) and Winer (1971), where more detailed and technical explanations are given. You will also find a book by Myers (1979) useful, particularly his treatment of Latin square design with repeated measures. Lindman (1974) provides a thorough discussion of complex experimental designs, including an excellent chapter on nested designs. Stevens (1986) illustrates how to use two comprehensive statistical software programs, SPSSX (the Statistical Package for the Social Sciences) and BMDP (the Biomedical Programs), to conduct many of the analyses we have covered in this book. Finally, I should mention Hays (for example, 1988), who makes accessible to the nonmathematically trained researcher the theory that lies behind the more common statistical procedures and tests.[7]

An important region toward which your future study perhaps should point is that of *experimental design*. A study of general principles of experimental design is useful in forcing you to examine your methods and procedures with a highly critical eye. Two older, but excellent, sources may be recommended: A discussion by Campbell and Stanley, which originally appeared as a chapter in a book (1963) but has been reprinted as a separate monograph (1966), and a book by Underwood (1957) in which Chaps. 4 and 5 are particularly relevant. A more recent book by Cook and Campbell (1979) offers advice and guidance in designing field research. Another book that considers issues relevant to the broad research needs of the behavioral scientist is by Neale and Liebert (1986). Finally, I should mention a book by Webb, Campbell, Schwartz, and Sechrest (1966), *Unobtrusive Measures*, which discusses the role of experimentation in changing the actual behavior under study.

General discussions that focus on experimental design or on the statistical analysis of experiments are only a first step in your training, however—you still must apply them in the laboratory. The success of any research attempt will depend in large part on the skill with which you accomplish this translation.

---

[7]Bruning and Kintz (1977) have prepared a useful chart providing cross references to a number of widely used statistics texts for a variety of experimental designs and procedures (pp. 301–304).

22.6 EXERCISES[8]

1. Consider the following interrelated studies reported as they might have appeared in an actual journal article.[9] Each describes a specific experiment conducted with different combinations of between- and within-subjects factors. The details of the manipulations are not important for this problem. In each case, (a) identify the factorial—that is, the nature of each independent variable, the levels of each factor, and the sample size—and (b) list the sources of variance you would expect to isolate in the statistical analysis. (c) Indicate also the error term for each factorial treatment effect.

Experiment A: Twenty-four subjects served in a 2 × 2 × 5 factorial. The main variable (generate versus read) was between subjects, as was the presentation rate (timed versus self-paced). The variable rules was within subjects.

Experiment B: There were 12 subjects. The design was a 2 × 2 × 5 factorial with generate versus read as a within-subjects factor, informed versus uninformed about a test as a between-subjects factor, and rules, again, as a within-subjects factor.

Experiment C: There were 24 subjects, employed in a 2 × 2 × 2 factorial design. The generate versus read variable was within subjects, the stimulus-versus-response recognition variable was between subjects, and a third variable of informed versus uninformed of a test was also between subjects.

Experiment D: There were 12 subjects. A "pure" within-subjects design was employed, consisting of a 2 × 3 × 5 factorial with generate versus read, rules, and five learning trials, all as within-subjects factors.

Experiment E: There were 24 subjects. The design was a 2 × 2 × 5 factorial with generate versus read as a within-subjects variable, stimulus-versus-response recall as a between-subjects variable, and the five trials as a within-subjects variable.

2. The following are descriptions of two actual experiments reported in the literature concerned with the effects of marijuana on memory. On the basis of the information provided, (a) identify the independent variables, indicating which represent between-subjects manipulations and which represent within-subjects manipulations; (b) identify the sources of variance normally extracted from this sort of design; and (c) indicate the error terms for each of the factorial treatment effects.

Experiment A:[10] Forty male volunteers were recruited for the study. On arrival in the laboratory, subjects were assigned to a marijuana (M) or placebo (P) condition. Taped instructions indicated that they would hear a series of word lists, with one word presented every three seconds. A given list of words was presented three times. Immediately following each presentation, subjects were required to write down as many words as they could remember. An answer sheet was provided with the initial letter of each word in the list printed in the order of presentation. These letters served as cues for recall. In the cued condition, subjects were told that these letter cues would be available during presentation of the lists and during the retention test and could be used in any way they wished to help them organize their thoughts for recall. In the uncued condition, the same instructions were given except that subjects were told that the recall cues would be removed before the recall test. The order of the cueing conditions was counterbalanced within the M and P groups.

---

[8]The answers to these problems are found in Appendix B.
[9]These descriptions are based on experiments reported by Slamecka and Graf (1978).
[10]Based on an experiment reported by Miller, Cornett, Brightwell, McFarland, Drew, and Wikler (1976).

Experiment B:[11] Sixteen male volunteers served as subjects. In each of the four sessions, subjects smoked a single marijuana cigarette containing one of three dosage levels of tetrahydrocannabinol (THC) or a placebo cigarette from which all THC had been removed. All sessions were separated by a one-week interval. The design was counterbalanced by assigning four subjects to each of the four possible orders of dosage. On arrival in the laboratory, subjects were randomly assigned to a dosage condition. In successive sessions, the dosage was changed so that each subject was eventually run under all treatment conditions. Following smoking, subjects were presented with two 40-item word lists. One list was presented at a two-second rate and the other at a four-second rate. New lists were used in each session, and both lists and presentation rates were counterbalanced as equally as possible from session to session. (The word lists themselves were disregarded in the statistical analysis.) Following presentation of each list, an immediate recall test was administered in which the subjects were required to write down all the words they could remember in any order. Subjects were allowed two minutes to recall each list. Following the recall interval, a new list was immediately presented.

3. Consider the following experiment reported by Slobin (1966). Subjects were shown pictures depicting some sort of activity together with a sentence describing the objects in the pictures. The subjects' task was to indicate whether or not the sentence accurately described the picture. There were four independent variables in the experiment, three of which involved repeated measures and one of which involved independent groups. Thus, the design could be represented as an $A \times (B \times C \times D \times S)$ factorial.

   The three independent variables based on repeated measures were (a) four types of sentences (factor B), (b) the truth or falsity of the descriptive sentences (factor C), and (c) the reversibility or nonreversibility of the subject and object depicted in the picture (factor D). For this latter independent variable, *reversibility* referred to situations in which the ". . . object of action could also serve as the subject . . ." and *nonreversibility* referred to situations in which ". . . the object could not normally serve as the subject" (p. 219). Factor A consisted of groups of subjects drawn from five different age groups—that is, groups of subjects whose ages were 6, 8, 10, 12, and 20 years.

   In short, then, the experiment was a "mixed" design, with four independent variables, three of which involved repeated measures, and it contained a total of $(a)(b)(c)(d) = (5)(4)(2)(2) = 80$ treatment combinations. There were $n = 16$ subjects in each of the age groupings. Your task is to identify the treatment sources of variance and the appropriate error terms with which to evaluate their significance.

4. Neal Johnson (1986) reported an experiment in which he studied the speed with which subjects could determine whether a predetermined target letter appeared as the first letter in either a word or a string of consonants. The design was a $2 \times 2 \times 2 \times 2$ factorial design in which subjects received all combinations of the four independent variables. Subjects received a series of displays, half of which were words and half of which were strings of consonants (factor A). On half of the trials, the target letter appeared in the display and on the other half it did not (factor B). The number of letters in the display was either three or six letters (factor C). The final independent variable (factor D) was the delay between the announcement of the target letter and the presentation of the display; this delay was either .5 seconds or 2 seconds. The order of these treatment conditions was counterbalanced over the $n = 32$ subjects. The design, then, is an $(A \times B \times C \times D \times S)$ "pure" within-subjects factorial.

   Your task is to identify the treatment sources of variance that may be extracted in this experiment and to indicate the appropriate error terms with which to evaluate their significance.

[11]Based on an experiment reported by Miller and Cornett (1978).

Appendix A

Statistical Tables

Table A-1 Critical Values of the F Distribution

df FOR NUMERATOR

df FOR DENOM.	α	1	2	3	4	5	6	7	8	9	10	12	15	20	24	30	40	60	∞
1	.25	5.83	7.50	8.20	8.58	8.82	8.98	9.10	9.19	9.26	9.32	9.41	9.49	9.58	9.63	9.67	9.71	9.76	9.85
	.10	39.9	49.5	53.6	55.8	57.2	58.2	58.9	59.4	59.9	60.2	60.7	61.2	61.7	62.0	62.3	62.5	62.8	63.3
	.05	161	200	216	225	230	234	237	239	240	242	244	246	248	249	250	251	252	254
	.025	648	800	864	900	922	937	948	957	963	969	977	985	993	997	1001	1006	1010	1018
	.01	4052	5000	5403	5625	5764	5859	5928	5982	6022	6056	6106	6157	6209	6235	6261	6287	6313	6366
	.001	4053*	5000*	5404*	5625*	5764*	5859*	5929*	5981*	6023*	6056*	6107*	6158*	6209*	6235*	6261*	6287*	6313*	6366*
2	.25	2.57	3.00	3.15	3.23	3.28	3.31	3.34	3.35	3.37	3.38	3.39	3.41	3.43	3.43	3.44	3.45	3.46	3.48
	.10	8.53	9.00	9.16	9.24	9.29	9.33	9.35	9.37	9.38	9.39	9.41	9.42	9.44	9.45	9.46	9.47	9.47	9.49
	.05	18.5	19.0	19.2	19.3	19.3	19.3	19.4	19.4	19.4	19.4	19.4	19.4	19.5	19.5	19.5	19.5	19.5	19.5
	.025	38.5	39.0	39.2	39.3	39.3	39.3	39.4	39.4	39.4	39.4	39.4	39.4	39.5	39.5	39.5	39.5	39.5	39.5
	.01	98.5	99.0	99.2	99.3	99.3	99.3	99.4	99.4	99.4	99.4	99.4	99.4	99.5	99.5	99.5	99.5	99.5	99.5
	.001	999	999	999	999	999	999	999	999	999	999	999	999	999	1000	1000	1000	1000	1000
3	.25	2.02	2.28	2.36	2.39	2.41	2.42	2.43	2.44	2.44	2.44	2.45	2.46	2.46	2.46	2.47	2.47	2.47	2.47
	.10	5.54	5.46	5.39	5.34	5.31	5.28	5.27	5.25	5.24	5.23	5.22	5.20	5.18	5.18	5.17	5.16	5.15	5.13
	.05	10.1	9.55	9.28	9.12	9.01	8.94	8.89	8.85	8.81	8.79	8.74	8.70	8.66	8.64	8.62	8.59	8.57	8.53
	.025	17.4	16.0	15.4	15.1	14.9	14.7	14.6	14.5	14.5	14.4	14.3	14.2	14.2	14.1	14.1	14.0	14.0	13.9
	.01	34.1	30.8	29.5	28.7	28.2	27.9	27.7	27.5	27.4	27.2	27.0	26.9	26.7	26.6	26.5	26.4	26.3	26.1
	.001	167	148	141	137	135	133	132	131	130	129	128	127	126	126	125	125	124	124
4	.25	1.81	2.00	2.05	2.06	2.07	2.08	2.08	2.08	2.08	2.08	2.08	2.08	2.08	2.08	2.08	2.08	2.08	2.08
	.10	4.54	4.32	4.19	4.11	4.05	4.01	3.98	3.95	3.94	3.92	3.90	3.87	3.84	3.83	3.82	3.80	3.79	3.76
	.05	7.71	6.94	6.59	6.39	6.26	6.16	6.09	6.04	6.00	5.96	5.91	5.86	5.80	5.77	5.75	5.72	5.69	5.63
	.025	12.2	10.6	9.98	9.60	9.36	9.20	9.07	8.98	8.90	8.84	8.75	8.66	8.56	8.51	8.46	8.41	8.36	8.26
	.01	21.2	18.0	16.7	16.0	15.5	15.2	15.0	14.8	14.7	14.6	14.4	14.2	14.0	13.9	13.8	13.8	13.6	13.5
	.001	74.1	61.2	56.2	53.4	51.7	50.5	49.7	49.0	48.5	48.0	47.4	46.8	46.1	45.8	45.4	45.1	44.8	44.0

*Multiply these entries by 100.

502

5	.25	1.69	1.85	1.88	1.89	1.89	1.89	1.89	1.89	1.89	1.89	1.89	1.88	1.88	1.88	1.88	1.88	1.87	1.87
	.10	4.06	3.78	3.62	3.52	3.45	3.40	3.37	3.34	3.32	3.30	3.27	3.24	3.21	3.19	3.17	3.16	3.14	3.10
	.05	6.61	5.79	5.41	5.19	5.05	4.95	4.88	4.82	4.77	4.74	4.68	4.62	4.56	4.53	4.50	4.46	4.43	4.36
	.025	10.0	8.43	7.76	7.39	7.15	6.98	6.85	6.76	6.68	6.62	6.52	6.43	6.33	6.28	6.23	6.18	6.12	6.02
	.01	16.3	13.3	12.1	11.4	11.0	10.7	10.5	10.3	10.2	10.0	9.89	9.72	9.55	9.47	9.38	9.29	9.20	9.02
	.001	47.2	37.1	33.2	31.1	29.8	28.8	28.2	27.6	27.2	26.9	26.4	25.9	25.4	25.1	24.9	24.6	24.3	23.8
6	.25	1.62	1.76	1.78	1.79	1.79	1.78	1.78	1.78	1.77	1.77	1.77	1.76	1.76	1.75	1.75	1.75	1.74	1.74
	.10	3.78	3.46	3.29	3.18	3.11	3.05	3.01	2.98	2.96	2.94	2.90	2.87	2.84	2.82	2.80	2.78	2.76	2.72
	.05	5.99	5.14	4.76	4.53	4.39	4.28	4.21	4.15	4.10	4.06	4.00	3.94	3.87	3.84	3.81	3.77	3.74	3.67
	.025	8.81	7.26	6.60	6.23	5.99	5.82	5.70	5.60	5.52	5.46	5.37	5.27	5.17	5.12	5.07	5.01	4.96	4.85
	.01	13.8	10.9	9.78	9.15	8.75	8.47	8.26	8.10	7.98	7.87	7.72	7.56	7.40	7.31	7.23	7.14	7.06	6.88
	.001	35.5	27.0	23.7	21.9	20.8	20.0	19.5	19.0	18.7	18.4	18.0	17.6	17.1	16.9	16.7	16.4	16.2	15.8
7	.25	1.57	1.70	1.72	1.72	1.71	1.71	1.70	1.70	1.69	1.69	1.68	1.68	1.67	1.67	1.66	1.66	1.65	1.65
	.10	3.59	3.26	3.07	2.96	2.88	2.83	2.78	2.75	2.72	2.70	2.67	2.63	2.59	2.58	2.56	2.54	2.51	2.47
	.05	5.59	4.74	4.35	4.12	3.97	3.87	3.79	3.73	3.68	3.64	3.57	3.51	3.44	3.41	3.38	3.34	3.30	3.23
	.025	8.07	6.54	5.89	5.52	5.29	5.12	4.99	4.90	4.82	4.76	4.67	4.57	4.47	4.42	4.36	4.31	4.25	4.14
	.01	12.2	9.55	8.45	7.85	7.46	7.19	6.99	6.84	6.72	6.62	6.47	6.31	6.16	6.07	5.99	5.91	5.82	5.65
	.001	29.2	21.7	18.8	17.2	16.2	15.5	15.0	14.6	14.3	14.1	13.7	13.3	12.9	12.7	12.5	12.3	12.1	11.7
8	.25	1.54	1.66	1.67	1.66	1.66	1.65	1.64	1.64	1.63	1.63	1.62	1.62	1.61	1.60	1.60	1.60	1.59	1.58
	.10	3.46	3.11	2.92	2.81	2.73	2.67	2.62	2.59	2.56	2.54	2.50	2.46	2.42	2.40	2.38	2.36	2.34	2.29
	.05	5.32	4.46	4.07	3.84	3.69	3.58	3.50	3.44	3.39	3.35	3.28	3.22	3.15	3.12	3.08	3.04	3.01	2.93
	.025	7.57	6.06	5.42	5.05	4.82	4.65	4.53	4.43	4.36	4.30	4.20	4.10	4.00	3.95	3.89	3.84	3.78	3.67
	.01	11.3	8.65	7.59	7.01	6.63	6.37	6.18	6.03	5.91	5.81	5.67	5.52	5.36	5.28	5.20	5.12	5.03	4.86
	.001	25.4	18.5	15.8	14.4	13.5	12.9	12.4	12.0	11.8	11.5	11.2	10.8	10.5	10.3	10.1	9.92	9.73	9.33
9	.25	1.51	1.62	1.63	1.63	1.62	1.61	1.60	1.60	1.59	1.59	1.58	1.57	1.56	1.56	1.55	1.54	1.54	1.53
	.10	3.36	3.01	2.81	2.69	2.61	2.55	2.51	2.47	2.44	2.42	2.38	2.34	2.30	2.28	2.25	2.23	2.21	2.16
	.05	5.12	4.26	3.86	3.63	3.48	3.37	3.29	3.23	3.18	3.14	3.07	3.01	2.94	2.90	2.86	2.83	2.79	2.71
	.025	7.21	5.71	5.08	4.72	4.48	4.32	4.20	4.10	4.03	3.96	3.87	3.77	3.67	3.61	3.56	3.51	3.45	3.33
	.01	10.6	8.02	6.99	6.42	6.06	5.80	5.61	5.47	5.35	5.26	5.11	4.96	4.81	4.73	4.65	4.57	4.48	4.31
	.001	22.9	16.4	13.9	12.6	11.7	11.1	10.7	10.4	10.1	9.57	9.39	9.24	8.90	8.72	8.55	8.37	8.19	7.81

Table A-1   (Cont.)

| df FOR DENOM. | α | \multicolumn{18}{c}{df FOR NUMERATOR} |
		1	2	3	4	5	6	7	8	9	10	12	15	20	24	30	40	60	∞
10	.25	1.49	1.60	1.60	1.59	1.59	1.58	1.57	1.56	1.56	1.55	1.54	1.53	1.52	1.52	1.51	1.51	1.50	1.48
	.10	3.29	2.92	2.73	2.61	2.52	2.46	2.41	2.38	2.35	2.32	2.28	2.24	2.20	2.18	2.16	2.13	2.11	2.06
	.05	4.96	4.10	3.71	3.48	3.33	3.22	3.14	3.07	3.02	2.98	2.91	2.85	2.77	2.74	2.70	2.66	2.62	2.54
	.025	6.94	5.46	4.83	4.47	4.24	4.07	3.95	3.85	3.78	3.72	3.62	3.52	3.42	3.37	3.31	3.26	3.20	3.08
	.01	10.0	7.56	6.55	5.99	5.64	5.39	5.20	5.06	4.94	4.85	4.71	4.56	4.41	4.33	4.25	4.17	4.08	3.91
	.001	21.0	14.9	12.6	11.3	10.5	9.92	9.52	9.20	8.96	8.75	8.45	8.13	7.80	7.64	7.47	7.30	7.12	6.76
11	.25	1.47	1.58	1.58	1.57	1.56	1.55	1.54	1.53	1.53	1.52	1.51	1.50	1.49	1.49	1.48	1.47	1.47	1.45
	.10	3.23	2.86	2.66	2.54	2.45	2.39	2.34	2.30	2.27	2.25	2.21	2.17	2.12	2.10	2.08	2.05	2.03	1.97
	.05	4.84	3.98	3.59	3.36	3.20	3.09	3.01	2.95	2.90	2.85	2.79	2.72	2.65	2.61	2.57	2.53	2.49	2.40
	.025	6.72	5.26	4.63	4.28	4.04	3.88	3.76	3.66	3.59	3.53	3.43	3.33	3.23	3.17	3.12	3.06	3.00	2.88
	.01	9.65	7.21	6.22	5.67	5.32	5.07	4.89	4.74	4.63	4.54	4.40	4.25	4.10	4.02	3.94	3.86	3.78	3.60
	.001	19.7	13.8	11.6	10.4	9.58	9.05	8.66	8.35	8.12	7.92	7.63	7.32	7.01	6.85	6.68	6.52	6.35	6.00
12	.25	1.46	1.56	1.56	1.55	1.54	1.53	1.52	1.51	1.51	1.50	1.49	1.48	1.47	1.46	1.45	1.45	1.44	1.42
	.10	3.18	2.81	2.61	2.48	2.39	2.33	2.28	2.24	2.21	2.19	2.15	2.10	2.06	2.04	2.01	1.99	1.96	1.90
	.05	4.75	3.89	3.49	3.26	3.11	3.00	2.91	2.85	2.80	2.75	2.69	2.62	2.54	2.51	2.47	2.43	2.38	2.30
	.025	6.55	5.10	4.47	4.12	3.89	3.73	3.61	3.51	3.44	3.37	3.28	3.18	3.07	3.02	2.96	2.91	2.85	2.72
	.01	9.33	6.93	5.95	5.41	5.06	4.82	4.64	4.50	4.39	4.30	4.16	4.01	3.86	3.78	3.70	3.62	3.54	3.36
	.001	18.6	13.0	10.8	9.63	8.89	8.38	8.00	7.71	7.48	7.29	7.00	6.71	6.40	6.25	6.09	5.93	5.76	5.42
13	.25	1.45	1.55	1.55	1.53	1.52	1.51	1.50	1.49	1.49	1.48	1.47	1.46	1.45	1.44	1.43	1.42	1.42	1.40
	.10	3.14	2.76	2.56	2.43	2.35	2.28	2.23	2.20	2.16	2.14	2.10	2.05	2.01	1.98	1.96	1.93	1.90	1.85
	.05	4.67	3.81	3.41	3.18	3.03	2.92	2.83	2.77	2.71	2.67	2.60	2.53	2.46	2.42	2.38	2.34	2.30	2.21
	.025	6.41	4.97	4.35	4.00	3.77	3.60	3.48	3.39	3.31	3.25	3.15	3.05	2.95	2.89	2.84	2.78	2.72	2.60
	.01	9.07	6.70	5.74	5.21	4.86	4.62	4.44	4.30	4.19	4.10	3.96	3.82	3.66	3.59	3.51	3.43	3.34	3.17
	.001	17.8	12.3	10.2	9.07	8.35	7.86	7.49	7.21	6.98	6.80	6.52	6.23	5.93	5.78	5.63	5.47	5.30	4.97

14	.25	1.38	1.40	1.41	1.41	1.42	1.43	1.44	1.45	1.46	1.47	1.48	1.49	1.50	1.51	1.52	1.53	1.53	1.44
	.10	1.80	1.86	1.89	1.91	1.94	1.96	2.01	2.05	2.10	2.12	2.15	2.19	2.24	2.31	2.39	2.52	2.73	3.10
	.05	2.13	2.22	2.27	2.31	2.35	2.39	2.46	2.53	2.60	2.65	2.70	2.76	2.85	2.96	3.11	3.34	3.74	4.60
	.025	2.49	2.61	2.67	2.73	2.79	2.84	2.95	3.05	3.15	3.21	3.29	3.38	3.50	3.66	3.89	4.24	4.86	6.30
	.01	3.00	3.18	3.27	3.35	3.43	3.51	3.66	3.80	3.94	4.03	4.14	4.28	4.46	4.69	5.04	5.56	6.51	8.86
	.001	4.60	4.94	5.10	5.25	5.41	5.56	5.85	6.13	6.40	6.58	6.80	7.08	7.43	7.92	8.62	9.73	11.8	17.1
15	.25	1.36	1.38	1.39	1.40	1.41	1.41	1.43	1.44	1.45	1.46	1.46	1.47	1.48	1.49	1.51	1.52	1.52	1.43
	.10	1.76	1.82	1.85	1.87	1.90	1.92	1.97	2.02	2.06	2.09	2.12	2.16	2.21	2.27	2.36	2.49	2.70	3.07
	.05	2.07	2.16	2.20	2.25	2.29	2.33	2.40	2.48	2.54	2.59	2.64	2.71	2.79	2.90	3.06	3.29	3.68	4.54
	.025	2.40	2.52	2.59	2.64	2.70	2.76	2.86	2.96	3.06	3.12	3.20	3.29	3.41	3.58	3.80	4.15	4.77	6.20
	.01	2.87	3.05	3.13	3.21	3.29	3.37	3.52	3.67	3.80	3.89	4.00	4.14	4.32	4.56	4.89	5.42	6.36	8.68
	.001	4.31	4.64	4.80	4.95	5.10	5.25	5.54	5.81	6.08	6.26	6.47	6.74	7.09	7.57	8.25	9.34	11.3	16.6
16	.25	1.34	1.36	1.37	1.38	1.39	1.40	1.41	1.43	1.44	1.44	1.45	1.46	1.47	1.48	1.50	1.51	1.51	1.42
	.10	1.72	1.78	1.81	1.84	1.87	1.89	1.94	1.99	2.03	2.06	2.09	2.13	2.18	2.24	2.33	2.46	2.67	3.05
	.05	2.01	2.11	2.15	2.19	2.24	2.28	2.35	2.42	2.49	2.54	2.59	2.66	2.74	2.85	3.01	3.24	3.63	4.49
	.025	2.32	2.45	2.51	2.57	2.63	2.68	2.79	2.89	2.99	3.05	3.12	3.22	3.34	3.50	3.73	4.08	4.69	6.12
	.01	2.75	2.93	3.02	3.10	3.18	3.26	3.41	3.55	3.69	3.78	3.89	4.03	4.20	4.44	4.77	5.29	6.23	8.53
	.001	4.06	4.39	4.54	4.70	4.85	4.99	5.27	5.55	5.8	5.98	6.19	6.46	6.81	7.27	7.94	9.00	11.0	16.1
17	.25	1.33	1.35	1.36	1.37	1.38	1.39	1.40	1.41	1.43	1.43	1.44	1.45	1.46	1.47	1.49	1.50	1.51	1.42
	.10	1.69	1.75	1.78	1.81	1.84	1.86	1.91	1.96	2.00	2.03	2.06	2.10	2.15	2.22	2.31	2.44	2.64	3.03
	.05	1.96	2.06	2.10	2.15	2.19	2.23	2.31	2.38	2.45	2.49	2.55	2.61	2.70	2.81	2.96	3.20	3.59	4.45
	.025	2.25	2.38	2.44	2.50	2.56	2.62	2.72	2.82	2.92	2.98	3.06	3.16	3.28	3.44	3.66	4.01	4.62	6.04
	.01	2.65	2.83	2.92	3.00	3.08	3.16	3.31	3.46	3.59	3.68	3.79	3.93	4.10	4.34	4.67	5.18	6.11	8.40
	.001	3.85	4.18	4.33	4.48	4.63	4.78	5.05	5.32	5.58	5.75	5.96	6.22	6.56	7.02	7.68	8.73	10.7	15.7
18	.25	1.32	1.34	1.35	1.36	1.37	1.38	1.39	1.40	1.42	1.42	1.43	1.44	1.45	1.46	1.48	1.49	1.50	1.41
	.10	1.66	1.72	1.75	1.78	1.81	1.84	1.89	1.93	1.98	2.00	2.04	2.08	2.13	2.20	2.29	2.42	2.62	3.01
	.05	1.92	2.02	2.06	2.11	2.15	2.19	2.27	2.34	2.41	2.46	2.51	2.58	2.66	2.77	2.93	3.16	3.55	4.41
	.025	2.19	2.32	2.38	2.44	2.50	2.56	2.67	2.77	2.87	2.93	3.01	3.10	3.22	3.38	3.61	3.95	4.56	5.98
	.01	2.57	2.75	2.84	2.92	3.00	3.08	3.23	3.37	3.5	3.60	3.71	3.84	4.01	4.25	4.58	5.09	6.01	8.29
	.001	3.67	4.00	4.15	4.30	4.45	4.59	4.87	5.13	5.39	5.56	5.76	6.02	6.35	6.81	7.46	8.49	10.4	15.4

Table A-1   (Cont.)

df FOR DENOM.	α	\multicolumn{18}{c}{df FOR NUMERATOR}
		1	2	3	4	5	6	7	8	9	10	12	15	20	24	30	40	60	∞
19	.25	1.41	1.49	1.49	1.47	1.46	1.44	1.43	1.42	1.41	1.41	1.40	1.38	1.37	1.36	1.35	1.34	1.33	1.30
	.10	2.99	2.61	2.40	2.27	2.18	2.11	2.06	2.02	1.98	1.96	1.91	1.86	1.81	1.79	1.76	1.73	1.70	1.63
	.05	4.38	3.52	3.13	2.90	2.74	2.63	2.54	2.48	2.42	2.38	2.31	2.23	2.16	2.11	2.07	2.03	1.98	1.88
	.025	5.92	4.51	3.90	3.56	3.33	3.17	3.05	2.96	2.88	2.82	2.72	2.62	2.51	2.45	2.39	2.33	2.27	2.13
	.01	8.18	5.93	5.01	4.50	4.17	3.94	3.77	3.63	3.52	3.43	3.30	3.15	3.00	2.92	2.84	2.76	2.67	2.49
	.001	15.1	10.2	8.28	7.26	6.62	6.18	5.85	5.59	5.39	5.22	4.97	4.70	4.43	4.29	4.14	3.99	3.84	3.51
20	.25	1.40	1.49	1.48	1.47	1.45	1.44	1.43	1.42	1.41	1.40	1.39	1.37	1.36	1.35	1.34	1.33	1.32	1.29
	.10	2.97	2.59	2.38	2.25	2.16	2.09	2.04	2.00	1.96	1.94	1.89	1.84	1.79	1.77	1.74	1.71	1.68	1.61
	.05	4.35	3.49	3.10	2.87	2.71	2.60	2.51	2.45	2.39	2.35	2.28	2.20	2.12	2.08	2.04	1.99	1.95	1.84
	.025	5.87	4.46	3.86	3.51	3.29	3.13	3.01	2.91	2.84	2.77	2.68	2.57	2.46	2.41	2.35	2.29	2.22	2.09
	.01	8.10	5.85	4.94	4.43	4.10	3.87	3.70	3.56	3.46	3.37	3.23	3.09	2.94	2.86	2.78	2.69	2.61	2.42
	.001	14.8	9.95	8.10	7.10	6.46	6.02	5.69	5.44	5.24	5.08	4.82	4.56	4.29	4.15	4.00	3.86	3.70	3.38
22	.25	1.40	1.48	1.47	1.45	1.44	1.42	1.41	1.40	1.39	1.39	1.37	1.36	1.34	1.33	1.32	1.31	1.30	1.28
	.10	2.95	2.56	2.35	2.22	2.13	2.06	2.01	1.97	1.93	1.90	1.86	1.81	1.76	1.73	1.70	1.67	1.64	1.57
	.05	4.30	3.44	3.05	2.82	2.66	2.55	2.46	2.40	2.34	2.30	2.23	2.15	2.07	2.03	1.98	1.94	1.89	1.78
	.025	5.79	4.38	3.78	3.44	3.22	3.05	2.93	2.84	2.76	2.70	2.60	2.50	2.39	2.33	2.27	2.21	2.14	2.00
	.01	7.95	5.72	4.82	4.31	3.99	3.76	3.59	3.45	3.35	3.26	3.12	2.98	2.83	2.75	2.67	2.58	2.50	2.31
	.001	14.4	9.61	7.80	6.81	6.19	5.76	5.44	5.19	4.99	4.83	4.58	4.33	4.06	3.92	3.78	3.63	3.48	3.15
24	.25	1.39	1.47	1.46	1.44	1.43	1.41	1.40	1.39	1.38	1.38	1.36	1.35	1.33	1.32	1.31	1.30	1.29	1.26
	.10	2.93	2.54	2.33	2.19	2.10	2.04	1.98	1.94	1.91	1.88	1.83	1.78	1.73	1.70	1.67	1.64	1.61	1.53
	.05	4.26	3.40	3.01	2.78	2.62	2.51	2.42	2.36	2.30	2.25	2.18	2.11	2.03	1.98	1.94	1.89	1.84	1.73
	.025	5.72	4.32	3.72	3.38	3.15	2.99	2.87	2.78	2.70	2.64	2.54	2.44	2.33	2.27	2.21	2.15	2.08	1.94
	.01	7.82	5.61	4.72	4.22	3.90	3.67	3.50	3.36	3.26	3.17	3.03	2.89	2.74	2.66	2.58	2.49	2.40	2.21
	.001	14.0	9.34	7.55	6.59	5.98	5.55	5.23	4.99	4.80	4.64	4.39	4.14	3.87	3.74	3.59	3.45	3.29	2.97

This table gives critical values of the F distribution. The denominator degrees of freedom (df_2) are shown at the left (26, 28, 30, 40, 60), each with rows for the upper-tail probability α (.25, .10, .05, .025, .01, .001). Columns give the numerator degrees of freedom (df_1).

df_2	α	1	2	3	4	5	6	7	8	9	10	12	15	20	24	30	40	60	∞
26	.25	1.38	1.46	1.45	1.44	1.42	1.41	1.39	1.38	1.37	1.37	1.35	1.34	1.32	1.31	1.30	1.29	1.28	1.25
	.10	2.91	2.52	2.31	2.17	2.08	2.01	1.96	1.92	1.88	1.86	1.81	1.76	1.71	1.68	1.65	1.61	1.58	1.50
	.05	4.23	3.37	2.98	2.74	2.59	2.47	2.39	2.32	2.27	2.22	2.15	2.07	1.99	1.95	1.90	1.85	1.80	1.69
	.025	5.66	4.27	3.67	3.33	3.10	2.94	2.82	2.73	2.65	2.59	2.49	2.39	2.28	2.22	2.16	2.09	2.03	1.88
	.01	7.72	5.53	4.64	4.14	3.82	3.59	3.42	3.29	3.18	3.09	2.96	2.81	2.66	2.58	2.50	2.42	2.33	2.13
	.001	13.7	9.12	7.36	6.41	5.80	5.38	5.07	4.83	4.64	4.48	4.24	3.59	3.72	3.60	3.44	3.30	3.15	2.82
28	.25	1.38	1.46	1.45	1.43	1.41	1.40	1.39	1.38	1.37	1.36	1.34	1.33	1.31	1.30	1.29	1.28	1.27	1.24
	.10	2.89	2.50	2.29	2.16	2.06	2.00	1.94	1.90	1.87	1.84	1.79	1.74	1.69	1.66	1.63	1.59	1.56	1.48
	.05	4.20	3.34	2.95	2.71	2.56	2.45	2.36	2.29	2.24	2.19	2.12	2.04	1.96	1.91	1.87	1.82	1.77	1.65
	.025	5.61	4.22	3.63	3.29	3.06	2.90	2.78	2.69	2.61	2.55	2.45	2.34	2.23	2.17	2.11	2.05	1.98	1.83
	.01	7.64	5.45	4.57	4.07	3.75	3.53	3.36	3.23	3.12	3.03	2.90	2.75	2.60	2.52	2.44	2.35	2.26	2.06
	.001	13.5	8.93	7.19	6.25	5.66	5.24	4.93	4.69	4.50	4.35	4.11	3.86	3.60	3.46	3.32	3.18	3.02	2.69
30	.25	1.38	1.45	1.44	1.42	1.41	1.39	1.38	1.37	1.36	1.35	1.34	1.32	1.30	1.29	1.28	1.27	1.26	1.23
	.10	2.88	2.49	2.28	2.14	2.05	1.98	1.93	1.88	1.85	1.82	1.77	1.72	1.67	1.64	1.61	1.57	1.54	1.46
	.05	4.17	3.32	2.92	2.69	2.53	2.42	2.33	2.27	2.21	2.16	2.09	2.01	1.93	1.89	1.84	1.79	1.74	1.62
	.025	5.57	4.18	3.59	3.25	3.03	2.87	2.75	2.65	2.57	2.51	2.41	2.31	2.20	2.14	2.07	2.01	1.94	1.79
	.01	7.56	5.39	4.51	4.02	3.70	3.47	3.30	3.17	3.07	2.98	2.84	2.70	2.55	2.47	2.39	2.30	2.21	2.01
	.001	13.3	8.77	7.05	6.12	5.53	5.12	4.82	4.58	4.39	4.24	4.00	3.75	3.49	3.36	3.22	3.07	2.92	2.59
40	.25	1.36	1.44	1.42	1.40	1.39	1.37	1.36	1.35	1.34	1.33	1.31	1.30	1.28	1.26	1.25	1.24	1.22	1.19
	.10	2.84	2.44	2.23	2.09	2.00	1.93	1.87	1.83	1.79	1.76	1.71	1.66	1.61	1.57	1.54	1.51	1.47	1.38
	.05	4.08	3.23	2.84	2.61	2.45	2.34	2.25	2.18	2.12	2.08	2.00	1.92	1.84	1.79	1.74	1.69	1.64	1.51
	.025	5.42	4.05	3.46	3.13	2.90	2.74	2.62	2.53	2.45	2.39	2.29	2.18	2.07	2.01	1.94	1.88	1.80	1.64
	.01	7.31	5.18	4.31	3.83	3.51	3.29	3.12	2.99	2.89	2.80	2.66	2.52	2.37	2.29	2.20	2.11	2.02	1.80
	.001	12.6	8.25	6.60	5.70	5.13	4.73	4.44	4.21	4.02	3.87	3.64	3.40	3.15	3.01	2.87	2.73	2.57	2.23
60	.25	1.35	1.42	1.41	1.38	1.37	1.35	1.33	1.32	1.31	1.30	1.29	1.27	1.25	1.24	1.22	1.21	1.19	1.15
	.10	2.79	2.39	2.18	2.04	1.95	1.87	1.82	1.77	1.74	1.71	1.66	1.60	1.54	1.51	1.48	1.44	1.40	1.29
	.05	4.00	3.15	2.76	2.53	2.37	2.25	2.17	2.10	2.04	1.99	1.92	1.84	1.75	1.70	1.65	1.59	1.53	1.39
	.025	5.29	3.93	3.34	3.01	2.79	2.63	2.51	2.41	2.33	2.27	2.17	2.06	1.94	1.88	1.82	1.74	1.67	1.48
	.01	7.08	4.98	4.13	3.65	3.34	3.12	2.95	2.82	2.72	2.63	2.50	2.35	2.20	2.12	2.03	1.94	1.84	1.60
	.001	12.0	7.76	6.17	5.31	4.76	4.37	4.09	3.87	3.69	3.54	3.31	3.08	2.83	2.69	2.55	2.41	2.25	1.89

Table A-1   (Cont.)

df FOR DENOM.	α																		
		1	**2**	**3**	**4**	**5**	**6**	**7**	**8**	**9**	**10**	**12**	**15**	**20**	**24**	**30**	**40**	**60**	**∞**
120	.25	1.34	1.40	1.39	1.37	1.35	1.33	1.31	1.30	1.29	1.28	1.26	1.24	1.22	1.21	1.19	1.18	1.16	1.10
	.10	2.75	2.35	2.13	1.99	1.90	1.82	1.77	1.72	1.68	1.65	1.60	1.55	1.48	1.45	1.41	1.37	1.32	1.19
	.05	3.92	3.07	2.68	2.45	2.29	2.17	2.09	2.02	1.96	1.91	1.83	1.75	1.66	1.61	1.55	1.50	1.43	1.25
	.025	5.15	3.80	3.23	2.89	2.67	2.52	2.39	2.30	2.22	2.16	2.05	1.94	1.82	1.76	1.69	1.61	1.53	1.31
	.01	6.85	4.79	3.95	3.48	3.17	2.96	2.79	2.66	2.56	2.47	2.34	2.19	2.03	1.95	1.86	1.76	1.66	1.38
	.001	11.4	7.32	5.79	4.95	4.42	4.04	3.77	3.55	3.38	3.24	3.02	2.78	2.53	2.40	2.26	2.11	1.95	1.54
∞	.25	1.32	1.39	1.37	1.35	1.33	1.31	1.29	1.28	1.27	1.25	1.24	1.22	1.19	1.18	1.16	1.14	1.12	1.00
	.10	2.71	2.30	2.08	1.94	1.85	1.77	1.72	1.67	1.63	1.60	1.55	1.49	1.42	1.38	1.34	1.30	1.24	1.00
	.05	3.84	3.00	2.60	2.37	2.21	2.10	2.01	1.94	1.88	1.83	1.75	1.67	1.57	1.52	1.46	1.39	1.32	1.00
	.025	5.02	3.69	3.12	2.79	2.57	2.41	2.29	2.19	2.11	2.05	1.94	1.83	1.71	1.64	1.57	1.48	1.39	1.00
	.01	6.63	4.61	3.78	3.32	3.02	2.80	2.64	2.51	2.41	2.32	2.18	2.04	1.88	1.79	1.70	1.59	1.47	1.00
	.001	10.8	6.91	5.42	4.62	4.10	3.74	3.47	3.27	3.10	2.96	2.74	2.51	2.27	2.13	1.99	1.84	1.66	1.00

df FOR NUMERATOR

This table is abridged from Table 18 in E. S. Pearson and H. O. Hartley (Eds.), *Biometrika tables for statisticians* (3rd ed., Vol. 1), Cambridge University Press, New York, 1970, by permission of the *Biometrika* Trustees.

Table A–2 Power Function for Analysis of Variance (Fixed-Effects Model)

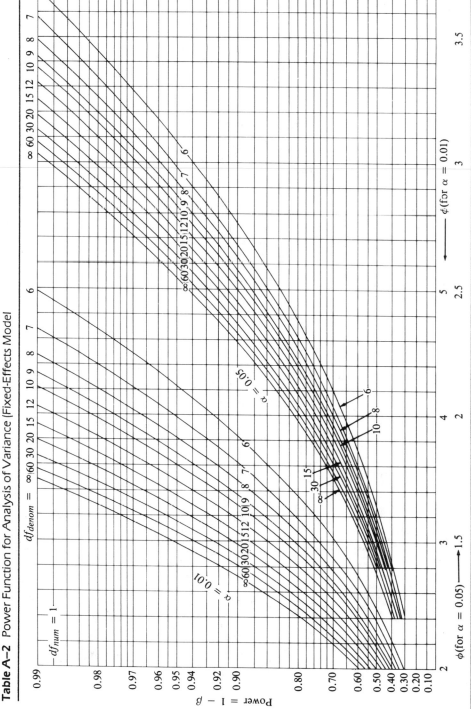

These charts are reproduced from Table 30 in E. S. Pearson and H. O. Hartley (Eds.), *Biometrika tables for statisticians* (Vol. II), Cambridge University Press, London, 1972, by permission of the *Biometrika* Trustees.

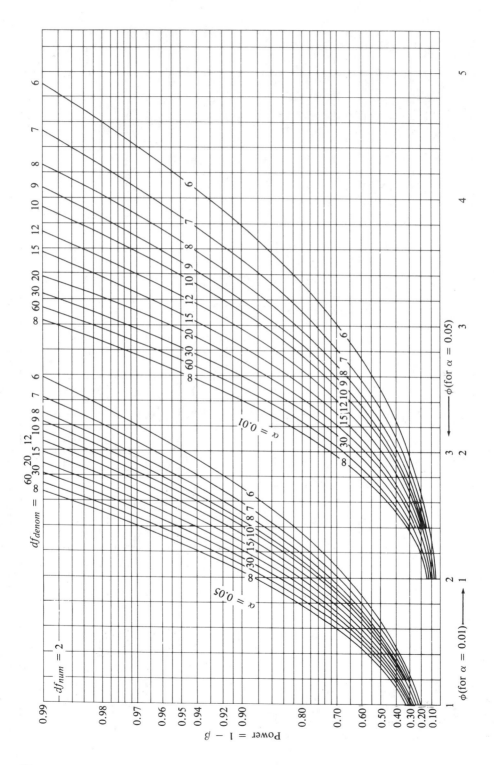

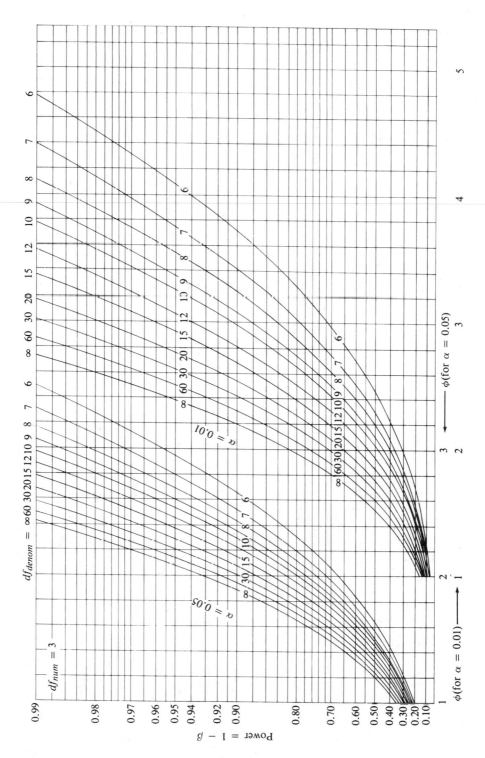

$df_{num} = 3$

$df_{denom} = \infty\ 60\ 30\ 20\ 15\ 12\ 10\ 9$

Power $= 1 - \beta$

$\alpha = 0.05$

$\alpha = 0.01$

ϕ (for $\alpha = 0.01$) ⟶

ϕ (for $\alpha = 0.05$)

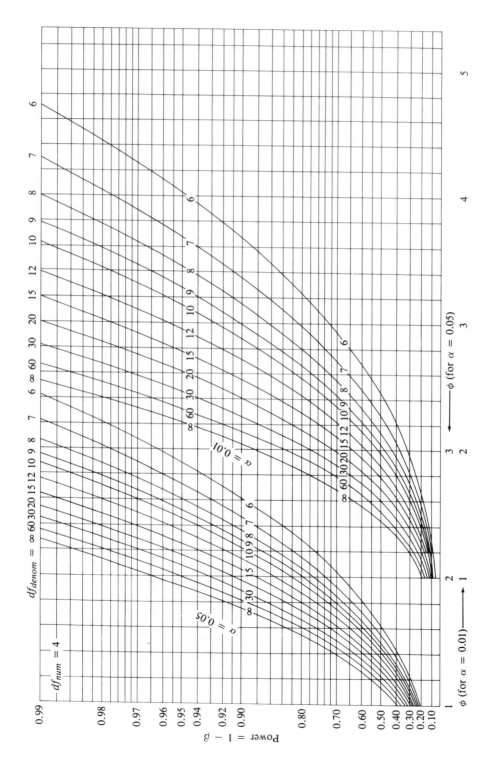

$df_{denom} = \infty\ 60\ 30\ 20\ 15\ 12\ 10\ 9\ 8$

$df_{num} = 4$

$\alpha = 0.01$

$\alpha = 0.05$

ϕ (for $\alpha = 0.05$)

ϕ (for $\alpha = 0.01$)

Power = $1 - \beta$

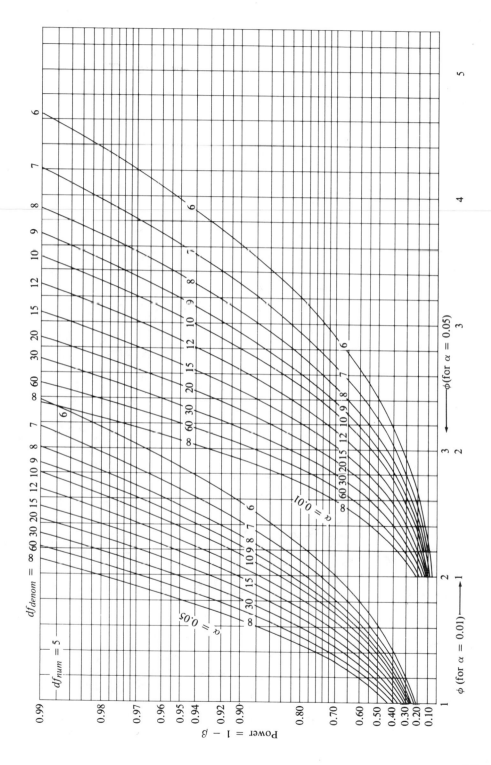

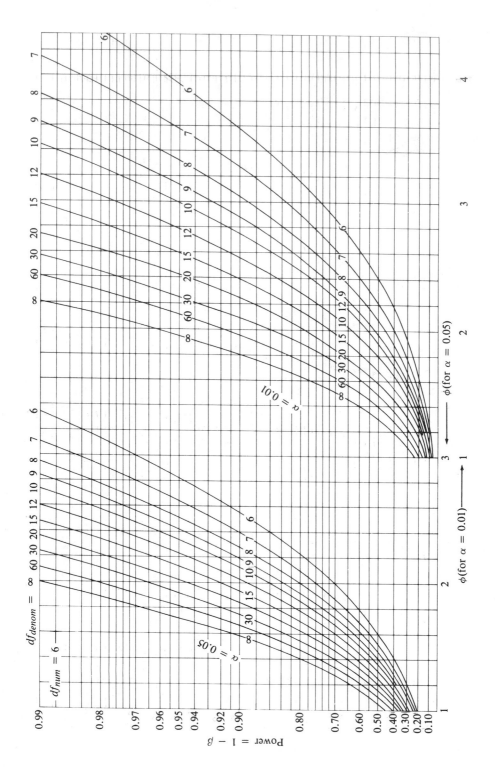

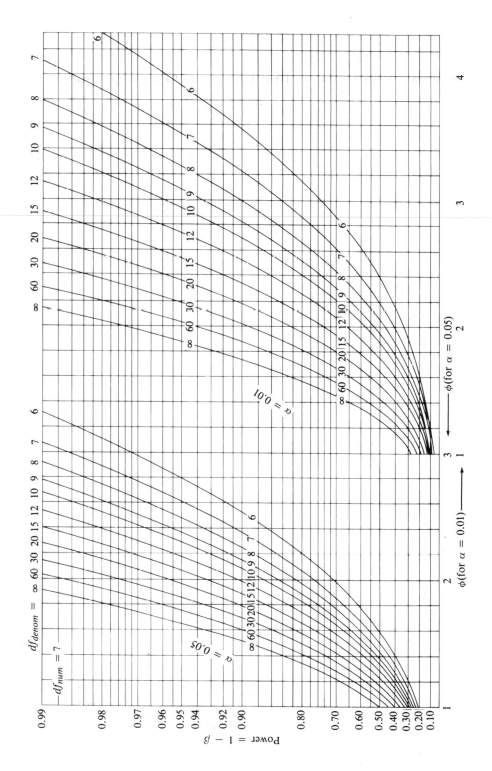

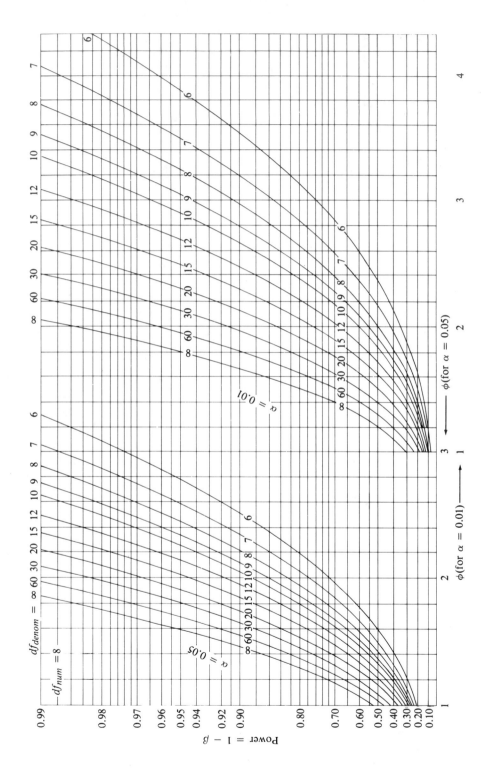

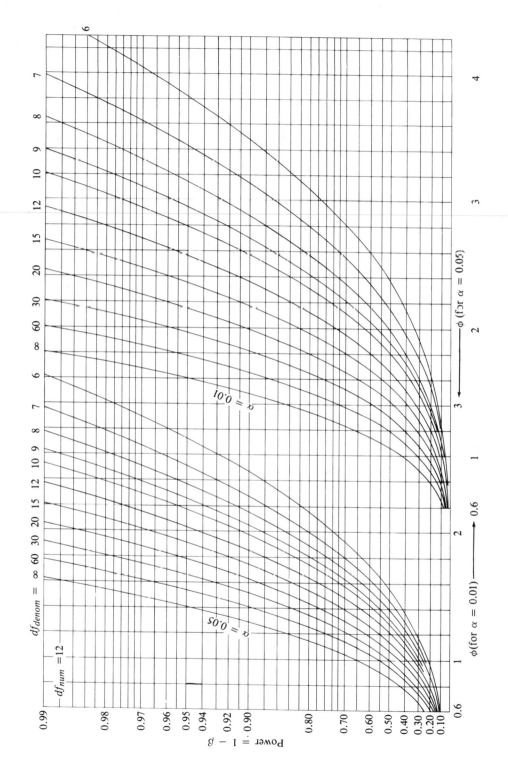

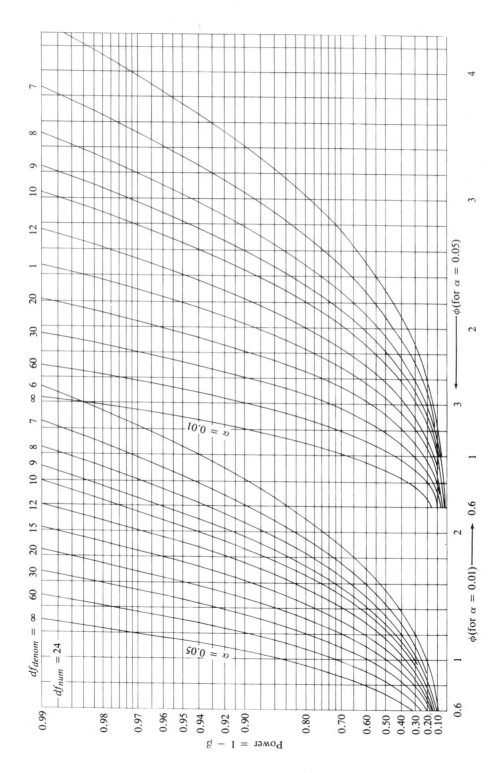

Table A-3   Selected Values from the t Distribution

df	$\alpha = .05$	$\alpha = .01$	df	$\alpha = .05$	$\alpha = .01$
1	12.71	63.66	18	2.10	2.88
2	4.30	9.92	19	2.09	2.86
3	3.18	5.84	20	2.09	2.84
4	2.78	4.60	21	2.08	2.83
5	2.57	4.03	22	2.07	2.82
6	2.45	3.71	23	2.07	2.81
7	2.36	3.50	24	2.06	2.80
8	2.31	3.36	25	2.06	2.79
9	2.26	3.25	26	2.06	2.78
10	2.23	3.17	27	2.05	2.77
11	2.20	3.11	28	2.05	2.76
12	2.18	3.06	29	2.04	2.76
13	2.16	3.01	30	2.04	2.75
14	2.14	2.98	40	2.02	2.70
15	2.13	2.95	60	2.00	2.66
16	2.12	2.92	120	1.98	2.62
17	2.11	2.90	∞	1.96	2.58

This table is abridged from Table 12 in E. S. Pearson and H. O. Hartley (Eds.), *Biometrika tables for statisticians* (3rd ed., Vol. 1), Cambridge University Press, New York, 1970, by permission of the *Biometrika* Trustees.

Table A–4 Coefficients of Orthogonal Polynomials

NUMBER OF LEVELS	POLYNOMIAL	COEFFICIENTS										$\Sigma (c_i)^2$
3	Linear	−1	0	1								2
	Quadratic	1	−2	1								6
4	Linear	−3	−1	1	3							20
	Quadratic	1	−1	−1	1							4
	Cubic	−1	3	−3	1							20
5	Linear	−2	−1	0	1	2						10
	Quadratic	2	−1	−2	−1	2						14
	Cubic	−1	2	0	−2	1						10
	Quartic	1	−4	6	−4	1						70
6	Linear	−5	−3	−1	1	3	5					70
	Quadratic	5	−1	−4	−4	−1	5					84
	Cubic	−5	7	4	−4	−7	5					180
	Quartic	1	−3	2	2	−3	1					28
	Quintic	−1	5	−10	10	−5	1					252
7	Linear	−3	−2	−1	0	1	2	3				28
	Quadratic	5	0	−3	−4	−3	0	5				84
	Cubic	−1	1	1	0	−1	−1	1				6
	Quartic	3	−7	1	6	1	−7	3				154
	Quintic	−1	4	−5	0	5	−4	1				84
8	Linear	−7	−5	−3	−1	1	3	5	7			168
	Quadratic	7	1	−3	−5	−5	−3	1	7			168
	Cubic	−7	5	7	3	−3	−7	−5	7			264
	Quartic	7	−13	−3	9	9	−3	−13	7			616
	Quintic	−7	23	−17	−15	15	17	−23	7			2,184
9	Linear	−4	−3	−2	−1	0	1	2	3	4		60
	Quadratic	28	7	−8	−17	−20	−17	−8	7	28		2,772
	Cubic	−14	7	13	9	0	−9	−13	−7	14		990
	Quartic	14	−21	−11	9	18	9	−11	−21	14		2,002
	Quintic	−4	11	−4	−9	0	9	4	−11	4		468
10	Linear	−9	−7	−5	−3	−1	1	3	5	7	9	330
	Quadratic	6	2	−1	−3	−4	−4	−3	−1	2	6	132
	Cubic	−42	14	35	31	12	−12	−31	−35	−14	42	8,580
	Quartic	18	−22	−17	3	18	18	3	−17	−22	18	2,860
	Quintic	−6	14	−1	−11	−6	6	11	1	−14	6	780

This table is abridged from Table 47 in E. S. Pearson and H. O. Hartley (Eds.), *Biometrika tables for statisticians* (3rd ed., Vol. 1), Cambridge University Press, New York, 1970, by permission of the *Biometrika* Trustees.

Table A-5   Critical Values of the Studentized Range Statistic

k = number of means (Tukey Test)

df_{error}	α_{FW}	2	3	4	5	6	7	8	9	10	11	12	13	14	15	16	17	18	19	20	α_{FW}	df_{error}
5	.05	3.64	4.60	5.22	5.67	6.03	6.33	6.58	6.80	6.99	7.17	7.32	7.47	7.60	7.72	7.83	7.93	8.03	8.12	8.21	.05	5
	.01	5.70	6.98	7.80	8.42	8.91	9.32	9.67	9.97	10.24	10.48	10.70	10.89	11.08	11.24	11.40	11.55	11.68	11.81	11.93	.01	
6	.05	3.46	4.34	4.90	5.30	5.63	5.90	6.12	6.32	6.49	6.65	6.79	6.92	7.03	7.14	7.24	7.34	7.43	7.51	7.59	.05	6
	.01	5.24	6.33	7.03	7.56	7.97	8.32	8.61	8.87	9.10	9.30	9.48	9.65	9.81	9.95	10.08	10.21	10.32	10.43	10.54	.01	
7	.05	3.34	4.16	4.68	5.06	5.36	5.61	5.82	6.00	6.16	6.30	6.43	6.55	6.65	6.76	6.85	6.94	7.02	7.10	7.17	.05	7
	.01	4.95	5.92	6.54	7.01	7.37	7.68	7.94	8.17	8.37	8.55	8.71	8.86	9.00	9.12	9.24	9.35	9.46	9.55	9.65	.01	
8	.05	3.26	4.04	4.53	4.89	5.17	5.40	5.60	5.77	5.92	6.05	6.18	6.29	6.39	6.48	6.57	6.65	6.73	6.80	6.87	.05	8
	.01	4.75	5.64	6.20	6.62	6.96	7.24	7.47	7.68	7.86	8.03	8.18	8.31	8.44	8.55	8.66	8.76	8.85	8.94	9.03	.01	
9	.05	3.20	3.95	4.41	4.76	5.02	5.24	5.43	5.59	5.74	5.87	5.98	6.09	6.19	6.28	6.36	6.44	6.51	6.58	6.64	.05	9
	.01	4.60	5.43	5.96	6.35	6.66	6.91	7.13	7.33	7.49	7.65	7.78	7.91	8.03	8.13	8.23	8.33	8.41	8.49	8.57	.01	
10	.05	3.15	3.88	4.33	4.65	4.91	5.12	5.30	5.46	5.60	5.72	5.83	5.93	6.03	6.11	6.19	6.27	6.34	6.40	6.47	.05	10
	.01	4.48	5.27	5.77	6.14	6.43	6.67	6.87	7.05	7.21	7.36	7.49	7.60	7.71	7.81	7.91	7.99	8.08	8.15	8.23	.01	
11	.05	3.11	3.82	4.26	4.57	4.82	5.03	5.20	5.35	5.49	5.61	5.71	5.81	5.90	5.98	6.06	6.13	6.20	6.27	6.33	.05	11
	.01	4.39	5.15	5.62	5.97	6.25	6.48	6.67	6.84	6.99	7.13	7.25	7.36	7.45	7.56	7.65	7.73	7.81	7.88	7.95	.01	
12	.05	3.08	3.77	4.20	4.51	4.75	4.95	5.12	5.27	5.39	5.51	5.61	5.71	5.80	5.88	5.95	6.02	6.09	6.15	6.21	.05	12
	.01	4.32	5.05	5.50	5.84	6.10	6.32	6.51	6.67	6.81	6.94	7.06	7.17	7.25	7.36	7.44	7.52	7.59	7.66	7.73	.01	
13	.05	3.06	3.73	4.15	4.45	4.69	4.88	5.05	5.19	5.32	5.43	5.53	5.63	5.71	5.79	5.86	5.93	5.99	6.05	6.11	.05	13
	.01	4.26	4.96	5.40	5.73	5.98	6.19	6.37	6.53	6.67	6.79	6.90	7.01	7.10	7.19	7.27	7.35	7.42	7.48	7.55	.01	
14	.05	3.03	3.70	4.11	4.41	4.64	4.83	4.99	5.13	5.25	5.36	5.46	5.55	5.64	5.71	5.79	5.85	5.91	5.97	6.03	.05	14
	.01	4.21	4.89	5.32	5.63	5.88	6.08	6.26	6.41	6.54	6.66	6.77	6.87	6.96	7.05	7.13	7.20	7.27	7.33	7.39	.01	
15	.05	3.01	3.67	4.08	4.37	4.59	4.78	4.94	5.08	5.20	5.31	5.40	5.49	5.57	5.65	5.72	5.78	5.85	5.90	5.96	.05	15
	.01	4.17	4.84	5.25	5.56	5.80	5.99	6.16	6.31	6.44	6.55	6.66	6.76	6.84	6.93	7.00	7.07	7.14	7.20	7.26	.01	

Table A-5 (Cont.)

k = number of means (Tukey Test)

df_{error}	α_{FW}	2	3	4	5	6	7	8	9	10	11	12	13	14	15	16	17	18	19	20	α_{FW}	df_{error}
16	.05	3.00	3.65	4.05	4.33	4.56	4.74	4.90	5.03	5.15	5.26	5.35	5.44	5.52	5.59	5.66	5.73	5.79	5.84	5.90	.05	16
	.01	4.13	4.79	5.19	5.49	5.72	5.92	6.08	6.22	6.35	6.46	6.56	6.66	6.74	6.82	6.90	6.97	7.03	7.09	7.15	.01	
17	.05	2.98	3.63	4.02	4.30	4.52	4.70	4.86	4.99	5.11	5.21	5.31	5.39	5.47	5.54	5.61	5.67	5.73	5.79	5.84	.05	17
	.01	4.10	4.74	5.14	5.43	5.66	5.85	6.01	6.15	6.27	6.38	6.48	6.57	6.66	6.73	6.81	6.87	6.94	7.00	7.05	.01	
18	.05	2.97	3.61	4.00	4.28	4.49	4.67	4.82	4.96	5.07	5.17	5.27	5.35	5.43	5.50	5.57	5.63	5.69	5.74	5.79	.05	18
	.01	4.07	4.70	5.09	5.38	5.60	5.79	5.94	6.08	6.20	6.31	6.41	6.50	6.58	6.65	6.73	6.79	6.85	6.91	6.97	.01	
19	.05	2.96	3.59	3.98	4.25	4.47	4.65	4.79	4.92	5.04	5.14	5.23	5.31	5.39	5.46	5.53	5.59	5.65	5.70	5.75	.05	19
	.01	4.05	4.67	5.05	5.33	5.55	5.73	5.89	6.02	6.14	6.25	6.34	6.43	6.51	6.58	6.65	6.72	6.78	6.84	6.89	.01	
20	.05	2.95	3.58	3.96	4.23	4.45	4.62	4.77	4.90	5.01	5.11	5.20	5.28	5.36	5.43	5.49	5.55	5.61	5.66	5.71	.05	20
	.01	4.02	4.64	5.02	5.29	5.51	5.69	5.84	5.97	6.09	6.19	6.28	6.37	6.45	6.52	6.59	6.65	6.71	6.77	6.82	.01	
24	.05	2.92	3.53	3.90	4.17	4.37	4.54	4.68	4.81	4.92	5.01	5.10	5.18	5.25	5.32	5.38	5.44	5.49	5.55	5.59	.05	24
	.01	3.96	4.55	4.91	5.17	5.37	5.54	5.69	5.81	5.92	6.02	6.11	6.19	6.26	6.33	6.39	6.45	6.51	6.56	6.61	.01	
30	.05	2.89	3.49	3.85	4.10	4.30	4.46	4.60	4.72	4.82	4.92	5.00	5.08	5.15	5.21	5.27	5.33	5.38	5.43	5.47	.05	30
	.01	3.89	4.45	4.80	5.05	5.24	5.40	5.54	5.65	5.76	5.85	5.93	6.01	6.08	6.14	6.20	6.26	6.31	6.36	6.41	.01	
40	.05	2.86	3.44	3.79	4.04	4.23	4.39	4.52	4.63	4.73	4.82	4.90	4.98	5.04	5.11	5.16	5.22	5.27	5.31	5.36	.05	40
	.01	3.82	4.37	4.70	4.93	5.11	5.26	5.39	5.50	5.60	5.69	5.76	5.83	5.90	5.96	6.02	6.07	6.12	6.16	6.21	.01	
60	.05	2.83	3.40	3.74	3.98	4.16	4.31	4.44	4.55	4.65	4.73	4.81	4.88	4.94	5.00	5.06	5.11	5.15	5.20	5.24	.05	60
	.01	3.76	4.28	4.59	4.82	4.99	5.13	5.25	5.36	5.45	5.53	5.60	5.67	5.73	5.78	5.84	5.89	5.93	5.97	6.01	.01	
120	.05	2.80	3.36	3.68	3.92	4.10	4.24	4.36	4.47	4.56	4.64	4.71	4.78	4.84	4.90	4.95	5.00	5.04	5.09	5.13	.05	120
	.01	3.70	4.20	4.50	4.71	4.87	5.01	5.12	5.21	5.30	5.37	5.44	5.50	5.56	5.61	5.66	5.71	5.75	5.79	5.83	.01	
∞	.05	2.77	3.31	3.63	3.86	4.03	4.17	4.29	4.39	4.47	4.55	4.62	4.68	4.74	4.80	4.85	4.89	4.93	4.97	5.01	.05	∞
	.01	3.64	4.12	4.40	4.60	4.76	4.88	4.99	5.08	5.16	5.23	5.29	5.35	5.40	5.45	5.49	5.54	5.57	5.61	5.65	.01	

This table is abridged from Table 29 in E. S. Pearson and H. O. Hartley (Eds.), *Biometrika tables for statisticians* (3rd ed., Vol. 1), Cambridge University Press, New York. 1970, by permission of the *Biometrika* Trustees.

Table A–6 Critical Values of the Dunnett Test for Comparing Treatment Means with a Control

TWO-TAILED COMPARISONS

k = number of treatment means, including control

df_{error}	α_{FW}	2	3	4	5	6	7	8	9	10
5	.05	2.57	3.03	3.29	3.48	3.62	3.73	3.82	3.90	3.97
	.01	4.03	4.63	4.98	5.22	5.41	5.56	5.69	5.80	5.89
6	.05	2.45	2.86	3.10	3.26	3.39	3.49	3.57	3.64	3.71
	.01	3.71	4.21	4.51	4.71	4.87	5.00	5.10	5.20	5.28
7	.05	2.36	2.75	2.97	3.12	3.24	3.33	3.41	3.47	3.53
	.01	3.50	3.95	4.21	4.39	4.53	4.64	4.74	4.82	4.89
8	.05	2.31	2.67	2.88	3.02	3.13	3.22	3.29	3.35	3.41
	.01	3.36	3.77	4.00	4.17	4.29	4.40	4.48	4.56	4.62
9	.05	2.26	2.61	2.81	2.95	3.05	3.14	3.20	3.26	3.32
	.01	3.25	3.63	3.85	4.01	4.12	4.22	4.30	4.37	4.43
10	.05	2.23	2.57	2.76	2.89	2.99	3.07	3.14	3.19	3.24
	.01	3.17	3.53	3.74	3.88	3.99	4.08	4.16	4.22	4.28
11	.05	2.20	2.53	2.72	2.84	2.94	3.02	3.08	3.14	3.19
	.01	3.11	3.45	3.65	3.79	3.89	3.98	4.05	4.11	4.16
12	.05	2.18	2.50	2.68	2.81	2.90	2.98	3.04	3.09	3.14
	.01	3.05	3.39	3.58	3.71	3.81	3.89	3.96	4.02	4.07
13	.05	2.16	2.48	2.65	2.78	2.87	2.94	3.00	3.06	3.10
	.01	3.01	3.33	3.52	3.65	3.74	3.82	3.89	3.94	3.99
14	.05	2.14	2.46	2.63	2.75	2.84	2.91	2.97	3.02	3.07
	.01	2.98	3.29	3.47	3.59	3.69	3.76	3.83	3.88	3.93
15	.05	2.13	2.44	2.61	2.73	2.82	2.89	2.95	3.00	3.04
	.01	2.95	3.25	3.43	3.55	3.64	3.71	3.78	3.83	3.88
16	.05	2.12	2.42	2.59	2.71	2.80	2.87	2.92	2.97	3.02
	.01	2.92	3.22	3.39	3.51	3.60	3.67	3.73	3.78	3.83
17	.05	2.11	2.41	2.58	2.69	2.78	2.85	2.90	2.95	3.00
	.01	2.90	3.19	3.36	3.47	3.56	3.63	3.69	3.74	3.79
18	.05	2.10	2.40	2.56	2.68	2.76	2.83	2.89	2.94	2.98
	.01	2.88	3.17	3.33	3.44	3.53	3.60	3.66	3.71	3.75
19	.05	2.09	2.39	2.55	2.66	2.75	2.81	2.87	2.92	2.96
	.01	2.86	3.15	3.31	3.42	3.50	3.57	3.63	3.68	3.72
20	.05	2.09	2.38	2.54	2.65	2.73	2.80	2.86	2.90	2.95
	.01	2.85	3.13	3.29	3.40	3.48	3.55	3.60	3.65	3.69
24	.05	2.06	2.35	2.51	2.61	2.70	2.76	2.81	2.86	2.90
	.01	2.80	3.07	3.22	3.32	3.40	3.47	3.52	3.57	3.61
30	.05	2.04	2.32	2.47	2.58	2.66	2.72	2.77	2.82	2.86
	.01	2.75	3.01	3.15	3.25	3.33	3.39	3.44	3.49	3.52
40	.05	2.02	2.29	2.44	2.54	2.62	2.68	2.73	2.77	2.81
	.01	2.70	2.95	3.09	3.19	3.26	3.32	3.37	3.41	3.44
60	.05	2.00	2.27	2.41	2.51	2.58	2.64	2.69	2.73	2.77
	.01	2.66	2.90	3.03	3.12	3.19	3.25	3.29	3.33	3.37

Table A–6 (Cont.)

TWO-TAILED COMPARISONS

k = number of treatment means, including control

df_{error}	α_{FW}	2	3	4	5	6	7	8	9	10
120	.05	1.98	2.24	2.38	2.47	2.55	2.60	2.65	2.69	2.73
	.01	2.62	2.85	2.97	3.06	3.12	3.18	3.22	3.26	3.29
∞	.05	1.96	2.21	2.35	2.44	2.51	2.57	2.61	2.65	2.69
	.01	2.58	2.79	2.92	3.00	3.06	3.11	3.15	3.19	3.22

This table is abridged from C. W. Dunnett, New tables for multiple comparisons with a control, *Biometrics*, 1964, *20*, 482–491, by permission of the author and the editor.

ONE-TAILED COMPARISONS

k = number of treatment means, including control

df_{error}	α_{FW}	2	3	4	5	6	7	8	9	10
5	.05	2.02	2.44	2.68	2.85	2.98	3.08	3.16	3.24	3.30
	.01	3.37	3.90	4.21	4.43	4.60	4.73	4.85	4.94	5.03
6	.05	1.94	2.34	2.56	2.71	2.83	2.92	3.00	3.07	3.12
	.01	3.14	3.61	3.88	4.07	4.21	4.33	4.43	4.51	4.59
7	.05	1.89	2.27	2.48	2.62	2.73	2.82	2.89	2.95	3.01
	.01	3.00	3.42	3.66	3.83	3.96	4.07	4.15	4.23	4.30
8	.05	1.86	2.22	2.42	2.55	2.66	2.74	2.81	2.87	2.92
	.01	2.90	3.29	3.51	3.67	3.79	3.88	3.96	4.03	4.09
9	.05	1.83	2.18	2.37	2.50	2.60	2.68	2.75	2.81	2.86
	.01	2.82	3.19	3.40	3.55	3.66	3.75	3.82	3.89	3.94
10	.05	1.81	2.15	2.34	2.47	2.56	2.64	2.70	2.76	2.81
	.01	2.76	3.11	3.31	3.45	3.56	3.64	3.71	3.78	3.83
11	.05	1.80	2.13	2.31	2.44	2.53	2.60	2.67	2.72	2.77
	.01	2.72	3.06	3.25	3.38	3.48	3.56	3.63	3.69	3.74
12	.05	1.78	2.11	2.29	2.41	2.50	2.58	2.64	2.69	2.74
	.01	2.68	3.01	3.19	3.32	3.42	3.50	3.56	3.62	2.67
13	.05	1.77	2.09	2.27	2.39	2.48	2.55	2.61	2.66	2.71
	.01	2.65	2.97	3.15	3.27	3.37	3.44	3.51	3.56	3.61
14	.05	1.76	2.08	2.25	2.37	2.46	2.53	2.59	2.64	2.69
	.01	2.62	2.94	3.11	3.23	3.32	3.40	3.46	3.51	3.56
15	.05	1.75	2.07	2.24	2.36	2.44	2.51	2.57	2.62	2.67
	.01	2.60	2.91	3.08	3.20	3.29	3.36	3.42	3.47	3.52
16	.05	1.75	2.06	2.23	2.34	2.43	2.50	2.56	2.61	2.65
	.01	2.58	2.88	3.05	3.17	3.26	3.33	3.39	3.44	3.48
17	.05	1.74	2.05	2.22	2.33	2.42	2.49	2.54	2.59	2.64
	.01	2.57	2.86	3.03	3.14	3.23	3.30	3.36	3.41	3.45
18	.05	1.73	2.04	2.21	2.32	2.41	2.48	2.53	2.58	2.62
	.01	2.55	2.84	3.01	3.12	3.21	3.27	3.33	3.38	3.42

ONE-TAILED COMPARISONS

k = number of treatment means, including control

df_{error}	α_{FW}	2	3	4	5	6	7	8	9	10
19	.05	1.73	2.03	2.20	2.31	2.40	2.47	2.52	2.57	2.61
	.01	2.54	2.83	2.99	3.10	3.18	3.25	3.31	3.36	3.40
20	.05	1.72	2.03	2.19	2.30	2.39	2.46	2.51	2.56	2.60
	.01	2.53	2.81	2.97	3.08	3.17	3.23	3.29	3.34	3.38
24	.05	1.71	2.01	2.17	2.28	2.36	2.43	2.48	2.53	2.57
	.01	2.49	2.77	2.92	3.03	3.11	3.17	3.22	3.27	3.31
30	.05	1.70	1.99	2.15	2.25	2.33	2.40	2.45	2.50	2.54
	.01	2.46	2.72	2.87	2.97	3.05	3.11	3.16	3.21	3.24
40	.05	1.68	1.97	2.13	2.23	2.31	2.37	2.42	2.47	2.51
	.01	2.42	2.68	2.82	2.92	2.99	3.05	3.10	3.14	3.18
60	.05	1.67	1.95	2.10	2.21	2.28	2.35	2.39	2.44	2.48
	.01	2.39	2.64	2.78	2.87	2.94	3.00	3.04	3.08	3.12
120	.05	1.66	1.93	2.08	2.18	2.26	2.32	2.37	2.41	2.45
	.01	2.36	2.60	2.73	2.82	2.89	2.94	2.99	3.03	3.06
∞	.05	1.64	1.92	2.06	2.16	2.23	2.29	2.34	2.38	2.42
	.01	2.33	2.56	2.68	2.77	2.84	2.89	2.93	2.97	3.00

This table is reproduced from C. W. Dunnett, A mulitple comparison procedure for comparing several treatments with a control, *Journal of the American Statistical Association*, 1955, *50*, 1,096–1,121, by permission of the author and the editor.

Appendix B

Answers to the Chapter Exercises

CHAPTER 2

1. a. and b.

	a_1	a_2	a_3	a_4	a_5
Sum	80	60	70	120	100
ΣY^2	684	426	600	1,524	1,096
Mean	8.00	6.00	7.00	12.00	10.00

c. $\quad [T] = \dfrac{(80 + 60 + 70 + 120 + 100)^2}{(5)(10)} = 3,698.00$

$\quad [A] = \dfrac{(80)^2 + (60)^2 + (70)^2 + (120)^2 + (100)^2}{10} = 3,930.00$

$\quad [Y] = 684 + 426 + 600 + 1,524 + 1,096 = 4,330$

$\quad SS_A = [A] - [T] = 232.00$

$\quad SS_{S/A} - [Y] - [A] = 400.00$

$\quad SS_T = [Y] - [T] = 632.00$

CHAPTER 3

1. a. $F(4,30) = 2.69, p = .05$
   b. $F(1, 120) = 11.4, p = .001$
   c. $df_{num.} = a - 1 = 7 - 1 = 6; df_{denom.} = (a)(n - 1) = 7(5 - 1) = 28;$
   $F(6, 28) = 2.00, p = .10$
   d. $df_{num.} = 3 - 1 = 2; df_{denom.} = 3(9 - 1) = 24; F(2, 24) = 1.47, p = .25$

2. Summary of the analysis:

Source	Calculations	SS	df	MS	F
A	$374.00 - 365.07 =$	8.93	2	4.47	.37
S/A	$518 - [A] =$	144.00	12	12.00	
Total	$[Y] - [T] =$	152.93	14		

3. Summary of the analysis:

Source	SS	df	MS	F
A	232.00	4	58.00	6.52*
S/A	400.00	45	8.89	
Total	632.00	49		

*$p < .05$.

4. a. Summary of the analysis:

Source	Calculations	SS	df	MS	F
A	$640.00 - 563.33 =$	76.67	5	15.33	3.14*
S/A	$757 - [A] =$	117.00	24	4.88	
Total	$[Y] - [T] =$	193.67	29		

*$p < .05$.

b. $MS_{S/A} = \dfrac{5.00 + 3.75 + 1.25 + 7.50 + 6.25 + 5.50}{6} = 4.88$

CHAPTER 4

1. a. $\hat{\omega}_A^2 = \dfrac{210.00 - (2)(14.17)}{380.00 + 14.17} = .461; \hat{\omega}_A^2 = \dfrac{2(7.41 - 1)}{2(7.41 - 1) + (3)(5)} = .461$

b. $R^2 = \dfrac{210.00}{380.00} = .553$

c. The experimental treatments account for somewhere between 46 percent to 55 percent of the total variability in the experiment. Using Cohen's (1977) terminology, we would say that this finding represents a "large" effect.

2. a. $\hat{\omega}_A^2 = \dfrac{8.93 - (2)(12.00)}{152.93 + 12.00} = -.091$

b. The presence of a negative value is interpreted to mean the absence of treatment effects. Negative values are obtained when $F < 1$.

3. a. $\hat{\omega}_A^2 = \dfrac{233.33 - (2)(17.90)}{609.33 + 17.90} = .315; \hat{\omega}_A^2 = \dfrac{233.33 - (2)(17.90)}{1,790.63 + 17.90} = .109$

b. As revealed by the F tests, the statistical conclusions drawn from the two experiments are the same, but the relative strengths of the treatment effects are quite different. With other factors held constant, a stronger treatment effect is associated with the experiment having the *smaller* sample size (that is, $n = 8$, rather than $n = 30$).

4. a. $\phi_A^2 = n' \dfrac{32/5}{15} = .4267\, n'; \phi_A = .653\sqrt{n'}$. For $n' = 7$, $\phi_A = (.653)\sqrt{7}$

$= 1.73$, $df_{denom.} = 5(7 - 1) = 30$, and power $= .83$. Any smaller sample size gives power $< .80$.

b. For $n' = 8$, we find $\phi_A = (.653)(2.828) = 1.85$, $df_{denom.} = 5(8 - 1) = 35$, and power $= .90$. (The chart is difficult to read exactly. More accurate computer programs indicate that for $n = 8$, power $= .89$ and for $n = 9$, power $= .93$).

c. For $n' = 10$, we find $\phi_A = (.653)(3.162) = 2.06$, $df_{denom.} = 5(10 - 1) = 45$, and power $= .84$; for $n' = 11$, we find $\phi_A = (.653)(3.317) = 2.17$, $df_{denom.} = 5(11 - 1) = 50$, and power $= .90$.

5. a. The means are 5, 8.5, 8.5, 8.5, 8.5, 8.5, 8.5, and 12; $\phi_A^2 = (9)\dfrac{24.50/8}{27.56}$

$= 1.000$; $\phi_A = 1.00$; $df_{denom.} = 8(9 - 1) = 64$; and power $= .45$.

b. The means are 5, 6, 7, 8, 9, 10, 11, and 12; $\phi_A^2 = (9)\dfrac{42.00/8}{27.56} = 1.714$;

$\phi_A = 1.31$; $df_{denom.} = 64$; and power $= .72$.

c. The means are 5, 5, 5, 5, 12, 12, 12, and 12; $\phi_A^2 = (9)\dfrac{98.00/8}{27.56} = 4.000$;

$\phi_A = 2.00$; $df_{denom.} = 64$ and power $> .98$. If this were a real situation, the researcher could probably afford to reduce sample size, given that power is so high in this particular case.

---

6. a. Using Eq. (4-7), we find $\phi_A^2 = n' \dfrac{.01}{1 - .01} = .0101\,n'$; $\phi_A = .1005\sqrt{n'}$. For

$n' = 356$, $\phi_A = (.1005)(18.868) = 1.90$, $df_{denom.} = \infty$, and power $= .90$. (The power charts are difficult to read accurately for this problem; any value around $n = 356$ is a reasonable approximation).

b. We find $\phi_A^2 = n' \dfrac{.06}{1 - .06} = .0638\,n'$ and $\phi_A = .253\sqrt{n'}$. For $n' = 56$,

$\phi_A = (.253)(7.483) = 1.89$, $df_{denom.} = \infty$, and power $= .90$.

CHAPTER 5

1. $\hat{\sigma}_M^2 = 4.88/5 = .976$; $\hat{\sigma}_M = .99$; $t(24) = 2.06$; $(t)(\hat{\sigma}_M) = (2.06)(.99) = 2.04$
Subtracting 2.04 from each mean gives the lower limit of each confidence interval and adding it gives the upper limit. For each mean,

$.96 \le \mu_1 \le 5.04$; $-.04 \le \mu_2 \le 4.04$; $2.96 \le \mu_3 \le 7.04$; $4.96 \le \mu_4 \le 9.04$; $2.96 \le \mu_5 \le 7.04$; $1.96 \le \mu_6 \le 6.04$

2. a. Summary of the analysis:

Source	Calculations	SS	df	MS	F
A	$1,371.50 - 1,225.00 =$	146.50	3	48.83	1.11
S/A	$1,901.00 - [A] =$	529.50	12	44.13	
Total	$[Y] - [T] =$	676.00	15		

Note: For this analysis, I used the following values for the four medians:

$Md_1 = \dfrac{22 + 25}{2} = 23.5$, $Md_2 = \dfrac{36 + 45}{2} = 40.5$, $Md_3 = \dfrac{46 + 66}{2}$

$= 56.0$, and $Md_4 = \dfrac{62 + 66}{2} = 64.0$.

b. The F associated with the Brown-Forsythe test is not significant. On the other hand, $F_{max.} = 240.33/51.00 = 4.71$, which might suggest the need for a slight correction in α.

CHAPTER 6

1. a. Summary of the analysis:

Source	Calculations	SS	df	MS	F
A	5,117.25 − 4,651.25 =	466.00	4	116.50	3.15*
S/A			15	37.00	

*$p < .05$.

b. Coefficients and sums of weighted means:

	a_1	a_2	a_3	a_4	a_5	$\hat{\psi}_A$	Σc_i^2
Mean	15.00	13.75	8.00	16.50	23.00		
Comp. 1	4	−1	−1	−1	−1	−1.25	20
Comp. 2	0	1	1	−1	−1	−17.75	4
Comp. 3	0	1	−1	0	0	5.75	2
Comp. 4	0	0	0	1	−1	−6.50	2

c. $\Sigma (c_i)(d_i) = 0$ for all pairs of comparisons.
d. Summary of the analysis:

Source	SS	df	MS	F
Comp. 1	.3125	1	.3125	.01
Comp. 2	315.0625	1	315.0625	8.52*
Comp. 3	66.1250	1	66.1250	1.79
Comp. 4	84.5000	1	84.5000	2.28
S/A		15	37.00	

*$p < .05$.

The analysis indicates that the main outcome of the experiment was a difference between the two drugs.
e. .3125 + 315.0625 + 66.1250 + 84.5000 = 466.0000 = SS_A
(The calculations were carried to four places to eliminate rounding error, which otherwise would detract from this demonstration.)
2. a. Summary of the analysis:

Source	SS	df	MS	F
Comp. 1	162.45	1	162.45	12.03*
Comp. 2	44.10	1	44.10	3.27
Comp. 3	3.60	1	3.60	.27
Comp. 4	.10	1	.10	.01
S/A		20	13.50	

*$p < .05$.

The main conclusion is that performance is significantly better when the material is presented all at once rather than when it is exposed one word at a time.

b. $\quad SS_A = 3{,}460.40 - 3{,}226.24 = 234.16$

$\Sigma \, SS_{A_{comp.}} = 162.45 + 44.10 + 3.60 + .10 = 210.25$

3. a. $\quad SS_{A_{set}} = \dfrac{(48)^2 + (53)^2 + (47)^2}{10} - \dfrac{(48 + 53 + 47)^2}{(3)(10)}$

$$= 732.20 - 730.13 = 2.07$$

$$MS_{A_{set}} = \frac{2.07}{2} = 1.04; \; F_{set} = \frac{1.04}{4.11} = .25$$

The three incentives did not influence performance differentially.

b. The average for the control condition is 3.20 problems and for the combined incentive conditions is $(4.8 + 5.3 + 4.7)/3 = 4.93$ problems. Using the coefficients $-1, -1, -1, 3$, we find

$$SS_{A_{comp.}} = \frac{10(-5.20)^2}{12} = 22.53$$

$$F = \frac{22.53}{4.11} = 5.48, p < .05$$

Although equally effective, the incentive conditions did facilitate problem solving in this experiment.

c. $\quad SS_A = \dfrac{(48)^2 + (53)^2 + (47)^2 + (32)^2}{10} - \dfrac{(48 + 53 + 47 + 32)^2}{(4)(10)}$

$$= 834.60 - 810.00 = 24.60$$

$$MS_A = \frac{24.60}{3} = 8.20; \; F = \frac{8.20}{4.11} = 2.00, p > .10$$

This problem illustrates one of the advantages of planned comparisons. The omnibus F test assesses the average differences among the treatment means and can "water down" specific differences in the data. In this case, the fact that the three incentive conditions did not differ helped to "average out" the significant single-*df* comparison between the control and the combined incentive conditions. The set of planned comparisons represented by parts (a) and (b) reflects a meaningful and logical way to analyze this experiment.

CHAPTER 7

1. a. *Linear component:*

$$\hat{\psi}_{linear} = (-3)(1.52) + (-2)(2.64) + (-1)(4.28) + (0)(3.86) + (1)(3.86)$$
$$+ (2)(2.79) + (3)(3.70) = 6.42$$

$$SS_{A_{linear}} = \frac{(14)(6.42)^2}{28} = 20.61; \; F = \frac{20.61}{5.84} = 3.53, p > .05$$

Quadratic component:

$$\hat{\psi}_{quadratic} = (5)(1.52) + (0)(2.64) + (-3)(4.28) + (-4)(3.86) + (-3)(3.86) \\ + (0)(2.79) + (5)(3.70) = -13.76$$

$$SS_{A_{quadratic}} = \frac{(14)(-13.76)^2}{84} = 31.56; F = \frac{31.56}{5.84} = 5.40, p < .05$$

b. *Linear component:*

$$\overline{Y}_T = (1.52 + 2.64 + 4.28 + 3.86 + 3.86 + 2.79 + 3.70)/7 = 3.24$$

$$\text{and } b_1 = \frac{6.42}{28} = .23$$

Regression equation: $\overline{Y}_{A_i}' = 3.24 + (.23)(c_i)$

Quadratic component:

$$b_2 = \frac{-13.76}{84} = -.16$$

Regression equation: $\overline{Y}_{A_i}' = 3.24 - (.16)(c_i)$

2. a. Summary of the analysis:

Source	Calculations	SS	df	MS	F
A	229.00 − 197.63 =	31.37	5	6.27	7.55*
S/A	249 − [A] =	20.00	24	.83	
Total	[Y] − [T] =	51.37	29		

*$p < .05$.

b. $\hat{\psi}_{quadratic} = (5)(.80) + (-1)(1.60) + (-4)(3.40) + (-4)(3.60) \\ + (-1)(3.20) + (5)(2.80) = -14.80$

$$SS_{A_{quadratic}} = \frac{5(-14.80)^2}{84} = 13.04; F = \frac{13.04}{.83} = 15.71, p < .05$$

c. $SS_{A_{residual}} = SS_A - SS_{A_{quadratic}} = 31.37 - 13.04 = 18.33$

$$df_{A_{residual}} = df_A - df_{A_{quadratic}} = 5 - 1 = 4$$

$$MS_{A_{residual}} = \frac{18.33}{4} = 4.58; F = \frac{4.58}{.83} = 5.52, p < .05$$

d. $\hat{\psi}_{linear} = (-5)(.80) + (-3)(1.60) + (-1)(3.40) + (1)(3.60) \\ + (3)(3.20) + (5)(2.80) = 15.00$

$$SS_{A_{linear}} = \frac{5(15.00)^2}{70} = 16.07; F = \frac{16.07}{.83} = 19.36, p < .05$$

There is no statistical basis for continuing the analysis further because the residual sum of squares is not significant; that is,

$$SS_{A_{residual}} = SS_A - SS_{A_{linear}} - SS_{A_{quadratic}} = 31.37 - 16.07 - 13.04 = 2.26$$

$$df_{A_{residual}} = df_A - df_{A_{linear}} - df_{A_{quadratic}} = 5 - 1 - 1 = 3$$

$$MS_{A_{residual}} = \frac{2.26}{3} = .75; \quad F = \frac{.75}{.83} = .90 \; p > .05$$

e. The theoretical expectations were supported by the experiment with a significant concave downward trend relating anxiety and backward memory span. In addition, there is a significant tendency for memory span to increase as a function of the anxiety level of the subjects.

CHAPTER 8

1. a. $\alpha_{FW} = (8)(.05) = .40$. Alternatively, we could use Eq. (8-1), in which case
   $\alpha_{FW} = 1 - (1 - .05)^8 - 1 - .66 - .34$
   b. $\alpha_B = .05/8 = .006$. The appropriate value for z is the point on the unit normal distribution above which $\frac{1}{2}(\alpha_B) \times 100$ = percent of the curve falls. In this example, that percentage is $.006/2 \times 100 = .3$ percent; the corresponding value of z $= 2.75$. Using Eq. (8-4), we find

   $$t(15) = 2.75 + \frac{(2.75)^3 + 2.75}{(4)(15 - 2)} = 2.75 + .45 = 3.20$$

   The corresponding value for $F = (3.20)^2 = 10.24$.
   c. If we assume that $\tilde{\alpha}_{FW_{planned}} = (4)(.05) = .20$, then $\tilde{\alpha}_{planned} = .20/8 = .025$. The percentage in this case is $.025/2 \times 100 = 1.25$ percent. Using Eq. (8-4), we find

   $$t(15) = 2.24 + \frac{(2.24)^3 + 2.24}{(4)(15 - 2)} = 2.24 + .26 = 2.50$$

   The corresponding value for $F = (2.50)^2 = 6.25$.
2. a. Summary of the analysis:

Source	Calculations	SS	df	MS	F
A	28,463.88 − 27,789.03 =	674.85	7	96.41	3.35*
S/A			120	28.75	

*$p < .05$.

b. The critical mean difference is

$$\bar{d}_D = 2.65\sqrt{\frac{2(28.75)}{16}} = (2.65)(1.90) = 5.04$$

Applying this value to the differences between the control and experimental groups, we find

	E_1	E_2	$\bar{E}_3$	E_4	E_5	E_6	E_7
$\bar{C} - \bar{E}$	1.18	3.00	.62	6.12*	4.75	5.25*	5.68*

*$p < .05$.

c. $F_S = (8 - 1)(2.09) = 14.63$. If we consider the largest difference, C versus E_4, and translate this comparison into a sum of squares, we have

$$SS_{A_{comp.}} = \frac{16(6.12)^2}{2} = 299.64$$

The $F = 299.64/28.75 = 10.42$ does not exceed $F_S = 14.63$. Thus, none of the control-experimental differences is significant, which demonstrates the marked advantage of specifying a restricted set of comparisons.

3. a. and b. To facilitate the evaluation of all pairwise differences, the means are ordered from smallest to largest in the following table. One way to evaluate these differences without correction is to use the standard formula for single-df comparisons, Eq. (6–5), to test the differences systematically, starting with the largest and continuing with the smaller differences until the first difference is *not* significant. Following this process, we find

$a_3\,\text{vs.}\,a_2: SS_{A_{comp.}} = 7(14.72)^2/2 = 758.37; F = 758.37/58.65 = 12.93, p < .05$

$a_1\,\text{vs.}\,a_2: SS_{A_{comp.}} = 7(9.29)^2/2 = 302.06; F = 302.06/58.65 = 5.15, p < .05$

$a_3\,\text{vs.}\,a_4: SS_{A_{comp.}} = 7(9.00)^2/2 = 283.50; F = 283.50/58.65 = 4.83, p < .05$

$a_4\,\text{vs.}\,a_2: SS_{A_{comp.}} = 7(5.72)^2/2 = 114.51; F = 114.51/58.65 = 1.95, p > .05$

The significance of the first three comparisons is indicated by an a superscript in the summary that follows. An easier way to proceed is to calculate the *mean critical difference* ($\bar{d}_{PC}$) rather than each sum of square. This value is easily calculated as follows:

$$\bar{d}_{PC} = \sqrt{F(1, df_{S/A})\,\frac{2(MS_{S/A})}{n}}$$

where $F(1, df_{S/A})$ is the critical value for a single-df comparison. In the present case,

$$\bar{d}_{PC} = \sqrt{4.26\,\frac{2(58.65)}{7}} = \sqrt{71.39} = 8.45$$

We simply compare this critical difference (8.45) with each pairwise difference; any pairwise difference that equals or exceeds this critical value is declared significant.

The critical mean difference for the Tukey test is $\bar{d}_T = 3.90 \sqrt{58.65/7} = (3.90)(2.89) = 11.27$. Only the largest difference (a_3 vs. a_2) is significant, which is indicated by a b superscript in the summary that follows.

	a_2	a_4	a_1	a_3
Means	47.57	53.29	56.86	62.29
$\bar{Y}_{A_2} = 47.57$	—	5.72	9.29[a]	14.72[a,b]
$\bar{Y}_{A_4} = 53.29$	—	—	3.57	9.00[a]
$\bar{Y}_{A_1} = 56.86$	—	—	—	5.43

[a]$p < .05$, no correction; [b]$p < .05$, Tukey test.

c. The new decision rules are

> If a pairwise difference $(\bar{d}) \geq 11.27$ (Tukey test), reject H_0.
> If $\bar{d}$ falls between 8.45 (no correction) and 11.27, suspend judgment.
> If $\bar{d} < 8.45$, retain H_0.

The comparison involving a_3 vs. a_2 is declared significant; we suspend judgment for the comparisons involving a_1 vs. a_2 and a_3 vs. a_4; and we retain H_0 for all other pairwise comparisions.

CHAPTER 9

1. **a.** One independent variable cannot influence another independent variable in a factorial design.
   b. This definition can apply to single-factor designs and to main effects, where independent variables influence behavior. What is missing is a specification of the way in which the two independent variables *combine* to influence behavior.
   c. This definition requires a specification of the effects of one of the *independent variables* and not one level of it. As stated, the effects being referred to could mean the simple effect of factor B at that level of factor A.
   d. The values of an independent variable refer to the *levels* of that variable. The definition again implies that one independent variable influences another independent variable.
2. **a.** A and B; **b.** A and B; **c.** A, B, and $A \times B$; **d.** B and $A \times B$; **e.** A, B, and $A \times B$; **f.** $A \times B$

CHAPTER 10

1. a. Summary of the analysis:

Source	Calculations	SS	df	MS	F
A	$12{,}892.00 - 12{,}701.01 =$	190.99	4	47.75	7.70*
B	$13{,}125.20 - [T] =$	424.19	2	212.10	34.21*
$A \times B$	$13{,}454.00 - [A] - [B] + [T] =$	137.81	8	17.23	2.78*
S/A	$13{,}826 - [AB] =$	372.00	60	6.20	
Total	$[Y] - [T] =$	1,124.99	74		

*$p < .05$.

b. $5.80 \pm (2.00)\sqrt{6.20/5} = 5.80 \pm (2.00)(1.11) = 5.80 \pm 2.22$

$11.13 \pm (2.00)\sqrt{6.20/15} = 11.13 \pm (2.00(.64)) = 11.13 \pm 1.28$

$15.48 \pm (2.00)\sqrt{6.20/25} = 15.48 \pm (2.00)(.50) = 15.48 \pm 1.00$

c. $\hat{\omega}_A^2 = 2.22/15.09 = .147$; $\hat{\omega}_B^2 = 5.49/15.09 = .364$; $\hat{\omega}_{A \times B}^2 = 1.18/15.09$
$= .078$

d. $\hat{\omega}_A^2 = 2.22/8.42 = .264$; $\hat{\omega}_B^2 = 5.49/11.69 = .470$; $\hat{\omega}_{A \times B}^2 = 1.18/7.38$
$= .160$

2. a. Summary of the analysis:

Source	Calculations	SS	df	MS	F
A	$3{,}777.56 - 3{,}468.00 =$	309.56	2	154.78	41.39*
B	$3{,}470.00 - [T] =$	2.00	2	1.00	.27
$A \times B$	$3{,}806.67 - [A] - [B] + [T] =$	27.11	4	6.78	1.81
S/AB	$3{,}874 - [AB] =$	67.33	18	3.74	
Total	$[Y] - [T] =$	406.00	26		

*$p < .05$.

b. *Standard omega squared:* $\hat{\omega}_A^2 = 11.19/15.18 = .737$; $\hat{\omega}_B^2 = -.20/15.18 = -.013$
(report as .000); $\hat{\omega}_{A \times B}^2 = .45/15.18 = .030$
Partial omega squared: $\hat{\omega}_A^2 = 11.19/14.93 = .749$; $\hat{\omega}_B^2 = -.20/3.54 = -.056$
(report as .000); $\hat{\omega}_{A \times B}^2 = .45/4.19 = .107$
Note: The estimated omega squared for the $A \times B$ interaction is of sufficient
size by either definition that one could question the power of the experiment for
detecting this effect (recall that $n = 3$). The experiment should be replicated with
a sample size large enough to detect an interaction effect of this magnitude.

3. First, convert the means to sums and calculate the treatment SS's. The resultant AB
matrix is

	a_1	a_2	a_3	Sum
b_1	44	48	40	132
b_2	12	40	56	108
Sum	56	88	96	240

We can now work out the SS's and df's, and MS's for the factorial effects, which are given in the summary table. We need the error term to complete the analysis. Since we are given the value of F for the interaction source of variance, we can solve for the $MS_{S/AB}$ with a bit of algebra.

$$F = \frac{MS_{A \times B}}{MS_{S/AB}} = 3.93$$

Solving for $MS_{S/AB}$, we find

$$MS_{S/AB} = \frac{MS_{A \times B}}{F} = \frac{72.00}{3.93} = 18.32$$

With this value, we can complete the analysis of variance, which is presented in the following summary table:

Source	Calculations	SS	df	MS	F
A	$2{,}512.00 - 2{,}400.00 =$	112.00	2	56.00	3.06
B	$2{,}424.00 - [T] =$	24.00	1	24.00	1.31
A × B	$2{,}680.00 - [A] - [B] + [T] =$	144.00	2	72.00	3.93*
S/AB			18	18.32	

*$p < .05$.

4. **a.** Summary of the analysis:

Source	SS	df	MS	F
A	55.80	2	27.90	1.90
B	3.33	1	3.33	.23
A × B	34.87	2	17.44	1.19
S/AB		24	14.66	

b. To calculate power (and to estimate sample size), we must estimate $\phi_{A \times B}$. Using Eq. (10–12), we find

$$\phi^2_{A \times B} = \left[\frac{n'}{5} \right]\left[\frac{(2)(1)}{(2)(1) + 1} \right]\left[1.19 - 1 \right] = n'\left[\frac{2}{(5)(3)} \right]\left[.19 \right] = .025n'$$

If we try $n' = 130$, $\phi^2_{A \times B} = (.025)(130) = 3.250$; $\phi_{A \times B} = \sqrt{3.250} = 1.80$; and power $= .80$ (use $df_{denom.} = \infty$).

CHAPTER 11

1. For some of the analyses, it is convenient to work with the AB matrix of sums, which is obtained easily by multiplying each cell mean by $n = 8$:

	a_1	a_2	a_3	Sum
b_1	28	32	60	120
b_2	30	62	88	180
Sum	58	94	148	300

a. Simple effects of B at each level of factor A:

$$SS_{B\ at\ a_1} = \frac{(28)^2 + (30)^2}{8} - \frac{(58)^2}{(2)(8)} = .25;\ df_{B\ at\ a_1} = 1;\ MS_{B\ at\ a_1} = .25$$

$$SS_{B\ at\ a_2} = \frac{(32)^2 + (62)^2}{8} - \frac{(94)^2}{(2)(8)} = 56.25;\ df_{B\ at\ a_2} = 1;\ MS_{B\ at\ a_2} = 56.25$$

$$SS_{B\ at\ a_3} = \frac{(60)^2 + (88)^2}{8} - \frac{(148)^2}{(2)(8)} = 49.00;\ df_{B\ at\ a_3} = 1;\ MS_{B\ at\ a_3} = 49.00$$

b. Simple effects of A at b_1

$$SS_{A\ at\ b_1} = \frac{(28)^2 + (32)^2 + (60)^2}{8} - \frac{(120)^2}{(3)(8)} = 76.00;\ df_{A\ at\ b_1} = 2;\ MS_{A\ at\ b_1} = 38.00$$

c. Simple comparison of A at b_1 (3.50 vs. 4.00):

$$\hat{\psi}_{A\ at\ b_1} = (1)(3.50) + (-1)(4.00) + (0)(7.50) = -.50$$

$$SS_{A_{comp.}\ at\ b_1} = \frac{8(-.50)^2}{2} = 1.00;\ df_{A_{comp.}\ at\ b_1} = 1;\ MS_{A_{comp.}\ at\ b_1} = 1.00$$

2. a. $\hat{\psi}_A = (1)(8.67) + (0)(16.11) + (-1)(9.22) = -.55$

$$SS_{A_{comp.}} = \frac{(3)(3)(-.55)^2}{2} = 1.36;\ df_{A_{comp.}} = 1;\ F = \frac{1.36}{3.74} = .36, p > .05$$

b. $\hat{\psi}_A = (-\frac{1}{2})(8.67) + (1)(16.11) + (-\frac{1}{2})(9.22) = 7.17$

$$SS_{A_{comp.}} = \frac{(3)(3)(7.17)^2}{1.5} = 308.45;\ F = \frac{308.45}{3.74} = 82.47, p < .05$$

3. a. Summary of the analysis:

Source	Calculations	SS	df	MS	F
B at a_1	520.00 − 392.00 =	128.00	1	128.00	6.98*
B at a_2	976.00 − 968.00 =	8.00	1	8.00	.44
B at a_3	1,184.00 − 1,152.00 =	32.00	1	32.00	1.75
S/AB			18	18.33	

*$p < .05$.

b. From Table 10–8, $SS_B = 24.00$ and $SS_{A \times B} = 144.00$.

24.00 + 144.00 = 168.00, and 128.00 + 8.00 + 32.00 = 168.00

4. a. Summary of the analysis:

Source	Calculations	SS	df	MS	F
A at b_1	2,688.20 − 2,401.00 =	287.20	4	71.80	11.58*
S/AB			60	6.20	

*$p < .05$.

b. $\hat{\psi}_{A \text{ at } b_1} = (1)(5.80) + (0)(6.80) + (0)(9.60) + (0)(11.60) +$
$$(-1)(15.20) = -9.40$$

$$SS_{A_{comp. \text{ at } b_1}} = \frac{5(-9.40)^2}{2} = 220.90; \ F = \frac{220.90}{6.20} = 35.63, p < .05$$

c. $\hat{\psi}_{A \text{ at } b_1} = (-2)(5.80) + (-1)(6.80) + (0)(9.60) + (1)(11.60) +$
$$(2)(15.20) = 23.60$$

$$SS_{A_{linear} \text{ at } b_1} = \frac{5(23.60)^2}{10} = 278.48; \ F = \frac{278.48}{6.20} = 44.92, p < .05$$

5. a. and b. Summary of the analyses:

Source	SS	df	MS	F
A at b_1	75.00	1	75.00	8.33*
A at b_2	27.00	1	27.00	3.00
$A \times B$	6.00	1	6.00	.67
S/AB		20	9.00	

$^*p < .05.$

CHAPTER 12

1. a. A logical first test is to compare the three alcohol conditions. If the three conditions do not differ significantly, we might be willing to combine them and to compare this average with the control condition. If the three conditions differ significantly, several interesting comparisons are possible. (Alternatively, we could test these comparisons directly, without a preliminary assessment of the three alcohol conditions.) For example, we might want to compare each of the alcohol conditions separately with the control to determine whether an effect of alcohol has been obtained. We will probably want to see what sorts of differential alcohol effects were found; for example, do the two whiskeys differ? Do the two whiskeys separately or in combination differ from the "pure" alcohol condition? All these comparisons ask meaningful questions of the data.

   b. Each comparison suggested in part a can be applied to the analysis of the interaction. These would have the form of an interaction between each of the comparisons involving the different alcohol conditions with the exposure variable.

2. *"Bright" vs. "dull"*: This interaction contrast compares the difference between the two strains raised in the "enriched" environment with the corresponding difference produced by the two strains in the "impoverished" environment; that is,

$$\hat{\psi}_{A \times B} = (3.50 - 7.50) - (3.75 - 11.00) = 3.25$$

$$SS_{A_{comp.} \times B_{comp.}} = \frac{8(3.25)^2}{(2)(2)} = 21.13$$

The interaction suggests that the difference between the "bright" and "dull" rats is greater for rats raised in the impoverished environment.

"Bright" vs. "mixed": This interaction contrast is similar to the first except that the comparison involves the "bright" and "mixed" rats.

$$\hat{\psi}_{A \times B} = (3.50 - 4.00) - (3.75 - 7.75) = 3.50$$

$$SS_{A_{comp.} \times B_{comp.}} = \frac{8(3.50)^2}{(2)(2)} = 24.50$$

The interaction suggests that the difference between the "bright" and "mixed" rats is greater for rats raised in the impoverished environment.

"Dull" vs. "mixed": This interaction contrast is similar to the first except that the comparison involves the "dull" and "mixed" rats.

$$\hat{\psi}_{A \times B} = (7.50 - 4.00) - (11.00 - 7.75) = .25$$

$$SS_{A_{comp.} \times B_{comp.}} = \frac{8(.25)^2}{(2)(2)} = .13$$

The interaction contrast suggests that the difference between the "dull" and "mixed" rats does not depend on the nature of the environment in which they were raised.

3. a. $\hat{\psi}_{A \times B} = (14.40 - 13.20) - (9.60 - 10.80) = 2.40;$ $SS_{A_{comp.} \times B_{comp.}}$

$$= \frac{5(2.40)^2}{(2)(2)} = 7.20; \quad F = \frac{7.20}{3.09} = 2.33, p > .05$$

The difference between verbal and monetary incentives does not depend on the complexity of the task.

b. $\hat{\psi}_{A \times B} = (13.80 - 14.00) - (10.20 - 6.40) = -4.00;$ $SS_{A_{comp.} \times B_{comp.}}$

$$= \frac{5(-4.00)^2}{(1.5)(2)} = 26.67; \quad F = \frac{26.67}{3.09} = 8.63, p < .05$$

The difference between the combined incentive groups and the group receiving no incentive depends on the complexity of the problems. Part c explores the nature of this interaction.

c. $\hat{\psi}_{A \text{ at } b_1} = 13.80 - 14.00 = -.20;$ $SS_{A \text{ at } b_1} = \frac{5(-.20)^2}{1.5} = .13;$

$$F = \frac{.13}{3.09} = .04, p > .05$$

$\hat{\psi}_{A \text{ at } b_2} = 10.20 - 6.40 = 3.80;$ $SS_{A \text{ at } b_1} = \frac{5(3.80)^2}{1.5} = 48.13;$

$$F = \frac{48.13}{3.09} = 15.58, p < .05$$

We see that the combined effects of the two incentives significantly increase the number of complex problems solved but have no effect on the number of simple problems solved.

4. a. Summary of the analysis:

Source	Calculations	SS	df	MS	F
A	1,244.70 − 1,243.23 =	1.47	3	.49	.10
B	1,407.25 − [*T*] =	164.02	1	164.02	33.89*
A × *B*	1,458.20 − [*A*] − [*B*] + [*T*] =	49.48	3	16.49	3.41*
S/AB			32	4.84	

*p < .05.

b. Summary of the analysis of trend components of the interaction:
Linear: The linear interaction coefficients (d_{ij}) are formed by crossing the linear coefficients (-3, -1, 1, 3) with the coefficients representing factor B (1, -1). Thus, $\hat{\psi}_{A \times B} = (-3)(5.80) + (-1)(8.40) + (1)(9.20) + (3)(7.00) + (3)(4.80) + (1)(3.00) + (-1)(2.40) + (-3)(4.00) = 7.40$; $SS_{A_{linear} \times B}$
$= \dfrac{5(7.40)^2}{40} = 6.85$; $F = \dfrac{6.85}{4.84} = 1.42, p > .05.$

Quadratic: The quadratic interaction coefficients are formed by crossing the quadratic coefficients (1, -1, -1, 1) with the coefficients representing factor B (1, -1). Thus, $\hat{\psi}_{A \times B} = (1)(5.80) + (-1)(8.40) + (-1)(9.20) + (1)(7.00) + (-1)(4.80) + (1)(3.00) + (1)(2.40) + (-1)(4.00) = -8.20$; $SS_{A_{linear} \times B} = $
$\dfrac{5(-8.20)^2}{8} = 42.03$; $F = \dfrac{42.03}{4.84} = 8.68, p < .05.$

Cubic: The cubic interaction coefficients are formed by crossing the cubic coefficients (-1, 3, -3, 1) with the coefficients representing factor B (1, 1). Thus, $\hat{\psi}_{A \times B} = (-1)(5.80) + (3)(8.40) + (-3)(9.20) + (1)(7.00) + (1)(4.80) + (-3)(3.00) + (3)(2.40) + (-1)(4.00) = -2.20$;
$SS_{A_{linear} \times B} = \dfrac{5(-2.20)^2}{40} = .61$; $F = \dfrac{.61}{4.84} = .13, p > .05.$

c. $\hat{\psi}_{quadratic \text{ at } b_1} = (1)(5.80) + (-1)(8.40) + (-1)(9.20) + (1)(7.00) = -4.80$
$SS_{A_{quadratic} \text{ at } b_1} = \dfrac{5(-4.80)^2}{4} = 28.80$; $F = \dfrac{28.80}{4.84} = 5.95, p < .05$

$\hat{\psi}_{A_{quadratic} \text{ at } b_2} = (-1)(4.80) + (1)(3.00) + (1)(2.40) + (-1)(4.00) = -3.40$
$SS_{A_{quadratic} \text{ at } b_2} = \dfrac{5(-3.40)^2}{4} = 14.45$; $F = \dfrac{14.45}{4.84} = 2.99, p > .05$

Only the quadratic trend at b_1 is significant.

5. a. Summary of the analysis:

Source	Calculations	SS	df	MS	F
A	408.10 − 276.03 =	132.07	2	66.04	24.01*
B	304.07 − [T] =	28.04	1	28.04	10.20*
A × B	452.60 − [A] − [B] + [T] =	16.46	2	8.23	2.99
S/AB			24	2.75	

*$p < .05.$

b. $\hat{\psi}_{A \times B} = (1.80 - 2.20) - (1.20 - 1.00) = -.60$; $SS_{A_{comp.} \times B} = \dfrac{5(-.60)^2}{4}$
$= .45$; $F = \dfrac{.45}{2.75} = .16, p > .05$

c. $\hat{\psi}_{A \times B} = (8.00 - 2.00) - (4.00 - 1.10) = 3.10$; $SS_{A_{comp.} \times B} = \dfrac{5(3.10)^2}{(1.5)(2)} = 16.02$;
$F = \dfrac{16.02}{2.75} = 5.83, p < .05$

CHAPTER 13

1. a. *Method of unweighted means:*

$$n_h = \frac{3}{\frac{1}{3} + \frac{1}{5} + \frac{1}{4}} = \frac{3}{.783} = 3.83$$

$$SS_A = (3.83)[(17.67 - 11.47)^2 + (6.00 - 11.47)^2 + (10.75 - 11.47)^2]$$
$$= (3.83)(68.88) = 263.81; MS_A = 263.81/2 = 131.91$$

$$SS_{S/A} = 4.67 + 40.00 + 8.75 = 53.42; MS_{S/A} = 53.42/9 = 5.94$$

$$F = 131.91/5.94 = 22.21, p < .05$$

Method of weighted means:

$$SS_A = 3(17.67 - 10.50)^2 + 5(6.00 - 10.50)^2 + 4(10.75 - 10.50)^2 = 154.23$$
$$+ 101.25 + .25 = 255.73; MS_A = 255.73/2 = 127.87$$

$$SS_{S/A} = 53.42; MS_{S/A} = 53.42/9 = 5.94$$

$$F = 127.87/5.94 = 21.53, p < .05$$

b. *Method of unweighted means:*

$$\hat{\psi} = (1)(17.67) + (-\tfrac{1}{2})(6.00) + (-\tfrac{1}{2})(10.75) = 9.30$$

$$SS_{A_{comp.}} = \frac{(3.83)(9.30)^2}{1.5} = 220.84$$

$$F = 220.84/5.94 = 37.18, p < .05$$

Method of weighted means:

$$SS_{A_{comp.}} = \frac{(9.30)^2}{\frac{(1)^2}{3} + \frac{(-.5)^2}{5} + \frac{(-.5)^2}{4}} = \frac{86.49}{.333 + .050 + .063} = 193.92$$
$$F = 193.92/5.94 = 32.65, p < .05$$

c. *Method of unweighted means:*

$$\hat{\psi} = (0)(17.67) + (1)(6.00) + (-1)(10.75) = -4.75$$

$$SS_{A_{comp.}} = \frac{(3.83)(-4.75)^2}{2} = 43.21$$

$$F = 43.21/5.94 = 7.27, p < .05$$

Method of weighted means:

$$SS_{A_{comp.}} = \frac{(-4.75)^2}{\frac{(0)^2}{3} + \frac{(1)^2}{5} + \frac{(-1)^2}{4}} = \frac{22.56}{.20 + .25} = 50.13$$
$$F = 50.13/5.94 = 8.44, p < .05$$

2. Summary of the analysis:

$$n_h = \frac{(3)(2)}{.25 + .333 + .333 + .25 + .50 + .25} = \frac{6}{1.916} = 3.13$$

$$SS_{S/AB} = 30.00 + 34.67 + 44.67 + 46.00 + 4.50 + 50.00 = 209.84$$

$$df_{S/AB} = 3 + 2 + 2 + 3 + 1 + 3 = 14$$

AB^* Matrix

	a_1	a_2	a_3	Sum
b_1	9.39	36.53	44.85	90.77
b_2	34.43	23.48	31.30	89.21
Sum	43.82	60.01	76.15	179.98

Source	Calculations	SS	df	MS	F
A	$1,808.34 - 1,724.86 =$	83.48	2	41.74	2.78
B	$1,724.99 - [T] =$	.13	1	.13	.01
$A \times B$	$1,965.04 - [A] - [B] + [T] =$	156.57	2	78.29	5.22*
S/AB		209.84	14	14.99	

$^*p < .05.$

3. a. $\quad \overline{Y}_{A_1} = \dfrac{3.00 + 11.00}{2} = 7.00; \; \overline{Y}_{A_2} = \dfrac{11.67 + 7.50}{2} = 9.59; \; \overline{Y}_{A_3} =$

$$\frac{14.33 + 10.00}{2} = 12.17$$

$$\hat{\psi}_A = (1)(7.00) + (0)(9.59) + (-1)(12.17) = -5.17$$

$$SS_{A_{comp.}} = \frac{(2)(3.13)(-5.17)^2}{2} = 83.66$$

$$F = 83.66/14.99 = 5.58, p < .05$$

b. Summary of the analysis:

Source	Calculations	SS	df	MS	F
A at b_1	$1,097.17 - 877.44 =$	219.73	2	109.87	7.33*
A at b_2	$867.87 - 847.54 =$	20.33	2	10.17	.68
S/AB			14	14.99	

$^*p < .05.$

c. $\quad \hat{\psi}_{A \text{ at } b_1} = (1)(3.00) + (-1)(11.67) + (0)(14.33)$
$$= -8.67$$

$$SS_{A_{comp. \text{ at } b_1}} = \frac{(3.13)(-8.67)^2}{2} = 117.64$$

$$F = 117.64/14.99 = 7.85, p < .05$$

d. $\hat{\psi}_{A \times B} = (11.67 - 14.33) - (7.50 - 10.00) = -.16$

$$SS_{A_{comp.} \times B_{comp.}} = \frac{(3.13)(-.16)^2}{(2)(2)} = .02$$

$$F = .02/14.99 = .001, p > .05$$

CHAPTER 14

1. a. Summary of the analysis:

Source	Calculations	SS	df	MS	F
A	3,930.00 − 3,698.00 =	232.00	4	58.00	8.79*
B	3,747.00 − [T] =	49.00	4	12.25	1.86
A × B	4,165.00 − [A] − [B] + [T] =	186.00	16	11.63	1.76
S/A	4,330 − [AB] =	165.00	25	6.60	
Total	[Y] − [T] =	632.00	49		

*p < .05.

b. The main gain from this analysis is the assurance that the same treatment effects were obtained by the five experimenters—revealed by the nonsignificant interaction. A second gain is the small reduction in the error term (6.60 versus 8.89), which came about by isolating the effects of the experimenters. The only loss is a reduction in the denominator *df* (25 versus 45); the small loss of power resulting from the reduction in *df* is easily compensated for by the reduction in the size of the error term.

2. a. Summary of the analysis of covariance:

Source	Calculations	$SS_{(adj.)}$	df	$MS_{(adj.)}$	F
A	284.08 − 72.62 =	211.46	2	105.73	20.37*
S/A	72.67 − .05[a] =	72.62	14	5.19	
Total	298.00 − 13.92[b] =	284.08	16		

*p < .05.
[a]$(-1.33)^2/36.00 = .05$; [b]$(23.33)^2/39.11 = 13.92$.

b. Summary of the analysis of variance:

Source	Calculations	SS	df	MS	F
A	2,537.33 − 2,312.00 =	225.33	2	112.67	23.28*
S/A	2,610 − [A_Y] =	72.67	15	4.84	
Total	[Y] − [T_Y] =	298.00	17		

*p < .05.

As you can see, only a small adjustment (.05) was applied to the within-groups error term. This fact clearly indicates that no precision was gained from the introduction of a covariate into the analysis. This lack of gain is reflected in the near-zero within-groups correlation between the covariate and the dependent variable:

$$r_{S/A} = \frac{-1.33}{\sqrt{(36.00)(72.67)}} = -.03$$

3. a. Summary of the analysis of covariance:

Source	Calculations	$SS_{adj.}$	df	$MS_{adj.}$	F
A	$138.83 - 31.99 =$	106.84	3	35.61	12.24^*
S/A	$48.50 - 16.51^a =$	31.99	11	2.91	
Total	$139.75 - .92^b =$	138.83	14		

$^*p < .05.$
$^a(-21.50)^2/28.00 = 16.51;$ $^b(-5.50)^2/33.00 = .92.$

b. $\overline{Y}'_{A_1} = 8.50 \quad (-.77)(3.00 - 3.25) - 8.50 - .19 = 8.31$

$\overline{Y}'_{A_2} = 8.75 - (-.77)(3.50 - 3.25) = 8.75 + .19 = 8.94$

$\overline{Y}'_{A_3} = 9.00 - (-.77)(2.50 - 3.25) = 9.00 - .58 = 8.42$

$\overline{Y}'_{A_4} = 14.25 - (-.77)(4.00 - 3.25) = 14.25 + .58 = 14.83$

c. $\quad MS'_{error} = 2.91 + (2.91)\left(\dfrac{5.00/3}{28.00}\right) = 2.91 + (2.91)(.06) = 3.08$

(1) $\quad \hat{\psi}' = (1)(8.31) + (-1)(8.94) + (0)(8.42) + (0)(14.83) = -.63$

$SS_{A_{comp.(adj.)}} = \dfrac{4(-.63)^2}{2} = .79$

$F = .79/3.08 = .26, p > .05$

(2) $\quad \hat{\psi}' = (-\tfrac{1}{3})(8.31) + (-\tfrac{1}{3})(8.94) + (-\tfrac{1}{3})(8.42) + (1)(14.83) = 6.27$

$SS_{A_{comp.(adj.)}} = \dfrac{4(6.27)^2}{1.33} = 118.23$

$F = 118.23/3.08 = 38.39, p < .05$

CHAPTER 16

1. a. Summary of the analysis:

Source	Calculations	SS	df	MS	F
A	$7,589.70 - 5,554.58 =$	$2,035.12$	4	508.78	8.81^*
S	$9,279.80 - [T] =$	$3,725.22$	9	413.91	
$A \times S$	$13,395 - [A] - [S] + [T] =$	$2,080.08$	36	57.78	
Total	$[Y] - [T] =$	$7,840.42$	49		

$^*p < .05.$

b. (1) Summary of the analysis:

Source	Calculations	SS^a	df	MS	F
$A_{comp.}$	$822.40 - 819.20 =$	3.20	1	3.20	.36
S	$1,492.00 - [T] =$	672.80	9	74.76	
$A_{comp.} \times S$	$1,576 - [A] - [S] + [T] =$	80.80	9	8.98	
Total	$[Y] - [T] =$	756.80	19		

[a]The adjustment factor $= 1$ for pairwise comparisons; no correction for the use of weighted Y scores is possible.

(2) Summary of the analysis:

Source	Calculations	SS^a	df	MS	F
$A_{comp.}$	$907.60 - 897.80 =$	9.80	1	9.80	.23
S	$2,189.00 - [T] =$	1,291.20	9	143.47	
$A_{comp.} \times S$	$2,580 - [A] - [S] + [T] =$	381.20	9	42.36	
Total	$[Y] - [T] =$	1,682.20	19		

[a]The adjustment factor $= 1$ for pairwise comparisons; no correction for the use of weighted Y scores is possible.

(3) Summary of the analysis:

Source	Calculations	SS^a	df	MS	F
$A_{comp.}$	$24,166.80 - 19,845.00 =$	4,321.80	1	4,321.80	11.27*
S	$32,137.00 - [T] =$	12,292.00	9	1,365.78	
$A_{comp.} \times S$	$39,910 - [A] - [S] \dotplus [T] =$	3,451.20	9	383.47	
Total	$[Y] - [T] =$	20,065.00	19		

*$p < .05$.

[a]The calculations are based on Y scores weighted by the coefficients $0, 0, 1, 1, -2$. You may compensate for the use of weighted Y scores by dividing each SS by the adjustment factor, $(\Sigma c_i^2)/2 = 6/2 = 3$. In any case, the final value of F remains unchanged.

2. a. Summary of the analysis:

Source	Calculations	SS	df	MS	F
A	$588.00 - 444.08 =$	143.92	5	28.78	10.32*
S	$498.33 - [T] =$	54.25	7	7.75	
$A \times S$	$740 - [A] - [S] + [T] =$	97.75	35	2.79	
Total	$[Y] - [T] =$	295.92	47		

*$p < .05$.

b. Analysis of the linear component:

Source	Calculations	SS^a	df	MS	F
A_{linear}	$19,472.00 - 15,376.00 =$	4,096.00	1	4,096.00	78.98*
S	$16,673.00 - [T] =$	1,297.00	7	185.29	
$A_{linear} \times S$	$21,132 - [A] - [S] + [T] =$	363.00	7	51.86	
Total	$[Y] - [T] =$	5,756.00	15		

*$p < .05$.

[a]The calculations are based on Y scores weighted by the coefficients $-5, -3, -1, 1, 3, 5$. You may compensate for the use of weighted Y scores by dividing each SS by the adjustment factor, $(\Sigma c_i^2)/2 = 70/2 = 35$. In any case, the final value of F remains unchanged.

Analysis of the quadratic component:

Source	Calculations	SS^a	df	MS	F
$A_{quadratic}$	$16,198.63 - 15,190.56 =$	1,008.07	1	1,008.07	6.16*
S	$16,563.50 - [T] =$	1,372.94	7	196.13	
$A_{quadratic} \times S$	$18,717 - [A] - [S] + [T] =$	1,145.43	7	163.63	
Total	$[Y] - [T] =$	3,526.44	15		

*$p < .05$.

[a]The calculations are based on Y scores weighted by the coefficients 5, -1, -4, -4, -1, 5. You may compensate for the use of weighted Y scores by dividing each SS by the adjustment factor, $(\Sigma c_i^2)/2 = 84/2 = 42$. In any case, the final value of F remains unchanged.

3. a. Summary of the analysis:

Source	Calculations	SS	df	MS	F
A	$1,690.80 - 1,632.16 =$	58.64	4	14.66	1.19
S	$1,646.00 - [T] =$	13.84	4	3.46	
$A \times S$	$1,902 - [A] - [S] + [T] =$	197.36	16	12.34	
Total	$[Y] - [T] =$	269.84	24		

b. Summary of the analysis:

Source	Calculations	SS	df	MS	F
Position	$1,804.00 - [T] =$	171.84	4	42.96	20.17*
Residual	$197.36 - 171.84 =$	25.52	12	2.13	

*$p < .05$.

c. The treatment main effect is now significant: $F = 14.66/2.13 = 6.88, p < .05$.

CHAPTER 17

1. a. Summary of the analysis:

Source	Calculations	SS	df	MS	F
A	$2,548.81 - 2,432.53 =$	116.28	1	116.28	2.51
S/A	$2,827.25 - [A] =$	278.44	6	46.41	
B	$2,562.13 - [T] =$	129.60	3	43.20	22.38*
$A \times B$	$2,681.75 - [A] - [B] + [T] =$	3.34	3	1.11	.58
$B \times S/A$	$2,995 - [AB] - [AS] + [A] =$	34.81	18	1.93	
Total	$[Y] - [T] =$	562.47	31		

*$p < .05$.

b. $SS_{B \times S/A \text{ at } a_1} = 949 - 794.25 - 875.75 + 742.56 = 21.56$

$SS_{B \times S/A \text{ at } a_2} = 2,046 - 1,887.50 - 1,951.50 + 1,806.25 = 13.25$

$21.56 + 13.25 = 34.81 = SS_{B \times S/A}$

c. (1) Summary of the analysis:

Source	Calculations	SS^a	df	MS	F
A	$854.50 - 812.25 =$	42.25	1	$—^b$	$—^b$
S/A	$1,014.00 - [A] =$	159.50	6	$—^b$	
$B_{comp.}$	$842.50 - [T] =$	30.25	1	30.25	15.76*
$A \times B_{comp.}$	$885.00 - [A] - [B] + [T] =$	.25	1	.25	.13
$B_{comp.} \times S/A$	$1,056 - [AB] - [AS] + A] =$	11.50	6	1.92	
Total	$[Y] - [T] =$	243.75	15		

*$p < .05$.

^{a}The adjustment factor = 1 for pairwise comparisons; no correction for the use of weighted Y scores is possible.

^{b}Not needed.

(2) Summary of the analysis:

Source	Calculations	SS^a	df	MS	F
A	$5,732.00 - 5,476.00 =$	256.00	1	$—^b$	$—^b$
S/A	$6,254.00 - [A] =$	522.00	6	$—^b$	
$B_{comp.}$	$5,765.00 - [T] =$	289.00	1	289.00	43.33*
$A \times B_{comp.}$	$6,030.00 - [A] - [B] + [T] =$	9.00	1	9.00	1.35
$B_{comp.} \times S/A$	$6,592 - [AB] - [AS] + [A] =$	40.00	6	6.67	
Total	$[Y] - [T] =$	1,116.00	15		

*$p < .05$.

^{a}The calculations are based on Y scores weighted by the coefficients 1, 1, -2. You may compensate for the use of weighted Y scores by dividing each SS by the adjustment factor, $(\Sigma c_i^2)/2 = 6/2 = 3$. In any case, the final value of F remains unchanged.

^{b}Not needed.

2. a. Summary of the analysis:

Source	Calculations	SS	df	MS	F
A	$24,992.17 - 24,753.78 =$	238.39	2	119.20	4.16*
S/A	$25,250.00 - [A] =$	257.83	9	28.65	
B	$25,512.83 - [T] =$	759.05	2	379.53	103.98*
$A \times B$	$25,854.50 - [A] - [B] + [T] =$	103.28	4	25.82	7.07*
$B \times S/A$	$26,178 - [AB] - [AS] + [A] =$	65.67	18	3.65	
Total	$[Y] - [T] =$	1,424.22	35		

*$p < .05$.

3. a. Summary of the analyses:

Source	Calculations	SS	df	MS	F
A at b_1	$4,924.25 - 4,920.75 =$	3.50	2	1.75	.12
S/A at b_1	$5,053 - 4,924.25 =$	128.75	9	14.31	
A at b_2	$8,874.00 - 8,748.00 =$	126.00	2	63.00	4.81*
S/A at b_2	$8,992 - 8,874.00 =$	118.00	9	13.11	
A at b_3	$12,056.25 - 11,844.08 =$	212.17	2	106.09	12.44*
S/A at b_3	$12,133 - 12,056.25 =$	76.75	9	8.53	

*$p < .05$.

b. $\hat{\psi}_{A \text{ at } b_3} = (1)(26.00) + (-1)(32.00) + (0)(36.25) = -6.00$

$$SS_{A_{comp. \text{ at } b_3}} = \frac{4(-6.00)^2}{2} = 72.00; F = 72.00/8.53 = 8.44, p < .05$$

4. a. Summary of the analyses:

Source	Calculations[a]	SS	df	MS	F
B at a_1	$6,608.00 - 6,533.33 =$	74.67	2	37.34	9.09*
S	$6,610.67 - [T] =$	77.34	3	25.78	
$B \times S$ at a_1	$6,710 - [B] - [S] + [T] =$	24.66	6	4.11	
B at a_2	$8,257.25 - 7,956.75 =$	300.50	2	150.25	58.24*
S	$8,093.00 - [T] =$	136.25	3	45.42	
$B \times S$ at a_2	$8,409 - [B] - [S] + [T] =$	15.50	6	2.58	
B at a_3	$10,989.25 - 10,502.08 =$	487.17	2	243.59	57.32*
S	$10,546.33 - [T] -$	44.25	3	14.75	
$B \times S$ at a_3	$11,059 - [B] - [S] + [T] =$	25.50	6	4.25	

*$p < .05$.
[a]For convenience, I have treated each analysis as if it were a separate $(B \times S)$ experiment for which the level of factor A was held constant.

b. (1) Summary of the analysis:

Source	Calculations	SS[a]	df	MS	F
$B_{comp.}$ at a_3	$7,020.25 - 6,555.13 =$	465.12	1	465.12	134.43*
S	$6,595.50 - [T] =$	40.37	3	13.46	
$B_{comp.} \times S$ at a_3	$7,071 - [B] - [S] + [T] =$	10.38	3	3.46	
Total	$[Y] - [T] =$	515.87	7		

*$p < .05$.
[a]The adjustment factor $= 1$ for pairwise comparisons; no correction for the use of weighted Y scores is possible.

(2) Summary of the analysis:

Source	Calculations	SS[a]	df	MS	F
$B_{comp.}$ at a_3	$25,416.25 - 24,090.13 =$	1,326.12	1	1,326.12	321.09*
S	$24,226.50 - [T] =$	136.37	3	45.46	
$B_{comp.} \times S$ at a_3	$25,565 - [B] - [S] + [T] =$	12.38	3	4.13	
Total	$[Y] - [T] =$	1,474.87	7		

*$p < .05$.
[a]The calculations are based on Y scores weighted by the coefficients 2, -1, -1. You may compensate for the use of weighted Y score by dividing each SS by the adjustment factor, $(\Sigma c_i^2)/2 = 6/2 = 3$. In any case, the final value of F remains unchanged.

CHAPTER 18

1. Summary of the analysis:

Source	Calculations	SS	df	MS	F
A	$5{,}554.75 - 5{,}504.08 =$	50.67	2	25.34	.60
S/A	$5{,}937.50 - [A] =$	382.75	9	42.53	
B	$5{,}567.50 - [T] =$	63.42	3	21.14	14.38*
$A \times B$	$5{,}743.50 - [A] - [B] + [T] =$	125.33	6	20.89	14.21*
$B \times S/A$	$6{,}166 - [AB] - [AS] + [A] =$	39.75	27	1.47	
Total	$[Y] - [T] =$	661.92	47		

*$p < .05$.

2. a. Summary of the analysis:

Source	Calculations	SS	df	MS	F
$A_{comp.}$	$3{,}298.50 - 3{,}280.50 =$	18.00	1	18.00	.50
S/A	$3{,}516.00 - [A] =$	217.50	6	36.25	
B	$3{,}292.75 - [T] =$	12.25	3	4.08	2.62
$A_{comp.} \times B$	$3{,}400.50 - [A] - [B] + [T] =$	89.75	3	29.92	19.18*
$B \times S/A$	$3{,}646 - [AB] - [AS] + [A] =$	28.00	18	1.56	
Total	$[Y] - [T] =$	365.50	31		

*$p < .05$.

b. The significant interaction indicates that the effects of removing brain tissue from the critical area depend on the particular test. An inspection of the means suggests that the effect is detected primarily by the test represented by level b_4.

c. Summary of the analysis:

Source	Calculations	SS	df	MS	F
$A_{comp.}$ at b_4	$845.00 - 760.50 =$	84.50	1	84.50	8.60*
$S/A_{comp.}$ at b_4	$904 - [A] =$	59.00	6	9.83	
Total	$[Y] - [T] =$	143.50	7		

*$p < .05$.

3. a. Summary of the analysis:

Source	Calculations	SS^a	df	MS	F
A	$2{,}390.63 - 2{,}340.38 =$	50.25	2	25.13	1.17
S/A	$2{,}584.50 - [A] =$	193.87	9	21.54	
$B_{comp.}$	$2{,}355.42 - [T] =$	15.04	1	15.04	7.16*
$A \times B_{comp.}$	$2{,}462.25 - [A] - [B] + [T] =$	56.58	2	28.29	13.47*
$B_{comp.} \times S/A$	$2{,}675 - [AB] - [AS] + [A] =$	18.88	9	2.10	
Total	$[Y] - [T] =$	334.62	23		

*$p < .05$.

[a]The adjustment factor = 1 for pairwise comparisons; no correction for the use of weighted Y scores is possible.

b. The difference between the two tests depends on the treatment a given group receives. An inspection of the means suggests that performance on the first test is considerably lower than on the fourth test, but this is true only for the control (a_1) and the noncritical (a_3) groups; the difference is reversed for the critical group (a_2).

c. Summary of the analysis:

Source	Calculations	SS^a	df	MS	F
$B_{comp.}$ at a_1	$914.00 - 882.00 =$	32.00	1	32.00	32.00*
S	$963.00 - [T] =$	81.00	3	27.00	
$B_{comp.} \times S$ at a_1	$998 - [B] - [S] + [T] =$	3.00	3	1.00	
Total	$[Y] - [T] =$	116.00	7		

*$p < .05$.

^{a}The adjustment factor $= 1$ for pairwise comparisons; no correction for the use of weighted Y scores is possible.

4. a. The interaction coefficients (d_{ij}) are as follows:

			(b_1)	(b_2)	(b_3)	(b_4)
	c_i	c_j:	0	0	$+1$	-1
(a_1)	0		0	0	0	0
(a_2)	$+1$		0	0	$+1$	-1
(a_3)	-1		0	0	-1	$+1$

Using these coefficients in conjunction with the individual means, we find

$$\hat{\psi}_{A \times B} = (0)(8.50) + (0)(11.50) + (0)(15.00) + (0)(12.50)$$
$$+ (0)(9.25) + (0)(11.75) + (1)(10.00) + (-1)(6.50)$$
$$+ (0)(9.50) + (0)(9.00) + (-1)(12.00) + (1)(13.00) = 4.50$$

$$SS_{A_{comp.} \times B_{comp.}} = \frac{4(4.50)^2}{4} = 20.25$$

$$SS_{B_{comp.} \times S/A_{comp.}} = SS_{B_{comp.} \times S/A_2} + SS_{B_{comp.} \times S/A_3}$$

$$= (660 - 569.00 - 635.00 + 544.50)$$
$$+ (1{,}276 - 1{,}252.00 - 1{,}271.00 + 1{,}250.00)$$

$$= .50 + 3.00 = 3.50$$

$$MS_{B_{comp.} \times S/A_{comp.}} = 3.50/6 = .58$$

$$F = 20.25/.58 = 34.91, p < .05$$

b. The effect of removing brain tissue from the critical area is detected differentially by the third and fourth tests. Simple comparisons would reveal that the effect is significant for only the fourth test.

5. a. Summary of the analysis:

Source	Calculations	SS^a	df	MS	F
A	$16{,}143.25 - 16{,}016.67 =$	126.58	2	—[b]	—[b]
S/A	$16{,}319.00 - [A] =$	175.75	9	—[b]	
B_{linear}	$16{,}764.83 - [T] =$	748.16	1	748.16	226.03*
$A \times B_{linear}$	$16{,}980.50 - [A] - [B] + [T] =$	89.09	2	44.55	13.46*
$B_{linear} \times S/A$	$17{,}186 - [AB] - [AS] + [A] =$	29.75	9	3.31	
Total	$[Y] - [T] =$	1,169.33	23		

*$p < .05$.

[a]The calculations are based on Y scores weighted by the coefficients -1, 0, 1, for which the adjustment factor $= 1$; no correction for the use of weighted Y scores is possible.
[b]Not needed.

b. The interaction coefficients (d_{ij}) are as follows:

	c_i	c_j:	(b_1) -1	(b_2) 0	(b_3) $+1$
(a_1)	0		0	0	0
(a_2)	$+1$		-1	0	$+1$
(a_3)	-1		$+1$	0	-1

Using these coefficients in conjunction with the individual means, we find

$$\hat{\psi}_{A \times B} = (0)(20.00) + (0)(24.00) + (0)(26.00)$$
$$+ (-1)(19.75) + (0)(25.50) + (1)(32.00)$$
$$+ (1)(21.00) + (0)(31.50) + (-1)(36.25) = -3.00$$

$$SS_{A_{comp.} \times B_{comp.}} = \frac{4(-3.00)^2}{4} = 9.00$$

$$SS_{B_{linear} \times S/A_{comp.}} = SS_{B_{linear} \times S/A_2} + SS_{B_{linear} \times S/A_3}$$

$$= (5{,}747 - 5{,}656.25 - 5{,}438.50 + 5{,}356.13)$$
$$+ (7{,}071 - 7{,}020.25 - 6{,}595.50 + 6{,}555.13)$$

$$= 8.38 + 10.38 = 18.76$$

$$MS_{B_{linear} \times S/A_{comp.}} = 18.76/6 = 3.13$$

$$F = 9.00/3.13 = 2.88, p > .05$$

Comment: If you plot the means for these two groups and draw a straight line through them, you will see that the two linear functions are parallel—that is, have the same slope—which is why the interaction contrast was not significant.

c. The interaction coefficients (d_{ij}) are as follows:

	c_i	c_j:	(b_1) -1	(b_2) 0	(b_3) $+1$
(a_1)	$+2$		-2	0	$+2$
(a_2)	-1		$+1$	0	-1
(a_3)	-1		$+1$	0	-1

Using these coefficients in conjunction with the individual means, we find

$$\hat{\psi}_{A \times B} = (-2)(20.00) + (0)(24.00) + (2)(26.00)$$
$$+ (1)(19.75) + (0)(25.50) + (-1)(32.00)$$
$$+ (1)(21.00) + (0)(31.50) + (-1)(36.25) = -15.50$$

$$SS_{A_{comp.} \times B_{linear}} = \frac{4(-15.50)^2}{12} = 80.08$$

$$SS_{B_{linear} \times S/A_{comp.}} = SS_{B_{linear} \times S/A_1} + SS_{B_{linear} \times S/A_2} + SS_{B_{linear} \times S/A_3}$$

We only need to calculate the first $SS(SS_{B_{linear} \times S/A_1})$ because we have already calculated the SS's for the last two groups in part b. For the first group, then,

$$SS_{B_{linear} \times S/A_1} = 4{,}368 - 4{,}304.00 - 4{,}285.00 + 4{,}232.00 = 11.00$$

Combining the three component SS's we find

$$SS_{B_{linear} \times S/A_{comp.}} = 11.00 + 8.38 + 10.38 = 29.76$$

$$MS_{B_{linear} \times S/A_{comp.}} = 29.76/9 = 3.31$$

$$F = 80.08/3.31 = 24.19, p < .05$$

Comment: If you plot the means for the group detecting targets on a white background (a_1) and for the combined groups detecting targets on a black background (a_2 and a_3) and draw a straight line through them, you will see that the two linear functions diverge substantially, which is why this interaction contrast is significant.

CHAPTER 19

1.

	Three-Way Interactions	Two-Way Interactions	Main Effects
Example 1:	No	None	A
Example 2:	No	None	A and B
Example 3:	No	None	A, B, and C
Example 4:	No	$A \times B$	None
Example 5:	No	$A \times B$	C^a
Example 6:	No	$B \times C$	A^a
Example 7:	No	$A \times B$ and $A \times C$	—
Example 8:	Yes	—	—
Example 9:	Yes	—	—
Example 10:	Yes	—	—

[a]This main effect is interpretable since it does not enter the two-way interaction.

2. a. Summary of the analysis:

Source	Calculations	SS	df	MS	F
A	$2,540.75 - 2,222.22 =$	318.53	2	159.27	91.01*
B	$2,431.25 - [T] =$	209.03	2	104.52	59.73*
C	$2,242.28 - [T] =$	20.06	1	20.06	11.46*
$A \times B$	$2,762.00 - [A] - [B] + [T] =$	12.22	4	3.06	1.75
$A \times C$	$2,575.83 - [A] - [C] + [T] =$	15.02	2	7.51	4.29*
$B \times C$	$2,456.00 - [B] - [C] + [T] =$	4.69	2	2.35	1.34
$A \times B \times C$	$2,815.50 - [AB] - [AC] - [BC]$				
	$+ [A] + [B + [C] - [T] =$	13.73	4	3.43	1.96
S/ABC	$2,910 - [ABC] =$	94.50	54	1.75	
Total	$[Y] - [T] =$	687.78	71		

*$p < .05$.

b. Since the three-way interaction is not significant, we can look at the two-way interactions and certain main effects for an adequate description of the results. For a more detailed comment on this problem, see problem 1 in the exercises for Chap. 20, where this example is examined further.

3. a. Summary of the analysis:

Source	Calculations	SS	df	MS	F
A	$8,643.40 - 8,534.53 =$	108.87	3	36.29	19.51*
B	$8,851.40 - [T] =$	316.87	2	158.44	85.18*
C	$8,624.67 - [T] =$	90.14	1	90.14	48.46*
$A \times B$	$9,006.60 - [A] - [B] + [T] =$	46.33	6	7.72	4.15*
$A \times C$	$8,765.33 - [A] - [C] + [T] =$	31.79	3	10.60	5.70*
$B \times C$	$9,076.40 - [B] - [C] + [T] =$	134.86	2	67.43	36.25*
$A \times B \times C$	$9,311.60 - [AB] - [AC] - [BC]$				
	$+ [A] + [B + [C] - [T] =$	48.21	6	8.04	4.32*
S/ABC			96	1.86	

*$p < .05$.

b. Since the three-way interaction is significant, we would usually direct our attention toward the detailed analysis of this effect. Examples of such analyses conducted with these data can be found in problem 2 in the exercises for Chap. 20.

CHAPTER 20

1. a. Summary of the analyses:

Source	Calculations	SS	df	MS	F
C at a_1	$301.42 - 301.04 =$	.38	1	.38	.22
C at a_2	$555.33 - 522.67 =$	32.66	1	32.66	18.66*
C at a_3	$1,719.08 - 1,717.04 =$	2.04	1	2.04	1.17
S/ABC			54	1.75	

*$p < .05$.

As a check, $\Sigma SS_{C \text{ at } a_i} = .38 + 32.66 + 2.04 = 35.08$ and $SS_{A \times C} + SS_C = 15.02 + 20.06 = 35.08$.

b. Summary of the two analyses:

	b_1	b_2	b_3		
$\overline{Y}_{B_j}$	7.92	4.79	3.96	$\hat{\psi}_B$	$\Sigma\, c_j^2$
Comp. 1	1	0	-1	3.96	2
Comp. 2	$-\frac{1}{2}$	1	$-\frac{1}{2}$	-1.15	1.5

$$SS_{B_{comp.\ 1}} = \frac{(3)(2)(4)(3.96)^2}{2}\ ;\ SS_{B_{comp.\ 2}} = \frac{(3)(2)(4)(-1.15)^2}{1.5}$$

Source	SS	df	MS	F
Comp. 1	188.18	1	188.18	107.53*
Comp. 2	21.16	1	21.16	12.09*
S/ABC		54	1.75	

*$p < .05$.

2. Summary of the analysis:

Source	Calculations	SS	df	MS	F
$A \times B$ at c_1	5,373.60 − 5,317.47 $-5,244.70 + 5,189.40 =$	.83	6	.14	.08
$A \times B$ at c_2	3,938.00 − 3,447.87 $-3,831.70 + 3,435.27 =$	93.70	6	15.62	8.40*
S/ABC			96	1.86	

*$p < .05$.

As a check, $\Sigma\, SS_{A \times B\ \text{at}\ c_k} = .83 + 93.70 = 94.53$ and $SS_{A \times B \times C} + SS_{A \times B} = 48.21 + 46.33 = 94.54$.

3. All three interaction contrasts are formed by crossing pairwise comparisons. The analyses may be accomplished by arranging the relevant means in the manner illustrated in Table 20–4, which facilitates the calculations of the relevant simple interactions.

a.
$$\hat{\psi}_{A \times B\ \text{at}\ c_1} = (8.0 - 7.6) - (4.4 - 3.8) = -.20$$
$$\hat{\psi}_{A \times B\ \text{at}\ c_2} = (8.4 - 8.0) - (7.4 - 7.2) = .20$$
$$\hat{\psi}_{A \times B \times C} = -.20 - .20 = -.40$$

$$SS_{A_{comp.} \times B_{comp.} \times C_{comp.}} = \frac{5(-.40)^2}{(2)(2)(2)} = .10$$

$$F = .10/1.75 = .06,\ p > .05$$

b.
$$\hat{\psi}_{A \times B\ \text{at}\ c_1} = (8.8 - 8.0) - (8.0 - 4.4) = -2.80$$
$$\hat{\psi}_{A \times B\ \text{at}\ c_2} = (9.0 - 8.4) - (7.8 - 7.4) = .20$$
$$\hat{\psi}_{A \times B \times C} = -2.80 - .20 = -3.00$$

$$SS_{A_{comp.} \times B_{comp.} \times C_{comp.}} = \frac{5(-3.00)^2}{(2)(2)(2)} = 5.63$$

$$F = 5.63/1.75 = 3.22,\ p > .05$$

c.

$$\hat{\psi}_{A \times B \text{ at } c_1} = (8.8 - 7.6) - (8.0 - 3.8) = -3.00$$
$$\hat{\psi}_{A \times B \text{ at } c_2} = (9.0 - 8.0) - (7.8 - 7.2) = .40$$

$$\hat{\psi}_{A \times B \times C} = -3.00 - .40 = -3.40$$

$$SS_{A_{comp.} \times B_{comp.} \times C_{comp.}} = \frac{5(-3.40)^2}{(2)(2)(2)} = 7.23$$

$$F = 7.23/1.75 = 4.13, p < .05$$

CHAPTER 21

1. Summary of the analysis:

Source	Calculations	SS	df	MS	F
A	$3,161.45 - 3,115.23 =$	46.22	1	46.22	25.82*
B	$3,290.30 - [T] =$	175.07	3	58.36	29.18*
$A \times B$	$3,339.80 - [A] - [B] + [T] =$	3.28	3	1.09	1.33
S	$3,497.38 - [T] =$	382.15	4	95.54	
$A \times S$	$3,550.75 - [A] - [S] + [T] =$	7.15	4	1.79	
$B \times S$	$3,696.50 - [B] - [S] + [T] =$	24.05	12	2.00	
$A \times B \times S$	$3,763 - [AB] - [AS] - [BS]$				
	$+ [A] + [B] + [S] - [T] =$	9.85	12	.82	
Total	$[Y] - [T] =$	647.77	39		

*$p < .05$.

2. a. Summary of the analysis:

Source	Calculations	SS[a]	df	MS	F
$B_{comp.}$	$1,164.50 - 1,110.05 =$	54.45	1	54.45	680.63*
S	$1,281.75 - [T] =$	171.70	4	42.93	
$B_{comp.} \times S$	$1,336.50 - [B] - [S] + [T] =$	.30	4	.08	
Total	$[Y] - [T] =$	226.45	9		

*$p < .05$.
[a]The adjustment factor $= 1$ for pairwise comparisons; no correction for the use of weighted Y scores is possible.

b. Summary of the analysis:

Source	Calculations	SS[a]	df	MS	F
$B_{comp.}$	$6,381.70 - 6,230.45 =$	151.25	1	151.25	63.55*
S	$6,994.75 - [T] =$	764.30	4	191.08	
$B_{comp.} \times S$	$7,155.50 - [B] - [S] + [T] =$	9.50	4	2.38	
Total	$[Y] - [T] =$	925.05	9		

*$p < .05$.
[a]The calculations are based on Y scores weighted by the coefficients 1, -1, -1, 1. You may compensate for the use of weighted Y scores by dividing each SS by the adjustment factor, $(\Sigma c_i^2)/2 = 4/2 = 2$. In any case, the final value of F remains unchanged.

3. a. Summary of the analysis:

Source	Calculations	SS	df	MS	F
B at a_1	$1{,}275.40 - 1{,}201.25 =$	74.15	3	24.72	41.90*
S	$1{,}395.75 - [T] =$	194.50	4	48.63	
$B \times S$ at a_1	$1{,}477 - [B] - [S] + [T] =$	7.10	12	.59	
Total	$[Y] - [T] =$	275.75	19		

*$p < .05$.

b. Summary of the analysis:

Source	Calculations	SS^a	df	MS	F
$B_{comp.}$ at a_1	$635.40 - 562.50 =$	72.90	1	72.90	112.15*
S	$647.50 - [T] =$	85.00	4	21.25	
$B_{comp.} \times S$ at a_1	$723 - [B] - [S] + [T] =$	2.60	4	.65	
Total	$[Y] - [T] =$	160.50	9		

*$p < .05$.
[a]The adjustment factor $= 1$ for pairwise comparisons; no correction for the use of weighted Y scores is possible.

CHAPTER 22

1. *Experiment A:* An $A \times B \times (C \times S)$ design, where

A consists of two levels (generate versus read)
B consists of two levels (timed versus self-paced)
C consists of five levels (rules)
$n = 6$ subjects in each of the $(a)(b) = 4$ independent groups

Source	Error Term
A	S/AB
B	S/AB
$A \times B$	S/AB
S/AB	—
C	$C \times S/AB$
$A \times C$	$C \times S/AB$
$B \times C$	$C \times S/AB$
$A \times B \times C$	$C \times S/AB$
$C \times S/AB$	—

Experiment B: An $A \times (B \times C \times S)$ design, where

A consists of two levels (informed versus uninformed)
B consists of two levels (generate versus read)
C consists of five levels (rules)
$n = 6$ subjects in each of the $a = 2$ independent groups

Source	Error Term
A	S/A
S/A	—
B	$B \times S/A$
$A \times B$	$B \times S/A$
$B \times S/A$	—
C	$C \times S/A$
$A \times C$	$C \times S/A$
$C \times S/A$	—
$B \times C$	$B \times C \times S/A$
$A \times B \times C$	$B \times C \times S/A$
$B \times C \times S/A$	—

Experiment C: An $A \times B \times (C \times S)$ design, where

A consists of two levels (stimulus versus response-recognition)
B consists of two levels (informed versus uninformed)
C consists of two levels (generate versus read)
$n = 6$ subjects in each of the $(a)(b) = 4$ independent groups

The analysis is the same as that for Experiment A.

Experiment D: An $(A \times B \times C \times S)$ design, where

A consists of two levels (generate versus read)
B consists of three levels (rules)
C consists of five levels (trials)
$n = 12$ subjects

Source	Error Term
A	$A \times S$
S	—
$A \times S$	—
B	$B \times S$
$B \times S$	—
C	$C \times S$
$C \times S$	—
$A \times B$	$A \times B \times S$
$A \times B \times S$	—
$A \times C$	$A \times C \times S$
$A \times C \times S$	—
$B \times C$	$B \times C \times S$
$B \times C \times S$	—
$A \times B \times C$	$A \times B \times C \times S$
$A \times B \times C \times S$	—

Experiment E: An $A \times (B \times C \times S)$ design, where

A consists of two levels (stimulus versus response-recall)
B consists of two levels (generate versus read)
C consists of five levels (trials)
$n = 12$ subjects in each of the $a = 2$ independent groups

The analysis is the same as that for Experiment B.

2. *Experiment A:* An $A \times (B \times C \times S)$ design, where

A consists of two levels (marijuana versus placebo)
B consists of three levels (trials)
C consists of two levels (cued versus uncued)
$n = 20$ subjects in each of the $a = 2$ independent groups

The analysis is identical to that for Experiment B, problem 1.

Experiment B: An $(A \times B \times S)$ design, where

A consists of four levels (placebo and three dosages)
B consists of two levels (rate of presentation)
$n = 16$ subjects

The analysis of this design is covered in Chap. 21.

3. Factorial treatment effects and error terms:

Treatment Source	Error Term	Treatment Source	Error Term
No Repeated Factors		Two Repeated Factors	
A	S/A	$B \times C$	$B \times C \times S/A$
		$A \times B \times C$	$B \times C \times S/A$
One Repeated Factor			
		$B \times D$	$B \times D \times S/A$
B	$B \times S/A$	$A \times B \times D$	$B \times D \times S/A$
$A \times B$	$B \times S/A$		
		$C \times D$	$C \times D \times S/A$
C	$C \times S/A$	$A \times C \times D$	$C \times D \times S/A$
$A \times C$	$C \times S/A$		
		Three Repeated Factors	
D	$D \times S/A$		
$A \times D$	$D \times S/A$	$B \times C \times D$	$B \times C \times D \times S/A$
		$A \times B \times C \times D$	$B \times C \times D \times S/A$

4. Factorial treatment effects and error terms:

Treatment Error	Error Term	Treatment Source	Error Term
One Repeated Factor		Three Repeated Factors	
A	$A \times S$	$A \times B \times C$	$A \times B \times C \times S$
B	$B \times S$	$A \times B \times D$	$A \times B \times D \times S$
C	$C \times S$	$A \times C \times D$	$A \times C \times D \times S$
D	$D \times S$	$B \times C \times D$	$B \times C \times D \times S$
Two Repeated Factors		Four Repeated Factors	
$A \times B$	$A \times B \times S$	$A \times B \times C \times D$	$A \times B \times C \times D \times S$
$A \times C$	$A \times C \times S$		
$A \times D$	$A \times D \times S$		
$B \times C$	$B \times C \times S$		
$B \times D$	$B \times D \times S$		
$C \times D$	$C \times D \times S$		

Appendix C

Analysis of Designs with Random Factors

Independent variables may be classified as *fixed* or *random*, depending on how the specific levels were selected. As discussed in Chap. 22, a factor is fixed if the selection is arbitrary, and random if the selection is unsystematic or random. Factors are fixed in most of the research reported in the behavioral sciences. Random factors are usually introduced as *control factors*—independent variables that help to broaden the generality of an experiment; typically, they are of little scientific interest to the researcher. Random factors complicate the statistical analysis, particularly when they are included in within-subjects designs. In this appendix I show how the analyses are different and offer some intuitive arguments concerning why. I present the discussion in the context of research in which investigators study the influence of semantic and linguistic factors on such cognitive processes as perception, learning, memory, problem solving, and thinking. Early papers by Coleman (1964) and Clark (1973) introduced the problem to psychologists. Both papers, which together provide a useful introduction to the issues, have sparked debate and controversy. Santa, Miller, and Shaw (1979) point out that random control factors are found in major fields of psychology outside the cognitive area, for example, clinical, developmental, educational, and social psychology (see pp. 37–40 of that article for examples and discussion).

AN EXAMPLE OF A RANDOM FACTOR

Let us consider a simple example of the complications that arise when a random factor is introduced into an experiment. The example comes from the Clark article (1973), which concentrated on a hypothetical experiment comparing reading speeds for two types of words, nouns and verbs; word type is the primary independent variable (factor A). Suppose random samples of five nouns and five verbs are selected from a dictionary or some other listing of words. The actual words in each sample constitute a second independent variable. Table C–1 illustrates the design. You will note that the five nouns (level a_1) are designated levels b_1 through b_5, whereas the five verbs (level a_2) are designated as levels b_6 through b_{10}. The levels of the second variable are numbered separately because the five instances of nouns are unrelated to the five instances of verbs. This is an example of an independent variable (factor B) that is **nested** within the levels of another independent variable (factor A). Factor A and factor B are not combined factorially in this design because the set of either type of word—noun or verb—is *uniquely defined* by the characteristics of that particular type. For all practical purposes, therefore, the set

Table C–1   An Example of a Nested Design

Instances	Nouns (a_1)	Instances	Verbs (a_2)
b_1		b_6	
b_2		b_7	
b_3		b_8	
b_4		b_9	
b_5		b_{10}	

of nouns is independent of the set of verbs. This same sort of independence is not present in the factorial design, however, because each factor is *consistently defined* at all levels of the other factor in the experiment. In this example, then, words are nested within word types; I will use the symbol B/A (read "*B* within *A*" or "*B* nested in *A*"), where the letter to the left of the diagonal designates the nested factor and the letter to the right designates the factor within which the nesting occurs.[1]

It may have occurred to you that we have already seen an example of a nested factor—namely, the within-groups factor. In a completely randomized single-factor design, for example, we can isolate the variability due to factor *A* and to the pooled variability of subjects treated alike. Although this latter source does not represent a true independent variable, "subjects" can be thought of as a factor consisting of n different levels (that is, n different subjects). "Subjects" does not cross with the levels of factor *A*—there is a different collection of n subjects in each of the *a* levels of the independent variable. Because the definition or meaning of "subjects" as a factor is different at each level of factor *A*, it, too, qualifies as a nested factor (which is why we refer to this source of variance as S/A, the variability of subjects nested within factor *A*).

Assume for the moment that the null hypothesis is true—that is, in the population, nouns and verbs do not differ in the speed with which they can be read by subjects. Although we would expect to find no difference in the reading speeds for the two types of words when the results are averaged over many independent experiments in which different random samples of nouns and verbs are obtained, we would certainly expect to find a difference between nouns and verbs in any *single* experiment. That is, we would expect the random sampling of materials to produce a set of nouns that on the average will be either easier to read than a set of verbs or more difficult to read. There is nothing mysterious about this process, just the operation of chance factors favoring one of the conditions over the other.

The problem, then, is to compare the variation between nouns and verbs (factor *A*) with an error term that specifically includes this particular consequence of sampling. To anticipate, this is accomplished by analyzing the data at the individual word level, using the variation among words of the same type to provide an estimate of the sampling error that is influencing the difference observed between the overall mean for the nouns and the overall mean for the verbs.

The Statistical Analysis

Suppose a researcher is interested in comparing two different concept-formation tasks, one involving a disjunctive concept and the other involving a conjunctive concept (factor A). To increase the generality of the experiment, the researcher includes $b = 4$ different examples of each of the two types of task (factor B/A). Subjects solved only one problem—either a disjunctive concept (a_1) or a conjunctive concept (a_2); $n = 2$ subjects were assigned randomly to each of the examples. The dependent variable is the number of minutes required to solve a problem. The

---

[1] In some references, this nested factor would be represented as $B(A)$.

individual Y scores are presented in the upper portion of Table C–2; $n = 2$ scores for each problem. As described, the design is a completely randomized, two-factor experiment, in which factor B is nested within the two levels of factor A. The data for the two subjects in each condition have been summed and placed in an AB matrix, which is more appropriately called a *nested AB* matrix. As you can see, the disjunctive concept was solved more quickly ($29/8 = 3.63$ minutes) than the conjunctive concept ($45/8 = 5.63$ minutes).

The formulas for the sums of squares are easily generated from df statements. The total sum of squares is divided into three sources of variability: the effect of the types of problem (A), the effect of examples nested within problem type (B/A), and the pooled variability of subjects treated alike (S/AB).[2] These sources are listed in column 1 of Table C–3. The degrees of freedom for each source are given in column 2. The rule for finding the df's for nested factors, originally presented in Chap. 17 (pp. 370–372), specified the following:

Multiply (1) the products of the df's of factors to the left of the diagonal by (2) the products of the levels of factors to the right of the diagonal.

Applying the rule to the nested factor, B/A, we find

$$df_{B/A} = (df_B)(a) = (b - 1)(a)$$

Table C–2   Numerical Example of a Completely Randomized Nested Design

Design and Data Matrix				
Disjunctive Concept (a_1)			**Conjunctive Concept (a_2)**	
Problems	**Y Scores**		**Problems**	**Y Scores**
b_1	3,2		b_5	10,10
b_2	1,1		b_6	3,3
b_3	5,3		b_7	6,6
b_4	5,9		b_8	4,3

Nested AB Matrix			
a_1		a_2	
b_1	5	b_5	20
b_2	2	b_6	6
b_3	8	b_7	12
b_4	14	b_8	7
Sum	29	Sum	45

[2]Technically, this term could be written $S/B/A$—subjects are nested within problems and problems in turn are nested in problem type—but this rearrangement does not change the nature of the nesting with regard to factor S. That is, the source refers to the pooled variability of subjects receiving a particular problem of a particular type. In any case, S/AB represents a source with which we are already familiar.

Table C–3 Calculating the Sums of Squares
for the Nested Design

(1) Source	(2) df	(3) Expanded df	(4) SS
A	$a - 1$	$a - 1$	$[A] - [T]$
B/A	$(a)(b - 1)$	$(a)(b) - a$	$[AB] - [A]$
S/AB	$(a)(b)(n - 1)$	$(a)(b)(n) - (a)(b)$	$[Y] - [AB]$
Total	$(a)(b)(n) - 1$	$(a)(b)(n) - 1$	$[Y] - [T]$

The rearranged version of this df statement is found in column 2 of Table C–3.
The df's for the effect of problem type (A), the within-groups source, and total,
which should all be familiar to you, are also presented in the table. The expanded
df statements (column 3) easily generate the computational formulas for the neces
sary sums of squares (column 4).[3]
    We are now ready to calculate the sums of squares. First, we will need the
basic ratios:

$$[T] = \frac{T^2}{(a)(b)(n)} = \frac{(74)^2}{(2)(4)(2)} = 342.25$$

$$[A] = \frac{\Sigma A^2}{(b)(n)} = \frac{(29)^2 + (45)^2}{(4)(2)} = 358.25$$

$$[AB] = \frac{\Sigma AB^2}{(n)} = \frac{(5)^2 + (2)^2 + \ldots + (12)^2 + (7)^2}{2} = 459.00$$

$$[Y] = \Sigma Y^2 = (3)^2 + (2)^2 + \ldots + (4)^2 + (3)^2 = 470$$

The sums of squares, which are calculated by combining the basic ratios in the
pattern specified in column 4 of Table C–3, are presented in an analysis summary
table (Table C–4). You should note that the sum of squares for the nested factor
($SS_{B/A}$) combines the variability of two subparts, the variation among the four disjunctive concepts (SS_{B/A_1}) and the variation among the four conjunctive concepts

Table C–4 Summary of the Analysis

Source	SS	df	MS	F
A	16.00	1	16.00	.95
B/A	100.75	6	16.79	12.17*
S/AB	11.00	8	1.38	
Total	127.75	15		

*$p < .05$.

---

[3]You will notice that we need the same basic ratios as are required for a completely randomized two-
way factorial, except for the absence of [B]. This basic ratio is undefined in this nested design because it makes no sense, for example, to combine the data for the first disjunctive concept (level a_1)
with the data for the first conjunctive concept (level a_2) to produce a B_1 subtotal.

(SS_{B/A_2}). We can verify this point by calculating the two sums of squares separately and then pooling them:

$$SS_{B/A_1} = \frac{(5)^2 + (2)^2 + (8)^2 + (14)^2}{2} - \frac{(29)^2}{(4)(2)}$$

$$= 144.50 - 105.13 = 39.37$$

$$SS_{B/A_2} = \frac{(20)^2 + (6)^2 + (12)^2 + (7)^2}{2} - \frac{(45)^2}{(4)(2)}$$

$$= 314.50 - 253.13 = 61.37$$

$$SS_{B/A} = 39.37 + 61.37 = 100.74$$

which equals the value in Table C–4 except for rounding error.

Selecting Error Terms.   The error term for any F ratio in the analysis of variance depends on the assumptions of the statistical model on which the analysis is based. In all analyses of completely randomized designs considered previously, we assumed that the levels of the independent variables are fixed factors—that is, they are selected arbitrarily and systematically—and thus we were justified in using the within-groups mean square as the error term. If we adopted the fixed-effects model in this particular example of nesting, we would use the $MS_{S/AB}$ as the error term with which to evaluate the significance of factor A.

However, the fixed-effects model is not appropriate for this type of design. Let's see why. The nested factor consists of $b = 4$ examples of disjunctive and of conjunctive problems. These examples constitute only a small proportion of all possible problems, some of which will be more difficult to solve than others. Since the researcher included in this experiment what in effect are two small samples of all possible problems, it is likely that either sample might be easier (or harder) than the average based on the total population of problems. Therefore, some unknown portion of the variability attributed to factor A is influenced by chance factors associated with the selection of the problems for each level of factor A. If the average difficulty of the four problems at a_1, say, is greater than the average based on the total population of disjunctive problems, the mean will be influenced adversely; on the other hand, if the average difficulty is less than the population average, the mean will be influenced positively. The same argument holds for the conjunctive problems. The point is that these chance differences resulting from the process by which the problems were selected contribute to the difference between the average reading speed for the nouns and that for the verbs.

You may have noticed that this argument is similar to the one we considered concerning the consequences of randomly assigning *subjects* to the different treatment conditions in a completely randomized single-factor design. In that case, it was argued that the groups would not be matched perfectly by this procedure and that some unknown part of the differences among the treatments was the result of uncontrolled chance factors introduced by the random assignment. As you know, we are able to take these chance differences into consideration by using an error term that estimates the effects of these uncontrolled chance factors directly—a mean square that is based on the pooled variability of subjects treated alike.

Let's see how we solve this problem when chance differences, which are introduced when we select task materials (for example, problems, words, and so on) for an experiment, contribute in some degree to the treatment effects. The treatment mean square, MS_A, is potentially influenced by *three*, rather than two, factors in this example of a nested design. More specifically, we have the null-hypothesis component—potential population treatment effects—and experimental error stemming from the random assignment of subjects to the treatment conditions and other uncontrolled factors. Up to this point, the situation is identical to that assumed for the completely randomized single-factor design. In addition to these two components, however, there is a third component, which represents the possible influence of the *nested factor*. This component reflects differences in the inherent difficulty of the particular sets of problems selected independently for each treatment condition. In symbols,

$$E(MS_A) = \sigma^2_{error} + (n)(\sigma^2_{B/A}) + (b)(n)(\theta^2_A) \tag{C-1}$$

where σ^2_{error} = population error variance
  $\sigma^2_{B/A}$ = variability due to the nested factor
  θ^2_A = population treatment effects

(The coefficients, n and b, represent sample size and the levels of the nested factor, respectively, which also influence the expected mean square.) Since the expected value of the usual error term, the within-groups mean square, is

$$E(MS_{S/AB}) = \sigma^2_{error}$$

you can see the problem, namely, that the $MS_{S/AB}$ is too small because it does not include the effects of the nested factor. This makes sense as soon as we remind ourselves that the within-groups mean square reflects the variability of subjects treated alike—that is, the variability of all subjects given the same problem to solve. Whereas this mean square adequately "captures" the usual experimental error, σ^2_{error}, it is uninfluenced by the differences in the difficulty of the different problems nested within factor A.

Fortunately, there is a simple way out of this problem: to use the nested mean square as the error term. This mean square, $MS_{B/A}$, is potentially influenced by two sources of variability, experimental error and differences among the problems of the same type. In symbols,

$$E(MS_{B/A}) = \sigma^2_{error} + (n)(\sigma^2_{B/A}) \tag{C-2}$$

Given this argument, then,

$$F = \frac{MS_A}{MS_{B/A}} \tag{C-3}$$

The expected value of the numerator term, Eq. (C-1), is exactly balanced by the expected value of the denominator term, Eq. (C-2), except for the null-hypothesis component, of course, which means that we can evaluate the significance of the F ratio in the usual manner. Continuing with this example,

$$F = \frac{16.00}{16.79} = .95$$

and is not significant. (The critical value of F is found with $df_{num.} = df_A = 1$ and $df_{denom.} = df_{B/A} = 6$.)

It is instructive to examine the consequences of using the usual, but *incorrect* error term, $MS_{S/AB}$, to evaluate the effects of factor A. With these data,

$$F = \frac{MS_A}{MS_{S/AB}} = \frac{16.00}{1.38} = 11.59$$

which is significant. This F is significant because the $MS_{S/AB}$ does not take into consideration the chance variation introduced by the random selection of problems that creates a positive bias in this F test. Monte Carlo studies verify the presence of this bias (for example, Forster & Dickinson, 1976; Santa, Miller, & Shaw, 1979).

It is also possible to evaluate the significance of the *nested* factor. In this case,

$$F = \frac{MS_{B/A}}{MS_{S/AB}} \tag{C–4}$$

With these data,

$$F = \frac{16.79}{1.38} = 12.17$$

which is significant. (In this case, $df_{num.} = df_{B/A} = 6$ and $df_{denom.} = df_{S/AB} = 8$.) This result tells us that the problems differ among themselves in difficulty.

Comments

The theoretical justification for the analysis of this nested design is based on a consideration of the expected mean squares associated with the sources of variance extracted in the statistical analysis. Consider again the expected mean squares for this design, which are presented in Table C–5. From this listing you can easily determine the correct error term by applying the following criterion:

> **A mean square qualifies as an error term if its expected value matches the expected value of the MS_{effect} in all respects except the null-hypothesis component.**

An inspection of the expected values in Table C–5 indicates that the nested factor (B/A) consists of the first two terms listed for factor A and thus becomes the error term for evaluating the significance of any difference of the primary independent variable. The $MS_{B/A}$ reflects the joint influence of two sets of chance factors, those stemming from the random assignment of subjects to the individual problems

Table C–5   Expected Mean Squares and Error Terms
for a Completely Randomized Design

Source	Expected Mean Square	Error Term
A	$\sigma^2_{error} + (n)(\sigma^2_{B/A}) + (b)(n)(\theta^2_A)$	B/A
B/A	$\sigma^2_{error} + (n)(\sigma^2_{B/A})$	S/AB
S/AB	σ^2_{error}	

(σ^2_{error}) and those stemming from the random selection of the levels of the nested factor ($\sigma^2_{B/A}$).

An examination of the expected values for MS_A and $MS_{B/A}$ reveals an important point concerning the power of rejecting the treatment null hypothesis. Consider first the consequences of increasing the subject sample size—the usual way of increasing power in this sort of design. You can see that increasing the number of subjects has *no major effect* on power because the coefficient associated with sample size, n, influences both the numerator and denominator terms of the F ratio. What about the consequences of increasing the number of problems? You will notice that the coefficient associated with the levels of the nested factor, b, affects only the numerator term of the F ratio, MS_A. Thus, any increase in the number of problems or words included in the experiment will produce an increase in power. From the point of view of experimental design, therefore, it makes far more sense to increase the levels of the nested factor than to increase the number of subjects per group in this type of experiment.[4]

A final point concerns the classification of independent variables as fixed or random. The issue frequently arises that control factors are not fixed, in the sense that they do not enumerate all levels of interest to the researcher, but they are not randomly selected from some clearly defined population, either. It is at this point that we must remind ourselves of the following: In the world of experimentation, structural models only approximate any given experimental application and it is up to us to determine whether it is better to view the factor as random or as fixed. Even if random sampling has not been followed, but the levels chosen clearly do not constitute the population, it is probably a good idea to treat the factor as random nevertheless. The reason for this advice is that there is a real possibility that the "random" factor will still intrude on treatment effects of interest, and this real possibility should be assessed statistically. Thus, from a practical point of view, error terms appropriate for random effects might be required even though the extent of the statistical generalization possible is limited by the failure to sample randomly. In any case, random factors, or "quasi-random" factors, pose serious problems for the statistical analysis and evaluation of treatment effects.

---

[4]See Wickens and Keppel (1983) for a detailed discussion of this important relationship between subject sample size and material or instance sample size.

ADDITIONAL EXAMPLES OF DESIGNS WITH NESTED RANDOM FACTORS

In this section, we consider additional complications that arise when nested random factors are included in within-subjects designs. Let's return to the experiment in which the reading speeds of nouns and verbs were compared. The original conceptualization of this experiment was as a completely randomized design in which subjects were assigned randomly to read only one of the words in the experiment—an uneconomical and unrealistic example but one that illustrates the effect of a nested random factor most clearly. You will recall that we extracted three sources of variation from this design: word type (A), word instances pooled over word type (B/A), and subjects reading a particular noun or verb (S/AB). (The expected values and error terms for the analysis of this design are found in Table C–5.) We now consider two designs that introduce repeated measures into this experiment.

A "Mixed" Repeated-Measures Design

A common way to design this particular experiment is to test one group of subjects on all the nouns and another group of subjects on all the verbs. This arrangement is diagrammed in the upper portion of Table C–6 in which $n = 2$ subjects receive all four nouns and two other subjects receive all four verbs. (In the completely randomized design, which we considered previously, subjects received only one noun or one verb.) The resulting design is a "mixed" or "split-plot" design, which includes both between-subjects variation and within-subjects variation. To understand the complications arising from this design, let's consider for a moment the expected values for the sources of variances normally extracted in the corresponding mixed *factorial* design, the $A \times (B \times S)$ design that we first discussed in Chap. 17.

The factorial arrangement of the $A \times (B \times S)$ design is presented in the lower portion of Table C–6. You will note that the two designs are identical except in the designation of factor B: In the nested design, the levels of the repeated factor (B) are b_1 through b_4 for level a_1 and b_5 through b_8 for level a_2; in the factorial design, the levels are the same—levels b_1 through b_4 for both levels of factor A. Table C–7 gives the sources of variance normally obtained from this design and their expected values. As you will recall, this design requires the use of two error terms, one to assess between-subjects differences ($MS_{S/A}$) and the other to assess within-subjects differences ($MS_{B \times S/A}$). An inspection of the expected mean squares indicates why. The expected mean square for the within-subjects error term contains two components, σ^2_{error} and $\sigma^2_{B \times S/A}$. The first is often referred to as *measurement error*, the variability that we would expect if a subject were repeatedly tested in the same treatment condition, together with so-called nuisance factors that vary randomly in an experiment. The second reflects the interaction of the B treatments with the subjects. In the usual design, these two components cannot be disentangled, even though they are assumed theoretically to exist apart. The expected values for the two factorial effects involving repeated measures, B and $A \times B$, contain these two error components plus the relevant null-hypothesis com-

Table C–6   Two Experimental Designs

Mixed Design with Factor B Nested

	a_1					a_2			
	b_1	b_2	b_3	b_4		b_5	b_6	b_7	b_8
s_1					s_3				
s_2					s_4				

Mixed Design with Factor B Crossed

	a_1					a_2			
	b_1	b_2	b_3	b_4		b_1	b_2	b_3	b_4
s_1					s_3				
s_2					s_4				

ponent, which indicates why $MS_{B \times S/A}$ is the error term for these two sources of variance.

The expected mean square for the between-subjects error term ($MS_{S/A}$) also contains two components, σ^2_{error} and $(b)(\sigma^2_{S/A})$. The first reflects measurement error and other uncontrolled factors, whereas the second reflects the variability among the subjects in the treatment populations assumed to exist for each level of factor A. Again, these two components cannot be disentangled. As you can see from Table C–7, this mean square qualifies as the error term for the A main effect because the two sets of expected values are matched except for the null-hypothesis component for A.

Let's return to the mixed design in which factor B is a random nested variable (the design in the upper portion of Table C–6). The sources of variance normally obtained from this design and the expected values for these sources are presented in Table C–8. An examination of the terms making up the expected value of the primary independent variable—that is, A main effect—indicates that the source

Table C–7   Expected Mean Squares and Error Terms
for the $A \times (B \times S)$ Design

Source	Expected Mean Square	Error Term
A	$\sigma^2_{error} + (b)(\sigma^2_{S/A}) + (b)(n)(\theta^2_A)$	S/A
S/A	$\sigma^2_{error} + (b)(\sigma^2_{S/A})$	
B	$\sigma^2_{error} + \sigma^2_{B \times S/A} + (a)(n)(\theta^2_B)$	$B \times S/A$
$A \times B$	$\sigma^2_{error} + \sigma^2_{B \times S/A} + (n)(\theta^2_{A \times B})$	$B \times S/A$
$B \times S/A$	$\sigma^2_{error} + \sigma^2_{B \times S/A}$	

Table C–8 Expected Mean Square for a Mixed Design with a Random Nested Factor

Source	Expected Mean Square
A	$\sigma^2_{error} + \sigma^2_{B \times S/A} + (n)(\sigma^2_{B/A}) + (b)(\sigma^2_{S/A}) + (b)(n)(\theta^2_A)$
S/A	$\sigma^2_{error} + \sigma^2_{B \times S/A} + (b)(\sigma^2_{S/A})$
B/A	$\sigma^2_{error} + \sigma^2_{B \times S/A} + (n)(\sigma^2_{B/A})$
$B \times S/A$	$\sigma^2_{error} + \sigma^2_{B \times S/A}$

contains five terms rather than the three that were specified for the $A \times (B \times S)$ design in Table C–7. One of the new terms, $(n)(\sigma^2_{B/A})$, is the nested factor, which we expect to exert an influence on the A main effect. The other new term, $\sigma^2_{B \times S/A}$, is included for certain theoretical reasons that are too complicated to explain in this discussion. In any case, an inspection of the expected value for the A main effect listed in Table C–8 indicates that the following *four* terms must be matched by the expected value of a source of variance if it is to serve as an error term:

$$\sigma^2_{error}, \quad \sigma^2_{B \times S/A}, \quad (n)(\sigma^2_{B/A}), \quad \text{and} \quad (b)(\sigma^2_{S/A})$$

A further inspection of the expected values of the remaining sources in the table reveals that none provides this necessary match. An F test cannot be found.

Although we are unable in this design to find a single source of variance to provide the matching of terms, we can find a match by combining several of them. More specifically, the $E(MS_{S/A})$ does include three of the four terms needed, and the $E(MS_{B/A})$ contains the remaining term. If we add these two mean squares, we will have a new mean square that contains the four critical terms and two terms that are included twice, that is, σ^2_{error} and $\sigma^2_{B \times S/A}$. These two extra terms can be eliminated by subtracting $MS_{B \times S/A}$ from the sum:

$$
\begin{aligned}
E(MS_{denom.}) &= E(MS_{S/A}) + E(MS_{B/A}) - E(MS_{B \times S/A}) \\
&= [\sigma^2_{error} + \sigma^2_{B \times S/A} + (b)(\sigma^2_{S/A})] \\
&\quad + [\sigma^2_{error} + \sigma^2_{B \times S/A} + (n)(\sigma^2_{B/A})] \\
&\quad - [\sigma^2_{error} + \sigma^2_{B \times S/A}] \\
&= \sigma^2_{error} + \sigma^2_{B \times S/A} + (n)(\sigma^2_{B/A}) + (b)(\sigma^2_{S/A})]
\end{aligned}
$$

which equals the expected value of MS_A except for the null-hypothesis component, $(b)(n)(\theta^2_A)$. We have an error term. On the basis of these arguments, then, we can form a ratio, F' to evaluate the significance of the A main effect:

$$F' = \frac{MS_A}{MS_{S/A} + MS_{B/A} - MS_{B \times S/A}} \tag{C–5}$$

The F ratio specified in Eq. (C–5) is called a **quasi F**—a statistic that is not distributed as F. As a consequence, we are not able to use the F table in any simple way to determine the critical values for the statistical test. Satterthwaite (1946) has provided a formula for calculating adjusted degrees of freedom that then permits the straightforward use of the F table. This adjustment formula can be used to calculate the degrees of freedom for any term that is a combination of mean squares; the df for terms representing single sources of variance are calculated in the usual way without adjustment. The adjustment formula is based on the mean squares contributing to the combination. If we represent these mean squares as MS_U, MS_V, MS_W, and so on, the adjustment formula becomes

$$df_{adj.} = \frac{(\text{combination of } MS_U, MS_V, MS_W, \ldots)^2}{(MS_U)^2/df_U + (MS_V)^2/df_V + (MS_W)^2/df_W + \ldots} \tag{C-6}$$

where the numerator consists of the square of the actual combination of mean squares, and the denominator consists of the sum of the mean squares contributing to the combination, which are squared and divided by their degrees of freedom. (The value obtained from this formula is rounded to the nearest whole number.) Applied to the present example, in which the denominator of the quasi F ratio consists of the combination $MS_{S/A} + MS_{B/A} - MS_{B \times S/A}$, Eq. (C-6) becomes

$$df_{adj.} = \frac{(MS_{S/A} + MS_{B/A} - MS_{B \times S/A})^2}{(MS_{S/A})^2/df_{S/A} + (MS_{B/A})^2/df_{B/A} + (MS_{B \times S/A})^2/df_{B \times S/A}} \tag{C-7}$$

Thus, we can test the significance of the A main effect by calculating the quasi F specified in Eq. (C-5) and finding the critical value of this statistic in the F table under $df_{num.} = df_A$ and $df_{denom.} = df_{adj.}$, calculated from Eq. (C-7).

Although the quasi F specified by Eq. (C-5) is preferred by some authors (see Myers, 1979, p. 192), there is the possibility of obtaining a denominator with a negative value, which can happen if the third mean square is larger than the sum of the other two mean squares. To avoid this potential problem, several statisticians recommend an alternative quasi F that avoids subtraction and negative numbers altogether. Consider, for example,

$$F'' = \frac{MS_A + MS_{B \times S/A}}{MS_{S/A} + MS_{B/A}} \tag{C-8}$$

Turning back to Table C-8, we find

$$E(MS_A + MS_{B \times S/A}) = [\sigma_{error}^2 + \sigma_{B \times S/A}^2 + (n)(\sigma_{B/A}^2) + (b)(\sigma_{S/A}^2) + (b)(n)(\theta_A^2)]$$
$$+ [\sigma_{error}^2 + \sigma_{B \times S/A}^2]$$

$$E(MS_{S/A} + MS_{B/A}) = [\sigma_{error}^2 + \sigma_{B \times S/A}^2 + (b)(\sigma_{S/A}^2)]$$
$$+ [\sigma_{error}^2 + \sigma_{B \times S/A}^2 + (n)(\sigma_{B/A}^2)]$$

A re-sorting of the terms for the numerator and denominator expected values will reveal a perfect match except for the null-hypothesis component, $(b)(n)(\theta_A^2)$, in the numerator of F'':

$$E(MS_A + MS_{B \times S/A}) = 2\sigma^2_{error} + 2\sigma^2_{B \times S/A} + (n)(\sigma^2_{B/A}) + (b)(\sigma^2_{S/A}) + (b)(n)(\theta^2_A)$$

$$E(MS_{S/A} + MS_{B/A}) = 2\sigma^2_{error} + 2\sigma^2_{B \times S/A} + (b)(\sigma^2_{B/A}) + (n)(\sigma^2_{S/A})$$

This means that F'' will be approximately 1.0 when the null hypothesis is true and greater than 1.0 when it is false. This quasi F test is distributed approximately as F if the numerator and denominator degrees of freedom are adjusted by means of Eq. (C–6). For the numerator, this adjustment is

$$df_{adj.} = \frac{(MS_A + MS_{B \times S/A})^2}{(MS_A)^2/df_A + (MS_{B \times S/A})^2/df_{B \times S/A}}$$

and for the denominator, it is

$$df_{adj.} = \frac{(MS_{S/A} + MS_{B/A})^2}{(MS_{S/A})^2/df_{S/A} + (MS_{B/A})^2/df_{B/A}}$$

A "Pure" Repeated-Measures Design

The final design we consider is the one discussed in detail by Clark (1973), an experiment in which each subject is tested on all the words in the study. This is a "pure" within-subjects design in the sense that both factors in the study, type of word (A) and instances of each type (B/A), are represented by repeated measures. The sources of variance and expected mean squares extracted from this particular design are presented in Table C–9. Again, you can see that no single source can serve as an error term for evaluating the A main effect. A quasi F that will provide a solution to this problem is seen at the bottom of the table. An alternative quasi F is

$$F'' = \frac{MS_A + MS_{B \times S/A}}{MS_{B/A} + MS_{A \times S}}$$

Table C–9   Expected Mean Squares and Error Terms for a "Pure" Within-Subjects Design with a Random Nested Factor

Source	Expected Mean Square	Error Term
A	$\sigma^2_{error} + \sigma^2_{B \times S/A} + (b)(\sigma^2_{A \times S}) + (n)(\sigma^2_{B/A}) + (b)(n)(\theta^2_A)$	See below
B/A	$\sigma^2_{error} + \sigma^2_{B \times S/A} + (n)(\sigma^2_{B/A})$	$B \times S/A$
S	$\sigma^2_{error} + \sigma^2_{B \times S/A} + (a)(b)(\sigma^2_S)$	
$A \times S$	$\sigma^2_{error} + \sigma^2_{B \times S/A} + (b)(\sigma^2_{A \times S})$	
$B \times S/A$	$\sigma^2_{error} + \sigma^2_{B \times S/A}$	

$$F' = \frac{MS_A}{MS_{B/A} + MS_{A \times S} - MS_{B \times S/A}}$$

Again, Eq. (C–6) must be used to calculate the adjusted df's for the denominator term of F' and for both terms of F''.

Comment

I mentioned earlier that the "pure" within subjects design formed the basis of Clark's (1973) paper on the analysis of experiments with random independent factors. Experiments of this sort are common in many fields of psychology. The important point of Clark's discussion is that the use of incorrect error terms, which do not take into consideration the random quality of one or more of the independent variables, frequently results in erroneous conclusions concerning the effects of these manipulations.

There is no denying the logic of the statistical analysis required when words are actually drawn at random from a large pool of instances. On the other hand, there are many cases in which this description of the selection of materials is completely inappropriate—situations in which words or problems are not chosen at random but with careful matching on dimensions known to influence the behavior under study. For example, a researcher might match nouns and verbs on the frequency with which the words occur in written and spoken prose, on the number of syllables, on the number of letters, and so on. The goal is not to study the reading speed of nouns and verbs as they exist in the linguistic environment, which presumably is the intent when one selects words randomly, but to study the cognitive effects of "nounness" and "verbness" with all other characteristics held constant.

This type of experimental design calls for a different kind of statistical analysis, one that substitutes matched pairs or matched blocks of words for random samples of words. Instead of the nested factor B/A (words within word type), we would have factor B (blocks of words), which *crosses* with factor A. Whereas this type of design still involves a random factor (blocks of words) and has to be analyzed with that assumption in mind, the analysis will generally result in a more sensitive assessment of the main independent variable (nounness versus verbness) than that provided by the nested design and the random selection of words. This occurs because variability among words is isolated in the analysis of the block design as the B main effect but remains unanalyzed in the error term in the analysis of the nested design. For this reason, then, the matching or block design will often prove to be a better choice in this type of investigation.[5]

EXTENDING THE ANALYSIS TO OTHER DESIGNS

There are many instances of random factors in the social sciences, typically masquerading as unanalyzed control variables. Ignoring the presence of these control variables will not eliminate the problem. This point was convincingly argued by Clark (1973), who demonstrated that previously significant findings, which were

[5]See Wickens and Keppel (1983) for a comparison of these designs.

established with incorrect error terms, are no longer significant once the appropriate analysis is conducted. The numerical example considered in this appendix also illustrates the point. Whereas the correct analysis of the difference in solving times for conjunctive and disjunctive problems was not significant (see Table C-4), an analysis using the within-groups mean square, which many researchers would instinctively choose, produced a significant F.

The key to the analysis of experiments with random factors is a listing of the expected values for the sources of variance extracted in the usual analysis of variance. Once you examine the terms specified for a treatment source of variance, you can scan the expected values for the other sources to see if one can serve as an error term. If no source satisfies the criterion for an error term—that is, there is no match of its expected value with that of the treatment source except for the null-hypothesis component—you will have to determine if you can construct a quasi F ratio in which the mean squares of several sources are combined to achieve an appropriate match.

Where can you find tables of expected values? Advanced statistics books such as Kirk (1982), Lindman (1974), Myers (1979), and Winer (1971) provide expected values for a variety of designs. Since it is not practical to present such tables for all complex experimental designs, most authors offer some sort of mechanical scheme for determining the expected values for each term listed in the analysis-of-variance summary table. You can find such schemes or "rules of thumb," in a variety of sources, including Glass and Stanley (1970, pp. 479–481), Keppel (1982, Appendix C-4), Kirk (1982, pp. 389–393), Lindman (1974, pp. 151–154), Myers (1979, pp. 205–206), and Winer (1971, pp. 371–375).

References

ANDERSON, R. B. (1981). *STAT POWER. An Apple computer program*. Cambridge, MA: Abt Associates.

BAKAN, D. (1966). The test of significance in psychological research. *Psychological Bulletin, 66*, 423–437.

BIRCH, H. G., & Lefford, A. (1967). Visual differentiation, intersensory integration, and voluntary motor control. *Monographs of the Society for Research in Child Development, 32* (2, Serial No. 110).

BISHOP, T. A., & DUDEWICZ, E. J. (1978). Exact analysis of variance with unequal variances: Test procedures and tables. *Technometrics, 20*, 419–430.

BOIK, R. J. (1979). Interactions, partial interactions, and interaction contrasts in the analysis of variance. *Psychological Bulletin, 86*, 1,084–1,089.

BOIK, R. J. (1981). A priori tests in repeated measures designs: Effects of nonsphericity. *Psychometrika, 46*, 241–255.

BORENSTEIN, M., & COHEN, J. (1988). *Statistical power analysis: A computer program*. Hillsdale, NJ: Erlbaum.

BOX, G. E. P. (1954a). Some theorems on quadratic forms applied in the study of analysis of variance problems, I. Effect of inequality of variance in the one-way classification. *Annals of Mathematical Statistics, 25*, 290–302.

BOX, G. E. P. (1954b). Some theorems on quadratic forms applied in the study of analysis of variance problems, II. Effect of inequality of variances and correlation between errors in the two-way classification. *Annals of Mathematical Statistics, 25*, 484–498.

BRADLEY, J. V. (1978). Robustness? *British Journal of Mathematical and Statistical Psychology, 31*, 144–152.

BRADLEY, J. V. (1980a). Nonrobustness in classical tests on means and variances: A large-scale sampling study. *Bulletin of the Psychonomic Society, 15*, 275–278.

BRADLEY, J. V. (1980b). Nonrobustness in Z, t, and F tests at large sample sizes. *Bulletin of the Psychonomic Society, 16*, 333–336.

BRECHT, M. L., WOODWARD, J. A., & BONETT, D. G. (1988). *GANOVA4.* (Available from Dr. J. A. Woodward, Department of Psychology, University of California, Los Angeles, CA, 90024)

BREWER, J. K. (1972). On the power of statistical tests in the *American Educational Research Journal. American Educational Research Journal, 9*, 391–401.

BROWN, M. B., & FORSYTHE, A. B. (1974a). The ANOVA and multiple comparisons for data with heterogeneous variances. *Biometrics, 30*, 719–724.

BROWN, M. B., & FORSYTHE, A. B. (1974b). Robust tests for equality of variances. *Journal of the American Statistical Association, 69*, 364–367.

BROWN, M. B., & FORSYTHE, A. B. (1974c). The small sample behavior of some statistics which test the equality of several means. *Technometrics, 16*, 129–132.

BRUNING, J. L., & KINTZ, B. L. (1977). *Computational handbook of statistics* (2nd ed.). Glenview, IL: Scott, Foresman.

CAMP, C. J., & MAXWELL, S. E. (1983). A comparison of various strengths of association measures commonly used in gerontological research. *Journal of Gerontology, 38*, 3–7.

CAMPBELL, D. T., & STANLEY, J. C. (1963). Experimental and quasi-experimental designs for research on teaching. In N. L. Gage (Ed.), *Handbook of research on teaching* (pp. 171–246). Chicago: Rand McNally.

CAMPBELL, D. T., & STANLEY, J. C. (1966). *Experimental and quasi-experimental designs for research*. Chicago: Rand McNally.

CARROLL, R. M., & NORDHOLM, L. A. (1975). Sampling characteristics of Kelley's ϵ^2 and Hays' $\hat{\omega}^2$. *Educational and Psychological Measurement, 35*, 541–554.

CHARTER, R. A. (1982). Practical formulas of strength of association measures. *Educational and Psychological Measurement, 42*, 969–974.

CHASE, L. J., & TUCKER, R. K. (1976). Statistical power: Derivation, development, and data-analytic implications. *The Psychological Record, 26*, 473–486.

CHURCH, J. D., & WIKE, E. L. (1976). The robustness of homogeneity of variance tests for asymmetric distributions: A Monte Carlo study. *Bulletin of the Psychonomic Society, 7*, 417–420.

CLARK, H. H. (1973). The language-as-fixed-effect fallacy: A critique of language statistics in psychological research. *Journal of Verbal Learning and Verbal Behavior, 12*, 335–359.

CLINCH, J. J., & KESELMAN, H. J. (1982). Parametric alternatives to the analysis of variance. *Journal of Educational Statistics, 7*, 207–214.

COHEN, J. (1962). The statistical power of abnormal-social psychological research: A review. *Journal of Abnormal and Social Psychology, 65*, 145–153.

COHEN, J. (1965). Some statistical issues in psychological research. In B. B. Wolman (Ed.), *Handbook of clinical psychology* (pp. 95–121). New York: McGraw-Hill.

COHEN, J. (1973). Eta-squared and partial eta-squared in fixed factor ANOVA designs. *Educational and Psychological Measurement, 33*, 107–112.

COHEN, J. (1977). *Statistical power analysis for the behavioral sciences* (rev. ed.). New York: Academic Press.

COHEN, J. (1980). Trend analysis the easy way. *Educational and Psychological Measurement, 40*, 565–568.

COHEN, J. (1988). *Statistical power analysis* (2nd ed.). Hillsdale, NJ: Erlbaum.

COHEN, J., & COHEN, P. (1983). *Applied multiple regression/correlation analysis for the behavioral sciences* (2nd ed.). Hillsdale, NJ: Erlbaum.

COLEMAN, E. B. (1964). Generalizing to a language population. *Psychological Reports, 14*, 219–226.

COLLIER, R. O., Jr., BAKER, F. B., MANDEVILLE, G. K., & HAYES, T. F. (1967). Estimates of test size for several test procedures based on conventional variance ratios in the repeated measures design. *Psychometrika, 32*, 339–353.

CONOVER, W. J., JOHNSON, M. E., & JOHNSON, M. M. (1981). A comparative study of tests for homogeneity of variances, with applications to the outer continental shelf bidding data. *Technometrics, 23*, 351–361.

COOK, T. D., & CAMPBELL, D. T. (1979). *Quasi-experimentation: Design and analysis issues for field settings*. Chicago: Rand McNally.

COOPER, H., & FINDLEY, M. (1982). Expected effect sizes: Estimates for statistical power analysis in social psychology. *Personality and Social Psychology Bulletin, 8*, 168–173.

CORNFIELD, J., & TUKEY, J. W. (1956). Average values of mean squares in factorials. *Annals of Mathematical Statistics, 27*, 907–949.

CRONBACH, L. J., & SNOW, R. E. (1977). *Aptitude and instructional methods: A handbook for research on interactions*. New York: Irvington Publishers.

DALLAL, G. E. (1986). PC-SIZE: A program for sample-size determinations. *The American Statistician, 40*, 52.

DAVIS, C., & GAITO, J. (1984). Multiple comparison procedures within experimental research. *Canadian Psychology, 25*, 1–13.

DAWES, R. M. (1969). Interaction effects in the presence of asymmetrical transfer. *Psychological Bulletin, 71*, 55–57.

DE CANI, J. S. (1984). Balancing type I risk and loss of power in ordered Bonferroni procedures. *Journal of Educational Psychology, 76*, 1,035–1,037.

DIXON, W. J., & MASSEY, F. J., Jr. (1957). *Introduction to statistical analysis* (2nd ed.). New York: McGraw-Hill.

DRETZKE, B. J., LEVIN, J. R., & SERLIN, R. C. (1982). Testing for regression homogeneity under variance heterogeneity. *Psychological Bulletin, 91*, 376–383.

DUNN, O. J. (1961). Multiple comparisons among means. *Journal of the American Statistical Association, 56*, 52–64.

DUNNETT, C. W. (1955). A multiple comparison procedure for comparing several treatments with a control. *Journal of the American Statistical Association, 50*, 1,096–1,121.

DUNNETT, C. W. (1964). New tables for multiple comparisons with a control. *Biometrics, 20*, 482–491.

DWYER, J. H. (1974). Analysis of variance and the magnitude of effects: A general approach. *Psychological Bulletin, 81*, 731–737.

EBBINGHAUS, H. (1885). *Memory*. Leipzig: Duncker.

EDGINGTON, E. S. (1966). Statistical inference and nonrandom samples. *Psychological Bulletin, 66*, 485–487.

EINOT, I., & GABRIEL, K. R. (1975). A study of the powers of several methods of multiple comparisons. *Journal of the American Statistical Association, 70*, 574–583.

ELASHOFF, J. D. (1969). Analysis of covariance: A delicate instrument. *American Educational Research Journal, 6*, 383–401.

ERICSSON, K. A., & POLSON, P. G. (1988). An experimental analysis of the mechanisms of a memory skill. *Journal of Experimental Psychology: Learning, Memory, and Cognition, 14*, 305–316.

ERLBACHER, A. (1977). Design and analysis of experiments contrasting the within- and between-subjects manipulation of the independent variable. *Psychological Bulletin, 84*, 212–219.

FELDT, L. S. (1958). A comparison of the precision of three experimental designs employing a concomitant variable. *Psychometrika, 23*, 335–353.

FELDT, L. S. (1973). What size samples for methods/materials experiments? *Journal of Educational Measurement, 10*, 221–226.

FISHER, R. A. (1935). *The design of experiments*. Edinburgh and London: Oliver & Boyd.

FISHER, R. A. (1951). *The design of experiments* (6th ed.). Edinburgh: Oliver & Boyd.

FISHER, R. A., & YATES, F. (1953). *Statistical tables for biological, agricultural and medical research* (4th ed.). Edinburgh: Oliver & Boyd.

FORSTER, K. I., & DICKINSON, R. G. (1976). More on the language-as-fixed-effect fallacy: Monte Carlo estimates of error rates for F_1, F_2, F', and min F''. *Journal of Verbal Learning and Verbal Behavior*, *15*, 135–142.

FOWLER, R. L. (1987). A general method for comparing effect magnitudes in ANOVA designs. *Educational and Psychological Measurement*, *47*, 361–367.

GAITO, J., & NOBREGA, J. N. (1981). A note on multiple comparisons as an ANOVA problem. *Bulletin of the Psychonomic Society*, *17*, 169–170.

GAMES, P. A. (1971a). Errata for "Multiple comparisons on means," *AERJ*, 1971, 531–565. *American Educational Research Journal*, *8*, 677–678.

GAMES, P. A. (1971b). Multiple comparisons of means. *American Educational Research Journal*, *8*, 531–565.

GAMES, P. A. (1978a). A four-factor structure for parametric tests on independent groups. *Psychological Bulletin*, *85*, 661–672.

GAMES, P. A. (1978b). A three-factor model encompassing many possible statistical tests on independent groups. *Psychological Bulletin*, *85*, 168–182.

GAMES, P. A., & HOWELL, J. F. (1976). Pairwise multiple comparison procedures with unequal N's and/or variances: A Monte Carlo study. *Journal of Educational Statistics*, *1*, 113–125.

GEISSER, S., & GREENHOUSE, S. W. (1958). An extension of Box's results on the use of the F distribution in multivariate analysis. *Annals of Mathematical Statistics*, *29*, 885–891.

GILLIG, P. M., & GREENWALD, A. G. (1974). Is it time to lay the sleeper effect to rest? *Journal of Personality and Social Psychology*, *29*, 132–139.

GLASS, G. V, & HAKSTIAN, A. R. (1969). Measures of association in comparative experiments: Their development and interpretation. *American Educational Research Journal*, *6*, 403–414.

GLASS, G. V, PECKHAM, P. D., & SANDERS, J. R. (1972). Consequences of failure to meet assumptions underlying the fixed effects analyses of variance and covariance. *Review of Educational Research*, *42*, 237–288.

GLASS, G. V, & STANLEY, J. C. (1970). *Statistical methods in education and psychology*. Englewood Cliffs, NJ: Prentice Hall.

GOLDSTEIN, R. (1989). Power and sample size via MS/PC-DOS computers. *The American Statistician*, *43*, 253–260.

GOLLIN, E. S. (1965). A developmental approach to learning and cognition. In L. P. Lipsitt & C. C. Spiker (Eds.), *Advances in child development and behavior* (Vol. II, pp. 159–186). New York: Academic Press.

GOSSLEE, D. G., & LUCAS, H. L. (1965). Analysis of variance of disproportionate data when interaction is present. *Biometrics*, *21*, 115–133.

GRANT, D. A. (1956). Analysis-of-variance tests in the analysis and comparison of curves. *Psychological Bulletin*, *53*, 141–154.

GRANT, D. A., & SCHILLER, J. J. (1953). Generalization of the conditioned galvanic skin response to visual stimuli. *Journal of Experimental Psychology*, *46*, 309–313.

GREENHOUSE, S. W., & GEISSER, S. (1959). On methods in the analysis of profile data. *Psychometrika*, *24*, 95–112.

GREENWALD, A. G. (1976). Consequences of prejudice against the null hypothesis. *Psychological Bulletin*, *82*, 1–20.

GREENWALD, A. G., PRATKANIS, A. R., LEIPPE, M. R., & Baumgardner, M. H. (1986). Under what conditions does theory obstruct research progress? *Psychological Review*, *93*, 216–229.

GRICE, G. R., & HUNTER, J. J. (1964). Stimulus intensity effects depend upon the type of experimental design. *Psychological Review*, *71*, 247–256.

HARTER, H. L. (1957). Error rates and sample sizes for range tests in multiple comparisons. *Biometrics*, *13*, 511–536.

HAYES-ROTH, B. (1977). Evolution of cognitive structures and processes. *Psychological Review*, *84*, 260–270.

HAYS, W. L. (1973). *Statistics for psychologists* (2nd ed.). New York: Holt, Rinehart & Winston.

HAYS, W. L. (1988). *Statistics for psychologists* (4th ed.). New York: Holt, Rinehart & Winston.

HAYTER, A. (1986). The maximum familywise error rate of Fisher's least significant difference test. *Journal of the American Statistical Association*, *81*, 1,000–1,004.

HEDGES, L. V., & OLKIN, I. (1985). *Statistical methods for meta-analysis*. New York: Academic Press.

HERR, D. G. (1986). On the history of ANOVA in unbalanced, factorial designs: The first 30 years. *The American Statistician*, *40*, 265–270.

HINKLE, D. E., & OLIVER, J. D. (1983). How large should the sample be? A question with no simple answer? Or. . . . *Educational and Psychological Measurement*, *43*, 1,051–1,060.

HOCHBERG, Y., & TAMHANE, A. C. (1987). *Multiple comparison procedures*. New York: Wiley.

HOLLAND, B. S., & COPENHAVER, M. D. (1988). Improved Bonferroni-type multiple testing procedures. *Psychological Bulletin*, *104*, 145–149.

HSU, L. M. (1980). On the power of multiple independent tests when the experimentwise error rate is controlled. *Educational and Psychological Measurement*, *40*, 31–40.

HUBERTY, C. J., & MORRIS, J. D. (1988). A single contrast test procedure. *Educational and Psychological Measurement*, *48*, 567–578.

HUCK, S. W., & SANDLER, H. M. (1979). *Rival hypotheses*. New York: Harper & Row.

HUITEMA, B. E. (1980). *The analysis of covariance and alternatives*. New York: Wiley.

HUNTER, J. E., & SCHMIDT, F. L. (1990). *Methods of meta-analysis: Correcting error and bias in research findings*. Newbury Park, CA: Sage.

HUYNH, H. (1978). Some approximate tests for repeated measurement designs. *Psychometrika*, *43*, 161–175.

HUYNH, H., & FELDT, L. S. (1970). Conditions under which mean square ratios in repeated measurements designs have exact F-distributions. *Journal of the American Statistical Association*, *65*, 1,582–1,589.

HUYNH, H., & FELDT, L. S. (1976). Estimation of the Box correction for degrees of freedom from sample data in the randomized block and split-plot designs. *Journal of Educational Statistics*, *1*, 69–82.

HUYNH, H., & MANDEVILLE, G. K. (1979). Validity conditions in repeated measures designs. *Psychological Bulletin*, 86, 964–973.

JACCARD, J., BECKER, M. A., & WOOD, G. (1984). Pairwise multiple comparison procedures: A review. *Psychological Bulletin*, 96, 589–596.

JAMES, G. S. (1951). The comparison of several groups of observations when the ratios of the population variances are unknown. *Biometrika*, 38, 324–329.

JOHNSON, E. S., & BAKER, R. F. (1973). The computer as experimenter: New results. *Behavioral Science*, 18, 377–385.

JOHNSON, H. H., & SOLSO, R. L. (1978). *An introduction to experimental design in psychology: A case approach* (2nd ed.). New York: Harper & Row.

JOHNSON, N. F. (1986). On looking at letters within words: Do we "see" them in memory? *Journal of Memory and Language*, 25, 558–570.

JOHNSON, P. O., & NEYMAN, J. (1936). Tests of certain linear hypotheses and their application to some educational problems. *Statistical Research Memoirs*, 1, 57–93.

KEPPEL, G. (1973). *Design and analysis: A researcher's handbook*. Englewood Cliffs, NJ: Prentice Hall.

KEPPEL, G. (1982). *Design and analysis: A researcher's handbook* (2nd ed.). Englewood Cliffs, NJ: Prentice Hall.

KEPPEL, G., POSTMAN, L., & ZAVORTINK, B. L. (1968). Studies of learning to learn: VIII. The influence of massive amounts of training upon the learning and retention of paired-associate lists. *Journal of Verbal Learning and Verbal Behavior*, 7, 790–796.

KEPPEL, G., & SAUFLEY, W. H., Jr. (1980). *Introduction to design and analysis: A student's handbook*. New York: W. H. Freeman.

KEPPEL, G., & UNDERWOOD, B. J. (1962). Proactive inhibition in short-term retention of single items. *Journal of Verbal Learning and Verbal Behavior*, 1, 153–161.

KEPPEL, G., & ZEDECK, S. (1989). *Data analysis for research designs: Analysis of variance and multiple regression/correlation approaches*. New York: W. H. Freeman.

KEREN, G., & LEWIS, C. (1979). Partial omega squared for ANOVA designs. *Educational and Psychological Measurement*, 39, 119–128.

KESELMAN, H. J., GAMES, P. A., & ROGAN, J. C. (1980). Type I and type II errors in simultaneous and two-stage multiple comparison procedures. *Psychological Bulletin*, 88, 356–358.

KESELMAN, H. J., & KESELMAN, J. C. (1988). Repeated measures multiple comparison procedures: Effects of violating multisample sphericity in unbalanced designs. *Journal of Educational Statistics*, 13, 215–226.

KESELMAN, H. J., ROGAN, J. C., & GAMES, P. A. (1981). Robust tests of repeated measures means in educational and psychological research. *Educational and Psychological Measurement*, 41, 163–173.

KESELMAN, H. J., ROGAN, J. C., MENDOZA, J. L., & BREEN, L. J. (1980). Testing the validity conditions of repeated measures F tests. *Psychological Bulletin*, 87, 479–481.

KIRK, R. E. (1968). *Experimental design: Procedures for the behavioral sciences*. Monterey, CA: Brooks/Cole.

KIRK, R. E. (1972). Classification of ANOVA designs. In R. E. Kirk (Ed.), *Statistical issues*. Monterey, CA: Brooks/Cole.

KIRK, R. E. (1982). *Experimental design: Procedures for the behavioral sciences* (2nd ed.). Monterey, CA: Brooks/Cole.

KOHR, R. L., & GAMES, P. A. (1977). Testing complex a priori contrasts on means from independent samples. *Journal of Educational Statistics*, 2, 207–216.

KRAEMER, H. C. (1985). A strategy to teach the concept and application of power of statistical tests. *Journal of Educational Statistics*, 10, 173–195.

KRAEMER, H. C., & THIEMANN, S. (1987). *How many subjects?: Statistical power analysis in research*. Newbury Park, CA: Sage.

LANE, D. M., & DUNLAP, W. P. (1978). Estimating effect size: Bias resulting from the significance criterion in editorial decisions. *The British Journal of Mathematical and Statistical Psychology*, 31, 107–112.

LASHLEY, K. S. (1929). *Brain mechanisms and intelligence: A quantitative study of injuries to the brain*. Chicago: University of Chicago Press.

LEVENE, H. (1960). Robust tests for equality of variances. In I. Olkin (Ed.), *Contributions to probability and statistics: Essays in honor of Harold Hotelling* (pp. 278–292). Stanford, CA: Stanford University Press.

LEVY, K. J. (1980). A Monte Carlo study of analysis of covariance under violations of normality and equal regression slopes. *Educational and Psychological Measurement*, 40, 835–840.

LINDMAN, H. R. (1974). *Analysis of variance in complex experimental designs*. New York: W. H. Freeman.

LOFTUS, G. R., & LOFTUS, E. F. (1988). *Essence of statistics* (2nd ed.). New York: Knopf.

MARASCUILO, L. A., & LEVIN, J. R. (1970). Appropriate post hoc comparisons for interaction and nested hypotheses in analysis of variance designs: The elimination of Type IV errors. *American Educational Research Journal*, 7, 397–421.

MARTIN, C. G., & GAMES, P. A. (1977). ANOVA tests for homogeneity: Non-normality and unequal samples. *Journal of Educational Statistics*, 2, 187–206.

MAXWELL, S. E., CAMP, C. J., & ARVEY, R. D. (1981). Measures of strength of association: A comparative examination. *Journal of Applied Psychology*, 66, 525–534.

MAXWELL, S. E., DELANEY, H. D., & DILL, C. A. (1984). Another look at ANCOVA versus blocking. *Psychological Bulletin*, 95, 136–147.

McFATTER, R. M., & GOLLOB, H. F. (1986). The power of hypothesis tests for comparisons. *Educational and Psychological Measurement*, 46, 883–886.

MILLER, L., & CORNETT, T. L. (1978). Marijuana: Dose effects on pulse rate, subjective estimates of intoxication, free recall and recognition memory. *Pharmacology Biochemistry and Behavior*, 9, 573–577.

MILLER, L., CORNETT, T. L., BRIGHTWELL, D., McFARLAND, D., DREW, W. G., & WIKLER, A. (1976). Marijuana and memory impairment: The effect of retrieval cues on free recall. *Pharmacology Biochemistry and Behavior*, 5, 639–643.

MILLER, R. G., Jr. (1981). *Simultaneous statistical inference* (2nd Ed.). New York: Springer-Verlag.

MILLIGAN, G. W., WONG, D. S., & THOMPSON, P. A. (1987). Robustness properties of nonorthogonal analysis of variance. *Psychological Bulletin*, 101, 464–470.

MULLER, K. E., & BARTON, C. N. (1989). Approximate power for repeated-measures ANOVA lacking sphericity. *Journal of the American Statistical Association*, 84, 549–555.

MYERS, J. L. (1979). *Fundamentals of experimental design* (3rd ed.). Boston: Allyn & Bacon.

NAMBOODIRI, N. K. (1972). Experimental designs in which each subject is used repeatedly. *Psychological Bulletin*, 77, 54–64.

NEALE, J. M., & LIEBERT, R. M. (1986). *Science and behavior: An introduction to methods of research* (3rd ed.). Englewood Cliffs, NJ: Prentice Hall.

O'BRIEN, P. C. (1983). The appropriateness of analysis of variance and multiple-comparison procedures. *Biometrics*, 39, 787–794.

O'GRADY, K. E. (1982). Measures of explained variance: Cautions and limitations. *Psychological Bulletin*, 92, 766–777.

PEARSON, E. S., & HARTLEY, H. O. (1951). Charts of the power function for analysis of variance tests, derived from the non-central F distribution. *Biometrika*, 38, 112–130.

PEARSON, E. S., & HARTLEY, H. O. (Eds.). (1970). *Biometrika tables for statisticians* (3rd ed., Vol. 1). New York: Cambridge University Press.

PEARSON, E. S., & HARTLEY, H. O. (Eds.). (1972). *Biometrika tables for statisticians* (Vol. II). London: Cambridge University Press.

PEDERSEN, J. M. (1988). Laboratory observations on the function of tongue extrusion in the desert iguana (*Dipsosaurus dorsalis*). *Journal of Comparative Psychology*, 102, 193–196.

PEDHAZUR, E. J. (1982). *Multiple regression in behavioral research: Explanation and prediction* (2nd ed.). New York: Holt, Rinehart & Winston.

POSTMAN, L., & RILEY, D. A. (1957). A critique of Köhler's theory of association. *Psychological Review*, 64, 61–72.

POULTON, E. C. (1973). Unwanted range effects from using within-subject experimental designs. *Psychological Bulletin*, 80, 113–121.

POULTON, E. C. (1974). Range effects are characteristic of a person serving in a within-subjects experimental design—A reply to Rothstein. *Psychological Bulletin*, 81, 201–202.

POULTON, E. C. (1975). Range effects in experiments on people. *American Journal of Psychology*, 88, 3–32.

POULTON, E. C., & FREEMAN, P. R. (1966). Unwanted asymmetrical transfer effects with balanced experimental designs. *Psychological Bulletin*, 66, 1–8.

RAMSEY, P. H. (1981). Power of univariate pairwise multiple comparison procedures. *Psychological Bulletin*, 90, 352–366.

RASMUSSEN, J. L., HEUMANN, K. A., HEUMANN, M. T., & BOTZUM, M. (1989). Univariate and multivariate groups by trials analysis under violation of variance-covariance and normality assumptions. *Multivariate Behavioral Research*, 24, 93–105.

ROGAN, J. C., & KESELMAN, H. J. (1977). Is the ANOVA F-test robust to variance heterogeneity when sample sizes are equal?: An investigation via a coefficient of variation. *American Educational Research Journal*, 14, 493–498.

ROGERS, W. T., & HOPKINS, K. D. (1988). Power estimates in the presence of a covariate and measurement error. *Educational and Psychological Measurement*, 48, 647–656.

ROGOSA, D. (1980). Comparing nonparallel regression lines. *Psychological Bulletin*, 88, 307–321.

RONIS, D. L. (1981). Comparing the magnitude of effects in ANOVA designs. *Educational and Psychological Measurement*, 41, 993–1,000.

ROSENTHAL, R., & GAITO, J. (1963). The interpretation of levels of significance by psychological researchers. *The Journal of Psychology*, 55, 33–38.

ROSENTHAL, R., & ROSNOW, R. L. (1984). *Essentials of behavioral research: Methods and data analysis*. New York: McGraw-Hill.

ROSENTHAL, R., & RUBIN, D. B. (1982). Comparing effect sizes of independent studies. *Psychological Bulletin*, 92, 500–504.

ROSENTHAL, R., & RUBIN, D. B. (1984). Multiple contrasts and ordered Bonferroni procedures. *Journal of Educational Psychology*, 76, 1,028–1,034.

ROSENTHAL, R., & RUBIN, D. B. (1985). Statistical analysis: Summarizing evidence versus establishing facts. *Psychological Bulletin*, 97, 527–529.

ROSNOW, R. L., & ROSENTHAL, R. (1989a). Definition and interpretation of interaction effects. *Psychological Bulletin*, 105, 143–146.

ROSNOW, R. L., & ROSENTHAL, R. (1989b). Statistical procedures and the justification of knowledge in psychological science. *American Psychologist*, 44, 1,276–1,284.

ROTHSTEIN, L. D. (1974). A reply to Poulton. *Psychological Bulletin*, 81, 199–200.

ROTTON, J., & Schönemann, P. H. (1978). Power tables for analysis of variance. *Educational and Psychological Measurement*, 38, 213–229.

ROUANET, H., & LÉPINE, D. (1970). Comparison between treatments in a repeated-measures design: ANOVA and multivariate methods. *The British Journal of Mathematical and Statistical Psychology*, 23, 147–163.

RULE, S. J. (1976). A general experimentwise error rate for multiple significance tests. *Perceptual and Motor Skills*, 43, 1,263–1,277.

RYAN, T. A. (1959). Multiple comparisons in psychological research. *Psychological Bulletin*, 56, 26–47.

RYAN, T. A. (1980). Comment on "Protecting the overall rate of type I errors for pairwise comparisons with an omnibus test statistic." *Psychological Bulletin*, 88, 354–355.

RYAN, T. A. (1985). Ensemble-adjusted p values: How are they to be weighted? *Psychological Bulletin*, *79*, 521–526.

SANTA, J. L., MILLER, J. J., & SHAW, M. L. (1979). Using quasi F to prevent alpha inflation due to stimulus variation. *Psychological Bulletin*, *86*, 37–46.

SATTERTHWAITE, F. E. (1946). An approximate distribution of estimates of variance components. *Biometrics Bulletin*, *2*, 110–114.

SCHEFFÉ, H. (1953). A method for judging all contrasts in the analysis of variance. *Biometrika*, *40*, 87–104.

SEDLMEIER, P., & GIGERENZER, G. (1989). Do studies of statistical power have an effect on the power of studies? *Psychological Bulletin*, *105*, 309–316.

SILVERSTEIN, A. B. (1986). Statistical power lost and statistical power regained: The Bonferroni procedure in exploratory research. *Educational and Psychological Measurement*, *46*, 303–307.

SLAMECKA, N. J., & GRAF, P. (1978). The generation effect: Delineation of a phenomenon. *Journal of Experimental Psychology: Human Learning and Memory*, *4*, 592–604.

SLOBIN, D. I. (1966). Grammatical transformations and sentence comprehension in childhood and adulthood. *Journal of Verbal Learning and Verbal Behavior*, *5*, 219–227.

SNEDECOR, G. W. (1956). *Statistical methods applied to experiments in agriculture and biology* (5th ed.). Ames: Iowa State University Press.

STEVENS, J. (1986). *Applied multivariate statistics for the social sciences*. Hillsdale, NJ: Erlbaum.

STOLOFF, M. L., & COUCH, J. V. (Eds.). (1988). *Computer use in psychology: A directory of software* (2nd ed.). Washington, DC: American Psychological Association.

TAN, W. Y. (1982). Sampling distributions and robustness of t, F and variance-ratio in two samples and ANOVA models with respect to departure from normality. *Communications in Statistics — Theory and Methods*, *11*, 2,485–2,511.

TOMARKEN, A. J., & SERLIN, R. C. (1986). Comparisons of ANOVA alternatives under variance heterogeneity and specific noncentrality structures. *Psychological Bulletin*, *99*, 90–99.

TUKEY, J. W. (1953). *The problem of multiple comparisons*. Unpublished paper, Princeton University, Princeton, NJ.

TUKEY, J. W. (1977). *Exploratory data analysis*. Reading, MA: Addison-Wesley.

TUKEY, J. W. (1980). We need both exploratory and confirmatory. *The American Statistician*, *34*, 23–25.

UNDERWOOD, B. J. (1957). *Psychological research*. Englewood Cliffs, NJ: Prentice Hall.

UNDERWOOD, B. J. (1961). Ten years of massed practice on distributed practice. *Psychological Review*, *68*, 229–247.

UNDERWOOD, B. J. (1975). Individual differences as a crucible in theory construction. *American Psychologist*, *30*, 128–143.

UNDERWOOD, B. J., & SHAUGHNESSY, J. J. (1975). *Experimentation in psychology*. New York: Wiley.

VAUGHAN, G. M., & CORBALLIS, M. C. (1969). Beyond tests of significance: Estimating strength of effects in selected ANOVA designs. *Psychological Bulletin*, *72*, 204–213.

WAGENAAR, W. A. (1969). A note on the construction of digram-balanced Latin squares. *Psychological Bulletin*, *72*, 384–386.

WALLACE, W. P., & UNDERWOOD, B. J. (1964). Implicit responses and the role of intralist similarity in verbal learning by normal and retarded subjects. *Journal of Educational Psychology*, *55*, 362–370.

WANG, M. D. (1982). Estimation of ω^2 for a one-way, fixed-effects model when sample sizes are disproportionate. *Educational and Psychological Measurement*, *42*, 167–179.

WEBB, E. J., CAMPBELL, D. T., SCHWARTZ, R. D., & SECHREST, L. (1966). *Unobtrusive measures: Nonreactive research in the social sciences*. Chicago: Rand McNally.

WELCH, B. L. (1947). The generalization of "Student's" problem when several different population variances are involved. *Biometrika*, *34*, 28–35.

WELCH, B. L. (1951). On the comparison of several mean values: An alternative approach. *Biometrika*, *38*, 330–336.

WICKENS, T. D., & KEPPEL, G. (1983). On the choice of design and of test statistic in the analysis of experiments with sampled materials. *Journal of Verbal Learning and Verbal Behavior*, *22*, 296–309.

WIKE, E. L., & CHURCH, J. D. (1982a). Nonrobustness in F tests: 1. A replication and extension of Bradley's study. *Bulletin of the Psychonomic Society*, *20*, 165–167.

WIKE, E. L., & CHURCH, J. D. (1982b). Nonrobustness in F tests: 2. Further extensions of Bradley's study. *Bulletin of the Psychonomic Society*, *20*, 168–170.

WILCOX, R. R. (1987a). New designs in analysis of variance. *Annual Review of Psychology*, *38*, 29–60.

WILCOX, R. R. (1987b). *New statistical procedures for the social sciences: Modern solutions for basic problems*. Hillsdale, NJ: Erlbaum.

WILCOX, R. R. (1988). A new alternative to the ANOVA F and new results on James's second-order method. *British Journal of Mathematical and Statistical Psychology*, *41*, 109–117.

WILCOX, R. R., CHARLIN, V. L., & THOMPSON, K. L. (1986). New Monte Carlo results on the robustness of the ANOVA F, W, and F* statistics. *Communication in Statistics — Simulation*, *15*, 933–943.

WILSON, W. (1962). A note on the inconsistency inherent in the necessity to perform multiple comparisons. *Psychological Bulletin*, *59*, 296–300.

WINER, B. J. (1971). *Statistical principles in experimental design* (2nd ed.). New York: McGraw-Hill.

WOODWARD, W. A., ELLIOTT, A. C., GRAY, H. L., & MATLOCK, D. C. (1988). *Directory of statistical microcomputer software*. New York: Marcel Dekker.

ZWICK, R., & MARASCUILO, L. A. (1984). Selection of pairwise multiple comparison procedures for parametric and nonparametric analysis of variance models. *Psychological Bulletin*, *95*, 148–155.

AUTHOR INDEX

SUBJECT INDEX